D0212155

Puritans and Puritanism
in Europe and America

Board of Advisors

Professor Lynn A. Botelho
Professor of History, Indiana University of Pennsylvania

Professor Patrick Collinson
Regius Professor of Modern History Emeritus, University of Cambridge

Professor Jacqueline Eales
Professor of History, Canterbury Christ Church University College, England

Professor Stephen Foster
Professor of History, Northern Illinois University

Professor Michael McGiffert
Editor Emeritus, *The William and Mary Quarterly*

Professor John Spurr
Professor of History, University of Swansea, United Kingdom

Professor Michael Winship
Professor of History, University of Georgia

Ref.
285.9
P974
v. 2

Puritans and Puritanism in Europe and America

A Comprehensive Encyclopedia

Editors

Francis J. Bremer
Tom Webster

Editorial Assistants

Susan Ortmann
W. Matthew Rice
Michael Spurr

A B C ⬤ C L I O

Santa Barbara, California   Denver, Colorado   Oxford, England

Nyack College Library

Copyright © 2006 by Francis J. Bremer and Tom Webster

All rights reserved. No part of this publication may be reproduced, stored in a
retrieval system, or transmitted, in any form or by any means, electronic, mechanical,
photocopying, recording, or otherwise, except for the inclusion of brief quotations in a
review, without prior permission in writing from the publishers.

Cataloging-in-Publication Data is available from the Library of Congress

09 08 07 06   10 9 8 7 6 5 4 3 2 1

This book is also available on the World Wide Web as an eBook. Visit abc-clio.com for
details.

ABC-CLIO, Inc.
130 Cremona Drive, P.O. Box 1911
Santa Barbara, California 93116-1911

This book is printed on acid-free paper.
Manufactured in the United States of America

Production Team:
Acquisitions Editor   Jim Ciment
Project Assistant   Wendy Roseth
Senior Media Editor   Ellen Rasmussen
Media Manager   Caroline Price
Production Editor   Anna R. Kaltenbach
Editorial Assistant   Alisha Martinez
Production Manager   Don Schmidt
Manufacturing Coordinator   George Smyser

Tom Webster would like to dedicate this to Ann Milović for so much support, understanding, and willingness to hear about the puritans.

Frank Bremer would like to dedicate this to his grandchildren—Adam, Keegan, Kristen, Luca, Lucy, Mac, Molly, Ryan, Taylor, and a player to be named later—who could care less about the puritans at this time, but nevertheless are very precious to him.

Contents

Contributors

Contributors

Simon Adams
Reader in History
University of Strathclyde
Glasgow
United Kingdom

David J. Appleby
Keele University
Staffordshire
United Kingdom

Margaret Aston
Independent Scholar
United Kingdom

Jeremy D. Bangs
Director
Leiden American Pilgrim
   Museum
Leiden
Netherlands

L. A. Botelho
Professor
Indiana University of
   Pennsylvania
Indiana, PA

Theodore Dwight Bozeman
Professor
University of Iowa
Iowa City, IA

Stephen Brachlow
Professor of Spirituality
Baptist Theological Seminary at
   Richmond
Richmond, VA

Sargent Bush
University of Wisconsin,
   Madison
Madison, WI

Andrew Cambers
Oxford Brookes University
Oxford
United Kingdom

Aaron F. Christensen
Oklahoma State University
Stillwater, OK

John Coffey
Reader in Early Modern History
University of Leicester
Leicester
United Kingdom

Patrick Collinson

David R. Como
Assistant Professor of History
Stanford University
Stanford, CA

James F. Cooper, Jr.
Professor
Oklahoma State University
Stillwater, OK

Will Coster
Department of History
De Montford University
Bedford
United Kingdom

John Craig
Professor, Department of
   History
Simon Fraser University
Burnaby, British Columbia
Canada

Bryan Crockett
Associate Professor, Department
   of English
Loyola College in Maryland
Baltimore, MD

Bruce C. Daniels
Professor of History
Texas Tech University
Lubbock, TX

Michael G. Ditmore
Associate Professor
Pepperdine University
Malibu, CA

David Dymond
University of Cambridge
Cambridge
United Kingdom

Simon Dyton
Cambridge University
Cambridge
United Kingdom

Jackie Eales
Canterbury Christ Church
    University College
Canterbury
United Kingdom

Lori Anne Ferrell
Professor
Claremont Graduate University
Claremont, CA

Amanda Flather

Alan Ford
Professor of Theology
University of Nottingham
Nottingham
United Kingdom

Stephen Foster
Distinguished Research
    Professor of History
    (Emeritus)
Northern Illinois University
DeKalb, IL

Rachelle E. Friedman
Coordinator, History and
    Geography
Lycée Français de New York
New York, NY

Malcolm Gaskill
Fellow and Director of Studies
    in History
Churchill College
Cambridge
United Kingdom

Richard Godbeer
Professor of History
University of Miami
Coral Gables, FL

Mark Goldie
Senior Lecturer in History
University of Cambridge
Cambridge
United Kingdom

Judith S. Graham
Independent Scholar
Newton, MA

Victoria Gregory
King's College, Cambridge
Cambridge
United Kingdom

Polly Ha
Research Fellow
Clare Hall
Cambridge
United Kingdom

Kate Harvey
Cambridge University
Cambridge
United Kingdom

Katherine A. Hermes
Associate Professor of History
Central Connecticut State
    University
New Britain, CT

Ann Hughes
Professor of Early Modern
    History
Keele University
Keele
United Kingdom

Nathan Johnstone
Canterbury Christ Church
    University
Canterbury
United Kingdom

Laura Luder
Dickinson College
Carlisle, PA

Diarmaid MacCulloch
Professor of the History of the
    Church
University of Oxford
United Kingdom

J. Sears McGee
Professor of History
University of California, Santa
    Barbara
Santa Barbara, CA

Michael McGiffert
Editor Emeritus
Omohundro Institute of Early
    American History and Culture
Williamsburg, VA

Jonathan D. Moore
Cambridge
United Kingdom

John Morrill
Professor of British and Irish
  History
Selwyn College, University of
  Cambridge
Cambridge
United Kingdom

David George Mullan
Professor
Cape Breton University
Sydney, Nova Scotia
Canada

Mary Beth Norton
Mary Donlon Alger Professor of
  American History
Cornell University
Ithaca, NY

Catherine Nunn
University of Manchester
Manchester
United Kingdom

Susan M. Ortmann
Graduate Student
University of Delaware
Newark, DE

Elizabeth Reis
Assistant Professor
University of Oregon
Eugene, OR

W. Matthew Rice
Millersville University
Millersville, PA

Sarah Rivett
Assistant Professor
Washington University
St. Louis, MO

Daryl Sasser
Union Theological Seminary
Richmond, VA

Paul S. Seaver
Professor of History Emeritus
Stanford University
Stanford, CA

William Sheils
University of York
York
United Kingdom

Larry A. Skillin
The Ohio State University
Columbus, OH

Stephanie Sleeper
Claremont Graduate University
Claremont, CA

Keith L. Sprunger
Professor of History
Bethel College
North Newton, KS

John Spurr
Professor
University of Swansea
Swansea
United Kingdom

Michael J. Spurr
Millersville University
Millersville, PA

Margo Todd
Walter H. Annenberg Professor
  of History
University of Pennsylvania
Philadelphia, PA

David E. Underdown
Professor Emeritus
Department of History
Yale University
New Haven, CT

Brett Usher

Elliot Vernon
London
United Kingdom

Claire Vivian
Swansea University
Swansea
United Kingdom

Susan Wabuda
Associate Professor of History
Fordham University
Bronx, NY

Dewey D. Wallace, Jr.
Professor of Religion
George Washington University
Washington, DC

James P. Walsh
Professor Emeritus
Central Connecticut State
  University
New Britain, CT

Cassandra Wargo
Dickinson College
Carlisle, PA

Peter Webster
Department of History
University of Sheffield
Sheffield
United Kingdom

Michael P. Winship
E. Merton Coulter Professor of
    History
University of Georgia
Athens, GA

Michelle Wolfe
Postdoctoral Research Fellow
Nottingham Trent University
Nottingham
United Kingdom

Walter W. Woodward
Assistant Professor
University of Connecticut
Hartford, CT

Ralph F. Young
Senior Lecturer, Department of
    History
Temple University
Philadelphia, PA

Introduction

In its broadest terms, puritanism in the sixteenth and seventeenth centuries was an agenda calling for furthering the perfection of Protestant reform, and it was to be found throughout the British Isles and in the English colonies abroad. Though often studied within the specific context of England or New England, it was a transatlantic movement, and this encyclopedia seeks to make more widely available recent scholarship that emphasizes the broader nature of the subject.

Over the years, claims have been made that credited puritanism with the origins of American democracy, the advancement of the spirit of capitalism, and much else that is cherished in the Western world. Puritans have also been blamed for censoriousness, intolerance, and much that is wrong with the Western world. Both sets of attributions distort the reality, but a proper appreciation of the world of John Winthrop, Oliver Cromwell, and their male and female peers will reveal that the footprints of puritanism are everywhere to be found in the centuries that have elapsed from their day to ours. These footprints are sometimes clearly detectable on the soil of history, and sometimes faint. It is not always clear what direction they are moving in. But the legacy of the puritans has clearly influenced many aspects of the culture of the United States, the British Isles, and some of the Caribbean societies that were part of the seventeenth-century British empire.

Yet historians who can agree on the importance of puritanism cannot agree on what precisely puritanism was. This is partially because for about the first century of the movement it had no institutional form. For the most part, men and women dissatisfied with the Protestant Church of Tudor England refused to leave it, preferring to attempt reform from within and thus joining on occasion with allies who supported them on a particular issue but disagreed with them on others. Where we draw the line between those whose agenda and zeal were sufficient to label them "puritan" and those who do not deserve the name is a question to which different historians will continue to offer different answers. In particular, historians have disagreed over whether Separatists, who clearly shared many of the hopes of other reformers, were puritans or whether their decision to leave the national church requires them to be classified as coming out of the puritan movement but not actually of it. This encyclopedia reflects that ongoing debate since the contributors have not been forced to accept a single definition of puritanism.

The imprecision about how to define puritanism even extends to the way the word is presented. Some scholars, including most of those who focus on American puritanism, capitalize "Puritan" and "Puritanism." Others, primarily students of British religion, use a lowercase *p*. This difference in usage might reflect the fact that the history of seventeenth-century New England does tell a story of a distinct people and ideas that are more clearly definable and thus capable of clearer categorization, while the British story is a less precise one, in which a common orientation, disposition, or temperament manifests itself in different ways at different times and in different circumstances. In editing this encyclopedia we have chosen to allow the individual contributors to decide on whether or not to capitalize the word in their individual essays.

Ironically, in the United States, where the existence of puritanism as a distinct phenomenon has never been in question, scholarship on the subject has been in decline in recent decades. The fascination with the religion of the New England colonists that was central to the work of scholars such as Perry Miller and Edmund S. Morgan has been replaced among most historians with interest in social and cultural aspects of the past. Intellectual history in general, and religious history in particular, are still pursued by researchers in divinity schools and literature departments, but less commonly in history departments. Even those engaged in recent public debates over the role of religion in U.S. life and government neglect the study of the puritan past that is so relevant to these issues.

It is in England, generally recognized as a nation where religion is less vital today than in the United States, that puritan studies have reached new levels of sophistication. Despite—or, perhaps, because of—the challenges of pinpointing exactly who the puritans were and what they believed, a new generation of scholars has embraced the subject. Following in the footsteps of scholars such as Christopher Hill and Patrick Collinson, younger researchers are exploring the relationship of religion in general and puritanism in particular to the shaping of sixteenth- and seventeenth-century England and the neighboring kingdoms of Ireland and Scotland.

This encyclopedia would not have been possible without the assistance of the many scholars on both sides of the Atlantic who still believe in the significance of puritan studies. Many of them have come together over the past decades at conferences on puritanism in England and America hosted in the United States by Thomas More College (1975) and Millersville University of Pennsylvania (1991 and 1999). It is the belief of the editors that those conferences helped shape a network of scholars who have been able to draw upon one another's expertise and generosity to help advance their own work and to show the relevance of American and British traditions of puritan scholarship for each other. Certainly, those connections have helped us to enlist the contributors to these volumes.

All this having been said, a true blending of American and British puritan studies would mean looking at all the various topics involved from a transatlantic perspective, but this has not always been possible. Some topics that have captured the enthusiasm of one group of scholars have simply not been investigated on the other side of the Atlantic. Thus, while some essays make insightful comparisons between the ways puritans in different places dealt with a particular issue or implemented a particular idea, others focus largely on topics from a purely American or purely English perspective. It is hoped that the encyclopedia itself, by demonstrating the value of transatlantic comparisons, will encourage more such work, which will perhaps be reflected in a later edition.

It should also be pointed out that the transatlantic approach is not merely something to be found in puritan studies. "Atlantic History" is one of the hot new approaches in historical studies. At the same time, this approach is not as novel as some of its proponents would claim. Indeed, much of puritan studies has always been transatlantic, from the work of the first puritan historians such as William Bradford, John Winthrop, and Cotton Mather, through eighteenth-century authors such as Daniel Neal, down to those who helped set the course for twentieth-century American puritan studies, such as Samuel Eliot Morison and Perry Miller. Through the sixties, seventies, eighties, and nineties, U.S. students of puritan ideas and institutions such as Edmund S. Morgan, David Hall, Stephen Foster, Michael McGiffert, and Michael Winship have placed their work in the broader contexts of not only Anglo-American religion but the Reformation in general. The approach is not new in this community of U.S. scholars, though British historians have been slower to recognize that New England's story may open new insights for them.

Puritans and Puritanism in Europe and America consists of a number of different, but related sections.

The collection of **Biographies** attempts to offer brief descriptions of the lives of the men and women who played key roles in the shaping of puritanism in England, New England, Scotland, Ireland, and other places where puritans settled. These are not complete lives, but rather focus on the "puritan" character or contributions of the individual. Included in this section are some who might not normally be thought of as puritans, such as Thomas Cranmer and Edmund Grindal, who helped advance positions that were then embraced by those more clearly puritan. Also included are men such as Matthew Wren and William Laud whose opposition to the movement helped define it or set it off in new directions. Unfortunately, there are relatively few women included in this section, though quite clearly women played an important part in advancing puritanism throughout the Atlantic world and came to be a majority of the formal church members in many New England and English congregations. Their underrepresentation is thus attributable not to their lack of significance but to the lack of surviving evidence that would allow them to speak to us over the centuries.

Given the impact of puritanism on virtually every aspect of life in this period, the section on **Ideas, Events, and Issues** could very well have been twice as long. We have tried to include the obvious topics that will be of interest to scholars and the general public, and we have also attempted to di-rect interest to areas that are rarely considered. In the process, there are undoubtedly some subjects that have been omitted, and we apologize for that. Readers who do not find a topic in this section are directed to the **Glossary**, where some subjects are explained more briefly.

The selection of **Primary Sources** presented another challenge, since there already exist numerous full volumes of puritan sources, and published puritan writings have become more available through published reprints and electronic access. We attempted a selection that gives some evidence of the puritan spirit as well as examples of advice, agreements, and official positions. We have also tried to include examples of private as well as public writings. Spelling has been modernized in all cases in order to facilitate use by nonspecialists though the hyphenation, capitalization, and punctuation of the original have been to some extent retained, to give the flavor of the period.

A complete bibliography of puritanism would be as long as this entire work. The **Bibliography** presented includes some older but still significant works, while focusing on works published since 1990. For references regarding specific topics, readers should look at the suggestions for **Further Reading** that follow each entry.

Francis J. Bremer

Acknowledgments

This work could not have been possible without the assistance of numerous individuals. First and foremost are the individual contributors, whose entries are evidence of their dedication and scholarship. The members of the Board of Advisors helped shape the content and offered advice when consulted, but are not responsible for the final decisions of the editors on what to include and what to leave out. Dr. Bremer would also like to acknowledge the invaluable assistance of Susan Ortmann, W. Matthew Rice, and Michael Spurr, who aided him in trying to maintain administrative control over the project, and who also contributed essays.

List of Entries

Biographies

Abbot, George — Larry Skillin
Abbot, Robert — Francis J. Bremer
Adams, Thomas — Dewey D. Wallace Jr.
Ainsworth, Henry — Francis J. Bremer
Alleine, Joseph — Dewey D. Wallace Jr.
Allen, Thomas — Ralph Young
Alsop, Vincent — John Spurr
Ames, William — Michael McGiffert
Andrewes, Bartimaeus — Patrick Collinson
Angier, John — Catherine Nunn
Annesley, Samuel — Mark Goldie
Archer, Isaac — Michelle Wolfe
Arminius, Jacobus — Francis J. Bremer
Arrowsmith, John — Francis J. Bremer
Ashe, Simeon — Ann Hughes
Aspinwall, William — Francis J. Bremer
Aylmer, John — Brett Usher
Bagshaw, William — Catherine Nunn
Baillie, Robert — John Coffey
Ball, John — Theodore Dwight Bozeman
Ball, Thomas — Theodore Dwight Bozeman
Balmford, Samuel — Francis J. Bremer
Bancroft, Richard — Brett Usher
Barker, Matthew — Francis J. Bremer
Barnardiston Family — Francis J. Bremer
Barrington Family — Francis J. Bremer
Barrow, Henry — Patrick Collinson
Bastwick, John — Francis J. Bremer
Bates, William — Dewey D. Wallace, Jr.

Baxter, Richard — John Spurr
Baynes, Paul — Victoria Gregory
Beadle, John — John Craig
Beaumont, Agnes — Claire Vivian
Bedell, William — Patrick Collinson
Benn, William — Francis J. Bremer
Bernard, Richard — Francis J. Bremer
Bird, Samuel — John Craig
Bird, William — Francis J. Bremer
Blackerby, Richard — Francis J. Bremer
Bolton, Robert — Francis J. Bremer
Bolton, Samuel — Francis J. Bremer
Bownd, Nicholas — John Craig
Bradford, William — Michael G. Ditmore
Bradshaw, William — Stephen Foster
Bradstreet, Anne Dudley — Michael G. Ditmore
Bradstreet, Simon — Susan Ortmann
Brearley, Roger — David Como
Brewster, William — David J. Appleby
Bridge, William — Ralph Young
Brightman, Thomas — Stephanie Sleeper
Brinsley, John — John Spurr
Brocklesby, Edward — Brett Usher
Brooks, Thomas — David J. Appleby
Browne, Robert — Francis J. Bremer
Bruen, John — Francis J. Bremer
Bulkeley, Peter — Michael McGiffert
Bunyan, John — Claire Vivian
Burgess, Anthony — Elliot Vernon
Burgess, Cornelius — Elliot Vernon
Burgess, John — John Craig

Goodwin, John	John Coffey	Hutchinson, Lucy	Francis J. Bremer
Goodwin, Thomas	Michael McGiffert	Jackson, Arthur	John Spurr
Gorton, Samuel	Michael G. Ditmore	Jacob, Henry	Keith L. Sprunger
Gouge, Robert	J. Sears McGee	Janeway, James	Dewey D. Wallace Jr.
Gouge, Thomas	Francis J. Bremer	Jeake, Samuel	Francis J. Bremer
Gouge, William	J. Sears McGee	Jermyn, Sir Robert	Francis J. Bremer
Gough, John	Brett Usher	Jessey, Henry	Stephanie Sleeper
Greenham, Richard	Francis J. Bremer	Johnson, Edward	Rachelle E. Friedman
Greenhill, William	Tom Webster	Johnson, Isaac	Francis J. Bremer
Greenwood, John	Francis J. Bremer	Jollie, Thomas	Dewey D. Wallace Jr.
Griffith, George	Francis J. Bremer	Jones, Samuel	Francis J. Bremer
Grindal, Edmund	Patrick Collinson	Josselin, Ralph	John Spurr
Hall, Joseph	Tom Webster	Keayne, Robert	Susan Ortmann
Hampden, John	David J. Appleby	Kiffin, William	Tom Webster
Harley Family	Jacqueline Eales	Knewstub, John	Francis J. Bremer
Harris, Richard	David Mullan	Knightley, Sir Richard	Paul Seaver
Harrison, Thomas	David J. Appleby	Knowles, John	Tom Webster
Harvard, John	Ralph Young	Knox, John	David Mullan
Henderson, Alexander	John Coffey	Lathrop, John	Francis J. Bremer
Henry, Philip	John Spurr	Laud, William	Francis J. Bremer
Herle, Charles	Francis J. Bremer	Lechford, Thomas	Francis J. Bremer
Herring, Julines	Francis J. Bremer	Lee, Samuel	Dewey D. Wallace Jr.
Heywood, Oliver	John Spurr	Leicester, Robert	
Hibbens, Anne	Mary Beth Norton	Dudley, Earl of	Simon Adams
Higginson, Francis	Francis J. Bremer	Leigh, William	Francis J. Bremer
Higham, Sir John	Francis J. Bremer	Leighton, Alexander	Francis J. Bremer
Hildersham, Arthur	Victoria Gregory	Lever, Thomas	Francis J. Bremer
Hill, Thomas	Francis J. Bremer	Leverett, John	Francis J. Bremer
Hoar, Leonard	Francis J. Bremer	Lobb, Stephen	Mark Goldie
Hobart, Peter	Aaron Christensen	Locke, Anne Vaughan	Francis J. Bremer
Hoby, Sir Edward	Andrew Cambers	Manton, Thomas	David J. Appleby
Holdsworth, Richard	Patrick Collinson	Marshall, Stephen	Tom Webster
Hooke, William	Francis J. Bremer	Martindale, Adam	Catherine Nunn
Hooker, Richard	Francis J. Bremer	Marvell, Andrew	Dewey D. Wallace Jr.
Hooker, Thomas	Stephen Foster	Mather, Cotton	Michael P. Winship
Hooper, John	Diarmaid MacCulloch	Mather, Increase	Michael G. Ditmore
Hopkins, Edward	James P. Walsh	Mather, Nathaniel	Francis J. Bremer
Hopkins, Matthew	Malcolm Gaskill	Mather, Richard	James F. Cooper
Howe, John	Francis J. Bremer	Mather, Samuel	Francis J. Bremer
Howie, Robert	David Mullan	Mayhew, Thomas Jr.	Francis J. Bremer
Hubbard, William	Michael G. Ditmore	Mead, Matthew	John Spurr
Hughes, George	Tom Webster	Mildmay, Lady Grace	Michelle Wolfe
Hughes, Lewis	Francis J. Bremer	Mildmay, Sir Walter	Patrick Collinson
Humphrey, Laurence	Francis J. Bremer	Milton, John	Simon Dyton
Hutchinson,		Mitchell, Jonathan	Francis J. Bremer
Anne Marbury	Michael G. Ditmore	More, John	Francis J. Bremer

Events & Ideas

Chronology

1485	Battle of Bosworth: death of Richard III and accession of Henry VII, marking the start of the Tudor dynasty
1494	Poynings' Law lays down that no legislation can be introduced into the Irish Parliament without prior consent of the King
1497	John Cabot, sailing from Bristol, lands in Newfoundland
1502	Treaty of Perpetual Peace between Henry VII and James IV sealed by marriage of James to Henry's elder daughter
1509	Death of Henry VII and accession of Henry VIII
1511	Henry VIII joins the Holy League, papal-led alliance against France
1513	Rise of Thomas Wolsey, who would eventually serve as chief minister in Church (Archbishop of York and Cardinal Legate) and State (Lord Chancellor)
1516	Publication of Sir Thomas More's *Utopia*
1521	Henry publishes *Assertio Septem Sacramentorum* and is given title "Defender of the Faith" by the Pope
1525	First edition of William Tyndale's New Testament in English published
1527	Henry VIII begins negotiations with Rome for an annulment of his marriage to Catherine of Aragon
1529	Wolsey dismissed from all his civil offices; he dies. Thomas More becomes Lord Chancellor
1529	Reformation Parliament meets in first of seven sessions that will extend to 1537
1532	Submission of the Clergy recognizes Henry's superiority over matters ecclesiastical if not matters theological
1532	Sir Thomas More resigns as Lord Chancellor
1532	Death of Archbishop Warham removes obstacle to settlement of Henry's divorce proceedings in England; Thomas Cranmer is appointed Archbishop by the King and approved by the Pope
1532	Anne Boleyn becomes pregnant
1532	Thomas Comwell becomes Henry's chief minister

1533	Cranmer married Henry to Anne Boleyn and subsequently annuls Henry's marriage to Catherine of Aragon; Princess Elizabeth born
1533	Parliament passes the Act in Restraint of Appeals which prevented Catherine appealing to Rome and proclaimed that "this realm of England is an Empire"
1534	Act of Supremacy ends all papal jurisdiction in England by identifying the monarch as head of the church in England
1535	Henry VIII and Thomas Cromwell order the *Valor Ecclesiaticus*, a survey of the wealth of all religious houses
1535	Publication of Miles Coverdale's English translation of the Bible
1535	Execution of Sir Thomas More and Bishop John Fisher for refusing to accept Henry's claim to be supreme Head of the Church
1536	Catherine of Aragon dies; Anne Boleyn executed on charges of treason; Henry marries Jane Seymour
1536	Royal Injunctions order all clergy to instruct youth in the Lord's Prayer; Ten Articles Act brings strong Lutheran influences to bear on religious practice
1536	Dissolution of the smaller monasteries
1536	Pilgrimage of Grace, the greatest of all sixteenth-century rebellions against royal policies; prompted in part by the religious changes of the regime
1537	Prince Edward born; Jane Seymour dies

1537	Thomas Cranmer publishes *The Institution of a Christian Man*
1538	Passage of Act requiring the registration of all baptisms, marriages, and burials in all parishes
1539	Act of Six Articles heralds a theological backlash toward a more Catholic perspective
1539	Dissolution of the Greater Monasteries
1540	Henry marries Anne of Cleves in January and following the annulment of that union in July, marries Catherine Howard
1540	Thomas Cromwell executed
1540	Completion of reforms that produced a new-style corporate Privy Council, combining deliberative and executive functions
1541	Act erecting Ireland into a Kingdom annexed to the Crown of England
1541	Catherine Howard executed for adultery
1542	Lord Deputy St. Leger announces policy of "Surrender and Regrant" in Ireland to bring Gaelic Lords into a feudal relationship with the King
1547	Death of Henry VIII and accession of Edward VI; Edward Seymour, Earl of Hertford, becomes Duke of Somerset and Lord Protector
1547	Dissolution of the Chantries; clerical marriage allowed; the first *Book of Homilies* published
1549	Act of Uniformity imposes first Prayer Book of Edward VI which creates a fully vernacular liturgy

1549   Somerset falls from power following rebellions in South-West and in East Anglia (Ket's Rebellion); power passes to John Dudley, Duke of Northumberland

1552   Second Prayer Book of Edward VI prepared by Cranmer draws on radical Continental Protestant models

1553   Death of Edward VI; Northumberland fails to place Lady Jane Grey on the throne; accession of Mary I

1553   Restoration of the Catholic Mass

1554   Marriage of Mary to Philip II of Spain; reconciliation of England and Rome and restoration of papal jurisdiction

1555   Wyatt's rebellion in Kent; a protest against the Spanish match

1555   Public executions of Protestant "heretics" begin (in all 282 men and women would be burned for heresy during Mary's reign); Cranmer deprived of his offices; over 800 English Protestants (Marian Exiles) go into exile on the Continent, in Protestant centers such as Geneva and Frankfurt

1556   Archbishop Cranmer executed by burning

1558   Marriage of Mary of Scotland to Francis, heir to French throne

1558   Militia Act, the basis of local defense for several centuries

1558   Publication of John Knox's *First Blast of the Trumpet against the Monstrous Regiment of Women*

1558   Death of Mary I and accession of Elizabeth I; France declares Mary of Scotland Queen of England

1559   Acts of Supremacy and Allegiance once more end papal jurisdiction in England and declare Elizabeth to be Supreme Governor of the church; The new Book of Common Prayer represents a step back from the Protestant expression of faith found in the 1552 Prayer Book. Similar provisions approved by the Irish Parliament for the Church of Ireland

1559   Matthew Parker appointed Archbishop of Canterbury

1559   John Knox returns to Scotland from Geneva

1559   Lords of the Congregation rebel against French Catholic domination of Scotland

1560   Elizabeth sends expeditionary force to Scotland and (by the treaty of Edinburgh) forces French to withdraw all troops; Scottish Protestant Lords of the Congregation secure power and the Scottish Parliament abolishes papal jurisdictions and the Mass

1560   Death of Francis II without a child being born to him and Mary

1560   Scots Confession and first Book of Discipline establish structure of a Reformed church

1561   Mary returns to Scotland

1562   Elizabeth nearly dies of smallpox

1563   Convocation approves the Thirty-Nine Articles, the doctrinal creed of the Church of England

1563   First edition of John Foxe's *Actes and Monuments* (or Book of Martyrs)

1566   Archbishop Parker's *Advertisements* require all clergy to wear the surplice

1567   Civil war in Scotland

1568   Mary Queen of Scots escapes to England and is imprisoned (until her execution in 1587)

1569   Northern Rising against Elizabeth I and in favor of Mary Queen of Scots and Catholicism

1570   Pope issues bull of excommunication against Elizabeth calling on her subjects to overthrow her

1570   English Plantation of East Ulster

1570   Thomas Cartwright preaches controversial lectures on the Acts of the Apostles and is removed as Professor of Divinity at Cambridge; he travels to the continent where he will be influenced by the Presbyterian views of Theodore Beza

1571   Ridolfi Plot to depose Elizabeth. Mary implicated but Elizabeth refuses to execute her

1571   Parliament officially approves the Thirty-Nine Articles

1572   An Act of Parliament makes the payment of poor relief mandatory on all householders not themselves in receipt of alms

1572   John Fields and Thomas Wilcox circulate their *Admonition to Parliament* calling for the further reform of the Church

1573   Privy council introduces the "trained bands" or specialist militia alongside the general militia

1573   Brief English invasion of Scotland to secure the position of the Protestant Regent

1576   Publication of William Lambarde's *Perambulation of Kent,* pioneering county history which inspired many others

1576   Edmund Grindal succeeds Matthew Parker as archbishop of Canterbury and relaxes pressures on religious reformers

1577   Archbishop Grindal suspended for opposing the Queen when she orders prophesying to be suppressed

1578   Walter Travers ordained by a synod of Walloon and Dutch ministers to be chaplain to the English Merchant Adventurers in Antwerp

1579   Major rebellion in Munster (the Desmond Rebellion, suppressed 1583)

1579   John Stubbs sentenced to have his hand cut off for criticizing Anglo-French marriage proposals

1580   Jesuit missionaries arrive in England

1580   Thomas Cartwright succeeds Travers as chaplain to the English Merchjant Adventurers in Antwerp

1580   Francis Drake completes a three-year circumnavigation of the globe and is knighted

1581   Parliament approves fines for non-attendance at church by "popish recusants"

1582   Act makes all Catholic clergy found in England liable to execution (more than 100 would be killed by 1603)

1583   Throckmorton Plot to assassinate Elizabeth

1583   First royal theater company established

1583   Edmund Grindal, suspended from his functions as archbishop since 1577, dies and is succeeded by John Whitgift

1583   Archbishop Whitgift's *Three Articles* aim to identify and prosecute Prebyterian minority in the Church

1584   Plantation of Munster begun

1584   The "Black Acts" in Scotland halt the advance of strict Presbyterianism

1585   First attempt to found a colony in North America (on Roanoke island)

1586   Privy Council introduces Books of Orders for regulating the work of local JPs, a policy repeated in crisis years until the 1630s

1586   First engagements involving English troops fighting Spanish troops in the Netherlands

1586   Babbington Plot uncovered; Mary implicated

1587   Execution of Mary Queen of Scots

1587   Walter Travers finishes his *Book of Discipline* as a model for the Presbyterian reforms advocated by some religious reformers. Cope's "Bill and Book," the most concerted Elizabethan attempt to persuade Parliament to reform the Church of England along Presbyterian lines

1588   Philip II sends the Grand Armada to invade England; it is dispersed by bad weather and the English Navy

1588   First of Shakespeare's plays staged (last one first staged in 1613)

1588   Publication of William Morgan's Welsh translation of the Bible

1588   Publication of the *Marprelate Tracts* attacking the bishops

1590   Thomas Cartwright and other Presbyterian leaders arrested for their efforts to change the church

1591   English troops sent to assist French Protestants in Brittany

1592   Scottish parliament passes "the Golden Acts" strengthening Presbyterianism

1592   Cartwright and other leaders released on their promise to desist from further efforts to alter the structure of the church

1593   Publication of Richard Hooker's *Of the Laws of Ecclesiastical Politie*

1593   Execution of John Greenwood and Henry Barrow, two leading Protestant separatists

1594   Nine Years War in Ireland begins

1594   Walter Travers appointed provost of the new Irish university, Trinity College, in Dublin

1597   Francis Johnson and a group of English Separatists attempt and fail to establish a colony at the mouth of the St. Lawrence River; Johnson joins the English Separatist congregation in Amsterdam that becomes known as the Ancient Church

1597   Major codification of the various acts for the relief of poverty into the systematic "Old Poor Law"

1599	Publication of King James VI's *Basilikon Doron*
1601	Spanish invasion of Ireland (3,500 troops land at Kinsale)
1601	Publication of William Perkins's *Treatise of the Vocations, or Callings of Men*
1603	Death of Elizabeth I and accession of James VI of Scotland to be James I of England and Ireland
1603	James presented with the "Millenary Petition" calling for religious reforms
1603	Surrender of Tyrone ends Nine Years War in Ireland
1604	Hampton Court Conference considers religious reform of the English Church
1604	Richard Bancroft succeeds John Whitgift as archbishop of Canterbury
1604	Treaty of London ends war with Spain
1605	Gunpowder Plot
1605	Publication of Francis Bacon's *Advancement of Learning*
1606	Act of Union of the Kingdoms debated in the Parliaments of England and Scotland but not approved
1606	Probable date of the formation of the Scrooby Separatist congregation under John Smyth and Richard Clifton
1607	Flight of the Irish Earls of Tyrone and Tyrconnel prepares way for English and Scottish plantations in Ulster
1607	Foundation of the Virginia Company
1607	English merchants in Amsterdam gain permission from city authorities to establish an English Reformed Church; John Paget becomes the first pastor of the congregation
1608	First Gaelic Irish translation of the Book of Common Prayer is published; too late to have a significant effect on the efforts to Protestantize Ireland
1608	Scrooby congregation decides to migrate to Amsterdam in the Netherlands; divisions in the Amsterdam Separatist community lead most to move to Leiden the following year with John Robinson as their pastor
1610	James VI and I achieves goal of restoring episcopacy in Scotland
1611	Publication of the Authorized (King James) Version of the Bible
1611	George Abbot succeeds Bancroft as archbishop of Canterbury
1611	Alexander Whitaker, son of the Cambridge puritan leader William Whitaker, arrives in Jamestown as the colony's first minister. He devoted considerable efforts to bringing Christianity to the native population (his most significant achievement in this regard being the conversion of Pocahontas in 1614). He died in 1617
1612	Death of Henry, Prince of Wales, leaving James's younger son, Charles, as heir to the throne
1613	Marriage of James's daughter Elizabeth to the Elector Palatine
1614	The puritan clergyman Lewis Hughes arrives in Bermuda. Three years later he undertakes a religious reformation on the

island that included abandoning the Book of Common Prayer

1615   Emergence of George Villers, later Duke of Buckingham (1623), as the new royal favorite

1616   Sir Edward Coke, Lord Chief Justice, is sacked as a judge, the first for more than a century; many more sackings follow later in the century

1617   James makes his only return visit to Scotland after becoming Kind of England

1617   Irish Articles promulgated (they are more unambiguously Calvinist than the English Thirty-Nine Articles of 1563)

1618   Synod of Dort at which British representatives affirm Calvinist teaching and condemn Arminianism

1618   Articles of Perth reform Scottish liturgy, including a demand that those who receive communion do so kneeling

1618   The Bohemian Revolt marks the outbreak of the Thirty Years War; James's son-in-law quickly ejected from his electorate by Spanish troops; James seeks Anglo-Spanish marriage treaty as part of a settlement of the disputes

1620   Members of the Scrooby-Leiden Separatist congregation depart from England in the *Mayflower* and plant the Plimouth colony on Cape Cod; the Pilgrims and the "strangers" who had joined them sign the Mayflower Compact as a voluntary commitment to self-government since they had landed outside the jurisdiction of the Virginia Company, which had granted them a patent

1621   Plymouth's first governor, John Carver, dies and is succeeded by William Bradford, who would hold the office for all but five years until his death in 1657

1623   Prince Charles and the Duke of Buckingham travel to Spain in a vain attempt to win the Infanta's daughter for Charles; they return humiliated and demand war with Spain

1623   Dorchester Company formed to establish fishing bases in New England

1623   Strawberry Bank (later to be Portsmouth, New Hampshire) settled by colonists sent by John Mason

1624   James declares war on Spain and pays Danish mercenaries under Count Mansfeld to recapture the Palatinate; the expedition fails

1625   Death of James VI and I and accession of Charles I

1625   Formation in England of the Feoffees for Impropriations, a group of clergy, merchants and lawyers seeking to purchase church livings and install preaching ministers

1625   Charles marries Henrietta Maria of France, but quickly falls out with France over the honoring of the marriage treaty and over Louis XIII's persecution of Protestants

1625   Charles seeks to cancel all the land grants made by his Stewart predecessors so that he can regrant them on terms more favorable to the Crown and the Church (the Act of Revocation)

1626   Buckingham leads failed expedition against Cadiz

1626   York House Conference upholds Arminian teaching, in effect reversing Dort

1626   Charles I prohibits predestinarian teaching at Cambridge (a similar prophibition applies to Oxford in 1628)

1626   Charles declares war on France

1626   Attempt by the House of Commons to impeach Buckingham; Charles forces to dissolve Parliament

1626   William Bradford and other Plymouth leaders arrange to purchase control of the enterprise from the London merchants who had underwritten the venture

1626   John Robinson dies in the Netherlands

1626   Roger Conant moves the small fishing outpost of the Dorchester Company from Cape Anne to Naumkeag (Salem)

1627   Buckingham leads failed expedition to Île de Rhé (near the besieged Protestant stronghold of La Rochelle)

1628   Parliament passes the Petition of Right, effectively limiting the Crown's right to imprison at will, to billet soldiers on civilians, and to punish those who refused to pay prerogative taxation or make prerogative loans

1628   Buckingham assassinated

1628   William Laud appointed bishop of London

1628   Rev. John White and other members of the Dorchester Company join with London merchants to form the New England Company; the New England Company sends John Endecott to assume control of the settlement at Salem

1628   Plymouth authorities send Miles Standish to break up Thomas Morton's settlement at Merrymount, where Morton is said to provide alcohol and guns to native Americans

1629   Violent scenes mark ending of Charles's third Parliament; seven MPs charged with sedition and imprisoned; Charles embarks on his "Eleven Years Personal Rule"

1629   New England Company reorganizes and receives a royal charter as the Massachusetts Bay Company; John Winthrop and other leaders sign the Cambridge Agreement, signifying their willingness to migrate to New England if they can bring the charter and powers of government with them

1630   Start of the Great Migration to New England as the *Arbella* and her sister ships sail for Massachusetts. Prior to departure Winthrop preaches the lay sermon, "A Model of Christian Charity."

1630   John Winthrop assumes control of Massachusetts Bay from Endecott and moves the center of government from Salem to Boston

1630   Formation of the Providence Island Company to establish a puritan colony off the coast of Nicaragua. Among the principal investors were John Pym, Viscount Saye and Sele, Sir Thomas Barrington, Sir Nathaniel Rich, and other prominent puritans. Their company meetings in the 1630s provided them an opportunity to exchange views and plans about public affairs during the personal rule of Charles I

1631   Freemanship expanded in Massachusetts so that all male church members are eligible for the colony franchise

1631   Clash over church polity in the English Church at Amsterdam between the pastor John Paget and the newly arrived Thomas Hooker

1632   Massachusetts General Court agrees that henceforth the governor will be elected by vote of the freemen and not the colony assistants

1633   William Laud becomes archbishop of Canterbury

1633   Feoffees for Impropriation disbanded by the courts in a case brought by William Laud

1633   Charles I visits Scotland, is crowned, and makes mischief

1633   Thomas Wentworth, later Earl of Strafford, takes up appointment as Lord Deputy in Ireland and begins to introduce his policies of "Thorough"

1633   William Prynne sentenced to lose his ears for libeling the Queen

1633   John Cotton and Thomas Hooker arrive in Massachusetts

1634   Ship Money levied on the coastal regions

1634   John Paget blocks the call of John Davenport to the ministry of the English Church at Amsterdam. The dispute between the two anticipated the divisions between English Presbyterians and Congregationalists in the 1640s

1634   Thomas Wentworth, Lord Deputy in Ireland, forces the Irish Convocation to adopt the English Thirty-Nine Articles and to require ministers to subscribe to them

1634   William and Anne Hutchinson and their family arrive in Boston, having decided to follow John Cotton to the New World

1635   Ship Money extended to inland countries

1635   Disputes between Roger Williams and the Massachusetts magistrates lead to William's banishment

1635   Early settlement of what will become Connecticut. Settlers from Dorchester, Massachusetts, settle the town of Windsor on the Connecticut River; an advance group from Newtown, Massachusetts settles Hartford; John Winthrop Jr., on behalf of a group of English grandees, founds a settlement at Saybrook, at the mouth of the Connecticut River

1636   New canons for the Scottish Church promulgated

1636   Roger Williams, warned off from Plymouth, settles Providence, in what will become Rhode Island

1636   Theophilus Eaton and John Davenport lead a group of mostly London puritans to New England, settling briefly in Boston

1636   Henry Vane is elected governor of Massachusetts

1636   Thomas Shepard's criticism of what he perceives as radical religious views emanating from the Boston, Massachusetts Church, marks the start of the free grace controversy (often misleading called the Antiniomian Controversy) that would divide the colony

1636	The Pequot War begins when John Endecott leads a military expedition against the tribe to punish them for failure to turn over those accused of the murder of English traders
1636	Massachusetts General Court authorized the establishment of a college, which will be named after John Harvard
1637	New Scottish Prayer Book promulgated by proclamation
1637	William Prynne sentenced to lose the stumps of his ears and others their ears for libeling the Bishops
1637	Sermon by the Rev. John Wheelwright inflames the divisions in Massachusetts. Synod at Cambridge defines religious errors presumably espoused by members of the Boston church; John Winthrop elected governor again in preference to Henry Vane. Wheelwright, Anne Hutchinson, and others associated with their views banished from Massachusetts
1637	Massachusetts and Connecticut forces under John Mason attack and destroy the main Pequot village, bringing that war to an end
1637	Davenport and Eaton lead their group in the settlement of New Haven
1638	John Wheelwright moves north and founds the town of Exeter (New Hampshire); William Coddington, William and Anne Hutchinson, and others settle Portsmouth (Rhode Island)
1638	Majority of Scottish political nation subscribe to the National Covenant to withstand religious innovations being advanced by Charles I that would bring the Scottish church into closer alignment with that of England
1638	Judges decide (in the case of *Rex v. Hampden*) in favor of the King's right to enforce the payment of Ship Money
1639	King plans to use English, Irish, and Scottish troops to impose his policies against the Scots. Planned invasion collapses
1639	Towns along the Connecticut River organize themselves under the Fundamental Orders
1639	William Coddington splits with the Hutchinsons and established the town of Newport (Rhode Island)
1639	Robert Keayne, merchant, is admonished by the Boston, Massachusetts church for selling wares at an excessive price
1639	Roger Williams and Ezekiel Holiman establish the first Baptist church in America at Providence
1639	Philip Nye and Thomas Goodwin minister to an independent gathered congregation at Arnhem in the Netherlands
1640	King fails to get support from a Short Parliament to raise troops against the Scots; he attacks Scotland anyway; the Scots defeat him and occupy northeast England; King forced to call the Long Parliament
1641	Constitutional reforms instituted; Strafford executed and other ministers and judges impeached or forced into exile; Triennial Act requiring regular parliaments passed, and prerogative courts and prerogative taxation abolished; Root and Branch Petition demands church reforms

1641 New Haven accepts jurisdiction over neighboring towns and the colony of New Haven adopts a frame of government

1641 Massachusetts General Court adopts the Body of Liberties, a law code

1641 *Bay Psalm Book,* prepared by Richard Mather, Thoams Welde, John Cotton, and John Eliot is published

1641 Massachusetts assumes jurisdiction over Strawberry Bank and Dover settlements in the future New Hampshire

1641 Irish Rebellion against the English Planters leads to widespread massacre of Protestants

1641 The Grand Remonstrance itemized royal misgovernment, remedies achieved, and remedies to be sought

1641 Leading English Presbyterians and Congregationalists agree in the Calamy House Accord to desist from attacking each other's viewpoints while concentrating on reforms of the national Church

1642 King attempts to arrest leading parliamentary critics and fails; King withdraws from London; military and political provocations escalate and the Civil War breaks out; first major battle, the Battle of Edgehill, fails to settle the dispute

1642 Parliament orders the closure of all theaters (ban lasts until 1660)

1642 Three New England puritan clergy arrive in Virginia, invited by Richard Bennett and other settlers of puritan inclination. They will meet discouragement from the colonial government. Many Virginia puritans will move to Maryland in 1648

1643 The English Parliamentarians and the Scottish Covenanters form an alliance formalized in the Solemn League and Covenant; the Scots promise to send 20,000 troops into England and the English promise a federal union of the English and Scottish states and a single system of church government and practice

1643 Parliament calls the Westminster Assembly of Divines to make recommendations for religious reform. New Englanders John Cotton, Thomas Hooker, and John Davenport are invited but decline

1643 The colonies of Massachusetts, New Haven, Connecticut, and Plymouth unite to form the New England Confederation (also United Colonies of New England) for mutual defense

1644 Battle of Marston Moor, the largest of all civil war battles, won by the Parliamentarians and the Scots

1644 Split between advocates of Presbyterianism and Congregationalists in the Westminster Assembly; Congregationalist minority published *An Apologetical Narration* to Parliament requesting toleration within any Presbyterian settlement

1644 Roger Williams's *The Bloody Tenent of Persecution* and John Cotton's *The Keys of the Kingdom of Heaven* are published

1644 Roger Williams, in England, obtains a parliamentary charter for Rhode Island, a colony uniting the settlements at Providence, Newport, and Portsmouth

1644 Publication of John Milton's defence of intellectual liberty, *Areopagitica*

1644   Parliament formally replaces the Book of Common Prayer with the Presbyterian oriented Directory of Worship

1644   Massachusetts General Court formally divides into two separately seated houses, with the Court of Assistants asserting veto rights over lower house (deputies) actions

1644   Parliamentary trial of Archbishop Laud (culminating in his attainder and public execution in Jan. 1645)

1645   New Model Army created and wins Battle of Naseby

1646   King surrenders and First Civil War ends; rise of the Leveller movement calling for more popular government

1646   George Fox begins his ministry; the start of the Quaker movement

1646   Robert Child and others petition the Massachusetts General Court for a broadening of church membership and the franchise, threatening to appeal to Parliament if their demands are not met; petition is rejected, the right of appeal denied, and the leading remonstrants jailed

1646   First session of the Cambridge Assembly in New England, charged with defining church faith and order

1646   John Eliot translates the Bible into the Massachusetts dialect of Algonquian language

1647   Failure of many attempts at peace; Leveller writings – *Heads of* Proposals, *Thwe Case of the* Army, *The Agreement of the* People – are published; Army leaders and Levellers debate the fundamentals of governance at Putney church

1647   Nathaniel Ward's *The Simple Cobbler of Agawam* and John Cotton's answer to Roger Williams, *The Bloody Tenent Washed,* are published

1647   William Sayle obtains a parliamentary charter to settle the island of Segatoo in the Bahamas, where he and other puritans who left Bermuda attempted to establish a colony they name Eleutheria. In 1649 they were joined by other puritans exiled from Bermuda by angry royalists following news of the execution of Charles I. In 1650, the church of Boston, Massachusetts raise £800 for the relief of the suffering colonists

1648   King signs an Engagement with dissident Scottish nobles and launches the Second Civil War which his supporters lose

1648   Pride's Purge excludes many of the remaining Presbyterians from Parliament, leaving in control an Independent coalition of Congregationalists, sectarians, and Erastians

1648   Thomas Hooker's *The Survey of the Summe of Church Discipline* is published

1648   Massachusetts adopts a detailed law code, the *Book of Laws and Liberties*

1648   The *Cambridge Platform* is promulgated, defining the New England Way; the platform endorses the Westminster Assembly's Confession of faith and outlines a Congregational form of church order

1648   Richard Bennett and up to six hundred fellow puritans will migrate from Virginia, where they had been subject to increasing government pressure, to the Severn River area of Maryland, where they establish the settlement of Providence

1649   Public trial and public execution of Charles I and abolition of monarchy in England and Ireland; the Scottish Estates proclaim Charles II King of Britain and Ireland

1649   Publication of *Eikon Basilike* begins the cult of Charles I as the martyr-king

1649   The Rump of the Long Parliament acts as interim government of England (until 1653), nominating its own executive Council of State

1649   Organization in England of the Society for the Propagation of the Gospel in New England for the advancement of missionary activities among the Indians

1649   Cromwell leads army of conquest against the Irish Confederates

1650   Cromwell breaks the back of Irish resistance, and returns home to lead invasion of Scotland; he defeats the army of the Covenanters at the battle of Dunbar

1650   Hartford Treaty between New England Confederation and New Netherland Director-General Peter Stuyvesant attempts to settle boundary disputes between the Dutch and English. Stuyvesant's arrest of New Haven colonists bound for the Delaware Bay in the following year leads to a renewal of tensions

1650   Anne Bradstreet's *The Tenth Muse Lately Sprung Up in America* published

1651   Charles II crowned King of Britain and Ireland at Scone; Scots invade England and are defeated at the battle of Worcester; Charles II flees to the Continent

1651   Failed Anglo-Dutch negotiation for a federal union of the two republics

1651   Massachusetts authorities fine and banish three Baptists

1651   John Eliot organizes village for Indian converts at Natick, Massachusetts; this is the first of the "Praying Towns."

1651   English Navigation Ordinances aimed at Dutch carrying trade

1651   Publication of Thomas Hobbes's *Leviathan*

1652   The Act of Settlement threatens to expropriate most Irish landowners and to confine the Catholic population in Connaught between the Shannon and the Atlantic

1652   Spurred by news of the outbreak of war between England and the Netherlands, New Netherland Director General Peter Stuyvesant threatens actions against the Connecticut and New Haven settlements

1653   Cromwell dissolves the Rump Parliament

1653   The Army Council summons a constituent assembly of 144 hand-picked men to prepare a longer-term settlement of the nations of Britain and Ireland (July); referred to as the Nominated or Barebon's Parliament, the Assembly resigns power back into Cromwell's hands (Dec.); he is installed as Lord Protector under *The Instrument of Government*

1654   Harvard president Henry Dunster acknowledges opposition to the practice of infant baptism and resigns

1654   Oliver Cromwell responds to requests for aid from the New Haven colony and commissions Robert Sedgwick and John Leverett (both natives of New England serving in England) to lead an expedition to cooperate with New Englanders in the conquest of New Netherland. When the Anglo-Dutch war ends before the combined force is ready to attack, Sedgwick and Leverett use their force to capture Acadia from the French

1655   Failure of a major Royalist attempt to overthrow Cromwell (Penruddock's Rising); Cromwell appoints the Major Generals

1655   Cromwell dispatches army and naval forces to capture Hispaniola: they fail, but captures Jamaica instead

1656   Cromwell declares war on Spain and makes a treaty with France

1656   Persecution of the Quakers peaks in England with the public torture of James Nayler, convicted by Parliament of "horrid blasphemy"

1656   First Quakers arrive in Massachusetts and are banished

1657   Cromwell declines a parliamentary invitation to become King but accepts a revised paper constitution – *The Humble Petition and Advice*

1657   Ministerial assembly with representatives from Massachusetts and Connecticut recommends what will become known as the Half-Way Covenant, which would allow the baptism of children whose parents were baptized but not full members of the church

1658   Savoy Conference, gathering of Congregationalist clergy in England, adopts *Savoy Declaration of Church and Order*, designed to be the basis for a Congregational national establishment

1658   Death of Cromwell; Richard Cromwell succeeds him as Lord Protector; Richard recalls the Long Parliament and resigns his position

1658   Troubled by reappearance of Quakers, Massachusetts enacts the death penalty for Quakers who return to the colony after banishment

1659   Collapse of the English Republic as political and military leaders struggle with each other for supremacy; the year ends in anarchy

1659   John Eliot's *The Christian Commonwealth,* expressing antimonarchical principles, published in England

1659   William Robinson and Marmaduke Stevenson hanged in Boston under the terms of the 1658 law against Quakers

1660   The General in charge of the Army in Scotland, George Monck, moves south at the head of his troops, occupies London, and calls for free elections; the resulting Parliament (the Convention) recalls Charles II unconditionally upon his issuance of the Declaration from Breda (promising to leave all disputed issues to be settled by Parliament); Restoration of Charles II; Individuals exempted from general pardon for their role in the trial and execution of Charles I (regicides) are tried and executed, including former New Englanders Hugh Peter and Henry Vane. Other regicides seek refuge in New England

1660   Mary Dyer, former "Antinomian" and Quaker, executed in Boston

1661	Savoy conference between Anglicans and Presbyterians fails to produce compromise on forms of worship
1661	Newly elected Parliament seeks a more partisan Cavalier and Anglican settlement
1661	Execution of Quakers in Massachusetts halted by order of Charles II
1661	Massachusetts general Court censures John Eliot for the sentiments expressed in his *Christian Commonwealth*
1662	Act of Uniformity restores Anglican church order and worship "lock, stock, and barrel" and imposes civil disabilities on dissenters; Charles II's attempts to secure liberty for tender consciences by perogative action stymied
1662	Michael Wigglesworth's *Day of Doom* published
1662	Charles II establishes the Royal Society by charter
1662	John Winthrop Jr. obtains a royal charter for the colony of Connecticut that absorbs the New Haven colony into Connecticut
1662	New England Synod of 1662 endorses the Half-Way Covenant and recommends it to the churches of the region, sparking grass-roots debates in many congregations
1663	Rhode Island receives a royal charter
1663	Group of Massachusetts puritans accept an invitation to settle in the Cape Fear area of the Carolinas
1664	First Conventicle Act lays penalties on those attending illegal Protestant services other than those established by law in the Act of Uniformity

1664	Charles II dispatches royal commission to settle boundary disputes and investigate charges against the various New England governments
1665	Great Plague hits London
1665	Five Mile Act bans the clergy who resigned or were ejected in 1662 from living in or even visiting their former parishes
1666	Great Fire of London destroys much of the city
1666	Third Dutch War. English fleet destroyed by the Dutch in the battle of the Medway
1667	Publication of John Milton's *Paradise Lost*
1670	Second Conventicle Act increases penalties on those attending illegal Protestant services other than those established by law in the Act of Uniformity
1672	Charles II issues the Declaration of Indulgence permitting Dissenters to hold licenses to worship outside the Anglican Church
1673	Parliament pressures the Kind to withdraw his promises of religious toleration and passes the First Test Act, imposing new and stringent oaths designed to prevent Catholics from remaining in public office
1675	Wampanoags under Metacom (King Philip) attack Swansea, initiating King Philip's War in New England
1676	Losses from Indian attacks continue to be heavy (estimates of ten percent of the population), but Metacom is killed and the war ends in southern New England.

Fighting continues in northern New England. Christian Indians interned on islands in Boston harbor. Mary Rowlandson taken captive

1676 Fire destroys much of Boston

1676 Edward Randolph arrives in Boston as special agent of the crown to report on enforcement of the Navigation Acts; he exploits divisions in the colony to build a faction favorable to crown intervention in New England affairs

1677 Marriage of James, Duke of York's elder daughter Mary to William of Orange, Stadtholder of the Netherlands

1677 Massachusetts buys out the rights of the Gorges heirs and incorporate what is now Maine into its jurisdiction

1678 Publication of John Bunyan's *Pilgrim's Progress*

1678 Titus Oates's revelations trigger the Popish Plot hysteria that will include efforts to exclude James Stuart (a Catholic) from the succession

1679 Exclusion Crisis peaks and breaks

1679 Reforming Synod in New England adopts the *Savoy Declaration* and urges a thorough reformation of morals and recommitment to the ideals of the founders

1680 New Hampshire separated from Massachusetts and made a royal colony

1681 Charles's opponents overreach themselves; popular concern about the Popish Plot wanes, leading to "the Tory reaction"

1681 Massachusetts General Court grants permission to Boston Baptists to worship in their own meetinghouse

1683 The Rye House Plot, an assassination plot, fails and cost the lives of several republican opponents of the regime, including Algernon Sidney

1684 Complaints against Massachusetts from Edward Randolph and others leads to the abrogration of the Massachusetts charter

1685 Joseph Dudley appointed acting governor of Massachusetts, New Hampshire, and Maine

1685 Death of Charles II and accession of James II; rebellions of the Duke of Monmouth in southwest England and the Earl of Argyll in southwest Scotland were brutally suppressed

1686 James seeks full religious and civil equality for Catholics; Anglicans protest and refuse to cooperate

1686 Royal government creates the Dominion of New England to incorporate the former colonies of Massachusetts (including Maine), New Hampshire, Plymouth, and Rhode Island. The Dominion eliminates the popular basis of government that had existed in most of these colonies. Sir Edmund Andros is appointed Governor General of the Dominion

1687 Connecticut is incorporated into the Dominion of New England (New York and New Jersey will be added in 1688). Andros antagonizes colonists by arbitrary rule, challenges to property titles, promotion of the Church of England, and the levying of taxes. Rev. John Wise is imprisoned for opposition to taxes levied without legislative involvement

1687   James attempts to win over the "Whig" opposition by appointing some to office, and begins a campaign to pack Parliament with supporter of religious liberty. James issues Declaration of Indulgence, attempting to establish toleration by royal prerogative

1687   Publication of Isaac Newton's *Philosophia naturalis principia mathematica*

1688   Seven Bishops tried for claiming the King's Declaration of Indulgence was illegal; they are acquitted of the charge of seditious libel

1688   Increase Mather eludes the Dominion authorities and sails for England to present to James II the colonists grievances against the Dominion

1688   James and his wife have a son after eleven years of marriage, opening up the prospect of a Catholic dynasty

1688   The Glorious Revolution; William of Orange invades England with the support of many Protestants and supporters of parliamentary rights. James flees to France

1689   Convention parliament declares that James's flight is an act of abdication, that the throne is vacant, and invites William and Mary to be joint rulers

1689   The Convention parliament passes the Bill of Rights

1689   Toleration Act grants rights of free religious assembly but no civil equality to Protestant Dissenters

1689   News of the Glorious Revolution leads to uprising in Boston that topples the Dominion of New England. Andros imprisoned

1689   John Locke's influential *Letter Concerning Toleration* published

1689   New England expedition under Sir William Phipps captures the French fortress of Port Royal on the coast of Canada

1690   Connecticut charter restored; Increase Mather lobbies for restoration of Massachusetts charter

1690   King William brings to an end the attempt of James II to regain control of Ireland by his victory at the Battle of the Boyne

1691   William and Mary grant Massachusetts a new charter that restores the popular basis of the General Court but provided for an appointed royal governor. The new charter incorporates the old Plymouth colony into the boundaries of Massachusetts. Increase Mather secures the appointment of Sir William Phipps as the first royal governor

1691   Increase Mather aids in securing a temporary alliance of English Congregationalists and Presbyterians signified by the signing of the Heads of Agreement

1692   Witchcraft episode in Salem Village and surrounding parts of Essex County, Massachusetts

1693   Rhode Island charter restored

1693   Cotton Mather's *Wonders of the Invisible World* published

1699   Publication of the Brattle Street
       Manifesto marks the appearance of a new
       liberal faction in New England Puritanism
       led by William and Thomas Brattle, John
       Leverett, and Rev. Benjamin Coleman of
       the Brattle Street Church

1700   Increase Mather forced out of the
       Harvard presidency

1701   Establishment of Yale College in
       Connecticut by orthodox clergy

1702   Cotton Mather's *Magnalia Christi
       Americana* published

Ideas, Events, and Issues

A

Adiaphora

A Greek word meaning "indifferent." In the context of the Reformation, it was used in a technical sense. Certain religious beliefs and practices were prescribed in the scriptures, but others were "indifferent," in the sense that they were matters over which believers could disagree without offending God. Early in the sixteenth century, Martin Luther and Erasmus engaged in a spirited debate over whether certain doctrines and actions were essential to Christian belief or were indifferent.

In England, the concept that certain matters were indifferent was present from the early days of the Reformation. The argument could cut two ways. During the late Elizabethan and early Stuart period, puritans argued that since some of the prescribed practices of the church (wearing vestments and signing with the cross in baptism) were not defined as essential to Christianity, they were free to follow their own beliefs and practices. But during the reign of Charles I, the debate shifted. On the one hand, Richard Hooker argued that God's will needed to be interpreted on the basis of reason and experience as well as scripture, in the process limiting the range of practices that were truly indifferent. At the same time, other church authorities, while still conceding that many such matters were indifferent, argued that there was no reason for puritans not to be forced to perform as required in the interests of uniformity to the dictates of the monarch and the church and used this logic to insist on conformity to practices where diversity had previously been tolerated in practice.

See also: Nonconformity, Vestments
Further Reading
Bernard Verkamp, *The Indifferent Mean: Adiaphorism in the English Reformation to 1555* (Athens, OH, 1977).

Francis J. Bremer

An Admonition to the Parliament (June 1572)

A pamphlet written and printed, clandestinely, by two young London preachers, John Field and Thomas Wilcox. It was less an appeal to Parliament than an appeal beyond Parliament to the people. The parliament that had met in that summer and the earlier parliament of 1571 both had failed to give the Puritans what they wanted, a "further reformation" on their own radical and Presbyterian terms. The real strategy of the *Admonition* was revealed when a witness in Star Chamber (twenty years later) reported Field as having said: "Seeing we cannot compass these things by suit or dispute, it is the multitude and people that must bring the discipline to pass which we desire." That was inflammatory. Archbishop Matthew Parker had passed sentence on the Scottish Reformation: "God keep us from such visitation as Knox have attempted in Scotland; the people to be orderers of things." The populism of the *Admonition* explains why it was taken so seriously, why there was a royal proclamation against a book "rashly set forth and by stealth imprinted," and why the authors spent the next year in prison. John Whitgift, the future archbishop, ignored advice to regard the *Admonition* as a nine days' wonder and wrote a book against it, which led to the definitive controversy between Elizabethan conformists and nonconformists, Whitgift versus Thomas Cartwright, known as the Admonition Controversy.

Whether Parliament or "the people" was the intended target, the *Admonition* could not have been more direct, in tone as well as content. "You should now . . . with all your main and might endeavor that Christ . . . might rule and reign in his church by the scepter of his word only." The little book consisted of two parts, the "Admonition" proper, and "A view of popish abuses yet remaining in the English Church, for the which godly ministers have refused to subscribe." When Archbishop Matthew Parker's chaplain interviewed Field and Wilcox in the Fleet prison and complained of "the bitterness of the style," the relatively emollient Wilcox pointed to Field, who was happy to admit that he was responsible for that. "As God hath his Moses, so he hath his Elijah. . . . We have used gentle words too long, and we perceive they have done no good. The wound groweth desperate. . . . It is no time to blench, nor to sew cushions under men's elbows, or to flatter them in their sins." Field was the leading Bolshevik, the Lenin of the further reformation that was destined never to be, as much opposed to the moderate Mensheviks as to the bishops.

This role of his suggests that it was Field who wrote the "view of popish abuses," the more stylistically vivid of the two essays. It is here that we read about such "abuses" as women arriving in church to be married bareheaded, with bagpipes and fiddlers and "divers other heathenish toys," making a "maygame" of marriage. "In all their order of service there is no edification . . . but confusion, they toss the Psalms in most places like tennis balls." As for the people, they were all over the place. "Now the people sit and now they stand up. . . . When Jesus is named, then off goeth the cap and down goeth the knees, with such a scraping on the ground that they cannot hear a good while after." Field's contribution to the *Admonition* is a mile-

stone in the history of English satire, and the next milestone was to be the Presbyterian pamphlets known as the Marprelate tracts.

But Wilcox was responsible for the sentence that said it all. "May it therefore please your wisdoms to understand, that we in England are so far off from having a church rightly reformed, according to the prescript of God's word, that as yet we are not come to the outward face of the same." That was to go rather too far. In the three surviving copies of the first edition of the *Admonition,* someone's pen has altered "not" to "scarce," and the correction was made in print in the second edition. If the English church had not acquired even the outward trappings, the infrastructure, of a truly reformed church, then it was Babylon, not Zion, and it would be a necessity to leave it and find the true church somewhere else. That is what the Separatists did. But that was not Puritanism, which was defined by that "scarce." The Church of England of the Elizabethan Settlement was not a false church like the church of Rome. It was permissible, and indeed necessary, to work within it, to turn its scarcity into a rightful reformation.

Before 1572 was out, there was *A second admonition to the Parliament*, often attributed, probably mistakenly, to Thomas Cartwright, but, like many sequels, it proved a damp squib, a stodgy essay in Presbyterian ecclesiology that no one read, then or since. To compare it with the original *Admonition* is to be persuaded that John Field was a satirist who deserves to be compared with Jonathan Swift.

See also: John Field, Thomas Wilcox
Further Reading
Patrick Collinson, *The Elizabethan Puritan Movement* (London, 1967).

Patrick Collinson

Altar Policy

Altar was the name used in the medieval church to describe the table where the sacrament of the Eucharist was performed. The term reflected the view that the liturgical ceremony centered there, the sacrifice of the Mass, was a reenactment of Christ's sacrifice on the cross to atone for the sins of man.

The traditional placement of the altar and the related organization of the church structure were designed to strengthen that symbolic link, as well as to reflect the belief that in the sacrament the elements of bread and wine became the actual body and blood of Christ. As Protestants challenged the meaning of the Eucharist, altar policies became contested.

The traditional placement of the altar was on a raised platform at the eastern end of the church. In many cases it was elaborately decorated with canopy and reredos (a decorative screen behind and above the altar). There the priest would celebrate the sacrifice of the Mass. Because this sanctuary (sometimes referred to as the chancel) was viewed as the place where Christ was actually present in the church, it was seen as a place of special holiness and was often separated from the nave of the church, where the worshippers gathered by a chancel screen made of carved stone or wood. In some churches the screen supported a carved and painted crucifix with the figure of Christ on the cross surrounded by figures of St. John and the Virgin Mary. In these cases, the screen was referred to as a rood screen, *rood* being the Old English word for cross. The screen was generally solid, with lower panels painted with images of the twelve apostles, saints, martyrs, prophets, and occasionally kings. The screens had a central opening (often with doors or gates). The effect of the screens was to preserve the sanctity of the chancel and to heighten the mystery of the priest's actions, particularly his consecration of the bread and wine. Following that consecration, he would bring the wafers of unleavened bread to the faithful, who would kneel reverently to receive their savior. In most churches, side altars also existed, where priests could celebrate masses for special intentions, but it was the "high altar" in the chancel that was the center of the parish's religious worship.

English Protestants rejected the doctrine of transubstantiation and accordingly sought to rebuild their churches to reflect a new understanding of the Eucharist. Though the exact nature of the understanding of what happened in this sacrament continued to be contested, from the time of Thomas Cranmer, the first archbishop of Canterbury after Henry VIII's split with Rome, to the time of William Laud, the archbishop of Canterbury whose return to old customs helped bring about the Puritan Revolution and his own beheading (in 1641), the altar policies were designed to downplay the sacrificial implications of the Eucharist and to emphasize the communion between those "saints" (as they sometimes called themselves) who were receiving the sacrament in a way that evoked the gathering of Christ's disciples at the Last Supper, when the Eucharist was believed to have been instituted. The chancel was no longer seen as a uniquely holy place. Rood screens were to be torn down. The altar itself was either replaced by a simple table or relabeled as a Communion table. Though in some churches the table remained in the chancel, Reformers preferred bringing it into the nave in the midst of the congregation. In either case, parishioners were to gather round the table for the distribution and consumption of ordinary bread. These new policies also were designed to demystify the sacrament, and many Reformers combined their altar policies with demands that the minister (no longer called a priest) should be divested of the elaborate ritual garb that was worn by Catholic clergy in presiding over the sacraments. Reformers also challenged the practice of kneeling at the Communion, believing that it symbolized the belief in Christ's actual presence in the bread being offered to them. Although the 1552 Book of Common Prayer did allow kneeling, a long explanation—referred to as the "black rubric"—was issued insisting that any kneeling was not to be interpreted as if "any adoration is done or ought to be done, either unto the sacramental bread or wine thereby bodily received, or unto any real and essential presence there being of Christ's natural flesh and blood."

For the most part, the reform position became the common practice of the Elizabethan church. Rood screens did disappear, and parishioners gathered around movable communion tables to receive the elements—more often than not sitting down. Some have argued that these changes was part of a puritan effort to elevate the importance of preaching and that in their parishes the pulpit rather than the communion table became the focus of worship, but this argument risks overlooking the fact that the Reformers clearly cared for and promoted the sacrament of the Eucharist.

These practices came to be challenged in the seventeenth century by a group of Church of England theologians and clergy often referred to as Laudians or anti-Calvinists. Concerned about restoring the dignity of the altar and citing its defilement by dogs and other creatures in its open location, William Laud and others restored altars to the east end of churches and ordered that they be railed in. But this restoration had as much to do with a desire to restore the "beauty of holiness" and in particular to make communion the centerpiece of worship and to reintroduce some of the ceremonial trappings of the pre-Reformation church. Puritans pointed to these new altar policies as evidence that Laud and his fellow anti-Calvinists were attempting to move the Church of England off its Elizabethan moorings and to return to popish practices. It is not surprising that with the outbreak of England's Civil War there was a new burst of iconoclasm that involved the tearing down of the hated altar rails.

See also: Anti-Calvinism, Book of Common Prayer, Vestments
Further Reading
Horton Davies, *Worship and Theology in England: From Andrewes to Baxter and Fox, 1603–1690* (Princeton, 1975); Horton Davies, *Worship and Theology in England: From Cranmer to Hooker, 1534–1603* (Princeton, 1970); Nicholas Tyacke, *Anti-Calvinists: The Rise of English Arminianism, c. 1590–1640* (Oxford, 1987).

Francis J. Bremer

Anabaptists

The Anabaptists were not only the radical vanguard of the Puritan Revolution in England, but the radical extreme of the European Reformation. Like puritans, they despised ecclesiastical excesses and tithes, and insisted on the abolition of the Mass and the right to choose their own preachers. They were united by their common insistence upon the invalidity of infant baptism and, on the continent, extended Martin Luther's revival of faith to a revival of piety, holiness, and "moral improvement": in this respect, they anticipated the puritan movement in England, where their commitment to reform gave radical impetus to the movement in the 1640s, and in America, where puritan colonists tolerated their baptismal differences because they also supported congregational church government.

On the Continent

The Anabaptist movement originated amid the zeal of the Reformation and made the most radical efforts to revitalize and renew Christianity by finding alternatives to both Rome and Reformed centers such as Zürich and Geneva. Catholic apologists accused Anabaptists of being reforming extremists; Lutheran and Zwinglian Reformers accused Anabaptists of deforming the broader Reformation. On the continent, to be an Anabaptist was to be a *Schwärmer* (fanatic), and their characteristic opposition to infant baptism and advocacy of baptism as a mark of faith, confession, and congregational membership caused them to be known as *Täuferen* (baptizers) or *Wiedertäuferen* (rebaptizers), which became in Latin *Anabaptistae* and in English "Anabaptists." These latter terms were derived from the Greek word for baptism. The prefix *ana-* (Greek for "re-") was added because men and women were baptized as true believers when they were adults and were therefore "rebaptized" (if they had been baptized before), though Anabaptists themselves insisted that any infant baptism was invalid because the New Testament, which superseded the Old, made no mention of it. Martin Luther, leader of the Reformation in Germany, justified infant baptism on the grounds of "hidden" (or temporarily "sleeping") faith; Martin Bucer, another important German leader, saw it as a parental pledge of a good Christian upbringing; Heinrich Bullinger, a Swiss Reformer, said that it was justified on the same grounds as the circumcision of infants mandated in the Old Testament.

Anabaptists, however, were united in their rigorous adherence to the New Testament, with its omission of infant baptism, and their subsequent refusal to admit validity of such baptism.

There were several Continental movements of this kind: men such as Conrad Grebel and Felix Manz in Zürich; Thomas Müntzer in Central Germany, whose ideas passed into the South with Hans Hut; and Melchior Hoffmann around Strasbourg, whose own strain of Anabaptism entered Lower Germany. Amid the disaffection of the Peasants' Wars, these movements, which originated among dissatisfied, literate Reformers, spread quickly into ever more uneducated, eccentric, and aggressively radical parts of the population. Baptisms not only took place in rivers and ponds, but also in taverns while even the baptized were drunk. In 1534, Anabaptists in Münster took control of the town (albeit legally) and introduced common ownership of goods and polygamy, executed their opponents, and exiled those who would not be rebaptized. In the 1540s in Central Germany, the Bloodfriends practiced *Christerie*, ritual sexual union, as an expression of Christian community. Anabaptists were persecuted ferociously: by the 1550s, Anabaptism had been eradicated from Central Germany and had splintered into numerous, exiled factions, which sought refuge elsewhere. Many gravitated toward Holland, from which they sailed to England.

In England

Anabaptists began arriving in England during the early 1530s, before a "puritan" movement emerged. They arrived upon ground that had already been prepared by native Lollardy (the fourteenth century reform movement in the church led by John Wyclif, the ideas of which still circulated underground). Anabaptists were not persecuted so rigorously in England as on the Continent and were not as denominationally distinct as on the European mainland. They campaigned against corruption in the English church rather than advocating their separation from it by the rite of rebaptism. The first royal decree against Anabaptists was issued in 1535, after news of Münster's seizure reached England. Several executions forced Anabaptists underground, to emerge as embodiments of the radi-

cal potential of puritanism during the mid-seventeenth century, when puritan radicalism could no longer be contained by the political and parliamentary advances made by Presbyterianism. The hostile label "Anabaptist" was used to describe a new generation of English sectaries who represented the sharp end of the puritan movement.

Accordingly, Robert Baillie entitled his refutation of the movement *Anabaptism, the True Fountaine of Independency, Brownisme, Antinomy, Familisme and Most of the Other Errours, Which for the Time Doe Trouble the Church of England, Unsealed* (1647). Many heresies of the 1640s were attributed to Anabaptists; Anabaptism was viewed as the "original" heresy. The atrocities of Münster were never forgotten and continually identified as representing the kind of threat posed by seventeenth-century Anabaptists. Daniel Featley identified fifteen kinds of Anabaptist on the frontispiece of his *Dippers Dipt. or, The Anabaptists Ducked and Plunged Over Head and Eares, at a Disputation in Southwarke* (1645); a translation of Frederick Spanheim's *England's Warning by Germany's Woe: or, An Historical Narration, of the Originall, Progresse, Tenets, Names, and Severall Sects of the Anabaptists in Germany, and the Low Countries* (1646) threatened to turn Continental sectaries into an English menace. The translation identified forty-four kinds of Anabaptist according to their leaders, places and cities of origin or habitation, behavior, and beliefs, and attributed to them a medley of anti-Trinitarian, Christological, and soteriological errors. In the early 1640s, the term *rantizing* (from the Greek *rantidzein*, "to sprinkle") was used to mean baptismal sprinkling (rather than submersion), and the word was related to the label applied to some of the most notorious radicals of the Puritan Revolution (though "sprinkling" was used by orthodox Protestants in infant baptisms), several of whom (such as Laurence Clarkson and Abiezer Coppe) were Baptists before turning "Ranter."

The origins of a distinctly English form of Anabaptism lie in a congregation that left England for Holland in 1608 and split into two groups. One group was influenced by Dutch Arminians and rejected the Calvinist conviction that Christ died for only the elect, and adopted the belief that all had the capacity to be saved. This group, upon returning to England in 1612, became known as General Baptists. Others refused to abandon their commitment to Calvinism and became known as Particular Baptists. Particular Baptists were a larger, looser group who could try to present themselves as moderate, orthodox Calvinists; General Baptists, however, laid greater emphasis upon human perfectibility (and thus accountability) and the goodness and equality of mankind. They provided a platform upon which the Levellers later built. Both kinds flourished in London and the Midlands. General Baptists were especially strong in Kent, Lincolnshire, and the Chilterns, where Lollardy had thrived; Particular Baptists predominated in areas of traditional puritan influence such as the West Country. The success of local Baptist congregations, however, largely relied upon local proselytizers such as Thomas Collier in the West Country, Samuel Oates and Henry Denne in Kent and the Midlands, and Thomas Lambe in London. Many Anabaptists prospered in the Parliamentarian armies of the English Civil War, and the Commonwealth tolerated them by abolishing compulsory attendance at parish churches. By the Restoration there were more than 250 Baptist churches, some 60 percent of them of the Particular kind.

In America

It was from England that Anabaptists reached America and influenced those there. The first president of Harvard College, Henry Dunster (a native of Lancashire, England) was forced to resign his position in 1654 when he refused to allow his newborn son to be baptized or to keep his Baptist convictions to himself. But the puritans of the New World were bringing the issue of infant baptism to the forefront of religious debate themselves. Membership of many churches was limited to those who could testify before the congregation to their belief that they were members of the elect, confident in themselves that their pre-elective behavior was reprehensible compared to their then current conduct. But as more and more individuals were brought up within these morally irreproachable communities, fewer and fewer had a sinful past against which they could measure their new behavior and thus be convinced of their election.

In 1662, a synod approved the Half-Way Covenant, which sought to modify what was known as "the New England way" by allowing for the baptism of children who had only one grandparent in full church membership. In adulthood, such individuals would retain partial membership, even if they were unsure of their own election. Each congregation was required to consider the issue, and many suggested that baptism was turning into a means of salvation rather than a seal of grace. Though this was a question of church polity rather than the nature of baptism, Baptists were indeed tolerated in New England as long as they did not seek to gather converts. Henry Dunster, for example, was treated far more civilly than Samuel Gorton the Seeker or Anne Hutchinson the reputed antinomian.

During the 1640s and 1650s, the twenty or thirty Baptists in the Massachusetts colony were never banished, despite the General Court's enactment of a penalty of banishment in 1642, because many non-Baptists were sympathetic to the Baptist cause. This law was enforced only in the 1660s, when Baptists attempted to establish their own church. Indeed, Baptists appeared to be defending the purity of the sacraments in the disputes over the Half-Way Covenant, and Baptists themselves shared the puritan congregationalism and saintliness of their fellow colonists.

Other Baptists in the Old World were encouraged to join their brethren in the New. One follower of Melchior Hoffman in Holland, Menno Simons, had created a further division in the movement by insisting upon the "ban" (that is, the practice of shunning, or "banning" those who fell away from the faith). Those of his followers who reached England had pretty much abandoned this practice, but others, led by one Jacob Ammann, had not. Both of these groups reached America in the late seventeenth century, settling first in Germantown and later moving to Schuylkill and Lancaster Counties, then to Virginia and the Carolinas. Today, the Mennonite Church remains in America, and Ammann's "Amish" still practice the exclusive introversion of the "ban" that allows these latter-day puritans to maintain the purity of their church.

See also: Ranters, Sects
Further Reading
Claus-Peter Clasen, *Anabaptism: A Social History* (Ithaca, NY, 1972); Hans Jürgen-Goertz, *The Anabaptists,* 2nd ed., trans. Trevor Johnson (London, 1996; first published in German, 1980); J. F. McGregor, "The Baptists: The Fount of All Heresy," in J. F. McGregor and B. Reay, eds. *Radical Religion in the English Revolution* (Oxford1984), pp. 23–63; James M. Stayer, *Anabaptists and the Sword* 2nd ed. (Lawrence, KS, 1976); George Huntston Williams, *The Radical Reformation,* 3rd ed. (Kirksville, MO, 1992).

Simon Dyton

Angels

It is curious that, though seventeenth-century Puritans lived in a world of wonders, a world filled with ghosts, devils, portents, signs, and monstrous births, earthly visits from heavenly angels were so rare. Puritans were hardly stodgy churchgoers, wedded mechanically to theological beliefs and practices with little sense of the supernatural. On the contrary, they attuned themselves to the nuances and implications of their natural surroundings and endowed them with supernatural power. Wonders and providences were God's messages. Puritans could explain and order their lives by observing and attending to such communications, which conveyed God's designs. Earthquakes, droughts, floods, thunderstorms, comets: they could explain all of these unusual occurrences as the mysterious manipulations of God. Likewise, *maleficia*—iniquitous acts magically perpetrated, implicitly or explicitly, with Satan's aid—represented the extraordinary distortion of the natural world by the devil.

But not all wonders were considered equal. Miracles seldom occurred, for example; seventeenth-century Protestants believed that the age of miracles had ceased in the biblical period, and they relied instead on the centrality of the text of Holy Scripture. Neither were visits by angels or direct revelations from God himself common. In the seventeenth century, Puritans looked to God's providences for knowledge and guidance, but they drew a distinction between these wonders, which they saw as emanating directly from God, and miracles, as in Roman Catholic tradition, which they interpreted as human or diabolical manipulations, not the work of God's divine goodness.

The revolutionary Swiss cleric John Calvin had emphasized the centrality of God in heaven and disparaged the medieval notion of angels' significance. In English Calvinist circles, not surprisingly, angels appeared infrequently in the lives or writings of either ministers or laypeople, though certainly angels remained part of the biblical panoply. Puritans worried about the fate of their souls after death and searched constantly for providential signs that would reveal to them God's final decree, but surprisingly their quest did not invite the appearance of benevolent angels who might have foretold their future. In fact, ministers and laity alike were much more apt to interpret providential signs negatively, as signs of God's displeasure. The rare angel appearance was regarded with skepticism, especially if received by a woman. For ministers, women's encounters with angels in the seventeenth century were suspect, probably delusions conjured by the evil angel, Satan, not visitations authorized by God.

By the Great Awakening in New England during the 1730s and 1740s, angel sightings became a more common feature of believers' writings. Angels appeared to people particularly to tell them about their future following death. These messengers from God—with their happy news of assurance—no longer carried the same negative connotations they had assumed in seventeenth-century New England. Frequent angel sightings suggest that an increased sense of access to the supernatural as a means of knowing one's ultimate destiny must be considered a part of the trend toward a popularization of religion in the eighteenth and nineteenth centuries. Angels increasingly signified and confirmed ordinary people's intimate and favorable relationship with the divine and affirmed the certainty of their salvation, a certainty that would have been anathema in the seventeenth-century Puritan world.

See also: Providence
Further Reading
David D. Hall, *Worlds of Wonder, Days of Judgment: Popular Religious Belief in Early New England* (New York, 1989); Robert Bruce Mullin, *Miracles and the Modern Religious Imagination* (New Haven, CT, 1996).

Elizabeth Reis

Antapologia

Antapologia, or a Full Answer to the Apologeticall Narration, published in July 1644, was a lengthy, detailed, and intemperate response to the manifesto produced by the leading Congregationalists of the Westminster Assembly the previous January. Fully ten times as long as the work it attacks, *Antapologia* was written by the zealous Presbyterian London lecturer Thomas Edwards, author also of *Reasons Against the Independant Government of Particular Congregations* (1641). In the interim, Edwards had very reluctantly accepted a 1641 agreement to forgo public controversy over church government, an agreement he now felt had been provocatively broken by the *Apologeticall Narration.* Edwards's work lacked the theological elaboration of other replies by Adam Stewart or Alexander Forbes; it was rather a lively challenge to the Apologists' self-presentation as moderate followers of a middle way between "Brownism" (the separatist position named after Robert Browne that called for absolute congregational autonomy) and Presbyterianism, and to their account of their church practice in their Dutch exile. Edwards provided long accounts of disorders in Arnhem's exile church and of disputes between William Bridge and Sidrach Simpson in Rotterdam, using these to argue that the congregational church way was no better than schism and that it offered no effective barrier to error and separation.

Antapologia's vivid "stories" were based on oral testimony, particularly from William Bridge, an old acquaintance from Cambridge, and printed sources, notably letters. Edwards's work is widely used as a source for the early conferences and debates over church government among English Puritans. Edwards himself, who had suffered for his nonconformity to Laudian ceremonial, did not accept that it was opposition to the ceremonies that prompted the Dutch exile, arguing that the Apologists were in fact moving to a separatist position. He bitterly rejected their account of themselves as suffering victims of oppression; for Edwards, harassment at home was a harder fate than living in "safety, plenty, pompe and ease" in Holland. *Antapologia* also burns with Edwards's anger at what he saw as the arrogant self-righteousness of Independents who refused to communicate with Reformed London parish churches in the 1640s. *Antapologia* made Edwards famous as an opponent of "Independency," which he saw as inevitably opening the door to sectarianism and horrifying error; it helped make possible his thoroughgoing assault on the "errors of the time," *Gangraena.*

See also: Thomas Edwards, *Gangraena,* Independency
Further Reading
Ann Hughes, *Gangraena and the Struggle for the English Revolution* (Oxford, 2004).

Ann Hughes

Anti-Calvinism

Anti-Calvinism is the term used by historian Nicholas Tyacke to describe the movement to alter the theological and liturgical character of the late Elizabethan church. It came to be identified with a group of bishops who came to the fore in early Stuart England, including William Laud, Richard Neile, John Cosin, and Richard Montague. Contemporaries attacked this movement as Arminianism, but though it was related to the efforts of the Dutch theologian Jacobus Arminius, none of the key figures can be shown to be true disciples of Arminius. The other common term for the movement, *Laudianism,* places too much emphasis on the role of William Laud.

Starting in the late sixteenth century a reaction developed against the dogmatic rigidity of the way Calvin's teachings had been interpreted by some of

Circa 1635, a cartoon showing the Archbishop of Canterbury, William Laud (1573–1645), at the dining table with a doctor and a lawyer. The inscription refers to the Archbishop choosing a meal of the ears of Puritans in preference to food fit for a prince. (Hulton Archive/Getty Images)

his disciples, most notably Theodore Beza, who stressed double and absolute predestination (the beliefs that God predestined those to go to hell as well as heaven and that these decrees were unchangeable). Double predestination had been endorsed by leading figures in the Elizabethan church, including archbishops John Whitgift and Richard Bancroft. One of the first challenges to this orthodoxy was launched by William Barrett, who challenged predestination at Cambridge in 1595. Having intervened against Barrett, Whitgift affirmed the Calvinist stance in the Lambeth Articles, a set of rulings that did not, however, become the official doctrine of the church. Others followed

in Barrett's path, however, some accepting the views of Arminius, others developing their own critique of predestinarian doctrines.

Closely related to the growing dissatisfaction with aspects of Calvinist doctrine was a suspicion of the implied egalitarianism of the Genevan system. Anti-Calvinists thus generally sought to modify some of the starkness of Calvinist doctrine and to assert hierarchical principles of church government. Furthermore, some sought to restore what William Laud called the beauty of holiness, reversing some of the liturgical reforms of the previous decades. While each of those whom historians refer to as anti-Calvinists had his own particular interests and agenda, they formed a party that sought to move the church in new directions that were seen by the orthodox as leading toward the reinstatement of discredited Catholic beliefs and practice.

These up-and-coming churchmen argued strongly in support of James I's claims for authority, and they played skillfully upon his suspicions of puritans. But there was no moving James from his Calvinist roots, and the delegation he sent to the Synod of Dort endorsed that body's rejection of the teachings of Arminius. Seeking to quiet the developing controversy, he forbade preaching on the doctrine of predestation, though many felt that this prohibition benefited the revisionists. Charles I was more sympathetic to the program urged upon him by Laud and his fellow bishops, and it was in his reign that concerns about the spread of "Arminianism" reached their peak.

See also: Jacobus Arminius, William Laud, Arminianism, Predestination, Synod of Dort
Further Reading
Julian Davies, *Caroline Captivity of the Church: Charles I and the Remoulding of Anglicanism, 1625–1641* (Oxford, 1992); Nicholas Tyacke, *Anti-Calvinists: The Rise of English Arminianism, c. 1590–1640* (Oxford, 1987); Nicholas Tyacke, *Aspects of English Protestantism, c. 1530–1700* (Manchester, Eng, 2001); Peter White, "The Rise of Arminianism Reconsidered," *Past & Present* 101 (1983), 34–54.

Francis J. Bremer

Antichrist

The implacable enemy of Christ and the harbinger of the end of the world. The concept of Antichrist owes much to the feverish imagery of biblical prophecy: for example, in the Book of Daniel, especially chapter 7 (which describes the battle of the "little horn" against the saints) or in the Book of Revelation, especially chapters 12–14 (which describe the battle between the archangel Michael and a seven-headed dragon, the rise of a seven-headed beast out of the sea, and the fall of the wicked city of Babylon). Pre-Reformation exegeses of these biblical passages identify the antichristian enemy as Satan.

Antichrist took on new and specific identities in the English reformations. The brief heyday of reforming Protestantism under Edward VI had given way to the Marian persecution so celebrated in the many revised Elizabethan editions of John Foxe's *Actes and Monuments.* The fragile state of Protestantism's subsequent reestablishment under Elizabeth, along with the political threat posed by the militant Catholicism of Spain and the papal excommunication of the queen, merely confirmed the Foxe-schooled ardor of English Protestants who considered their church purified by the blood of martyrs.

Little wonder, then, that the first half century of post-Reformation discourse (as befits the impatient, dangerous, and apocalyptic tenor of the times) is one of almost routine discussion of the evils and threats of a personalized religious enemy, and we find bishops and clergy of unimpeachable conformity and sobriety denouncing Rome as Babylon and the Pope as Antichrist with impunity throughout the last half of the sixteenth century. Revelation chapters 12 and 13, for example, are explained in the margins of the highly influential Geneva Bible (1560) as visions wherein "is declared how the Church which is compassed about by Jesus Christ the son of righteousness is persecuted of Antichrist." A broadside ballad of the period wittily explained: "The Pope his [Satan's] Vicar commands all estates/Kings, Emperors, and Potentates/And turns his power to furious tyranny/Against that Christ and all his company/And by his rage they now abide affliction/He's *Antichrist* without all contradiction" (*A True and Plaine Genealogy or Pedigree of Antichrist*, 1561–1562).

The early seventeenth century, however, witnessed the secure tenure of Protestantism in England after a century of Tudor vacillations, the cessation of Anglo-Spanish hostilities, the desire of James I to maintain diplomatic relations with Catholic countries, and the replacement of the Geneva Bible with the less provocatively glossed Authorized Version. Association of the Pope with Antichrist (and, indeed, the apocalyptic impulse altogether) was on the wane in the language of mainstream Protestantism in England. But the denunciation of the papal Antichrist continued among the "hotter sort of Protestants." By the early seventeenth century, the labeling of things as "antichristian" or persons as "Antichrist" was considered so characteristic of puritan culture that playwrights like Ben Jonson could parody such turns of phrase on the Jacobean stage: in *Bartholomew Fair* (1614), for example, the puritan Zeal-of-the-Land Busy addresses a puppet as "Dagon," defies a tray of gingerbread as the "merchandise of Babylon," and denigrates Smithfield Market as "the seat of the beast."

The language of Antichrist, delivered in earnest, may be said to have reached an apogee in the 1650s, as the experience of the English Civil Wars, the execution of Charles I, and the unprecedented and revolutionary experience of the Interregnum fuelled increasingly luxuriant chiliastic imaginations. As the discredited Rump Parliament gave way to the Cromwellian Protectorate, what was once labeled an indiscriminate puritanism continued its fragmentation into myriad radical sects. Of these the Quakers and the Fifth Monarchists may be said to be the most enthusiastic and prolific wielders of the language of Antichrist. Their writings record a raging disappointment that the reign of the saints was not instituted after the fall of the Caroline government and a profound disillusionment with Cromwell's rule. Having once identified Charles I with the Beast spoken of in prophetic scripture, Fifth Monarchists now cast Oliver Cromwell in that unenviable leading role in their ongoing apocalyptic drama. The language of these extreme sectarians may have been as metaphoric as it was martial, but it was sufficient to frighten London and dismay less radical but nonetheless godly English Protestants.

The most skillful and memorable denunciations of Antichrist in this period were penned by John Milton, whose own fervent belief in the cause of godly revolution led him to denounce its enemies, wherever he found them, as agents of Satan. In *Paradise Lost,* Milton found the enemies of godly revolution most often in the Presbyterian party. But this epic poem generally resists such crude correspondence, and its well-known description of Satan's revolt can also be read as a more general indictment of the polemical as well as political confusion that characterize the period.

See also: Antipopery, Sects
Further Reading
Christopher Hill, *Antichrist in Seventeenth Century England* (London, 1971); David Loewenstein (according to COPAC, the online catalogue of 24 UK institutions), *Representing Revolution in Milton and his Contemporaries* (New York, 2001).

Lori Anne Ferrell

Antinomianism

Simply defined, antinomianism is a tendency to exalt the transformative power of free grace on believers and to denigrate, or even deny, the role and use of the Moral law as revealed in the Old Testament in the lives of converted Christians. The word was used by Luther to denounce Johann Agricola and his followers in the 1530s. In its Anglo-American context, the term *antinomian* (from the Latin *anti* and the Greek *nomos,* "law") was first widely used to describe a theological protest movement that evolved at the margins of the English puritan community in the early decades of the seventeenth century. Spearheaded by ministers such as John Eaton, Roger Brearley, and John Traske, this protest movement called into question prevailing forms of godly pastoral divinity, objecting to what antinomian ministers and their followers perceived as the legalism and overweening moral rigorism that had crept into puritan piety in the decades after the Reformation. The word *antinomian* was itself a term of abuse, and was rarely if ever accepted by those to whom it was applied. Yet it is clear that by the early 1630s, the various proponents of antilegal divinity and their lay followers had come to develop a relatively discrete core of beliefs and arguments, which set them apart from their godly opponents and furnished them with a sense of group identity or solidarity. Though England's antinomian enthusiasts did not constitute a sect or church in any formal way, they did form a clear and identifiable ideological grouping, one that was in certain respects pitted against the broader godly community and the English church as a whole.

Naturally, at the core of the antinomian style of divinity was the claim that the Moral Law, including the Ten Commandments, had little or no role to play in the salvation and lives of true believers. True Christians were in some sense free of the Law as it had been handed down at Sinai. Yet this claim represented only the most obvious manifestation of a more thoroughgoing critique of contemporary modes of religiosity. For in denying the role of the Law, antinomians were primarily denying the obsession with sanctification, fierce self-examination, and outward holiness that had come to characterize puritan practice as elaborated by famous pastoral theorists such as John Dod and Richard Rogers. Antinomians argued that this obsession with legal observance obscured the true Protestant message of free grace, which they claimed to be restoring against their pharisaical godly opponents. Thus, antinomians denounced the ubiquitous puritan habit of inferring grace from works. So likewise, they emphasized the absolute passivity of the believer, ascribing all agency in the process of salvation to God, while denigrating works of the Law as useless and deceptive.

On the face of it, then, antinomians positioned themselves as true bearers of Luther's message of free justification by Christ alone; the reality was more complicated. For in many ways, antinomian theorists pushed beyond the realms of acceptable Protestant theological argument. Thus, although they all emphasized the fact that true believers would do good works despite their freedom from the Law, their claims concerning the putative sinlessness of converted believers, their intense hostility toward the Mosaic Law, and their tendency to argue for a radical, indeed supernatural, transformation in those who had been touched by free grace, all went far beyond anything sanctioned by the canons of respectable Protestant divinity. In fact, at times, antinomian theorists were so extravagant in their claims for the effects of divine grace and the inhabitation of God's spirit that they implied that believers were in some sense rendered perfect, indeed divine, in this life.

Such extreme claims were partly a result of the fact that for all their declared allegiance to Luther, antinomian enthusiasts were often also under the influence of sectarian, mystical sources, including (but not limited to) the *Theologia Germanica* (a work of mystical meditation that had been discovered and published by Luther), the Familist writings of Hendrik Niclaes, and the writings of the German mystic Sebastian Franck. Thus, while English antinomianism was first and foremost a development that emerged out of mainstream Reformed divinity, the tradition as it had taken shape by 1630 or so was also indebted to subcurrents of radical Reformation theology, which had always been viewed with abhorrence by magisterial Protestant authorities.

The stage was thus set for fierce conflict with fellow Protestants. The first signs of widespread dispute over these issues can be traced to London in the late 1620s, when leading antinomians found themselves under attack from an unlikely coalition of mainstream puritans and Laudian churchmen. While this bout of contestation resulted in the temporary suppression of antinomian ideas in London, conflicts over grace and the Moral Law continued to trouble the puritan community, the most famous outbreak taking place in New England between 1636 and 1638. Here, in the well-known events usually known as the antinomian controversy, the supposedly antinomian doctrines espoused by John Cotton, John Wheelwright, Anne Hutchinson, and their followers threatened to tear the Massachusetts Bay Colony apart. Once again, the antilegal critique was suppressed, but only after a protracted series of debates, heated denunciations, and show trials, which saw Wheelwright, Hutchinson, and others banished from the colony. It was in the 1640s in England, however, that antinomianism emerged as a truly serious challenge to the integrity of the godly community.

In the newly uncensored civil war public sphere, the proscribed ideas of Eaton, Traske, and others could now be published, while eloquent spokesmen such as Tobias Crisp, John Simpson, and John Saltmarsh climbed into prominent pulpits to expound previously forbidden messages. In this way, antinomian theology (reworked and often radicalized) came to exert a powerful influence over some of the more startling forms of religiosity that emerged during the revolutionary decades. Many notorious radicals—William Walwyn, Gerard Winstanley, Lawrence Clarkson, and Anna Trapnel, to name a few—were directly influenced by versions of antilegal thought that had been worked out in the previous decades. Now, in the intellectual cauldron of the Civil War, such antinomian ideas were applied to new situations, producing corrosive critiques not just of mainstream piety, but of the basic ecclesiastical and political institutions of English society. While the Restoration replaced the lid on such radical intellectual experimentation, it did not entirely eradicate the antinomian strand from puritan culture—the Quakers appear to have carried on certain aspects of the antinomian tradition, while even less heterodox members of the Dissenting community continued to be plagued by occasional controversies over issues of grace and the Moral Law into the 1690s, when the so-called neo-nomian controversy, sparked by the republication of the sermons of Tobias Crisp, threatened once again to divide and fragment the English nonconformist community.

See also: Roger Brearley, Tobias Crisp, John Eaton, Anne Marbury Hutchinson, Grace, Sin

Further Reading

Theodore Dwight Bozeman, *The Precisianist Strain: Disciplinary Religion & Antinomian Backlash in Puritanism to 1638* (Chapel Hill, 2004); David Como, *Blown by the Spirit: Puritanism and the Emergence of an Antinomian Underground in Pre–Civil War England* (Stanford, 2004); Michael Winship, *Making Heretics* (Princeton, 2002).

David Como

Antipopery

Most early modern English people, upon hearing the word *Antichrist,* would have immediately understood it to refer to the pope; the "Whore of Babylon" was the Roman Catholic Church. So pervasive was anti-Catholic rhetoric in Reformation England, so vast the body of polemical writing devoted to the topic (over five hundred tracts from 1605 to 1625 alone), that some scholars are at a loss to explain why. In view of the tremendous amount of common ground between Protestantism and Catholicism—a fact systematically ignored during much of the period—antipopery can seem, as it does to some scholars, an irrational mystery, perhaps some sort of collective Protestant paranoia. In fact there are theological, psychological, and political factors that provide a coherent context, if not a complete explanation, of Reformation anti-Catholicism.

Theological and Psychological Factors

Sixteenth-century Protestantism, Calvinism in particular, depended upon and in turn fostered a binary sensibility. The cosmos was divided into watertight oppositional categories: the divine and the demonic; Christ and Antichrist; the elect and the reprobate; the true church and the false. In an age of rapid cultural change involving a shift from a medieval, communal way of thinking to a modern, individualist mentality, the self tended to be defined by what it opposed: the vast amount of fiercely polemical rhetoric during the period bears witness to the fact. For Protestants, whose faith had been born in opposition to the Church of Rome, membership in the true church continued to be defined by the symbolic rejection of all things Catholic—even if in fact many of the doctrines, liturgical practices, and devotional habits of the two groups were shared.

The doctrine of election, or the way it was perceived by many puritans, no doubt played a role in anti-Catholic rhetoric. As the sixteenth century progressed, the doctrine seems to have caused increasing amounts of anxiety among Calvinists, especially puritans. If the elect were a small minority whose membership had been determined by God from the beginning, how could one know whether one belonged among their number? Since a number of puritan writers identified doubt on this score as a sign of reprobation, assurance of election was essential; the stakes were high. The result was a tendency to conflate the visible body of puritan believers with the invisible body of the elect. It was the believer's own group that was saved, and it was easy to identify the opposition: the Church of Rome. The tendency, conscious or unconscious, was to see antipopery as divinely ordained.

Political Factors

There were also political motives for anti-Catholicism. After Henry VIII's break from Rome, Catholics posed political threats—or so it seemed to the court. While in fact very few English Catholics were insurrectionary, adherence to the Church of Rome meant adherence to the belief that the pope had the power to depose monarchs. Suspicions of Catholic plots against the English monarch grew through the sixteenth and early seventeenth centuries. Spain seemed a particular threat: the second half of Elizabeth's reign saw the emergence of the "black legend" of Spanish cruelty, cunning, and tyranny. The great myth of a popish plot, from Spain or elsewhere, did much to obscure the common ground between Protestants and Catholics.

On the other hand, Spain did pose a genuine political threat to England, and the persecution of Protestants under Queen Mary had been very real. Tensions increased in 1570, when Pope Pius V excommunicated Elizabeth and absolved her subjects from obedience to her. In the 1570s, then, English Catholics who had been "church papists" during the 1560s (that is, Catholics who retained allegiance to Rome but attended Church of England services) organized themselves into a separate, underground church. In the early years of Elizabeth's reign there had been a measure of tolerance for Catholic priests remaining from the days of her predecessors, but as these priests died and were replaced by English priests educated on the Continent, especially at the seminary in Douai, the queen began to take a harder line. It was in the interest of the court to depict these foreign-educated Catholics as missionaries bent on reconverting England and overthrowing the Crown. The priests themselves usually saw their role as pastoral rather than missionary, but they began to experience persecution nonetheless. Executions of priests increased through the late 1570s, and in 1585 a law made it treason for a priest ordained abroad to enter the country. Anyone who aided or sheltered such priests likewise committed treason. By that time the Jesuits, more missionary-minded and more deeply feared than their predecessors, had begun to arrive. As executions increased (thirty-one during six months of 1588 alone), so did anti-Catholic rhetoric. During the last half of Elizabeth's reign and the first half of James's, all prominent members of the episcopate engaged in antipapal invectives, as did many other preachers and writers.

Voices calling for moderation were few. When the great English theologian of the late sixteenth century Richard Hooker argued that antipopery had reached immoderate proportions, it was only to point out that fear of the Catholic obscured the more pressing threat posed by the puritan. When Archbishop William Laud called for a reduction in the heat of the controversy, he opened himself to charges of crypto-Catholicism. In 1622 King James attempted to assert a degree of control over the situation by issuing his *Instructions regarding Preaching:* "no preacher of what title or denomination soever, shall consciously and without invitation from the text, fall into bitter invectives, and indecent railing speeches against the person of either papists or puritans." But anti-Catholic polemics continued to fill the air and pour from the presses.

Further Reading
Christopher Haigh, *English Reformations: Religion, Politics, and Society under the Tudors* (Oxford, 1993); Peter Lake, "Anti-popery: The Structure of a Prejudice," in Richard Cust and Ann Hughes, eds., *Conflict in Early Stuart England* (Harlow, Eng., 1989), pp. 72–106; Arthur F. Marotti, ed., *Catholicism and Anti-Catholicism in Early Modern English Texts* (Basingstoke, Eng., 1999); Anthony Milton, *Catholic and Reformed: The Roman and Protestant Churches in English Protestant Thought, 1600–1640* (Cambridge, Eng., 1995).

Bryan Crockett

Anti-Trinitarianism

Anti-Trinitarianism is a general term for various views that denied the orthodox doctrine of the Trinity formulated in the Nicene Creed, that God was a single essence subsisting in three coequal, co-essential, and coeternal persons, as Father, Son, and Holy Spirit. In the sixteenth and seventeenth centuries, anti-Trinitarianism appeared among some theological radicals, usually by the names Arianism and Socinianism. Although these terms were sometimes used interchangeably, the former harked back to a fourth-century theological dispute named after Arius, an Alexandrian theologian, for whom the Son and Spirit were divine but not coequal or coeternal with the Father. As revived in seventeenth-century England, what was called Arianism is more accurately designated subordinationism, because it rarely replicated the views of Arius apart from the subordination of Son and Spirit to the Father. Socinianism was named after Faustus Socinus, a sixteenth-century Italian anti-Trinitarian, whose followers, while acknowledging that divine honors were rightly paid to Christ after his resurrection and ascension, rejected his preexistence, his atoning death as a satisfaction of God's justice, the imputation of his righteousness to believers, and original sin. Rejection of the Reformed doctrine of salvation was often the main thing meant by Socinianism to its seventeenth-century opponents. Many controversialists, however, used the term *Socinian* loosely to refer to all kinds of heterodoxy. The term *Unitarian* was first used in 1687 to refer to anti-Trinitarians. Puritans were prominent among the orthodox opponents of Arian and Socinian ideas, at the same time that some radicals on the margins of the Puritan movement gravitated to these same ideas.

Early English "Arianism"

In late Elizabethan and early Jacobean England, several persons were executed as Arian heretics, the last persons tried and executed for heresy in England. Between 1579 and 1589, four were burnt at the stake in Norwich, the last of whom was Francis Kett. Kett had been educated at Cambridge and shared the eschatological interest of many Puritans, but he denied that Christ was divine in his first coming, although he thought he would be at his second coming, when he would atone for sin and establish a true church. In 1612 Bartholomew

Legate and Edward Wightman were executed as Arians, the former deeming Jesus a mere man and sharing Kett's view that no true church yet existed, the latter believing himself to be the Holy Spirit. These radicals also held some Anabaptist ideas. Applied to these cases of eccentric heresy, *Arianism* was used imprecisely.

Fear of Socinianism

In the seventeenth century, Puritan and Calvinist theologians expressed great alarm over Socinianism. Copies of the Latin version of the Socinian Racovian Catechism were publicly burnt in England in 1614; in the 1640s and 1650s, when Socinian books circulated freely in England, alarm increased. In 1642 George Walker accused John Goodwin of Socinianism for denying the imputation of Christ's righteousness to believers. Francis Cheynell in 1643 and Thomas Edwards in his *Gangraena* (1646) expressed the fear that Socinianism lurked among the Arminians, especially singling out William Chillingworth. In 1654 the Council of State requested John Owen to refute Socinianism, and the result was his *Vindiciae Evangelicae* of 1655, directed against the Socinian John Biddle and the Racovian Catechism. Other writings of Owen focused on this heresy: his work on the Holy Spirit vindicated the Spirit's divinity as essential for its regenerating work, and his huge commentary on the epistle to the Hebrews stressed, against the Socinians, the atonement of Christ as a satisfaction for sin. John Bunyan accused Edward Fowler, soon to be a Church of England bishop, of Socinianism, and the staunch Calvinist John Edwards made the same charge against John Locke in 1695. In New England, Cotton Mather feared Rhode Island was harboring Socinians. In 1697 a deputation of Dissenting ministers asked William III to forbid the printing of Socinian books. Puritans also excoriated Quakers as Socinian for denying the vicarious atonement.

Later Socinianism and Arianism

In the 1640s and 1650s, some religious radicals on the margins of the Puritan movement took advantage of their newfound freedom to express Socinian ideas. The Seeker William Erbery and the Baptist

Paul Hobson apparently read and sympathized with Socinian books, but the first important English Socinian was John Biddle. Educated at Oxford, Biddle was imprisoned in 1644 for denying the divinity of the Holy Spirit. In 1647 he published the first of many Socinian tracts (it was proscribed and burnt by order of Parliament), and he was in and out of prison until he died there in 1662. His *A Twofold Catechism* (1654) denied predestination, justification by faith, original sin, and the resurrection of the body, as well as the Trinity, none of which, he claimed, were taught in scripture. Paul Best was another early Socinian. He served in the parliamentary army and picked up Socinian ideas while traveling on the continent. Imprisoned for heresy, he smuggled manuscripts out of prison; his *Mysteries Discovered* (1647) rejected the Trinity. A leading Socinian of the next generation was Thomas Firmin, scion of a Puritan family and member of John Goodwin's congregation before becoming a follower of Biddle. In New England William Pynchon, who came to Massachusetts in 1630, was the author of *The Meritorious Price of our Redemption* (1650), which denied imputation and the vicarious atonement; returning to England in 1652, he was accused of Socinianism. No Socinian congregations were formed, though there were informal meetings gathered around leaders. By the end of the seventeenth century some Socinians were beginning to describe themselves as Unitarians.

In the second half of the seventeenth century, some continued to maintain the Reformed theology of redemption, but adopted a subordinationist view of Christ, though without denying his preexistence. Unknown to his contemporaries, John Milton may have been one of these, as he was probably the author of a theological manuscript not discovered until 1823 that, denying Christ's coequality and coeternity with the Father, nonetheless affirmed his preexistence and consubstantiality with the Father. John Knowles, a Dissenting lay preacher, was also a subordinationist, but unlike Milton, held a Socinian view of redemption. Responding to rumors of Arian subordinationism among fellow Dissenters, a group of London ministers nonetheless decided against doctrinal tests other than scripture in the Salters' Hall Conference of 1719. Thereafter some English Presbyterians became Arians, as did later some New Englanders. In the Church of England Arthur Bury, rector of Exeter College, declared Arian belief sufficient for salvation in his *Naked Gospel* (1689); William Whiston was expelled from Cambridge in 1710 for claiming that earliest Christianity was Arian; and Samuel Clarke, author of *The Scripture Doctrine of the Trinity* (1712), cast doubt on orthodox Trinitarianism.

See also: Sects

Further Reading

J. Hay Colligan, *The Arian Movement in England* (Manchester, Eng., 1913); Philip S. Gura, *A Glimpse of Sion's Glory: Puritan Radicalism in New England, 1620–1660* (Chapel Hill, 1984); H. John McLachlan. *Socinianism in Seventeenth-Century England* (1951); Dewey D. Wallace Jr., "From Eschatology to Arian Heresy: The Case of Francis Kett (d. 1589)," *Harvard Theological Review* 67 (October 1974).

Dewey D. Wallace Jr.

An Apologeticall Narration

Published in January 1644, *An Apologeticall Narration* articulated the mainstream Congregationalist position and was signed by five Dissenting Brethren in the Westminster Assembly—Thomas Goodwin, Philip Nye, Jeremiah Burroughes, William Bridge, and Sidrach Simpson. The document set out "a middle way betwixt that which is falsely charged on us, Brownism; and that which is the contention of these times, the authoritative Presbyteriall Government."

The *Apologeticall Narration* brought into the open disagreements that had been festering for several years. At a meeting in late 1641, a distinguished group of puritan divines—including all five future signatories of the *Narration*—had agreed to put aside their ecclesiological differences in order to cooperate against both episcopacy and sectarianism. This agreement was effective for so long as puritans were simply engaged in

An Apologeticall Narration

negative campaigning against episcopacy, but once the Westminster Assembly of Divines was established in July 1643, they had to turn to the constructive project of deciding on a new form of church government. It soon became apparent that the majority of the Westminster divines supported a Presbyterian system, in which individual congregations would be subject to an ascending hierarchy of local, regional, and national assemblies. For a few months, the Congregationalists hoped that the assembly might permit the establishment of independent gathered churches (those organized by the consent of the members rather than by geography) within the national church, and they vigorously condemned sectarianism. As late as December 1643, they joined the Presbyterians in publishing *Certaine Considerations to Dis-swade Men from Further Gathering of Churches*, arguing that the godly should wait for the assembly's recommendations on church government.

The publication of the *Apologeticall Narration*, therefore, marked a significant turning point, for with it the Congregationalists broke their diplomatic silence over their disagreements with the Presbyterians. It may have been provoked by the Scottish Covenanter, Alexander Henderson, whose sermon to the Commons on 27 December 1643 made it clear that the Scots would not accept independent congregations within a national church. Whatever the immediate cause, the Congregationalists now felt that they had to speak out, though they stressed that they had restrained themselves hitherto because they had no wish to divide the godly. They explained that they had been forced into exile by the Laudians and had made it their business to discover the primitive New Testament pattern for the church. Inspired by England's "old Nonconformists" and the New England puritans, but keen to avoid the Brownist error of separation from the national Church, they had rejected schism with "the Calvinian Reformed Churches," while believing that they required "a further reformation." They concluded that the elders of each congregation should have "complete power of jurisdiction" over its affairs. Although there was a place for synods, their role was advisory, not authoritative.

The Dissenting Brethren knew that they were appealing to Parliament and a wider public beyond the assembly, and they finished by requesting an "allowance of a latitude to some lesser differences," so that they could enjoy the ordinances of Christ in self-governing congregations.

Although this public appeal brought the Presbyterian-Independent dispute into the open, the *Apologeticall Narration* did not mark a complete break with the Congregationalists' earlier strategy. Indeed, it was a finely balanced statement. While it explained the differences between Congregationalists and Presbyterians, it also stressed their common ground. While it rejected authoritative assemblies, it recognized their role as advisory bodies. Although it requested a limited toleration for orthodox Congregationalist churches, it rejected a broader toleration for the sects. It repudiated full-blown Presbyterianism, but also condemned separatism and rejected "the odious name of Brownism" and "That proud and insolent title of Independencie." The authors insisted that they recognized the Church of England as a true church; had maintained communion with it and the Dutch Reformed Church; and would continue to associate with the parish churches.

The Dissenting Brethren's *via media* pleased neither Presbyterians nor sectarians. 1644 saw the publication of a number of major Presbyterian responses to the Dissenting Brethren, including Thomas Edwards's *Antapologia*. From the radical Independent side, William Walwyn attacked the Dissenting Brethren for abandoning their sectarian brothers and only requesting toleration for themselves. In the toleration debate of 1644, it became increasingly obvious that sectarians wanted a far wider religious liberty than the Congregationalists were willing to contemplate. But although it was controversial, no one doubted the significance of the *Apologeticall Narration*. It had exposed the deep division between the Westminster Assembly's Presbyterian majority and its Independent minority, and it inaugurated a bitter ecclesiastical conflict that was played out in the assembly, the City of London, Parliament, and the press.

See also: Thomas Goodwin, Philip Nye, Calamy House Accord, Dissenting Brethren

Further Reading

John Coffey, *Religious Toleration in Seventeenth-Century England* (Harlow, Eng., 2000); Robert S. Paul, ed., *An Apologeticall Narration* (Philadelphia, 1963).

John Coffey

Arminianism

A theological view that rejected absolute predestination and upheld free will, the possibility of falling from grace, and the death of Christ for all, not just the elect. Arminianism was named for Jacobus (in English, James) Arminius, a Reformed theologian of the Netherlands (1560–1609). Arminius, troubled by the extreme predestinarianism of some Calvinist theologians, argued that predestination was based on God's foreknowledge of those who would freely choose to believe. The ideas of Arminius were condemned in 1618 at the Synod of Dort in the Netherlands. Puritan preachers and theologians attacked Arminianism, fearing that it was hijacking the hitherto Calvinist Church of England; nevertheless, Arminianism also appeared on the margins of the Puritan movement in both Old and New England.

Varieties of Arminianism

In the seventeenth century, three different though sometimes overlapping kinds of Arminianism can be distinguished. In the Netherlands, Arminianism came to designate a liberal and tolerant Protestantism that rejected strict Calvinism. Called the Remonstrants after 1610, these Dutch followers of Arminius had roots, as did Arminius himself, in the Christian Humanism of Desiderius Erasmus, the great Dutch Humanist and opponent of Luther of the early sixteenth century. This liberal Arminianism appealed to certain aristocratic circles in England, such as that gathered around Lord Falkland at Great Tew, which included John Hales (who had been present at Dort and there "bid goodnight" to Calvin) and William Chillingworth. This liberal Arminianism was also characteristic of some of the later Cambridge Platonists and of yet later Latitudinarians.

A second kind of Arminianism, which usually rejected the name, was that eventually led by William Laud and sometimes called Laudianism. Beginning in the 1590s with Lancelot Andrewes and John Overall, these Arminians became more outspoken in the years surrounding the Synod of Dort and gained dominance in the Church of England with the patronage of King Charles I after 1625 and with Laud as archbishop of Canterbury after 1633. They carried out a sustained anti-Calvinist attack in many parishes and in the universities. They promoted the refurbishing of church interiors (replacing communion tables with railed altars) to accommodate ceremonial and sacramental worship as a substitute for the Calvinism that had been prevalent in the Church of England. They were dubbed Arminians because they rejected the predestinarian theology of grace in favor of a freedom of the will that made room for sacramental grace; for if salvation is God's gift by predestination, it is not at the disposal of the church as an institution through the sacraments. By the 1650s, some spokesmen for the by then defeated Laudian program were acknowledging and defending Arminius, and after the Restoration in 1660, Arminianism became widespread in the Church of England, with Calvinists, especially after the ejection of many Puritans in 1662, remaining an embattled minority.

A third Arminianism was that of various sectarian and dissenting deniers of predestination who sprang up on the margins of Puritanism. These Arminians shared Puritan piety and perhaps prefigured the later evangelical Arminianism of Methodism. In the 1540s there appeared a group of "freewillers," typified by Henry Hart, who balked at the predestinarian formulas of the learned English Protestant mainstream. Some later English Separatists in the Netherlands, led by John Smyth and Thomas Helwys, coming under Mennonite influence, rejected infant baptism and adopted a free-will theology. These General Baptists, believing in a general atonement for all, are to be distinguished from the Calvinistic Particular Baptists (who believed in the predestination of particular persons), who were closer to the Puritan mainstream. There was a congregation of General Baptists in London in the 1620s led by John Murton, who published his views in 1620. A number of such congregations flourished during the 1640s and 1650s, especially in London, suffering persecution after the restoration of the monarchy in 1660. General Baptists also appeared in Rhode Island, in spite of Roger Williams's Calvinism; Cotton Mather later listed Arminians among the heretics of that colony. Closer to the Puritan mainstream were John Goodwin, a leading London Puritan during the Interregnum, and the poet John Milton, freedom of the will being central to the theodicy of *Paradise Lost.*

Even such a leading Puritan as Richard Baxter came under suspicion of Arminianism because of incautious remarks made in early publications, and later English Presbyterians such as he and Daniel Williams are often regarded as having opened the door to Arminian ideas among later English Presbyterians. Arminianism also appeared among New England Puritans: an attempt to gather a church in Dorchester was aborted because some prospective members were Arminian, and the radical Samuel Gorton was reputed an Arminian. Both in England and New England, this Arminianism in the course of the eighteenth century sometimes metamorphosed into a liberalized Protestantism comfortable in an age of reason.

The Calvinist Attack upon Arminianism

It was a consistent refrain of Calvinists that Arminianism revived the Pelagian heresy, making salvation the result of human effort rather than of divine grace. Grace to the Puritans was efficacious, really effecting what it promised; nothing else could redeem persons from the power of sin. Calvinists associated Arminianism with Roman Catholic salvation by works and thought that it provided an opening for Rome, the anti-Arminian writer William Prynne being convinced that the Laudians were plotting to undo the Reformation. Intense opposition to Arminianism appeared in the theology of William Perkins, in Calvinist theologians at the universities such as Samuel Ward and John Prideaux, in the protests of parliamentary Puritans

such as Francis Rous and John Pym in 1629, and in the works of the high Calvinist theologians William Pemble and William Twisse. John Owen made the refutation of Arminianism his theological lifework. In the eighteenth century in New England, Jonathan Edwards devoted a major treatise to its refutation. When it appeared in the Church of England, Arminianism was an innovative and disruptive force that created theological division between Puritans and their opponents, where earlier divisions had been over ritual and discipline. Calvinism in England was thereby redefined as Puritan, and Puritans were more alienated from the established church than they had formerly been; the alienation caused by Arminianism was a factor in the immigration of Puritans to New England.

See also: Jacobus Arminius, Anti-Calvinism, Predestination
Further Reading
Philip F. Gura, *A Glimpse of Sion's Glory: Puritan Radicalism in New England, 1620–1660* (Chapel Hill, 1984); Murray Tolmie, *The Triumph of the Saints: The Separate Churches of London, 1616–1649* (Cambridge, Eng., 1977); Nicholas Tyacke, *Anti-Calvinists: The Rise of English Arminianism, c. 1590–1640* (Oxford, 1987); Dewey D. Wallace Jr., *Puritans and Predestination: Grace in English Protestant Theology, 1525–1695* (Chapel Hill, 1982).

Dewey D. Wallace Jr.

Articles of Religion

The Church of England promulgated the Ten Articles of Religion in 1536, the Forty-two Articles of Religion in 1553, and the Thirty-nine Articles of Religion in 1563. The Church of Ireland promulgated its own articles in 1615.

The Ten Articles

The Ten Articles were developed while the nature of Henry VIII's church was very much under dispute and were probably spurred by disputations held in the previous year over questions such as the existence of purgatory and other disputed beliefs. They were developed by a committee of theologians and bishops that included Thomas Cranmer, the first archbishop of Canterbury after Henry VIII's split with Rome, and the conservative humanist bishop of Durham, Cuthbert Tunstall. They were intensely debated in convocation, requiring the intervention of the king, who ordered them published. The first five of the articles dealt with doctrinal matters such as the sacraments and justification. The second five focused on images, honoring saints, praying to saints, rites and ceremonies, and purgatory. The positions expressed reflected the influence of the Lutheran Augsburg Confession of 1530 and the Wittenberg Articles that had been worked out by the spring of 1536. The first five articles generally angered those conservative churchman who were committed to traditional views, particular in their recognition of only three sacraments (baptism, penance, and the Eucharist). The second five reflected a compromise that neither conservatives nor evangelical Reformers were to be happy with.

The Forty-two Articles

By 1553 Thomas Cranmer and the evangelical reformers of the church were in the ascendant, and fully supported by the young King Edward VI. Consequently the Forty-two Articles reflected a more advanced Protestant vision of English faith. They appear to have been part of a general restructuring of the church that included revision of the Book of Common Prayer and an uncompleted revision of canon law. Though they were never approved by the two archdiocesan convocations, they were officially published.

Cranmer had been considering the issues since the promulgation of the Ten Articles, even as he worked in those intervening years to help broker a doctrinal agreement among all Protestants. In all of these labors he was influenced by the views of the noted Continental theologians Martin Bucer and Peter Martyr, both of whom he had helped to resettle in England. Others, including the Scottish Reformer John Knox, were asked to critique a draft in October 1552, leading to a reduction from forty-five to forty-two articles as well as other modifications. The Privy Council also took a role in shaping the document, and it was the Privy Council that promulgated the articles.

If the Ten Articles showed a Lutheran influence, the Forty-two Articles aligned England with Calvinism. The articles strongly condemned Catholic doctrines such as transubstantiation, the efficacy of good works, and purgatory. Anabaptist views were also signaled out for repudiation. On many issues where English Protestants were divided—such as predestination—the articles were ambiguous, allowing the internal debates in the church to continue. Article 6 affirmed the sufficiency of scripture for salvation.

The Thirty-nine Articles

The Forty-two Articles were barely promulgated before Edward VI died, and the church he had governed was swept away in the Marian reaction of 1553–1558. Following the accession of Queen Elizabeth, it was imperative to define anew what England's church stood for. This was accomplished by passage of a series of measures. The Act of Supremacy (1559) proclaimed the monarch as head of the church, repealed Marian legislation regarding the church and revived many of the statutes of Henry VIII's reign regarding the organization of the church. The Act of Uniformity (1559) authorized the newly issued Book of Common Prayer (revised in a slightly conservative direction from its last Edwardian version) and set penalties for those who refused to use it and for those who absented themselves from church services. The Thirty-nine Articles (1563) differed little in their essence from the Forty-two Articles of a decade earlier, though Archbishop Matthew Parker did temper them somewhat in an effort to steer a moderate course. While Article 11 clearly asserted that "we are justified by faith alone," Article 12 emphasized that good works, though they "cannot put away our sins," were nevertheless "pleasing and acceptable to God." Like the Forty-two Articles, they steered the church away from Catholicism and Anabaptism, but avoided trying to define standard Protestant doctrine too precisely.

Some bishops and members of Parliament wished to see the Thirty-nine Articles enacted by legislation, but Elizabeth initially opposed such action. Following a papal bull excommunicating the queen, the government's position changed. In 1571 Parliament passed legislation that required all clergy not ordained under the Protestant Ordinal to subscribe to the Thirty-nine Articles. This was designed primarily to put pressure on Catholics. In 1583 John Whitgift, the new archbishop of Canterbury, demanded that all clergy subscribe to three articles: acknowledging the royal supremacy (that is, acknowledging that the monarch of England was the head of the Church of England), accepting the Book of Common Prayer as "containing nothing contrary to the word of God," and accepting the Thirty-nine Articles. The second of these was primarily intended to identify and curb puritan nonconformists.

See also: Irish Articles

Further Reading

H. G. Alexander, *Religion in England 1558–1662* (London, 1968); Patrick Collinson, *The Elizabethan Puritan Movement* (1967); Diarmaid MacCulloch, *Reformation: Europe's House Divided, 1490–1700* (London, 2003).

Francis J. Bremer

Assurance of Salvation

Predestination and assurance of salvation were intimately connected Reformed doctrines. Those whom God chose from eternity for salvation were predestined to never fall from grace. Therefore, once believers knew they were saved, they could be assured that they would inevitably go to heaven. The Reformed laid great stress on the doctrine of assurance, contrasting it favorably with Catholic doctrine, which, they argued, kept believers in a constant state of uncertainty about their eternal destination.

Putting the doctrine of assurance into practice, however, proved tricky. The earliest puritan ministers in the sixteenth century tended to treat assurance as an inevitable by-product of the experience of faith in Jesus. Faith was self-validating, and if you had faith, you would by definition have assurance. Two problems arose from this assumption. Some listeners, "weak Christians," proved unable to believe that the Lord could possibly have predestined such sinners as they were to salvation. Their faith, being wracked with uncertainty, was not accompanied by any sense of assurance. Their lack of assurance, in turn, made them doubt that their faith was genuine, and they fell easily into a despair that could reach suicidal intensity. Other listeners, however, were quite happy to take for granted that they had faith in Jesus and were therefore assured of salvation without feeling any further need for rigorous piety.

In response to these poles of despair and complacency, near the end of the sixteenth century English puritan ministers began developing their famous practical divinity. Pioneered by ministers like Richard Rogers and William Perkins, this divinity methodically stressed the intense work people needed to do before they could take assurance in the first place. It further stressed that true assurance was always accompanied by, and could be measured by, a lifelong course of piety and soul-searching. It thereby provided a concrete program of action for those weak Christians who were unable to find assurance through the strength of their faith alone. At the same time, by its ongoing strenuousness, it warned off the complacent. Indeed, ministers often stressed that complacency about salvation was a sure sign that one was among the damned. The widespread diffusion of this divinity on the continent indicates that it was responding to a generally felt need in the Reformed world.

Historians have argued over the extent to which this emphasis on assurance through the methodical generation and scrutiny of visible signs of piety represented a departure from the intentions of the first generation of Reformers. Did it substitute a kind of imitation Catholic works righteousness for the pristine apprehension of the miracle of justification, and did the ministers' emphasis on introspection for salvation come at the expense of a focus on Christ? Those questions feed into a larger debate about the continuity or discontinuity of Calvinism, and many of the historians in these debates have had their own personal religious stake in them. Whatever the quarrels of historians, it surely counts for something that the original promulgators of puritan practical divinity perceived what they were offering as both new and necessary, and as required by the pastoral limitations of the original conception of assurance.

How successful this divinity was is not simple to measure, given that it had the conflicting goals of crushing complacency and providing comfort. Some historians portray puritan preaching on assurance as fostering a near-psychotic anxiety in listeners, while others argue that puritans usually eventually found peace from the techniques their ministers promoted. Obviously, any attempt to make broad generalizations about long-ago mental states faces formidable problems. There are, however, ample indications that the doctrine of assurance remained a difficult one to put into practice. It is telling that puritan ministers complained steadily from the beginning of the century to its end that few of those whom they considered godly achieved a reliable assurance.

Meanwhile, mainstream puritan preaching on assurance came under intense attack for its perceived limitations. Radical puritan preachers angrily dismissed the requirement of a heavy dosage of piety for proof of salvation as a betrayal of God's free grace. They attacked the argument that the assurance that came from justification had to be preceded by a lengthy and visible period of intense struggle; they stressed the importance of retaining confidence in one's assurance, regardless of how much one thought one was coming up short in terms of personal holiness; and some of them spoke of assurance as coming through the Holy Spirit in a kind of intense illumination. To mainstream preachers, such ministers were heretical Familists (the followers of the Dutch radical Heinrich Niclaes who believed that they were part of the Godhead) and antinomians. Bitter clashes between partisans of these different approaches in both England and New England broke out among the godly throughout the seventeenth century and beyond.

Dismay over the pastoral results of preaching predestination also seems to have prodded a number of ministers toward anti-Calvinism in the early seventeenth century. While comforting laity who were convinced that God had predestined them to hell, they assured them that they had some control over their salvation. At the same time, anti-Calvinists had a rock-hard argument against antinomianism, since by their teaching, believers could fall from grace and be damned if they behaved wickedly.

The doctrine of assurance was at the center of a famous theory advanced by the German sociologist Max Weber in *The Protestant Ethic and the Spirit of Capitalism* (1904). Weber argued that the Calvinist (by which he meant puritan) doctrine of assurance produced what he called an "inner-directed worldly asceticism." Puritan practical divinity encouraged a spirit of introspective rational calculation, and the godly confirmed their salvation through disciplined hard work at their callings, coupled with the virtuous avoidance of luxurious consumption. The accumulation of wealth was an almost inevitable by-product of this activity. Thus, the doctrine of assurance played a vital role in the development of early modern capitalism. Other historians, however, have had difficulty finding case studies that support the thesis that Calvinism produced exceptional economic development, and there is some indication that the strenuous pursuit of Calvinist piety distracted from the accumulation of wealth.

See also: Grace, Predestination, Soteriology
Further Reading
Philip Benedict, *Christ's Churches Purely Reformed: A Social History of Calvinism* (New Haven, 2002); Charles Lloyd Cohen, *God's Caress: The Psychology of Puritan Religious Experience* (New York, 1986); John Stachniewski, *The Persecutory Imagination: English Puritanism and the Literature of Religious Despair* (Oxford, 1991); Michael P. Winship, "Weak Christians, Backsliders, and Carnal Gospelers: Assurance of Salvation and the Pastoral Origins of Puritan Practical Divinity in the 1580s," *Church History* 70 (2001), 462–481.

Michael Winship

Atonement

The divine reconciliation of God and man through the sacrifice of Jesus Christ. One of the critical issues of the Reformation involved how human beings received the benefits of the atonement. Luther and other Reformers emphasized that Christ's atonement was the sole condition for the forgiveness of sins, rejecting the Catholic notion that man also had to atone for his transgressions in this world and then in purgatory. Calvin likewise proclaimed the sufficiency of Christ's sacrifice. His followers, particularly Theodore Beza, elaborated on what this meant for the doctrine of predestination. Beza and his fellow Reformed theologians of the late sixteenth century believed in a double predestination of those chosen for salvation and those relegated to hell and thus argued that Christ's atonement was limited to the first group. The Synod of Dort ruled that though Christ's death was sufficient for the salvation of all human beings, it was efficient only for the elect. In England William Perkins emphasized double predestination and limited atonement in the sixteenth century, as did John Owen in the seventeenth.

See also: Predestination, Soteriology
Further Reading
A. C. Clifford, *Atonement and Justification: English Evangelical Theology, 1640–1790* (Oxford, 1990).

Francis J. Bremer

B

Ballads

Narrative poems suitable for singing. Ballads were among the most popular of publications: from 1550 to 1600, between three and four million were printed in England in the form of broadsides, while others formed part of larger works. As well as providing the words of the songs, printed ballads were often illustrated with woodcuts and accompanied with (often nonsensical) music or directions that they were were intended to be sung to a particular tune, such as the "hanging tune" commonly used for ballads with moral and religious overtones. Many were printed in "black letter," the most accessible of all typefaces. Sold in shops and throughout the land by peddlers, ballads extended beyond the literate: they were commonly pasted to the walls of houses and alehouses and read aloud or sung in company. The ballads were short and cheap, costing about half a penny. The socially humble may have been able to buy them as luxuries, though collections that survive were compiled by the rich. It is likely that the more humble buyers found subsequent uses for the paper ballads were printed on, from lining pie tins to use as toilet paper.

Many that survive contain religious content, notably those classed as "godly ballads."

These had titles such as *The gude and godlie ballatis* (Edinburgh, 1567) and *A right Godly and Chresteane a.b.c. shewinge the dewty of every degre* (1624). Though not concerned with Puritan theology, such ballads were often preoccupied with examples of God's interventions in the world and judgments on individuals. Some were written by those on the fringes of the clergy, sometimes recycling longer Puritan works: *Youths warning peice* (1636) was a summary of a godly funeral sermon, and the best-selling *Christs teares over Jerusalem* abridged a tract by Thomas Nashe. These ballads, in particular in their morality, were often consistent with the message of Puritan pamphlets and not necessarily at odds with the messages expressed from puritan pulpits. The pamphlets themselves were used in attempts to evangelize the poor in the seventeenth century.

Puritan attitudes toward ballads changed over time: from the mid-sixteenth century, attempts were made to harness their power to spread the reforming message and to mock Catholic practices; from the 1570s, Puritans distanced themselves from such popular print, especially after the Psalms, which had often been printed along with ballads, came to be printed separately. In the seventeenth century, there was a revival in the production of godly ballads, but Puritan preachers consistently preached against ballads and their singers. Despite the obvious religious aspirations of publications such as John Rhodes's *The contrie mans comfort. Or religious recreations*, a collection that versified the Apostles' Creed and Ten Commandments to ballad tunes, Puritan preachers insisted that ballads went against true religion, both in their message and in their very existence as popular recreation, detracting from worship.

Circa 1628, people drinking in an alehouse, illustrating the old ballad "Jack Had-Land's Lamentation." (Hulton Archive/Getty Images)

See also: Broadsides, Leisure Time, Theology of, Sports and Recreation

Further Reading

Adam Fox, *Oral and Literate Culture in England, 1500–1700* (Cambridge, Eng., 2000); Tessa Watt, *Cheap Print and Popular Piety, 1550–1640* (Cambridge, Eng., 1991).

Andrew Cambers

Baptism

Baptism was one of the sacraments retained in the Church of England after the Reformation. Through its rituals, an individual was transformed from sinner to recipient of grace and welcomed into the Christian community. In that church it was to be administered to infants by the Sunday after they were born. Because of the importance placed upon this sacrament, the church allowed private baptism and even baptism by a midwife in an emergency. The rite of baptism in the first Book of Common Prayer retained a number of medieval Catholic practices, including a rite of exorcism and anointing with oil. Some of these elements were dropped in the second Book of Common Prayer and the Elizabethan rite. Normally the sacrament was celebrated at the traditional baptismal font located at the west end of the church, near the south door. The Reformed ceremony began with the clergyman reminding those in attendance that all men were born in sin and noting that Christ had asserted that none could enter the kingdom of heaven unless he was regenerate and "born anew of water and the Holy Ghost." The minister asked the name given to the child and then dipped the infant in water, signing with the cross and stating that he baptized the infant "in the name of the Father, and the Son, and the Holy Ghost." Godparents were asked to speak on behalf of the child and to pledge themselves to see that the child was raised in the Christian faith.

Theologically, the official position of the Church of England was that the sacrament of baptism itself did not automatically wash away all sin. But the exact meaning of the ceremony was disputed. Some, particularly those who were later associated with the Arminian, or anti-Calvinist, movement in the Stuart church, stressed the regenerative elements of the sacrament. Others—especially puritans—preferred to see it as an initiation into the Christian community and as an affirmation of a covenant between the child and Christ.

Some English Protestants felt that the rituals of baptism were not sufficiently reformed. Reflecting their general disapprobation of special vestments, puritans rejected the rubric that required that the presiding clergyman wear vestments. Some also preferred the sacrament to be conducted at the front of the church. They objected to the practice of signing with the cross, seeing in this a papist ritual akin to a spell.

Viewing baptism as a rite of initiation into the community of faith, they rejected the practice of private baptism. In New England, puritans were able to introduce these further reforms, and they also did away with the requirement of godparents, allowing the parents to bring the child to the sacrament.

A far more serious challenge to the practice of baptism came from those who rejected the notion of infant baptism entirely. Rare in the sixteenth century in England, Anabaptists gained some momentum in the seventeenth century, particularly during the turmoil of the midcentury. Such individuals believed that baptism was a seal of the transformation wrought on the soul by Christ and argued therefore that only born-again adult believers ought to be baptized.

See also: Anabaptism
Further Reading
David Cressy, *Birth, Marriage, and Death: Ritual, Religion, and the Life Cycle in Tudor and Stuart England* (Oxford, 1997).

Francis J. Bremer

Baptismal Names

One of the major functions of the ceremony of baptism in the early modern period was to provide an individual with a name and therefore an identity, but these names and the method by which they were given became bones of contention between traditionalists and Puritans in the late sixteenth and early seventeenth centuries. It is now widely accepted that in the late medieval period, names were not given by the parents of a child, but by its godparents. As Puritans objected to the office of godparent and emphasized the role of the parents (particularly the father) in the naming process, both debate and dispute grew up around roles in naming and in baptism. There was also a further disagreement about the suitability of some of the names chosen for children, which echoed and occasionally clashed with concerns among more conservative divines. The results were disputes over both the process and product of baptism in the giving of names. This led to an attempt to give or impose Puritan "grace" names, an attempt that was significant only in some localized areas for short periods, and a more successful campaign to move the naming function in baptism from the spiritual to the natural parents. This campaign can be seen as an important contribution of Puritanism to the subsequent wider culture of family life.

The absence of parents from baptism and the centrality of godparents in naming in medieval England, linked to the fact that godparents usually gave their own names to children, has been seen as leading to a gradual reduction of the pool of forenames available to individuals and may have contributed to the rise of surnames from the fourteenth century, as greater clarity in identification was needed. Thus only five male forenames (Henry, John, Richard, Thomas, and William) made up two-thirds of all those used by the fourteenth century, and three female forenames (Elizabeth, Mary, and Anne) were over half of all those used by the end of the medieval period. In the early stages of the Reformation, this picture had already begun to break down with the adoption of a limited number of classical names, such as Julius and Horatio, and, more successfully, with the use of relatively large numbers of biblical names that had not been widely distributed through the medieval cult of the saints, including Abraham, Daniel, Judith, and Ruth, a phenomenon that has unusually been attributed to the introduction of the Geneva Bible from 1560. Because of the lack of associations with popery in these names, they seem to have been preferred by those with Puritan leanings, although they also had a wider currency outside of these circles. More peculiar to Puritans was the adoption from the 1580s of "grace names," which were not only divorced from the contamination of popery, but also could provide statements of belief in line with Protestant and specifically Reformed theology. These included names such as Reformation, Delivery, Tribulation, Thankful, and Love-God. These were condemned by conservative divines and elicited disapproval from the first important commentator on English names, the sixteenth-century historian and herald William Camden. The most famous case remains that of Praise-God "Barebones" Barbon, called in derision Praise-God Barebones. He was a member of the parliament that resulted from Cromwell's attempt to bring order by nominating his own parliament in 1653; it was called the Barebones Parliament by mockers, and the name stuck.

In the dissemination of these names, the role of local clergy with Puritan leanings seems to have been instrumental. However, it is clear from English parish registers that the practice was never widespread and seems to have been confined to a handful of parishes in Kent, later spreading to Sussex and southern Northamptonshire. Although in some parishes in these areas a majority of children being baptized were given such names, the practice failed to penetrate further, even into what are usually thought of as particularly Puritan areas such as Essex, nor did it last far into the seventeenth century. There are later isolated examples of the practice further afield, particularly for the years of the Civil Wars in Lancashire and Yorkshire, but in general this Puritan revolution in English baptismal names was stillborn. A handful of these names did make it into the general pool, most obviously the female forenames of Grace, Prudence, and Faith, but in general the popular medieval names reasserted themselves in the seventeenth century.

The more significant contribution of Puritanism to English, and wider, naming practices was in the debate over the role of parents. The position of Reformed Protestantism, exemplified by Calvin, was that, as infant baptism was to be retained, the father should act as the godparent, promising to look after the child's spiritual welfare. English prayer books from 1552 were ambiguous on the role of the father, who may have been able to be present, but they were clear that he should not be the godparent. In the Interregnum, under the Directory of Public Worship, godparents were abolished, and the father was elevated to be sole sponsor, although there is considerable evidence that this directive was disregarded in some quarters. After the Restoration, godparents were reinstated, but the father seems to have continued to be present, and from 1662 the mother could also attend. The evidence from parish registers strongly indicates that in this period there was a collapse of the role of the godparents as the givers of names. Very much in line with Puritan aims, the father and even the mother seem to have taken over this function, with name sharing with godparents declining and the practice of naming children after parents (particularly fathers) growing. The result was the virtual completion of a process that had begun at the Reformation of a transfer of functions to the natural parents and thus, arguably, an increased emphasis on the role of the family, a development that has been seen as central to Puritanism.

See also: Family Piety

Further Reading

Scott Smith Bannister, *Names and Naming Patterns in England, 1538–1700* (Oxford, 1997); Will Coster, *Baptism and Spiritual Kinship in Early Modern England* (Aldershot, Eng., 2002); David Cressy, *Birth, Marriage, and Death: Ritual, Religion, and the Life Cycle in Tudor and Stuart England* (Oxford, 1997); Nicolas Tyacke, "Popular Puritan Mentality in late Elizabethan England," in P. Clark, G. T. Smith, and N. Tyacke, eds., *The English Commonwealth 1547–1640, Essays in Politics and Society Presented to Joel Hurstfield* (New York, 1979), pp. 77–92.

Will Coster

Bay Psalm Book

The Whole Book of Psalmes Faithfully Translated into English Metre (commonly known as the Bay Psalm Book because it was published in the Massachusetts Bay Colony in 1640) was the first English book to be published in America. The work of the ministers Thomas Weld, John Eliot, and Richard Mather, the first edition of 1,700 copies was produced on a press belonging to Harvard College. As stated in the preface, its production was inspired by a dissatisfaction with the Sternhold and Hopkins version, the dominant translation in England. That "Old Version," although held in great reverence, was felt to depart from the literal sense of the Psalms too often and was liable to cause offense to those capable of comparing it with the original. The Bay Psalm Book was designed as a more literal translation, plain and familiar in style, with the minimum of poetic elaboration. The compilers also rendered a higher proportion of the Psalms into the simple "common meter" for greater ease of singing and memorization. It was soon adopted almost universally in New England, using for the most part the tunes of the Old Version. (A tune supplement to the book did not appear until the ninth edition of 1698, and all thirteen of the tunes used there were standard English tunes.) It remained in that position of dominance until it was superseded by later translations, including the English New Version of Tate and Brady of 1696.

The preface of the book has generally been attributed to Richard Mather, though most scholars now attribute it to John Cotton. It displays many of the characteristic concerns of contemporary writers in England. Written explicitly to counter objections made by others (presumably in New England, although unnamed) to psalm singing, it deals with the same scriptural commonplaces as writers in England, and the title page of the 1697 edition (printed in London) bears the two central New Testament references to music (Colossians 3:16 and Ephesians 5:19). (That there was some dispute is also evident from John Cotton's *Singing of Psalmes a Gospel Ordinance* [London, 1650]). The concluding sentence of the preface, with its references to the saints' "eternal Hallelujahs," is also a highly characteristic godly vision of the music of heaven.

See also: Thomas Sternhold, Psalms
Further Reading
Perry Miller and Thomas Johnson, eds., *The Puritans. A Sourcebook of Their Writings* (New York, 1963); Stanley Sadie, ed., *The New Grove Dictionary of Music and Musicians*, 2nd ed. (London, 2001).

Peter Webster

Bible

The Bible has traditionally been viewed by Christians as the inspired word of God. At the time of the Reformation, Protestants placed it at the center of their attempts to understand God's will and commands. They asserted that the Bible was the ultimate authority in matters of religion. Written originally in Hebrew, Greek, and Aramaic, the Bible included the books of the Old, or Hebrew, Testament and the New Testament. An early Greek translation of the Old Testament, called the Septuagint, had included a number of books that were not found in the Hebrew Bible. Those books are referred to as Apocrypha. The entire Bible, including the Apocrypha, had been translated into Latin by St. Jerome, who finished his task in the year 405. That version, the Vulgate, was the principle tool used by clergy, theologians, and other churchmen through the Middle Ages. Luther and the other Reformers believed that the Bible deserved to be made available to all Christians. This required the publication of the Bible in inexpensive editions in vernacular languages.

The earliest English translation of the Vulgate Bible was prepared by the fourteenth century religious reformer John Wyclif, prior to the development of printing. It was circulated in manuscript among the Lollards, who were followers of Wyclif's teachings. Following the Reformation, William Tyndale translated the Bible into English from the Greek and Hebrew. Because of official opposition to his efforts, he left England and settled in the German states, finishing the first printed New Testament in 1525 and finishing the Old Testament nine years later. Tyndale did not see the publication of the latter, since he was arrested in 1535 and executed in the following year. His graceful translation not only made the Bible more accessible to the English, but also helped to shape the English language itself. Miles Coverdale published a complete English Bible in 1535. The attitude of the authorities was changing, and Coverdale's Great Bible (1537) was accepted by the king and bishops.

During the Marian exile, English Reformers prepared the English-language Geneva Bible, which was published in 1560. This version was notable for its extensive marginal commentary, which gave a clear Protestant and anti-Catholic interpretation of the scripture. The Calvinist orientation of this translation has led many to assert that it was the favored Bible among puritans in England and New England, but an examination of Bible ownership and the actual words cited in sermons and recorded in sermon notes would indicate that this is an exaggeration.

In fact, puritans believed that the Geneva translation was imperfect, and one of their petitions to King James I at the start of his reign was that a new translation be authorized. The king granted that request at the Hampton Court Conference, and fifty-four scholars from several universities were charged with the task, working in six committees. They turned back to the Greek and Hebrew rather than using the Latin Vulgate as the basis for their translation, though they did make extensive use of Tyndale's efforts. This Authorized Version, also called the King James Bible, was published in 1611. It quickly became the preferred English Bible, and like Tyndale's work, it had a great influence on the English language, used by almost all Christian English-speaking writers for several centuries and Milton among others.

See also: Geneva Bible, Soldier's Bible
Further Reading
S. L. Greenslade, *The Cambridge History of the Bible,* 3 vols. (Cambridge, Eng., 1963–1970); Alistair McGrath, *In the Beginning: The Story of the King James Bible* (London, 2001).

Francis J. Bremer

Bishops' Wars

Two failed attempts by Charles I to use military force to impose his will on the Scots in 1639 and in 1640. Each was called a Bishops' War (or, in Latin, *bellum episcopale*) at the time, reflecting the widespread puritan belief that Charles was trying to impose a plan hatched by the English bishops to impose their policies for church government, discipline, and worship on the Scots, with their proud tradition of episcopacy-in-presbytery (whereby the office of bishop was incorporated into a Presbyterian church system). The culmination of attempts to centralize the Scottish Church had indeed been the new Scottish Prayer Book of 1637, based on the first Book of Common Prayer of Edward VI (1549). The attempt to impose this prayer book had led to mass protests by Scots, many of whom signed the National Covenant committing them passively to resist all innovation in church and state. Charles I was determined to have his way and planned to use dissident Highlanders, troops from Ireland, and an invasion force of 20,000 men raised in England to impose his will by force. The Scots (recalling many veterans from the Continental wars) mobilized more effectively than Charles, whose plans proved overcomplicated. So when he reached the borders, he realized he lacked the strength to achieve his purposes, and he signed a truce on 18 June 1639 at Berwick that restored the status quo ante. But resentment on both sides smoldered over the next twelve months.

The king made sullen and patently insincere concessions to a Scottish parliament and General Assembly and called an English parliament, hoping it would support him against the still much disliked Scots. But this "Short Parliament" wanted more concessions over the way Charles was governing England before they would back his war; and he dissolved it after only three weeks. Yet he still went ahead with mobilizing a new army for a second assault on Scotland. This one was even less well managed, and its move north was accompanied by many acts of vandalism and iconoclasm. The Scots again mobilized first and did not wait for Charles to arrive. They

English troops retreat from the Scottish in 1641 during the Bishops' Wars, the prelude to the English Civil War. Two conflicts, collectively known as the Bishops' Wars, were precipitated when English king Charles I tried to force his religious views on the people of Scotland. (North Wind Picture Archives)

occupied the eastern part of the North of England as far south as Newcastle, and the king's disintegrating army had no hope of dislodging them. Charles was forced into humiliating concessions that led to the elimination of all his personal authority in Scotland and the summoning of the Long Parliament in England, which he could not dissolve, because he had agreed that the Scots would remain in Newcastle until their war costs were met by that parliament. This agreement gave the puritans and their allies the leverage to reform England, or, in the event, to force the country into civil war.

See also: Anti-Calvinism, National Covenant
Further Reading
Mark Fissel, *The Bishops' Wars: Charles I's Campaigns against Scotland, 1638–1640* (Cambridge, Eng., 1994).

John Morrill

Book of Common Prayer

The Book of Common Prayer has been the official form of public worship in the Church of England since the sixteenth century. It contains the daily service of morning and evening prayer, the forms for the administration of the sacraments of baptism and Holy Communion, and the services for baptism, marriage, burial, the churching of women after childbirth, the ordination of deacons and priests, and the consecration of bishops. It also includes the Psalter, the Catechism, and the scripture readings for the collects (a specific collect, or short prayer, is provided for each Sunday of the year), and the portions from the Gospels and Epistles appointed for each Sunday. It has been revised several times and has in the past included forms of service for specific occasions, such as that acknowledging England's delivery from the Gunpowder Plot of 5 November 1605.

The Book of Common Prayer was introduced in 1549 when Edward VI's Act of Uniformity made it the mandatory form of national worship. The work of Archbishop Thomas Cranmer, this prayer book was intended to replace the Latin Mass with a collective form of worship in English and to embody the Protestant theology of the Church of England. Cranmer trod carefully around political difficulties and differences in public opinion, but his 1552 revision of the Prayer Book marked a more decisive turn to Protestantism of a Zwinglian kind: all references to the "mass" and "altar" were excised; the surplice was enjoined as the standard vestment; and explanatory notes were added, such as "the declaration on kneeling" (known since the nineteenth century as the "black rubric"), which stated that kneeling at the communion did not imply adoration. The 1559 Book of Common Prayer issued by Queen Elizabeth was based on the 1552 Book. However, it omitted "the declaration on kneeling" and conflated the formulae used at the reception of the bread and wine in the 1549 and 1552 prayer books so as to allow worshippers and celebrants more freedom of interpretation about the theology of the Eucharist. It included a rubric that restored the ornaments of the church and minister as they had been in the second year of Edward VI until the queen or archbishop made "other order." This order was never forthcoming, and many saw the rubric as allowing "popish" ornaments.

It is no exaggeration to say that English Puritanism was a reaction to the 1559 Book of Common Prayer. Other issues—such as the role of bishops or predestination—became equally important, but the conviction that the prayer book was redolent of popery and that its imposition was a burden on the godly consciences both of ministers and their flocks formed a persistent strand in English Puritanism until at least the end of the seventeenth century. Specific complaints ranged from the retention of the term *priest* to the readings taken from apocryphal books of the Bible. Puritans objected to the cap and surplice worn by the minister, standing at the reading of the Gospel, bowing at the name of Jesus, kneeling to receive the sacrament, the use of a ring in marriage, the making of the sign of the cross at baptism, and the burial service's confident hope that the deceased would rise again to eternal life. Beyond these particular "inconveniences," Puritans resented the principle of such a minutely prescribed form of worship. Elizabethan Puritans such as John Field and Thomas Cartwright argued that the clergy were simply reading prayers rather than praying with the Spirit as St. Paul demanded. They complained that set forms thwarted ministers in the exercise of their "gifts" for extemporized prayer and deadened devotion among the congregation. Prayer book worship in the sixteenth and seventeenth centuries may have justified these complaints. Few among the congregation owned a copy of the prayer book, and many were illiterate, so the parish clerk led the laity's responses. Although many may have learned the liturgy aurally, there were frequent laments from both Puritans and conformists about the mumbled or inaudible prayer, the passivity of the congregation, and the lack of emphasis on the intelligent preaching they believed the laity were hungry for and needed.

Elizabethan Puritans campaigned against the prayer book in several ways. They produced their own alternative liturgy, A *Booke of the Forme of Common Prayers* (1584). They lobbied Convocation and Parliament for relaxation of uniformity and for specific modifications of the prayer book. In their own parishes they adapted the liturgy and omitted parts of it. The authorities responded by making conformity to the prayer book into a shibboleth by which to identify and penalize Puritan clergy. Archbishop Whitgift's articles of 1583 demanded among other things that ministers acknowledge that the Book of Common Prayer was lawful and consonant with the word of God and that they promise to use it. This requirement was extended to all those entering the ministry by the canons of 1604. Although the drive to enforce clerical subscription at the beginning of James I's reign claimed some notable Puritan victims, the king generally turned a blind eye to those modifying or omitting prayer book worship once they had subscribed. The millenary petition presented to James I in 1603 demanded revision of the Book of

Common Prayer, and the consequent Hampton Court Conference led to minor amendments to the liturgy.

Migrating to New England, Puritans abandoned use of the Book of Common Prayer in their services. Official tolerance or pragmatism in England had evaporated by the 1630s when Charles I and Archbishop Laud demanded conformity to the Book of Common Prayer and attempted to impose a new version on Scotland. Liturgical issues, now combined with charges of "popish" practices and Arminian theology, were a major factor in the political crisis that led England into civil war. In 1645 the Book of Common Prayer was banned, and the Westminster Assembly's *Directory for the Public Worship of God,* prefaced by an indictment of the Book of Common Prayer, was issued as a guide to ministers on how to structure their services. The Book of Common Prayer returned with the monarchy: the 1661 Savoy Conference was a golden opportunity for revision, but the changes were minor; the readings from the Gospels and Epistles were taken from the Authorized Version, and a modified "black rubric" was reinstated. The 1662 Act of Uniformity required clergy to offer their "assent and consent" to the Prayer Book. As hopes of reunion with the Church of England dwindled and Nonconformists grasped the opportunities presented by the 1689 Toleration Act, Puritan distaste for the Book of Common Prayer became irrelevant to the movement.

See also: Antipopery, Surplice, Vestments, Westminster Assembly

Further Reading

F. E. Brightman, *The English Rite,* 2 vols. (London, 1915); F. Proctor, *A History of the Book of Common Prayer,* revised by W. H. Frere, (London, 1901).

John Spurr

Book of Discipline

The First Book of Discipline is the name used to refer to the document that provided the blueprint for the government of the Church of Scotland. Having been considered but not adopted by the Scottish parliament that in 1560 abolished the Mass and accepted a new confession of faith, it was accepted by an assembly of clergymen called by John Knox. Knox played the principal role in the drafting of the proposals, which were an essential part of the construction of the Presbyterian Church in Scotland. The document suppressed monasteries and chantries, but insisted that tithes should continue to be paid for the support of the parish ministry and schools. It called for parish grammar schools and higher level schools in every principal town. The Book established regional superintendents to oversee the implementation of reforms; originally appointed, the superintendents were after three years to be elected by the clergy of their region in consultation with neighboring superintendents. Prophesyings were required to be regularly held as a means of raising the quality of the clergy. Parish clergy were to be elected by their congregations, with the assistance of ministers of neighboring communities. The parish was also to elect elders, who were charged with supervising discipline and managing the parish finances.

Ambitious in the extreme, the First Book of Discipline was never formally approved by Parliament nor the monarch and was not fully implemented. Over the next decades, debate continued over how the church in Scotland was to be structured. A Second Book of Discipline was proposed in 1578. Whereas the First Book of Discipline had reflected a general Reformed outlook, the new proposal drew more specifically upon a Genevan model. Andrew Melville was the strongest proponent of the reform. Whereas the earlier work had accepted the role of bishops in the church, the new document was more critical of episcopacy and called for a more specifically Presbyterian and synodical church government. Its discussion of the proper relationship between church and state was drawn from Calvin's *Institutes.* Because it demanded clerical autonomy and denied any lay claims to church property, it too was never adopted by Crown or Parliament. However, its provisions were gradually implemented by the General Assembly of the church.

Inspired by the efforts of the Scottish church, English Reformers of the 1580s attempted to implement a similar reform in their own country.

Rebuffed in their efforts to turn the English parliament into the vehicle for reform, leading Reformers such as Thomas Cartwright, John Field, and Thomas Wilcox drafted their own proposals, which were also called the Book of Discipline. This document went through various drafts before it was eventually submitted to existing clerical conferences for endorsement in 1586. Reflecting the Scottish influence, the Book called for parish consistories, local clerical conferences, and provincial and national synods. It appears to have been formally endorsed by few of the regional conferences that considered it, but it did provide an impetus for an effort to elect Reformed candidates to the parliament of 1586, in the hope that they would replace the Book of Common Prayer with a Genevan order of service and would also debate reforms in church structure. Queen Elizabeth and her bishops prevented that from happening, and the English Book of Discipline had no immediate influence on reform.

See also: Thomas Cartwright, John Field, John Knox, Thomas Wilcox, Conference Movement, International Puritanism.
Further Reading
Philip Benedict, *Christ's Churches Purely Reformed: A Social History of Calvinism* (New Haven, 2002); Patrick Collinson, *The Elizabethan Puritan Movement* (1967); David Mullan, *Scottish Puritanism, 1590–1638* (Oxford, 2000); Margo Todd, *The Culture of Protestantism in Early Modern Scotland* (New Haven, 2002).

Francis J. Bremer

Book of Martyrs

The popular name for *The Actes and Monuments of the English Martyrs,* first published in 1563. It was the major work of John Foxe and told the history of Christianity in England, while memorializing those who gave their lives for their faith during the reign of the Roman Catholic Mary Tudor.

Foxe had first begun to consider a work that would establish the pre-Reformation roots of the Church of England during the reign of Edward VI. When Mary came to the throne, Foxe left England, along with many others, called Marian exiles. He journeyed first to the Netherlands and then moved on to Strasbourg, Frankfurt, and Basel. Over the next five years, approximately three hundred English men and women were burned as heretics. Foxe began to gather reports of their suffering. He considered adding some of these tales to an earlier work he had published on the persecution of the Lollards in England during an earlier time.

Following the death of Mary and the accession of Elizabeth to the English throne, leaders of the restored Protestant Church of England, including London's bishop Edmund Grindal, urged Foxe to expand the project he had been considering to make it into a full collection of the lives of the English martyrs. This is essentially what Foxe did, and his first edition of the *Acts and Monuments* began with the Lollards and told the story of the Marian persecutions. He drew material not only from official documents but also from the testimony of eyewitnesses and the writings of the martyrs themselves from prison.

The *Acts and Monuments* went through a number of editions during Foxe's lifetime. In each he worked to correct earlier editions and to expand the work by including the martyrdom of Continental saints and by going back in time to the early days of Christianity. New editions also featured a growing number of illustrations, over 150 in the latter editions. The work was an unequalled work of anti-Catholic propaganda, which had been the intention of those who supported Foxe. It was set up in many English churches and helped shape the Elizabethan sense of Protestant identity. Its influence extended to the English settlements in the New World, particularly New England.

See also: John Foxe, Marian Exiles, Marian Martyrs
Further Reading
David Loades, ed., *John Foxe and the English Reformation* (Aldershot, Eng., 1997); David Loades, ed., *John Foxe: An Historical Perspective* (Aldershot, Eng., 1999); J. F. Mozley, *John Foxe and His Book* (London, 1940).

Francis J. Bremer

Book of Sports

"The King's Book of Sports," also known as "The King's Declaration," was issued by James I in August 1617. When passing through Lancashire, the king had learned of bitter disputes between the defenders of customary entertainments on Sundays and puritan justices eager to ban such "profanations." At first the declaration applied solely to Lancashire, which the king saw as "much infested" by two extreme groups, puritans and papists. On 24 May 1618, James authorized the printing and nationwide distribution of the document, with a new introduction. Much later, in 1633 and 1634, Charles I republished "his blessed father's Declaration," with slight differences and his own addenda. It was ordered to be read in every parish church. It has been reprinted among the Primary Sources in this work in its entirety.

The central message of the declaration was that, providing good order was kept, a range of honest and healthy entertainments could be pursued on Sunday, but only after afternoon service had been attended. The tone was permissive rather than dictatorial. However, the first two versions contained important discrepancies. Piping was allowed in 1617 but not in 1618, and only in 1618 was there specific permission for May games, Whitsun ales, morris dances, and maypoles. When reissued in 1633–1634, the text was not updated or tightened to meet changing circumstances.

Since the 1570s, the puritan attack on popular recreations had resulted in various acts, royal proclamations, and court judgments imposing tighter controls or bans on Sundays. The Declaration of 1617 was a significant landmark in this controversy, though defenders and opponents interpreted it differently. Most local disputes were argued out in ecclesiastical and civil courts: some, for example, insisted that their celebrations had not actually coincided with divine service, though they had taken place before morning or afternoon worship. Lengthy diatribes were also written by both sides. Christopher Windle of Bisley (Oxfordshire) wrote a Latin commentary (1618) in fulsome support of the declaration. By contrast, Henry Burton's *Divine Tragedy* (1641) documented fifty-six examples of God's judgment "upon Sabbath breakers . . . in their unlawful sports." Thus, at Battersea near London, a young piper who played when a maypole was garlanded, "with the pipe in his mouth, fell down dead."

The greatest acrimony followed the declaration's republication in 1633–1634, which coincided with William Laud's appointment as archbishop of Canterbury. His ritualism and insistence on liturgical uniformity was seen by his enemies as an attempt to reimpose Catholicism. Though important fiscal, political, and constitutional factors were by now involved in the worsening relationship between king and Parliament, the reissued declaration was a provocation in two ways. It emboldened local communities into revitalizing traditional entertainments, and it simultaneously infuriated puritan clergy and laity, who saw this as godless flouting of the fourth commandment. Ministers who refused to read the book publicly, or who prevented such customs as morris dancing on Sundays, were suspended or ejected by Laudian bishops. Finally, during the Civil War, the puritan parliament of 1644 ordered that all copies of the Book of Sports were to be seized and publicly burned.

See also: Leisure Time, Theology of, Sports and Recreation
Further Reading
Julian Davies, *The Caroline Captivity of the Church* (Oxford, 1992); Christopher Durston and Jacqueline Eales, ed., *The Culture of English Puritanism, 1560–1700* (Manchester, Eng.,1996); Ronald Hutton, *The Rise and Fall of Merry England: The Ritual Year, 1400–1700* (Oxford, 1993); Kenneth Parker, *The English Sabbath* (New York, 1988).

David Dymond

Brattle Street Church

The Brattle Street Church, sometimes called the Church on Brattle Square, or, derisively, the Manifesto Church, first opened its doors in Boston on 24 December 1699. It was the fourth Congregational Church of Boston and the seventh church in the city (Quakers, Baptists, and Anglicans each had a meetinghouse). The founders sought to create a different kind of church, a congregation that was Calvinist and Congregational but also sympathetic to Anglican modes of worship and with a less publicly confessional membership requirement.

Being certain about what they wanted, the church's founders, who called themselves "the undertakers" (that is, those who were "undertaking" this new endeavor), published *A Manifesto or Declaration Set forth by the Undertakers of the New Church* in 1699, which staked out their new church's theological and ecclesiastical territory. These founders included Thomas Brattle (treasurer of Harvard College and donor of the land on which the church was built), William Brattle (tutor at Harvard), John Mico (a successful merchant), John Leverett (tutor at and future president of Harvard College), Thomas Banister (another wealthy merchant), and Benjamin Colman (first minister of Brattle Street and a student of Leverett). The founders of the church were generally merchants and at odds theologically and politically with Increase and Cotton Mather, who embodied New England's Puritan order. The Brattle Street's founders and the Mathers fought over control of Harvard College and the establishment of the new church.

The founder's manifesto simultaneously tied the Brattle Street Church to New England's Puritan Congregationalism and alienated it by asserting boldly a heterodox set of practices of worship and polity. They wanted a cosmopolitan church steeped in a culture of social reserve and politeness. But they also wanted to be part of the religious, commercial, and civil life of New England's most important port. Thus, they undertook the task of founding a new church that could meet all their needs.

A Different Sort of Congregationalism
Published in 1699, the manifesto was intended to "prevent all misapprehensions and jealousies" by declaring to both the church's prospective members and ecclesiastical peers its "aims, designs, principles and rules." The author or authors (probably Benjamin Colman) were aware of the impending controversy that their innovations would incite in orthodox New England. The aim of the document was to avoid tension. In publishing the manifesto, the undertakers attempted to lessen the shock waves they knew the founding of their new church would create.

The first of sixteen statements in the manifesto associated the Brattle Street Church with the Westminster Confession, the statement of orthodox puritan faith developed by the Westminster Assembly in the 1640s. This allegiance was not controversial; all Boston Congregational churches would have done the same at that time. The second declaration claimed that the new congregation would practice a "true and pure" worship of God. By so asserting, they partially allied themselves with the United Brethren in London. The United Brethren were an alliance that brought together Presbyterians and Independents (Congregationalists) in an effort to create a united Dissenting movement. However, the United Brethren were rejected by some Congregationalists in New England because they believed the agreement started Congregational churches down the path of Presbyterianism. In fact, the undertakers were not interested in Presbyterianism, and their decision to become part of the United Brethren was less about theology and polity and more about practice. The Brattle Street Church wanted scripture, chosen by the minister, to be read aloud without explication or comment to the congregation each Sabbath. The established New England Congregational churches were opposed to this form of worship, because it was too reminiscent of Anglican and Catholic practices.

Increase Mather, who at the time embodied the traditionalist impulse in New England Congregationalism, protested against the plain reading of scripture to the congregation, as well as against the new church's alliance with the United Brethren. But his opposition was tempered, because while in England he had been one of the architects of the United Brethren. He approved of the United Brethren as a force for reforming the Church of England, but he did not support their actual worship practices—especially in his hometown.

The manifesto went on to distinguish the new church in several other ways, including the saying of the Lord's Prayer at every meeting, the baptism of all children whose parents professed a faith in

Christ (as opposed to requiring church membership), no requirement to publicly relate a conversion experience in order to be a member, and the ability of all church members (even women) to vote on the calling and installation of a new minister. The manifesto also declared that the church body was a mutual voluntary society that was to meet regularly in the same place with the same minister. This distinction brought them back into alignment with the established New England Congregationalists by illustrating that they were neither Catholics nor Quakers.

Increase Mather published *The Order of the Gospel* in 1700 to refute the manifesto's theology, polity, and practice. Not to be outdone, the undertakers of Brattle Street Church published the *Gospel Order Revived* as a rebuttal. It was probably written by Benjamin Colman, but he did not sign it. (Boston printers claimed they could not print it because of a lack of signature, and so it was published in New York.) Cotton Mather entered the fray and published several pamphlets denouncing the Brattle Street Church's ideas and innovations. In response to these attacks, the members of Brattle Street Church invited their detractors to jointly observe a day of prayer on 31 January 1700. The Mathers, for both civil and religious reasons, could not refuse, and thus they symbolically accepted Brattle Street as an institutional peer. Despite the initial strident rhetoric and the actual differences, the Brattle Street Church became a genuine option for Boston Congregationalists who wanted a different style of worship and ecclesiastical organization. In short order, the church became a popular option for liberal-minded, cosmopolitan, and mercantile Bostonians. This acceptance and popularity was due in large part to the moderating and diplomatic efforts of Brattle Street's first minister, Benjamin Colman.

After the Founding

The church became the religious home of many of Boston's most successful merchants, largely due to its minimal membership requirements and its style of worship. Their controversial theology and practices became unremarkable in the face of the ever-evolving religious landscape of New England. Within two decades of the church's founding, other churches had instituted similar reforms. Colman served as senior pastor until his death in 1747. He had as his assistant William Cooper and then Samuel Cooper, who became senior minister after Colman's death. The Brattle Street Church participated in the Great Awakening by inviting George Whitfield, a prominent figure in that revival movement, to speak in their church. Both Colman and William Cooper took a public pro-revival stand, which created some tension with other Boston churches. During the latter part of the eighteenth century, Brattle Street Church became a center of American patriotism. The congregation and its ministers were so adamant in their patriot views that General Gage ordered his British Regular troops to use the church as their barracks during their occupation of Boston in the early stages of the Revolutionary War.

See also: Benjamin Colman
Further Reading
Samuel Kirkland Lothrop, *History of the Church in Brattle Street Boston . . .* (Boston, 1851); Perry Miller, *The New England Mind: From Colony to Province* (Cambridge, MA, 1953).

Daryl Sasser

Bridewell

The bridewell, a kind of corrective institution, was a product of sixteenth-century England's innovative overhaul of its means and methods of alleviating poverty. Inspired by the writings of Christian Humanism, with their emphasis on improving the welfare of all subjects, the bridewell was designed to receive individuals, specifically the poor, who were, or were likely to become, a drain upon the parish purse, such as "the riotous and prodigal person, that consumeth all with play and drinking;" "the dissolute person, as the strumpet, pilferer &c.;" "the slothful person, that refuseth to work;" "all such as wilfully spoil or embezzle their work;" and "the vagabond that will abide in no service or place" (Michael Dalton, *The Countery Justice* [1631], p. 101). Bridewells were to punish their behavior and instill a proper regard for the orderly and godly life through enforced labor. Thus, bridewells were to be a place of correction and reformation for the laboring poor. Ultimately, they failed, the bridewell slowly becoming conflated with the workhouse, until in 1865 the institution officially merged with the prison system to form the "local prison."

The first bridewell—Bridewell Hospital—was established in London during the early 1550s as the fifth and final hospital designed to control London's poverty problem. (The others were for the old, the sick, the mentally ill, and orphans.) In addition to its traditional use of stocks, whipping post, and loss of freedom, Bridewell Hospital set out to reclaim these lost souls through regular work and steady religious observance, with the added hope that, in a pioneering attempt at setting the poor to work, the inmates themselves might defray the costs of their incarceration through the sale of their own handiwork. Within a decade, London's Bridewell was a divided institution, with a small portion devoted to the training of poor boys and the greater part used as a corrective facility for the disorderly and idle, most of whom had been engaged in "prostitution, . . . , adultery, bigamy, profane swearing, dice-playing, drunkenness, slander, and running away from a master" (Innes, pp. 57–58). Other urban areas followed London's lead, with Oxford (1562), Salisbury (1564), Norwich (1565), Gloucester (1569), Ipswich (1569), plus as many as ten other areas, each establishing its own bridewell by the close of the sixteenth century. In nearly all cases, the erection of a bridewell was only one part of a comprehensive attempt to put an end to local poverty.

Between 1575 and 1630, a network of bridewells was established across England, including rural areas. Significantly, the distribution of individuals admitted to the bridewells differed between the urban and rural settings, with urban areas more concerned with clearing disorderly streets and rural ones preoccupied with enforcing the subordination of the lower orders, particularly those who violated labor and poor laws. Justices of the peace (JPs) were the linchpin in the establishment and filling of rural bridewells, and it is here, at the local level, that the role of Puritanism can most plainly be seen.

Bridewells figure prominently in the creation of England's most famous godly villages and towns, such as Sudbury, Suffolk, and the cities of Dorchester and Salisbury. In Sudbury, work was matched by prayer. Each inmate said "the General Confession, the Lord's Prayer, and a special prayer acknowledging that 'the punishment wherewith we be now scourged is much less than our deserts; but we humbly beseech Thee that it may work in us a reformation of our former life and true obedience [to] his Majesty's Laws'" (Slack, *Poverty*, p. 151). In Salisbury the appearance of the plague in 1627 sparked the town's leaders and leading Puritans, such as Henry Sherfield, to follow the course of its godly counterpart Dorchester, and strive for a "reformation, a true and real reformation of this city." This effort at reformation included the municipal control of poor relief to ensure the fair distribution of the poor rate; the establishment of a municipal storehouse to provided wood and food to the city's poor; the creation of a civic brew house in order to generate income (plus control consumption); and the workhouse, with its "careful supervision 'for avoiding of all prophaneness and vice whatsoever' (Slack, *Poverty*, p. 152)." As in London, Salisbury's workhouse was split between the manual training of children and the punishment of the idle. In this case, the children were to be "continually lodged dieted and kept to work in the said house and not be permitted . . . to resort home to their parents or else to wander up and down the streets." And, lest there be any confusion of identification, they were to wear blue caps and badges with the city arms "whereby they might be known the children of the workhouse and distinguished from all other children." Upon entering the bridewell, the idle of Salisbury were to be whipped, and "to be kept prisoners and not to have any come to them" (Slack, "Salisbury," p. 192).

The desire to curb the problems of poverty, to discipline the idle, and to reform the disorderly was not the sole domain of Puritans. Indeed, the impetus behind such social activism predates the rise of this hotter brand of Protestantism in England. Yet in the seventeenth century, it was the Puritans who were the heirs of Christian Humanism's social goals, if not its theology, providing a renewed enthusiasm for older ideas, as they strove to shape their local environments into parochial cities upon hills and minuscule new Jerusalems. The bridewell became, at least in the hearts and hopes of the godly, household-sized Genevas. It seems likely that Puritan JPs and parish elites would "have been especially anxious to promote the establishment of bridewells," given Puritanism's emphasis on public edification and wholesale reform, and as Joanna Innes points out, there were "more bridewells in West Suffolk, a notably Puritan district, than in any other county" (Innes, p. 72). The difference between Puritan and non-Puritan uses of the bridewell may well have been a degree of intensity rather than a change of form.

See also: Crime and Punishment
Further Reading

Joanna Innes, "Prisons for the Poor: English Bridewells, 1550–1800," in F. Snyder and D. Hay, eds., *Labour, Law, and Crime: An historical perspective* (London, 1987), pp. 42–122; Paul Slack, *From Reformation to Improvement: Public Welfare in Early Modern England* (Oxford, 1999); Paul Slack, *Poverty and Policy in Tudor and Stuart England* (1988); Paul Slack, "Poverty and Politics in Salisbury 1590–1666," in P. Clark and P. Slack, eds., *Crisis and Order in English Towns, 1500–1700: Essays in Urban History* (Toronto, 1972), pp. 164–203; Margo Todd, *Christian Humanism and the Puritan Social Order* (Cambridge, Eng., 1987).

Lynn A. Botelho

Broadsides

Large sheets of paper that were printed on one side only. They were among the most popular of printed formats, especially for ballads. Broadsides often contained a mixture of media: many contained woodcut pictures and songs, while some were intended to be read aloud. They were cheap (retailing for less than one penny), easily understood, and very popular. They were posted in public places and read aloud and found in homes, pasted up on chimneypieces for edification and entertainment. They were popular in town and countryside among all sorts of people, and those that survive represent a fraction of those originally printed. They were especially popular in England, from the mid-sixteenth century, and, though they continued to be popular with an increasing pictorial element in the early seventeenth century, from that time more radical political and religious ideas tended to be expressed in the form of news books. As the broadside was a format rather than a genre, there was considerable variation in subject, complexity, and audience. A significant proportion contained religious material that, while relatively light on theology, related to Puritanism in the realms of politics and domestic piety. Many others were far from spiritual and were condemned by preachers (and perhaps enjoyed by their readers) for their bawdiness.

Broadsides were never as overtly political as they were in the German Reformation, partly because English woodcut technology lagged behind that of its European neighbors, but as the period progressed, they touched on political issues and were manipulated in propagandist efforts, usually in conjunction with religion. Several were antipopish, such as *A table briefly pointing out such places of Scripture as condemn the principall points of popery* (1625), and produced in the aftermath of the Spanish match, the unsuccessfull effort to marry Charles Stuart, the heir to the throne, to a Catholic Spanish princess. During the Civil Wars, broadsides promoted the reputations of godly Parliamentarian heroes; at the Restoration, they were used to attack Puritanism. Later, during the Exclusion Crisis, propagandist broadsides highlighted the dangers of having a Catholic king.

Many broadsides bolstered Protestant piety, especially the godly "tables," complex broadsides containing pictures, poems, and prayers, all with domestic devotional purposes. Some were broadly puritan, such as *A godly meditation day and night to be exercised* (ca. 1600), while others combined the devotional with the educational, such as *Finch his Alphabet, or, A Godly direction, fit to be perused of each true Christian* (ca. 1635). Though rarely explicitly Puritan in their theology, many tables flaunted godly reputations, for instance *Old Mr Dod's Sayings* (1667), which purported to be the sayings of the Puritan divine John Dod. Others provided edification and entertainment in their description of providential occurrences. Though they contained scandalous news, often detailing monstrous births, these were compatible with broadly Puritan ideas about the interventions of God in the world. Puritan clergy rarely countenanced broadsides, especially their vivid woodcuts, but shared common theological ground with the godly tables.

See also: Ballads
Further Reading
Alexandra Walsham, *Providence in Early Modern England* (Oxford, 1999); Tessa Watt, *Cheap Print and Popular Piety, 1550–1640* (Cambridge, Eng., 1991).

Andrew Cambers

Brownism
See Separatists

Burial Practices

After the Reformation, the great majority of English people were still buried in a traditional manner in ancient churchyards, but behind this apparent continuity from the past lay fundamental changes of belief, liturgy, and practice. Most revolutionary was the decisive rejection of the Catholic concept of purgatory, the after-death realm where souls were supposedly purged of their pardonable sins before entering heaven. Elaborate funerary masses, prayers, and commemorations could no longer be justified, and the old cyclical relationship between the living and dead had lost its meaning. Now it was believed that the soul at death went instantly to its eternal reward: heaven for the righteous, hell for the sinful. Funerals could only benefit the living, for the fate of the dead was already sealed.

The second Book of Common Prayer, issued in 1552 and readopted after Elizabeth's succession to the throne in 1558, provided a burial service that was shorter and more Calvinistic than its predecessor of 1549. Gone were the communion, the commendation of the soul, and several psalms. The minister merely met the burial party at the churchyard stile, escorted it to the graveside (or church), said or sang a few short passages, and read a lesson and collect. While he intoned the powerful words of the committal, earth was cast upon the corpse by "some standing by." The keynote was respect and decency, without superstition.

All this was not radical enough for the puritan writers of *An Admonition to the Parliament* (1572). To them burial was simply a pious and charitable duty incumbent on everyone. Any form of "prescript" (prescribed) service was unscriptural and superstitious, and nothing could justify the involvement of ministers, pealing of bells, or use of surplices, funeral sermons, and doles. Consecrated graveyards were not needed, nor were particular ways of digging graves. Corpses were viewed as "loathsome carrion," yet paradoxically they were destined, it was believed, to be reassembled whole and perfect for the Last Judgment. To people convinced that humankind was divided into the saved and the damned, the most objectionable part of the prayer book's service were the all-inclusive words, "in sure and certain hope of resurrection to eternal life;" several substitutes were proposed such as, "some to joy and some to punishment." The most extreme statement of puritan thinking came in the Presbyterian Directory of Public Worship, officially adopted in 1653. Pointing out that praying, reading, and singing had been "grossly abused," it demanded burial "without any ceremony," "decently attended" by Christian friends.

In the burial service, stoutly defended by John Whitgift and others, puritan preachers and writers constantly saw idolatry and popish praying for the dead. Equally reprehensible in their eyes were surviving popular superstitions and folk beliefs of a quasi-Catholic kind, such as watching the corpse, sprinkling it, and holding wakes after funerals. In this fevered atmosphere, local zealots physically attacked pre-Reformation tombs in churches, particularly when they bore religious images or popish inscriptions such as "Pray for the soul of . . .." Some iconoclasts went so far as to smash purely secular images and inscriptions, although Elizabeth had is-

An eighteenth-century puritan gravestone depicting a crude death figure struggling with an angel in an attempt to extinguish the light of the spirit in the form of a candle. (MPI/Getty Images)

sued a proclamation in 1560 forbidding this senseless destruction.

Believing that burials should be simple and sober, the godly fiercely criticized all kinds of costly "pomp," for example mourning clothes or "blacks," heraldic displays and processions, the custom of embalmment, and large-scale consumption of food and drink. Funeral sermons were originally put into this category, but by 1600 were accepted as a convenient means of celebrating godly lives. The irony, however, is that in the late sixteenth and seventeenth centuries the wealthier ranks of society probably indulged in more secular display and expenditure at funerals than ever before. Simultane-

ously their monuments proliferated greatly, using new kinds of non-Christian symbolism, while the interiors of churches became ever more strictly divided into zones, determined by social class for both the living and the dead. Indeed, social status was a major reason for the variable nature of Protestant funerals, and even the directory allowed due deference to rank.

No single, distinctively puritan form of burial emerged in England. At one end of the spectrum, most of the godly tolerated the prayer book, if only grudgingly. Samuel Clarke, puritan biographer, described the church funerals of many godly divines, which were attended by huge numbers of mourners, both ministers and laity, expressing "much sorrow and lamentation." A substantial number, however, viewed the prayer book more critically, and in doing so risked prosecution. Ministers like Richard Greenham used the text selectively; others refused to greet the corpse at the stile or to wear a surplice. Sometimes the duty of burial was diplomatically avoided. In about 1607, a layman conducted several burials in the churchyard of Coggeshall (Essex), without a minister or the prayer book. Another strategy, in order to escape churchyards and the official service, was to use newly established extramural graveyards; for example the new Bethlehem (Bedlam) cemetery outside London was used by "divers fantastical persons" from at least 1584.

Small numbers of extremists broke away from the established church altogether and set up their own independent congregations. They buried their dead where they pleased, and one burial soon attracted others. For example, at Walsham-le-Willows (Suffolk) in 1656, at least three individuals were "put into a hole in Thomas Cooke's orchard" by a group known as "Brethren of the Separation." Similarly the Quakers, from the 1650s onward, created many new graveyards in different parts of the country, most of which lasted for generations. In the New World too, the earliest burials were as simple and unceremonious as the admonition had demanded, and burial grounds were separated from churches. Within a few decades, however, New Englanders were beginning to adopt elaborately carved headstones, mourning clothes, and funeral sermons.

See also: Death and Dying

Further Reading

David Cressy, *Birth, Marriage, and Death: Ritual, Religion, and the Life Cycle in Tudor and Stuart England* (Oxford, 1997); Ralph Houlbrooke, ed., *Death, Ritual and Bereavement* (Oxford, 1989); Peter Jupp and Clare Gittings, eds., *Death in England: An Illustrated History* (Manchester, Eng., 1999); David Stannard, *The Puritan Way of Death: A Study in Religion, Culture and Social Change* (New York, 1977).

David Dymond

C

Calamy House Accord

Also known as the Aldermanbury Accord, this is the name given to an agreement reached between leading Congregationalists and Presbyterians in late 1641. Thomas Goodwin, Philip Nye, and other Congregationalists newly returned to England met with English Presybyterians at the Aldermnabury, London, home of Edmund Calamy. The two reformist groups agreed to neither write, speak, nor take action against the views of the opposing side while they joined together to dismantle those parts of the Church of England most in need of reform and also to combat the spread of sectarianism. Over the next few years this amity was generally maintained and some of the publications of leaders on each side were commended by clergy on the other side. The unity began to fragment as the divisions between Congregationalists and Presybterians in the Westminster Assembly became more evident. While not taking to the lists against Congregationalism themselves, English Presbyterians aided the attacks on New England Congregationalism penned by Scottish Presbyterian authors such as Robert Baillie. On their side, Goodwin, Nye, and their colleagues facilitated the publication of tracts by John Cotton, John Davenport, and other colonial authors advocating and defending the "New England Way." The agreement finally collapsed in 1644 with the publication of the Congregationalists' *An Apologeticall Narration,* openly calling for the accommodation of their views in any Presbyterian religious settlement.

See also: *An Apologeticall Narration,* Independency, Smectymnuus, Westminster Assembly
Further Reading
Francis J. Bremer, *Congregational Communion: Clerical Friendship in the Anglo-American Puritan Community, 1610–1692* (Boston, 1994).

Francis J. Bremer

Cambridge Agreement

An agreement signed at Cambridge, England, by twelve members of the Massachusetts Bay Company pledging themselves to migrate to New England, to bring the charter of the company with them and to thus transfer the company headquarters from England to Massachusetts. The signatories included Sir Richard Saltonstall, Thomas Dudley, John Winthrop, William Pynchon, and Isaac Johnson.

For the agreement to take effect, the plan had to be approved by the General Court of the company, where it was debated and approved later that month. The significance of the agreement and its subsequent implementation is that it changed the nature of the colony being established. Whereas all other such ventures involved a corporation sending colonists and controlling their activities from England, Massachusetts would be governed by men living in the colony. Furthermore, by transferring the corporation charter to America, the leaders of the colony made it more difficult for the royal government to seize or revoke the charter, thus making the colony more autonomous than it would otherwise have been.

See also: Massachusetts Bay Company
Further Reading
Francis J. Bremer, *John Winthrop: America's Forgotten Founding Father* (New York, 2003); Frances Rose-Troup, *The Massachusetts Bay Company and Its Predecessors* (New York, 1930).

Francis J. Bremer

Cambridge Assembly

The Cambridge Assembly, or Synod, was a gathering of representatives of the New England church convened on an invitation of the Massachusetts General Court issued in May of 1646. The stated purpose was to craft a formal statement of the New England system of church government for the benefit of Englishmen who were still debating the reform of their national church. But other factors undoubtedly played a part in the decision. Though it was being challenged by English Congregationalists, Parliament had recently adopted a Presbyterian system of church government, as recommended by the Westminster Assembly, and some feared that, in the absence of a set colonial system, there might be an attempt to extend the Presbyterian system to the colonies. Also of concern to some of the New England leaders was the emergence of colonial calls for Presbyterianism in the Massachusetts towns of Newbury and Hingham. It appeared time to formally set out what the majority of New Englanders practiced and were committed to.

The assembly first met in Cambridge in September in the buildings of Harvard College. Some churches had been torn over whether such a gathering was tolerable in a congregational system, and at the first meeting there were no representatives from the churches of Salem, Boston, Hingham, and Concord. All but Hingham soon relented, however. Joining the representatives of the churches of Massachusetts were laymen and clergy sent by churches in New Hampshire, the colony of Plymouth, the Connecticut Colony, and the New Haven Colony. The assembly discussed the role of the civil magistrate in religious matters, the nature and power of synods, and the authority of the civil power to call for such assemblies. After two weeks of deliberations, the reverends John Cotton of Boston, Richard Mather of Dorchester, Massachusetts, and Ralph Partridge of Plymouth's Duxbury Church were appointed to prepare drafts of a model of church government, and then the assembly was adjourned till the following June.

The June 1647 session of the assembly was attended by Plymouth's Governor William Bradford, among others, but adjourned quickly due to the ravages of a regional epidemic, which caused the death of Connecticut's Thomas Hooker and Governor John Winthrop's wife, Margaret. The assembly convened for its final session in August 1648. The delegates affirmed their unity with international puritanism by adopting the Confession of Faith drawn up by the Westminster Assembly. They refined the model prepared by Richard Mather and offered it, with a preface by John Cotton, as their platform of church government.

See also: Cambridge Platform, Westminster Confession of Faith
Further Reading
Francis J. Bremer, *Congregational Communion: Clerical Friendship in the Anglo-American Puritan Community, 1610–1692* (Boston, 1994); Williston Walker, ed., *The Creeds and Platforms of Congregationalism* (Philadelphia, 1960).

Francis J. Bremer

Cambridge Platform

The Cambridge Platform (1648) was prepared by delegates from the churches of New England to be their official statement of faith and policy. It was prepared by the Cambridge Assembly, which was called into being by the Massachusetts General Court and met in three sessions between 1646 and 1648. It was intended to affirm the congregational system of church government at a time when some New Englanders were challenging that order and petitioning for Presbyterian practices. It was also hoped that the promulgation of the platform would aid those who were advocating congregationalism in England.

The preface to the declaration was prepared by Boston's John Cotton and sought to emphasize the colonists' commitment to maintaining unity and harmony with the best reformed churches in Europe and to demonstrate that the assembly endorsed the Confession of Faith previously issued by England's Westminster Assembly. It also defended the New England Way against Presbyterian charges that congregationalism fostered sectarianism.

The platform was based largely on a draft model prepared by Richard Mather. It asserted that a congregational church was "a company of saints . . . united into one body by a holy covenant, for the public worship of God and the mutual edification one of another." Each such congregation was to choose its own clerical and lay officers. Ministers were not only to be selected by the congregation but ordained by the congregation through imposition of hands. Each congregation was a self-governing unit. In terms of the power granted by Christ unto the "brotherhood of the church . . . it resembles a democracy," while in respect of the authority committed to the clerical and lay officers it was an aristocracy. Those who were admitted to membership in the congregational brotherhood were required to show "repentance from sin and faith in Jesus Christ." The platform justified the requirement of a personal and public confession of faith by those seeking membership, as had become the practice in most of the region's churches. It was ambiguous on the question of eligibility for baptism, which was beginning to prove troublesome and eventually lead to the controversy centered on the Half-Way Covenant.

Drawing on the experience of clerical associations in England and New England, the assembly allowed the calling of synods and granted the civil magistrates the right to call such gatherings. Synods were allowed to debate and determine matters of faith, to discuss and recommend church practices, to censure corrupt churches and doctrine, and to propose means for reformation. But the synods were advisory only and could not exercise authority over or impose discipline on any church or individual.

The Cambridge Platform became the foundation document for New England churches and for the congregational denominations that evolved from those roots. It influenced the Declaration of Faith and Order adopted by England's Congregationalists at the Savoy Assembly of 1658.

Further Readings:
Williston Walker, editor, *The Creeds and Platforms of Congregationalism* (Boston, 1960).

Francis J. Bremer

Catechisms

Summaries of religious doctrine in a form designed to teach those beliefs, often as a series of questions with answers. They generally include or focus on the Ten Commandments, the Apostles' Creed, and the Lord's Prayer. In the Middle Ages, catechisms were developed as means of preparing youth for confession, confirmation, and Holy Communion. Sometimes these catechisms were in the form of oral instruction, such as a series of catechetical sermons. Later, book forms were developed.

Protestants made the most of the development of printing by preparing instructional catechismal booklets to assist in the propagation of their faiths. Close to 200 separate catechisms were published in Germany alone in the 1520s. Calvin published a catechism for Geneva in the mid-1530s.

The Book of Common Prayer of 1549 contained a catechism, which was enlarged in 1604 and was the official shorter catechism of the Church of England. Numerous unofficial publications elaborated on the official catechism, making it easier to use by adapting it to the needs of particular age groups and elaborating on the message it contained. The simplest focused on short responses to be memorized. Others, particularly those designed for adults, elaborated on the answers and set forth their implications for the Christian life. Orthodox churchmen prepared catechisms, as did Reformers such as Eusebius Pagit and John Ball, but the form was such that most English Protestant catechisms presented a common doctrinal ground. Some clergymen prepared their own (unpublished) catechisms as an aid in instructing the youth of their parish, and some laymen may have adapted published catechisms for family instruction.

Puritans who came to New England used catechisms in the New World as they had in the Old World. John Cotton prepared an extensively used catechism titled *Milk for Babes, Drawn Out of the Breasts of both Testaments* (1646), which was popular on both sides of the Atlantic and went through nine printings in the seventeenth century. The Westminster Assembly of Divines drew up its own catechisms during the 1640s.

See also: Westminster Catechisms, Cotton's Catechism (in Primary Sources)
Further Reading
Ian Green, *The Christian's ABC: Catechisms and Catechizing in England, c. 1530–1740* (Oxford, 1996).

Francis J. Bremer

Censorship

The publication of printed books in England began in the late fifteenth century. The number of printers increased in the reign of Edward VI, was reduced by Mary Tudor, and grew again in Elizabeth's reign. But the number was still small and the output subject to regulation, both by the Stationers Company (the guild of printers) and the government. Licensing of printed books was introduced in 1553, and in 1559 a license from a bishop or university chancellor was made necessary for a book to be published. In 1557 the Stationers Company was placed in charge of the printing business and in 1566 authorized to search workshops as part of its regulatory function. In 1586 printing was restricted to London, Oxford, and Cambridge.

Despite these efforts at controlling the dissemination of ideas, controversial ideas still were able to reach the reading public. Before the invention of printing, Lollard "books" had circulated, and copies of handwritten manuscripts (scribal publication) continued to be one way of disseminating subversive ideas. Printed books that could not be published in England were published abroad and easily smuggled into the country. Authors and publishers found ways to cast their arguments that might evade the attention of censors. And illegal presses, such as the one that issued the Presbyterian pamphlets known as the Marprelate tracts, were difficult to detect and suppress.

There were sporadic attempts to achieve more effective regulation of the press in the 1620s and 1630s, largely associated with (or at least blamed on) William Laud. The outbreak of the wars of the 1640s led to the collapse of censorship. Earlier scribal publications critical of church and government policies were now able to be printed, and new radical voices were able to reach print.

In New England a press was established at Cambridge in 1639. In the first ten years, the only items published were ten almanacs, five college commencement broadsides, a catechism, two editions of the Bay Psalm Book, and *The Book of the General Laws and Liberties* of Massachusetts. There was no formal system of censorship, but the press was clearly controlled by the orthodox so that criticisms of the civil or church authorities of the region were either published in England or circulated in manuscript form.

See also: Marprelate Tracts
Further Reading
David Hall and Alexandra Walsham, "'Justification by Print Alone?' Protestantism, Literacy, and Communications in the Anglo-American World of John Winthrop," in Francis J. Bremer and Lynn Botelho, eds., *The World of John Winthrop, 1588–1649* (Boston, 2005); Samuel Eliot Morison, *The Intellectual Life of Colonial New England* (New York, 1936); Nigel Wheale, *Writing and Society: Literacy, Print and Politics in Britain, 1590–1660* (London, 1999).

Francis J. Bremer

Christmas

The traditional festival celebrating Christ's nativity, observed by Catholics, Anglican Protestants, and many non-Christians, but considered by strict Puritans to be superstitious hedonism with no basis in scripture. The concept of Christmas appears to have emerged during the second century, reflecting the influence of pagan festivals such as the Saturnalia

(17–24 December), the Calends (1 January), and the central festival of the Mithraic cult, Dies Natalis Invicti Solis (Birthday of the Unconquered Sun), held on 25 December. In northern Europe there was a move to assimilate Yuletide celebrations connected with the midwinter solstice, including decorations such as holly, ivy, and mistletoe. Despite an Eastern tradition that Christ had been born on 6 January, enthusiasm for a December nativity proved overwhelming. The date of 25 December was officially adopted by the Papacy at some time between 354 and 360, although the term "Christ-mass" does not appear to have entered common usage until the ninth century. The character of Father Christmas and the custom of giving children presents are of medieval Dutch-German origin, centered on the cult of the fourth-century saint Nicholas and a character known as the Knecht Ruprecht. Dutch Protestant émigrés to America later merged Nicholas-Ruprecht with a magician from Nordic folklore who rewarded good children. In medieval and early modern Europe, Father Christmas was often pictured as an old white-bearded man dressed in a long white robe, while the equally traditional Lord of Misrule was red-robed. The prevailing modern image of Santa Claus, encapsulated in the Coca-Cola advertising images created by Haddon Sundblom between 1930 and 1950, therefore has considerable precedent.

The Christmas Act of 1448 required businesses in England to close on Christmas Day and to remove their goods from public display. Religious festivities included carols, poetry, and mystery plays. At the same time, however, Christmas in England was characterized by the reign of the "Lord of Misrule" (often a servant appointed to act as master of ceremonies), whose appearance in the houses of the nobility and gentry heralded a period of feasting and drinking, disorder and excess, which continued until Twelfth Night. The Scottish equivalent, the "Abbot of Unreason," was banned by Mary, Queen of Scots, in 1555. Henry VIII passed a law in 1511 proscribing mummers' plays, as the masked players themselves, moving from house to house, were believed to be responsible for an increasing amount of seasonal crime. Despite the

threat of heavy fines and imprisonment, the plays continued to be performed. In the first of several editions of *The Anatomie of Abuses* (1583), the Puritan Philip Stubbes railed against "masking and mumming, whereby robbery, whoredom, murder and what not is committed," as well as gambling and excessive eating and drinking, "to the great dishonor of God and the impoverishing of the realm."

Since their emergence within English Protestantism in the 1560s, Puritans had viewed Christmas and its various traditions as evidence of continuing popish influence within the Church of England. English Catholics did indeed retain a notable fondness and reverence for the festival, as did the English royal household. The ostentatious Christmas celebrations of the early Stuart monarchy, particularly the sumptuous and incredibly expensive Christmas masques, were a particular point of tension between Puritans and the court. These two issues combined with the appearance of Charles I's Catholic consort, Queen Henrietta-Maria, as an earth goddess in a Christmas masque. The performance was condemned by William Prynne, who in *Histrio-Mastix: The Player's Scourge* (1633) attacked both Christmas and (by implication) the queen. The Puritan reminded his readers of the pagan origins of the festivities, and urged "all pious Christians eternally to abominate them." Prynne's subsequent fine, imprisonment, and mutilation at the hands of the royal judiciary only served to emphasize the divide.

During the English Civil War, strenuous efforts were made in areas under Parliamentarian control to treat 25 December as a normal day. In 1645, a new Directory of Public Worship was published, which declared that "holy days, having no warrant in the Word of God are not to be continued." In 1647 Parliament passed an ordinance specifically banning the feasts of Christmas, Easter, and Whitsun. The proscription proved difficult to enforce: Christmas Day 1647 witnessed serious civil disorder in London and many English towns. A particularly violent riot in Canterbury led to a full-scale uprising and a second civil war. Measures to repress Christmas services and sermons appear to have been largely effective throughout the 1650s, although it proved almost impossible to enforce laws against private celebrations. Even Thomas Fairfax, former commander of the New Model Army, was fined for attending a Christmas play in 1655. There was also a steady stream of clandestine literature promoting Christmas festivities and deriding Puritan killjoys. These pamphlets were attacked in their turn by Puritan ministers, who defended the ban on the grounds that Christmas was a human invention and a relic of paganism and popery. However, shops in London had continued to close on 25 December in defiance of the ban, and in 1657 the Anglican John Evelyn was able to record a "grand assembly" held to celebrate Christmas in a London chapel. The failure to change the habits of the nation had political as well as religious consequences: the repression of Christmas contributed significantly to the unpopularity of Puritan rule under Cromwell, and the conspicuous resumption of Christmas festivities after the Restoration of 1660 helped propagate the merry image of the restored monarchy.

In America the Puritan rejection of Christmas was epitomized by the Pilgrim Fathers, who spent 25 December 1620 erecting their first building, before returning to the *Mayflower*. Their influence appears to have remained in some areas until the late nineteenth century: until at least 1870, public schools in Boston held classes on Christmas Day and punished absenteeism. However, magazines such as *St. Nicholas Magazine* (1887) and *Harper's Young People* (1894) countered with short stories in which dour seventeenth-century Puritan characters attempted to repress their children's jollity, before succumbing to the temptation to delight them with presents and festive greenery. The story of Christmas since then has been one of increasing secularization and consumerism.

Further Reading
Christopher Durston, "Lords of Misrule: The Puritan War on Christmas 1642–60," *History Today*, 35 (December 1985), 7–14; Karal Ann Marling, *Merry Christmas!: Celebrating America's Greatest Holiday* (Cambridge, MA, 2000); Daniel Miller, ed., *Unwrapping Christmas* (Oxford, 1993); Ralph Pimlott, *An Englishman's Christmas* (Hassocks, Eng., 1978); David Underdown, *Revel, Riot and Rebellion: Popular Politics and Culture in England, 1603–1660* (Oxford, 1987).

David J. Appleby

Christology

Teaching on the person, nature, and role of Christ. Traditional Christian teaching, adopted in general by the churches of the Reformation, including the Church of England, emphasizes the fact that Jesus Christ is both human and divine. On the one hand Christ is the eternal son of God, and on the other hand he is also a human being who suffered and died for the salvation of human beings. The essence of the union of these two natures—the incarnation—has traditionally been seen as a mystery, acceptance of which rests on faith, but this has not prevented theologians from elaborating on and attempting to tease out the meaning of the doctrine. During the long history of Christology, some theologians have been perceived as making too much of a separation between Christ's divine and human natures, while others have been seen as tending to emphasize his divinity at the expense of his humanity.

The leading churchmen of the Church of England in the sixteenth and seventeenth centuries, puritans included, held traditional beliefs about the dual nature of Christ, seeing him as fully human and fully divine at the same time. Claims that puritans focused more on the Old Testament in their preaching and thus did not make Christ central to their teaching are false, as analyses of sermons clearly demonstrate. Numerous puritans made Christ central to their teaching.

These traditional views were challenged by Socinianism, which originated in the writings of Faustus Socinus, who, in the sixteenth century, questioned the doctrine of the Trinity and argued that Christ was simply a man to whom God gave divine powers. Other Socinians denied the redemptive role of Christ, rejecting as well the doctrine of original sin and arguing that Christ's role was merely to show humanity the path to follow to be saved. Rakow, a town in Poland, became the center of this teaching, and the Racovian Catechism

(1605; English editions 1614 and 1624) an important means of its dissemination. John Hales and William Chillingworth were among the English thinkers who took up these ideas in the 1630s.

Socinianism appeared to be spreading in England following the erosion of church authority during the wars of the 1640s. Responding to this danger, Parliament reacted to an English publication of the Racovian Catechism in 1651 by ordering it burnt and appointing a committee headed by John Owen that was charged with drawing up a list of fundamentals of the faith. The committee prepared a document known as *The Humble Proposals,* but it was defeated through protests by Roger Williams, founder of Rhode Island and advocate of toleration, among others. John Biddle and other Socinians appeared to be gaining support in the following years, and Parliament responded by imprisoning Biddle, ordering his books burnt, and jailing him in 1655 under the terms of the Blasphemy Act. Such efforts did nothing to diminish the attraction of Socinianism for many, and these beliefs continued to trouble orthodox Englishmen through the seventeenth century and beyond. John Owen continued his efforts to defend orthodox Christology, emphasizing the role of the Holy Spirit, the third person of the Trinity, as the motive force of Christ's actions.

See also: Anti-Trinitarianism, Atonement, Soteriology
Further Reading
John Coffey, *Persecution and Toleration in Protestant England, 1558–1689* (Harlow, Eng., 2000); H. R. Mackintosh, *The Doctrine of the Person of Jesus* (Edinburgh, 2000 edition of work originally published in 1912).

Francis J. Bremer

Church Covenants

Agreements on which local Congregational churches were grounded.

Many puritans, including most of those who settled in America, desired to limit church membership to those perceived as saints (those chosen by God for salvation) and to give greater freedom to individual congregations than was given by other forms of church government. These "Congregationalists" believed that a true church consisted of a voluntary association of believers who contracted with God and each other to adhere to scriptural rules of government and church organization. At the heart of their ecclesiastical theory was the local church covenant, a document prepared by those recognized by their fellow believers as especially godly—"pillars" upon whom a church could be erected—and in which they pledged to form a church. These covenants, which differed in some degree from church to church, contained written promises to unite in faith and brotherly love, to serve as communal watchmen over each other, to partake together the ordinances of God, to worship him, to edify one another, and to live the gospel as required in the scriptures. Subsequent candidates for admittance, once judged by the elders and congregation to be of the visibly elect, were sanctioned under the covenant as members. Only those who satisfied these strict requirements were granted the privileges of formal church membership, which included the right to elect ministers and other officers, appropriate funds, determine church policy, and admit, dismiss, or discipline other members. Since the covenant represented an agreement between God and the local congregation, outside human authority, including synods, assemblies, councils, and civil government, held no jurisdiction over the local church. Nonmembers were compelled to submit to the rule of the pious in church affairs.

In New England, the covenant was considered the scriptural foundation of social order. It was based on theological principles from the Bible, contractualism, and mutual consent. Violations of the covenant were thought to be both violations of scripture and contrary to the ideals of common consent. Through consent the covenant was created and through consent the church was governed. The covenant, then, institutionalized popular participation in local church government.

Throughout the colonial period and beyond, Congregationalists continued to base their churches on written covenants. As they began to struggle with issues of church government in the eighteenth century, churches began to vary over the specific practices that commitment to the church covenant entailed. This new development, however, did not alter the fundamental belief that churches were grounded on the written consent of the governed. The consent of the people continued to be expressed in these covenants. As generations passed from the founding of a church, "covenant renewals" were employed to continually maintain the consent of the members and to preserve the idea of the covenant.

See also: Independency
Further Reading
James F. Cooper Jr., *Tenacious of their Liberties: Congregationalists in Colonial Massachusetts* (New York, 1995); Perry Miller, *The New England Mind: The Seventeenth Century* (Cambridge, MA, 1939); Edmund S. Morgan, *Visible Saints: The History of a Puritan Idea* (Ithaca, 1963).

Aaron Christensen

Churching of Women

The ceremony of the churching of women was performed approximately one month after childbirth to mark the reentry of a mother into the church. It was one of the many Catholic rites retained by the English church at the Reformation, which became a flashpoint in conflicts between traditionalists and those with Puritan sympathies well into the late seventeenth century, reaching its apogee in the abolition of the ceremony in the Interregnum. The rite, also known as the "Purification of Women" and as the "Thanksgiving of Women after Childbirth," can be seen as removing the stigma of sexuality and childbirth from a mother, as presenting an opportunity for an interaction that placed motherhood at the center of social theater, or as marking the end of a period of ritual separation by a process of reincorporation. This ambiguity of purpose fed the intellectual debate in the sixteenth and seventeenth centuries, making it both a popular social ritual and a rite that for Puritans carried intimations of superstition, popery, and Judaism. The result was an intellectual debate that exemplified many of the is-

sues that divided Puritans and traditionalists and was an occasion for conflict in churches across England, as parents and clergy clashed over the performance of the ritual. The ambiguity surrounding the ritual has also created a less acrimonious modern intellectual debate between those who see the ritual as an affirmation of motherhood and those who have stressed its penitential aspects, a debate that feeds into a larger discussion about the nature of gender, family life, and religion.

The ceremony itself, as it survived in the 1552 and subsequent Book of Common Prayer, was relatively brief, involving a procession through the church, kneeling "in some convenient place," and the recitation of Psalm 121. Puritans objected to some of these elements, not least the kneeling, which had traditionally been before the rood screen; although it was now directed to be close to the communion table, it could still be in the same place. They also disliked the use of the psalmist's observation that "the Sun shall not burn thee by day: neither the Moon by night," out of context, which they saw as introducing elements of paganism or Jewish traditions into the church. Similar objections were also raised to the giving of offerings at the end of the ceremony, mentioned in the prayer book; the offering had originally consisted of the christening, or "chrisom," cloth of the child, but it seems to have metamorphosed into the veil worn by women in the ceremony, or simple offerings of cloths. There were also objections to the idea that "green women," as new mothers were called between the birth and churching, could not enter the church, that they were inherently dangerous and should even be buried outside of consecrated ground. Not least of the Puritan protests may have been against the celebrations, or "gossipings," that accompanied the event, which by this time included not only the parents and "godsibs" (godparents), but the women who had been present at the childbirth. As these celebrations often involved feasting and alcohol (and were principally located in the local tavern or alehouse), objections to this custom constituted part of a wider objection to drunkenness and Sabbath breaking.

Historians have debated whether the traditionalist or Puritan standpoints on the ceremony better exemplify a "feminist" perspective: some see the traditionalists as upholding a ceremony that marked an unusual moment of female centrality; others see the Puritans as attempting to remove an oppressive view of childbirth as a social evil. Either may have contributed to more positive views of women that later emerged, but this was certainly not the intention, or the central theme of the dispute over the ceremony. Rather it was the contest between those who upheld established practice and those who saw such practice as a Trojan horse admitting superstition into the church that excited most debate. *An Admonition to the Parliament,* a clandestine pamphlet issued in 1572 calling for more drastic reform of the church, stated that the rite "smelleth of Jewish purification." Thomas Cartwright objected to the offering as "most Jewish." Henry Barrow saw it at one point as "a mixed action of Judaism and popery." Most Puritan writers objected along these lines, often reiterating the rather confused objections to the rite on the basis of its origins.

There is considerable evidence from court and visitation records that these objections to the ritual permeated the popular Puritan consciousness. It is notable that this controversy, unlike many other points of contention such as element of the rites of baptism and communion, provided women with an opportunity to protest, which some clearly availed themselves of, either by avoiding the ceremony altogether, or by engaging in staged objections or satires. On the other side it has been argued that most women welcomed the ceremony and that it was not, as might, but rarely has, been assumed, a simply oppressive institution. However, although it might be noted that female participation and popularity do not necessarily negate the effects of part of a patriarchal system and indeed the acquiescence or enthusiasm of the suppressed in their suppression is often a vital element in such systems.

The practice of churching should have officially come to an end in 1645, when the Directory of Public Worship replaced the existing Elizabethan Book of Common Prayer. However, continuation of the practice is evident in the diaries of the some of the royalist elite. Widespread popular defiance of the directory has yet to be uncovered, but the adoption of ceremonies of thanksgiving, naturally stripped of all superstitious elements, like that created by Richard Baxter for the mothers of Kidderminster in the 1650s, suggests that a social imperative to commemorate childbirth still existed. Popular objections to the reinstatement of the ceremony are much clearer, when, in the decade after the Restoration of 1660, visitation returns contain relatively large numbers of cases concerning the failure of women to participate in the ceremony. Much of this increase in numbers of those not participating may simply be part of the inability to close the Pandora's Box of separatism that had been opened in the years of war and commonwealth; it may also reflect a genuine attempt to enforce the rites of the church.

Like many other elements of established ritual that were debated in the century and a quarter after the break with Rome, the issue of churching seems to have gradually declined in importance as enforcement loosened and perhaps consequently resentment of the ritual decreased. Churching continued to be widely performed by the Anglican Church, perhaps particularly in strongly working-class areas of the country, well into the twentieth century, but for Puritans, and their intellectual descendants, the disappearance of an element of compulsion reduced the heat of the debate long before feminism and liturgical reform removed it from the liturgy of the established church.

Further Reading
Will Coster, "Purity, Profanity and Puritanism: The Churching of Women 1500–1700," in W. J. Sheils and D. Wood, eds., *Women in the Church,* Studies in Church History, vol. 27 (Oxford, 1990), pp. 377–387; David Cressy, *Birth, Marriage, and Death: Ritual, Religion, and the Life Cycle in Tudor and Stuart England* (New York, 1997); Keith Thomas, *Religion and the Decline of Magic: Studies in the Popular Beliefs in Sixteenth- and Seventeenth-Century England* (Oxford, 1971); Adrian Wilson, "'The Ceremony of Childbirth and Its Interpretation," in V. Fildes, ed., *Women and Mothers in Pre-Industrial England: Essays in Memory of Dorothy McLare* (London, 1990).

Will Coster

Clarendon Code

A series of acts of Parliament that penalized Protestant Dissenters in the years following the restoration of the monarchy. These were the Corporation Act (1661), the Act of Uniformity (1662), the Conventicles Act (1664) (which was succeeded by a second Conventicles Act in 1670), and the Five Mile Act (1665). Each of the acts had a distinct purpose. The Corporation Act empowered commissioners to purge municipal officeholders by requiring them to abjure the Solemn League and Covenant by which men had committed themselves to oppose Charles I, swear the oaths of allegiance and nonresistance, and receive the Anglican communion. It was supplemented in 1663 by an act for regulating select vestries. The Uniformity Act restricted ecclesiastical benefices to those who conformed to the Book of Common Prayer, subscribed to the Thirty-nine Articles, received episcopal ordination, and repudiated the Covenant. The first Conventicles Act forbade meetings for worship of more than five people other than members of the same household. After expiring in 1668, it was succeeded by the 1670 Conventicles Act, which Andrew Marvell described as "the quintessence of arbitrary malice." The new act focused attention on the clerical leaders of Nonconformity and sought to encourage prosecution by rewarding informers and penalizing negligent local justices. The Five Mile Act prohibited Nonconformist clergy from preaching and teaching in or even coming within five miles of any corporate town, or any parish in which they had previously served, unless they took an oath of nonresistance.

The Clarendon Code was an assertion that England had only one form of religion, the Church of England, and that it was illegal to attend, practice, or minister in other forms. Dissenters were punished for meeting in "conventicles"; ministers who preached and prayed at such gatherings were liable to drastic penalties; and civil office, education, and other opportunities were denied to those who were not conformists. Designed to break up the congregations of ejected ministers and other Nonconformists, it was of course a tacit acknowledgment of the existence of this separate Protestant community.

The attribution of these acts to the malign influence of Edward Hyde, Earl of Clarendon, Charles II's lord chancellor in the 1660s, is unjust. Clarendon may well have preferred a more moderate approach. However, prominent among those who were pushing for such legislation was Archbishop Gilbert Sheldon. Although some of the earlier acts were security measures designed to ensure that urban corporations and hence parliamentary elections were under the control of loyal men, later legislation demonstrates the conviction among churchmen and members of Parliament that the Nonconformist clergy were the root of the problem. The Five Mile Act, for example, was designed to cut the links between ejected clergy and their former flocks, while the 1670 Conventicles Act increased the penalties for ministers and decreased them for lay conventiclers. There was little popular enthusiasm for this legislation, and many disliked the use of paid informers. Neither central government nor local authorities enforced the acts consistently or effectively, although some groups, such as the Quakers, suffered more than others for their Nonconformity. The operation of these and earlier penal laws was suspended by the various Declarations of Indulgence (1672, 1687, 1688) and by the 1689 Toleration Act.

See also: Conventicles, Dissenters, Nonconformity
Further Reading
John P. Kenyon, ed., *The Stuart Constitution 1603–1688,* 2nd edition (Cambridge, Eng., 1986).

John Spurr

Classical Movement

See Conference Movement

Clothing

The image of the ubiquitously black-clad Puritan is, like much of Puritan mythology, inaccurate. Yes, both men and women did wear the high steeple hat and had shiny buckles on their shoes, but both of these were part of a whole set of contemporary fashions imported from the east of England. Nonetheless, proper apparel was critical to the Pu-

Circa 1630, woodcut of a Puritan couple in daily dress. (MPI/Getty Images)

ritans, as an expression of their sober and orderly life, but also as an outward sign of their particular piety.

Most people avoided wearing black, reserving that distinctive color for the ruling elite, governors, and the elder-saint. Black was one of the most expensive dyes to produce. Suitable for such dignitaries as John Winthrop, the first governor of Massachusetts, who was painted (ca. 1629) wearing a black velvet suit with neck ruff and lace cuffs. While clearly demonstrating his gentlemanly status (holding translucent gossamer gloves that were incapable of surviving any manual labor), he was also markedly more restrained in his apparel than his non-Puritan, English contemporaries. This portrait at once marks Winthrop as both gentry and Puritan.

Though black was not considered a plain enough color for the bulk of the Puritan population, there was a wide range of "sadd colours" available for the common Puritan. Drawn from the traditional clothing of East Anglia, a 1638 list specifically mentions "liver colour, de Boys, tawney, russet, purple, French green, ginger-lyne, deer colour, orange" (Fischer, *Albion's Seed,* p. 140). Russet and *feuille morte* (dead leaf) were particularly popular in New England, creating a striking match with their autumnal leaves.

More colorfully dressed than in myth, albeit in subdued shades, the average Puritan male was also better outfitted than in the popular view of the thrifty, one-suited Puritan. The Massachusetts Bay Company specified—among other items—that the common male immigrant bring four pair of shoes, four shirts, two suits of doublet and hose, and the above-mentioned black felt steeple hat. What distinguished the ordinary Puritan male's attire from his less godly counterpart was not so much the color of his clothes, but their cut: plain, simple, and relatively unadorned.

To guarantee that Puritan clothing would remain distinctively plain, Massachusetts passed a set of "sumptuary laws" that, as in England, regulated clothing by social rank. But, unlike in England, the earliest Bay Colony sumptuary laws sought to control the everyday dress of men and women, the high and the low. These codes outlawed the manufacture, and even sale, of fancy clothing, including items with short sleeves, "whereby the nakedness of the arm may be discovered" (Fischer, *Albion's Seed*, p. 143). Everyday wear was to be restricted to the traditional styles of the early colonies, avoiding the latest change of fashions, including clothing with more than one slash (designed to show off underclothing) in the sleeve, as well as "immoderate great sleeves . . . great rayles, long wings, etc." (Fischer, *Albion's Seed*, p. 143). Hatbands and fancy cuffs were also legislated against for everyday wear. Underclothing, however, was not regulated by the sumptuary laws, allowing for both more color and individual style, including red petticoats and aprons with a little lace.

Long hair was also in violation of the Puritan standard of plain dress, especially long curly hair worn by the young. Wigs too faced the full force of magisterial furor. Josiah Willard, a Puritan preacher, received a visit from his local magistrate after he cut his hair and began wearing a wig. He was told that "God seems to have ordained our hair as a test, to see whether we can bring our minds to be content to be at his finding: or whether we would be our own carvers" (Fischer, *Albion's Seed*, p. 143). Cosmetic aids, such as wigs, false teeth, and female makeup, were not merely a violation of the plain dress code of Puritan lifestyles, but an act of blasphemy.

Women's clothing was also made up in "sad colors," but with seemingly more outward ornamentation, such as bright ribbons on their sleeves and small lace caps. Women's clothing—because of early modern views of women in general—may have also been watched more closely for violations of seemliness and decency. In 1676, thirty-six Northampton young women were criminally charged for inappropriate wearing of hoods, including one Hannah Lyman, who also wore "silk in a flaunting manner, in an offensive way, not only before but when she stood presented" (Fischer, *Albion's Seed*, p. 145). Even John Winthrop's niece, Mary Downing, was not immune to sartorial censorship for the wearing of too much lace.

Puritans were not against changes of fashion per se, as hose and doublet eventually gave way to a series of modifications the eventually resulted in the suit. But the key to distinctive Puritan dress was plainness and modesty.

Further Reading
David Hackett Fischer, *Albion's Seed: Four British Folkways in America* (Oxford, 1989).

Lynn A. Botelho

Commandment Boards

The provision of the text of the Ten Commandments, prominently displayed in churches, reflected both the displacement of religious imagery by the word and the enhanced respect for the law of Moses, which constituted so important a part of the moral code of sixteenth-century Reformers.

Boards bearing texts of one kind or another, sometimes including the Decalogue, were not unknown before the Reformation, but the replacement of painted images by admonitory scriptural texts began in earnest in England during the reign of Edward VI. Under Elizabeth I, the display of the commandments was officially enjoined by royal orders, the queen's direction to Archbishop Parker on this score in January 1561 being followed up in October that year by printed instructions addressed to the queen's ecclesiastical commissioners. The commandment tables were to be placed at the east end of chancels, on the wall over the communion table, and they were regarded as decorative as well as instructive. Printed versions were to be produced for this purpose, though it was accepted that larger and more expensive painted texts would be required for display in cathedral churches. The instructions made explicit that churchgoers should edified through reading; hence the need for suitably large script to facilitate the learning of the Decalogue, which, in 1547 and more rigorously in 1559, formed part of the learning deemed essential for admission to the sacrament. The placing of the commandment text over the communion table was therefore a critical advertisement of the Reformed church order, in which worship of the host (the bread used in Holy Communion) and the figure of Christ on the rood was superseded by fidelity to the law and text of scripture, with words replacing the carved and painted images of reredos and altarpiece. Bishop Bentham of Coventry and Lichfield, a purifying member of Elizabeth's bench, ordered in 1565 that the table of commandments should be set up in the place where the reserved sacrament used to hang.

From this time on commandment boards were an accepted part of church furnishing. The maintenance of freshly whitewashed walls adorned with scriptural texts for godly learning was among the obligations of churchwardens in the Canons of 1571, and in 1604 Canon 82 specified that these chosen sentences, written legibly on church walls, must include the Ten Commandments on the east end of every church and chapel. The Stationers' Registers reflect the production of the needed prints in 1594 and 1612, and as time went on these boards dominating the east end, which might be quite ornate painted versions, sometimes shaped like the stone tables of law received by Moses on Mount Sinai, often came to include in addition the Lord's Prayer and the Apostles' Creed, and perhaps supporting figures of Moses and Aaron. Even if we lack evidence of parishioners' rote learning of the commandments being aided by this means, the opportunity was omnipresent in these conspicuous affirmations of the divinity of the word.

Though there is no evidence that English puritans criticized the use of such boards in England, there is also no evidence of their placement in colonial meetinghouses.

Further Reading
Margaret Aston, *England's Iconoclasts: Laws against Images* (Oxford, 1988); H. Munro Cautley, *Royal Arms and Commandments in Our Churches* (Ipswich, Eng., 1934, reprinted 1974).

Margaret Aston

Comprehension
The term used to describe the possible reunion of Dissenters with the Church of England. Comprehension was a goal of various groups between 1662 and 1689, but it failed because of the disunity of the Dissenters and opposition from Anglicans. A comprehension would have required Parliament to revise the 1662 Act of Uniformity so that "moderate" Nonconformist ministers could conform to the Church of England and become eligible for appointment as parish ministers. It was assumed that these ministers would bring their lay followers with them into the national church.

The first step would have been to revise the Act of Uniformity to meet the Nonconformist clergy's objections. The obligation for all incumbents to have been ordained by a bishop was unacceptable to those with Presbyterian orders. Although many such ministers were prepared to pursue their vocations under episcopacy, they could not accept "re-ordination" at the hands of a bishop, particularly if it cast doubt on the validity of their past ministries. Nonconformists resented the oath of canonical obedience to the bishop and the obligation to subscribe to the Thirty-nine Articles because of the articles on church government. Nor would they declare their "unfeigned assent and consent" to the Book of Common Prayer. They disliked its repetitions, obsolete words, implicit theological errors (especially in the baptism and burial services), and offensive rubrics requiring the wearing of the surplice, the sign of the cross at baptism, and kneeling to receive the sacrament. A fourth—and for many an insuperable—obstacle to conformity was the renunciation of the Solemn League and Covenant. Not only was a solemn oath before God inviolable, but the renunciation required the conformist to swear never "to endeavour any change or alteration of government either in church or state." All of these issues were addressed in the various comprehension schemes.

Yet comprehension may never have been a realistic goal. The leaders of the Church of England were unlikely to accept the drastic changes it would have involved. Nor would they welcome the resulting double standard within the clergy, some of whom would have subscribed under the terms of 1662 and others under revised terms. Once Nonconformist ministers had been comprehended, they would still find themselves confronted by unpalatable liturgical and disciplinary demands. Nor was it clear that lay Nonconformists would automatically follow their pastors into the parish church and abandon their conventicles. The younger generation of Presbyterian clergy, brought up after 1662, did not dream of a role in a national church but saw their future in terms of an autonomous denomination. The rival attraction of religious toleration was perhaps the key to the failure of comprehension. Comprehension proposals were usually twinned with plans for a toleration or "indulgence" of the irreconcilable minority. Those, such as Presbyterians, who sought comprehension, generally welcomed toleration for others, but those who sought toleration feared that a comprehension would simply leave them as an isolated and vulnerable minority. Whether the Congregationalists consciously sought to prevent comprehension is a matter of interpretation, but in practice their determination, under the leadership of the redoubtable John Owen, to achieve a toleration repeatedly thwarted the delicate political negotiations for a comprehension. Comprehension and toleration were raised in Parliament in 1663, in 1667 and 1668, in 1673 and 1674, and in 1680 when two bills were prepared that were to be dusted off and reintroduced in 1689. Political jockeying and mistakes in 1689 led to the shelving of the comprehension bill and the Toleration Act, which covered far more non-Anglican Protestants than had been intended.

See also: Clarendon Code, Dissenters, Nonconformity
Further Reading
John Spurr, "The Church of England, Comprehension and the Toleration Act of 1689," *English Historical Review*, 104 (1989), 927–946.

John Spurr

Conference Movement

The term used to refer to the effort by godly reformers to establish formal clerical conferences in the Elizabethan church during the 1580s. Though this effort has sometimes been judged as an attempt to establish a Presbyterian church within a church, that interpretation has recently been challenged for too broadly assuming a clear Presbyterian intent on the part of those involved.

A tradition of joining in informal associations or conferences with likeminded reformers in order to discuss how the church could better be reformed dated to the earliest days of the English Reformation. Such gatherings enabled these individuals to both strive for agreement among themselves and to then benefit from the fact that what they advocated was not the view of one man but had been authorized by the judgment of a group of godly clergy. Such meetings were held in college rooms at Oxford and Cambridge universities, where students joined with fellows and in the process learned the value of such associations.

The prophesyings of the early Elizabethan period were more formal expressions of the effort to bring clergy together for discussions that would create greater unity while also educating those clerical members who were less well trained. It is likely that these gatherings became the occasion for informal meetings of the more reform-minded clergy who had come together for the formal exercises. When the queen, fearful of the direction that these discussions might take, ordered that the prophesyings be brought to an end, the godly were forced to rely entirely on informal gatherings. These could take many forms, such as the coming together of a group of regional clergy to hear one of their number preaching in a combination lecture, followed by the ministers present re-

and some at least reported to John Field in London, who seems to have coordinated the effort.

These conferences did not have the authority that one would expect to find in a Presbyterian church structure, but more closely resembled the type of assemblies that were later employed by Congregationalists to achieve agreement on issues. The Dedham Conference members also explored the possibility of working in conjunction with sympathetic archdeacons and other church officials.

After the death of John Field in 1588, much of the reformer's correspondence came into the possession of Richard Bancroft, the archbishop of Canterbury. Further evidence of the movement came to the hands of the church authorities when clerical studies were raided in 1589 in an attempt to track down the authors of the Presbyterian pamphlets known as the Marprelate tracts. The authorities soon cracked down on the conferences, forcing their dissolution. This action did not bring an end to associations of clergy, however, but merely forced greater reliance on other mechanisms such as combination lectureships.

See also: John Field, John Knewstub, Dedham Conference, Lectures and Lectureships, Prophesyings, Combination Lecture (Gloss.)
Further Reading
Francis J. Bremer, *Congregational Communion* (Boston, 1994); Patrick Collinson, John Craig, and Brett Usher, eds., *Conferences and Combination Lectures in the Elizabethan Church, 1582–1590* (Woodbridge, Eng., 2003).

Francis J. Bremer

The parish church of Cockfield in Suffolk, England, where the Reverend John Knewstub convened the gathering of clergy that sparked the Conference Movement in East Anglia. (Courtesy Francis J. Bremer)

tiring to dine and discuss issues of reform and conformity.

In 1582 John Knewstub invited godly clergy from East Anglia to a conference at his parish of Cockfield, in Suffolk. News of this conference was conveyed to John Field in London, and it is at least possible that the original call was prompted by Field and other nationally prominent godly clergy. The result was the formation of a series of local conferences in East Anglia. The most famous of these was centered on Dedham. Others in the Stour Valley region along the Essex-Suffolk border included one at Braintree, Essex, and one at Cockfield itself. Other similar conferences were established in other parts of the nation. They were connected with one another through informal means,

Confirmation

In the ceremony of confirmation, individuals confirmed the baptismal pledges that had been made on their behalf by their godparents when they were baptized. In the Roman Catholic Church, this rite was considered to be a sacrament and was administered by a bishop. The ceremony involved a laying-on of hands by the bishop and the anointing of the individual being confirmed with chrism.

Reformers tended to accept confirmation in some form, while rejecting the idea that it was a sacrament. Luther allowed for pastors to examine the faith of children, lay hands on them, and confirm them. Calvin disapproved of the Catholic rite, particularly the act of anointing with chrism. Though he did not develop a specific rite for confirmation, he allowed for the catechetical questioning of youth before the congregation as a confirmation of the covenant promises signified in their baptism.

The Church of England did retain a rite of confirmation from its inception, but did not regard it as a sacrament. Martin Bucer, a Continental Reformer whom Thomas Cranmer had invited to Cambridge, was a strong proponent of confirmation, and this may have influenced Cranmer as he prepared the Book of Common Prayer. As in the Catholic Church, the rite was administered by a bishop. Children who could demonstrate knowledge of the Apostles' Creed, the Lord's Prayer, and the Ten Commandments, as well as answer questions from the catechism, were brought before the bishop by a godparent. The rite as contained in the Book of Common Prayer recognized that baptism had brought regeneration, but asked that the faith of the individual being confirmed be strengthened by the work of the Holy Spirit. Confirmation was required for admission to Holy Communion.

Puritans are not known to have objected to the rite of confirmation as such, and in England presumably they brought their children to be confirmed on episcopal visitations. There was no observation of the rite in New England. Obviously there was no bishop to perform the rite in the colonies, but there also seems to have been no regret about the absence of confirmation. This is a subject that has not been investigated by scholars, but it is possible that the test for membership (and the right to receive Communion) imposed for membership in the colonial churches took the place of the rite of confirmation.

Further Reading
Hans Hillerbrand, ed., *The Encyclopedia of Protestantism* (New York, 2004).

Francis J. Bremer

Congregationalism

Congregationalism was founded on the notion of a gathered church (one organized by the consent of the members rather than by geography) in which the normative experience of Christian life lay not in diocesan, national, or international ecclesiastical structures but in the particular congregation. In common with other Protestant traditions, Congregationalism considered itself rooted in the precepts of the New Testament, but saw its historical origins in the establishment of the congregation of foreign Protestants led by John a Lasco, which was allowed to worship in London in 1550 independent of episcopal jurisdiction. Soon after this, the circumstances of persecution under Queen Mary I, when secret and gathered congregations were the best means of keeping Protestantism alive in England, provided the political context in which this form of churchmanship, where the godly few kept themselves separate from the corrupt institutional church, was considered essential to the preservation of the gospel. A few congregations survived into Elizabeth's reign, most notably the congregation meeting in Plumbers' Hall in London in the 1560s, but the religious settlement of 1559 changed the political context entirely, and thereafter Christian life for English men and women was to be organized on a national scale within an established church. These earlier experiences, therefore, became submerged in the debate about the character of the national church. Submerged, but not entirely lost, as the foreign exile churches in London, though supervised by the bishops, continued to enjoy a considerable degree of independence in worship and discipline, including the election of their own ministers, all matters that later became hallmarks of Congregational churchmanship.

The first comprehensive theological expression of Congregational churchmanship in English came in the writings of the Separatists Robert Browne and Henry Barrow, in the late 1580s. Like the Marian Protestants, they withdrew from any communion with the established church, which they considered irredeemably corrupt, confining the church solely "to the worthiest, be they never so few." This degree of exclusiveness, although the logical extension of the gathered church theology, rarely operated in practice, and in the context of the Elizabethan and Jacobean Church, in which jurisdictional compromise and local patronage structures conspired to permit a degree of local, not to say congregational, independence in some parts of the country, separatism remained the choice of a small minority. The "semi-Separatist" churches of Henry Jessey and Henry Jacob in London in the early seventeenth century held to a congregational view of the church, as did some of the English congregations in the Netherlands, but most dissenters at this time espoused some form of Presbyterianism, in theory at least. This did not always work out in practice, however, and more common was the experience of the puritan ministers of Essex, who organized themselves into a classis at Dedham in the 1580s. Though they were formally committed to a Presbyterian style of discipline, the records of their meetings reveal that the key element in the churchmanship of this neighborhood was the close relationship between individual congregations and their pastors, some of whom, notwithstanding their episcopal ordination, saw the validity of their ministry as resting on the call they had received from their congregations.

Support from the prosperous clothiers of Essex, or the patronage of the puritan gentry of Northamptonshire, rendered many puritan clergy immune not only from episcopal censure but also from discipline by the classis where they existed, and this story was repeated in other parts of the country. What emerged in these contexts, in which the prosperous laity managed the appointment and supported the maintenance of the local clergy, was a de facto form of congregationalism before the name existed, which existed uneasily within the structures of the national church. In addition, there was another, more exclusive tendency within puritanism that merged into congregationalism, that of conventicling. Conventicles, in which the godly withdrew from the wider community into "private" extraliturgical gatherings for worship and study, became a prominent feature of puritan life, both in places served by puritan clergy and in places where they were absent. Cutting across parochial struc-

tures, they were regarded with suspicion by the authorities, who viewed them as gathered congregations with potentially separatist tendencies, but they became widespread by the 1620s. In these circumstances, the ecclesiological implications of a gathered church did not need full articulation, as many of its characteristics existed. All this changed from the mid-1620s onward.

The drive for uniformity pursued by the Arminians from the late 1620s made the position of puritans within the established church, those "non-separating Congregationalists," or "semi-separatists," untenable, and within England puritan congregations increasingly withdrew into conventicles where ministers in trouble with ecclesiastical authority could preach and teach. Even more important, however, was the experience of exile, or emigration, which a number of puritans undertook in the face of persecution. The already existing congregations in the Netherlands provided a welcome for these exiles, especially that at Rotterdam where Hugh Peter was pastor in the 1630s and where William Ames, a scholar of European reputation who formed a link with the earlier generation of Separatists, worshipped immediately prior to his death in 1633. Even here though, congregational values were challenged by the Presbyterians, and, having been criticized by English Presbyterian exiles for introducing a covenant into the Rotterdam church, Peter emigrated to New England in 1635.

In New England the circumstances of setting up new churches in a territory without well-established civil or ecclesiastical structures altered the circumstances in which puritan ministers had previously worked. The decision to migrate was never easy; Cotton had served his Boston, Lincolnshire, parish for over twenty years, and most of the emigrant clergy had been working within the established church before the Laudian drive for conformity forced them out. Like Cotton, a number were accompanied by former parishioners. While still in Lincolnshire, Cotton had gathered godly members of his parish in old Boston into a covenant, but he rejected separatism and preached against the covenant undertaken in 1629 by the church in Salem, Massachusetts. On arriving in that colony himself, though still opposed to separatism, he admitted that he had been wrong, and that covenants were vital to the church. In what lay the change? Clearly radical lay initiatives played some part in this shift and point to separatist influence, but perhaps more important was the need to bind settled populations together in a stable community in an otherwise unfamiliar and potentially hostile environment. So the covenant became a means of coping with, in Ames's words, "the special difficulties" of a new plantation and owed as much to the drive to reinforce community as to the desire to make it exclusive. The covenant added a civil, or political, dimension to Congregationalism in the New World, New England churches became autonomous, local, and voluntary, the antithesis of the hierarchical church left behind in England. The earliest full statement of this ecclesiological position was expressed in 1644 in John Cotton's *Keys to the Kingdom of Heaven*, which was also an important influence on English Congregationalism.

If the New England experience was critical to the refining of congregational ideas in the 1630s, it was five ministers from the Netherlands, now returned to England—Thomas Goodwin, Philip Nye, Sidrach Simpson, William Bridge, and Jeremiah Burroughes—who set out the Congregationalist agenda in the *Apologeticall Narration* of 1644. Representing the minority in the Westminster Assembly, they were keen to distance themselves from the Separatists, eschewed the name of Independent, which some more separatist churches espoused, and stressed the common cause with the Presbyterians on many issues, while disagreeing with them on church government. Despite this, they were denounced by Presbyterians like Thomas Edwards, who charged them with separatism despite the fact that many of them tried to work within the established church in the tradition of Henry Jacob.

With the emergence of the radical sects during the course of the Civil Wars, the Congregationalists became progressively more conservative, holding firmly to a Calvinist theology, while at the same time being outflanked on the left by groups such as the Baptists. Under the Interregnum, the Congre-

gationalists did achieve a significant role in the national church for a short time when they provided the largest group among the Triers established to test the suitability of would-be clergymen, and certainly Oliver Cromwell was sympathetic to the gathered churches. During the 1650s, the surviving records of the Congregational churches reveal a vigorous, if loose, exchange of ideas: the church at Norwich gave advice to the "Christians" at North Walsham and sent representatives to churches at Bury St. Edmunds, Beccles, Wymondham, Guestwick, and Denton. Other churches were in correspondence with the Netherlands and New England, from where some ministers had returned. These contacts led to a meeting at the Savoy in 1658 of over one hundred Congregational ministers, which produced a statement of Congregational principles composed by, among others, Thomas Goodwin and Philip Nye, authors of the 1644 *Apologeticall Narration*. The declaration advocated a comprehensive churchmanship that allowed both Presbyterian and Congregational forms to coexist, broadly confirmed the Calvinism of the Westminster Confession, and affirmed the autonomy of individual congregations in matters of discipline.

Congregationalism remained at the heart of New England churchmanship as it developed in the later seventeenth century, and its democratic traditions played a significant part in the political development of the New England states. But the hopes for comprehension in the English church expressed at the Savoy were dashed by the Act of Uniformity of 1662, after which many ministers, both Congregational and Presbyterian, left the established church to form Dissenting congregations, eventually achieving toleration under the Act of 1688.

See also: William Bradshaw, John Cotton, Cambridge Assembly, Conventicles, Dissenters, Independency, Separatism

Further Readings

Francis J. Bremer, ed., *Puritanism: Transatlantic Perspectives* (Boston, 1994); Patrick Collinson, "Towards a Broader Understanding of the Early Dissenting Tradition," in *Godly People* (London, 1983); Perry Miller, *The New England Mind*, 2 vols. (New York, 1939; Cambridge, MA, 1953);

A. P. F. Sell, *Saints: Visible, Orderly, and Catholic—the Congregational Idea of the Church* (Allison Park, PA, 1986); Michael Watts, *The Dissenters*, vol. 1 (Oxford, 1978); G. Nuttall, *Visible Saints: The Congregational Way, 1640–1660* (Oxford, 1957).

William Sheils

Connecticut

Connecticut is considered by some to have been the most successful Puritan colony in British America. Unlike Providence Island, Plymouth, and New Haven, it has sustained its legal and political existence down to the present. It supported a larger population than Rhode Island and New Hampshire, and it developed its institutions less hampered by imperial supervision than Massachusetts. Because Connecticut never produced an agricultural staple, it attracted few immigrants and never became a market for the Atlantic slave trade. Because it had no major seaport, it had no significant transient population, and no great extremes of wealth and poverty. Its covenanted villages, bound together by ties of family and neighborhood, amply supplied by a preaching ministry, came closer to the Puritan vision of a godly community than any other Puritan society in New or Old England.

The history of Puritanism in Connecticut traditionally begins in 1636 with the emigration of Thomas Hooker and most of his congregation from Massachusetts Bay to Hartford, but advance parties had already established themselves in Hartford, Wethersfield, and Windsor a few years earlier. In 1638, the three river towns adopted the Fundamental Orders, setting up a general court, elected by the admitted inhabitants of each town. Except for a brief interlude in 1687 when Connecticut was

A salt marsh in Saybrook, Connecticut, illustrates the coastal geography of the region in the seventeenth century. (Courtesy Francis J. Bremer)

thrown into the Dominion of New England, that government remained in force until the constitution of 1818 replaced it.

The Connecticut colony might easily have disappeared. It had no basis in English law, and separate Puritan colonies were planned at Saybrook and New Haven. Connecticut was saved by John Winthrop Jr., leader of the Saybrook colony, when he accepted Hartford's jurisdiction and agreed to serve Connecticut as its governor. More importantly, Winthrop secured a royal charter in 1662 that legitimated the Fundamental Orders, annexed the New Haven colony, and gave Connecticut a boundary on the "South Sea." That claim was unenforceable, but it encouraged later emigrants from Connecticut to carry their institutions and ideals westward through New York and Pennsylvania, into the Midwest.

Puritanism in Connecticut did not fundamentally differ from Puritanism elsewhere. Puritans in Connecticut, like all Puritans, struggled with the question of whether it was possible to reform the Church of England, or whether separation from it was necessary. During the English Civil Wars, the Connecticut Puritan clergy fully participated in the creation of a church that was neither episcopal nor Presbyterian, but Congregational. Thomas Hooker wrote the definitive defense of such a polity in his *Survey of the Sum of Church Discipline,* and Connecticut clergymen attended the conferences that resulted in the Cambridge Platform of 1648, the basic statement of church discipline for all New England Congregationalists. The Connecticut clergy took the lead in working out the Half-Way Covenant, which allowed not yet regenerate parents to have their children baptized, and most Connecticut churches had adopted that practice by 1700. Connecticut, like Massachusetts, felt threatened by witches and Quakers in the seventeenth century, and sometimes shed blood in the name of orthodoxy. Puritans in Connecticut were as dismayed as Puritans everywhere by the Restoration, and Puritan intellectuals in Connecticut, like their counterparts elsewhere, attempted to reconcile Reformed theology with the Enlightenment philosophy of the eighteenth century. Congregationalists

in all of New England supported the American war for independence, in part because they interpreted it as a continuation of the struggle against King Charles I and Archbishop Laud. The first warship launched by Connecticut after 1776 was named the *Oliver Cromwell.*

If Connecticut Puritanism differed from Puritanism elsewhere, it was in its greater sense of security and confidence. For over two centuries, the great majority of the people born in Connecticut were baptized into a Congregational church, and remained under the watch and care of that church for the rest of their lives. There was, as a result, a relationship between church, state, and people that was built upon mutual trust. The Fundamental Orders required that the governor belong to a Congregational church, but the law was unnecessary in a society that rarely elected non-Congregationalists to positions of political power, and that once elected a serving minister, Gurdon Saltonstall, to be governor. The law required all taxpayers to support the Congregational clergy, but in practice ministers relied upon the voluntary and generous support usually provided by their congregations. The alliance of state and church in Connecticut was demonstrated in 1708, when the general court enacted the Saybrook Platform, establishing ministerial associations with supervisory authority over ecclesiastical matters, but Connecticut Congregationalism was always comfortable with a union of church and state that was designed, as the Fundamental Orders declared, to preserve the way of worship "now practiced amongst us."

The placidity of Connecticut Congregationalism was only occasionally disturbed by outsiders. Quakers, no matter how few, were always resented, but Anglicans seemed the greater threat in the eighteenth century. The Church of England financed an active missionary effort in Connecticut, with some success, most spectacularly so in 1722, when the president and both tutors at Yale College suddenly announced their conversion to episcopacy. The Congregational establishment was shaken to its roots, but Yale survived.

The greatest threat to Congregationalism in the eighteenth century came from within the ranks during the Great Awakening of the 1740s. Two of the most famous revivals of the Awakening took place in Connecticut, one when Jonathan Edwards set off a frenzy of fits and fainting at Enfield when he preached *Sinners in the Hands of an Angry God,* and the other when James Davenport, temporarily insane, presided over a bonfire of the vanities in New London, where books, wigs, and other objects were flung into the flames. It was also a Connecticut resident, Nathan Cole, who most vividly described the effect George Whitefield had on an audience and the agony of being spiritually reborn. Of greater consequence was the split between New Lights, who championed the revivals, and Old Lights, who questioned their validity. The most extreme New Lights separated from ministers and congregations that were deemed unregenerate, and formed "Strict Congregational" churches in defiance of the general court. It took decades for Connecticut Congregationalism to recover its bearings, but in time the clergy and their parishioners joined together in common allegiance to the New Light, revivalist theology of Jonathan Edwards, whose most important disciple was Joseph Bellamy of Bethlehem, Connecticut. By 1800, with a second Great Awakening flooding the churches with born-again saints, the Congregational churches of Connecticut had generally renounced the Half-Way Covenant and had made it necessary to profess a conversion experience to become a communicant.

Connecticut is no longer Puritan, but it is difficult to say when it ceased to be so. It has been argued that Puritans became "Yankees" in Connecticut starting in the late seventeenth century, as increasing wealth sapped vital piety, but Congregationalism remained at the center of Connecticut life through the eighteenth century, and even past 1818, when the Congregational Church was disestablished. Perhaps Connecticut ceased to be Puritan in the mid-nineteenth century, when Congregationalism was given a new direction by Horace Bushnell, who argued that the "Christian nurture" of baptized children was more important than the reborn experience of baptized adults. Bushnell, however, may be considered the rightful heir of Thomas Hooker, the foremost Puritan champion of

"preparationist" theology that encouraged men to prepare for the gift of salvation. Or perhaps Puritanism never died in Connecticut, but was simply overwhelmed by the immigration of non-Protestants beginning in the late nineteenth century, an immigration that eventually made the Roman Catholic Church the largest in the state. It may be that the white-steepled Congregational churches that still grace so many village greens in Connecticut testify to a faith not just rich in history, but to a Puritanism that yet survives.

See also: Dominion of New England
Further Reading
Richard Bushman, *From Puritan to Yankee: Character and the Social Order, 1690–1765* (Cambridge, MA, 1967); Christopher Grasso, *A Speaking Aristocracy: Transforming Public Discourse in Eighteenth-Century Connecticut* (Chapel Hill, 1999); Mary Jones, *Congregational Commonwealth: Connecticut, 1636–1662* (Middletown, CT, 1968); Robert Taylor, *Colonial Connecticut: A History* (Milwood, NY, 1979).

James P. Walsh

Conscience

Conscience may be defined as the human capacity to understand God's requirements, and thereby the difference between right and wrong. In the early modern period, conscience was most often characterized as a form of "inward assent" to the moral law and as such the word took on two distinct but related meanings, both of which were deeply important to puritan thought. One definition was theological: conscience was seen as the inner knowing that gave one the capacity to obtain assurance of salvation. The other definition was more specifically political: conscience was the inner arbiter of truth that could give one the strength to trust one's personal judgment and stand against the intolerable demands of religious conformity.

The confrontation between religiously conscientious subjects and a government that took as its duty the regulation of national religion could be strongly polarizing and dramatic in the fitful progress of England's sixteenth-century reformations. Henrician and Marian Protestants defended their conversions to Protestantism by appeals to their own consciences—at the scaffold, or, most often, in controversial tracts and sermons. By the beginning of the seventeenth century, however, the tenure of Protestantism in England was of a half century's duration. Theologies of conscience became essential methodological strategies for those minorities still left outside the bounds of the established church: either confessionally, as with English Catholics; or in matters of polity and ecclesiology, as with English puritans.

The connection between the theological and political definitions of the term *conscience* was forged, in part, in puritan experience. It originates in characteristic puritan glosses on Calvinist theology that center on the doctrine of assurance. In their quest to "make their election sure" (the oft-quoted expression is from 1 Peter 1:10), Calvinists carefully examined their lives for signs of regeneration. One important sign was confidence in God's promise: an inward assent to the truth of God's election as described in the scriptures.

The techniques for this work of discernment could be taught. The seventeenth century abounds in texts called "cases of conscience." Case divinity was not an exclusively puritan enterprise, but in the hands of puritan writers it took on certain identifying characteristics. Puritan casuistry, wherein passages of scripture were marshaled to prove the truth of the divine work of election, found its best and most prolific expression in the writings of William Perkins (whose *A Discourse of Conscience* was first published in 1592 and reprinted more than a dozen times before 1640). The remarkable popularity of Perkins's and others' works on conscience (for example, William Ames's *Conscience and Cases Thereof* of 1639) suggests that case divinity provided essential underpinning for puritan religious culture. For if only the regenerate conscience could reliably know the difference between right and wrong, then human will—prompted by the word preached and trusting in the providential act of God's election—in effect *became* that inward assent: the still, small voice of Christian conscience.

By the 1630s, the conflict between a Protestant culture that privileged inward assent and preaching-centered piety and a Protestant culture that privileged outward conformity and sacramental piety could no longer be reconciled within the bounds of the Church of England. The Caroline government and the most powerful wing of its ecclesiastical regime (led by Archbishop William Laud) were themselves sacramentalists, and to that end they placed an unprecedented emphasis on the enforcement of outward conformity. Their actions (which included the railing of altars, the strict enforcement of prayer-book liturgical practice, and the public repudiation of Calvinist doctrine in sermons and treatises) imposed a burden many puritan consciences could no longer endure, thus leading to the catastrophic and rapid dissolution of the structures of church and state in the early 1640s.

Puritan response to intolerable Caroline ecclesiastical policy thus provides the necessary and logical link between the conscience of casuistry and the conscience that was to play a supporting role in later seventeenth-century political debates on the granting of religious toleration. In the 1640s, parliamentarians demanded the return of the English church to its Calvinist theological beliefs and reformed practice. They claimed the authority of their own consciences in resisting and overturning the authority of Charles I and Archbishop Laud, but at first they were not prepared to tolerate the offended consciences of English Protestants who disagreed with them: those who loved the English prayer book, for example, or those who did not love a Presbyterian polity.

However, the bitter experience of England's wars of religion, along with concerns in the 1650s over the authority of the state to compel religious conformity, led to the design of a remarkably tolerant religious system under the Protectorate of Oliver Cromwell (1653–1658). Himself a religious Independent, and once head of an army renowned for its Independency, the Lord Protector tolerated most peaceable Protestant dissent and championed the liberty of tender consciences—so long as the consciences were neither Catholic nor Episcopal. But even this brief summer of religious liberty for Protestant sectarians was, like English summers in general, all too short.

See also: Sects, Toleration Act
Further Reading
David Martin Jones, *Conscience and Allegiance in Seventeenth Century England* (Rochester, NY, 1999); Andrew R. Murphy, *Conscience and Community* (University Park, PA, 2001).

Lori Anne Ferrell

See also: Clarendon Code, Conference Movement, Conventicles Act
Further Reading
Patrick Collinson, *The Elizabethan Puritan Movement* (London, 1967); John Spurr, *English Puritanism* (Basingstoke, Eng, 1998).

Tom Webster

Conventicle

Whether a meeting is defined as a "conventicle" or as a more neutral "religious exercise" is partly a legal issue, partly in the eye of the beholder. From the most positive perspective, such a meeting was a gathering intended to supplement public worship, as a helpful adjunct to it, not to challenge it. The activities would include sermon repetition, prayer, and psalm-singing. The practice was often led by a minister, but this was by no means necessary. Lay empowerment could be limited to sermon repetition, but there was the opportunity, sometimes taken, for a member of the laity to effectively conduct worship, a fine distinction but an important one. The 1593 Conventicles Act had assumed that such meetings had a conspiratorial motive, but open definition left it in the hands of the magistrates to decide whether a meeting was or was not a conventicle. The 1604 Canons required that exercises criticize the government or liturgy of the church to be defined as conventicles, but ecclesiastical courts could interpret this requirement broadly or narrowly.

Scholarly knowledge of such exercises comes predominantly through the legal system, and they have thus tended to be seen inaccurately as proto-sectarian gatherings. This tendency finds support in the Conventicles Acts of 1664 and 1670, which assumed guilt rather than innocence and constituted an important element of the Clarendon Code that sought to impose conformity to the established church; Dissenters' meetings were often stormed by troops or mobs, leading to substantial periods of imprisonment. Conventicles were usually solely pious exercises, but the changed context fostered a perception of implicit disloyalty, a perception that was often acted upon with vigor.

Conventicles Act (1664, 1670)

Statutes outlawing meetings for worship by Protestant Dissenters, passed in the aftermath of the restoration of the episcopal Church of England in 1662. They were part of a larger body of legislation known as the Clarendon Code, designed to suppress the puritan movement. The first Conventicle Act (16 Car. II, c.4) lapsed in 1669; the second (22 Car. II, c.1) remained in force until the Toleration Act of 1689. The acts were similar, but the second was more irksome. Both were motivated by fear and revenge on the part of the Cavalier Parliament. The 1670 act earned from Andrew Marvell the immortal and often quoted rebuke that it was "the quintessence of arbitrary malice."

A conventicle was a gathering for worship outside the official parish worship of the Church of England. Whereas the Uniformity Act (1662) required attendance at parish worship, the Conventicles Act went further and made alternative assemblies illegal. The acts defined a conventicle as any religious meeting of five or more persons, over the age of sixteen, other than members of the same household. The acts declared that "seditious sectaries . . . under pretence of tender consciences do at their meetings contrive insurrections." The penalties in the 1664 Act were on a scale, beginning with a £5 fine or three months' imprisonment for a first offense, £10 or six months for a second, and, for a third, £100 or seven years transportation to the colonies. A transported person who absconded or returned was subject to the death penalty. Magistrates and militia might "break open and enter into any house or other place where they shall be informed any such conventicle . . . is or shall be held."

The 1670 act was in some measure more lenient. It specified a five shilling fine for a first offense and then ten shillings for repeat offenses. Transportation was dropped. However, the later act was much more vexatious in other ways. It specified that if a convicted person could not pay the fine, then it could be levied on any other worshipper present and convicted. It imposed a fine of £20 (rising to £40 for a repeat offense) upon anyone who preached, again to be levied if necessary on anyone present. Any person who allowed their property to be used for conventicling was liable to a £20 fine. Husbands were liable for their wives' fines. Convictions required only the word of two witnesses, or merely "notorious evidence and circumstance of fact," before a single justice. Under the first act, only the transportation clause required a jury trial; under the second, only appeals against conviction were tried before a jury. The 1670 act imposed a fine on constables and churchwardens who withheld information about conventicles and upon magistrates who "wilfully and wittingly omit" the execution of the act, a clause plainly reflecting the sympathy of many officials for Dissent. A special iniquity of the 1670 Act was the clause by which a third of the fine was to be paid to the "informer or informers . . . having regard to their diligence and industry in the discovery, dispersing, and punishing of the said conventicles." It was an open invitation to people to turn professional informers. Both acts were resisted tooth and nail by puritan-inclined members of Parliament, especially in the House of Lords, but the Cavalier majority and the bishops pushed the legislation through. The lack of jury trial, the power of summary conviction before a single justice, and the right to break into and search dwellings on suspicion were all regarded as gross violations of legal traditions.

Under the first act, the Quakers were especially targeted, though it often took bullying of juries by judges to ensure convictions on the third offense. About 250 people were sentenced to transportation, but ships' crews frequently obstructed the process, and in the event probably no more than 20 Quakers reached the Americas; one became a slave in Virginia.

Many thousands of Dissenters were fined under the acts or had their goods distrained for nonpay-ment. The acts ruined the livelihoods of puritan clergy and laity through crippling accumulations of fines. Ministers who preached in their own homes were doubly liable as preacher and householder. Complicated modifications were made to buildings, involving trapdoors, partitions, and holes in walls, in order to evade the letter of the law. Thomas Ellwood's *Caution to Constables and Other Inferior Officers Concerned in the Execution of the Conventicle Act* (1683) offered advice on how to evade the law. Prosecutions peaked during the "Tory reaction" in the first half of the 1680s, at which time the militias were used to destroy meetinghouses. By 1685 almost all of London's meetinghouses had ceased to function. Informers were widely used by militant Anglican magistrates. In London in the early 1680s, the Hilton Gang practically monopolized the prosecution of Dissent, imposing a regime of fear and extortion, until, in the new political climate under King James II, the Hiltons' perjuries and peculation were exposed.

The effects of this "horrid law" were poignantly summed up by the Presbyterian minister John Howe in 1689: "Our Magna Carta was torn in pieces; the worst and most infamous of mankind, at our own expense, hired to accuse us; multitudes of perjuries committed; convictions made without a jury, and without any hearing of the persons accused; penalties inflicted; goods rifled; estates seized and embezzled; houses broken up; families disturbed, often at most unseasonable hours of the night, without any cause, or shadow of a cause, if only a malicious villain could pretend to suspect a meeting there."

See also: Clarendon Code, Conventicles, Dissenters
Further Reading
C. R. Horle, *The Quakers and the English Legal System, 1660–1688* (Philadelphia, 1988).

Mark Goldie

Conversion Process

For Puritans, conversion involved a process of intense, inward self-scrutiny. Puritans engaged in a daily quest for signs of the action of grace upon their hearts in order to intuit whether they were

The cover of John Davenport's Profession of Faith. *Those seeking church membership in New England were asked to make a public profession such as this. (Courtesy Francis J. Bremer)*

tivate a community of followers around the teaching that God's dealings were completely arbitrary and that humans could do nothing to affect the state of their souls.

From the 1570s through the mid-seventeenth century, Puritans responded to this dilemma by adopting a "doctrine of preparation," which taught that potential converts could exercise their will by undergoing a period of introspection and self-analysis, accompanied by the rigorous study of scriptural truths. Through self and scriptural study, the prospective convert became aware of his or her own sins; this awareness led to the discovery of an innately sinful self through self-identification with Adam's original sin. Identification with Adam induced an experience known as "humiliation." Humiliation initiated the process of preparation, as the individual underwent more meditations on sin and depravity, which "softened" and "broke" the heart by inculcating a need and desire for saving grace. True humility came when the Puritan realized that original sin created a debt between sinner and God that could not be repaid by engaging in good works. Paradoxically, recognizing this condition of complete debility before God was the first step that the Puritan took toward salvation. Puritans believed that a hard heart would resist grace, while a broken heart would be more receptive to divine dispensation.

Ministers emphasized repeatedly that this process of preparation did not guarantee salvation. The individual was not converted through the softening of the heart alone. Instead this initial phase lead to more introspection and self-examination, as the individual became aware of an intense desire for God's saving grace. After humiliation, conversion became a process of emptying out all private feelings and ideas about individual agency. In his sermon, *The Sincere Convert,* Puritan minister Thomas Shepard describes this process through the metaphor of melting down the tarnished inner self.

The three phases described thus far (conviction of sin, humiliation, and then this process of self-emptying) prepared the Puritan for communion with Christ. The Puritan began to see him- or herself as a hollow cast of Adam. It was within this hollow space that the euphoric, reassuring moment of

among the elect. The Puritans believed that grace came from personal experience, supplying the convert with an "indwelling" spirit that had to be "entertained" by persons familiar with the Bible. A mark of divine election was the convert's ability to unite experiential and biblical religion.

The theology of Puritan conversion was largely based on Reformation interpretations of the Epistles of Paul, in which they found a belief in human depravity and the consequent human inability to know the state of the soul or initiate the conversion process. In practice, this theology of conversion proved difficult to maintain. In Old England and particularly in New England, it was difficult to cul-

Puritan conversion occurred. God's "seed" flowed into the unregenerate saint, "pricked" the sinful heart, and partially redeemed the convert from the irreparably destructive Fall. Some ministers described this euphoria through the metaphor of the convert as Christ's bride, drawing an analogy between this blissful spiritual moment and an idealized marital union.

Once the Puritan had experienced this feeling of assurance, he or she had hope, but not proof, of divine election. The elect, referred to as "visible saints" by the Puritans, consisted of those community members included in God's covenant of grace. Puritan covenant theology taught that the contract between God and humans was based solely on faith. Since Adam's rebellion, the covenant of works was no longer valid. The Puritan belief in the breach of this original covenant reinforced their understanding that humans could do nothing to affect their conversion. Only the experience of saving grace could give Puritans a clue as to whether they might be part of the covenant of grace guaranteeing salvation for the elect. The experience of assurance necessarily recurred throughout the life of a saint, coupled with opposing yet paradoxically complementary feelings of deep anxiety. Because the saint could never fully know the status of his or her own soul, anxiety and even despair frequently followed the experience of assurance. Through more inward searching and self-scrutiny, the saint would question the experience of assurance, wondering whether he or she had just been deluded into thinking that the experience had been authentic. Puritan conversion was an open-ended process, patterned by a "dynamic relation of hopeful and fearful emotions."

Even though grace was characteristically elusive and ineffable, the Puritans strove to develop a system of signs through which they could study the experience in others. What was the *ordo salutis,* or way of salvation, by which an individual realized his or her faith? Reformed interpretations of Pauline theology and the doctrine of preparation only partially answered this question. Yet the answer was central to Puritan evangelical and proselytizing goals, as they tried to promote the experience of

conversion in English and Native American communities. The testimony of faith, which became a requirement for church membership in 1635, fostered the communal study of the *ordo salutis.* It was not enough for prospective members to attest to their scriptural knowledge or belief in God, they had to display evidence of the effects of grace upon their soul before church members and ministers. Visible saints were called upon to translate the intensely inward experience of conversion and self-scrutiny into a series of signs that others could recognize. The testimony of faith marked an attempt to work out the *ordo salutis* in practice, reflecting the theology of the conversion's status as an interpretive process rather than a set doctrine.

See also: Grace, Soteriology

Further Reading

Patricia Caldwell, *The Puritan Conversion Narrative: The Beginnings of American Expression* (Cambridge, Eng., 1983); Charles Cohen, *God's Caress: The Psychology of Puritan Religious Experience* (New York, 1986); Janice Knight, *Orthodoxies in Massachusetts: Rereading American Puritanism* (Cambridge, MA, 1994); Edmund Morgan, *Visible Saints: The History of a Puritan Idea* (New York, 1966); Norman Petit, *The Heart Prepared: Grace and Conversion in Puritan Spiritual Life* (New Haven, 1966); Charles Hambrick Stowe, *The Practise of Piety: Puritan Devotional Disciplines in Seventeenth-Century New England* (Chapel Hill, 1982).

Sarah Rivett

Court of High Commission

A prerogative court—that is, one established by the king's prerogative—that functioned as the supreme court in ecclesiastical matters. Its authority was challenged by the common law courts early in the seventeenth century, but in 1611 James I issued new letters reestablishing its authority. Two years later James charged the court with enforcing an earlier ban on unlicensed books. The use of this and other prerogative courts to implement Charles I's personal rule (that is, his eleven years of governing without Parliament) was very unpopular. In particular, Archbishop William Laud's extensive use of it to enforce conformity to the canons of the church and his ecclesiastical policies became highly controversial. Due to its reputation of suppressing Puritanism, the Long Parliament abolished the court in 1641.

Further Reading
Kevin Sharpe, *The Personal Rule of Charles I* (New Haven, 1992); R. G. Usher, *The Rise and Fall of the High Commission* (Oxford, 1913).

Francis J. Bremer

Covenant Theology

See Federal Theology

Crime and Punishment

For frequently challenging civil and religious authority, puritans were prosecuted throughout the early modern period. The history of puritanism as a crime and the punishment of puritans must be appreciated by not only examining the legislation against those believed to be puritans but by acknowledging that puritanism indeed gave rise to numerous heresies and dangerous political ideas, whose proponents were persecuted and imprisoned by their more conservative brethren in authority. Subject to popular and judicial prejudice, the term *puritan* became identified with and included within the "heretical" and the "schismatic," but puritanism, in this respect, must also be examined in the context of an evolving historical context and a changing notion of what "Puritanism" itself was.

Elizabethan "Heresy"

The Elizabethan Settlement repealed the eighty-eight heresies recorded in canon law, leaving common law with jurisdiction over the prosecution and imprisonment of "heretics." In practice, this approach gave ecclesiastical courts the responsibility for dealing with religious error by the writ *de heretico comburendo,* which was itself repealed in 1677, along with the death penalty, after which "heresy" was punishable only by ecclesiastical censures. The Act of Supremacy of 1559 defined

Colonel John Lilburne, English pamphleteer who fought in the Parliamentary Army during the Civil War. A Puritan, he belonged to a group called the Levellers who believed in liberty of conscience and an extended franchise to all Englishmen and was imprisoned for his agitation. (Hulton Archive/Getty Images)

heresy according to the authority of the scriptures, Parliament with the assent of an ecclesiastical convocation, or the first four church councils (Nicaea in 325, Constantinople in 381, Ephesus in 431, and Chalcedon in 451).

Numerous Protestant martyrs met the flames during Mary's reign (and several Lollards before that), but Protestant England sought to avoid making martyrs of puritan zealots. However, the primacy of scriptural authority and individual conscience, which puritanism encouraged, created a religious culture in which "puritan" heresies grew rapidly. Though Elizabeth had abolished the burning of heretics when she claimed the throne, the fires were lit once again in the 1560s. Two Brownists were executed in 1567 for sedition, having compared Queen Elizabeth I to Jezebel. In 1612 James I suspended the burning of heretics (though not of their books), preferring to lock religious radicals up in prisons. The last two heretics burned at the stake in England were Bartholomew Legate and Edward Wightman, both of whom denied the Trinity.

During Elizabeth's reign, the primary means of suppressing the puritan movement were legislation and imprisonment. John Whitgift assumed the archbishopric of Canterbury in 1583, taking a far harder line against the puritans than his predecessor Edmund Grindal. In his Eleven Articles, Whitgift banned private congregations and enforced the use of the Bishop's Bible over the Geneva translation. The sixth article concerned ministerial subscription, stating that no man was permitted to administer the sacraments unless he subscribed to three further articles of belief, by acknowledging under oath royal supremacy (that is, acknowledging that the monarch of England was the proper head of the Church of England), the legitimacy of episcopacy and the Book of Common Prayer, and the doctrinal rectitude of the Thirty-nine Articles. Many puritans refused to accept these oaths, exposing themselves to prosecution before ecclesiastical courts. Many puritans were interrogated under the "ex officio" oath, which demanded that those questioned respond to incriminating questions or be prosecuted for refusing to take the oath, rather than for their beliefs.

Jacobean Confinement

By the reign of James I, religious radicals were quietly confined rather than publicly executed. This had the effect of integrating "puritan" prisoners with the debtors, pickpockets, and prostitutes who populated county jails and, in London, prisons such as the Gatehouse, the Fleet, the Clink, and Bridewell. The exception to this was the New Prison, Maiden Lane, which was devoted exclusively to the incarceration of religious prisoners. Here, as in Bridewell, whipping and other hardships accompanied strict religious observance, along with lots of work, such as weaving, spinning, packing, grinding chalk or corn, and beating hemp, the purpose of which was not to punish, but to improve the prisoners. The New Prison, Maiden Lane, was established during the first quarter of the seventeenth century, during the reign of James I, but fell into disuse due to a succession of escapes and a thriving Roman Catholic community within the prison, which caused much resentment among its puritan inmates and brought the prison itself into disrepute.

Another reason for the decline of this prison is that it was full. Though Whitgift's suppression of the Presbyterian movement silenced many puritans during the 1620s and 1630s and forced others to leave the country for the more legislatively hospitable New World, the increasing "Laudian" and "Arminian" momentum of the English Church prompted a puritan revival in opposition to its alleged incipient Roman Catholicism. Laud himself, as Bishop of London, was responsible for sentencing many puritans who now chose to separate from the English church and pursue their own religious inclinations. The New Prison, along with the Gatehouse, the Fleet, and Bridewell, received notorious puritan zealots such as John Vicars and Nathaniel Bernard; the Sabbatarians Theophilus Braborne, John Traske, and Dorothy Traske; the Familist Richard Lane; and the antinomian John Eachard. In April 1632, a large number of Separatists were captured at a private conventicle in Blackfriars. Until several escaped, they were confined in the New Prison, Maiden Lane.

Not all puritans, of course, were imprisoned in the New Prison. One of the most notorious puritans of this period, William Prynne, was held away from the metropolis so that he could serve his sentence in isolation. Prynne was prosecuted for his *Histrio-Mastix* in 1634, a pamphlet that railed against stage plays and obliquely criticized both Charles I and the queen, Henrietta Maria. Such high-profile cases were tried before the Star Chamber, an extension of the royal council, made up of Privy Counsellors as well as judges. It was involved in the activities of the common law and equity courts in both civil and criminal matters; it also dealt with cases referred to it by the High Commission and consulted the High Commission in cases of religious indictment. Prynne was fined £5,000, expelled from the Inns of Court where he was a lawyer, and pilloried; he had both his ears cropped and was imprisoned for life. The fine was never exacted; imprisonment proved only temporary; and the earless Prynne soon offended the authorities once more. In 1637, his ears were again cropped (the stumps were sawn off), and he was branded on his cheek with "S.L." (for "Schismatic Libeller") and imprisoned far away from London (until released by the Long Parliament in 1640), first in Caernarvon, Wales, and then in the grim Castle Orgeuil on Jersey. Tried alongside Prynne in 1637 were the puritans John Bastwick and Henry Burton, who received similarly harsh punishments.

American Liberty

Many puritans sought to escape persecution by fleeing to the Netherlands and America. New England consisted of puritan colonies amid an untamed and unknown wilderness, quite beyond the reach of Laudian authorities and legislation aimed at suppressing the puritan movement. Those who offended the "puritan" authorities of the New World were therefore punished by the congregational authority of the colonists themselves, who punished those they considered heretical by banishing them from their communities. In 1636, Anne Hutchinson maintained that legally prescribing right religion was unnecessary for those in whom God's grace operated. Because the puritan leaders of Boston held that conduct and piety were valid signs of inner sanctification, she was unfairly charged with antinomianism, excommunicated, and banished from the First Church of Boston in Massachusetts. Roger Williams was a member of the church at Salem and repeatedly claimed that the church should separate ever further from the English church. In 1635, when he denounced land grants from Charles I, arguing that the land belonged to the Indians, he was exiled from the community and founded Providence, Rhode Island, rather than face deportation.

The Civil War, Interregnum, and Beyond

In the early 1640s, many puritans who remained in England were still being persecuted by the ecclesiastical authorities, both for their beliefs and the actions that those beliefs prompted them to take (such as the withholding of tithes). But when Parliament abolished episcopacy, the High Commission, and the Star Chamber in 1641, Parliament assumed the responsibility of examining "puritan" radicals and, along with the Stationers' Company, committing men and women to jails such as the New Prison. The Stationers' Company had become an increasingly bitter opponent of the puritan movement after the surreptitious publication of the Presbyterian pamphlets known as the Marprelate tracts in the late 1580s. After 1586, printing was only permitted in London; in 1596, licensing was placed under the jurisdiction of the archbishop of Canterbury and the bishop of London; in 1637, only twenty printers in London could print books legally. The increasing regulation of the presses collapsed when episcopacy was abolished, and Parliament, with the assistance of the Stationers' Company, sought out and imprisoned radical authors and their printers who no longer railed against their old enemies the bishops, but the king, Parliament, and the now powerful Presbyterian party. During this period, many shades of "puritanism" were pitted against one another, which, in turn, disintegrated into separating congregations of godly believers.

The radicalization of puritanism during the English Civil War makes it difficult to examine a judicial and penal world of "crime" and corresponding "punishment." Insofar as Parliament was dominated by Presbyterians and, in 1648, members who were sympathetic to the Army, the "puritans" had won: it was Charles I whose crime was the bloodshed of the Civil War and whose punishment was execution. During this period, one zealot's deed or opinion was another zealot's crime or heresy. In 1646, for example, Thomas Edwards, the Presbyterian, railed against soldiers who mocked the sacrament of baptism by urinating in a font and baptizing a horse, but the punishment they received was little more than trial by paper and condemnation in print. Later in the decade, however, John Lilburne, who had inspired much political unrest in the army by spearheading the Leveller movement, was in conflict with the top Army leadership who were far more powerful than the waning Presbyterians. Lilburne spent, in total, half of his adult life in prison: in the Fleet, in the Tower of London (where he spent so much time that one of his children was christened "Tower") and the same Castle Orgeuil in which Prynne had been confined.

The most notorious legislative response to the puritan extremists of the 1640s and 1650s were the Blasphemy Acts, which were promulgated against the perceived threat of the Ranters. Though the tide of Independency that swept London in the late 1640s elicited a "Draconick" Presbyterian ordinance for "the punishing of Blasphemies and Heresies" in May 1648, acts against "the detestable sins of Incest, Adultery and Fornication" (10 May 1650) and "severall Atheistical, Blasphemous and Execrable Opinions" (9 August 1650) turned the Ranters into social deviants. These acts imposed punishments of six months in a house of correction (maintaining the same purpose of moral reformation instituted by the bridewells), with second offenses eliciting banishment or, in the case of adultery, death. Many of the so-called Ranters convicted under this legislation, such as John Robins, Elizabeth Haygood, and Joshua and Joan Garment, were imprisoned in the New Prison, Clerkenwell, which burned down in 1679.

The other "puritan" sect that was prosecuted during the Interregnum and the Restoration (and sometimes as Ranters) was the Quakers. Cromwell's sympathy toward religious diversity was not reflected in the actions of local courts, and many Quakers were prosecuted in Quarter Sessions and Assizes around the country. A *Proclamation Prohibiting the Disturbing of Ministers* was made in 1654, specifically against offending Quakers, in order to supplement Marian legislation on the matter. Parliament also extended Elizabethan vagrancy legislation to prevent Quakers proselytizing cross country, as George Fox had so effectively done, and passed an act for observing the Lord's Day that prosecuted Quakers for not attending church or for traveling on the Sabbath. James Nayler received the harshest punishment imposed upon a Quaker (he escaped death by fourteen votes in Parliament) when he was branded, bored through the tongue, whipped, and pilloried after riding into Bristol on an ass in October 1656, emu-

lating Christ. Quakers were prosecuted with widespread ferocity after Thomas Venner's armed Fifth Monarchist uprising in January 1661. Though Venner and about 20 of his accomplices were executed and 100 imprisoned, nearly 5,000 Quakers were imprisoned within six weeks of his revolt.

The Restoration sought to reestablish the Church of England, and the Clarendon Code, as the laws passed to that end were called, restricted Nonconformists' meetings, limited their political rights, and excluded them from universities. Dissenting clergymen were deprived of their livings and imprisoned. In May 1662, the Act of Uniformity demanded that clergymen and schoolmasters renounce the Solemn League and Covenant and accept the Book of Common Prayer. After a series of rumored plots, the Conventicles Acts of 1664 and 1670 reiterated that of 1593 by forbidding "any Assembly, Conventicle or Meeting under colour or pretence of any exercise of religion in other manner than is allowed." Nonconformists continued to flee the Old World for the New, and it is an irony of history that the Quakers, persecuted and imprisoned so relentlessly after the Restoration, built the first modern prisons in America during the early eighteenth century: the puritan movement, whose "crimes" did so much to dissolve the religious absolutism of the early modern period and usher in modernity's secular diversity, also ultimately produced the first modern prisons, in which confinement involved regimented supervision rather than punishing isolation as a means of personal reformation.

See also: Bridewell, Clarendon Code, Conventicles Act, Toleration

Further Reading

Simon Dyton, "Fabricating Radicalism: Ephraim Pagitt and Seventeenth-Century Heresiology" (Ph.D. dissertation, University of Cambridge, 2002); Joanna Innes, "Prisons for the Poor: English Bridewells, 1555–1800," in Douglas Hay and Francis Snyder, eds. *Labour, Law, and Crime: An Historical Perspective* (London, 1987), pp. 42–122; J. F. MacGregor and Barry Reay, eds., *Radical Religion in the English Revolution* (Oxford, 1984); E. D. Pendry, *Elizabethan Prisons and Prison Scenes*, 2 vols. (Salzburg, 1974).

Simon Dyton

D

Death and Dying

The period between 1558 and 1660, arguably a time of particular Puritan activity in England, was characterized by the increasing secularization of death. Manifested and reinforced by Protestant doctrinal changes, this era witnessed a reduction in funeral splendor. It also was a time of a constant threat of death and moments of abnormally high mortality. One-third of all infants did not live until their first birthday, and 2–3 percent of their mothers did not survive childbirth. Puritan children were taught young the lessons of death, often memorizing simple verses such as "if I should die before I wake, I pray the Lord my soul to take" and "In the burying place [you] may see / Graves shorter there than I / From death's arrest no age is free / Young children too must die." (*New England Primer*, 1777) For those past adolescence, the English Civil Wars accounted for its share of premature deaths. Plague, however, may be the most famous of the period's epidemic killers—killing 60–80 percent of those who were infected and nearly half of those within the week—but the "sweating sickness" of 1557–1559 did the most damage, resulting in roughly of 6 percent loss of England's population. The omnipresence of death found voice in the secular image of the memento mori (be mindful of dying)—the skeleton with hourglass raised in one hand, a dart raised in the other.

While death found visual expression agreeable to the Puritan doctrine, an image of the afterlife could not be used (part of the puritan resistance to fixing images of spiritual beings). Instead the secular image of Fame, looking remarkably like an angel, was forced into double duty. In deathbed paintings of the era, Fame descends into the frame (implying, but not articulating, her descent from Heaven) with a trumpet and wreath to crown the deceased. Once departed, worthy souls "are at their death made perfect in holiness" and "do immediately pass into glory" (*The New England Primer*, 1777); such a soul rests in the Bosom of Abraham, "lodge[d] in Everlasting arms, and Solacing it self in the full possession of endless and inexpressible Glories" (Willard, *Compleat Body of Divinity*, p. 535). Viewed from the Puritan perspective of an omnipresent and omnipotent God, death was an act of God's will, and to question the justness of death was to question God's purpose. Therefore, one needed only to accept the will of God and recognize that nothing could be done either to prevent death or to help the soul of the departed. The fate of the soul was sealed at death.

Death was a particularly fearful and uncertain time for Puritans, and a period during which competing ideas were required to be held in an agonizing tension. First, Puritans held that death was a punishment for sins on earth, as well as a reward for their time of suffering in the "wilderness" and a release from the trials of the world. Second, and most troubling to the dying person, was the theological concept of assurance, and the set of uncertainties that followed from it. As the critical step toward conversion, assurance came from receiving signs of God's mercy. Yet, assurance was not a guarantee of salvation; men can be deceived by the devil into a false sense of salvation. Those who did not doubt their spiritual worth and passed easily into death were viewed with suspicion. Therefore, doubt was the best sign of election. The result for many of such religious and cultural contradictions was a fear-filled death.

Given its unpredictability and spiritual importance, Puritans were constantly reminded to prepare themselves for death, and given detailed instruction as to how to die. Illness, wrote Richard Baxter, was death's "harbinger," designed to "wean us from the world, and make us willing to be gone; that the unwilling flesh has the help of pain." At the same time, "you must judge yourselves on your sick beds as near as you can as God will judge you." Baxter's *Directions for a Peaceful Death* has seventeen points to help achieve a godly death, most of which are variations upon the theme of the joys of heaven: "Look up to the blessed society of angels and saints with Christ, and remember their blessedness and joy, and that you also belong to the same society, and are going to be numbered with them (Direction VII)." For those troubled in mind, Baxter recommends choosing two or three "promises" to think about ("a sick man is not [usually] fit to think of very many things.") For those troubled by the number of his sins, Baxter suggests three verses to meditate on: one, "God so loved the world, that he gave his only begotten Son, that whosoever believes in him should not perish, but have everlasting life" (John 3:16); two, "And by him all that believe are justified from all things, from which you could not be justified by the law of Moses" (Acts 13:39); and three, "For I will be merciful unto their unrighteousness, and their sins and iniquities will I remember no more" (Hebrews 8:12).

Upon the soul's departure, the body of the elect appeared no different from those of the wicked, "nor," according to Massachusetts Reverend Samuel Willard, "do the Bodies of the Saints bear any Character upon them, by which men may distinguish them from the Bodies of other men" (Willard, p. 535). Yet, according to Willard, the saints' bodies rest in a state of "happiness," which "makes a vast difference between the Bodies of the Godly and the Wicked, though it be secret and not discerned by sensible Observation." The believer's body then "rests," in "happiness," until the Glorious Resurrection. Puritan divines were quick to point out that resting in the grave was not necessarily meant in the literal sense, because history made clear that earthly remains of God's chosen have not always lain undisturbed.

The wicked, too, got a rest from their labors: "not only a ceasing of the toil, and travail, of the Employments of this Life, but the putting an end to all the bodily Troubles of this World." "This deed belongs to the state of Humanity, and the ungodly Sinner hath this Rest as well as the Saint," yet, explains Samuel Willard, "it is a poor Rest, which is only a dark Interval, and a Prologue to more dismal Troubles" (Willard, p. 537). The rest of the damned lasts only until the Judgment Day; the rest of the elect for eternity.

Logically, therefore, Puritan theology should result in a funeral utterly lacking in any spiritual function. It should be a secular event around the task of disposing of the corpse. In 1644, with Parliament's establishment of *A Directory for the Public Worship of God*, England was momentarily obliged to follow quintessentially Puritan—and secular—funeral practices. A minister was not required at the burial, and should one be present, his role was confined to simply reminding those gathered of their obligation to bury the body "without any ceremony" (*Directory*, pp. 73–74), or, put more forcefully, the deceased should be buried without "the exorbitance of superstitious exiquies . . . as in their [Roman Catholic] bel-ringings, lamp-lighting, dirge and such other gear" (Spicer, p. 168). Ideally, departed Puritans were "carried to the church without singing or clerks and at the church a psalm was sung after Geneva and a sermon" as Henry Machyn recorded in 1561 (Gittings, p. 154). Early New England Puritan divines did not preach funeral sermons; only later did this practice develop, with the first North American funeral sermon printed in 1672. This change reflects a general softening of the Puritan attitude toward death around

1650, which resulted in larger and more elaborate funerals and increasingly decorated tombstones. New England gravestones offer especially graphic representations of the unpredictability of death.

Most people were buried within the churchyard in unmarked graves. In accordance with Geneva's example, kirk burial was forbidden in Scotland, for example, by the First Book of Discipline (1560), although with mixed results: even the noted John Knox preached at one. William Birnie, in his *The Blame of Kirk-buriall* (1606), continued to rail against it in the seventeenth century, calling it just one of "many of the Papistical punks . . . secretly slipped in the Kirk" (Spicer, p. 171).

Yet, even the *Directory* recognized that not all funerals would be the same and that "civil respects and difference" in rank would be recognized. For the aristocracy, the heraldic funeral was extremely complex, typically involving embalming (although frowned upon by Puritan teaching), long-distance transportation (from across the country or across the Channel), and conveyance by a black draped cart. Large numbers of mourners, in matching black liveries during the sixteenth century, and matching cloaks, gloves, and hats during the seventeenth century; banners; and other devices of heraldry accompanied the coffin to the grave site. The poor's winding sheeting and a trip to the grave in a communal coffin, accompanied by friends and neighbors, marked the other end of the social spectrum, as well as of funeral practices. The intervening social orders had correspondingly intervening styles of funerals. Parliamentarians were noted for the splendor of their funerals.

See also: Burial Practices, Death and Dying (in Primary Sources)

Further Reading

Clare Gittings, "Sacred and Secular: 1558–1660," in P. C. Jupp and C. Gittings, eds., *Death in England* (Manchester, Eng., 1999), pp. 147–173; Andrew Spicer, "'Rest of their Bones': Fear of Death and Reformed Burial Practices," in W. G. Naphy and P. Roberts, eds. *Fear in Early Modern Society* (Manchester, Eng., 1997); David E. Stannard, "Death and Dying in Puritan New England," *American Historical Review* 78 (1973), 1305–1330; David E. Stannard, *The Puritan Way of Death. A Study in Religion, Culture, and Social Change* (New York, 1977).

Lynn A. Botelho

Declaration of Indulgence

A royal proclamation or edict suspending the operation of the laws that enforce worship in the Church of England and proscribe other forms of worship. Such proclamations were acts of the royal prerogative suspending the operation of parliamentary statutes. They effectively granted religious toleration to Protestant Dissenters and, in some cases, to Roman Catholics. They were therefore contentious on constitutional and religious grounds. There were three such proclamations in the later seventeenth century: Charles II made a feint at one in December 1662 and issued a full-scale indulgence in 1672; James II issued his Declaration of Indulgence on 4 April 1687 and repeated it on 27 April 1688.

In the Declaration of Breda (1660), issued on the eve of his restoration, Charles II had promised liberty to tender consciences, but political suspicion and maneuvering had by 1662 resulted in an Act of Uniformity, which permitted no religious freedom to those who did not conform to the Church of England. On 26 December 1662, Charles announced his intention of asking Parliament to find a way in which he might exercise his power to dispense with the penalties of the act. The following February he received a very unsatisfactory answer, as Parliament told him that he had no such power and that any concessions would end in the return of intolerant Roman Catholicism. Parliament feared that the king's ulterior motive was to allow freedom to Catholics as well as Protestant Dissenters.

This proved to be true when on 15 March 1672 Charles issued his Declaration of Indulgence suspending all penalties in matters ecclesiastical against Dissenters and Popish recusants. Protestant Nonconformists were granted freedom of public worship if their ministers and places of worship were licensed, and Roman Catholics were allowed to worship in private. The Church of England, meanwhile, was to remain the "standard of the general and public worship of God." This sudden reversal of over a decade of official religious policy was justified in terms of the failure of the effort to impose uniformity, but it was also motivated by Charles's audacious new foreign policy, an alliance with Catholic France to wage war against the Protestant Netherlands. In pursuit of this alliance Charles had made a secret and rather vague commitment to convert to Catholicism and reintroduce that religion in his kingdoms. Once again, it was Parliament that forced Charles to back down and cancel the Declaration in 1673. Nevertheless many of the Nonconformist congregations that had taken out licenses continued to worship quite openly, and many meetings later regarded 1672 as their date of foundation. Several Protestants, both Anglican and Nonconformist, disliked the Declaration because of the freedom it had extended to Roman Catholics. In 1673 Parliament tried to underline the difference between Catholic and Protestant by passing the Test Act to drive Catholics from public office and by promoting a bill "for the ease of dissenters." Although the latter did not succeed, it did indicate a greater political willingness to consider constitutional measures of comprehension and toleration for Protestant Dissenters.

As an open Roman Catholic, James II did not disguise his hopes of dismantling the laws against Catholics and Nonconformists. When it became apparent that the Anglican majority in Parliament would not aid him in legislating a repeal, he began to dangle the bait of a toleration before the Dissenters. On 4 April 1687, he issued a Declaration of Indulgence suspending all penal laws in matters ecclesiastical, allowing freedom of public worship, and removing all civil disabilities from non-Anglicans. This was the most far-reaching religious freedom attempted in the seventeenth century. James even promised to seek parliamentary approval in due course, which may have drawn the unconstitutional sting of this royal setting aside of the laws of the land. But if the Declaration sounded less arbitrary than the 1672 Indulgence, it was blatantly pro-Catholic: James stated that he could not "but heartily wish" that all his subjects were members of the Catholic Church.

James obtained the "thankful acceptance" of Dissenters in the form of eighty addresses of thanks for the Declaration. Presbyterian ministers such as Vincent Alsop, Joseph Read, and Daniel Burgess put their hand to these addresses, but some of their brethren were troubled by this. William Bates and John Howe, the Presbyterian leaders, Stretton the Congregationalist, and William Kiffin the Baptist, refused to offer their thanks. Richard Baxter explained his refusal on several grounds, but one of them was that he did not want to offend the conforming clergy of the Church of England, and he lacked the skill to compose an address that would displease neither the king nor these clergy. Dissent was torn between taking advantage of this Catholic-inspired generosity and closing ranks with the Protestant Church of England. Matters came to a head when, disappointed by the initial response, James reissued the Declaration in April 1688 and required the clergy of the Church of England to read it from their pulpits. This was a step too far for the church and its leaders, and it was their resistance and the subsequent trial of the seven bishops who led that resistance that led to a rapprochement between Protestant Dissenters and the Church of England. After the Revolution of 1688, a parliamentary "Toleration Act" (1689) formally recognized the freedom of Protestant worship established by the Declaration of Indulgence and denied that same freedom to Roman Catholics.

See also: Antipopery, Dissenters
Further Reading
John Spurr, *The Restoration Church of England, 1646–1689* (New Haven, 1991).

John Spurr

Dedham Conference

One of many meetings of ministers in the 1580s that made up what is sometimes called the Classical Movement, sometimes the Conference Movement. Dedham is a small town on the River Stour, on the borders of Essex and Suffolk, a protoindustrial center of cloth manufacture, and a relatively safe zone for nonconformists, as far as one could get from the diocesan machinery in London and Norwich. However, it is far from clear that the Dedham Conference was one of the more powerful or influential of puritan conferences. With the exception of Dr. Edmund Chapman, the first tenant of an endowed lectureship in the town, its leadership was less distinguished than that of a neighboring conference meeting in and around Braintree, which included Richard Rogers of Wethersfield and George Gifford of Maldon. The commitment of Dedham to the cause of presbyterian militancy was also more limited than that of other conferences, particularly that in Northamptonshire. But, uniquely, the "minutes" and other papers relating to the Dedham Conference survive, written up many years after its dissolution by the sometime vicar of Dedham, Richard Parker, who had acted as its secretary. Much of this material was published for the Royal Historical Society in 1905 by Roland Green Usher in a not very satisfactory edition (Camden 3rd Series, vol. 8), and the archive of the Dedham Conference in its entirety has now been published for the Church of England Record Society. It tells us most of what we know about the Conference Movement.

Dedham as a parish was most peculiar. The vicarage was so poorly endowed that in the early Elizabethan years it proved impossible to fill it, and it took fifty years for the pastoral care of the place to find a safe pair of hands. Yet there was godly money about, especially the resources of the rich clothier and gentleman William Cardinal, a native of Dedham with commanding interests in the neighboring township of East Bergholt and Chapman's brother-in-law. Toward 1580 one of several transient vicars of Dedham, John Keltridge, was complaining, in print, of what in religious circles is called "sheep-stealing," "vain glorious men" who were creating "sects and divisions." This could only refer to the arrival in the parish of Chapman and the setting up of his lectureship, mainly through Cardinal's initiative. Chapman had arrived as a refugee from an anti-puritan reaction in Norwich, and with him came two other Norwich asylum seekers, Dr. Richard Crick, who settled in East Bergholt, and Richard Dow, who found a berth in Stratford St. Mary, two neighboring parishes.

This was the nucleus of the Dedham Conference, which was instituted in October 1582. That it was set up as part of a concerted plan, orchestrated by John Field in London, is suggested by what happened at Cockfield in Suffolk (the parish of John Knewstub) in May of that year, when large numbers of ministers met at a conference of which Field was fully informed. John Whitgift was not yet archbishop of Canterbury, but his promotion was anticipated. The moment that Whitgift was in his post, in November 1583, and had launched his campaign to secure subscription to articles that were a denial of all that the puritans stood for, resistance to the archbishop became a major raison d'être for conferences like that now meeting every month in and around Dedham, its members drawn from as far away as Ipswich and Boxford in Suffolk and Coggeshall and Colchester in Essex. As the subscription crisis of 1584 deepened and battle lines were drawn between nonconformists and the conformist establishment, the Dedham minutes are full of references to the predicament of members from whom subscription was demanded, attempts to achieve solidarity in the puritan ranks, petitions and other initiatives aimed at "further reformation," and liaison with sympathetic gentlemen and Parliamentarians. But lest we should regard the conference as a piece of ecclesiopolitical machinery, the first business at all its meetings was scriptural exposition, and many conference days were spent in prayer and fasting, the main weapons in the puritan armory. Much time was devoted in the early years of the conference to a learned but inconclusive debate about the Sabbath.

The Dedham Conference was more than a talking shop. It assumed the authority to resolve a variety of pastoral and other contentious issues in the church life of its members, and to exercise its own discipline, almost as if the bishops and archdeacons and their courts did not exist. Yet it would be wrong to call Dedham a Presbyterian classis. For one thing, it was a conference only of ministers, without the element of ruling elders that we find in the theoretical presbyterian literature and in the Scottish presbytery. For another, the conference was deeply divided between moderates, who were anxious to come to reasonable terms with the bishops, notably Chapman, and harder men, such as the gentleman minister William Tey, for whom the bishops were anti-Christian, no longer to be regarded as brethren. And the repeated failure of the conference to control its own members, or to be bound by decisions taken above and beyond the conference in London, suggest that although it would be an anachronism to credit it with the invention of Independency, that rather than Presbyterianism was the direction in which it was headed. And again and again the conference declined to endorse the Presbyterian Book of Discipline, whether for ideological reasons or from simple caution is not clear.

The Dedham Conference came to an end in the summer of 1589, after its eightieth meeting. Following the affair of the Marprelate tracts, Presbyterian pamphlets clandestinely published, storm clouds were gathering. Richard Parker was summoned to London, where he sang like a canary, confessing to meetings that were supposed to be secret and naming names. But the demise of the conference had its murky side. Parker was involved in more than one sexual scandal involving women of the town and a neighboring parish, and he was soon forced out of Dedham and into yet another exile in Norfolk. Naturally his account of the last days of the conference tells us nothing about this.

See also: Conference Movement
Further Reading
Patrick Collinson, *The Elizabethan Puritan Movement* (London, 1967); Patrick Collinson, John Craig, and Brett Usher, eds., *Conferences and Combination Lectures in the Elizabethan Church: Dedham and Bury St. Edmunds, 1582–1590* (Woodbridge, Eng., 2003).

Patrick Collinson

Devil

The perceived agency of the devil, and especially his ability to tempt internally, was central to Puritan devotional culture, reflecting a perception that the godly life was characterized by a constant struggle with the demonic subversion of faith. In this, Puritans were the main exponents of a characteristically Protestant concept of the devil that was shaped, in the sixteenth century, by the experience of the Reformation. Traditionally, diabolic agency had encompassed a wide range of physical and spiritual activity, but Protestants elevated temptation as its defining characteristic. This was a consequence of the Reformers' perception of the ubiquitous existence of sin within mankind and of their concern, in the wake of their progressive disillusionment with Catholicism, that diabolic false religion could be hidden within the superficially benign and pious.

The profound consequences of this change of emphasis for Protestant culture were most evident in the devotional writings and practices of Puritans in England and New England. Works of practical divinity described the godly as besieged by a continuous satanic assault. The devil was master of the reprobate majority, who resisted Puritan attempts at reformation, and he sought constantly to subvert individuals' faith through temptation. Temptation was understood as a mechanism by which the devil triggered the innate sinfulness inherited by every man as a consequence of the fall of Adam. Satan "injected" blasphemous and sinful thoughts directly into the mind, to tempt men to sin, and, in the case of the godly, to undermine their assurance by suggesting that they were reprobate. This concept reflected the profound difficulties many of the godly suffered in living up to ideals of personal piety, and the continued experience of doubt in the face of strenuous efforts to gain assurance gave an especial tangibility to the notion that the conscience was being intruded upon by a demonic tempter. But Puritan demonism was prescriptive rather than simply descriptive. It sought to aid afflicted consciences by maximizing the potential for a positive soteriological interpretation of temptation. God allowed the faithful to be tested by the devil, who reserved his greatest efforts for the most godly. Thus, by extension, temptation itself could be taken as a sign of election. Moreover, Puritan ministers became the main contributors to a genre of dialogue writing that sought to guide parishioners through temptation by rehearsing the debates over salvation that could take place between the conscience and the thoughts introduced into the mind by the devil.

Accounts left by individual Puritans testify to the depth to which this picture of diabolic temptation was assimilated into their lives. Some of the godly, such as the New England minister Michael Wigglesworth (whose diary survives for 1653–1657), accorded the devil relatively little influence. Others, such as Nehemiah Wallington or Hannah Allen, experienced profound isolation and despair as they interpreted their intense experiences of temptation as symptoms of reprobation. But most of the godly both experienced temptation and were able to understand its soteriological potential. Thus Lady Margaret Hoby (1599–1602) or Sir Simonds D'Ewes (1621) noted diabolic affliction in their diaries as a routine part of their religious experiences, while Lady Brilliana Harley (1622) drew up a model of temptation in her commonplace book so that she might judge if her response to it was consistent with election. Indeed, temptation became central to the narratives of spiritual progress that ensured mutual identification among the godly. Thus the Oxford Puritan Elizabeth Wilkinson was accepted into Robert Harris's public assembly as the result of her submitting a spiritual autobiography, which was then used by the minister as an exemplar of the temptation of the godly. The Baptist John Bunyan, writing in the 1660s, even noted that, on overhearing a group of women discussing their experiences of diabolic affliction, he had felt isolated by his own lack of temptation. The godly laity also assimilated the characterization of temptation as an internal dialogue with Satan. For many, the most terrifying aspect of diabolic affliction was the lack of control they experienced over their thoughts. The dialogue, in which the soteriological potential of temptation could be rehearsed, allowed a certain reimposition of control, and in some celebrated cases, such as the deathbed afflictions of Katherine Stubbs (1591) or Katherine Brettergh (1601), could be a profound religious experience contributing to an experiential attainment of assurance.

The Puritan understanding of diabolic agency also had a far wider social and political significance.

A powerful analogy could be drawn between the temptation of the individual human body and the temptation of the body politic, in which Satan intruded unseen into the commonwealth as he did into the mind. The attempted Puritan reformation of manners in England was informed by an understanding that Satan employed the devices of popular culture—the stage and the maypole—to subvert the commonwealth. In their reassuring familiarity, such activities offered an enticing, but false, equation between physical and spiritual comfort. Moreover, as the "schools of Satan" they activated the sinful potential of the body politic by encouraging their audiences to emulate the lascivious activities that were depicted. This provocative analogy was also widely used by Puritans in their conflicts with the established church. In the debates over Presbyterianism in England in the 1580s and 1590s, and in the attacks on Laudianism in the 1630s and 1640s, Puritans argued that the continuance of episcopacy and other "popish remnants" as pollutants within the English church was a temptation of the body politic. They made wide use of 2 Corinthians 6:14–15—"What concord hath Christ with Belial?"—to argue that any Catholic/diabolic survival within the English church inherently worked its subversion. As the diabolic invasion of the individual triggered that individual's innate sinfulness, so unreformed remnants threatened to trigger the corrupt potential of the body politic, conceived as the existence of the reprobate majority. Responsibility to be vigilant against the diabolic invasion of the commonwealth lay with the church hierarchy, the magistracy, and the government. Thus, though Puritan criticisms were aimed primarily at the Elizabethan and Laudian bishops, they were implicitly extended to the English Protestant monarchs, and on occasion this was openly stated by Puritans such as Peter Wentworth (in parliament in 1576) or William Prynne (in *Histrio-Mastix* in 1633).

But though Puritans emphasized the spiritual agency of the devil, they were also concerned with his physical manifestations. Providential appearances, in which Satan punished sinners on God's behalf, interested Puritans as demonstrations of the consequences of sin. Writers such as Thomas

Beard appropriated this traditional genre of exemplar tale for the purposes of Puritan moralizing. Similarly, despite denouncing the Catholic practice of exorcism, Puritans concerned themselves with cases of demonic possession in order to both answer a need among their parishioners and exploit the polemical potential of individual ministers' victories over Satan. Finally, Puritans were highly concerned with cases of witchcraft, which they understood to involve an explicit contract between a witch and the devil, and which they argued demonstrated the increasing prevalence of the devil's agency in the Last Days.

See also: Witchcraft

Further Reading

Richard Godbeer, *The Devil's Dominion: Magic and Religion in Early New England* (Cambridge, Eng., 1992); Nathan Johnstone, *The Devil in Early Modern England* (forthcoming); Frank Luttmer, "Persecutors, Tempters and Vassals of the Devil: The Unregenerate in Puritan Practical Divinity," *Journal of Ecclesiastical History* 51 (2000), 37–68; Darren Oldridge, *The Devil in Early Modern England* (Stroud, Eng., 2000).

Nathan Johnstone

Dissenters

Dissenters in the late seventeenth century were those Protestants who refused to worship with the Church of England. It was perhaps the most general term in use and was applied to all those Protestants, whether lay or clerical, and of whatever denomination, who rejected the doctrine, discipline, and worship of the Church of England as laid down in the 1662 Act of Uniformity. *Nonconformity* was a near synonym. Dissenters were also described by their opponents as fanatics, enthusiasts, sectaries, and, less frequently, as puritans. Dissent effectively acquired a legal identity as the Clarendon Code and other legislation persecuted all non-Anglican Protestants for their religious preferences and excluded them from full participation in civil and political life.

The category of Dissent embraced the full range of non-Anglican Protestantism from the "ejected clergy" (that is, those who had been forced out

their benefices by the Clarendon Code) and moderate Presbyterian divines to the Baptists and sects such as the Quakers. Restoration Dissent was a diverse body. In the countryside, especially, Dissenters were often scattered widely, a family or a few individuals in each parish: the Dissenters' church at Rothwell, Northamptonshire, drew members from sixteen distinct places. Some communities boasted several congregations. The Cambridgeshire village of Over had Baptists, Quakers, Congregationalists, and visits from the sectarian leader Ludowick Muggleton, while the city of Bristol enjoyed three Independent churches, two Baptist, and a Presbyterian, as well as a Quaker congregation. Religious choice was clearly a fact of Dissenting life. Charles Doe described how, as a fifteen-year-old apprentice in the late 1660s, he heard the General (Arminian) Baptists while his father-in-law attended a Presbyterian meeting; in the 1680s William Hone promiscuously attended Baptist, Independent, and Presbyterian meetings. Such diversity implies that religious allegiances could be hazy. On the other hand, those described as Dissenters by the authorities did not always recognize other denominations as their brethren. The overriding question for Dissent in Restoration England was whether it had sufficient common purpose to act as a body.

Dissent had political influence. There were Presbyterian and Independent sympathizers among both members of Parliament and peers in the Cavalier Parliament (1661–1679), and the "Dissenting interest" was strong within the mercantile community and the City of London. The consequent political support for improving Dissenters' legal position was squandered because Dissenters lacked a common goal: some aspired to "comprehension," or reunion with the Church of England, while others were interested only in religious toleration. Dissent also suffered by its association with radical politics. Tainted by its Cromwellian past, Dissent was suspect in the eyes of the government and subject to persecution on grounds of subversion and disloyalty. Radical elements among Dissent, including Baptists and Independents, did exploit the Exclusion Crisis to plot the overthrow of Charles II and/or his brother. The conspiracies exposed by the investigation of the supposed Rye House Plot in 1683 and the Monmouth rebellion of 1685 against James II confirmed the existence of this extreme wing within Dissent.

In the later 1680s James II courted the Dissenters, in the hope that they would support a religious toleration that would include Roman Catholics as well as Protestants. Once again, Dissenters were divided over strategy. Was it desirable or even safe to ally with an idolatrous false religion like popery in pursuit of their own religious freedom? Although some Dissenters offered their thanks for the 1687 Declaration of Indulgence, the majority rallied to the Protestant cause and reaped their reward after the Glorious Revolution of 1688. The Toleration Act of 1689 confirmed the legal identity of Dissent by providing freedom of worship for all non-Anglican Protestants. The future of Dissent seemed to lie in collaboration between the different denominations. The 1690s saw progress in this direction. Although the Common Fund and "Happy Union" failed, other cooperative ventures, often at the local level, between Presbyterians, Congregationalists (as Independents were increasingly known), and Baptists flourished. Yet in the early eighteenth century, theological realignment over fundamental issues like the Trinity, justification by faith alone, and predestination was leading to a reconfiguration of Dissent. The Presbyterians moved toward Arminianism and Unitarianism, while antinomianism gained ground in other quarters. There is also some evidence of the "routinization" of the Dissenting experience in these years. "Old Dissent," as it was soon to be known, eventually found itself outflanked by the zeal of the Evangelical Revival and the Methodists.

See also: Clarendon Code, Comprehension, Ejections of Clergy, Independency, Nonconformity, Subscription
Further Reading
Neil H. Keeble, *The Literary Culture of Nonconformity in Later Seventeenth-Century England* (Leicester, Eng., 1987).

John Spurr

Dissenting Brethren

The Independents in the Westminster Assembly of Divines, particularly the five signatories to *An Apologeticall Narration*—Thomas Goodwin, Philip Nye, Jeremiah Burroughes, William Bridge, and Sidrach Simpson. The term was also used to denote the seven Independents (the original five plus William Carter and William Greenhill) who later dissented from the majority conclusions of the Westminster Assembly.

Goodwin, Nye, Burroughes, Bridge, and Simpson had all migrated to the Netherlands in the mid-1630s after suffering under the Laudian drive for conformity within the Church of England. Nye became pastor of the English church at Arnhem in 1633 and was joined by Thomas Goodwin, the former vicar of Trinity Church in Cambridge, in the late 1630s. Bridge succeeded John Davenport as pastor of the English church at Rotterdam after being silenced and excommunicated from his ministry in Norwich. They were joined by both Burroughes, suspended from his ministry in Norfolk in 1636, and Simpson, a former curate at St. Margaret's, Fish Street, London. Like the New England Congregationalists, the future Dissenting Brethren denied that they were Separatists, and continued to see the Church of England as a true church. Disillusioned by episcopacy, however, they came to reject ecclesiastical hierarchies and embrace a congregational polity.

After the calling of the Long Parliament in November 1640, all five men returned to England to participate in the campaign for further reformation. Bridge became the pastor of a gathered church at Norwich and Yarmouth, and Goodwin established a gathered church in London. The other three accepted appointments within the Church of England—Burroughes was made a lecturer to congregations in Stepney and Cripplegate; Nye became a vicar in Huntingdonshire and then a rector in Middlesex; and Simpson was appointed lecturer in his old parish of St. Margaret's, Fish Street. All became enthusiastic Parliamentarians, with Burroughes and Bridge writing pamphlets in defense of Parliament's resistance to the king in 1642–1643.

In 1643, all five men were appointed to the Westminster Assembly, appointments that reflected their willingness to cooperate with moderate Presbyterians, and contrasted with the exclusion of the more aggressive Henry Burton and his Presbyterian opponent, Thomas Edwards. During the early months of the assembly, the Westminster Independents supported the Presbyterians in condemning separatism and sectarianism, and in December they joined sixteen other members in subscribing a declaration entitled, *Certaine Considerations to Dis-swade Men from Further Gathering of Churches*. However, it was rapidly becoming clear that the assembly was likely to support a Presbyterian settlement of the Church of England, and the Independents feared that their own congregations would be threatened by the imposition of Presbyterian uniformity. Thus, in January 1644, they published *An Apologeticall Narration,* which called for a limited toleration of orthodox Independent churches. The Apologists argued that they represented a middle way between Brownism and "the authoritative Presbyterial government."

The publication of the *Apologeticall Narration* marked the beginning of a protracted rearguard action by the Dissenting Brethren against the Presbyterians. On some minor issues debated in the assembly (e.g., distribution of communion, selection of pastors, ruling elders), the Independents did form temporary alliances with some English Presbyterians or the Scottish Covenanters. But only a small minority of their fellow divines endorsed Independency—Carter and Greenhill, Joseph Caryl, John Phillips, and Peter Sterry. Although John Cotton, John Davenport, and Thomas Hooker had been invited to attend the assembly, all three declined, though they did support the Dissenting Brethren with their publications on "the Congregationall way." In the assembly's debates, Independents spoke often but to little avail, and were outvoted on all the key issues, including the congregation's right to ordain its own minister and its freedom to govern itself independent of the authority of classical (referring to a group of local congregations), provincial, and national assemblies.

The Dissenting Brethren did not deny the value of such assemblies, but they granted them an advisory role only. When the assembly finalized its recommendations on church government in April 1645, it gave its firm backing to Presbyterian reform of the Church of England. The seven Dissenting Brethren issued various statements explaining their dissent, culminating with *The Reasons presented by the Dissenting Brethren against certain Propositions concerning Presbyteriall Government* (1648).

Although they had lost the battle, they went on to win the war. The implementation of the Presbyterian settlement was painfully slow and piecemeal, and Independents were in the ascendant in the New Model Army. After the Second Civil War, Parliament was purged of many of its Presbyterian members, and an Independent coup led to the execution of the king and the establishment of a commonwealth. The remaining Dissenting Brethren were Dissenters no more, and during the Interregnum they were to become leading figures in the Cromwellian church. Although Burroughes had died in 1646, the others lived on. Goodwin and Nye, in particular, rose to great prominence under Cromwell. Goodwin became president of Magdalen College, Oxford, in 1649, and was present at Cromwell's deathbed. He organized a Congregational church at Oxford, but continued to be heavily involved in the established church too, an arrangement typical of the Dissenting Brethren. Nye played a leading role in organizing the Savoy Conference of Independent churches in 1658, and he was ironically dubbed Cromwell's archbishop of Canterbury. In contrast to more radical Independents, the conservative Independents only supported a limited toleration and refused to countenance the abolition of tithes. They also supported the establishment of the commissions of Triers and Ejectors to monitor the clergy of the established church. At the Restoration, Bridge, Goodwin, Greenhill, Nye, and Simpson were all ejected from their livings (Carter had died in 1658), but they continued to be active leaders of Restoration Congregationalism.

See also: An Apologeticall Narration, Independency, Triers and Ejectors

Further Reading
Francis J. Bremer, *Congregational Communion* (Boston, 1994); Berndt Gustafsson, *The Five Dissenting Brethren: A Study on the Dutch Background of their Independentism* (Lund, Sweden, 1955); Robert Paul, *The Assembly of the Lord* (Edinburgh, 1985).

John Coffey

Domestic Relations

Domestic relations in the Puritan family, if the term is understood to mean the nature of the bonds between husband and wife, parents and children, and nuclear family and extended family, can be glimpsed in the diary and letters of Samuel Sewall (1652–1730), the Boston judge, merchant, and councillor.

As one who enjoyed a privileged place in Puritan society, Sewall must be taken to be an exceptional Puritan and not a representative one, if indeed any individual could be characterized as representative. The very term *Puritan family* is a convenience, encompassing ways of life that varied according to time, place, socioeconomic level, church membership status, and personal qualities, among many other characteristics of particular families. But Sewall's work projected him into every stratum of his community, and he observed his world with endless curiosity, making his diary a valuable repository of information about family life in Puritan New England. The record of domestic relations that Sewall left behind generally is in accord with that of two other Puritans whose lives are well documented, the Boston minister Cotton Mather and the minister in Earls Colne, Essex, Ralph Josselin. Barely a

A Puritan family in England, 1563. (TopFoto.co.uk/AAAC)

trace of Hannah (Hull) Sewall's (1658–1717) writings survives, so she must remain an obscure figure, whose ideas and deeds can be known only as they have been selected by and filtered through her husband in his diary and letters.

The family life that Sewall revealed in his writings was one in which husband and wife enjoyed the loving, mutually respectful relationship that was prescribed by the Puritan divines. Hannah lived mostly in her domestic world, her days framed by the constant demands of bearing, nursing, weaning, and, often, burying children. Busy as Sewall was with his judicial, civic, and religious responsibilities, he did not relegate household matters to Hannah and her helpers, but was engaged in every aspect of the children's care. Sewall joyously, if anxiously, awaited their births, took pains with the important rituals of baptism and naming, observed their progress in nursing and weaning, attended to them in their illnesses, prayed and watched with those who were dying, and grieved deeply at their deaths. Of the Sewalls' fourteen children, seven died in infancy, one was stillborn, and only six survived to adulthood.

Hannah and Samuel delighted in the gradual progress of their children from the condition of helplessness through stages of increasingly greater intellectual, physical, and moral capacity. They weaned the children gradually; marked their first words, first teeth, and precocious ideas; called them by affectionate diminutive names; and never mistook them for "miniature adults," or forced them to prematurely assume the demeanor or full religious responsibilities of adulthood. The parents led by example and persuasion, and Sewall notes only one occasion when he chose to strike a misbehaving child.

Hannah was a partner to her husband in the crises that affected her family. Though the children's religious education was largely directed by their father, Hannah too helped to guide the family's daily readings of the scriptures and to address the terror of damnation engendered in the course of Puritan indoctrination. Throughout the nearly irrevocable breakdown of their son Samuel Jr.'s marriage to the willful Rebeckah, daughter of Governor Joseph Dudley, Hannah was an outspoken defender of her not entirely blameless son. While Sewall applied patience and tact to the distressing situation, Hannah was willing to have "very sharp discourse" with Rebeckah and to stand "vehemently against" Sam's ending his estrangement from his wife until matters of contention were put right, a position that even put Hannah at odds with the counsel of the pastor to the younger Sewalls.

Hannah's many pregnancies and frequent indispositions caused her to miss some family gatherings, outings to Hog Island, and dinner parties, and she was unable to attend the Harvard commencement ceremonies at which her son Joseph took his first and then his second degree. Nonetheless, there is evidence to be found in Sewall's diary of a companionable and affectionate marriage. Besides going to Sabbath meetings and Thursday lectures together, Samuel and Hannah visited with kin, socialized with friends, and spent fall days enjoying cider and apples at their rural properties. Sewall trusted Hannah's judgment above his own in managing household expenditures, one day handing his cash over to her because "She has a better faculty than I at managing Affairs."

At times Sewall was troubled that his work might have caused him to be insufficiently attentive to his wife. He recorded disturbing dreams in which Hannah had suffered because of his neglect, and noted in Latin after one such account that when he "shook off sleep, I embraced my wife for joy as if I had newly married her." Several days after embarking on a long voyage to England, Sewall wrote, with more than a hint of passion, that he "ait my wives Pasty, the remembrance of whom is ready to cut me to the heart."

Samuel and Hannah resided in John and Judith Hull's Boston home, so for as long as the maternal grandparents lived, they were on hand to help raise their grandchildren and to provide the family with a sense of continuity with the ways of New England's second generation of Puritans. Grandmother Judith Hull was deeply involved in her grandchildren's birth and early years. Grandmother Jane Sewall also came to help at times of birth and weaning, and several of her ailing grandchildren

Part of a letter of Margaret Winthrop to her husband, John. (Courtesy Francis J. Bremer)

were sent to Newbury in the hope that the paternal grandparents could cure their "convulsions." Aunts, uncles, and cousins often came for visits, and several young people, some kin and some who were not relatives, came to live with the Sewalls as servants or hopeful scholars.

On occasion, and for specific purposes, the parents relied on others to care for their children. They arranged for Sam Jr. and Joseph to live with a distinguished schoolmaster for a time and sent some of their ailing children to be nursed not only by grandparents, but also by healers. The Sewall daughters visited the homes of relatives, where they enjoyed the company of their many cousins, and found opportunities to practice domestic skills and expand their social experiences in preparation for marriage. Hannah and Samuel never sought to relegate to others the responsibility for raising their children. Rather, they entrusted their sons and daughters to persons they judged to be the best teachers, the most effective healers, the most suit-

able masters, and the most congenial kin. Sewall regularly visited his absent children. He was closely joined to Sam Jr. as the indifferent scholar struggled through several failed apprenticeships until finally he succeeded as a bookseller; and he followed Joseph's progress through college and zealously monitored that son's spiritually and physically agonizing rise to the ministry of the Third (South) Church.

When the time came for each of the Sewall children to take a husband or wife, Samuel and Hannah steered but did not force their offspring into courtship with a proper partner. While the parents accorded the courting couple a measure of privacy, they kept a keen eye on their activities, and did not hesitate to intervene if youthful judgment and the course of nature seemed in need of correction. Sewall urged his daughter Elizabeth to reconsider a rejected suitor, the merchant Grove Hirst, but he never suggested that she suppress her natural feelings to make a match that was merely judicious:

"[I]f you find in yourself an immovable, incurable Antipathy from him, and cannot love, and honour, and obey him, I shall say no more." Hirst's persistence, and Sewall's wisdom in advising, and not dictating, a course of action proved effective. When he found reason to doubt the intentions of Sam Gerrish, a suitor to his daughter Mary, Sewall made pointed inquiries and closely observed the young bookseller's behavior until he was convinced of his good faith. Joseph, preoccupied with his religious duties, seems to have had a rather inconspicuous role in the wooing of Elizabeth Walley, leaving to his indefatigable father much of the business of securing her hand. Sewall helped his daughter Judith to fend off two distinguished but unwanted admirers, until she made a romantic match with William Cooper, minister at the Brattle Street Church.

Samuel and Hannah remained deeply involved in the lives of their married children and their grandchildren. Their unmarried invalid daughter, Hannah, found comfort, affection, and honor in her life at home. The Sewalls steered Sam Jr. through his marital difficulties, in the course of which their daughter-in-law gave birth to an illegitimate child; but throughout this turbulent period, they did not flinch at the pain, the humiliation, and the spiritual dangers that Sam's weaknesses and Rebeckah's indiscretions inflicted on the family. Shortly after Hannah's death in October 1717, when Sewall was sixty-five years old, he was called upon to care for several of his orphaned Hirst grandchildren.

Sewall was profoundly saddened by the loss of his "dear Yokefellow" Hannah, but he was, as always, resigned to the will of Divine Providence. Four months later the lonely widower reported that he was "wandering in my mind whether to live a Single or a Married Life." Urged on by friends and ministers, he began his awkward pursuit of eligible widows, undertakings often more fraught with material considerations than romance. He soon took a second wife, who died in a matter of months. In 1722, after suffering humiliation and dashed hopes in his effort to court the widow of Wait Still Winthrop, Sewall entered into a comfortable marriage with Mary (Shrimpton) Gibbs, who survived him. But he never laid aside the memory of Hannah, and in her honor he set up a "Connecticut stone post in Elm pasture," and made a deed of land in the pasture as an annuity to the South End writing-school. Not long before his own death, Sewall was "much affected" by marking the "same day of the week and Moneth that the Wife of my youth expired Eleven years agoe," and he asked his son Joseph to join in his "Condolence."

The Puritan religion firmly set the expectations for domestic relations in the Sewall family. It demanded of parents that they strive unceasingly to lead their children away from their innate sinfulness and bring them into a covenant with God. Samuel Sewall took the chief role in family governance, while Hannah was his helpmate. But even within the stern dictates and constraints of Puritan ways, it seems that the members of the Sewall household, adults and children alike, viewed and thus related to one another as worthy and interesting individuals.

See also: Family Piety

Further Reading

Judith S. Graham, *Puritan Family Life: The Diary of Samuel Sewall* (Boston, 2000); Philip J. Greven, *The Protestant Temperament: Patterns of Child-Rearing, Religious Experience, and the Self in Early America* (New York, 1977); Alan Macfarlane, *The Family Life of Ralph Josselin, a Seventeenth-Century Clergyman: An Essay in Historical Anthropology* (London, 1970); Edmund S. Morgan, *The Puritan Family: Religion and Domestic Relations in Seventeenth-Century New England* (Boston, 1944); Linda A. Pollock, *Forgotten Children: Parent-Child Relations from 1500 to 1900* (Cambridge, Eng., 1983); Kenneth Silverman, *The Life and Times of Cotton Mather* (New York, 1984); Roger Thompson, *Sex in Middlesex: Popular Mores in a Massachusetts County, 1649–1699* (Amherst, 1986); Laurel Thatcher Ulrich, *Good Wives: Image and Reality in the Lives of Women in Northern New England, 1650–1750* (New York, 1982).

Judith Graham

Dominion of New England

From the restoration of the monarchy in 1660 forward, the English monarch sought overtly and covertly to exercise greater authority over the Puritan colonies in British North America. These efforts met with limited success during the reign of Charles II. Upon his accession to the throne in 1685, James II moved forcefully to implement direct royal control over New England governments. On 3 June 1686, he appointed Sir Edmund Andros captain general and governor of the Territory and Dominion of New England, which included all the New England territories except for Connecticut and part of present-day Rhode Island. Andros and a newly created king's council were given total authority to create laws, establish courts, control militia, validate contracts (including real estate deeds), and set and collect taxes. James later expanded the Dominion, incorporating Connecticut, the rest of Rhode Island, East and West Jersey, and New York.

Connecticut and Massachusetts actively resisted Andros's assertion of royal control. Connecticut sought to impede Andros's assumption of the government by refusing to surrender its colonial charter to him, hiding it in an oak tree near the state house. As The Charter Oak, this tree became one of Connecticut's most treasured symbols. Massachusetts, after unhappily accepting Andros as the governor, became increasingly restive under his heavy-handed implementation of legal, commercial, and religious policies antithetical to Massachusetts Puritans' understanding of their rights. Word of the Glorious Revolution in England led Massachusetts colonists to depose Andros in a bloodless coup on 19 April 1689, an act that effectively brought an end to the Dominion of New England.

Further Reading
David Sherman Lovejoy, *The Glorious Revolution in America* (New York, 1972).

Walter Woodward

E

Ejections of Clergy (1660–1662)

In the first two years of the Restoration, about 1,760 clergymen were "ejected" from their parishes in England. Another 120 clergy in Wales and 200 university dons, parish lecturers, and schoolmasters also lost their jobs. In broad terms, these clergymen were deprived of their livings because they refused to conform to the new religious settlement, and especially to the 1662 Act of Uniformity. Closer examination, however, shows that others factors were also involved.

The parish clergy of the 1650s were a diverse group. Some ministers had remained in place since before the Civil Wars, some had filled vacancies that arose naturally, others had replaced deprived royalist clergy, and yet others were theologically averse to the institution of a national church but happy to serve their own flock in a parish setting. In 1660 political uncertainty surrounded the religious settlement that would accompany the restored monarchy. The first signs were that a compromise between the Presbyterian and Episcopalian parties would create a broad and pluralistic national church in which many of the existing clergy would happily serve. While these negotiations were under way, it was also necessary to provide security for those parish clergy who held only a tenuous legal title to their livings after the upheaval of the 1640s and 1650s. Clerical mobility, the absence of diocesan authorities to institute, induct, or license, the seizure of advowsons, and the sequestration and ejection of previous incumbents had left many clergy without a title to their living recognizable in law. In the county of Derbyshire, for example, the majority of parish clergy were in this position. Meanwhile those ejected royalist ministers who were still alive clamored for reinstatement.

A royal proclamation of June 1660 forbade the ejection of any minister until Parliament had resolved the issue. William Prynne was the leading advocate of the Act for Settling Ministers of September 1660, which confirmed all incumbents, except those who denied infant baptism, or had lobbied for the regicide (the execution of Charles I) or against the restoration of Charles II, or held the livings of sequestered ministers who were still alive. This act produced the first wave of "ejections": 695 parish ministers were ousted, and in almost 300 of these cases this was due to the survival of the original incumbent. At Kidderminster, for example, Richard Baxter was replaced by his predecessor.

By the winter of 1660–1661, then, the ministers who had left their parish churches were either simple victims of uncertain legal title to their benefices or, as in the case of some Baptists and Independents, fundamentally opposed to any form of national church. It should not be forgotten that many of the leading puritan divines occupied no benefice in 1660 from which to be removed. And it still seemed likely that many of the godly ministers, especially the Presbyterians, would find a place within the national church that was being slowly constructed. This hope came to naught due to the failure of the 1661 Savoy Conference and the determination and chicanery of the Anglican leadership in the newly elected "Cavalier Parliament." In March 1662, Parliament agreed to a Bill of Uniformity, and this received the royal assent on 19 May. The Act of Uniformity was the antithesis of earlier hopes. It provided for a single, narrowly defined national church and made no allowance for "tender consciences." The act came into force on St. Bartholomew's Day, 24 August 1662, and in due course its requirements led to the "ejection" of 936 ministers from their livings: 59 of these had first been ejected in 1660 but had since found another living (benefice).

The ejected clergy varied in their objections to the Uniformity Act. Some resented the obligation to use and acknowledge the Book of Common Prayer or the Thirty-nine Articles, others were more troubled by the renunciation of the Solemn League and Covenant or of their previous ministry under Presbyterian ordination. Many of these were personal clerical scruples of conscience that did not affect the same individual's ability to attend the Church of England as a layman, nor did they have any relevance to the minister's flock. Thus the ejected Presbyterian Thomas Manton went to St. Paul's Covent Garden to hear the sermons of his successor, Simon Patrick. John Corbet also participated in Anglican public worship, according to his friend Richard Baxter, who himself attended his parish church. Such ministers would lead their followers to the parish church and would advise them to attend prayers and hear the best preachers in the Church of England. Other ejected ministers, like the Congregationalists Thomas Jollie or Matthew Mead, would have no truck with the restored church.

What united the ejected clergy was their common suffering. A conscious attempt to portray the ejected ministers as Bartolomeans, that is, as a group of martyrs, may have begun as early as their "farewell sermons," preached for the most part on 17 August and published soon after. Some ministers continued to live in their former parishes; others moved to puritan centers such as the huge London parish of St. Giles Cripplegate, and others took up chaplaincies with sympathetic gentry. Talk of a

mass exodus to New England came to nothing. These increasingly elderly ministers found themselves dependent upon the generosity of their followers and patrons, or forced to earn a living as schoolmasters, tutors, or physicians. If they maintained a congregation and worshipped in a "conventicle" or broke the terms of the Five Mile Act, they were open to prosecution and harassment. The ejected clergy, especially the Presbyterians, formed the backbone of moderate Dissent: they came to be venerated for their conscientious stance, respected for their courage (especially those who remained in London during the Great Plague); and courted by those who hoped to modify the religious settlement of 1662. Their lives were recorded by Edmund Calamy in his *Abridgement of Mr Baxter's History of His Life and Times* (1702; revised 1713) and its *Continuation* (1727).

See also: Clarendon Code, Conventicles, Dissenters, Subscription
Further Reading
Ian Green, *The Re-establishment of the Church of England 1660–1663* (Oxford, 1978); A. G. Matthews, *Calamy Revised: Being a Revision of Edmund Calamy's Account of the Ministers and others Ejected and Silenced, 1660–2* (1934; reprinted 1988).

John Spurr

Emmanuel College

Emmanuel was a strange creation, replete with what Marxists call internal contradictions. Within forty years of its foundation in 1584, it had grown to be the largest college in Cambridge, yet it was poorly endowed. The intention of its founder, Sir Walter Mildmay, was that it should be devoted to the sole purpose of sending out preachers into the parishes and pulpits of England. This mission was built into the statutes, including the notorious statute "De Mora" requiring Emmanuel men to proceed to the degree of Doctor of Divinity, and then to leave the college. Yet in its early years, the percentage of its members who entered the ordained ministry (38 percent) was lower than the roughly 43 percent who were ordained from Jesus,

King's and St. John's Colleges. By the same token, and for reasons attributable to the endowment, Emmanuel admitted a higher than average proportion of fellow commoners and pensioners (who in effect paid fees), so that the impact of the college on seventeenth-century England was as much in nurturing a new generation of godly magistrates (the generation of the Civil War) as in training preachers and divines, although of course many preachers and divines, including some famous names, were products of Emmanuel. They included William Bedell, John Cotton, Giles Firmin, Thomas Hooker, Stephen Marshall, John Rogers, Nathaniel Rogers, Thomas Shepard, and Samuel Ward.

The final contradiction was that in the mid-seventeenth century Emmanuel diverged from the "orthodoxy" of its founding fathers, which is to say, Calvinism, and a practical, "experimental" Calvinism at that, in two directions: a reactive High Churchmanship, and the rational-spiritual tendency of the Cambridge Platonists. Both sea changes may be regarded as generational. The third master, William Sancroft (1628–1637), was persuaded to serve in order to preserve the Calvinist tradition established by Laurence Chaderton (1584–1622) and continued, high profile, by John Preston (1622–1628), but seen to be at risk. His nephew, another William Sancroft (master of Emmanuel, 1662–1665), who went on to become the archbishop of Canterbury deprived after the Glorious Revolution of 1688, was the staunchest of Church and King men; he commissioned the chapel by Sir Christopher Wren, which is a monument to what the college had become. William Law, author of *The Serious Call to a Devout and Holy Life*, was a product of this new Emmanuel. In between the first Sancroft and the second, the Platonists Benjamin Whichcote and Ralph Cudworth horrified Anthony Tuckney, fifth master (1644–1653), by betraying the "spiritual, plain, powerful" tradition of the college with a divinity "which my heart riseth against." But long before this, Emmanuel had called a new world into being to redress the balance of the old. Of the 129 Oxford and Cambridge men who settled in New England be-fore 1650, no less than 35 had been at Emmanuel. They included a relatively obscure student called John Harvard who went on to give his money and his name to Harvard College.

Further Reading

S. Bendall, C. Brooke, and P. Collinson, *A History of Emmanuel College Cambridge* (Woodbridge, Eng., 1999); *The Statutes of Sir Walter Mildmay . . . for Emmanuel College* (Cambridge, Eng., 1983).

Patrick Collinson

English Puritanism in the Netherlands

Puritan refugees in the Low Countries established around thirty churches, developing alternative forms of church order, arguing about the relation of congregational authority to that of the consistory, and disputing the eligibility of nonmembers' children for baptism, as well as writing and publishing, free from English episcopal and government supervision. Their discussions and anathemas defined the differences between Separatism, Independentism, and Presbyterianism before similar experimentation could take place extensively elsewhere. Their churches ranged from small, temporary Separatist house groups led by laymen to congregations whose consistories and clergy were incorporated into the Dutch Reformed structures of classis and synod. Military chaplaincies served several British regiments aiding the Dutch revolt; the chaplains were mostly nonconforming clergy.

The first English chaplaincy in the Low Countries was that of the Merchant Adventurers in Antwerp, where William Tyndale, Myles Coverdale, and John Frith enjoyed protection in the 1530s. Later, some of the "Marian exiles" found refuge in Antwerp. They in turn were succeeded by Puritans, including Walter Travers (1578–1580), whose ordination came from a "synod" of Walloon and Dutch ministers, and Thomas Cartwright (1580–1585). The English merchants moved with their church to Middelburg in 1582, there competing with the refugee Separatist congregation of Robert Browne (1582–1585). Richard Schilders, an

English printer in Middelburg, published both Puritan and Separatist writings, including Browne's *Treatise of Reformation without Tarrying for Anie* (1582). Opposing not only Separatists, but also Catholics and by implication liturgical Anglicans, Cartwright began his *Confutation of the Rhemists* (an attack on the translation of the New Testament done in 1582 by English Jesuits at Rheims) about 1582–1583, This was finally published by the Pilgrims (that is, the Separatists who later founded the colony of Plymouth in the New England) in Leiden (1618). Among Cartwright's successors at Middelburg were Francis Johnson (1590–1592), Henry Jacob (late 1590s), Hugh Broughton (1605–1611), and John Forbes (1610–1634), who took the church along when the Merchant Adventurers removed to Delft (1621).

In 1585, arrangements for chaplains for the garrisons of English soldiers in the Netherlands were negotiated when the Earl of Leicester became governor-general. The regiments remained until 1616. Garrison chaplaincies were established at The Hague, Utrecht, Leiden, Bergen op Zoom, Vlissingen ("Flushing"), and Den Briel. Salaries were administered as part of the army budget; clergy wanting transfers, salary increases, and the like petitioned the Dutch government. The Earl of Leicester patronized Puritanism in the garrison churches and sponsored a synod in 1586, attempting to impose a more rigid form of Calvinism in the Netherlands than had developed until then.

Having converted to separatism in 1592, Francis Johnson joined a Separatist congregation in London, some of whose members emigrated to Amsterdam in 1593, removing to Kampen, then Naarden, and finally back to Amsterdam in 1596, where they eventually became known as the Ancient Church. Jacobus Arminius and other Dutch clergy admonished the group for meeting in private houses without official approval. Johnson arrived from London in 1597, remaining their pastor until his death in 1618. Henry Ainsworth, the author of *The Book of Psalmes: Englished both in Prose and Meter* (1612), became the congregation's teacher. The congregation constructed its own church building in 1607. Their numbers were soon aug-

mented by the arrival of the Gainsborough and Scrooby refugees, led by John Smyth, Richard Clifton, and John Robinson. Separatist writings were published by Giles Thorp (active in Amsterdam, ca. 1604–1622). Famous schismatic rivalry was expressed in luridly accusatory pamphlets that were read in the Netherlands and England and taken as proof of the unsoundness of Separation. Relations with the Dutch Reformed Church, never friendly, soured further. Smyth's conversion to Anabaptism led to the decision of Robinson's group to leave Amsterdam for Leiden. Disagreements about Smyth's application to join the Amsterdam Mennonites inspired Thomas Helwys and some adherents to return to England, where in London they founded a Baptist congregation. By 1630, the remaining Amsterdam Separatist groups reunited under John Canne, a preacher and printer who returned to England in 1647 as an Independent, becoming a Fifth Monarchist. The Amsterdam Separatist congregation survived till 1701.

Worried about being misidentified with these troublemakers and their new building, in 1607 Puritan merchants in Amsterdam applied to the city government to establish an English Reformed Church that, like the French (Walloon) and German Reformed churches, would be conceived as a foreign-language sister of the Dutch Reformed Church. Their application was granted, and accordingly the Amsterdam magistrates had a final decisive choice regarding candidates for the positions of minister, teacher, and deacon within this English congregation, just as they did in the other Reformed churches. The Dutch consistory asserted a certain supervisory authority, presumably in reaction to their unsuccessful experiences attempting to discipline Amsterdam's Separatists.

John Paget, chaplain to Colonel Sir Horace Vere, accepted a call to be their minister, remaining in office until 1637 (d. 1638). Paget strongly opposed the Separatists, forbidding attendance at their preaching. Paget also resisted the attempt led by John Forbes to establish an English classis, or synod, distinct from the local Dutch structure. Paget found fault with Hugh Peter, William Ames, Thomas Hooker, and John Davenport, when these men were proposed for the position of teacher. Hooker's views that a Reformed member might attend Brownist preaching occasionally, that only children of members of the congregation should be baptized, and that the congregation had full authority to call a minister without participation by the classis or the magistrates found support within Paget's congregation, but such ideas were not approved by Paget or Dutch authorities. To outmaneuver congregational favor for Hooker, Paget enlisted the support of the opinionated Jacob Trigland, a Reformed minister famous for his intemperate opposition to the more liberal Remonstrants and important in Amsterdam's ecclesiastical factionalism. Davenport, although invited by the Amsterdam English Reformed and approved by the burgomasters, could not agree with baptizing infants of nonmembers and declined. Paget was opposed to Davenport in any case. The controversy erupted in print with *A Just Complaint . . . [against] the tirannical government and corrupt doctrine of Mr. John Pagett* (Amsterdam, 1634).

During the Cromwellian period, the Amsterdam congregation preserved an apparent neutrality, resisting innovation. The minister from 1648 to 1659 was William Price, an anti-Cromwellian Presbyterian who had been at the Westminster Assembly. Now affiliated with the Church of Scotland, Amsterdam's English Reformed Church still worships in the medieval Beguinage chapel granted to it in 1607.

As in Amsterdam, Leiden's British community of merchants, soldiers, and university members petitioned the town in 1607 to form an English Reformed Church. First served by visiting preachers, including Franciscus Gomarus, the anti-Arminian professor, the congregation responded to the arrival in Leiden of Robinson's group by finally calling its own minister, Robert Dury (father of John Dury the ecumenicist). After Dury's death (1616), Hugh Goodyear served as pastor (1617–1661). Among the congregation's leaders was Thomas Brewer, a supporter of William Brewster's antiepiscopal printing and later a Fifth Monarchist. Remarkably irenic for the time, Goodyear maintained friendship with William Ames, John Robinson, and William Brewster, even acting as the business agent of some of the Pilgrims who had emigrated. Numerous visitors from England stopped by Leiden, including Sir Thomas Browne, Sir William Brereton, and William Aspinwall, Goodyear's relative through marriage.

The English Church in The Hague was initially (from 1586) a military and ambassadorial chaplaincy, but it was organized more formally with a minister and consistory in 1627. Despite attempts led by Stephen Goffe (1633–1634) to introduce conformity to the Book of Common Prayer, most of the ministers were Puritans. Among them were John Paget, William Ames (1611–1619), John Wing (1627–1629), and Samuel Balmford (1630–1650), who successfully resisted attempts to enforce conformity, having himself been imprisoned briefly by William Laud in 1635. The church also served as the chapel of Elizabeth Stuart, Queen of Bohemia, the daughter of James I, and of Princess Mary, daughter of Charles I. Their chaplains introduced Laudian innovations, but Balmford obtained the aid of Dutch Reformed antagonism to ceremonialism in resisting successfully. The Hague's English Church was placed under the "protection" of the Dutch classis, although not officially a member. The English Parliament, paying the salary, dismissed Elizabeth Stuart's Laudian chaplain Sampson Johnson and appointed William Cooper (1644–1648). After the execution of her brother, Elizabeth defiantly appointed Charles's former chaplain William Stamp (1650–1653), making the church half Puritan, half Chapel Royal. Stamp was succeeded by George Morley, later Bishop of Winchester. Princess Mary's chaplains included Thomas Browne and John Dury. With a congregation mixing royalty, ambassadors Sir Ralph Winwood, Sir Dudley Carleton, Sir William Boswell, and George Downing, and Puritan merchants and craftsmen, the church in The Hague played out national tensions on a small scale. It continues as the English and American Episcopal Church of Saints John and Philip.

Rotterdam's English Church began in 1611, but first called a minister in 1620. Thomas Barkely, a garrison chaplain, was succeeded by Hugh Peter (1629–1635), assisted by William Ames in 1633. John Davenport (1636–1637?), William Bridge

(1636–1641 or 1642), John Ward (1636–1641), Jeremiah Burroughes (1639–1641), Sidrach Simpson (1639–1641), and Nathaniel Mather (1663–1671) were among Rotterdam's ministers. Thomas Hooker was a member. Under Barkely, the church followed Dutch practice. Hugh Peter reorganized the congregation in 1633 with a covenant signing by which many of the previous members were excluded; nonetheless, during that period the congregation numbered about a thousand members. Noteworthy was the participation of women in congregational decisions. Plans to open a Puritan college collapsed with the death of Ames. Three congregations split from each other, but were reunited by the 1640s, when, however, a separate Scots church was officially founded, whose first minister, Alexander Petrie, arrived in 1643.

Churches at Dordrecht, Vianen, Arnhem, and elsewhere served similar populations of soldiers and merchants, with university students also at Utrecht. The Utrecht church, arising from military chaplaincies, took form in 1622. Among its ministers were Thomas Scott (1622–1626), Alexander Leighton (1629), and Paul Amyraut (1637–1638). Leighton published *An Appeal to the Parliament; or Sions Plea against the Prelacie* (Amsterdam, 1628); he left Utrecht because of disagreement with the Dutch classis about feast days. Factions in the congregation reflected social rifts between English and Scots and between officers and soldiers. Under Thomas Potts (1651–1655) and his successor, the Dutchman John Best (1655–1696), church life was quiet if not entirely harmonious, with numerous royalist preachers now refugees in Utrecht. The English Church achieved foreign-language equality with other Reformed churches, as at Amsterdam, Leiden, and The Hague.

See also: Dissenting Brethren, Separatism
Further Reading
Keith L. Sprunger, *Dutch Puritanism: A History of English and Scottish Churches of the Netherlands in the Sixteenth and Seventeenth Centuries* (Leiden, 1982); Keith L. Sprunger, *Trumpets from the Tower: English Puritan Printing in The Netherlands, 1600–1640* (Leiden, 1994).

Jeremy Bangs

Erastianism

A doctrine associated with the Swiss-born Reformer Thomas Erastus (1524–1583). Erastus studied theology at Basel and medicine at Bologna and Padua. In 1558 he was appointed personal physician to the Elector of the Palatinate. Relied on as a spiritual advisor as well, he advocated the abolition of the death penalty for witches and fought the introduction of Lutheranism into the Palatinate.

During his life, Erastus appeared to have supported the model of church-state relations that the sixteenth-century Swiss Reformer Huldrych Zwingli had introduced in Zurich. However, in his posthumously published book *Explicatio* (1598), Erastus argued that the civil government was sovereign within a state and that the secular authority was superior to that of the church, which had to be submissive to the state. This doctrine became known as Erastianism and was popular among some of the members of England's Parliament in the 1640s.

Further Reading
J. Neville Figgis, "Erastus and Erastianism," *Journal of Theological Studies*, 2 (1901), 66–101.

Francis J. Bremer

Espousal Imagery

Within puritan piety, both in sermons and private devotional writings, espousal imagery occurred most often as exegeses or adaptations of the Canticle of Canticles, also known as the Song of Songs and the Song of Solomon, an extended love poem in the Old Testament. The forms of adaptation were myriad, and the image of espousal, or marriage, could apply on an institutional level or a personal one, or a mixture of the two. The marriage could be seen as between Christ and the church, offering membership as a guarantee of Christ's love. The marriage could be between the church as Christ's representative on earth and the individual Christian. Use of such imagery related to ways of understanding the covenant of grace, with the espousal image between God and individual Christians bringing confidence in His love but also requisite faithfulness on the part of the Christian.

In sermons, treatises, and pastoral epistles, the imagery of marriage could provide a space for a more sensual piety. Such expressions of piety can be found in the works of ministers like John Cotton, Richard Sibbes, and, perhaps most famously, the letters of the similarly minded Scottish radical Samuel Rutherford. One of the main sources, beyond scripture, was the piety of the twelfth-century monk Bernard of Clairvaux. The different relationships played into images of clerical service and vocation. The clergy were part of the feminized church, both institutionally and individually, but the clergy could also take on the part of the masculinized church to the believer when the church was Christ's representative. The minister could be the best man or even the panderer, wooing individuals to be the spouse of Christ. This almost mystical devotion can be seen as the flip side of fear of the distant, judgmental, patriarchal figure of God the Father, providing a more intimate, cherishing, and protective figure of Christ, God made male flesh, as bridegroom. Robert Harris on his deathbed offered comfort to his wife, writing that after his death she could resign herself to "the Husband of Husbands, the Lord Jesus."

The sensual, almost erotic application of espousal imagery taken from Canticles can be found in spiritual journals. Such imagery provides a constant refrain in the diary of Samuel Rogers and was probably his primary way of pleading for comfort and expressing his all too rare times of assurance. The language of gender inversion need cause no surprise, as it fitted in with the goals of the journal. Within early modern gender discourse, feminine capacities were seen to be lesser than those of masculinities and more prone to succumb to temptations. With proper discipline, however, femininity could also be the epitome of passivity and humility. Thus gender inversion opened a space for male writers to expand their ability for passivity, humility, and a greater intimacy with Christ, intended to provide a route to assurance. Espousal imagery oscillated between the personal and the institutional. This profitable tension created a space for the negotiation of the huge vertical gap between human and divine. Reading the sense of confidence di-

arists like Rogers found through Canticles helps us to understand why Sibbes referred to the image as a "wondrous comfort."

See also: Marriage, Sexuality
Further Reading
John Coffey, *Politics, Religion and the British Revolutions: The Mind of Samuel Rutherford* (Cambridge, Eng., 1997); Richard Godbeer, "'Love Raptures': Marital, Romantic and Erotic Images of Jesus Christ in Puritan New England," in Laura McCall and Donald Yacovone, eds., *A Shared Experience: Men, Women, and the History of Gender* (New York, 1998); S. Hardman Moore, "Sexing the Soul: Gender and the Rhetoric of Puritan Piety," in R. N. Swanson, ed., *Gender and Christian Religion*, Studies in Church History, vol. 34 (Rochester, NY, 1998); Tom Webster, "'Kiss me with the kisses of his mouth': Gender Inversion and Canticles in Godly Spirituality," in Thomas Betteridge, ed., *Sodomy in Early Modern Europe* (Manchester, Eng., 2002).

Tom Webster

Exorcism

A major controversy surrounded the continued use of exorcism by a number of Puritan ministers in England around the turn of the seventeenth century. Exorcism—which traditionally emphasized the priest's power of command over the devil, and the quasi-magical efficacy of holy artifacts—had been attacked as superstitious during the Reformation. The exorcism of the unbaptized infant was removed from the Book of Common Prayer in 1552, and Protestant orthodoxy stated that the power to cast out devils had been given only as a special dispensation to the fathers of the primitive church in an "age of miracles" that was long past. Nevertheless, belief in possession continued, and indeed it may have been encouraged further by the Protestant emphasis on temptation, in which the devil was believed to enter directly into the mind. Moreover, there was perhaps a connection between possession cases and the more intensive regimes of religious observance in Puritan congregational and household settings. In a number of prominent cases in Elizabethan and early Stuart England, as well as in the witchcraft outbreak in Salem in 1692, possession may have allowed its victims to react violently to highly restrictive Puritan domestic environments in a way that was often licensed rather than punished. As victims of possession had fits and blasphemed, they became the objects of public concern, and, for the godly, their plight was a tangible demonstration of the ubiquity of satanic activity.

Despite clerical misgivings, Puritan ministers such as John Foxe and John Darrell were at the forefront of the development of a Protestant form of exorcism that emerged in Elizabethan England in response to two related factors. First, as cases of possession continued to proliferate, ministers felt impelled to meet the needs of their parishioners. Secondly, dispossession became a contested area with the concerted polemical use made of exorcism by Catholic priests from the 1580s: they claimed that the ability to cast out devils evidenced that theirs was the true faith. From the 1560s a number of Protestant dispossessions gained a high profile. Divines were able to use Mark 9:14–29—a story of an exorcism by Christ in which he explains that devils "can come forth by nothing except prayer and fasting"—as the basis of an alternative method that avoided the use of mechanistic ritual. Though a minister could no longer command a devil to depart, he could lead the faithful in lengthy exercises of prayer and fasting that entreated God to cast it out. These occasions developed a theater to rival that of the Catholic ceremonies, often apparently including theological debates between devils and the assembled ministers. Successful exorcisms greatly enhanced the reputation of the Puritan ministry. The services of figures such as John Darrell became extensively sought after, and the suggestion that Puritans had the ability to dispossess had considerable propaganda value in the context of the debates over church government in the 1580s.

As a result, Protestant dispossession became a focus of the anti-Puritan campaign spearheaded by Richard Bancroft, the bishop of London. John Darrell was imprisoned for a year after being exposed as a fraud on the evidence of one his demoniacs, and a fierce pamphlet war erupted between him and skeptical writers sponsored by Bancroft. These skeptics not only restated that the end of the age of miracles made vain all attempts at exorcism, but also challenged the actual reality of corporeal possession. When in 1602 the alleged possession of a girl in London sparked a witch trial, Bancroft encouraged a physician, Edmund Jorden, to dispute the demonic origin of her symptoms. A group of Puritan ministers who met to attempt to dispossess the girl, Mary Glover, were imprisoned and suspended from their offices, and Bancroft instituted a program of preaching in London in which exorcism was denounced. Finally, the new Church Canons of 1604 ruled that a minister would now only be allowed to attempt dispossession with the permission of his bishop. However, though conforming ministers were thus prevented from practicing dispossession, many Puritans continued to accept the efficacy of prayer and fasting. In the so-called Godly Lives, which developed as a Puritan form of exemplar in the mid-seventeenth century, dispossessions were rendered as edifying personal conflicts between Satan and heroic ministers such as Richard Rothwell and Robert Balsom. Moreover, diaries, such as that of the Lancashire minister Henry Newcome, suggest that the Puritan clergy continued to view dispossession by prayer and fasting as a routine aspect of their duties.

See also: Devil
Further Reading
M. MacDonald, ed., *Witchcraft and Hysteria in Elizabethan London: Edward Jorden and the Mary Glover Case* (London, 1990); D. P. Walker, *Unclean Spirits: Possession and Exorcism in France and England in the Late Sixteenth and Early Seventeenth Centuries* (Philadelphia, 1981).

Nathan Johnstone

F

Familists

See Family of Love

Family of Love

The Family of Love (also Haus der Liebe, Familia caritatis, Hüsgesinn der Lieften, Domus armoris, Famille de la Charité, Huis der Liefde), was a radical spiritist underground movement emphasizing the work of the spirit that began on the European continent in the 1540s before spreading to England in the 1550s. Although the Continental groups had virtually disappeared in the early 1600s and its existence was largely subterranean, it survived in England at least until the Glorious Revolution of 1688 and influenced various radical English sects. Originating under the charismatic leadership of one Hendrick Niclaes (variously spelled, often abbreviated "H.N.") in Emden, East Friesland, in the 1540s, the Familists promoted religious perfectionism, communal property (with rumors of sexual libertinism), and anti-institutional salvation. A central tenet is that true believers will experience a full indwelling of the Spirit (when the believer will be "godded with God"), thereby eliminating dependence on both church and Bible. Familist belief is reflected in Niclaes's several ambiguous prophetic writings that stem from his own revelations.

In practice, Familist groups tended to be highly secretive (they have been characterized as Nicodemian for their willingness to recant or equivocate under pressure) and thus both limited in size and difficult to trace. Niclaes originally composed in Low German, but his works were translated into Latin, French, English, and High German. In organization, the group was structured into an episcopal hierarchy. The various Continental Familist groups seem to have disappeared in the early 1600s.

The first known adherent in England was Christopher Vitel (or Vittels) in the 1550s, but the first definite English connection came in a 1561 confession of two ex-Familists before a Surrey magistrate. Familism seems to have flourished in the areas of Cambridge, Balsham, Surrey, the Isle of Ely, London, and elsewhere, and by the late 1570s, it had attracted stringent opposition from the likes of John Knewstub, William Wilkinson, and John Rogers and had become notorious enough that in 1580 Elizabeth I issued a proclamation against it; it was believed that Familists had attained influential positions in the Queen's Guard. Familism seems to have resurged in the early 1600s in groups such as the Family of the Mount and the Grindletonians, and then again during the 1640s, when Niclaes's writings were once again reprinted in England. Familists survived until at least the late 1680s, after which whatever was left was probably absorbed into other radical groups.

The actual numbers of Familists must remain a matter of conjecture, but perhaps never more than several hundred were active at any one time in England, although it is not unlikely that that some members became influential in the courts of the monarchs. Because of their limited size and covert nature, *Familism* became a term often used somewhat indiscriminately as a convenient smear invective by those who sought out and attacked heresies from the 1570s through the 1640s. Anne Hutchinson and her supporters in colonial Massachusetts were tarred with this brush. Historians have sometimes credited Familism with spreading occult and alchemical theories as well as with contributing to the English Civil War, but perhaps its more obvious influence is reflected in its emphasis on mystical revelation and individual perfection.

See also: Roger Brearley, Sects

Further Reading

Christopher Marsh, *The Family of Love in English Society, 1550–1630* (Cambridge, Eng., 1993).

Michael Ditmore

Family Piety

Puritanism in Britain and America has long been associated with a new form of familial organization based on the conjugal or nuclear unit, of parents and children, and centered on the idea of this limited family as a religious unit. The family has been seen as being strengthened by divinely created bonds of authority and responsibility between a husband and wife, and a parent and child, and by the mutual affection expected between siblings. These bonds were to be reinforced in many branches of Puritanism by the growth of collective acts of religious devotion, including prayer, catechizing, and, most obviously, Bible reading. The act of sharing these religious experiences not only meant a constant reiteration of these bonds and obligations, but is often thought to have created a mentality that has been characterized (somewhat confusingly) as individualistic. In this view the Puritan family differed from what had come before (and what existed in parallel in other areas of society) in that the emphasis on religious experience did not primarily involve interaction and participation with the wider community or kin, but was internal and domestic. It has been much noted that this model of family life was widely adopted in British and North American society by the nine-

teenth century, even outside of religious groups that owed their origins to Puritanism, and the emphasis on family solidarity and individualism in this sense has been seen as a cornerstone of successful economic development in these countries.

The vision of the godly household sitting grouped around the father and studying the scriptures was a very common one in both illustration and Puritan literature of the late sixteenth and early seventeenth centuries, and similar images can be found to echo these ideals well into the modern period. The tendency to see the family as the essential building block of religious and indeed social life, was hardly a new one in the early modern period. It can be seen in medieval literature and in particular in works with a Humanist bias. However, it seems to have enjoyed a renewed emphasis in most branches of Puritanism. The analogies between a godly household and church and state were also particularly marked in this literature. Thus the parallels between authority of secular and religious governments (already present in medieval polemic) and the authority of the father in the family was further underlined in Puritan rhetoric. This was often described, as by John Cotton in *The Way of Life* in 1641, as a covenant between God and man and between a man and his family.

The many Puritan-leaning instruction manuals of this period thus placed a stress on the role of the father in leading his family in its devotions. Commonly these were expected to follow immediately on rising, with prayers, readings, and the singing of psalms, which would occur again in the day and certainly be reiterated at night before sleep. Children and servants were to be frequently catechized. This activity was naturally to be particularly marked on Sunday, and one major effect of the strict Sabbatarianism adopted by many branches of Puritanism was to clear the day for exactly such activities. In this way the practice of family piety did not present a rival to the congregational worship of the church but was designed to continue and magnify it. Typical advice was that members of the household would discuss the sermon and readings of Sunday services and pray on the themes that they illuminated. Thus Puritan families were steeped in a biblical milieu and conditioned by the necessity of reflection and virtually continual prayer. Naturally all this activity demanded the acquisition of literary, mental, and theological skills and has often been seen as making the Puritan family both a model church and a little school and may help to account for the relatively high levels of literacy among some groups of Puritans.

Evidence from diaries and other materials from both England and North America strongly suggests that many Puritans attempted to encourage this kind of family life. However, these efforts were not unproblematic. The emphasis on, and elevation of, the family in Puritan thinking, led to a concerted attack on aspects that threatened it, most obviously the double standard in sexual conduct; it also meant that all sexual offenses were to be punished much more harshly. Patriarchal authority in the family could not simply be supplied by rhetoric alone, it had to be reinforced, often with punishment, and there is some evidence that the Puritan family regime was particularly harsh in this respect. The inclusion of servants in many households meant that the rhetoric of a family covenant was often explicitly extended to them, helping to underline the authority of a master, but it was in the nature of service that it was often a short-term relationship and that servants were highly mobile and only transitory members of a household. By definition many servants were of lower social status than their masters, which increased the likelihood that they would lack the literary or mental skills (not to mention enthusiasm) necessary for religious activity of this kind. Evidence from diaries occasionally indicates frustration with the failure of servants to participate in this regime, and their role was evidently often limited to simple repetition of a catechism. However, catechizing was a very widespread instructional tool, and it seems that until recently historians have tended to underestimate both its extent and importance. It may have played a large part in instilling a basic theological knowledge and reinforcing the social order. It is also possible that this system helped in the social diffusion of literacy so marked in the sixteenth and seventeenth centuries.

A second set of problems revolved around the difficulties created when fathers were absent (either permanently or temporarily) or were unable or unwilling to pursue the mental rigor necessary for high-level family piety. In some cases, like that of the first English female diarist, Lady Margaret Hoby of Hackness in Yorkshire, at the end of the sixteenth century, it was possible for women with absent husbands to take over these responsibilities, although it could be argued that their doing so undermined the concept of patriarchy. The case of Anne Hutchinson, who became embroiled in the celebrated antinomian controversy, demonstrates some of the limits of such arrangements, as the fact that her Boston Bible classes from 1635 began to include male participants meant that she was seen as subverting the covenant and patriarchy.

These problems, and the limitations of family-based religious and literary education, have been seen as leading to a shift in emphasis in the mid-seventeenth century, where the need to educate children was gradually moved away from the family toward organized communal educational institutions. Distrust of the established schools in England, which were dominated by the church, meant that this trend was more marked in the North American colonies, where the continual influx of new servants may have made it a necessity, but it did begin to be seen in England. The result was further concentration of religious devotion in the conjugal family, which now might exclude servants, but the intensity and frequency of family devotion and piety were also beginning to wane. Diaries begin to be less notable for the regularity and intensity of private devotions. This trend might have owed something to the rise of sects like the Baptists and Quakers, where collective communal worship was again emphasized. There is also the much noted "feminization of religion" on both sides of the Atlantic, as the trend is called by which women began to predominate in numbers in congregations of all denominations from the late seventeenth century. The passive participation of many adult males in religious life may therefore have seriously undermined the practice of family piety. However, the ideal and image of the family worshiping together was a more lasting one. Shorn of some of its Puritan associations, it seems to have been widely adopted by all Protestant groups, perhaps not least because of the implications it had for reinforcing the authority of fathers. The potential gap between image and reality may therefore have grown even wider, but the concept of family piety did provide an important pillar to support the familial systems of the modern era in both Britain and North America, and it still has considerable currency in Protestant circles.

See also: Domestic Relations, Old Age, Puritan Best-Sellers, Puritan Childrearing

Further Reading

Ian Green, *The Christian's ABC: Catechisms and Catechizing in England, c. 1530–1740* (Oxford, 1996); Ralph Houlbrooke, *English Family Life, 1450–1700* (Oxford, 1984); Edmund S. Morgan, *The Puritan Family: Religious and Domestic Relations in Seventeenth-Century New England* (Boston, 1966 printing of 1944 work); Rosemary O'Day, *The Family and Family Relationships, 1500–1900: England, France and the United States of America* (Basingstoke, Eng., 1994); Leven L. Schucking, *The Puritan Family: A Social Study from the Literature Sources*, trans. Brian Battershaw (London, 1969); Lawrence Stone, *The Family, Sex and Marriage in England, 1500–1800* (Oxford, 1977).

Will Coster

Fasting

Public or private fasts were a search for humility and a plea for mercy, always including ex tempore prayer and psalm singing and frequently including the collection of alms. All public fasts and most private ones were focused on sermons, sometimes having up to six hours of preaching. An agenda might be established, with prayers made for public matters, such as reformation, education, or the protection of godly ministers, and private, such as spiritually troubled saints or those preparing for communion. The pleas for mercy and support could be on an international, national, parochial, or individual level. We have scraps of evidence for the actual physical practice of fasting. Abstinence from food was recommended, but meant eating plain food rather than utterly refraining from eating. Practitioners were encouraged to "dress down" for the occasion. Some sought humility by lying face down in the dust, but this seems to have been rare.

For the puritans, the practice of fasting had an uneasy relationship with the established church. They had little interest in the regular fasts of the ecclesiastical calendar, the Ember Days and so on. They had a greater commitment to the publicly ordained fasts, public services called in response to actual or threatened calamities such as plague, dearth, or potential invasion. Puritans gave fasting the credit for the failure of the Spanish Match (between the heir to the throne and a Spanish princess) in the 1620s, and such occasions were called to protect the Feoffees for Impropriations (a puritan effort to install godly preachers in English pulpits) and to hinder the imposition of discipline by unpopular bishops. Indeed a common puritan complaint in the early seventeenth century was that such occasions were not called often enough. The delay of and subsequent restraint placed on public fasts was an important element in William Prynne's criticism of the Laudian regime.

Puritans were well known for private fasts, observed by groups drawn from across an area, within a single household or by the solitary saint. The most famous public fasts were during the Long Parliament. These were part of an established tradition, opposed by Queen Elizabeth but an expectation by the 1620s. They were, however, merely the most visible part of the means of beginning, or sustaining, worthy causes. Fasts were so frequently part of the arrival of a new godly minister in a parish, for instance, that it became part of a minister's ordination, a practice already established in New England. Fasting and prayer was usually at the center of the puritan replacement for exorcism. Disapproval of such puritan ceremonies was thus part of the motivation for the greater control of fasting enacted in the 1604 Canons.

The most important consequences of private fasts were social. They aided the mutual recognition of the godly and provided a theater for the establishment of a saint's reputation. Their voluntary nature meant that they were theoretically inclusive.

However, their practical selectivity meant that they drew attention to the absentees, who were therefore implicitly ungodly. Thus they were an important contribution to the separation of the saints and sinners.

Further Reading
Richard Gildrie, "The Ceremonial Puritan Days of Humiliation and Thanksgiving," *New England Historical and Genealogical Register*, 136 (1982), 3–16; Tom Webster, *Godly Clergy in Early Stuart England: The Caroline Puritan Movement, c. 1620–1643* (Cambridge, Eng., 1997).

Tom Webster

Federal Theology

Federal Theology, or federalism, affirms that God's relations with humanity are fully comprehended under the aspect of covenant (in Latin, *foedus*, whence *federal*), either by the covenant of works (or nature), or by the covenant of grace. In one or other of these domains, all human creatures were believed to have their being here and hereafter. The first covenant aligns with the letter of the moral law; the second, with the spirit of the gospel. In soteriological principle, these modalities are antithetical; in scriptural history and evangelical practice they are sequential though disjunct, with the covenant of (gratuitous) grace superseding and abrogating, for the elect, the covenant of (meritorious) works. The covenant of works originates as command and promise in God's prelapsarian protocol for Adam; the covenant of saving grace culminates in the redemptive work of Christ, which fulfills the requirements of the broken covenant of works. Federalism centers Christian experience in the dynamic of Adamic rupture and Christic reconciliation.

Federal theology emerged within Reformed Protestant orthodoxy of the late sixteenth century with the propagation of the formulation of the covenant of works by Caspar Olevianus at Heidelberg, Dudley Fenner (who was the first to use the term *covenant of works*) and William Perkins in England, and Robert Rollock in Scotland. Covering

the entire human race by birth, the covenant offered to aspiring reformers the benefit of universal leverage. It gained creedal presence in the Irish Articles of 1615 and the Westminster Confession of Faith of 1647. In Britain under puritan auspices, the combination of covenants furnished a dual rationale for directing morality, channeling piety, and forging religious community. On the European continent in the 1640s, mature federal theory found an acute if controversial exponent in Johannes Cocceius.

The two-covenant formula in its early or classical form, 1580s–1620s, paralleled the Calvinistic structure of double predestination, with the covenants implementing the decrees in the sense that everyone who was predestined to hell was justly condemned under the covenant of works, but that those God chose to bring under the covenant of grace were saved, but the connection was loosened by the conversionist divines who were mainly responsible for federalism's British development. Their dividing of God's federal ways tended to shift the inflection of federal discourse from ethical control to evangelical inspiration and helped puritan ministers to free the covenant of grace from the taint and drag of legalism.

Keying on the evangelical covenant, mid-seventeenth-century puritans such as John Preston, John Ball, John Cotton, Peter Bulkeley, and Samuel Rutherford set federal theology on its own base and course. Their efforts extended the theological concept of grace through covenant to every facet of religious life and found richest expression, not in a contractual rhetoric of quid pro quo, but in images of God's parental and Christ's marital love to elect souls. Such unconditioned love empowered recipients to make the covenantal commitment and to perform, however imperfectly, the consequent obligations of faith, repentance, and obedience. God was accordingly said to enact not only his part of the covenant but that of the human parties as well.

First and last, federal development was driven by desire to enhance believers' confidence in the allsufficiency of God and their own state of grace by restricting or vitiating their active role in meeting the terms of salvation. Pursuing this purpose, the high federal theology of the later seventeenth century appropriated and elaborated as its signature idea the concept of an eternal, foundational pact among the Persons of the Trinity. British federalists such as Thomas Goodwin, Francis Roberts, and Patrick Gillespie used this doctrine to undergird believers' trust by excluding them from any role in making and managing the federal means of grace. Possibly inspired by Goodwin, Milton wrote elements of the intra-Trinitarian accord into the dialogue in heaven between the Father and the Son in book 3 of *Paradise Lost*. Most of the theologians who championed this initiative belonged to the puritan movement's Congregational, or Independent, wing.

As the covenant of redemption or *pactum salutis*, the high covenant redefined Christ's federal role from that of God's agent in providing and applying grace to that of coauthor of the grand plan of salvation, now newly worked out along fully federal lines on fully federal grounds. The divine design was made to rest upon the Three Persons' contract for the souls of the elect, who then enter the domain of grace by imputation of the merits of the Redeemer's sacrifice. The covenant of grace, recast as unilateral and irresistible gift, continued, though with differences of emphasis, to support the affective practice of piety. Magnifying the transcendental architecture of federal faith and building the transactive principle into the expanded blueprint of salvation at the highest level, the Trinitarian consensus capped the creation of a theology that was at once federal, evangelical, and puritan.

Federal theology was perhaps puritanism's greatest and most characteristic doctrinal construction. In relatively intact versions, it remains vital in certain Protestant communions of the present day.

Key puritan texts for the rise of federalism include Preston's *The New Covenant* (1629), Ball's *A Treatise of the Covenant of Grace* (1645, but written before 1640), Bulkeley's *The Gospel-Covenant* (1646), and Thomas Goodwin's *Christ the Mediator* (1692, but written in the early 1650s).

See also: Christology, Grace, Soteriology
Further Reading
Theodore Dwight Bozeman, "Federal Theology and the 'National Covenant': An Elizabethan

Presbyterian Case Study," *Church History* 61 (1992), 394–407; Michael McGiffert, "Grace and Works: The Rise and Division of Covenant Divinity in Elizabethan Puritanism," *Harvard Theological Review* 75 (1982) 463–502; Perry Miller, *The New England Mind: The Seventeenth Century* (New York, 1939); D. A. Weir, *The Origins of Federal Theology in Sixteenth-Century Reformation Thought* (Oxford, 1990).

Michael McGiffert

Feoffees for Impropriations (1626–1633)

A group that functioned as a trusteeship created in London in early 1626 to buy impropriations and advowsons in order to provide income and access to important pulpits lacking godly preachers, as well as to provide additional endowment for the St. Antholin's early morning lectures in the City of London. Impropriations gave to a lay owner the property rights of a benefice, normally the rectorial tithes, and the advowson was the right to nominate to the bishop a candidate for a benefice with cure of souls; the two together gave the possessor control over both the personnel and property of a parochial living (benefice).

The group known as the Feoffees for Impropriations, which had been meeting informally from about 1613, was formalized in the very week when the York House Conference took place, when it was evident that John Preston, said to "govern" the Puritans, could no longer depend on the support of the Duke of Buckingham, and when William Laud, still only the Bishop of St. David's, had become King Charles's principal ecclesiastical advisor. The feoffees, or trustees, were to number twelve, four clerics, four lawyers, and four merchants, all prominent in godly circles.

The initial trustees were Richard Stock, rector and lecturer at All Hallows Bread Street; Richard Sibbes, preacher at Gray's Inn and master of St. Catherine's Hall, Cambridge; Charles Offspring, rector and lecturer at St. Antholin's; John Davenport, vicar and lecturer at St. Stephen's Coleman Street; Christopher Sherland of Gray's Inn; Samuel Brown and Robert Eyre of Lincoln's Inn; John White of the Middle Temple; Francis Bridges,

Salter; Richard Davies, Vintner; John Gearing, Grocer; and George Harwood, haberdasher. Bridges, Davenport, Davies, White, and Harwood were members of the Massachusetts Bay Company; Gearing and White were members of the Dorchester Company; and Harwood and Sherland were members of the Providence Island Company. Brown later sat in the Long Parliament and was a member of the prosecutorial team that tried Archbishop Laud. When Stock died later that first year, William Gouge, curate and lecturer at St. Anne's Blackfriars, was elected in his place, and when Sherland died in 1632, Sir Thomas Crewe, Sergeant at Law and of Gray's Inn, replaced him. Crewe had been elected Speaker of the House of Commons in 1625 against the wishes of the Crown. To supply a casting vote, should the feoffees split, Rowland Heylyn, ironmonger and alderman, was elected, and when he died in 1632, he was replaced by Nicholas Rainton, haberdasher and lord mayor. Until 1629 Hugh Peter, who was preaching at various churches in the City of London, served as an agent of the Feoffees for Impropriation, as did John Vicars, usher at Christ Church Hospital. Thomas Foxley, one of the early morning lecturers at St. Antholin's, was so closely identified with the feoffees' affairs that he was named in the indictment that led to the dissolving of the trusteeship in 1633.

The connection with St. Antholin's was not accidental. Offspring used the early morning lectures as a training ground for young godly clergy, who were then sent out to preach where such preaching was lacking and provided with an income by the feoffees. In turn, the feoffees sometimes termed themselves "the Collectors of St. Antholin's," and £1,500 of the £6,300 raised went to help endow the St. Antholin's lectureships. By comparison, the initial working capital of the Providence Island Company in 1630 was only £3,800. Altogether by 1631 the feoffees acquired eight impropriations and eight advowsons, along with leased tithes and other contributions in twenty-six parishes, eleven in Parliamentary boroughs, and managed to place lecturers in four: Hertford, Cirencester, High Wycombe, and Bridgnorth. Another fourteen vicars, curates,

and lecturers had been installed elsewhere before the scheme was declared illegal in 1633.

Proposals to purchase lay impropriations as a means of solving the pervasive poverty of many parochial incumbents had been discussed not only by Puritans but by Archbishop Richard Bancroft in 1610, but neither the church nor the Crown possessed the financial means for such a vast undertaking. Henry Burton had proposed a scheme to Parliament by which a proportion of all impropriations, particularly of underfunded vicarages, would go to augment such livings, but in 1625 Parliament was preoccupied with issues of war finance, and the Puritans perforce had to turn to private initiatives. Private individuals were prepared to act, even before the Feoffees for Impropriations were formally constituted; in 1623 Dame Mary Weld, the wealthy widow of Alderman Sir Humphrey Weld, bequeathed £2,000 to be administered by the Haberdashers Company for the purchase of impropriations, the income to be spent on securing learned and diligent ministers prepared to preach twice on the Sabbath. The scheme, probably unknown to the authorities, continued through the years when the feoffees were prosecuted and in fact was not interfered with at any time during the 1630s.

In 1630 Peter Heylyn, the nephew of Alderman Heylyn and a future chaplain of Archbishop Laud's, preached from a university pulpit at Oxford where he was a fellow that the Feoffees for Impropriations were engaged in a conspiracy to take over the church. Heylyn had the sermon printed and dispatched to Laud, who encouraged him to pursue his investigations. By 1632 enough information had been gathered and turned over by Laud to Attorney General William Noy, who presented information about what he argued was an illegal corporation, bent on creating a church within the church but outside the control and authority of the king, to the Equity Side of the Exchequer Court. The Feoffees for Impropriations were defended by a team of lawyers, including William Lenthall, the future Speaker of the House of Commons during the Long Parliament, but the Exchequer barons found that the Feoffees for Impropriations were operating as a corporation but without the sanction of a letter patent, and in early 1633 the Feoffees for Impropriations were dissolved and their properties confiscated to the disposition of a royal commission.

See also: Lectures and Lectureships, St. Antholin's, Tithes
Further Reading
Isabel M. Calder, ed., Activities of the Puritan Faction of the Church of England, 1625–1633 (London, 1957); Christopher Hill, Economic Problems of the Church from Archbishop Whitgift to the Long Parliament (Oxford, 1971).

Paul Seaver

Fifth Monarchists

The Puritan Revolution saw the rise of many political and religious parties. The economic crisis of the sixteenth and early seventeenth centuries, as well as the religious questioning that burgeoned at the time, helped create a revolutionary form of anarchism known as the Fifth Monarchy Men. They supported the republic formed in 1649 after the execution of Charles II and advocated following the laws of Moses until the prophecy of a fifth monarchy, the coming of Jesus as king, was fulfilled. The name of the party came from a biblical reference in the Book of Daniel to a dream of Nebuchadnezzar in which the great "kingdoms" of Assyria (Babylonia), Persia, Greece, and Rome were followed by a fifth monarchy, presumed to be the reign of Christ. As supporters of Oliver Cromwell, they encouraged him to allow the Jews to return to England, which he did in 1655. The conversion of the Jews was a prerequisite for the return of Christ in the eyes of many apocalyptic believers, including the Fifth Monarchy. The party began to turn against Cromwell when he established the Protectorate, and its members occasionally tried to overthrow the government.

Called Fifth Monarchy Men, the group itself had a mixed following of men and women in various congregations across England, Scotland, and Ireland. Women were often attracted to Quakerism and so-called antinomianism, which offered greater equality and freedom for their sex. Anna Trapnell was a famous English visionary who embraced the Fifth Monarchists and made dramatic predictions. The group also cut across class lines, involving aristocrats as well as the poor. Although the Fifth Monarchy was never a party per se in New England, there were many sympathizers, particularly in the colony of New Haven. New Haven embraced the Mosaic code, incorporating biblical references into its legal code. Other settlements, such as Anne Hutchinson's group in Portsmouth, Rhode Island, held certain millennialist ideas that later became common among Fifth Monarchists in England. John Cotton's ideas incorporated many of the various beliefs of the Fifth Monarchists, but predated the party's formation. Works such as Henry Archer's *The Personal Reign of Christ upon Earth,* a work on the coming of the millennium published in 1642, became popular during the period and set the stage for the group's coalescence in England, while New England was at the same time reacting against further sectarianism. Thus, despite the fact that New Englanders embraced many of the ideas of the Fifth Monarchy, the Puritan authorities there turned away from radicalism.

The Fifth Monarchists saw the demise of the English monarchy and the establishment of the republic as signs of the coming of the New Jerusalem. Earthly kings were demystified by the execution of Charles I in 1649, and ordinary men saw that they could shape political events. They hoped to be instruments of anticipated heavenly events. The Fifth Monarchists' public leaders in England were Major-General Thomas Harrison, later a member of Parliament, and preachers Christopher Feake of Newgate's Christ Church, John Rogers of Dublin, Vavsor Powell, and the cooper Thomas Venner. Cromwell took Harrison's army commission from him after Harrison protested the creation of the Protectorate. Harrison was later executed by Charles II for being a regicide, because he had signed the death warrant of Charles I. John Rogers wrote a pamphlet in 1654 in which he decried the loss of liberty under the "Norman Yoke," the oppression by kings descended from William the Conqueror who had stolen the birthright of the Anglo-Saxons, and the oppressive and unrighteous laws of the "Babylonian Yoke," secular law that had replaced the laws of Moses. Opposed to lawyers, the Fifth Monarchists were sometimes labeled as antinomians, even though they advocated following Mosaic law. This belief that they were "lawless" combined with their own sometimes violent actions brought down the wrath of both the Protectorate and the Crown. Fifty men under Venner attempted to take London after the Restoration of Charles II, and in 1661 Venner and several of his men were executed for high treason.

The Fifth Monarchy drew support from many different religious sects and used Cromwell's New Model Army as a vehicle for spreading their beliefs. Independents, also called Congregationalists, and Baptist laymen and ministers joined the New Model Army during the Civil War and became influential. In addition to the New Model Army itself, many of these same soldiers also came from various General and Particular Baptist congregations, such as the Seventh-Day Men, also known as Sabbatarians, who worshiped God on Saturday rather than on Sunday, following the Jewish tradition. Seventh Day Men were often assumed by the Protectorate and later by the Crown to be Fifth Monarchists, and thus were subject to persecution as a dangerous group. Between 1650 and 1660, there had been strong ties of support between the various groups of Baptists, Independents, Sabbatarians, and Fifth Monarchists, but being a member of one of these congregations did not mean one subscribed to Fifth Monarchy beliefs. John Jones, a Sabbatarian, was executed and his head displayed on a pike outside of his church because it was wrongly assumed he belonged to the Fifth Monarchy party. Quakers and Levellers also supported the Fifth Monarchy, because they shared ideas of the equality of human beings, the redistribution of land, and the restructuring of society. After Venner's Uprising, over four thousand Quakers were put in prison as threats to the restoration of the king. After the uprising, the Fifth Monarchy Men disappeared as a group, but their millenarian ideas remained among Dissenters.

See also: Sects

Further Reading

Louise Fargo Brown, *The Political Activities of the Baptists and Fifth Monarchy Men in England during the Interregnum* (New York, 1911); Stephen Foster, *The Long Argument: English Puritanism and the Shaping of New England Culture, 1570–1700* (Chapel Hill, 1996); Christopher Hill, *Puritanism and Revolution: Studies in Interpretation of the English Revolution of the 17th Century* (London, 1997); Daniel Loewenstein, *Representing Revolution in Milton and his Contemporaries: Religion, Politics, and Polemics in Radical Puritanism* (Cambridge, Eng., 2001); James P. Maclear, "New England and the Fifth Monarchy," *William and Mary Quarterly* (1975), 223–260.

Katherine Hermes

G

Gangraena

The first part of *Gangraena: or a Catalogue and Discovery of many of the Errours, Heresies, Blasphemies and Pernicious Practices of the Sectaries of this time, vented and acted in England in these four last years,* was published in February 1646; Part Two, *A Fresh and Further Discovery* followed in May, with Part Three, *A New and Higher Discovery,* in December. These massive composite tracts were the work of Thomas Edwards, a controversial London lecturer and zealous Presbyterian polemicist. Together they made one of the most notorious and one of the most influential books to emerge from the vibrant print culture of the English Revolution. In over 800 pages Edwards listed the outrageous errors spread by contemporary sectaries, described their disorderly and often immoral behavior, and offered the orthodox a program to resist the sectarian onslaught. *Gangraena* was one of many surveys of the errors of the times, but it was the most comprehensive account of contemporary developments and the most compelling, offering vivid narratives of women preachers, notorious "dippers" like Samuel Oates, political radicals such as John Lilburne, and mystical preachers such as John Saltmarsh and William Dell.

Edwards's account included eyewitness testimony, depositions from law courts and committees, and many letters sent in by his allies. Extracts from the sectaries' own books were offered along with printed denunciations by orthodox writers. Part Two of *Gangraena* concentrated on responses to Edwards's critics, particularly to John Goodwin's *Cretensis,* a forthright attack on Part One. Goodwin and his London congregation, a potent force in radical parliamentary politics, were Edwards's major targets. Part Three showed an intensified concern with political radicalism, centered on Lilburne and others shortly to be dubbed Levellers, and included long extracts from *The Remonstrance of Many Thousand Citizens* that protested the treatment of John Lillburne. Throughout, but especially in Part Three, Edwards denounced the malign impact of Parliament's New Model Army as a promoter of "toleration" and "independency" and described the soldiers' blasphemous transgressions (such as the baptism of horses) and assaults on orthodox clergy. Edwards deliberately elided Independency with sectarianism in *Gangraena.*

The exotic stories usually concern the most radical and unorthodox Separatists, but in his general comments Edwards held the mainstream Calvinist Independents to blame for religious division and confusion. He was a bitter opponent of toleration, believing that any degree of religious liberty inevitably opened the door to fundamental error and chaotic separation. Hence the respectable Independents, calling for liberty for their own church way, were acting as the "nurse and patronesse" of sects.

Gangraena was of course a profoundly controversial text. For its subjects and opponents, it was a call for ruthless persecution of the godly, and Edwards provoked many angry pamphlet responses.

Gangraena was a work of "shameless untruths" (John Goodwin); its author "the father of lyes" (the Baptist Edward Drapes). For Edwards and his Presbyterian allies, such as Robert Baillie, John Bastwick, John Vicars, and William Prynne, it was an urgent defense of truth against heresy and schism. For these men Edwards was a new Augustine, "a faithful friend of truth." *Gangraena* has been widely, although controversially, used as a source for 1640s radicalism. Despite his obvious biases and his London-centered outlook, Edwards's presentation of evidence in an elaborate and disorganized fashion does offer valuable material for historians. Nonetheless, *Gangraena* is perhaps best studied as text in its own right, with an enormous influence in the mid-1640s, helping to intensify polarization among parliamentarians on religious and political grounds. It helped to rally Presbyterian zealots, especially in the city of London, to campaign against religious liberty and the perceived inadequacies of Parliament's church settlement, and to agitate for peace and the disbanding of the New Model Army. It also worked to cement a precarious radical alliance of sectaries and Independents, drawing together members of John Goodwin's congregation, proto-Levellers, members of the army, and Independents in both Houses of Parliament.

See also: Thomas Edwards, *Antapologia*
Further Reading
Ann Hughes, *Gangraena and the Struggle for the English Revolution* (Oxford, 2004).

Ann Hughes

Geneva Bible

The Bible of Shakespeare as well as John Bunyan (author of *Pilgrim's Progress,* 1678), Cromwell's army, and the Pilgrims on the *Mayflower,* the Genevan translation saw widespread use in England and the New World for several generations after its first printing in 1560. Both Queen Elizabeth and King James resisted the promulgation of the Geneva Bible, with its decidedly Calvinist marginal annotations, refusing to appoint it for use in the English churches. Yet it went through some 180 editions, either as a whole or in parts, between 1560 and 1644. This is the translation known also as the Breeches Bible, after its rendering of Genesis 3:7: "they sewed figtree leaves together, and made themselves breeches." While this usage seems today a quaint anachronism, it had already been employed in the Wycliffite versions and other sources predating the Geneva Bible by nearly two centuries. In fact the Genevan translation was developed by careful scholars thoroughly conversant in Hebrew and Greek. It strongly influenced later translations, including not only King James's Authorized Version of 1611 but also the Catholic Rheims-Douay translation of 1609.

Authorship and Format

The Geneva Bible of 1560 was preceded by William Whittingham's translation of the New Testament in 1557. A Marian exile who eventually settled in Geneva, Whittingham largely followed Tyndale's translation. Shortly after the volume's publication, he collaborated with others, including Anthony Gilby, Thomas Sampson, and perhaps Miles Coverdale, in improving his version of the New Testament and producing a new translation of the Old. The result was the 1560 Geneva Bible.

Initial publication expenses appear to have been furnished by John Bodley, father of the founder of the Bodleian Library at Oxford. The Geneva Bible was clearly designed for practicality. Its quarto-sized format made it relatively inexpensive to purchase and easy to handle. It soon supplanted in popularity the 1539 Great Bible, so named for its unwieldy size. For ease of reading, the Geneva Bible replaced the usual black-letter type with roman. The Genevan version was the first English translation to number the verses, improving precision of reference. In fidelity to the original languages, English words that were not direct translations from the original languages were set in italics—a practice that persisted over the next three centuries.

A dedicatory epistle to Queen Elizabeth follows the title page and a list of the books of the Old and New Testaments. In view of the usual sixteenth-century practice of offering fulsome praise in dedicatory addresses, the epistle in the Geneva Bible seems remarkably straightforward, even blunt. While Elizabeth is hailed as "our Zerubbabel" (from the governor of the Babylonian exiles allowed to return to Jerusalem and rebuild the temple), the message is clear: she is warned of "Papistes, who under pretence of favoring Gods worde, traiterously seak to erect idolatry and destroy your majesty"; "above strength you must show your self strong and bold in God's matters." Elizabeth is to reform the English church along Genevan lines, to "build up the ruins of God's house." The translators, of course, were disappointed in their hopes for a thoroughly reformed Church of England modeled on that of Geneva.

Some editions of the Geneva Bible contained Calvin's concise "Sum of the Whole Scripture of the Old and New Testament" and the French Reformer Theodore Beza's "Certain questions and answers touching the doctrine of predestination, the use of God's word and Sacraments." Needless to say, the predestinarian emphasis of this catechism was emphatic. One exchange, for example, reads, "Question. Are all ordained unto eternal life? Answer. Some are vessels of wrath ordained unto destruction, as others are vessels of mercy prepared to glory." In addition to these doctrinal statements, some editions had concordances, maps, woodcuts, lists of Old Testament names to be used in naming children, and brief "arguments" prefacing biblical books and summarizing their contents.

The Geneva Bible contains the Apocrypha, with a prefatory note that the books are "to be read for the advancement and furtherance of the knowledge of the history, & for the instruction of godly maners" and are not strictly part of the canon; the books are suitable for proving points of Christian doctrine only when those points are confirmed by canonical books. The marginal note on 2 Maccabees 12:44, a verse that advocates prayer for the dead, says that the passage "was not written by the holy Gost" and "is not sufficient to establish a doctrine." After the Apocrypha was dropped by the Synod of Dort in 1618, the books were eliminated from the edition of 1633.

Marginal Notes

Arguably the most influential aspect of this translation was not its generally sensible and accurate rendering of Hebrew and Greek but its controversial marginalia. Though a good many of these marginal notes provide the sorts of aids to study one might find in a modern Bible, such as cross-references and historical or geographical clarifications, others are doctrinal. As might be expected, these annotations are thoroughly Calvinist. The note on Matthew 26:26 ("this is my body," said by Christ after he blesses the bread at the Last Supper), for example, reads, "That is, a true sign and testimony that my body is made yours." The following note adds that the blood of Christ is "spiritually received." On Christ's words as recorded in John 19:30, "It is finished," the antecedent of "It" is supplied with precision: "Man's salvation is perfected by the onelie sacrifice of Christ: & all ye ceremonies of the Law are ended."

While the notes on the Gospels, Acts, and Epistles are generally not militantly anti-Catholic in tone, they do insistently outline the differences between Geneva and Rome. In its comment on Matthew 16:19, for example, which records Christ's giving the keys of the kingdom to Peter, the note makes it clear that it is the preachers, not a succession of popes, who open the gates of heaven. Clerical celibacy is implicitly denounced in the note on Matthew 19:11, in which Christ tells his disciples, "All men can not receive this thing [celibacy], save they to whome it is given"; the gift of celibacy is "very rare," say the translators, "and given to few: therefore men may not rashly abstain from marriage."

The notes to Revelation are decidedly anti-Roman, often scathingly so. The locusts of Revelation 9:3, who are "given power, as the scorpions of the earth have power," are glossed as "false teachers, heretics, and worldly subtle Prelates, with Monks, Friars, Cardinals, Patriarches, Archbishops, Bishops, Doctors, Bachelors, and Masters which forsake Christ to maintain false doctrine." The "beast that cometh out of the bottomless pit" of Revelation 11:7 is "the Pope which hath his power out of hell and cometh thence." The Sodom of the next verse is "the whole jurisdiction of the

Pope, which is compared to Sodom for their abominable sinne." The "mark of the beast" of Rev. 13:16 consists of popish "chrismatories, graisings, vows, oaths & shavings."

The anti-Catholic rhetoric became even more strident in Laurence Tomson's editions of the Geneva Bible, of which there were many after 1576—and yet more pronounced after Francis Junius replaced Tomson's notes to Revelation with his own in 1598. In Junius's annotation to Revelation 9:4, for example, Pope Gregory VII is singled out as "a most monstrous Necromancer," his followers "most expert cut-throats." Such rhetoric in the family Bibles of ordinary English people no doubt played its part in exacerbating the hostilities between the Protestants and Catholics of the time.

Despite their own anti-Roman sentiments, neither Queen Elizabeth nor King James endorsed the Geneva Bible. Elizabeth responded to its publication by authorizing Archbishop Matthew Parker to produce a rival translation, the Bishops' Bible of 1568. This version was to be kept uncontroversial. Accordingly, Parker instructed his translators "to make no bitter notice upon any text, or yet to set down any determination in places of controversy." Yet even as preparations for the Bishops' Bible were under way, Parker granted Bodley a twelve-year extension of his license to print the Geneva Bible, saying that it would "nothing hinder but rather do much good to have diversity of translation and readings."

King James was even less enthusiastic than Elizabeth, remarking that the Genevan version was the worst yet. Some of the notes, he said, were "very partial, untrue, seditious, and savouring too much of dangerous and traitorous conceits." James cited the note to Exodus 1:19, which allowed disobedience to royalty under certain circumstances, and the note to 2 Chronicles 15:16, in which the annotator takes King Asa to task for not putting his idolatrous queen mother to death. Such notes are one reason James readily agreed, in 1604, to a new translation. The result, the Authorized Version of 1611, of course proved highly influential on both sides of the Atlantic. But it did not supplant the Geneva Bible in popularity until the 1640s.

See also: Antipopery, Bible, Marian Exiles, Soldier's Bible
Further Reading
The Geneva Bible: A Facsimile of the 1560 Edition (Madison, WI, 1969); Basil Hall, "The Genevan Version of the English Bible: Its Aims and Achievements," in W. P. Stephens, ed., *The Bible, the Reformation, and the Church,* (Sheffield, Eng., 1995); Naseeb Shaheen, "Misconceptions about the Geneva Bible," *Studies in Bibliography* 37 (1984) 156–158.

Bryan Crockett

Glorification

A term used in Puritan theology for the consummation of salvation in heavenly blessedness. Puritan theologians regarded glorification as one of the steps in the order of salvation (see Soteriology), such as justification and sanctification, of which it was the culmination. Glorification changed redeemed persons from sinners whose sins had been forgiven by God's grace but would never be free from sin in this life to a state of perfection. The righteousness that had been imputed to the believer in justification became the believer's true character in glorification, and the believer was delivered from sin, death, and hell, and glorified by the taking away of all imperfections of soul and body.

In his *Discourse of the Glory to which God hath called Believers by Jesus Christ,* the American Puritan Jonathan Mitchell thought there might be "inchoate" beginnings of glorification in this life, prior to the perfect glorification of the heavenly rest. But perfect glorification began when the soul of a believer was separated from the body at death and passed into heavenly rest. However, the body would not be glorified as a spiritual body until reunited with the soul at the second coming of Christ, the resurrection from the dead, and the Last Judgment. Some Reformed theologians asserted that the separated soul experienced a blessed expectation of that final reunion with the glorified body before the resurrection. When soul and body were reunited, they would mutually experience, in Mitchell's words, "the joy of the whole." In heaven there would also be the joy of communion with the saints and angels, and with the Persons of the Trinity. The climax of heavenly blessedness would be the *beatific vision,* a term Puritans used in common with medieval theologians. William Perkins described this as beholding the face of God, that is, his glory and majesty, and being transformed into the likeness of Christ. The happiness of beatitude included the absence of all evils, such as the temptations and molestations of Satan. The glorified wills of the blessed would have the true freedom of willing only the good. Beatitude would be not only perfect joy, but also an eternity of service to God through praise and thanksgiving. Thus, echoing the words of the Westminster Shorter Catechism, the redeemed will "glorify God and enjoy him forever." Puritan theology, in accordance with I Corinthians 15:41–42, generally also held that there would be degrees of glory in the heavenly rest, not according to merit, but based on the variety of graces given to the redeemed in their earthly lives.

In William Ames's treatment of glorification in *The Marrow of Sacred Divinity* (his *Medulla Theologiae* of 1623, translated into English from the Latin in 1642), more attention was given to the significance of glorification in this life than its nature in the next life. He described future glorification as an encouragement to holy living and a source of assurance of salvation, since those whom God had predestined to glorification could not fail to come to that goal. Mitchell encouraged believers to grow in grace that they might be "ripe for heaven" and the persecuted to recall that the glory of the saints would be manifested to the wicked in hell who scorned them on earth. He also thought consideration of heaven sweetened death for the godly. This "heavenly mindedness" became prominent in Puritan piety; it was achieved by meditation on heaven, fortifying the devout against earthly misfortunes and providing a foretaste of bliss. John Bunyan introduced a "Mr. Heavenly-Mind" into his allegory *The Holy War* (written 1681–1682) and had his pilgrims in *The Pilgrim's Progress* (1678) engrossed in discussion of heaven. Richard Baxter's *The Saints' Everlasting Rest* (1650), one of the most widely read of Puritan devotional writings, stressed meditation on heaven, and contemporary biographies of Puritan ministers frequently praised their heavenly mindedness, whereby they lived as pilgrims and strangers on earth.

See also: Grace, Soteriology
Further Reading
William Ames, *The Marrow of Theology,* trans. from the third Latin edition of 1629 and ed. John Dykstra Eusden (Boston, 1983).

Dewey D. Wallace Jr.

God

Puritan beliefs about God restated traditional Christian concepts drawn from scripture, creeds, ancient church fathers, and medieval theologians, as filtered through the Protestant reformers, especially Calvinist theologians with their distinctive emphases. For the Puritans, it was certain that God existed: William Perkins, writing in 1592, thought God's existence evident to human conscience from the moral sense, to human reason from the necessity of a first cause and from the unanimous consent of rational beings. A larger place was given to this kind of natural theology in the later seventeenth century in the writings of Richard Baxter, William Bates, and John Howe. They so strongly emphasized the evidence in nature of intricate design pointing to an omnipotent designer that they considered atheism an irrational rebellion against God. Puritans thought that God was revealed in both creation and scripture, though more completely in scripture, especially since, as the New England minister James Fitch said, the book of nature had been "blurred by sin."

Whether based on scripture or nature, however, human language about God was considered analogical, the explanation of divine things in a limited human fashion. Ultimately the Puritans thought God was characterized by incomprehensibility. For the essence of God is understood fully only by God, although pointed to in the affirmation that God is first being, absolute being, and necessary being existing in itself and needing nothing outside itself. From this divine essence proceed God's attributes: as explained by Samuel Willard, some attributes are incommunicable, belonging only to God, such as eternity, infinity, omnipotence, omniscience, and immutability, and some are communicable to human beings, such as life or goodness. These latter attributes exist in creatures in imperfect degree. All these attributes in God are aspects of a single divine essence, though appearing diversely to humans.

God, however, is not a static abstraction: as the living God, God enjoys himself in infinite self-love, and the divine essence, according to the puritan theologian William Ames, subsists as three "relative properties," which may be called persons and are three "individual forces" in the one essence. The relative property of the Father is to beget, of the Son to be begotten, and of the Holy Spirit to proceed from Father and Son. These divine persons are coessential, coequal, and coeternal, but have a relational order, the Son begotten by the Father as an act of intellection, and the Spirit proceeding from Father and Son as an act of love. Thus Puritan theology was thoroughly Trinitarian. Each person of the Trinity has a particular role in creation and salvation, even as it can be said that what one person effects is effected by all. And thus the divine being, perfect in itself, goes outside of itself in the works of creation and redemption. Puritan theologians employed the medieval distinction of God's absolute and ordaining power: by the first God can do all things that are possible (that is, that do not deny the divine nature; thus, for example, God cannot lie), and by the second God ordains what he has actually ordained. However, all that is in God's ordained power (his works or effects by which he goes outside of himself) is known immediately to God in one absolutely simple act of decreeing creation and redemption. As Calvinists, Puritans gave special emphasis to God's greatness and sovereignty and to the absoluteness of the divine decrees, God doing all things of his mere good pleasure and without reference to any external cause. In piety, this emphasis on God's absolute sovereignty entailed abhorrence of all idolatry.

Further Reading
William Ames, *The Marrow of Theology*, trans. from the 1629 Latin edition and ed. John Dykstra

Eusden (Boston, 1983); Ernest Benson Lowrie, *The Shape of the Puritan Mind: The Thought of Samuel Willard* (New Haven, 1974).

Dewey D. Wallace Jr.

Gospel

The term used to identify the doctrines taught by Jesus Christ as set down in the records of the four evangelists, *gospel,* derived from the Old English *godspel,* "good news," a translation of the Greek *euangelion,* was also used to identify the New Testament and its "good news" of salvation through faith in Christ generally. In more evangelically minded early modern writings, therefore, it was employed to distinguish New Testament teachings from those of the "Law" (i.e., the commandments set out in the Hebrew Bible). Calling themselves "Minister(s) of the Gospel" on the title pages of their sermons and other writings, many puritan writers used the word *gospel* to mean, in effect, "Protestant," a polemical strategy that efficiently conveyed their contention that Roman Catholicism was corruptly based upon a doctrine of salvation that depended on the works of the law rather than on the merits of Christ's death and resurrection.

Lori Anne Ferrell

Grace

Grace as a theological term refers to God's favor and mercy freely given. Salvation by grace alone was central to Reformation Protestantism and to the piety and theology of the Puritans. For them, grace was first of all the forensic act of justification by which the sins of those who have faith are pardoned in God's declaratory act of free mercy. This pardon was through the atoning death of Christ whereby he took the place of sinners, satisfying offended divine justice and reconciling them to God. By grace the righteousness of Christ was imputed to sinners and Christ united to the souls of believers, apart from any human merit or deserving. The salvation of believers continued in a process of sanctification by grace, whereby the believer increased in holiness of life through the working of the Holy Spirit.

In the Reformed, or Calvinist, theology that prevailed among Puritans, God's grace was closely connected to the doctrine of predestination, which guaranteed the freeness and unconditionality of the role of grace in salvation. It is for this reason that predestination came to play such a large part in Puritan thought. Understanding of the nature of God's grace was also connected in Reformed theology to the doctrine of limited atonement, the belief that the death of Christ was only for the elect, because God's grace was a goodness that always effected its purpose. Grace was not a general offer of salvation depending on human response, but an effective salvation for those whom God had predestined and for whom Christ had died. Otherwise it would not be "free grace," a phrase constant in Puritan theology and sermons, but grace dependent on some readiness, choice, or merit in human beings. Although Calvinist theologians did not rule out cooperation of the human will with grace, that cooperation itself was made possible by grace, and they referred to grace as irresistible, since it would inevitably accomplish its purpose. Reformed theology emphasized a covenant of grace as the story of God's grace unfolding in the Bible (see Federal Theology), as well as an order of salvation that was the consequence of gracious acts of God in believers and the means of grace by which believers came to salvation (discussed under the heading "Soteriology").

Puritans wrote and preached extensively about grace. William Perkins defined it as the goodness and mercy of God, the first being God's free exercise of his liberality toward his creation, the second God's help given to creatures. Thomas Goodwin described grace as the dominant and most absolute principle in God. John Owen's theology stressed that every stage in the process of salvation was by grace alone: his massive *Pneumatologia or a Discourse Concerning the Holy Spirit* (1674) insisted on the irresistibility of the regenerating grace effected by the Holy Spirit in believers.

Kinds of Grace

Reformed and Puritan theologians distinguished between various kinds of grace. Common grace was God's universal favor in bestowing his blessings on the created world and in granting a moral sense to humankind. Some Puritan theologians also included in common grace the revelation of God's word in scripture and some illuminations of the conscience with regard to it, thereby constituting it a kind of entry for special grace. Such common grace was, however, to be distinguished from special, or saving, grace, which was subdivided into various types. Preventing, or prevenient, grace (grace coming before), granted to sinners in the word of the gospel, incited them toward salvation; preparing grace made them aware of their sin and open to the gospel; operating grace regenerated the will and illumined the mind, enabling faith, repentance, and conversion. Cooperating grace, in which the renewed will cooperates with the indwelling grace of the Holy Spirit to do good works, sanctified the believer, and was sometimes described, in a phrase echoing medieval Scholastic conceptions, as an indwelling habit or disposition. Persevering grace enabled the believer to continue to the end.

Controversies over Grace

Many of the theological controversies that occupied Puritans concerned grace. This was true of the various controversies about Arminianism, in which the assertion that predestination followed God's foreknowledge of human choices and that human will was free, that human beings had freedom of choice, was taken as denial of the greatness and effectiveness of God's grace and a return to the idea that human merit played a role in salvation. The Laudian Arminians in the Church of England were thought by their Calvinist opponents to be supplanting the free grace of predestination with sacramental grace, that is, with grace coming through the sacraments of the church. Puritan and Calvinist attacks upon Socinianism represented it as denying the free grace of God in the atonement and in justification by faith. Later in the seventeenth century, Puritans worried about "moralism," the substitution in the process of salvation of a mere morality for grace, which they considered a complete denial of the saving grace of God. Puritan controversialists assailed Arminianism, Socinianism, and moralism as Pelagian heresy, which they thought also tainted Roman Catholicism. The antinomian controversies in New England in the 1630s and in England in the 1640s and 1690s also involved grace. The antinomians exalted free grace but were understood by the mainstream of Calvinist and Puritan theologians to err in their denial that sanctification was needed for assurance and in their belief that the elect were justified when they believed, and not from eternity.

Grace in Puritan Piety

The Puritan emphasis on free grace played a definitive role in works of Puritan piety and spirituality. In these works, the Christian life was represented as continual thankfulness toward God for mercy and grace. Such works were filled with effusive praise acknowledging divine grace; Peter Sterry for example wrote that the saints and angels in heaven continually cry out "free grace" in raptures of joy. But the Christian life was also the consequence of the supernatural regeneration of the believer by grace and the gracious union of the believer with Christ, which led to a higher goodness and a deeper spirituality than was possible apart from grace. Biographies of Puritan saints extolled the holiness of their lives as possible only through grace. It is thus characteristic of this grace-centered piety that what is perhaps the greatest of Puritan spiritual autobiographies, that of John Bunyan, is entitled *Grace Abounding to the Chief of Sinners* (1666).

> *See also:* Antinomianism, Federal Theology, Predestination, Sin, Soteriology
> *Further Reading*
> John Von Rohr, *The Covenant of Grace in Puritan Thought* (Atlanta, 1986); Dewey D. Wallace Jr., *Puritans and Predestination: Grace in English Protestant Theology, 1525–1695* (Chapel Hill, 1982).
>
> *Dewey D. Wallace Jr.*

Grand Remonstrance

This document of formal protest was a major step by the puritan members of the Long Parliament to force King Charles I to accept the reform of the English Church. Drafted by John Pym and passed by the House of Commons in November 1641 by only eleven votes, it listed religious grievances requiring reform, demanded that the king appoint no new ministers to livings (as benefices were called) unless they were approved by Parliament, and called upon the king to pledge his support of recommendations that would derive from the Westminster Assembly of Divines. It struck a strongly antipapal stance and was strongly critical of the policies of bishops.

The Grand Remonstrance came as something of a culmination of steps taken to reform the church. In February 1641 Parliament had begun debate on the Root and Branch Petition, which had demanded thorough church reforms. In March of that year, Archbishop Laud had been imprisoned and shortly thereafter he was brought to trial by the House of Lords. In May the Protestation of the House of Commons revived the Elizabethan Oath of Association, pledging to support the true Protestant faith against popery. In July the Court of High Commission was dissolved.

> *Further Reading*
> John Morrill, *The Nature of the English Revolution* (London, 1993); Conrad Russell, *The Fall of the British Monarchies, 1637–1642* (Oxford, 1991).
>
> *Francis J. Bremer*

Great Migration

The *Great Migration* is the term used for the emigration of English puritans to New England in the 1630s. It is generally seen as starting with John Winthrop's voyage to the New World in the *Arbella* at the head of a fleet in 1630. In all it is estimated that some 21,000 men, women, and children left England and settled in the puritan colonies during the 1630s. Most came for religious reasons, though in deciding to migrate they also believed that they would be able to sustain a reasonable level of prosperity in their new homes. Social influences such as the decision to accompany family or friends also played a part.

The ongoing migration was important in sustaining the economic vitality of the region. Newcomers brought money with them and purchased cattle and other commodities from established settlers. The migration slowed significantly with the outbreak of the wars of the three kingdoms in the 1640s. Many who might have been inclined to emigrate remained in England, in the hope that the long awaited reforms of church and state might at last occur. Soon there was a reverse migration, with established clergy and Harvard graduates returning to England to take up the ministry there. Laymen returned as well, with some serving in the Parliamentary Army and others chosen to Parliament or appointed to government positions. With the reduction in immigrants, the colonists faced an economic challenge. This challenge actually fostered the development of new trade links with other British colonies, as the New Englanders sought to find new sources of wealth.

Further Reading

Virginia Anderson, *New England's Generation* (New York, 1991); Francis J. Bremer, *John Winthrop* (New York, 2003); Carl Bridenbaugh, *Vexed and Troubled Englishmen: 1590–1640* (London, 1968); David Cressy, *Coming Over: Migration and Communication between England and New England in the Seventeenth Century* (Cambridge, Eng., 1987); Roger Thompson, *Mobility and Migration* (Amherst, 1994).

Francis J. Bremer

Gunpowder Plot

The Gunpowder Plot of November 1605. A group of disaffected young Catholics, disappointed by King James I's backtracking on earlier concession to Catholics, attempted to blow up the king and Parliament; the plot was uncovered on 5 November, the eve of the opening of Parliament, as a result of a letter from one plotter, Francis Tresham, to a kinsman, Lord Monteagle, warning him to absent himself from the opening. The letter came into the hands of Robert Cecil, who allowed the affair to proceed until the evening of 5 November, when Guy Fawkes was discovered in the cellars of Parliament ready to ignite barrels of gunpowder. Some of the plotters, led by a Warwickshire gentle-

Guy Fawkes is caught conspiring to blow up King James I and both houses of Parliament in an English Roman Catholic conspiracy, 5 November 1605. (Hulton Archive/Getty Images)

man named Robert Catesby, were killed in the skirmish that followed its discovery, and Fawkes, after torture in the Tower, was executed on 31 January 1606. Protestant preachers were quick to interpret the plot as evidence of the Jesuits' implacable determination to overthrow the regime, and one Jesuit, Henry Garnet, was executed for his complicity in the affair.

The discovery of the Gunpowder Plot, like the defeat of the Armada, became a landmark in the belief that Providence was acting to save England from the Roman Catholics that was a central feature of England's Protestant identity. The anniversary was marked by sermons at court, the first being preached by Lancelot Andrewes in 1606, and was taken up by civic corporations and parochial elites throughout the country, so that by the 1620s rejoicings in the forms of processions, sermons, bell ringing, and bonfires were commonplace, and several places had special sermons endowed. These sermons reminded the leaders of local society of the ever-present threat from popery and sat, sometimes uncomfortably, alongside the popular manifestations of anti-Catholicism that marked the day in the eyes of the multitude, so often twinned with papists as the objects of preachers' condemnation. By the later 1620s the vigorous antipopery that marked the anniversary itself was a source of division, as Laudian churchmen sought to reshape the past on lines different from those previously mapped out by John Foxe, the author of the Book of Martyrs. On the one hand, the Laudians sought to curtail the religious dimensions of the anniversary and, in reissuing the liturgy for 5 November in 1635, stressed the sin of rebellion in general rather than the wickedness of Catholics in particular. On the other hand, to puritan preachers such as Samuel Ward the anniversary became the opportunity to remind his audience of the need to remain true to England's Protestant past and, by implication, to criticize the current ecclesiastical policy of the hierarchy. Thus, commemoration of the event itself became an occasion of conflict between puritans and their opponents, and this continued with the outbreak of war in the 1640s, when Parliament drew a parallel between the atrocities committed in Ireland and the actions of the plotters in order to demonstrate the fundamentally treasonable acts of Catholics, while royalists likened the rebellion of Parliament against the king to the plotters' attempt to assassinate his father.

See also: Antipopery, Providence
Further Reading
David Cressy, *Bonfires and Bells: National Memory and the Protestant Calendar in Elizabethan and Stuart England* (London, 1989); A. Walsham, *Providence in Early Modern England* (Oxford, 1999).

William Sheils

H

Half-Way Covenant

In colonial New England, the early colonists gradually adopted church membership criteria that required the applicant to demonstrate a knowledge of the faith, evidence of a life without serious blemish, and public testimony about the way the experience of God's grace had left a conviction that the person was of the elect. The congregation would then evaluate the candidate and vote to admit him or her. While all townsfolk were expected to attend services and hearken to the preached word of God, only those who passed these tests were admitted to membership. Only members could share in the Lord's Supper and present their children for baptism.

By the late 1640s the number of individuals presenting themselves for membership was diminishing. There is no evidence that the colonists were less committed to their faith, but some evidence that they were becoming more scrupulous. The type of born-again experience that would have been offered by early colonists as evidence of election was not sufficient to persuade this new generation that they were indeed saved, and lest they falsely lay claim to election they deferred joining the church and waited for greater assurance. But among the consequences of this scrupulosity was a growing number of townsfolk who were not members and thus not subject to the discipline of the congregation, and a growing number of unbaptized children.

The question this situation posed was whether the original membership standards had been set too high, or whether the declining membership was a sign of the decline of adequate piety among the new generation of colonists. A number of clergymen decided that the former was the case and began to investigate ways of expanding membership. Richard Mather of Dorchester proposed a new form of partial membership. Called the Half-Way Covenant, this new policy called for allowing the child of any baptized parent to be admitted to a limited membership, even if the parent had not been accepted into full church membership. This "half-way" membership brought the individual into a formal relationship with the church and thus under its discipline. It also conveyed to the individual the right to eventually have his or her own children baptized if, upon reaching maturity, he or she (the parent) demonstrated knowledge of the faith and agreed to swear to the church covenant. But it did not allow the "half-way" member to participate in the Lord's Supper, or, as eventually adopted in most churches, to exercise a vote in the church.

Mather's congregation adopted the innovation in 1655, and Thomas Cobbet's Ipswich congregation did so in the following year. But then, on the urging of neighbor churches, Dorchester reversed itself. Other congregations were confused, and so the Massachusetts General Court called a ministerial assembly to debate the issue. Meeting in 1657, the assembly consisted of representatives of thirteen Bay Colony churches and four from Connecticut. New Haven, whose John Davenport was opposed to the plan, did not participate. The assembly recommended the proposed change, but in a congregational system, this recommendation was advice that each individual congregation could accept or reject.

In 1661, the growing diversity in membership standards led the Massachusetts General Court to once again beseech the churches to address the issue. Over eighty lay and clerical delegates gathered at the synod of 1662, the most notable absentee again being John Davenport—though on this occasion his absence was likely explained by his preoccupation with preventing his colony from being incorporated into Connecticut. The synod overwhelming endorsed the Half-Way Covenant, and the Massachusetts General Court added its recommendation. But because the decision was still in the hands of each individual congregation, the battle had only just begun.

Among the leading advocates of the innovation were prominent clergy of the founding generation such as Richard Mather, John Wilson, John Eliot, and Thomas Cobbet. Arrayed with Davenport against the proposal were a number of younger clergy, including Mather's own sons Increase and Eleazer. Because of these divisions, the ensuing debate helped to erode clerical authority, as some clergy wrote and preached urging laypeople to oppose their ministers of they supported the wrong side. Eventually, the supporters of the change won out. But in the process of the debate, other, more radical proposals began to emerge. Some called for the adoption of a parish-style system, in which all town residents could present themselves or their children for baptism. Some threw up their hands and adopted the Baptist position of rejecting all infant baptism.

See also: Congregationalism
Further Reading
Robert Pope, *The Half-Way Covenant: Church Membership in Puritan New England* (Princeton, 1969).

Francis J. Bremer

Hampton Court Conference

A conference to discuss religion called early in his reign by James I (James VI of Scotland). While James was traveling south in 1603, having inherited the throne of England, he was presented with the millenary petition, setting out puritan complaints against the ceremonies, abuses, and practices in the church. James promised a conference, and after a short delay caused by an outbreak of the plague it was called in January 1604. Puritan representatives were to be there, but they were more likely to have been selected by the Privy Council than by the puritans themselves. This decision ensured not only that they were learned and respected clergymen but also that they were chosen rather from the moderates than from the radicals. In addition, the primary records are the official accounts, written and published by the bishops, so they have to be carefully weighed. James was willing to talk, but the conference was also an opportunity for him to make plain what he was willing to do and where the limits lay.

The first day dealt with the Book of Common Prayer, and some issues were clarified, such as absolution and confirmation, so that any popish reading of the ceremonies would be made much more difficult. Private baptism was still allowed, although its performance was to be limited to ministers and curates, excluding midwives. Excommunication was to be limited to serious offenses, not imposed for "trifles" that were felt to devalue the sentence. The second day opened with consensus on good doctrine and worthy ministers. The third issue is the most famous: the issue of church government. When John Reynolds, the puritan representative, mentioned "the bishop, with his presbytery," James seems to have taken the opportunity to deliberately misunderstand him and give a lengthy response, which plainly ruled Presbyterianism out of court, regardless of the fact that Reynolds was not proposing Presbyterianism as a form of government. It seems to have been too good a chance to pass up for James to make it plain that he was willing to clean up aspects of the church but not to change anything structurally.

The rest of the day produced little regarding reform of the ceremonies, but it did produce what became the most lasting legacy of the conference. James agreed that existing translations of the Bible were inadequate. The conference established the project of providing a new translation, much of which was to be based on the Geneva Bible, but without the pointed marginal comments, which James saw as far too partial and seditious. The translation was to be undertaken by the best, most learned scholars from both universities, and the Authorized Version, popularly known as the King James Bible, owes a great deal to puritan scholarship.

The purpose of the final day was to determine the implementation of the resolutions. James discussed the matter with the bishops and councillors, dividing the work into committees, some to draft the necessary statutory changes. These steps were reported to the puritan representatives. For James the conference had been a success, in that it had built the image of him as a reasonable man, willing to discuss these issues and to make reasonable compromises and it had shown the complaints to be relatively little cause for concern. For the excluded radicals it was seen as less of a success, as there were many matters of ceremony that were not changed or even discussed. As far as James was concerned, the lack of discussion on these matters was fine, in that it made such reformers look demanding and beyond the pale in terms of negotiation.

See also: Geneva Bible
Further Reading
P. Collinson, "The Jacobean Religious Settlement: The Hampton Court Conference," in H. Tomlinson, ed., *Before the English Civil War: Essays in Early Stuart Politics and Government* (London, 1983); F. Shriver, "Hampton Court Revisited: James I and the Puritans," *Journal of Ecclesiastical History* 33 (1982), 48–71.

Tom Webster

Happy Union

An agreement reached between the Presbyterians and Congregationalists (hitherto known as the Independents) in the early 1690s. A paper of agreement was approved in a general meeting of London Presbyterian and Congregational ministers at Stepney on 6 March 1691, when Matthew Mead fa-

mously preached on "two sticks made one" (taking as his text Ezekiel 37:19, where that metaphor was used). Subscribed by between 80 and 100 ministers, this paper was read to congregations on 15 March, and published with some alterations in April as the *Heads of Agreement assented to by the United Ministers in and about London: formerly called Presbyterian and Congregational.* It laid the basis for close cooperation between the two denominations without trespassing on congregational independence. It was explicitly designed to preserve order in congregations, not to provide a national constitution. Scripture was to be the rule of faith, but congregations could follow the Savoy or Westminster Assembly confessions or even the doctrinal parts of the Thirty-nine Articles. Communion between the congregations was allowed where it was possible. The union was rapidly adopted by assemblies of clergy in Cheshire, Somerset, Devon, Dorset, and Gloucestershire, and subsequently in Lancashire and Yorkshire, and it is believed in various other counties of the North, the Midlands and East Anglia.

The Happy Union was the culmination of earlier attempts at union between the two churches. Some see precedents in the Worcestershire Association sponsored by Richard Baxter in 1652 or even in the "Antrim Meeting" in Ulster in the 1620s. The Pinners' Hall Lecture established in 1672 had provided a forum for cooperation between the denominations. By 1680 London Dissenters had produced a proposal for union, which was discussed and revised by ministers in Bristol, the West Country, and the capital. Although what subsequently became of these proposals is unclear, by 1690 they were once again under consideration. For by then it was apparent that the "comprehension" of some Presbyterian clergy within a revised Church of England was a lost cause, and that, in the new circumstances created by the Toleration Act of 1689, the Presbyterians and Congregationalists needed to sink their differences and organize themselves. In the provinces, some ministers were already leading the way. In June 1690, after six months of discussion, the clergy of Gloucestershire, Somerset, and Wiltshire had agreed to an "accommodation" based on the 1680 agreement. In London in July 1690, Presbyterians and Congregationalists established the "Common Fund," a national fund managed by lay and clerical representatives of both denominations to provide financial aid to ministers, churches, and students for the ministry, and to centralize charitable donations. The Happy Union was the next and welcome step: although for some Presbyterians, it represented the final abandonment of hopes of reunion with the national church, and for others, especially Congregationalists, it seemed to fudge some of the differences of principle between the denominations.

In London, the Union was short-lived. The Congregationalists were troubled by attempts to control the heterodox minister Richard Davis of Northamptonshire. Davis had offended against the spirit of the Union by sending out preachers to poach followers from existing congregations. Moreover he was alleged to teach antinomianism, an accusation that reflected a growing difference of theological tone between the Presbyterians, who taught that assurance of salvation depended on "the divine truth of the promise of salvation," and the more emotive Congregationalists, who relied on "the blood and righteousness of Christ." Davis, who received support from the Common Fund, refused to cooperate with its inquiry, and when Daniel Williams, a Presbyterian acolyte of Richard Baxter, attacked Davis in print, Isaac Chauncy and five other Congregational ministers seceded from the Union (October 1692). In November 1694 the Presbyterian clergy left the Pinners' Hall lecture and set up the rival Salters' Hall lecture. The following autumn, the Congregational ministers withdrew from the Common Fund and set up a separate fund. The Union in London was at an end and was succeeded by a loose coalition, the General Body of Protestant Dissenting Ministers, which concentrated on the civil rights of Dissenters. Yet unions were, of necessity, local institutions and evolved in different ways: in parts of eighteenth-century England, Presbyterian and Congregational meetings did worship together or share chapels; and some unions, such as those in Devon and Lancashire, survived into the nineteenth century.

See also: Comprehension, Congregationalism, Dissenters
Further Reading
C. G. Bolam, J. Goring, H. L. Short, and T. Thomas, eds., The English Presbyterians (London, 1968); Alexander Gordon, Freedom after Ejection (Manchester, Eng., 1917); Michael Watts, The Dissenters from the Reformation to the French Revolution (Oxford, 1978).

John Spurr

Harvard College

"After God had carried us safe to *New England*, and we had builded our houses, provided necessaries for our livli-hood, rear'd convenient places for Gods worship, and settled the Civill Government: One of the next things we longed for, and looked after was to advance *Learning . . ..*" states the first Harvard commencement program, *New Englands First Fruits* (1643). Shortly after settling in Massachusetts, the Puritans sought to create a university, largely to train ministers. Initial plans were disrupted by the antinomian controversy, but in November 1637, a college was ordered "to be at Newetowne," the original name of Cambridge. By the summer of 1638, Nathaniel Eaton was named professor, and the first class of nine students began attending. Receiving the bequest—half of the estate (approximately £1,700) and the library—of a Charlestown settler who died in September 1638, the college was named for the donor, John Harvard.

Harvard College's first decades were fraught with difficulty. Eaton proved to be a tyrant, going so far as to beat students. Students also complained about Mrs. Eaton's poor hospitality, including serving spoiled food. Tried by the General Court, Eaton was removed, and in its second year, Harvard College was closed.

Henry Dunster was chosen president. He instituted several changes, which enabled the college to meet with greater success. During his administration (1640–1654), he built a library of over one thousand volumes, oversaw the construction of three buildings and obtained a charter. He, too, was forced to resign as a result of controversies surrounding his decision to change the curriculum from three to four years, financial questions, and ultimately, his unpopular stance against infant baptism. Other presidents followed (though many men turned down the position), with varying degrees of success. The final seventeenth-century president, Increase Mather, was forced from office after sixteen years, for he refused to live in Cambridge.

Despite such problems of governance, education proceeded. The president was assisted in teaching by several tutors. The curriculum consisted of logic, physics, metaphysics, Greek grammar, Hebrew grammar, rhetoric, ethics and politics, and divinity. It was assumed that students would come in with knowledge of Latin, an understanding of Cicero, and an elementary knowledge of Greek grammar. Although the college was ostensibly begun to train the clergy, just over half entered the ministry, with the remainder becoming teachers, doctors, lawyers, businessmen, and farmers. As originally intended, Harvard did not limit its student body to Puritans, nor to boys from New England. In the seventeenth century, a few young scholars came from Virginia, Great Britain, Bermuda, and New Netherland. An impressive library was built. The volumes were mostly theological, and included works by Luther, Calvin, Aquinas, and Augustine; the library also included ancient classics and some English poetry.

Harvard College was a great source of pride to Massachusetts. That it should remain so, the colony's government took steps to ensure its smooth governance and financial success. A Board of Overseers was chosen. The General Court gave the college the Boston-Charlestown ferry rents, a financial agreement that provided the most important source of funding from the colony. In 1641, every family was asked to contribute a quarter bushel of corn for the college's maintenance. Harvard College also received private donations.

Further Reading
Lawrence A. Cremin, *American Education: The Colonial Experience, 1607–1783* (New York, 1973); Samuel Eliot Morison, *The Founding of Harvard College* (Cambridge, MA, 1935).

Rachelle E. Friedman

Holidays and Holy Days

In pre-Reformation Europe, the annual calendar was filled with days commemorating particular saints, as well as with holy days marking the major events in the life and mission of Christ. Protestant reformers were critical of the pagan elements they saw underlying many of these celebrations and also attacked them as providing occasions for idleness, drinking, and other sins.

In England Henry VIII reduced the number of holy days, but kept some such as Easter, the Nativity, and the feasts of the Apostles as high holy days (with no work allowed), and relegated others to a lesser status. During the reign of Edward VI, some of those eliminated were restored, so that in all there were twenty-seven holy days in addition to the fifty-two Sundays of the year that were ordered to be kept holy by prayer, worship, and abstention from all work. The Book of Common Prayer printed the holy days in red letters and stipulated that days sacred to saints and angels (such as St. George and the Archangel Michael) were kept to honor the saints, rather than as occasions to seek their favor.

Many reformers, including Scottish Presbyterians and English puritans, felt that these English reforms did not go far enough. They sought to abolish all holy days, including Christmas, and to leave only the weekly Sabbath as a day set aside to abandon work for prayer and worship. This complete abrogation of saints days and holy days was instituted in the New England colonies.

See also: Christmas
Further Reading
David Cressy, *Bonfires and Bells: National Memory and the Protestant Calendar in Elizabethan and Stuart England* (London, 1989).

Francis J. Bremer

Hourglasses in the Church

The hourglass, the symbol of fleeting life and of the infinite, was a common accessory for pulpits between the late fifteenth and the nineteenth centuries. An hourglass was made of two joined matching bulbs of clear glass, set into a frame, and partially filled with tinted sand. When inverted, it provided onlookers with a rough indication of time's passage, as the sand strained slowly from one bulb to the other. Large hourglasses were placed on the railings of pulpits, or upon nearby pillars, in easy reach of the preacher or his assistant, as at Paul's Cross (England's premier preaching place, in the churchyard of London's great Gothic cathedral). The Bishops' Bible of 1569 portrayed an hourglass at the very elbow of Archbishop Matthew Parker as he gestured to his hearers. Few pulpits could have been better outfitted than the imposing example at Kedington in Suffolk (the seat of the Bernardiston family), which bristles with elaborate features: its high sounding-board, a stand for the preacher's wig, and its hourglass. Miniature hourglasses for personal use or travel were also known (Martin Luther carried one in a small case). Before the standardization of materials and means, the "hour" of an hourglass was only an approximation of sixty minutes, and usually measured a shorter span than a full hour. Until pendulum clocks and pocket watches became more available, hourglasses were the chief public timekeepers in their association with the sermon, and they symbolized new expectations concerning its length.

The turning of the hourglass became one of the small ceremonies associated with preaching. The preacher (or his associate, who carried his books to the pulpit for him) turned the glass to start the running of the sand at the beginning of the sermon, and again at least once in the midst of the flow of eloquence. Longer sermons were a concomitant of the new importance that had been invested in preaching, encouraged by Erasmus and other Humanists, then by the Protestant reformers from the sixteenth century onward. While poor preachers were dreaded, as their sermons (with the crawling sand) seemed to stretch into an eternity, fine speakers were begged to turn the glass again and again.

Never as exact as a clock, the hourglass suggested the infinite, through the inexorable passage of time. An hourglass increased the sense of awe that was associated with the pulpit as the august meeting place of humanity with the divine, and the sermon as the word of God. As it sifted its hour, the glass paradoxically came to represent a species of sacred timelessness, of time-without-time, as the sermon was meant to be a moment of eternity, when the faithful were absorbed in listening to God's own voice, spoken through the preacher. Thus hourglasses became the symbol also of life and the soul, death and salvation, meanings that were conveyed by their carved representations on the evocative slate tombstones of the Old Granary Burying Ground in Boston and elsewhere in early eighteenth-century New England.

See also: Preaching

Further Reading

J. Charles Cox, *Pulpits, Lecterns, and Organs in English Churches* (London, 1915); Susan Wabuda, "Triple Deckers and Eagle Lecterns: Church Furniture for the Book in Late Medieval and Early Modern England," in R. N. Swanson, ed., *The Church and the Book*, Studies in Church History, vol. 38 (Woodbridge, Eng., 2004), pp. 143–152.

Susan Wabuda

Household Seminaries

An ad hoc institution that developed out of the suppression of the prophesying movement of the 1570s. Once this semiofficial means of training younger, less experienced ministers was gone, it was felt that this responsibility should be met within the households of gifted ministers. Fresh graduates were taken into residence, and spiritual and practical experience was added to "mere" academic training. What might have seemed almost indulgent in an Elizabethan context was almost requisite by the second decade of the seventeenth century, although it is noteworthy that such seminaries were more common in the south than in the north of England, where there were fewer godly ministers.

The ministers who provided the crucial charismatic leadership for such seminaries almost reads as a roll call of the most famous preachers, including such figures as John Dod, Arthur Hildersham, John Cotton, Thomas Hooker, and William Whately. An account of Whately's seminary gives details of such regimes. The day began with prayer and a passage of scripture, which was to be the set topic of conversation at the communal meal. As well as attending the seminary and delivering and discussing sermons, students learned their trade with pastoral, catechetical, and disciplinary duties within the town. We cannot know how many ministers attended such seminaries, but on an individual level they were clearly influential. Such a context could prove a critical environment for spiritual and vocational growth, as well as a further induction into the formative lifestyle of the painful (in the sense of "diligent") ministry.

See also: Richard Blackerby, Prophesyings
Further Reading
Francis J. Bremer, *Congregational Communion: Clerical Friendship in the Anglo-American Puritan Community, 1610–1692* (Boston, 1994); Tom Webster, *Godly Clergy in Early Stuart England: The Caroline Puritan Movement, c. 1620–1643* (Cambridge, Eng., 1997).

Tom Webster

Human Nature

The basic structures that were believed to form the human person, whether as created by God, fallen into sin, or in a state of grace. Puritans generally thought about human nature in ways derived from Greek philosophy (especially Aristotle), as preserved and developed in patristic and medieval theology, and continued by Renaissance Christian Humanists and Protestant theologians. Important to all of these thinkers were the human as combining body and soul, the soul as divided into various faculties, and the control of the passions by reason.

Puritans praised the excellence of humanity as God's creation, and following Calvin, thought it stood midway in the chain of being as a microcosm of the whole creation. Thus the human included an inanimate body made out of the elements (especially earth), a vegetative soul with the power of growth, a locomotive soul with the power of motion like the soul of a star, a sensitive soul like the soul of an animal, and a rational soul like the soul of an angel. Sharing all but the rational soul with animals, humans were properly characterized as animals.

The sensitive soul, which perceived through the five senses, was itself subdivided into several faculties: imagination, forming images from sensory experience; cogitation, drawing conclusions about images; memory, storing up images and cogitations; and affections, desiring or fearing what the images, cogitations, and memory presented.

The rational soul, on the other hand, distinguished the human from animals. It was divided into intellect (or understanding) and will (or rational appetite), and was the aspect of humanity that was created in the image of God (even after the fall, an impaired image remained). The rational soul was immortal; however, humans were mortal because they conjoined body and soul (including the rational soul), and death dissolved that relationship. The rational soul was "spirit," like the angels and God, though some Puritans spoke as though the affections were also spirit, and part of the rational soul. The animal and vital spirits quickened the body and held body and soul together. There was some disagreement as to exactly how spirit fit into the duality of body and soul, and some identified spirit with the intellect and soul with will, considering humans to be tripartite, body, soul, and spirit. The rational soul was thought by Calvinists to be an immediate creation of God at each person's beginning, and not derived from the parents (a view of the Lutherans that they considered an error). Because they possessed a rational soul, human beings were moral agents, with the faculties of knowing and choosing corresponding to intellect and will. The intellect determined the good as that which would lead to happiness, and then the will chose it, naturally choosing what was taken to be the good by the intellect. The will's choice was then executed by the affections, which subserved the will. In this choosing, the will acts freely, even though that which it freely elects will be quite different, depending on whether the person is in a state of sin or grace. God was regarded as ordinarily working through the structures of human nature by the means of secondary causes, thus not violating the order of things established at Creation.

This basic scheme of human nature was modified in the course of the sixteenth and seventeenth centuries. A revived Augustinianism emphasized the heart as distinct from reason (the will was often identified with the heart and the intellect with the brain) and the affections as an aspect of the heart. This way of thinking seems clearly to be behind the "affectionate" divinity of many Puritan preachers and writers, with Richard Sibbes maintaining that God designed the heart to be central to humanity. The bodily senses also came to be more highly regarded, perhaps in the case of hearing because of the great weight given to the hearing of the preached word in the Protestant world.

A standard Puritan treatise dealing with human nature was Edward Reynolds's *A Treatise of the Passions and Faculties of the Soul of Man* (1640). Samuel Willard gave extensive treatment to the subject in *A Compleat Body of Divinity*, published posthumously in 1726. Charles Morton's *The Spirit of Man* (1692) discussed the relationship of spirit and soul and, integrating a modified humoral theory with the structures of soul and body, probed the impact of different human temperaments upon Christian piety.

See also: Sin, Soteriology

Further Reading

William Bouwsma, *The Waning of the Renaissance, 1550–1640* (New Haven, 2000); Charles Lloyd Cohen, *God's Caress: The Psychology of Puritan Religious Experience* (New York, 1986); Mark E. Dever, *Richard Sibbes* (Macon, GA, 2000); Ernest Benson Lowrie, *The Shape of the Puritan Mind: The Thought of Samuel Willard* (New Haven, 1974).

Dewey D. Wallace Jr.

Iconoclasm and Iconography

In recent years the importance of Reformation iconoclasm has come to be fully recognized. Puritans undoubtedly became deeply involved in iconoclastic initiatives, but the campaign to reform church images started in England a generation before the arrival of the name *puritan* in the mid-1560s, and it cannot be assumed that all those stigmatized by that term were necessarily committed to this cause.

Continental centers of reform set examples of iconoclastic change that affected England during the reign of Henry VIII. In 1547–1548, England's parishes were given their first traumatic experience of physical change when orders were given for the removal of imagery of all kinds from their churches. This involved the disappearance of roods, carvings of saints, reredoses, and altarpieces. The regime of Protector Somerset during the reign of Edward VI endorsed the most extreme form of church purification, and men like John Hooper and William Turner, who had personal experience of Zürich in the 1540s, could understand the meaning of Archbishop Thomas Cranmer's claim in 1548 that Englishmen had no images in their churches. This statement long remained an idealistic claim rather than an accurate description, but it set an aspirational benchmark that prompted action, both official and illicit, through the following century. Puritans tried to spur the church to live up to its own image-denying character.

Calvin's pronouncements carried great weight for Elizabethan iconomachs. By 1559 successive editions of Calvin's Institutes presented a fully argued case against the supreme danger of idolatry and the peril of having imagery of any kind in churches. The only true images were the living symbols of the two sacraments of baptism and the Lord's Supper. This teaching, transmitted to English believers through catechetical instruction and the Homilies prepared to be read from the nation's pulpits, established the presumption of an image-free church, and the duty of church governors and churchgoers was to create and inhabit a whitewashed state of walls and minds. But it is important to remember that this prescription was for places of worship. There was no bar (witness the theologian William Perkins) on scriptural histories in private places, and religious imagery painted on cloth or wall or in printed form remained visible in gentry residence, farmhouse, inn, and cottage. Sixteenth-century iconoclasts concentrated their efforts on the idolatry of places of worship.

Calvin also offered guidance on the kinds of image that were most reprehensible. Central here were images of the Trinity. The worst offense of all was to attempt any portrayal of God the Father. It was also quite contrary to divine law to suppose that the Holy Spirit could be delineated in the form of a dove. And Christ should be represented not by the erection of crosses but through preaching the gospel.

The case against traditional iconography of God as a bearded ancient started early in the Reformation, and in England, as elsewhere, there was much

Iconoclasts burn religious symbols during the Reformation period. (Bettman/Corbis)

destruction of such images. The heinous offense of portraying God in human form was accepted among all Reformed Protestants and gave rise to a new iconography, as the Tetragrammaton, the four Hebrew letters for God's name, was used to convey the presence of the invisible Godhead. In 1572 the *Admonition to Parliament* publicly objected to the blasphemous pictures of God the Father included in the 1568 Bishops' Bible. This book did indeed contain woodcuts showing God as the old man in the clouds, though in fact Archbishop Parker had made sure that several of the Continental woodblocks used for this Bible replaced the Creator by the Tetragrammaton. His critics found that the task had not been completed. This incident is a representative example of how the more rigid purifiers pressurized the church authorities. The Bishops' Bible was itself exceptional among English Bibles of the period in the fullness of its illustrations. That did not last. Illustrative matter was purged from the pages of printed Bibles, starting with the departure of portraits of leading courtiers, and continuing with the removal of the royal head of the church from the title page and of any pictorial matter in the scriptural text.

The imagery still to be seen in church windows long remained provocative. The bishops of Winchester and St. David's were unusually zealous in taking steps, the first to purge the glass of the cathedral church of Trinity of its images and the other to purge the whole diocese of the crucifixions in parish chancels. Elsewhere Puritan activists such as John Bruen and Henry Sherfield pressed on with destruction that the authorities had failed to accomplish. Such initiatives, however, even against notoriously forbidden images, incurred legal penalties, as Sherfield discovered to his cost. Unauthorized iconoclasts might end up in Star Chamber. The authority to proceed against proscribed images belonged to the church, and to break down a window without ecclesiastical sanction was, until 1641, to court prosecution.

Controversy over images of Christ came to the forefront at the very time when the phenomenon of puritanism was recognized. Between the 1560s and 1643, when, after years of contention, Cheapside Cross was finally pulled down, the presence of crosses everywhere was called in question, bare cross as well as crucifix, and not only in places of worship but also in public places and by roadsides, in the form of monumental crosses. Even the gestured sign of the cross and the uttered name of Jesus were construed as idols.

It was under the aegis of the most extreme reformers that this process culminated. The iconoclasm sanctioned in the 1640s reached new levels: for the first time it was Parliament, not the church or the monarch, supreme head of the church, who took command. Specific imagery was proscribed at large (all persons of the Trinity, crosses and crucifixes, the Virgin, saints and angels), and in 1644 the destruction was not limited to places of worship but extended to any open place throughout the kingdom. The most zealous of puritan iconoclasts had no hesitation about taking their mission into private houses, where hitherto religious art had been relatively free from intrusive destroyers. If a revival of militant puritanism is discernible by 1640, its genesis owed much to the provocation of church imagery—old and new.

See also: William Dowsing, Henry Sherfield, Idolatry
Further Reading
Margaret Aston, "Iconoclasm in England: Official and Clandestine" (1989), in Peter Marshall, ed., *The Impact of the English Reformation, 1500–1640* (London, 1997); Margaret Aston, "Puritans and Iconoclasm," in Christopher Durston and Jacqueline Eales, eds., *The Culture of English Puritanism, 1560–1700* (Basingstoke, Eng., 1996); Patrick Collinson, "From Iconoclasm to Iconophobia: the Cultural Impact of the Second English Reformation" in Peter Marshall, ed., *The Impact of the English Reformation, 1500–1640* (1997).

Margaret Aston

Idolatry

Idolatry, the transgression of the second commandment, was very much a Reformation sin. It was central to the scriptural moral code of the English church and the puritans.

The placing of idolatry at the forefront of divine transgressions rested in part on better understanding of the Old Testament that came with improved Hebrew learning. In the medieval Western church the image prohibition was included in the first commandment. Expositions of the sins against this precept might include idolatry, but the service of alien gods was more likely to be interpreted in terms of worldly desires than false worship of the multiplying images sanctioned by the church. A critical change took place on the Continent in the 1520s and 1530s, which resulted in the clauses against graven images being made into a separate second commandment throughout the reformed churches. In England the image prohibition was an unavoidable fact of religious life after 1547.

Earnestly inculcating the perils of this leading sin, Protestants claimed that the Church of Rome was guilty of deliberate obfuscation by screening out the commandment against idolatry. They also went out of their way to attack the ecclesiastical theory that there was an equivalence between learning from words and learning from images. Their own impassioned teaching of the evils of this sin and the threat to pure worship posed by images is evident in the large volume of contemporary catechetical literature. The second commandment was given its full due in a wide range of catechisms, from Thomas Cranmer's and Alexander Nowell's to those of John Dod and Robert Cleaver, of the Westminster Assembly and beyond. The long tripartite "Homily against Peril of Idolatry," which first appeared in 1563, became for some a critical touchstone of the Church of England's probity. The greater the commitment of the purifier, the greater the fidelity to this Old Testament proscription. But although forward hotheads were certainly most zealous in expounding the sin of idolatry, there was a wide consensus on the importance of this issue.

The battle to eliminate idolatry was part of the Elizabethan settlement and not peculiar to puritans. But in the early seventeenth century, new defenders of religious images argued that churchgoers had outgrown the peril of idolatry and that the homily was no longer applicable, having been composed for the dangers of different times. This was highly contentious. Abhorrence of idolatry, the subject of so much teaching and learning, was too deeply embedded in godly hearts to allow any diminution of the dangers posed by religious imagery. Idolatry—still papal idolatry but now more insidious—poisoned the air in the 1640s as it had in the 1540s.

See also: Iconoclasm and Iconography
Further Reading
Margaret Aston, *England's Iconoclasts: Laws against Images* (Oxford, 1988); Ian Green, *The Christian's ABC: Catechisms and Catechizing in England, c. 1530–1740* (Oxford, 1996).

Margaret Aston

Illegitimacy

Illegitimacy was condemned by all religious groups in the early modern period, but a campaign against this product of sexual incontinency has been particularly associated with Puritanism. Illegitimacy was only one element of a wider picture of sexual misdemeanor that included rape, sodomy, incest, and bestiality, but it was the most obvious manifestation of the phenomenon and the easiest to prove and punish. As a result, Puritan polemic and action was particularly powerful in this area and for obvious reasons has been seen as directed largely at the women, who were the identifiable transgressors. This arc of Puritan thinking reached its apogee during the Interregnum (1649–1660), with the passing of the Massachusetts Code in 1648 in America and in England the notorious so-called Adultery Act of 1650. These both made adultery (and other sexual crimes) capital offenses. The English law made fornication a capital offense on the second occasion, while in Massachusetts it was punishable by public humiliation or whipping. However, these laws have been seen as evidence of the failure to enforce Puritan values through legal structures as opposed to simply church procedures.

Although there was considerable concern about the problem of illegitimacy in early modern England, records demonstrate that extramarital births were historically low, remaining below 3 percent for every decade between the 1540s and 1750, except for the demographic crisis years of the 1590s. This compares with a rate twice that in the nineteenth century. The level of anxiety can be seen in the very fact that ministers kept such records in parish registers, to which we largely owe these figures. This anxiety was partly the product of financial concerns, since the Tudor Poor Law made the bastards of the poor chargeable to the parish where they were born. It is also true to say that producing illegitimate children was not activity that was approved or condoned by any religious group. There is some evidence, however, that ministers with Puritan leanings were particularly concerned with the problem of bastardy. Remarkably, English civil law in the sixteenth and early seventeenth centuries prescribed no punishment for bearing an illegitimate child as such, though under an act of 1610 (7 James, cap 4) a woman who bore a bastard chargeable on the parish was to be sent to the house of correction. The only punishments were the penance that could be prescribed by the church courts, which were generally resented by those with Puritan leanings. As a result, there were frequent attempts in the early seventeenth century, often seen as spearheaded by the Puritan movement in Parliament, to pass harsher civil punishments for sexual incontinence, all of which failed until the Interregnum. Therefore the concern with illegitimacy among Puritans can be seen as part of a wider desire to decrease the power of the church over such matters as marriage (reflected in attempts to make it a civil ceremony) and to protect the institution of marriage more strictly.

These aims were fulfilled in the Massachusetts Code of 1648, and under the English Commonwealth in 1650 with the passing of the Adultery Act, both of which made various forms of sexual incontinence and particularly adultery capital offenses. Court records indicate that both sets of laws resulted in almost no successful prosecutions. In England there was a virtual disappearance of illegitimacy from the historical record (the so-called nadir of English illegitimacy) and only a handful of prosecutions for what was considered to be a widespread crime. These laws were directed at offenders of both sexes, but given the difficulty of proving male adultery and the ease of proving that a woman was carrying an illegitimate child, it was on unmarried mothers that the strictures fell. It is generally thought that harshness of punishment on a number of women who could be seen as victims meant that there was a marked reluctance to report this new crime. Given the large proportion of clergy who had Puritan sympathies in this period, this reluctance must have included considerable willful disregard for the law, even among the committed. However, the fall in the records of English illegitimacy was marked before the 1650s, and this trend has led some historians to suggest that the advent of Puritan elites in local communities before and during the Civil Wars may have had a real effect in suppressing illegitimacy, although others point to demographic and economic changes in this period.

It is also important to note that the ferocity of Puritan treatment of illegitimacy was part of a wider picture: marriage was held in particularly high regard, and the sexual double standard was consistently attacked. The Puritan position on the married state as a positive good can be seen in countless conduct manuals, though more conservative commentators seem to have retained a view, as Richard Hooker put it, of the single state as "a thing more angelical and divine." In contrast William Gouge, the most successful of all Puritan writers of conduct books, saw the family as "a little Church, and a little Commonwealth, at least a lively representation thereof, whereby trial may be made of such as are fit for any place of authority, or of subjection in Church or Commonwealth." as a result his final conclusion on comparing adultery by husbands and wives was that, "If difference be made, it is meet that adulterous husbands be so much the more severely punished, by how much the more it appertaineth to them to excel in virtue, and to govern their wives by example."

See also: Domestic Relations, Marriage, Reformation of Manners, Sexuality
Further Reading
Bernard Capp, "The Double Standard Revisited: Plebeian Women and Male Sexual Reputation in Early Modern England," Past and Present, 162 (1999), 70–100; Peter Laslett, Household and Family in Past Time (Cambridge, Eng., 1972); Peter Laslett, Karla Oosterveen, and Richard M. Smith, eds., Bastardy and Its Comparative History: Studies in the History of Illegitimacy and Marital Nonconformism in Britain, France,

Germany, Sweden, North America, Jamaica and Japan (London, 1980); Eric Monkkonen, Crime and Justice in American History: The Colonies and Early Republic, 2 vols. (Westport, CT, 1991); Keith Thomas, "The Puritans and Adultery: The Act of 1650 Reconsidered," in D. Pennington and K. Thomas, eds., Puritans and Revolutionaries, Essays in Seventeenth-Century History Presented to Christopher Hill (Oxford, 1978).

Will Coster

Incarnation

The term used to refer to the doctrine that Jesus Christ was God himself, or, to be more specific, the second person of the triune God, that is, the Son of God, born in human flesh (incarnate) of Mary. As formulated in the early days of the Christian church, the doctrine claimed that this incarnation had taken place through the power of the Holy Spirit. This belief was formalized by decisions made in the fourth and fifth centuries at the church councils held at Nicaea (325) and Chalcedon (451). As expressed in the Nicene Creed, which became an important part of the liturgy of many Christian churches, the doctrine affirmed a single God with three persons, and the dual divinity and humanity of Christ. Most Puritans accepted this orthodox doctrine.

See also: Christology, God, Soteriology
Further Reading
Diarmaid MacCulloch, Reformation: Europe's House Divided, 1490–1700 (London, 2003).

Francis J. Bremer

Independency

A term popularized in the 1640s to denote the opponents of Presbyterianism. Independents maintained that authentic New Testament churches were self-governing congregations of "visible saints" not subject to the authority of synods or higher assemblies. Bound together by this ecclesiology and by their fear of a Presbyterian settlement, Congregationalists, Separatists, and Baptists formed a powerful coalition in defense of Independency, though their temporary alliance against a common enemy masked profound differences.

The first use of the term *Independent* can be traced back to the pamphlets of Henry Burton in 1641, which spoke of "Independent congregations," "Independent churches," and "the church-way of Independency." Burton's neologisms quickly took hold, although contemporary usage was somewhat varied. At times, Independency referred only to mainstream Congregationalists who maintained fellowship with parish churches, while at other times the term covered Separatists and Baptists as well. Despite their disagreements over the status of the Church of England, Separatists and Congregationalists shared common ecclesiological ideals. They agreed that the membership of their "gathered" churches should be limited to the truly godly, those who were "visible saints," and they denied that higher assemblies or synods had authority over self-governing congregations. However, both the New England Congregationalists and the Dissenting Brethren in the Westminster Assembly rejected the "Independent" label, with its connotations of stubborn isolation and hostility to authority. They much preferred to call themselves followers of "the Congregationall way." Certainly the term was used pejoratively by Presbyterians like William Prynne and Thomas Edwards, but radical puritans like Burton and John Goodwin proudly adopted it.

Origins

The origins of Independency lie in Elizabethan and early Stuart England, where various radical puritans established independent congregations of the godly outside the parish system. Separatists and Baptists denounced the Church of England as a false church and refused to attend parish worship. Other puritans were far more reluctant to separate from the Church of England, but in the early years of the seventeenth century they began to develop a non-separating Congregationalism. The key theorists of this movement were Henry Jacob, Robert Parker, Paul Baynes, William Ames, and William Bradshaw, who argued that covenanted congregations could maintain communion with parish churches. Their middle way between Separatists and mainstream Church of England puritans has been variously described as "semi-Separatist" or "non-separating Congregationalist." By 1640, Separatists, Baptists, and Congregationalists had established underground churches in London and southern England, were meeting openly in the Netherlands, and had planted five distinct colonies in New England (Massachusetts, Connecticut, New Haven, Plymouth, and Rhode Island). Despite their deep differences over the status of the established church, baptism, and even predestination, these various congregational movements were now poised to participate in the campaign for "further reformation" of English Christianity.

The 1640s

With the establishment of the Long Parliament in November 1640, a number of congregational leaders returned from exile in the Netherlands and New England, and although there were attacks on Separatist congregations in 1641, the "godly" were on the offensive. Some puritans advocated reduced or primitive episcopacy (as they perceived it was in the early church), but many called for root-and-branch reform of the church, and most came to support the abolition of bishops. The problem was what to put in their place. Gradually, two broad alternatives emerged, though both disguised considerable internal complexities. The first was the Presbyterianism exemplified by the Scottish Kirk and other European Reformed churches, which gave considerable authority to national synods. The second was the "Independency" associated with New England. Throughout the 1640s, "Independency" was to be defined in opposition to "Presbyterianism."

When the Long Parliament established the Westminster Assembly of Divines in 1643 to settle the issue of church government, it was not long before the assembly witnessed a clash of ecclesiologies. The majority of the divines inclined toward a Presbyterian system, though they were often wary of *jure divino* claims (literally, claims that such a system was mandated "by divine law," that is, by the Bible) and were noticeably more Erastian than the Scottish Covenanters. A minority within the assembly, however, known as the Dissenting Brethren, vigorously defended the independence of the covenanted congregation from higher ecclesiastical authority. Although they conceded the value of synods, they insisted that these bodies should have no compulsive power over congregations. In January 1644, five of the Westminster Independents—William Bridge, Jeremiah Burroughes, Thomas Goodwin, Philip Nye, and Sidrach Simpson—issued *An Apologeticall Narration,* in which they proposed "a middle way" between "Brownism" (separatism) and "the authoritative Presbyterial government." They pleaded for toleration for their congregations, but were careful to denounce separatism and recognize the Church of England as a true church.

Outside the assembly, Independency was growing apace. By 1646, there were at least a dozen Congregationalist gathered churches in London, pastored by eminent figures such as Henry Jessey, Thomas Goodwin, John Goodwin, Sidrach Simpson, Henry Burton, and William Greenhill. In addition, it seems that the General Baptists had five congregations in the capital, the Particular Baptists seven, and the Separatists eight or nine. Members of these churches were active in London politics, and by 1644, the various Independent movements were orchestrating a highly vocal campaign against Presbyterian uniformity. That year saw the publication of eloquent tolerationist tracts by pro-Independent pamphleteers, including John Goodwin, Henry Robinson, William Walwyn, and John Milton. The Westminster Independents refused to endorse a broad toleration, and they tried to distance themselves from heresy and sectarianism, but they were forced to make common cause with the sects against Presbyterianism.

So central did the Presbyterian-Independent controversy become during the 1640s, that historians have attempted to divide members of Parliament (MPs) into "political Presbyterians" and "political Independents." There were, of course, puritan politicians in both houses with a firm commitment to religious Presbyterianism or to religious Independency (e.g., Sir Henry Vane the younger, an Independent), but often there was no close correspondence between the political and religious views of MPs. Political Independents were MPs who favored a hard line against the king, worked closely with the army leadership, and supported toleration for Protestant minorities. Political Presbyterians were more conservative MPs who advocated a softer line toward Charles I, distrusted the army, championed the Scots alliance, and feared religious and social anarchy.

Ultimately, political and religious Independents were to be the victors, and the single most important factor in their triumph was the support of the army. Although only a minority of soldiers were members of gathered churches, that minority exercised a disproportionate influence and were fostered by leading commanders like Oliver Cromwell. By April 1644, the Covenanter Robert Baillie had identified Cromwell as "the great Independent," and Presbyterians were disturbed by his patronage of Congregationalists, Separatists, and Baptists. Although Presbyterians had the upper hand in Parliament, the City of London, and the Westminster Assembly, they risked losing everything because of the army. In 1645, following the creation of the New Model Army, Cromwell consolidated his reputation with a decisive victory over the royalists at the battle of Naseby. Although Parliament agreed to establish a Presbyterian settlement, its progress was delayed by Independent and Erastian politicians who feared a clericalist church along Scottish lines. Moves to set up Presbyterian organization in London and Lancashire began in the second half of 1646, but in the following year the army rose up in revolt over Parliament's attempts to disband it. When Charles I formed an alliance with the moderate wing of the Scottish Covenanters—the Engagers—in 1648, inaugurating the Second Civil War, it was the army that once again saved the Parliamentarian cause, and Presbyterianism was damaged by its association with royalism. In December 1648, Colonel Pride purged Parliament of political Presbyterians and left the way open for the Independents' revolution. The army had become convinced that Charles I was a "man of blood," responsible for plunging the nation into two terrible wars, and in January 1649, led by

Cromwell, the "Rump" Parliament put the king on trial and executed him for treason.

The Interregnum

The regicide was denounced by the Presbyterians, who understandably depicted it as an Independent coup. Some Independents, including Thomas Goodwin and Philip Nye, were uneasy about regicide and revolution, but by and large the Congregationalist, Separatist, and Baptist churches were distinguished by their enthusiasm for the new order. The Independent coalition had not simply forestalled a Presbyterian settlement; it had also toppled the king and the House of Lords. For the next decade, England was to be a puritan republic, but one dominated not by the majority puritan movement (the Presbyterians) but by the minority Independents. As Lord Protector from 1653, Cromwell guaranteed freedom of religion for the religious sects, and under him Congregationalist leaders like John Owen and Philip Nye became the most influential clergy in the land.

Yet the Independent coalition of the 1640s had disguised deep rifts over the national church, tithes, and toleration, and by the mid-1650s the coalition was disintegrating. Congregationalists were now more willing to attack the heterodoxy and radical tolerationism of their erstwhile sectarian allies, and they cemented their partnership with moderate Presbyterians. Cromwell himself polarized opinions, for while many Congregationalists and Baptists supported his Protectorate, Fifth Monarchists denounced him as a usurper standing in the way of Christ's millennial rule. Practically all Independents counseled Cromwell to refuse the crown in 1657, but even though he did refuse it, there was widespread disillusionment with the Lord Protector, and Cromwell was criticized by old allies like Sir Henry Vane. After his death, radical Independents argued vigorously for the resurrection of the "good old cause" of civil and religious liberty, but they were to be bitterly disappointed. With support from the Presbyterians, the Convention Parliament recalled the king, and in May 1660 Charles II returned to London. Independency as a political force was exhausted, and from this point on, "Independency" was an ecclesiastical label, largely synonymous with Congregationalism.

See also: Oliver Cromwell, John Owen, Congregationalism, Dissenting Brethren
Further Reading
Francis J. Bremer, *Congregational Communion: Clerical Friendship in the Anglo-American Puritan Community, 1610–1692* (Boston, 1994); Murray Tolmie, *The Triumph of the Saints: The Separate Churches of London, 1616–1649* (Cambridge, Eng., 1977); David Underdown, *Pride's Purge: Politics in the Puritan Revolution* (Oxford, 1971); Michael Watts, *The Dissenters*, vol. 1 (Oxford, 1978); George Yule, *The Independents in the English Civil War* (Cambridge, Eng., 1958).

John Coffey

Indian Bible

The Indian Bible, produced by John Eliot with the help of native interpreters, was intended as a vehicle for conversion of Massachusetts Indians to Christianity. Its production in 1663 was the result of over a decade of work on the translation itself and a culmination of several other efforts at printing materials to assist missionary work. When the Puritans settled New England in the 1630s, there was little missionary effort toward the native peoples. A few dedicated ministers and some educated colonists compiled glossaries of English words, and even set out Christian phrases in various Algonquian dialects. In 1643 Roger Williams published an annotated dictionary, *A Key to the Language*, and Abraham Pierson in New Haven published *Some Helps for the Indians* in 1649. Nevertheless, the scripture was unavailable in any Algonquian language in New England. The Society for the Propagation of the Gospel was formed in England in 1649 at the height of the Puritan revolution, and its members corresponded regularly with Eliot, a minister in Roxbury, Massachusetts. The society decided to finance the printing of a Bible in the Massachusetts language. Eliot studied for nearly a decade to prepare the translation of the whole text. He was tutored by Job Nesutan, a native convert to Christianity, and perhaps also assisted by John Sassamon, another "praying Indian," whose mysterious death in 1675 helped sparked King Philip's War.

Work on translating the scriptures into the Massachusetts language was incremental. Eliot began his teaching at the praying town of Natick with a simple catechism, published in 1654. With the help of Native American associates, Eliot produced a book of metrical psalms in the winter of 1652–1653, though it was not printed until 1658 or 1659. Eliot's translations of the Gospel of Matthew and the Book of Genesis were printed in 1655. These editions were probably only a sample run, to show how a completed work would look. English words below the Massachusetts text were removed in the final editions to save on publication costs. In 1660 the London Commissioners sent a professional printer, Marmaduke Johnson, who finished printing the Bible within his three-year contract. Abraham Pierson, a knowledgeable translator, probably reviewed the final proofs. Fifteen hundred copies of the first New Testament printed in New England were printed in September of 1661. It was followed by a thousand-copy run of the Old Testament between 1660 and 1663. Two years after the first New Testament appeared, the complete Eliot Indian Bible was printed by Samuel Green, assisted by Marmaduke Johnson, at Cambridge, Massachusetts. They were also aided by James Printer, a praying Indian who learned the trade and who subsequently worked on many of Eliot's tracts. The Bible contained a preface composed by Simon Bradstreet and Thomas Danforth, both of whom then served as commissioners of the United Colonies.

The translation of the Bible into a native language was a feat that earned Eliot praise among other linguists, such as Roger Williams and later James Hammond Trumbull. There were untranslatable terms and grammatical inventions. Eliot could not translate terms that had no Indian meanings, such as "book" or "horse," but he declined the nouns as any Indian noun would have been declined, and incorporated them into the Bible. More significant is the cultural impact his translation had. He tinkered with meanings and changed stories.

Trumbull noted that Eliot took a story about ten wise and foolish virgins in the Gospel of Matthew and turned them into men, because in native Massachusetts culture chastity was a virtue most highly valued in men.

With over a thousand complete Bibles in circulation in the 1660s among an Indian population of only a few thousand souls, there were more than enough copies to educate the converts and spread the word. Yet by 1676 Eliot told some Dutch missionaries that finding a copy would be difficult. During King Philip's War, from 1675 to 1676, many of the Bibles were destroyed. Indians were certainly responsible for some of the burnings, for the symbolism of the Bible was not lost on them. In a tract called *Indian Dialogues* written to help Indian missionaries proselytize among their unconverted kinfolk, Eliot reported that Indian sachems hostile to Christianity often pointed to the Bible as a book meant to trick them into selling their land. During the war, Puritan captives like Mary Rowlandson clung to their own Bibles if they had them, while unconverted Indians vented hostility not just toward Puritans but to the Indians who had become Christians. At the same time, colonists also became hostile to Christianized Indians. There is some evidence that Puritans burned these books to remove what they considered to be corrupt versions of the scripture, that is, scripture printed in a heathen language. By 1679, English-language instruction was a requirement for Indians who desired to embrace Christianity. Daniel Gookin, an advocate of English-language instruction, preached in the English language to the Indians at Natick, the town founded by Eliot.

Eliot did raise enough funds for a second printing of the Indian Bible in 1685, but a third printing divided the New England Commissioners, two-thirds of whom favored English-language instruction for Indians. One argument for preserving the English put forward by the commissioners was that Eliot's use of certain words that he had tried to put into their language never made sense to the Indians. Thus, only total immersion in English, the commissioners believed, could make Indians think like Christians. By the 1720s no Indian texts were being printed. Nevertheless, missionaries to the Indians continued to raise the question of publishing Bibles in Native American languages, and the idea continued to be shot down. Reverend Jedediah Morse was arguing as late as 1850 that only English instruction could give Indians useful knowledge of scripture. That he had to make the argument demonstrates the power of Eliot's publication of an Indian Bible and his mission to put the vernacular word into Indian hands and minds.

See also: King Philip's War, Praying Towns, Society for the Propagation of the Gospel in New England
Further Reading
Richard Cogley, *John Eliot's Mission to the Indians Before King Philip's War* (Cambridge, MA, 1999); Edward G. Gray, *New World Babel: Languages and Nations in Early America* (Princeton, 1999).

Katherine Hermes

International Puritanism

The term *puritan* was first used in the 1560s. It is not an exact term, and as early as 1655 Thomas Fuller desired its banishment, "because so various in the acceptations thereof." However, historians can now hardly avoid its use, so deeply has it fixed itself in the English language. *Puritanism* purports to identify a form of Protestant religion, comprehending theology, discipline, piety, and perhaps other practices and patterns of thinking. Even though some, even all, of these are clearly recognizable in other states and societies, the term refers specifically to the English-speaking peoples. *Puritanism,* and its synonym *precisianism*, appeared initially as terms of abuse; adherents of this mood or movement preferred to think of themselves as the "godly," in that they were seeking only to live out divine precepts they had found in the Bible.

Puritanism had both native and foreign origins. Its iconoclasm and attachment to the authority of the Bible can be traced in Lollard culture in the fifteenth century. However, foreign origins figure more largely, and even though some features of Puritanism can be seen in the work of William Tyndale, the early sixteenth-century translator of the Bible, M. M. Knappen writes that "the story of En-

glish Puritanism is best begun in 1524." The role of the Marian exiles, as those who fled to the Continent during the reign of the Catholic Mary Tudor were called, and others who came under the sway of the Swiss Reformation cannot be overestimated. Upon their return to England after the death of Queen Mary Tudor, they were drafted into the Elizabethan Church of England, where their radical tendencies generated a number of controversies that were only with difficulty controlled, but not finally uprooted. First came the Vestiarian Controversy over the wearing of "popish" vestments in worship; this was followed by rejection of features of the Book of Common Prayer and, finally, by a struggle against episcopacy and an abortive attempt to institute Presbyterian, or "classical," church government (as in the Dedham Classis in the county of Essex). Elizabeth fought successfully against all these trajectories of dissent, silencing Walter Travers and Thomas Cartwright, leaving men like Francis Johnson, John Robinson, Robert Browne, and John Smyth to depart the country and to organize varying forms of separatism, which is probably to be regarded as an offshoot of Puritanism rather than the thing itself. English-speaking exiles and others in the Netherlands, notably merchants, established their own communities, which historian Keith L. Sprunger has studied under the heading of "Dutch Puritanism."

There occurred, in the later Elizabethan era, what T. D. Bozeman terms "the great pietistic turn." Augustus Lang described William Perkins as "the father of pietism," and men who shared the same effort to focus on pious behavior, such as Lewis Bayly, John Abernethy, George Downame, and James Ussher, were elevated to the various episcopates of the British Isles. At the accession of James I of England, while puritans grumbled over certain features of the English church, they could at least find a theological home there and carry on with their traditional emphases upon the authority of the Bible, the importance of the sermon, and the imposition of a rigid discipline, including Sabbatarianism. But though members of the landed classes might prove good friends to puritan preachers, King James's rule witnessed the rise and indeed royal encouragement of a new breed of clergy. Lancelot Andrewes was among the first to appropriate more Catholic forms of worship, and he was followed by Archbishop William Laud, John Cosin, and a number of others whose alleged Arminianism consisted especially of a renewed emphasis upon ceremonial and an elevation of sacrament over preaching the word. This created an upheaval within the Church of England that eventually brought church and state into civil war and ultimately led to regicide and constitutional experimentation.

However, because the two kingdoms shared a single monach, what happened in England hinged directly upon contemporary events in Scotland. Scotland was a rather poorer country than England and had long lived in the shadow of its more powerful southern neighbor, but the peculiarities of reform north of the Tweed meant that Presbyterianism had been implemented nationally in the 1580s with the advent of the Second Book of Discipline. There was considerable conflict surrounding this polity, and from the late 1590s King James VI (who became James I of England in 1603) set about the restoration of episcopacy; he achieved his goal in 1610, though the Presbyterian structure remained in attenuated form. What was ultimately fatal to the royal supremacy in the Church of Scotland was the imposition of liturgical reforms in 1618, the Five Articles of Perth, most notoriously among them, the demand for kneeling at communion. James was less than fervent in demanding conformity, but his son Charles I was not inclined toward compromise. He imposed new canons and constitutions upon the country, and with the introduction of a Scottish Book of Common Prayer in 1637, public disaffection appeared on the streets, and indeed in the churches. On 28 February 1638, the National Covenant was signed, drawing together the religious impulses of what may well be called "Scottish Puritanism" and the political grievances of the aristocracy.

The content of Scottish Protestantism was similar to what is known as puritanism in England, and indeed the term was used in seventeenth-century Scotland. Robert Rollock had achieved fame for his federal theology, similar to that of English divines like Edward Dering, and Scottish divinity practiced

the same kind of physic for burdened souls as one identifies with English puritanism. Scottish divinity was sometimes published in London, and English puritan works were also issued in Edinburgh as well as imported into the country. The countries' divines recognized each other as kindred spirits, and once rebellion had begun in the north, these contacts quickly produced a growing sense of a united political destiny.

The public manifestation of this alliance was the Scottish participation in the Westminster Assembly and the drafting of common instruments (Catechisms, Confession, Directory of Worship). The assembly also recognized the puritan contributions of English Protestant culture in Ireland, basing the confession on the Irish Articles of 1615. Not only had English divines of puritan sympathies been at work in Ireland, they also made it possible for nonconforming Scottish clergy like Robert Blair and John Livingstone to find work there, before returning to Scotland in the 1630s, where they helped to radicalize the Church of Scotland before and after the National Covenant.

In the 1620s, some English puritans began to feel the pinch of government action to curtail their attempts at reformation of the church. Their meetings in the late 1620s resulted in the formation of the Massachusetts Bay Company, 1628, and by removing the charter and the board of directors to the colony, they allowed it to become virtually self-governing, with practically no government control from London until the end of the century. Plymouth Colony had been founded by Separatists from Robinson's exiles in Leiden in 1620, but the Massachusetts Bay Colony was established by nonseparating Congregationalists under the control of men like John Winthrop (governor) and John Cotton (minister of the Boston church). They set sail in quest of freedom from the control of their religious practices by men like Laud, and indeed freedom was a significant rubric in puritan thought, though more for themselves than for others. Roger Williams discovered this in 1636 when he had to flee the Massachusetts Bay Colony rather than be returned to England. He established Rhode Island Colony with the intention of forming a refuge from all religious constraint. But Williams, though sharing much of puritan thought, also traveled beyond it, as did others dependent upon puritanism, including George Fox, the Quaker founder, whose emphasis on the Holy Spirit was thoroughly rooted in puritanism but unconstrained by its emphasis on the written word.

English puritanism reached its political apogee in the 1640s when it rose up against Charles I, and with Scottish help began the process of redefining England, and indeed Britain. However, the forces of religious radicalism, however, and the social and political freedom that it unleashed, which found a supportive structure in the New Model Army, helped to defeat English puritanism's institutional pretensions, and after the Restoration, with all hope of reformulating the Church of England gone, saw its influence reduced to a sometimes persecuted religious minority. In Scotland, it managed through many a vicissitude to remain the leading social force for generations to come. In its Biblicism, moral earnestness, emotional religious experience, providentialism, and resistance to all forms of human absolutism, puritanism left an immense cultural legacy on both sides of the Atlantic, where its pulse can be easily felt 350–400 years after its flowering.

> See also: English Puritanism in the Netherlands, Irish Puritanism, Marian Exiles, Westminster Assembly
> *Further Reading*
> Francis J. Bremer, ed. *Puritanism: Transatlantic Perspectives on a Seventeenth-Century Anglo-American Faith* (Boston, 1993); Patrick Collinson, *The Elizabethan Puritan Movement* (London, 1967); Christopher Hill, *Society and Puritanism in Pre-Revolutionary England* (New York, 1964); Perry Miller, *The New England Mind: The Seventeenth Century* (Cambridge, MA, 1939); David George Mullan, *Scottish Puritanism, 1590–1638* (Oxford, 2000); Geoffrey F. Nuttall, *The Holy Spirit in Puritan Faith and Experience* (Oxford, 1992).

David Mullan

Irish Articles (1615)

The Irish Articles of 1615 form a significant, but rather neglected link between the Thirty-nine Articles and the Westminster Confession. Almost nothing is known of how they were composed or approved, bar a reference by Nicholas Bernard, writing in 1656, that Archbishop Ussher was appointed by the Irish convocation of 1613–1615 to draw them up. Whether this meant he wrote them or merely wrote them out as secretary is unclear. In the absence of further information, therefore, it is to the text of the articles that one must turn for enlightenment.

The Church of Ireland was, from the beginning, modeled upon the Church of England: thus the Irish Act of Supremacy in 1537 was largely copied from the English Act of 1534, and the Irish religious legislation of 1560 was similarly based upon the English Elizabethan settlement of 1559. Hence it is not surprising that the text of the Irish Articles of 1615 should be modeled closely on the English Thirty-nine Articles. It is, of course, true that, reflecting the inevitably tendency of Reformed confessions to grow ever more detailed over time, the Irish version—with a total of 104 articles—were much longer than its English prototype. But comparison of the two demonstrates that the backbone for the Irish creed was provided by the English one. All but one of the English Articles was included in some form or other. And much of the additional material was in any case taken from that other official source of English church doctrine, the two sets of homilies. Thus on the subject of the sacraments, English Article 25 appears as Irish Articles 85–88. Equally, English Article 9 on original sin is largely incorporated into Irish Articles 23 and 24. And Irish Articles 63 and 64, which deal with matters such as our duty to our neighbors and matrimony, can be seen as paralleling material in the homilies. Hence the most detailed modern analysis of the stance of the Irish Articles comes to the conclusion that "what is novel in the Irish Articles does not seriously diverge from the Thirty Nine Articles, let alone contradict them."

And yet, closer comparison of the two formularies makes it difficult to endorse this interpretation of them as an "Anglican" confession, little different from the English Articles. First, there is in the Irish Articles new material that is not paralleled in either the English Articles or the English homilies. Thus there is a much more aggressive approach to Catholicism, with specific Catholic doctrines and practices explicitly condemned (Irish Articles 67, 79, 91, 100) and, most notably, the pope is declared (in Irish Article 80) to be "that man of sin," that is, Antichrist. It is of course true that after the excommunication of Elizabeth by the pope in 1570, Protestant attitudes toward Catholicism hardened considerably: thus the Irish Articles can be seen as reflecting this changed context. But the inclusion of such a reference in the national confessions of faith was in itself highly significant, since it formally bound the church to a particular view of the Roman Catholic Church, thus preventing future flexibility on this issue. The most notable addition to the English Articles was the inclusion in Irish Articles 12, 14, 15, 32, and 37 of the Lambeth Articles of 1595. The purpose of the Lambeth Articles had been to end the attacks in Cambridge on the doctrine of double predestination, which had exploited the ambiguities of English Article 17 on the subject of predestination. Despite pressure from Archbishop Whitgift, Elizabeth had refused to allow them to be incorporated into the English confession. Their inclusion in the Irish Articles, therefore, marks a major departure, identifying the Irish church unequivocally with the Calvinist doctrine of predestination.

Second, a small amount of material from the English Articles was omitted. The most obvious and significant was English Article 36 "Of consecration of bishops and ministers," introduced into the Elizabethan formulary in 1563 as a riposte to puritan objections to episcopacy. The Church of Ireland was episcopalian, and content to remain so, but it saw no need to define itself as such in its articles, which thus contain no mention of the threefold ministry of bishops, priests, and deacons—indeed, the only time the Irish Articles refer to episcopacy is when they mention the bishop of Rome. Ministers opposed to episcopacy could still therefore in good conscience work within the Church of Ireland. Thirdly, even where the Irish Articles adopted the English Articles, it was often with changes that significantly altered the meaning. Thus on the

question of the authority of the church, again an issue on which puritans were particularly sensitive, the Irish Articles diluted their English counterpart by dropping the opening of English Article 20, "The church hath power to decree rites or ceremonies and authority in controversies of faith." English Article 34, "Of the traditions of the church," was also subtly altered. Finally, though the Irish Articles concluded with a synodical decree that any minister publicly teaching doctrine contrary to the articles was to be deprived, there was no requirement in Ireland, in marked contrast to England, that all ministers subscribe to the confession of faith.

What the Irish Articles did, therefore, was to reposition the Church of Ireland both theologically and ecclesiologically, and so to distinguish it from the Church of England, without radically breaking from the latter's confession. The Irish Articles were fuller, more hostile to Rome, and more reformed than the English Articles, ending many of the latter's ambiguities, while at the same time being more accommodating of those on the left wing of the established church. They offered, as a result, the possibility of a more inclusive Church of Ireland, united in the task of attacking and confuting Roman Catholicism. And, indeed, during the 1610s and 1620s, Scottish Presbyterians and English puritans in many cases fled to Ireland, where they were accommodated within its Protestant church. Similarly, when in the late 1620s, English Parliamentarians sought to attack the Arminian proclivities of leading English clergy, it was to the Irish Articles that they pointed as evidence of the fundamentally Calvinist character of the English Articles. Not surprisingly, William Laud, and his Irish allies, Bishop Bramhall of Derry and Lord Deputy Wentworth, were not enamored of the Irish Articles and sought, in the Irish Convocation of 1634, to replace them with the English Articles. The attachment of the Irish church to its independence led, however, to a rebellion by the members of Convocation, suppressed only by Wentworth's firmness, and a compromise whereby the English Articles were adopted, but the Irish Articles were not formally rescinded. Archbishop Ussher, for one, insisted that clergy subscribe to both sets of articles, but the Irish Articles soon fell into disuse, and the Thirty-nine Articles remain the formal confession of the Church of Ireland to this day. But they did have an afterlife in the Presbyterian tradition, since the Westminster Assembly, when drawing up its Confession in 1645–1646, started from the Irish Articles, which thus provide not only its structure but in many instances the wording of individual articles. The Irish Articles thus act as a bridge from the reformed but ambiguous Thirty-nine Articles to the classic Presbyterian formulary.

See also: Articles of Religion, Westminster Confession of Faith

Further Reading

Gerald Bray, ed., *Documents of the English Reformation* (Cambridge, Eng., 1994); Alan Ford, *The Protestant Reformation in Ireland,* 2nd ed. (Dublin, 1997); R. B. Knox, "The Ecclesiastical Policy of James Ussher, Archbishop of Armagh" (London University, Ph.D. diss., 1956); R. B. Knox, *James Ussher, Archbishop of Armagh* (Cardiff, 1967); Philip Schaff, ed., *The Creeds of Christendom,* 6th ed., 3 vols. (New York, 1919).

Alan Ford

Irish Puritanism

Though the Irish Acts of Supremacy and Uniformity of 1560 parroted, almost word for word, their English counterparts, the way in which the Elizabethan settlement in Ireland developed was rather different from the way it developed in England. In the latter, the queen set her face firmly against any further reform and insisted that clergy knuckle under, wearing the surplice and subscribing to the Thirty-nine Articles. In Ireland, however, the church was desperately in need of clergy and so was prepared to be much more flexible, welcoming puritan and conformist alike.

Thus Adam Loftus (archbishop of Armagh, 1562–1657; archbishop of Dublin, 1567–1605) had strong puritan leanings when he first arrived in Ireland: sympathizing with the godly ministers in London who refused to wear what they called "antichristian apparel," complaining about the Elizabethan church settlement as a "mixed and mingled religion, neither plainly against, nor wholly with God's word," and, with delightful incongruity, recommending Thomas Cartwright for an archbishopric. After the collapse of the classis movement in England in the early 1590s, one of its leading figures, Walter Travers, found refuge in Ireland, becoming provost in 1594 of the new Irish university, Trinity College, Dublin, and inviting over his fellow Presbyterian, Humphrey Fenn. Travers was succeeded in 1601 by Henry Alvey, and he in 1609 by another strong puritan sympathizer, William Temple. In short, in Ireland as in Lancashire and other "dark corners of the land," the church was prepared to be flexible about conformity in order to secure the services of evangelical pastors.

In 1615, when the Irish church set about drawing up its confession of faith, it sought to formalize this unofficial tolerance. The standard interpretation of the Irish Articles, by Buick Knox, is that they were thoroughly "Anglican," adopting or adapting most of the Thirty-nine Articles. In fact they are much more subversive, seeking to amend the English formulary in such a way as to create a broader-based Irish church. Thus the Lambeth Articles were included, copper-fastening a double predestinarian interpretation of English Article 17. English Article 36 on the ordination of bishops was dropped; all mention of the threefold ministry of bishops, priests, and deacons was omitted, as was the opening to English Article 20 asserting the power of the church to impose ceremonies, another bête noire for puritans. Nor was there any requirement that clergy subscribe to the articles.

The results of this inclusiveness became evident in the 1620s and 1630s, when the plantation of the north of Ireland got under way. As large numbers of lowland Scots settled in Ulster, they inevitably brought with them Presbyterian clergy. Under the tolerant eyes of Scottish bishops, these ministers were incorporated into the Church of Ireland: some seeking ordination even obtained the right to edit the ritual used at ordination. It was clergy such as these who led the great Six Mile Water revival of 1625, during which thousands of people gathered for open-air preaching and communions, serving as

Crowds watching the execution of the Lord Lieutenant of Ireland, Thomas Wentworth, first Earl of Strafford, 12 May 1641. He was declared guilty of crimes against the state by a parliamentary act of attainder and was beheaded. (Hulton Archive/Getty Images)

an early model for later revivals in Ireland, Scotland, and America.

By the early 1630s, it appeared that in Ireland the Elizabethan settlement had been turned into a far more flexible polity than in England. But Irish exceptionalism did not last. As early as 1594 an older and more cautious Archbishop Loftus had warned Provost Travers not to promote Presbyterianism while in Ireland, lest he blemish "our reformation with the reproachful blots of innovation and dissension . . . for I dread the hostility of innovation as being a thing laboured by too many in England already." And indeed, as information flowed more freely across the Irish Sea in the early seventeenth century, it became increasingly difficult to conceal the ways in which the Irish church diverged from its English counterpart. In 1614 rumors of puritanism in Trinity College reached England, leading Archbishop Abbot to intervene in the affairs of the college. And in the same year the new archbishop of Armagh, Christo-

pher Hampton, preached a sermon in which he warned of the dangers of innovation and asserted, as had Richard Hooker, the great Anglican apologist of the late sixteenth century, the right of the church to legislate concerning *adiaphora* ("things indifferent"; that is, matters not covered in the Bible). Hampton raised his concerns again in 1621, writing to England to complain of "certain factious and irregular puritans . . . [in Antrim and Down] entertaining the Scottish discipline and liturgy so strongly, that they offer wrong to the church government here established." Action was finally taken in 1634–1636, when the new Lord Deputy, Wentworth, acting on the advice of Archbishop Laud, and with the help of Bishop Bramhall, finally set about rooting out puritanism from the Church of Ireland. Their first steps were constitutional: Wentworth and Bramhall forced Irish Convocation in 1634 to adopt the Thirty-nine Articles as the Irish confession and then to adopt articles that required ministers to subscribe to the new articles. Bramhall, with the help of the bishop of Down and Connor, Henry Leslie, then proceeded, in a series of visitations in Ulster, to weed out Presbyterian clergy and expel them from their livings. The brief and unique ecclesiological experiment, which sought to include conformists, puritans, and Presbyterians in the same church, was over. Henceforth in Ireland, puritanism was to operate outside the established church, as nonconformity.

See also: Irish Articles

Further Reading

Alan Ford, "The Church of Ireland 1558–1641: A Puritan Church?" in Alan Ford, James McGuire, and Kenneth Milne, eds., *As by Law Established: The Church of Ireland since the Reformation* (Dublin, 1995); St. J. D. Seymour, *The Puritans in Ireland 1647–1661* (Oxford, 1912).

Alan Ford

J

Justification

The Protestant doctrine of the remission of sins by God's free grace (*sola gratia*), dependent on faith in Christ alone (*sola fide*), not on works or human merit. In puritan theology, justification is God's forgiveness of the sins of the elect, which makes them righteous (acceptable to God) and begins the process of *sanctification,* or growth in holiness. Although all Protestants held that faith, not works, was the necessary condition of salvation, the unique importance of this doctrine for puritan theology and religious experience lies in its relationship to other strongly Calvinist doctrines of *original sin, election, works, grace,* and *sanctification.*

Medieval Doctrines of Justification

Justification (the making of something or someone "just," in the sense of "right" or "lawful") is a legal term for payment (or acceptance of nonpayment) for a debt, in this case, sin. In late medieval Catholicism, earthly justification was part of a cyclical and incomplete process of debt and repayment: born with original sin, which was only partially "repaid" through baptism, humans sin, perform the sacrament of penance, receive absolution, and sin again. At the point of death, confession and absolution (extreme unction, or the "last rites") paid the debt for sins committed since the last act of penance. In Catholic doctrine, justification occurred through God's gift of grace in the sacrament of penance, a system of reciprocal, ritual repayment through the penitent's saying of prayers or acts of charity. But grace did not permanently eliminate this cycle due to the burden of original sin—humans could not help sinning again and again throughout their lifetimes, continuing the cycle of debt and repayment.

Justification by Faith Alone

The Protestant doctrine of justification by faith alone attempted to counter what Protestants saw as "works-based" doctrines, which gave too much agency to humans, too much efficacy to their works (including the structures of the church), and too little to God's ultimate power and majesty. Notably, Martin Luther's doctrine of *sola fide* (faith alone), a centerpiece of Protestant reform, asserts that the burden of original sin leaves humans incapable of doing any work that would be acceptable to God and could "pay" the debt of original sin, or even personal sins: "Nothing in the labor done in one's vocation, or in the good deeds performed for one's neighbors, or in the special religious works done for the church saved anybody; faith only sufficed, but completely." Only God could step in to "pay" the debt of human sin. This ultimate, once-and-for-all payment was the incarnation of Christ. Faith in Christ, meaning faith in God's forgiveness of human sin through Christ, was the only means to justification in Luther's theology: no works were required, nor could they possibly repay human sin.

Likewise, for the French Reformer John Calvin, belief in Christ meant the acceptance of one's own "utter depravity" and the knowledge that God's free gift, Christ, is the only solution to this wormlike state. Faith in Christ prompts the two-part process of (1) the forgiveness of sins, *justification,* and (2) the "clothing" in the righteousness of Christ, or *sanctification* for the elect. In this latter process of sanctification, good works can appear as "fruits" of the Holy Spirit in the regenerated person, but good works do not precede justification or somehow cause it.

For both Luther and Calvin, then, good works could (and should) *stem from* true faith and righteousness, but they should never be considered the *cause* of salvation—they could never *justify* a human being. Clearly, the doctrine of justification by faith alone, in contrast with one in which works could also merit salvation, was not in question among Protestants. Justification occurs supernaturally, by God's own free act of forgiveness, outside of any human will, action, or preparation. This classically Protestant doctrine of justification is stated in the Thirty-nine Articles (1563): "We are accounted righteous before God, only for the merit of Our Lord and Saviour Jesus Christ, by faith, and not for our own works or deservings." In practice, however, the temporal relationship between faith, works, and justification was a chicken-and-egg dilemma that led to difficult questions: is faith a kind of *work* a believer does that God rewards with justification, as it seems in Luther's explanation, or does faith itself come from God's grace, as Calvin argues? Many puritan theologians took the latter viewpoint—God alone could provide justifying faith, though the moral problem of the role of human merit and "preparation" for faith and justification remained.

The Puritans on Justification

As Luther and Calvin argued, many English Reformers affirmed that a justified person would perform good works, but further added that these could be signs, or proof, that justification had indeed occurred. As Calvin and many puritans remarked, these signs could be great comfort to those who were anxious about the state of their souls. This pastoral focus was not without hindrance, however, as the signs could be misleading. William

Perkins, puritan theologian and preacher, argued that some reprobates (elected to damnation) nevertheless demonstrated an "ineffectual call," which was only a taste of faith, grace, justification, and sanctification, but was not true "justifying" faith: a lapse was inevitable. Such a person appeared to be justified "in the eyes of men," but never in the eyes of God. Additionally, God sent trials and temptations to test his elect, who would, because they were still fallen humans, continue to sin and might appear to have "lost" the signs of election. Though Perkins's rigid assertion of double predestination and the possibility that reprobates may receive a false sense of election was later replaced with notions of a "covenant" between humans and God that focused less on predestination and more on preparation for grace, the connection between works and faith remained blurred in much puritan theology. How was one to know that one's faith was true, saving faith, not a delusion? Clearly, the assurance that one had been justified, that one was a member of the elect, was difficult to achieve in such a theological system, and many argued that assurance was never beyond doubt. Constant reexamination of conscience, one's "works," for signs of election was essential.

These and other more practical and pastoral questions, were of central importance for puritans because of their calls for reform within the larger English church, their positions within religiously mixed parishes and communities, and the need to understand their own religious experiences. Were the sacraments necessary, and if so, why, if faith alone justifies? What did justification feel like? Was it a specific occurrence, a moment of conversion? How did it change a person? Should one prepare for it with feelings of repentance, reading the scriptures, and listening to sermons, or did God provide all that was necessary? If one felt assured of election, should one attend church with those who were "obviously" reprobate, or even associate with them? There were no uniform, definite answers to these questions. The central debates over the application of the doctrine of justification influenced puritan behavior and experience as well as belief.

Justification and Antinomianism

Although the formal doctrine of justification itself was not necessarily at issue, many puritans would have agreed with Calvin's statement that justification is "the main hinge on which religion turns." The central issue for many puritans regarding the process of justification and salvation was practical: how did the saints behave? What should one do, if anything, in order to prepare to receive faith and the grace of justification? The antinomian crisis in seventeenth-century England and Massachusetts stemmed directly from these theological questions: did God give faith to those who appeared to be unprepared for it, even though they behaved in a manner inappropriate for Christians (as church leaders saw it)? Once a person felt assured of salvation, did it matter how that person behaved? Could one claim inspiration directly from God as a result of grace received through justification? Many more mainstream or moderate puritans, including New England church leaders, answered a strong "no" to all of these questions. Though grace was freely given, only those who showed signs that God was beginning to favor them (who acted in a righteous manner by listening to sermons, reading scripture, examining their consciences, and obeying God and magistrate by following the law) would receive the grace of justification. Good works came from true faith—a saint must continually examine his or her conscience for these signs throughout his or her life. Lapses could mean that a person had been deluded into assurance or might be a hypocrite. Although justification occurred supernaturally, by God's action only outside of human agency, it had to be "demonstrated" in practice. It did not give excuses for immoral behavior or disobedience. Some more radical puritan thinkers interpreted Paul's letter to the Romans differently and saw that although justification made them "dead" to the law ("antinomian" is from the Greek *anti-nomos,* literally, "against the law") and gave them a special status and connection to God and their fellow elect, it did not give them liberty to sin.

The practical, pastoral questions asked above preoccupied the treatises and sermons of puritan divines who struggled to understand the doctrines of predestination and election, faith, justification, and sanctification, the place of good works within this system of salvation, and the implications for church government and discipline. In addition to theological debates, individual puritans' personal experiences of assurance and tribulation—what historian Peter Lake calls the "intense evangelical experience of justification"—also informed the answers to these questions. Debates over central doctrines like justification provided puritans with a foundation for disputes over more worldly concerns such as order, discipline, ceremonies, and the ethical consequences of justification in an unregenerate world.

See also: Antinomianism, Atonement, Federal Theology, Grace

Further Reading

R. T. Kendall, *Calvin and English Calvinism to 1649* (Oxford, 1979); Peter Lake, *Moderate Puritans and the Elizabethan Church* (Cambridge, Eng., 1982); Steven Ozment, *The Age of Reform, 1250–1550: An Intellectual and Religious History of Late Medieval and Reformation Europe* (New Haven, 1980).

Stephanie Sleeper

K

King Philip's War

King Philip's War, the most significant struggle between natives and colonists in seventeenth-century New England, began in the Plymouth Colony town of Swansea in 1675, when a group of Wampanoag Indians attacked the colonists. Lasting one year, the war spread north into New Hampshire, across Massachusetts and Rhode Island, and south into Connecticut. King Philip, grand sachem of the Wampanoag and either the second son or the grandson of Massasoit, began a military campaign, the purpose of which was to drive every last colonist from New England.

Philip, or Metacom (or Metacomet) as he was also known, succeeded his brother, Alexander, also called Wamsutta, to the sachemship in 1662. The Plymouth Court had summoned Wamsutta to Plymouth to answer questions about native conduct, and it had sent forth Major Josiah Winslow and a small force to back up the summons by force of arms. Wamsutta became sick and died suddenly. Philip was enraged by the cruel and disrespectful treatment of his brother, and he began to distrust the colonists with whom the Wampanoag had had long and peaceful relations under Massasoit. At first Metacom had sought to accommodate to a life alongside the colonists. As sachem, he took the lead in much of his tribe's trade with the colonies. He adopted the European name of Philip, and wore some English-style clothing. Although he never embraced Christianity and was wary of missionary efforts by Indian converts from the praying towns,

he occasionally allowed them to visit his people. His complaints about colonists' interference with Indian livestock, for example, resulted in serious clashes with the colonial leaders. Despite Philip's best efforts at maintaining his relationship with the colonial authorities, they continued to suspect him of planning acts of war. Finally, in 1671 the colonial leaders of the Plymouth Colony forced major concessions from Philip. He gave up much of his tribe's arms, and according to colonial authorities, agreed that he and his tribe were subject to English law.

In March of 1675, after more than a decade of mounting tensions with colonists and with Indians who had converted to Christianity, a single incident tipped Philip toward war. John Sassamon, a Christian Indian from Cambridge, Massachusetts, was making his way home when he disappeared through the ice into a lake in the marshlands. At first colonial authorities deemed Sassamon's death accidental, but rumors began to circulate that three Wampanoag Indians had murdered the young convert. The men were arrested, tried, found guilty by a jury of Indians and colonists, and hanged. Philip declared that the colonies had no power to hang his people.

Philip had been negotiating with the Narragansetts of Rhode Island and other tribes in southern New England whose contact with the colonists was also strained by constant demands for land, the poverty of the native peoples, and escalating trading difficulties. He wanted their assurances of assistance if he went to war, and for the most part, he received them. Not all Indians sided with Philip. Those who had converted to Christianity generally fought with the English or remained neutral, although the English also imprisoned many of these praying Indians on Deer Island in Boston Harbor to keep them from waging war. Some native communities on Cape Cod, Martha's Vineyard, and Block Island did not participate in the war. Indian soldiers fighting with the colonists helped turn the tide of the war. Governor Edmund Andros of New York convinced the Mohawk tribe to attack some of Philip's winter camps, and in April 1676, the Mohegan and Pequot tribes succeeded in defeating the Narragansetts under the sachem Canonchet, whom the Mohegan sachem, Uncas, executed. On 12 August 1676, Philip was killed in the great Assowamset Swamp in Rhode Island by a Wampanoag fighting with Captain Benjamin Church. Soldiers dismembered the sachem's body, cutting off his hands and head, and displayed the parts on trees. While this death brought the main conflict to an end, fighting continued on the northern frontiers of New England.

The war left colonial communities in the western regions of New England particularly traumatized. The mortality rate on both sides was probably 10 percent of all soldiers, one of the bloodiest wars in American history. The Indians burned over a dozen Massachusetts Colony towns, including Brookfield, Deerfield, Northfield, Springfield, and Lancaster. Western towns were abandoned and not resettled until much later. Mary Rowlandson's famous 1682 narrative, *The Sovereignty and Goodness of God, together with the faithfulness of his promises displayed, being a narrative of the captivity and restoration of Mrs. Mary Rowlandson,* described her travels with the Indians as a captive from Lancaster in the war. During her captivity she moved with the Indians over 150 miles.

Worse, though, was the fate of the Indians. It had become common to take Indians into servitude since the Pequot War of 1637, but after King Philip's War, many native peoples never knew freedom again. Philip's young son and many of the warriors were sent to the Caribbean, where they were sold into slavery. Trust between Indians and colonists was broken, and even Indian praying towns suffered as a result. They lost financial support, and colonists appointed overseers to the Indians, who lived now on reserved land. Colonists viewed the war as a dreadful judgment upon them, not for their conduct toward Indians, but for their materialism and lack of faith. The end of the war resulted in a short-lived burst of piety among the victorious colonists and a precarious sovereignty for Indian tribes in southeastern New England.

The war remained a significant cultural memory for both Indians and whites in the centuries to come. In historical literature it has been variously referred to as Metacom's Rebellion, a series of skirmishes between colonists and Indians, and a pan-Indian movement for liberation. By the eighteenth century, many Anglo-Europeans treated the war as the end of Indian existence in New England. The war was the subject of plays in the nineteenth century, and a U.S. warship was christened *Metacom*.

See also: Indian Bible, Pequot War, Praying Towns

Further Reading

Colin Calloway, *After King Philip's War: Presence and Persistence in Indian New England* (Hanover, NH; 1997); Yasuhide Kawashima, *Igniting King Philip's War: The John Sassamon Murder Trial* (Lawrence, KS, 2001); Jill Lepore, *The Name of War: King Philip's War and the Origins of American Identity* (Middletown, CT, 1998); Eric B. Scholtz and Michael J. Tougias, *King Philip's War: The History and Legacy of America's Forgotten Conflict* (Woodstock, VT, 2000).

Katherine Hermes

L

Lambeth Articles

The Lambeth Articles were prepared by Archbishop John Whitgift in 1595 in response to attacks on the doctrine of predestination that had arisen in Cambridge University. In April of that year, William Barrett, chaplain of Gonville and Caius College, preached a university sermon that criticized the deterministic predestinarianism of many Calvinists. This criticism flew in the face of what was the informal orthodoxy of the Church of England, though Barrett believed that his views were consistent with the language on predestination found in the church's Articles of Religion, or Thirty-nine Articles. Despite his defense, the university Consistory Court called upon Barrett to recant his views. Instead, he appealed to Archbishop Whitgift. After considering the matter, Whitgift issued the Lambeth Articles in November 1595.

Whitgift's articles came down strongly on the side of double predestination. He stated that God had from eternity predestined some to salvation and reprobated others to death. The efficient cause of predestination was not to be found in God's forseeing of faith, perseverance, or good works, but stemmed purely from the will of God. The number of predestined was certain and could not be increased or diminished. Those not predestined were rightfully condemned because of their sins. A true and justifying faith, which is found in those elected by God, could not be lost. Those upon whom God bestows this justifying faith were sure of the remission of sins and eternal salvation. Obviously, then, saving grace was not granted to all men. Only those called to Christ by the Father were saved. And it was not in the power of any individual to influence whether or not that individual was saved. These assertions of what had become Calvinist orthodoxy were stated by Whitgift to be "uniformly professed in this Church of England and agreeable to the Articles of Religion established by authority."

Though they carried the personal authority of the archbishop of Canterbury, Queen Elizabeth rejected requests that the Lambeth Articles be officially incorporated into the Articles of Religion. Again, at the Hampton Court Conference of 1604, the puritan spokesmen requested of the new monarch, James I, that the Lambeth Articles be made official policy of the Church of England, but the king rejected the request. However, the Church of Ireland did incorporate the Lambeth Articles in its 1615 Articles of Religion, generally credited to Archbishop James Ussher. Because of this acceptance of the articles, as Arminian views gained greater currency in England in the early seventeenth century, many puritans perceived the Irish Protestant Church as more orthodox.

See also: Anti-Calvinism, Arminianism, Articles of Religion, Irish Articles, Predestination
Further Reading
Nicholas Tyacke, *Anti-Calvinists: The Rise of English Arminianism, c. 1590–1640* (Oxford, 1987).

Francis J. Bremer

Law in Puritan New England

The Puritans of New England came to their new settlements with reform of religion and law uppermost in their minds. They introduced ideas, all the while fighting about them, that became increasingly important and even took on new meanings by the time the United States was established, ideas such as the separation of church and state, legal toleration of dissent, and codification of the laws. Knowledge of the law, and thus its printing and widespread distribution, were paramount to the Puritan legal ethic. They practiced a consensus form of governance that lent itself to bitter arguments, at the same time that it provided a foundation for mediation rather than purely adversarial practice of law. This latter contribution helped ease a legal transition with the native Algonquian population, however difficult it made life for Dissenters in New England itself. It also contributed to a persistence of a sense of substantive or actual justice, rather than the increasingly procedural and formal justice of the common law.

The legal practice of the indigenous Algonquian people was rule by council and consensus. During the colonial period, especially in its early days, referred to as the contact period between Indians and Europeans, legal relations between native groups and the settlers were characterized by mediation. The English Puritans who formed the colonial governments of Plymouth (1620), Massachusetts (1630), New Haven (1636), and Connecticut (1636) experimented with legal institutions. They used both biblical and equitable principles and rules. The Massachusetts Bay Company Charter and the Mayflower Compact provided some guidance and legal authority, as did John Winthrop's sermon "Model of Christian Charity." Several colonial leaders, including Winthrop, had been trained at the Inns of Court in England, and they exchanged letters on legal matters, especially in capital cases. The laws were codified, published, and distributed. Rhode Island (settled in 1635), on the other hand, remained firmly attached to the emerging English emphasis on common law. Vermont and New Hampshire had colonial legal systems similar to those of their parent colonies. New Hampshire, for example, codified its laws as early as 1679. The legal landscape from 1620 to 1690 was reform-minded and consensus-oriented, in general. This period was followed by the re-anglicization of legal institutions in the eighteenth century, which removed much of the Puritan character of the law and its goal of substantive over procedural justice.

The concept of law, that is, the idea that there are systematic means by which to regulate human behavior and make decisions regarding problems between human beings, predates written history. According to European accounts from the sixteenth century onward, the early native inhabitants of New England had a system of law that relied on such principles as reciprocity and compensation for harm. The Algonquian Native Americans governed themselves through personal jurisdiction, which lay in the hands of a paramount chief and his or her council. As Indians faced the colonization of their land, they developed legal strategies to handle relations with the Europeans. They formed an idea of subject-matter jurisdiction to address such problems as the introductions of livestock, alcohol, and guns—matters that they took to the settlers' own colonial courts. In all other respects, however, they retained personal jurisdiction over themselves until, successively, they were defeated in wars or incorporated into colonial societies. The experience with the native population and its impact on Puritan jurisprudence in New England cannot be underestimated. By settling differences with the nations around them using some of the same concepts that they had imported, the colonists were able to see a benefit that they could parlay into a public relations coup. They claimed they treated the Indians with the same justice as they had among themselves.

Perhaps the most important legal document composed in New England was the Mayflower Compact of 1620. At that time in coastal waters, 102 passengers were making their way to Virginia in the ship when it was blown off course. The passengers who were Adventurers, that is, coming to the New World in quest of material advantages, threatened the Pilgrims, or Separatists, with mutiny if they

Quakers Mary Dyer, William Robinson, and Marmaduke Stevenson are led to their execution. Robinson and Stevenson were hanged, but Dyer was reprieved on condition that she never return to Massachusetts. When she violated that condition she was later hanged. (Bettmann/Corbis)

could come to no agreement on governance, and thus the group drew up the Mayflower Compact. The compact was a constitution of sorts, in that it laid the foundation for self-government and gave rights of participation to the non-Separatist males on the ship. The other New England colonies had charters obtained from the Crown, which often served as models for their state constitutions after the American Revolution. Each colony, thus, had some legal document that brought it into existence and gave it authority from the king to govern itself.

The English colonists who settled southern New England in the seventeenth century had been exposed in England to diverse theories of law reform, and each colony tried to use various legal theories to set up its government under the authority of a royal charter. All the New England colonies drew a distinction between the church and state, even though Puritan magistrates and ministers consulted closely on issues of polity. There were no church courts in New England as there had been in old England. In 1630 Massachusetts interpreted their charter to set up a legal system that included a General Court, which acted both as a legislature elected by the freemen and as an appellate court; a Court of Assistants, which advised the governor and also acted as an appellate court; and in 1636, a system of county courts that heard cases at trial. There was trial by jury, and in 1641 the laws, called the "Body of Liberties," were codified, to be published and read aloud in each town. In 1648 Massachusetts revised its code, called the *Laws and Liberties,* and updated it periodically after that.

The other New England colonies had systems that resembled that of Massachusetts, but there were variations. New Haven elected to establish a Mosaic Code for its criminal laws based on Reverend John Cotton's treatise *Moses His Judicials.*

New Haven had twenty-three capital offenses in its 1656 code, while Massachusetts had twelve in 1641, and Plymouth only nine in 1636. When Connecticut merged with New Haven Colony, it too pronounced the authority of the Mosaic Code, but its laws were in fact more moderate than New Haven's. There was no trial by jury in New Haven Colony, and only adult male church members could be freemen. Thus the separation of church and state existed technically in New Haven but was not as clear as it was in Plymouth Colony, Massachusetts Bay, or Connecticut. In Connecticut, all men of property could vote for the General Court, serve on juries, and hold office, irrespective of church membership.

In all the New England colonies except Rhode Island, lawyers were legally prevented from practicing in courtrooms in an effort to keep procedure uncomplicated and, according to legislators, to more readily get to the truth. Each colony had law books brought from England to consult, such as John Cowell's legal dictionary, Michael Dalton's *Country Justice,* and Edward Coke's *On Littleton,* a set of court reports. Private citizens also had law books in their possession, but they were forbidden to bring these to court or to argue from them. The emphasis on substance over form was consistent with Puritan beliefs. Rhode Island followed English law to a large extent, although it had no separate ecclesiastical courts and was officially tolerant of all religions, unlike the other colonies, which punished people deemed heretical, such as Baptists and Quakers. The New England colonies also set several precedents in the area of slavery, with the first colonial law defining slavery included in the Massachusetts Body of Liberties of 1641. The enslavement of Native Americans taken in war was also included in this statute.

Several legal cases in the seventeenth century have since become infamous and are generally seen as a sign of Puritan intolerance, although the reality was more complex. In each of these cases—the expulsion of Roger Williams (1636), the antinomian controversy (1637), the heresy trials of the Quaker missionaries (1659–1660), and the Salem witch trials (1692)—the Puritan desire for consensus and stability overrode the community's ability to tolerate debate or dissent. Roger Williams was expelled from Massachusetts for his political beliefs, which included support of the desecration of the English flag by cutting out the king's cross and the argument that the king had no right to grant land in North America because it belonged to the Indians. Williams moved to Providence Plantations in Rhode Island, which became a refuge for others who were banished.

In the antinomian controversy, Anne Hutchinson and her followers were "convented," that is, brought before the community assembled as a court and questioned about their beliefs in religious doctrines. Conventing was a procedure derived from Roman law, called *libellus conventionis,* to air complaints that threatened the stability of the community. The antinomians, who were alleged to believe that moral law did not apply to the elect of God, were banished when no reconciliation was possible. They moved to Aquidneck in Rhode Island and to Exeter and Dover, New Hampshire. Some of the so-called antinomians were accepted back into Massachusetts after recanting, but others joined dissenting religious sects such as the Quakers. One such individual was Mary Dyer, who with two men came to preach in Massachusetts in 1659. The three Quakers had previously been banished from the colony and were condemned under the terms of a law that set the death penalty for Quakers who returned after banishment. The two men were hanged on Boston Common, while Dyer was reprieved. When she returned yet again in the next year, she was again sentenced to death, and this time the penalty was inflicted on her. This was the last execution for religious heresy in New England.

Finally, in the Salem witch trials, which occurred simultaneously with witch trials in Fairfield, Connecticut, seventeen people were hanged by order of a special Court of Oyer and Terminer called by Governor William Phips to handle the hundreds of complaints of witchcraft that awaited him on his arrival in the colony. Another was pressed to death in an attempt to extract a plea, and yet another died in jail. Spectral evidence, or visitations by images of witches to the accusers, was admitted as evidence against the accused witches to accommodate the rule of two independent witnesses. Two prominent ministers, father and son, Increase and Cotton Mather, both of whom believed in witches, urged the judges to refuse to admit spectral evidence. Later, one of the judges, Samuel Sewall, offered a public apology for his role in the trials. The Mathers and Sewall represent the transition from a premodern to a modern mind-set. Though all believed in witchcraft, the Mathers also embraced Newtonian physics, and Sewall wrote the first antislavery tract published in North America, called *The Selling of Joseph* (1700).

Although the seventeenth century was marked by legal reform and experimentation with unusual legal procedures, in the eighteenth century the region returned to more standard English legal institutions. In 1685 King James established the Dominion of New England, hoping to envelop all of New England under one royal government. The dominion's planned jurisdiction included the colonies of southern New England, plus the two New Jersey colonies and New York. However, the dominion fell with the Glorious Revolution of 1688; in 1689 the colonists rose up upon hearing the news of the English revolution's success. King William and Queen Mary restored charter government to the colonies, but they retained the right to appoint royal governors and established a more uniform system of courts throughout New England. It was the end of Puritan rule in the formal sense, but society's transition from Puritan to Yankee was by no means complete. Even though the legal systems of the New England colonies reflected the emerging dominance of the common law system, the Puritans' legacy to the future United States was its preference for substantive justice over mere form.

See also: Laws and Liberties, Mayflower Compact, *Moses His Judicials* and Mosaic Law, Salem Witchcraft
Further Reading
P. S. Atiyah and R. S. Summers, *Form and Substance in Anglo-American Law: A Comparative Study of Legal Reasoning, Legal Theory, and Legal Institutions* (Oxford, 1991); Cornelia Hughes Dayton, *Women before the Bar*

(Chapel Hill, 1995); George Lee Haskins, *Law and Authority in Early Massachusetts* (New York, 1961); Edgar J. McManus, *Law and Liberty in Early New England: Criminal Justice and Due Process, 1620–1692* (Amherst, 1993); Christopher L. Tomlins and Bruce H. Mann, eds., *The Many Legalities of Early America* (Chapel Hill, 2001).

Katherine Hermes

Laws and Liberties

The Massachusetts *Laws and Liberties,* published at the General Court's direction in 1648, marked the first comprehensive effort at fixing in public written form the various positive statutory laws for the colony. Prior to its publication, the magistrates had ruled with broad discretionary authority, but by 1634 the court's deputies pressed for comprehensive publication of enacted laws for common reference and to restrict discretionary rule. Various appointed committees failed to produce material, but two important documents preceded the *Laws.* Boston teacher John Cotton submitted *Moses His Judicials* in 1636; although not accepted, this work influenced the eventual formation of law and seems to have been influential on both New Haven and Rhode Island legal codes. A draft by Ipswich minister Nathaniel Ward had a greater impact on the formulation of the Masschusetts "Body of Liberties." Although more a bill of rights than a body of laws, eighty-six of its one hundred clauses were adopted for the *Laws and Liberties.*

Two other incidents prompted the publication: the Hingham military controversy of 1645 and Robert Child's Remonstrance of 1646. Led by John Hills, a committee formed in 1645 succeeded in producing the required laws. Arranged alphabetically, *Laws and Liberties* lists most laws "of general concernment" that had been enacted by the General Court and covers a wide range of areas and behaviors, including criminal, civil, and inheritance law. Among the controversial laws is the list of capital laws (including offenses such as idolatry, witchcraft, blasphemy, bestiality, homosexuality, adultery, parent cursing, and the like) as well as a law specifically targeting Anabaptists.

See also: Law in Puritan New England, *Moses His Judicials* and Mosaic Law, Massachusetts Body of Liberties of 1641 (in Primary Sources)
Further Reading
Daniel Coquillette, ed., *Law in Colonial Massachusetts, 1630–1800* (Boston, 1985); Richard Ross, "The Legal Past of Early New England: Notes for the Study of Law, Legal Culture, and Intellectual History," *William and Mary Quarterly* 50 (1993), 28–41; Ronald Walters, "New England Society and the *Laws and Liberties* of Massachusetts, 1648," *Essex Institute Historical Collections* 106 (1970), 145–168.

Michael G. Ditmore

Lectures and Lectureships

This refers to sermons preached at times other than the regular service of morning prayer, in most cases by parochial incumbents, but occasionally by independent ministers who lacked a benefice and were prepared to live by their preaching. There were essentially three types of lectureship, but despite their institutional differences, all three stemmed from a common conviction among Reformed, Protestant churchmen of the centrality of the preached word to the process of conversion and the economy of grace. Only with the rise of Arminianism in the 1590s and the conviction among some churchmen that the sacraments, rather than the word preached, were the principal vehicles of grace did the importance of lectures come to be questioned and ultimately to be seen as dangerous because so difficult for the Crown and hierarchy to control. Town preachers and parish lecturers had much in common; the third institutional type, the lecture by combination, came largely from clerical and in many cases episcopal initiative.

Although sermons were in increasing demand in the late medieval church, most priests, unlike the preaching friars, lacked the education necessary to become competent preachers, a situation the Catholic Church found tolerable, given the central role assigned to the Mass. For the new Protestant Church, preaching was essential as a tool of evangelization and as a means, now that the Bible was available in the vernacular, to explain what that complex work had to do with the process of salvation by faith alone. In the 1622 Directions Concerning Preachers, James I defined lecturers as "a new body severed from he ancient clergy of England, as being neither parsons, vicars, or curates," but in fact most lecturers were rectors, vicars, or curates; virtually all were ordained priests licensed to preach; and the institution dates back at least to the beginning of Elizabeth's reign, more than sixty years before. Thomas Lever, the Edwardian reformer, had no sooner returned in 1559 from exile in Zürich, where he had sought safety during Catholic Queen Mary's reign, than he was invited by the town of Coventry "to proclaim the gospel to them." By 1562, if not a year or two earlier, the corporation of the town of Leicester provided lectures on Wednesdays and Fridays and required one from every household to attend, a kind of forced evangelization that attests to the awareness that much of the population was still Catholic. The town lecturer at Ipswich appears to date back to the 1540s, and this Protestant institution may in turn have been based on the earlier guild priest. In London Whittington College, dating from the fifteenth century, had an endowed divinity lecture in addition to an almshouse located in the parish of St. Michael Paternoster Royal. Although Whittington's chantry was suppressed in King Edward's reign, the divinity lecture entrusted to the Mercers' and Clothworkers' Companies continued at St. Michael's as a parish lecture. In 1559 the early morning lectures at St. Antholin's in London were being preached by three well-known nonconformists, and in 1560 Christ Church Newgate instituted lectures on Wednesdays and Fridays. By 1640 there were town lectures in 74 Parliamentary boroughs, at least 52 of which were controlled by the borough corporation. By that year, 117 London urban parishes had hired lecturers at one time or another. In the diocese of London alone outside the city, another 65 parishes had had lecturers by that date. Lectureships were thick on the ground in the southeast, East Anglia, and parts of the Midlands where there was a powerful Puritan presence, such as Northamptonshire, but like the borough corporation lectureships, which were scattered across the breadth and length of the land from Newcastle upon Tyne in the north to Bristol in the West, parish lectures were found everywhere. In 1637 John Tombes, one of Sir Robert Harley's Puritan clerical clients, bragged that he had lectured at Leominster, Herefordshire, for the past decade. In 1614 William Jones, a godly merchant and London haberdasher, left a bequest that provided for lectureships in Newland, Gloucestershire, and Monmouth across the border in Wales.

Since lectureships existed before there was a self-conscious Puritan movement and continued after Puritan Dissenters were removed from the restored Church of England in 1662, the connection between Puritanism and lectureships was obviously not an exclusive one. There was, however, an affinity. Although much of the early Protestant leadership of the Elizabethan Church recognized the centrality of preaching—it was Archbishop Grindal who claimed that "Public and continual preaching of God's word is the ordinary mean and instrument of the salvation of mankind"—in fact the liturgy in the Book of Common Prayer allowed little time for a sermon. The Elizabethan Settlement required only that a quarterly sermon be preached in every parish; the Canons of 1604 imposed a requirement of a monthly sermon. Clearly the official church did not set a high priority on preaching, although individual bishops both preached themselves and encouraged the training of priests who lacked the ability, by sponsoring prophesyings and later ministerial conferences. In the early years of the Elizabethan Settlement, there were too few educated clergy prepared to preach the kind of sermon acceptable to Protestants to staff the approximately 9,000 parishes in England, and in any event the queen preferred that her clergy read the sermons contained in the Book of Homilies, safely orthodox statements that contained no challenge to the ecclesiastical order by law established. If "without the preaching of the word," as the Puritan Edward Dering insisted, "we can never have faith," and if preaching was "even the very way to bring people into a state of salvation," as the House of Commons' order "for the Establishing of Preaching Lecturers," insisted in 1641, then a way had to be found to remedy the paucity of preachers and the poverty of many parochial livings, whose benefices were too poor to attract a university-trained preaching minister. The solution was found largely in the lectureship, although lectureships were never preached exclusively by Puritans.

The solution, however, was not without its problems. Lecturers expected to be paid for their skill in preaching, and such salaries, which were initially small (the St. Antholin's lecturers were paid as little as £6 in 1559), soon rose (the lecturer at St. Lawrence Jewry was paid £10 in 1570 but £60 in 1631). In Lincoln, where the two vicarages and the rectory all had incomes of less than £6 per annum, the lecturer was paid £40 in 1590. Providing what the godly laity considered an adequate number of sermons by godly preachers was expensive, and both contributions and bequests mounted throughout the period to support an apparently insatiable demand for sermons. The very fact that lecturers were paid by the laity gave the lay godly the power to appoint and dismiss a lecturer and to a degree to defy ecclesiastical censures on those preachers they favored. When Bishop Godfrey Goodman prohibited John Workman from preaching his lectures at Gloucester in 1633, the city council simply continued his salary until a suit in High Commission against the magistrates in 1635 stopped such defiance.

Lectures by combination were less problematic. Normally preached in a market town by beneficed clergy in the neighborhood gratis, they did not involve the lay control that a salaried lectureship did. Further, the fact that the ministers were beneficed was to a degree a guarantee that those preaching were not nonconformists. Such combinations seem to have arisen out of the early Elizabethan prophesyings or exercises, in part as a mechanism enabling unskilled clerics to learn from their better-educated peers how to preach an exegetical and evangelical sermon; the preaching and teaching at these exercises stretched over two or three days, frequently under the supervision of the archdeacon or bishop. Prophesyings were suppressed officially in 1577 in the province of Canterbury by order of Queen Elizabeth, but similar exercises were begun in various towns in the province of York and survived so long as they had the blessing and license of the bishop. Even in the south, such exercises and lectures by combination survived with the blessing of the more evangelical bishops and in some cases with their active encouragement, although usually with some proviso that those preaching be conformable and peaceable. The royal instructions of 1629 that required that Sunday afternoon sermons be turned into catechetical exercises nevertheless permitted combination lectures so long as they were preached by "grave and orthodox divines." At least eighty-five such lectures by combination have been identified, and a number of them—as at Banbury, Kettering, and Bury St. Edmunds—were to all intents dominated by local Puritan ministers. These were essentially collegial institutions, and attempts to impose a combination lecture against local wishes could be a prescription for failure. After the suspension and departure of the popular Thomas Hooker from Chelmsford, Jeffrey Watt, rector of Leigh Magna, wrote to Dr. Arthur Duck, Laud's commissary, that while he and others were willing "to uphold that lecture, upon your appointment," nevertheless to be "(as some say) thrust upon them without any desires on their parts" was bound to produce "small success of our preaching to a people nothing desiring it." Watt went on to say that he would rather face the censure of the bishop than the anger of the people.

Lectureships existed before there were Puritans and after, but lectureships came to be identified as a Puritan institution, peculiarly suited to their demand for a church centered on a preaching ministry.

See also: Feoffees for Impropriations, Pinners' Hall, Prophesyings, Salters' Hall, St. Antholin's
Further Reading
Patrick Collinson, "Lectures by Combination," in Patrick Collinson, Godly People (London, 1983), 467–498; Paul S. Seaver, The Puritan Lectureships (Stanford, 1970).

Paul Seaver

Leisure Time, Theology of

Considering the long-standing popular opinion that they were pleasure-hating killjoys and joyless fanatics, Puritans expressed rhetorical beliefs about leisure that were surprisingly supportive of it. Time spent away from work was essential, Puritan ministers preached, in order to refresh and strengthen God's elect as they pursued earthly piety in preparation for eternal afterlife. Puritan ministers argued that grim-faced ascetics or solitary celibates perverted rather than celebrated the true meaning of Christianity. "God has given us temporals to enjoy," the minister, Joshua Moody, told his congregation: "we should therefore suck the sweet of them, and so slake our thirst with them, as not to be insatiably craving after more."

Moody's words reveal explicitly the psychological and sociological importance Puritans attached to their theological concept of leisure. Original sin produced a flawed human nature in all people that made them require some pleasure in their earthly life. By engaging in appropriate leisure activities, however, one could ward off the temptations of engaging in inappropriate ones. Thus, godly leisure became one of the most dependable shields against the ungodly pursuit of excess. Denial of all pleasures would only work for a short time, and then the unnatural dam would burst with sinful violence.

Once having established the theoretical legitimacy of leisure, Puritans hedged the actual practice of relaxing activities with caveats and restrictions that betrayed an uneasiness that lay just beneath the rhetoric of acceptance. Most obviously, they forbade any conduct that either detracted from God or was condemned by scripture. So, too, they proscribed many apparently innocent diversions such as dancing between men and women, because these activities, although not harmful in themselves, could lead to collateral sins such as fornication. Activities popular with people the Puritans regarded as morally impure—Catholics, Italians, the idle rich—were often condemned as guilty of sinfulness by historical association. Puritans regarded violent and competitive sports that could produce injuries or hostilities as antisocial and thus contrary to the public good. Activities associated with an enhanced sensuality or immoral thought—theater, for example—fell outside of the acceptable limits for God's saints.

The ideal form of leisure, endorsed by virtually all Puritans, would be moderate, truly relaxing, devoid of temptation, and productive. Berry-picking and fishing were favorite Puritan pastimes. If these activities took place in groups, were educational, and made people more aware of God, so much the better. Puritans liked communal fun—dinner parties and conversation, group readings, house raisings, and harvest parties. Some activities they endorsed tentatively, always a little afraid that "sober mirths," as Reverend Benjamin Colman called these double-edged leisure activities, could easily degenerate into unacceptable behaviors—"carnal mirths." Thus, the appropriate pleasure associated with sexual intercourse between husband and wife could easily slide into wantonness; or the productive relaxation that came with a glass of beer could lead to the sin of drunkenness. Puritans required righteous men and women to be ever vigilant when pursuing leisure to prevent the devil from snaring their souls when their guards were down.

The caveats, restrictions, and ambivalence with which they surrounded their support for leisure gave rise to the popular perception that developed in Elizabethan England and has persisted across the centuries that Puritans were hostile to fun. They were not. Puritan preachers and writers, however, spent so much time worrying in their pulpits and in print about bad leisure activities, that they drowned their endorsement of good leisure in their own chorus of fears.

See also: Ballads, Music, Sports and Recreation, Theater and Opposition
Further Reading
Bruce C. Daniels, *Puritans at Play: Leisure and Recreation in Colonial New England* (New York, 1995); Alice Morse Earle, *Stage Coach and Tavern Days* (1900); Perry Miller, *The New England Mind in the Seventeenth Century* (New York, 1939).

Bruce C. Daniels

Literacy

Puritans believed that literacy, alongside listening to sermons, was desirable and important: it was almost a qualification for salvation. Placing the Bible at the center of their faith and shunning sacramental rituals, Puritans placed added emphasis on reading God's word. Their preachers regularly complained of ignorance and illiteracy as impediments to further reformation.

However, *literacy* was not easily defined. Contemporaries used the term to refer to the ability to read a variety of different, professionally distinct forms of handwriting and typefaces. Notably, it meant the ability to read Latin. Such a litmus test conceals those who could read their own language and those more at home with italic type ("black letter"), which was learned from childhood, than roman type or the abbreviated handwriting used by officials. Low estimates of literacy, based on the ability to write one's name, suggest that the Reformation coincided with a significant rise in literacy: from about 20 percent of men and 5 percent of women in England in 1558 to about 30 percent of men and 10 percent of women in 1642. However, as writing was taught at a later age than reading and usually to boys and not girls, it is likely than many more had reading skills. In addition, more prosperous urban areas had higher rates than rural ones, and regions that welcomed Puritanism, such as Essex, often had rates higher than average. Individual Puritan communities, which often invested heavily in education, appear to have had exceptionally high literacy rates.

Puritan preachers urged reading both at home and in church. Many advised the following of the biblical texts that were read in church and the making of sermon notes. Puritan towns, such as Bury St. Edmunds and Halifax, were among the first to have parish libraries, for the use of clergy and laity. Personal collections circulated in networks of godly sociability: Archbishop Tobie Matthew allowed godly clergy to use his library to inform their sermons and printed books. Reading was also a standard feature of conventicles, where the Bible was read in groups.

Literacy was a feature of domestic devotion, where as well as the Bible, Puritans read books such as John Foxe's Book of Martyrs, sermons, and other Puritan texts. Such reading was usually practiced aloud and in company: fathers read to their children and servants as a domestic religious exercise. Puritans regularly donated books in their wills; many, such as Richard Baxter and John Shaw, distributed numerous Bibles among the poor. Puritan books demonstrated that literacy was central to their faith. Some books, including Nicholas Bownd's *Doctrine of the Sabbath* (1595) and Alexander Nowell's *Catechism* (1591), presented it as part of a wider program; others, such as Henry Webley, whose manuscript was entitled *A breef and godly exhortatione to the daylye reedinge of the Holye Scriptures* (1603), taught that literacy was central to Puritan devotion.

See also: Bible, Family Piety
Further Reading
David Cressy, *Literacy and the Social Order: Reading and Writing in Tudor and Stuart England* (Cambridge, Eng., 1980); Adam Fox, *Oral and Literate Culture in England, 1500–1700* (Oxford, 2000).

Andrew Cambers

M

Magnalia Christi Americana

The modern scholar Perry Miller noted, perceptively, that though Cotton Mather spent only three years writing the *Magnalia Christi Americana*, it took "all the country's experience to produce." When Mather began to write his masterful history of New England in the 1690s, the status of New England was much in doubt. The Massachusetts charter had been annulled, and Puritans were enduring the tyrannies delivered by Dominion Governor Edmund Andros. Mather sought to demonstrate that despite appearances, New England had not been defeated and was worthy of a grand history illustrating its glory. Indeed, at over one thousand pages, the *Magnalia* gave Mather the opportunity not only to write a history of New England but also to express his family's version of history. With its accounts of ordinary and remarkable events as well as famous and infamous individuals, it is the most comprehensive, original, and visionary seventeenth-century American Puritan history.

Although Mather discussed many of the same themes as his first- and second-generation predecessors had, the *Magnalia* differed from other histories both quantitatively and qualitatively. More than any other Puritan historian, he demonstrated his extraordinary, unparalleled passion for New England. At the heart of Mather's story was New England itself, rather than a colony with a connection, however tentative, to England. The *Magnalia* expressed a sense of New England's role, potential, uniqueness, and wonder unlike that found in any other Puritan writing. It was crucial to show that the experiment was succeeding, and to defend this premise, Mather recounted the lives of clergy and rulers, the history of Harvard, and stories of remarkable providences. All of these supported Mather's idea that New England had already become worthy of merit in the eyes of God and that it still held great potential to become a New Israel.

At the same time, Mather could not be completely certain that America would become the elect nation he hoped for. He was especially concerned that his generation and their children were less pious than their forebears and lacked respect for the clergy. Mather showed how God responded to this declension: the colonists were punished harshly with various misfortunes. Despite such misgivings, Mather desired to write his own generation into history and indicated that they might reform themselves and revive their dying piety. The *Magnalia* has, because of this message, been compared to a jeremiad. Mather's efforts to redeem his own times were self-serving; as well as being a history, the work gave him the opportunity to explain his controversial positions and justify his actions.

Ultimately, Mather concludes his work unsure if he should be optimistic or pessimistic about the Puritans' prospects in America, and he thus shares much in common with first-generation New England historians. While he identified himself more as a New England Puritan than the historians who preceded him, he did not end the *Magnalia* on the confident note on which he began it. As original and as grand as the *Magnalia* may seem, Mather showed how deeply he had imbibed the founders' myths as well as their trepidations about New England's future. Yet it is a grand work, set apart by Mather's imagination and eighty years of history behind him as well as a motivating passion unseen in any other Puritan.

Further Reading
Christopher Felker, *Reinventing Cotton Mather in the American Renaissance: Magnalia Christi Americana in Hawthorne, Stowe, and Stoddard* (Boston, 1993); Kenneth Silverman, *The Life and Times of Cotton Mather* (New York, 1984).

Rachelle E. Friedman

Major-Generals

The rule of the major-generals, Oliver Cromwell's experiment with direct military dictatorship, lasted a little over sixteen months, but even today the memory of that period shapes a very pervasive image of English Puritanism. Cromwell's decision to appoint a number of his most trusted military commanders (several of whom were related to him by blood or marriage) as regional governors was motivated partly by his failure to achieve a stable political system, but equally by the alarm caused by royalist uprisings in England in the summer of 1655.

By the time the major-generals took up their posts in late 1655, England and Wales had been divided into ten military administrative units. Northern England was allotted to John Lambert (Yorkshire, Westmorland, Cumberland, Northumberland, Durham). Charles Worsley was given charge of Lancashire, Cheshire, and Staffordshire (which, after his death in June 1656, passed to Tobias Bridge). In the Midlands, Cromwell placed his cousin Edward Whalley (Lincolnshire, Leicestershire, Derbyshire, Nottinghamshire, and Warwickshire), William Boteler (Bedfordshire, Huntingdonshire, Rutland, and Northamptonshire), and James Berry (Worcestershire, Herefordshire, Shropshire, Monmouthshire, and Wales). The West Country was entrusted by Cromwell to his brother-in-law John Desborough (Gloucestershire, Somerset, Wiltshire, Dorset, Devon, Cornwall). Southern and eastern England was divided between Cromwell's son-in-law, Charles Fleetwood (Oxfordshire, Buckinghamshire, Hertfordshire, Cambridgeshire, Essex, Norfolk, and Suffolk), "Praying William" Goffe (Sussex, Hampshire, and Berkshire), and Thomas Kelsey (Kent and Surrey). The administration of London and Middlesex was shared between the elderly Philip Skippon and John Barkstead.

Within these regions were smaller administrative units, overseen by subordinates. Fleetwood's deputy in East Anglia, for example, was Major-General Hezekiah Haynes. Ireland was ruled by Henry Cromwell, Oliver's second surviving son, although he was technically subordinate to Fleetwood. The government of Scotland was supervised by George Monck.

The major-generals were coordinated by Cromwell's secretary of state, John Thurloe, and supported by regional authorities in the shape of county commissions. These were formally in place by October 1655, and effective military government commenced that November. The origins of many commissioners were distinctly humble, although a few came from traditional county families. In general, however, it is thought that most were comparatively inexperienced in wielding power. Their lack of experience and status was resented by many of the older gentry, even Puritans, who considered themselves the natural local rulers. The fact that the military governors were distinctly Independent in hue, however, did not prevent Presbyterians from sitting as commissioners, even though a few refused the honor. Thus, just as the characters of the individual major-generals varied, so did those of the county commissions. Whereas in Somerset the persecution of royalists and levying of taxes appears to have been comparatively mild, zealous Essex commissioners even "decimated" the estate of Major-General Haynes's brother. The central authorities in London, including Cromwell himself, often found themselves more moderate than county commissions. Such radicalism sometimes resulted in the intimidation of not only royalists, but also of moderate Puritans such as Ralph Josselin, who reported some Essex commissioners had threatened him with transportation to Barbados.

Surprisingly, the machinery by which the major-generals enforced their rule was not primarily through the New Model Army. Although the Army numbered some 53,000 in 1655, only 11,000 were stationed in England and Wales—3,000 around London. Not only were the remainder too scattered to police a population in excess of 5 million, but the soldiers themselves were far from homogeneously Puritan. A significant proportion of the infantry were conscripts, while many others were former royalist prisoners of war. Many officers were not well disposed to the idea of a Protectorate. Instead, the major-generals utilized newly raised local militias, who, being volunteers, were largely combat veterans and ideologically committed.

The duties of the major-generals were wide-ranging, principally concerned with the maintenance of national security and the promotion of godly morality. They were required to disarm individuals disaffected from the state and to monitor their subsequent activities. An example of the care with which this was done can be seen in Major-General Haynes's returns for Essex, preserved in the British Library. The major-generals were to supervise the collection of a "decimation" tax, levied on landowners known to have supported the Stuart cause since 1641. In pursuance of their duty to "encourage and promote godliness and virtue and discourage and discountenance all profanes and ungodliness," the major-generals were to detect and close places of ill repute, such as brothels, gaming houses, and unlicensed alehouses. They were to deal with idle persons, suppress proscribed sports such as horseracing, bearbaiting, and cockfighting, enforce the observance of the Sabbath, and prevent swearing and fornication. They were to punish those married by religious, rather than civil ceremony, and to prohibit Christmas and Easter celebrations. They were to supervise committees of "Triers" and "Ejectors," who vetted sitting and prospective ministers and schoolteachers. Most of these duties, however, were no more than what had been required of civilian magistrates, and even the Puritan-inspired legislation against festivals and re-

ligious marriage had been in place long before 1655.

The major-generals excited considerable resentment, but whether their unpopularity has been exaggerated by propaganda disseminated after the restoration of the monarchy, and by subsequent historians, is a matter of debate. Against those who have claimed (with some validity) that the major-generals were detested in the localities, others have pointed out that the military governors found considerable support among Puritan gentry and committed godly among the general population. Such people saw the major-generals as the spearhead of the godly reformation that had been expected and prayed for after the defeat of the royalist armies in the Civil Wars. Without doubt, however, the cost of maintaining such large military forces was huge, and the heavy taxation required was deeply resented. Even if their reputation as arrogant killjoys was exaggerated, the traditional English resentment of arbitrary government and of standing armies was echoed even in the writings of committed Puritans such as William Prynne.

When in January 1657 a militia bill designed to provide permanent revenue for the local militias was defeated in Parliament, Cromwell promptly abandoned the experiment and began to reassign his major-generals to other duties.

See also: New Model Army
Further Reading
Christopher Durston, *Cromwell's Major-Generals* (Manchester, Eng., 2001); Anthony Fletcher, "The Religious Motivation of Cromwell's Major-Generals," in D. Baker, ed., *Religious Motivation: Biographical and Social Problems for the Church Historian,* Studies in Church History, vol. 15 (Oxford, 1978).

David J. Appleby

Marian Exiles

After the death of her brother, King Edward VI, Mary Tudor acceded to the throne of England. Under Edward's rule, England had retained and further reformed the Protestant faith that Edward's father, King Henry VIII, had imposed upon the nation. Henry had overthrown Catholicism and become head of England's Protestant Church in order to obtain a divorce from Mary Tudor's mother, Catherine of Aragon. Thus, Mary identified the Protestant faith with the dishonoring of her mother and the loss of her claim to inherit the English throne as Henry's oldest child.

Upon her accession to the throne in 1553, Queen Mary restored Catholicism to England and instituted repressive measures against Protestants. Threatened by the queen's insistence that they repudiate their beliefs, about 800 Protestants fled England. Referred to as the Marian exiles, many of those Protestants, who escaped from England to the Continent, settled in Geneva or Zürich. The refugees that lived in Geneva fell under the influence of John Calvin, while those who resided in Zürich benefited from the teachings and practices of Henry Bullinger. Under these influences, the Marian exiles further developed their own religious ideas while they engaged in practices they witnessed in their adopted Protestant communities. On the Continent, English Protestants enjoyed an even greater ability to work out their theological beliefs than they had experienced under the rule of Edward VI.

When Mary Tudor died in 1558, her half sister Elizabeth inherited the crown. With Queen Mary dead, many of the refugees felt free to return to England. The returning exiles brought home with them plans for completely reforming the Protestant Church of England with the religious beliefs and practices acquired during their time abroad. The resistance of Queen Elizabeth to more radical religious reform, however, stalled their efforts. The queen's decision to follow a more moderate path of religious reform meant that the insistence on deeper reforms made by Marian exiles and committed Protestants who had remained in England during the reign of Queen Mary formed the basis of what became the Puritan movement.

See also: Marian Martyrs, Marian Underground, International Puritanism
Further Reading
C. H. Garrett, *The Marian Exiles* (Oxford, 1938); M. M. Knappen, *Tudor Puritanism* (Chicago,

1939); Andrew Pettegree, ed., *Marian Protestantism: Six Studies* (Brookfield, VT, 1996).

Susan Ortmann

Marian Martyrs

King Henry VIII renounced Roman Catholicism and the papacy in order to obtain a divorce from Mary Tudor's mother, Catherine of Aragon. Henry became head of England's Protestant Church and with his archbishop of Canterbury, Thomas Cranmer, set about reforming the new Church of England. Under the rule of Edward VI, Henry's son, England retained the Protestant faith. Archbishop Cranmer with Edward's support continued to remodel the English church. After the death of her brother King Edward VI, Mary Tudor acceded to the throne of England.

Mary identified the Protestant faith with the dishonoring of her mother Catherine and the loss of her claim to inherit the English throne as the first of Henry's children. English crown in hand, Queen Mary resolved to restore Catholicism to England. Her marriage to Philip of Spain and persecution of Protestants cost her support. While the Marian exiles fled from England to the Continent in order to practice their faith, others remained under Mary's rule, and some of those who stayed in England proved ready to die for their faith.

In December of 1555 the first group of the approximately 300 Marian martyrs were executed under Queen Mary's rule. Charged with and found guilty of heresy, some of those burnt at the stake included Bishops Hugh Latimore and Nicholas Ridley, and Thomas Cranmer, the archbishop of Canterbury. The deaths of the Marian martyrs earned Queen Mary the nickname of "Bloody Mary." Queen Mary died in 1558. Her half sister Elizabeth succeeded her on the throne.

Queen Elizabeth's moderate approach to religious reform and the return of the Marian exiles helped promote the growth of the Puritan movement and also advanced the importance of the Marian martyrs. John Foxe's Book of Martyrs, in particular, helped to shape the depiction of Mary's rule as ruthless and Catholic corruption as the root cause of unjust Protestant martyrdom. Richard Rogers's *Seven Treatises for Living a Godly Life,* also used the martyrdom of Protestants living under Queen Mary's rule to encourage godly citizens (Puritans) to zealously practice their faith and remain committed to properly reforming the English Protestant Church.

See also: Book of Martyrs, Marian Exiles, Marian Underground

Further Reading
C. H. Garrett, *The Marian Exiles* (Oxford, 1938); M. M. Knappen, *Tudor Puritanism* (Chicago, 1939); Andrew Pettegree, ed., *Marian Protestantism: Six Studies* (Brookfield, VT, 1996).

Susan Ortmann

Marian Underground

Shortly after the accession of Mary Tudor to the English throne in 1553, Parliament approved legislation restoring the Mass and reinstating legal penalties for heresy. Catholicism was being restored, and Protestants were faced with stark choices. Perhaps as many as a thousand went into exile. Hundreds were arrested and imprisoned, with approximately three hundred being executed. An unknown number of Englishmen who had come to believe in Protestantism during the reigns of Henry VIII and Edward VI chose a different course. Such individuals sought to remain in England and live under the radar of the authorities. Just as many loyal Catholics had hidden their religious treasures during the previous regimes in hope of a better day, so a London merchant, Edward Underhill, sealed his Protestant books "in a brick wall by the chimney side of my chamber, where they were preserved from mold or mice until the first year of our most gracious queen Elizabeth." Some—including the princess Elizabeth—publicly worshipped in accord with the new dispensation while keeping their true views secret. But there were other options.

The Marian regime relied upon parish officials to report those who were not attending required worship. Not all clergy were as eager as others to do so,

and it can be imagined that in parishes where a majority were sympathetic to Protestantism and parishes that were geographically removed from the seats of zealous Catholic bishops, it would have been relatively easy to go one's own way. Indeed, this is likely what led Adam Winthrop, the master of the Clothworkers' Company and thus a prominent Londoner, to leave the city and relocate on his rural Suffolk manor where he was patron of the church living. A slightly different strategy was employed by his son, William, who shortly after the accession of Mary moved a few blocks from a residence in the parish of St. Peter's Cornhill to the neighboring parish of St. Michael's. The rector of St. Peter's no longer had responsibility for him; and the odds were that he would be able to hide his presence in his new parish.

Those who wished to continue Protestant worship could draw hope from the long success of the Lollards in maintaining their faith underground over the centuries. There were clearly secret congregations that met in private rooms, in ships, and elsewhere to worship. Evidence exists, for instance, that on the first two Easter Sundays of Mary's reign, William Winthrop, Christopher Goodman, and Michael Reniger celebrated Holy Communion in the home of John Pulleyne. London was large enough in size and population for the Protestant underground to survive undetected. Edward Underhill reported that there was no better "place to shift in this realm . . ., notwithstanding the great spying and searching." Pulleyne also traveled into the countryside, nurturing underground congregations in Colchester, Essex, and elsewhere. Members of the underground were able to offer some level of material support to those who were imprisoned. Papers of those who were martyred were preserved by such secret Protestants.

Those in exile were frequently critical of those in England who hid their faith under a bushel, but the fact is that many of those then helped rebuild Protestantism during the reign of Queen Elizabeth. Not the least of these was Matthew Parker, Elizabeth's first archbishop of Canterbury.

See also: William Winthrop, Marian Exiles, Marian Martyrs

Further Reading

Andrew Pettegree, *Marian Protestantism: Six Studies* (Brookfield, VT, 1996).

Francis J. Bremer

Marprelate Tracts

The Marprelate tracts are seven Presbyterian pseudonymous pamphlets important to both English religious and literary history, published between October 1588 and September 1589. By 1588, the cause of Presbyterian reform appeared bleak. Queen Elizabeth had blocked all efforts at ecclesiastical reform through parliament, and with her angry speeches and imprisonment of unduly assertive members, she left no doubt that she would continue to do so. The appointment to her Privy Council of the puritans' archenemy Archbishop John Whitgift in 1586 and the death of their protector the Earl of Leicester in early 1588 signaled the growing dearth of friends in high places to protect and promote their cause. It was looking increasingly improbable that reform would take place through official channels.

As a result, Presbyterian activists resorted to more unconventional and desperate measures. In 1587 and 1588, informal provincial classes and synods began meeting and started debating how much, if any, respect and validity was to be accorded the bishops and nonpuritan ministers of the Church of England. Some of their members seem to have envisioned England gradually becoming Presbyterian through the irresistible but peaceful force of a growing movement, while some even toyed with the idea of implementing Presbyterianism against Elizabeth's will.

The Presbyterian organization was furtive and, in its own eyes at least, nonconfrontational and within legal bounds. The Marprelate tracts were neither. In 1587 the dean of Salisbury, Dr. John Bridges, wrote a large volume attacking Presbyterianism and defending episcopal government. A response to an earlier Presbyterian treatise, it received two sober responses from Presbyterian divines. It also received a response of a very different nature by an author who identified himself as Martin Marprelate—a response

almost stream-of-consciousness in structure, far more interested in scurrilous gossip and jokes than in analysis of Bridges's works, and frequently wandering off into lively and very entertaining personal attacks on various bishops and other foes of the Presbyterians. Two months later, another, slightly less giddy follow-up pamphlet under Martin's name appeared. Martin's fresh inventive satire is regarded as a landmark in English literature.

By this time the Marprelate affair took on a life of its own. Thomas Cooper, bishop of Winchester, responded and thereby provided Martin with a fresh target. More pamphlets followed. The government launched a two-pronged attack. Its agents scoured the Midlands for the press, while it fought fire with fire. It paid its own satirists to attack Martin, while Martin became a figure of crude abuse on the London stage. Martin's printers were caught, on 14 August 1589, and tortured. One angry short last pamphlet under Martin's name appeared at the end of September.

Apart from the personal attacks and wit, Martin's was a conventional Presbyterianism, distinctive only in its uncompromising urgency. The struggle between the Presbyterians and the bishops would tear England apart if the government did not intervene to end it, Martin warned, and should the government support the bishops, the outcome would be apostasy and the wrath of God. The pamphlets made a variety of suggestions as to ways to end the dispute. In one of his tracts, Martin suggested that Parliament had the authority to institute reformation even over the monarch's objection. He did not pursue this truly revolutionary line of thought, although hostile critics made much of it. His other suggestions were standard Presbyterian appeals. He called for a great supplication to the queen, a supplication that would draw its force not only from the righteousness of the cause of the godly, but also from their strength—"lords, knights, gentlemen, ministers and people" a hundred thousand signatures, "the strength of our land, and the sinew of her Majesty's royal government." Elizabeth was under the sway of evil counselors, and if she could only be reached by this impressive demonstration of the will of the people, then Presbyterianism would be installed. He also wanted the defenders and opponents of Presbyterianism to have a winner-decides-all debate.

The Marprelate tracts could not have had press runs in more than three figures, but that small figure scarcely conveys the extent of their distribution. Copies were said to have been read to pieces, and we have one account of a puritan minister gathering the godly together in a house to share with them the latest product of the Marprelate press. The frantic efforts of the government to track down the press seem to have been based on a realistic appraisal of the pamphlets' appeal.

Some Presbyterians thought that Martin's appeal to the people through ridicule was worth a try and that the defamation of the bishops could be seen as a just judgment of God upon them. But his tactics were far from universally appreciated among Presbyterians. Leading puritans like Thomas Cartwright showed a great deal of unhappiness about the Marprelate tracts. The tracts, they felt, displayed a less than godly scurrility, and mockery was a less than godly substitute for argument. Furthermore, Presbyterians liked to project themselves as the rightful religious establishment in England, the rightful monitors of order and decorum. Martin's guerrilla and gutter tactics, completely severed from the respectable traditions of learned exchange and severed even from conventional venues of change like Parliament, neatly played into their opponents' preferred portrayal of them as "popular" and seditious sectaries promoting social instability. Martin, in turn, denounced his puritan critics as cowards.

Martin certainly did not help the Presbyterian cause, but it might be doubted that he did much damage to a movement that was already pretty much dead in the water. It has been argued, however, that by bringing the debate over church government into the gutter, Martin licensed the creation of the "puritan" as a figure of abuse. He was thus indirectly responsible, this argument goes, for the standard "stage" puritan who began appearing in the 1590s, a hypocritical, oversexed, greedy fraud. However little direct damage Martin may have done, the search he precipitated did have se-

rious consequences. It uncovered the secret classis organization, and the trials that followed effectively killed Presbyterianism as an organized movement in England.

See also: Censorship, Crime and Punishment, Martin Marprelate

Further Reading

Leland H. Carlson, *Martin Marprelate, Gentleman: Master Job Throkmorton Laid Open in His Colors* (Los Angeles, 1981); Patrick Collinson, "Ecclesiastical Vitriol: Religious Satire in the 1590s and the Invention of Puritanism," in John Guy, ed., *The Reign of Elizabeth I: Court and Culture in the Last Decade* (Cambridge, Eng. 1995), 150–170; *The Marprelate Tracts [1588–1589]* (facsimile edition, Leeds, Eng., 1967).

Michael P. Winship

Marriage

Marriage was the central institution structuring sexuality, intimacy, and everyday adult life in the early modern English Atlantic world. In most areas, puritans and conforming English Protestants shared the same understanding of marriage as a Christian ordinance, a social rite of passage, and a social and sexual partnership. Puritan attitudes did diverge from the established church position on some points, particularly in regard to the Church of England's retention of Catholic calendrical regulations and the church's continued prohibition of remarriage after divorce. Finally, marriage played a significant role in puritan ideology and practice, as a vehicle for reforming personal conduct, and as a singular and central relationship in the conduct and experience of domestic piety.

Doctrine and Ritual

Pre- and post-Tridentine Catholic doctrine (that is, doctrine before and after the Council of Trent, 1545–1563) designated marriage as a sacrament. This designation had practical and ritual implications. As a transaction conferring interior grace and figuring the union with Christ, marriage was viewed by the Catholic Church as indissoluble. Technically, in all cases where the marriage was proved to be valid, this rendered divorce impossible. Practical separations (termed divorce *a mensa et thoro:* "from table and bed") could be granted in the case of adultery or excessive cruelty. Such a separation relieved spouses of the requirement of cohabitation, but it did not free them from the union itself; neither spouse could remarry. As a church rite, the pre-Tridentine Catholic marriage ritual was restricted to periods during the ritual year deemed appropriate for a celebration of a union both spiritual and carnal. In the pre-Tridentine calendar, marriage was forbidden during Lent, Rogationtide, Trinity, and Advent.

Both Lutheran and Calvinist reform of the sacraments downgraded marriage to a Christian ordinance. According to Reformers, marriage was instituted by God; both the marriage ritual and the marriage relationship should honor God and reflect God's will. But neither the marriage rite nor the relationship conferred grace. Protestant revision of marriage doctrine allowed for the loosening of ritual requirements and made full divorce with remarriage (release *a vinculo matrimonio:* literally, "from the matrimonial bond"; dissolving the marital bond) a possibility in many Protestant states; it also opened the door for greater civil jurisdiction in the regulation of marriage.

Clerical marriage and the value of celibacy were further points of dramatic confessional difference. Both pre- and post-Tridentine Catholic doctrine continued to validate celibacy and virginity as higher spiritual states; it also upheld clerical celibacy as intrinsic to the sacramental state of the priesthood. Protestant reformers abolished the formal institution of spiritual celibacy, the monastic system; in their writings, many Reformers attempted to legitimize marriage as a condition equal with celibacy in social and spiritual value. Concurring with the Catholic view that marriage was divinely instituted for human reproduction and the avoidance of fornication, Protestant theorists more heavily emphasized companionship as an ordained end of marriage as well.

English Reform and Puritan Critique

Protestant theology opened many doors to possible changes in theory, ritual, and practice; the Church of England sometimes closed them. The Elizabethan settlement followed Protestant formulations of marriage as an ordinance rather than a sacrament. It also upheld the Tudor monastic dissolutions and permitted clerical marriage, which became a widespread practice by the end of the Elizabethan era. However, the Elizabethan canons retained the pre-Tridentine calendrical restrictions, and the English homily on marriage continued to utilize the sacramental language of a union with Christ. It also continued to treat the marriage bond as indissoluble under all circumstances. Only a separation *a mensa et thoro* could be obtained from an adulterous or abusive spouse. Separated spouses were guilty of adultery if they attempted to remarry.

The retention of these pre-Tridentine practices invited puritan critique and experiments in puritan reform. Caroline enforcement of the calendrical restrictions became a mild point of liturgical conflict between ceremonialists and evangelicals. There was a failed attempt by the 1628 Parliament to abolish the restrictions and a temporarily successful attempt in the 1645 Presbyterian Directory of Public Worship. Although the Restoration church revived the calendar of prohibited days, historian David Cressy has noted a gradual decline of both calendrical enforcement and calendrical compliance in the late seventeenth century.

From the Elizabethan period onward, Puritan domestic theorists raised objections against Church of England policy on divorce. Claiming that separation without remarriage negated the reproductive and protective purposes of marriage, Thomas Becon and Robert Cleaver argued, in *Golden Boke of Christian Matrimonye* (1542) and *A Godlie Form of Household Government* (1612), respectively, that full divorce with right to remarriage should be permitted to innocent spouses with adulterous partners. In *Christian Oeconomie* (1609), William Perkins extended the argument to cases of desertion, a phenomenon especially afflicting to early modern wives. Theophilus Eaton, a founder and magistrate of New Haven colony, put these arguments into action in 1639. As part of a puritan experiment in both civil and spiritual regulation that lasted until the colony was subsumed by Connecticut in 1665, the New Haven code placed fornication and adultery under civil jurisdiction and legalized divorce *a vinculo matrimonio* in the case of adultery or desertion.

Printed Advice and Private Piety

Across liturgical preferences and reform commitments, early modern English lay attitudes toward the marital relationship reflected a consensus of emotional and social pragmatism, valuing financial solidity, rough similarity in social rank and harmony, and friendship between spouses. However, in the culture of Elizabethan and Stuart printed sermons, puritan clergy disproportionately dominated the discourse. Puritan preaching luminaries such as Robert Cleaver, William Perkins, William Gouge, Thomas Gataker, and Richard Baxter developed marriage and domestic advice sermons into puritan and Dissenting genres. Puritan divines took common values of household order, mutual companionship, and joint domestic duties, and repackaged them as an evangelical practice, linking them to a puritan model of household piety and religious voluntarism.

The preponderance of puritan and dissenting clerical voices in the Elizabethan and Stuart domestic literature prompted earlier historians to partially attribute the origins of companionate marriage (a marital relationship based on mutual affection and heterosexual companionship) and early modern regimes of domestic piety (often termed "spiritualized households" by historians) to puritanism. Finding both to be more broadly based in Continental Humanist thought and in ordinary English practice, current scholarship has highlighted a unique puritan emphasis upon, rather than attitude toward, marriage and domestic mores. Puritan disillusionment with established worship shifted a significant portion of energy toward personal godliness and household religion. Evangelical impulses were channeled into the moral reform of sexual behavior and the religious reform of marriage and the family, as personal and domestic conduct became a venue for articulating puritan and dissenting ideals and identities.

This led to especially harsh objections among puritans to aspects of sexual misconduct, such as the morally ambiguous practice of prenuptial intercourse between betrothed men and women. In New England this approach extended to social policy; the first decades of the Massachusetts and New Haven colonies saw a heightened and far more gender-egalitarian prosecution of fornication, as mid-seventeenth-century New England magistrates were unusually evenhanded in punishing men as well as women.

Puritan attitudes toward gender roles in marriage and in society were generally conventional. However, the puritan emphasis on marriage as a venue for reforming personal conduct mildly mitigated certain aspects of the sexual double standard, as men were pressured in proscriptive discourse to adhere to equal standards of fidelity and chastity. The mutuality of sexual responsibilities also stemmed from the puritan conceptualization of marriage as a covenant. A binding and mutual contract directed toward Christian ends and sealed with spiritual force, the marriage covenant was an evangelical partnership. This understanding placed the married couple at the center of puritan models of domestic and personal reform; wives and husbands contracted to jointly govern a Christian household and facilitate each other's spiritual improvement, through encouragement, admonition, and dyadic sessions of religious conversation, reading, and prayer.

See also: Domestic Relations, Espousal Imagery, Family Piety, Sexuality

Further Reading

Eric Josef Carlson, *Marriage and the English Reformation* (Oxford, 1994); David Cressy, *Birth, Marriage, and Death: Religion, Ritual, and the Life Cycle in Tudor and Stuart England* (Oxford, 1997); Cornelia Hughes Dayton, *Women before the Bar: Gender, Law and Society in Connecticut, 1639–1789* (Chapel Hill, 1995); Richard Greaves, *Society and Religion in Elizabethan England* (Minneapolis, 1981); Mary Beth Norton, *Founding Mothers and Fathers: Gendered Power and the Forming of American Society* (New York, 1996).

Michelle Wolfe

Martin Marprelate

The Marprelate tracts (1588–1589) were seven pseudonymous pamphlets produced by a clandestine printing press, based first at East Molesey on the Thames west of London and then at more than one location in the English Midlands. The identity of the printer is known. He was Robert Waldegrave, whose press was at the service of the most radical of puritan propagandists until its destruction by order of the Court of High Commission. The identity of "Martin Marprelate" ("Marprelate" meaning literally "spoil bishop") is less certain and is the topic on which most of the scholarship devoted to the subject has focused. Among the various names proposed, the more plausible include the radical Welsh preacher John Penry, whose acknowledged attacks on the bishops and Separatist principles were to take him to the gallows in 1593; among the less likely, another Welshman, the soldier of fortune Sir Roger Williams. It is now accepted that if Martin was a single author, then he was the Warwickshire gentleman and member of Parliament (MP) Job Throckmorton. This identification is suggested both by circumstantial evidence and by comparison with Throckmorton's other utterances, including his parliamentary speeches of 1587. The case for Penry (who was certainly collusively involved) is weakened when the tracts are compared with what he is known to have written, which is in an altogether more pedantic and humorless style. But nowadays the game of "hunt the author" has been followed by the postmodernist "death of the author," and we are less resistant to the possibility that the tracts were the work of more than one hand. That being the case, it is hard to resist the suggestion that Throckmorton's fellow MP George Carleton was one of those hands. In 1589 Carleton married the widow Elizabeth Crane, in whose house the first tracts were printed, and the first of all, the "Epistle to the right puisante and terrible priests, my clergie masters of the Convocation house," was subscribed: "Given at my Castle between two wales [or walls]." Now Carleton was keeper of the recusant prisoners at Wisbech Castle, a place surrounded by place-names with the prefix "wal," referring to a Roman wall or bank, such as more than one parish called Walpole.

The case for a single author, whether or not Throckmorton, is favored by the extraordinary and distinctive quality of the satire that the tracts deploy, which makes them a defining moment in the history of satire. The "Epistle" professed to be a response to a ponderous and tedious tome of anti-puritan polemic recently published by Dr. John Bridges, dean of Salisbury, which Martin described as "a very portable booke, a horse may car[r]y it if he be not too weake." Bishops and other senior churchmen were savaged as malevolent prelatical despots, but also as figures of fun: bowling on a Sunday, sending the wood of its way with "the Devil go with thee," and straight away trotting after it themselves. An episcopal sermon preached on St. John's Day goes like this: "John / John / the grace of God / the grace of God / the grace of God: gracious John / not graceles John / but gracious John. John / holy John / holy John / not John ful of holes / but holy John."

We find this as hilarious as Monty Python. But in the perception of the authorities this was rank and dangerous sedition. In the words of a royal proclamation the tracts were "schismatical and seditious books, defamatory libels." The police operation mounted to discover the secret Marprelate press and Marprelate himself, which we may compare to the search for Osama bin Laden, uncovered the network of puritan conferences, or *classes*, and led directly to the trial in the High Commission and Star Chamber of Thomas Cartwright and other leading Presbyterians. As the puritans looked back, toward the end of Elizabeth's reign, they saw the whole episode as a calamity that had destroyed their cause politically. Indeed Martin knew that he was not speaking for majority puritan opinion, which would repudiate him. The authorities responded not only penally and judicially but by answering Martin in his own vein, commissioning anti-Martinist tracts by Thomas Nashe and other denizens of Grub Street, and even mounting crude entertainments on the stage, "jigs" that "lanced and wormed" Martin, a tactic of the future archbishop, Richard Bancroft. It was a little like employing poison gas in modern warfare. The gas is always liable to blow back into the faces of those who have used it.

The question of who Martin Marprelate was is less important than investigation of the genres that fed into and out of the tracts. One significant source was the tradition of satirical polemic, expressed for example in Field and Wilcox's *Admonition to the Parliament* (1572), and especially in the one-liners that appeared in the margins of such books, properly the reader's space. Another was the practice of "registering" the sufferings of the faithful, deployed on a massive scale in John Foxe's *Actes and monuments* (the Book of Martyrs) and in John Field's collections, *A parte of a register* (1593) and the manuscripts preserved as "The Seconde Parte of a Register," which were a source for some of Martin's best stories. But the tracts also belong to a culture of attacking enemies through libelous ballads, "cast abroad" in the streets of provincial towns, or stuck up in public places. They were also inherently theatrical, and Martin adopts the "rap" of the popular comedians of the day, such as Dick Tarleton. It was just recompense that he should himself be lampooned on the stage. The abiding significance of the Marprelate tracts is that they inspired the anti-puritan drama, a genre with which Shakespeare was able to experiment ten years on from the tracts, in *Twelfth Night*, and which received its definitive treatment in Ben Jonson's *Bartholomew Fair*. In a certain sense the anti-Martinist reaction invented Puritanism itself, in the polemical media of the seventeenth century.

See also: Censorship, Crime and Punishment, Marprelate Tracts

Further Reading

Leland H. Carlson, *Martin Marprelate, Gentleman* (Los Angeles, 1981); Patrick Collinson, "Ecclesiastical Vitriol: Religious Satire in the 1590s and the Invention of Puritanism," in John Guy, ed., *The Reign of Elizabeth I: Court and Culture in the Last Decade* (Cambridge, Eng., 1995); *The Marprelate Tracts [1588–1589]* (facsimile edition, Leeds, Eng., 1967).

Patrick Collinson

Massachusetts Bay Company

A company chartered by the king of England, giving commercial rights to those who would settle in New England. The original charter was granted to the New England Company in 1628, which had taken over the Dorchester Company, a short-lived fishing colony in Cape Ann, Massachusetts, established in 1623. The Massachusetts Bay Company received its charter in 1629. Under this patent, Puritan Matthew Craddock was governor and Thomas Goffe, lieutenant governor. The Massachusetts Bay Colony became more than a royal colony authorized by the Crown to conduct trade. The Puritan founders of the colony regarded it as a covenanted society. They strove to implement practices and institutions that would foster its godliness, creating what the first governor, John Winthrop, so famously termed "a City Upon a Hill." The charter specified, "That the said Governour and Companye, and their Successors, maie have forever one comon Seale, to be used in all Causes and Occasions of the said Company, and the same Seale may alter, chaunge, breake, and newe make, from tyme to tyme, at their pleasures."

The Massachusetts Bay Colony came into existence when English Puritans decided to immigrate to the New World. Growing difficulties for Puritans in England along with positive reports from Salem aroused interest in settling in Massachusetts, and in August 1629, serious talk began among those who later emigrated. Those involved in discussions included John Winthrop, Thomas Dudley, and John Saltonstall. Along with others, they signed the Cambridge Agreement, promising to sail for Massachusetts the next year, pending the General Court's approval of the transfer of the company's government and charter to the colony. (The Puritans would thus completely control the colony and charter). Leadership was transferred to Winthrop as governor and John Humphrey as lieutenant governor. Though the Crown had not anticipated that the Puritans would use their patent as more than a commercial charter, the emigrants quickly used the opportunity to create a civil constitution and godly commonwealth immune from England's religious, social, and political ills.

In 1630, the first Puritans arrived in Massachusetts, choosing to settle in Boston. Though the Crown had not anticipated that the Puritans would use their patent as more than a commercial charter, the emigrants quickly used the opportunity to create a civil constitution and society based on their notion of what a godly commonwealth should be. Once in Massachusetts, questions of governance immediately emerged. The Puritans agreed that "freemanship"—bringing along with it the right to vote and hold office—was no longer determined by stockholding, but by church membership. As the charter did not indicate that the colony was subject to the rule of the Board of Governors in England, the New England Puritans quickly assumed exclusive authority. Still, disagreements arose over the nature of power. Governor Winthrop believed that the rule's office was imbued with a divine nature and that the freemen did not have the right to play an active role in the colony's government. Much of Winthrop's *Journal* is a discussion of the colony's early political struggles.

After decades of either benign neglect or failure to assume control, the Crown began to question the prerogatives assumed by the Massachusetts Bay Company. Sir Fernando Gorges attempted to retract the colony's land claims without success. In the 1660s, the king attempted to regain control and regulate the colonies. In 1684 the charter was withdrawn, and the company was driven out of existence. At first the impact was only slight, as the Lords of Trade and the Privy Council did not introduce another form of government. In 1685 a Provisional Government ruled by Sir Edmund Andros was implemented. Massachusetts was made a royal colony in 1691 as part of the Dominion of New England.

> *See also:* Cambridge Agreement, Massachusetts Bay Colony
> *Further Reading*
> John Eric Adair, *Puritans: Religion and Politics in Seventeenth-Century England and America* (Stroud, Eng., 1998); T. H. Breen, *The Character of the Good Ruler: Puritan Political Ideas in New England, 1630–1730* (New Haven, 1974); Francis J. Bremer, *The Puritan Experiment: New England*

Society from Bradford to Edwards (New York, 1978).

Rachelle E. Friedman

Mayflower Compact

Aboard the *Mayflower* on 11 November 1620, 41 men, representing 102 "Pilgrim" and "non-Pilgrim" passengers, signed the Mayflower Compact. This compact bound the signers to covenant and combine themselves into a civil body politic, which would enact just and equal laws for the general good of the colony.

Blown north on their voyage from England to present-day Provincetown in Cape Cod, the *Mayflower* passengers realized that there, their patent from the Virginia Company was invalid. Several men threatened disobedience and expressed a desire to exercise their own liberties. To prevent such behavior, the leading men, drawing upon their English beliefs in social contracts and Puritan concepts of covenants, composed the Mayflower Compact, which contracted the settlers to submit to and obey the government that they would establish. Though the compact did not directly create the framework of government, it acknowledged that a government is legitimate if it derives from the consent of the governed. This was the first example of a "plantation covenant," a model followed subsequently by many New England towns. The settlers of Plymouth established a democracy, in which all adult men voted in a General Court. At least one historian argues that independent women (mostly widows) also voted. Ten years later, the General Court of Massachusetts limited the franchise in its colony only to church members admitted as freemen. Until King James II formed the Dominion of New England in 1686, The Mayflower Compact remained Plymouth Colony's authorizing source of governmental power and is considered by some to be America's first constitution.

> *See also:* Law in Puritan New England
> *Further Reading*
> Jeremy Bangs, *Seventeenth-Century Records of Scituate, Massachusetts,* vol. 3 (Boston, 2001); William Bradford, *Of Plymouth Plantation* (New

Pilgrims aboard the Mayflower *in 1620 sign the Mayflower Compact, a document that set an important precedent for the constitutions that would later be written in America. (Library of Congress)*

York, 1952); William Bradford and Edward Winslow, *Mourt's Relation: Or Journal of the Plantation at Plymouth* (1969); George D. Langdon Jr., *Pilgrim Colony: A History of New Plymouth, 1620–1691* (New Haven, 1966).

Cassandra Wargo

Millenary Petition

The millenary petition, formally entitled "The humble petition of the ministers of the Churche of England desiringe reformation of certaine ceremonies and abuses of the Church," was presented to King James I in May 1603 as he rode from Edinburgh to London to take possession of the English throne. The petition was submitted in the name of a thousand puritan ministers, and although it bore no signatories, Arthur Hildersham and Stephen Egerton were among its chief promoters.

The millenary petition was just one of several petitions presented to the king between the years 1603 and 1606. Its central aim was to highlight widespread discontent with the "corruptions" that remained within the established Church of England, which, in the view of the petitioners, had not been fully reformed during the reign of Elizabeth I and had retained many remnants of its Catholic heritage. Historians have traditionally cited it as evidence that puritanism remained strong at James's accession, despite a government crackdown on puritan nonconformity in the 1580s and 1590s.

The petition requested reform of the Church of England in four key areas. First, it requested that liturgical abuses such as signing with the cross in baptism, bowing at the name of Jesus, and the use of the ring in marriage should be banished from church services. Second, it urged that the caliber of ministers should be improved, in particular that ministers who were not qualified to preach should be ejected and barred from the ministry. Third, it requested that financial abuses, including the double-beneficing of ministers, should be eradicated. And lastly, that church discipline should imitate more closely that of "Christ's own institution," including a stricter enforcement of the sentence of excommunication and restraint in the use of the "ex officio" oath (whereby clergy could be required to incriminate themselves). In addition, the petitioners asked King James to convene a conference—subsequently staged at Hampton Court in January 1604—at which the issues might be resolved in proper scholastic debating fashion.

Prior to his accession, James had made encouraging overtures to the godly community and had actively solicited their support, both in his printed works and through petitions to Queen Elizabeth on behalf of imprisoned puritan ministers. His penchant for scholarly debate was well known, and the hopes of the puritan community were high. However, James came to disapprove highly of the petitions presented to him by the godly and declared in the Court of Star Chamber that petitioning was a serious offense, "finable at discretion, and very near to treason and felony in the punishment."

The concerns highlighted in the millenary petition did not represent the views of more radical puritans, many of whom were involved in its composition. Its innocuous content indicates that a tentative consensus had been forged between moderates and radicals, in order to convey a united front to the new king. The consensus did not hold, and the cracks were clearly on display at the Hampton Court Conference, which witnessed the virtual failure of the puritan program and which was a bitter disappointment to many puritans who sought more substantial reform.

See also: Hampton Court Conference, Tithes
Further Reading
Nicholas Tyacke, *Anti-Calvinists: The Rise of English Arminianism, c. 1590–1640* (Oxford, 1987).

Victoria Gregory

"Model of Christian Charity"

The title given to the lay sermon that John Winthrop preached to the group of colonists accompanying him to New England in 1630. Though it is often stated that this sermon was delivered on the flagship *Arbella* while crossing the Atlantic, this is not likely. The address is clearly designed to inform and inspire all those preparing to undertake the migration, and a mid-Atlantic delivery would only have been heard by the small portion on the flagship. It is more likely that it was delivered in Southampton, before the fleet set sail.

No copy of the text survives in Winthrop's own hand, and there is only one contemporary copy, currently in the possession of the New York Historical Society. A single contemporary reference to the governor's "Christian Charity" does sustain the tradition that Winthrop did deliver the sermon. Lack of other contemporary comment or descriptions of the occasion tells us that rather than articulating a novel message, Winthrop was drawing upon the tradition of social Christianity in which his audience had been raised and applying it to their circumstances.

There are two major parts to the sermon. The first articulates a corporate view of society and explores the implications of this view for members of the new society. Though all men were equally creatures of God, they were created with different talents to fill different functions so that no one was self-sufficient and all had need of the skills of others. Because every man in the community had "need of other, . . . hence they might all be knit more nearly together in the bond of brotherly affection." In establishing in America a "place of cohabitation and consortship," the colonists were to see to it that "the care of the public must oversway all private respects." They were to "delight in each other, make others' condition our own; rejoice together, mourn together, labor and suffer together—always having before our eyes our commission and community in the work, our community as members of the same body."

The second theme in the sermon was Winthrop's assertion that in emigrating the colonists were following God's will and had entered into a covenant with him. On their part, he reminded them, "whatsoever we did or ought to have done in England, the same must we do and more also where we go." That which most Christians professed, the colonists "must bring into familiar and constant practice, as in this duty of love." If they lived exemplary lives and thus upheld their part of the covenant, "the Lord will be our God and delight to dwell among us as his own people, and will command a blessing upon us in all our ways, so that we shall see much more of his wisdom, power, goodness and truth than formerly we have been acquainted with." But if they failed, neglected their obligations and pursued their own individual selfish interests, then "the Lord will surely break out in wrath against us, be revenged on such a perjured people, and make us know the price of the breach of such a covenant." In this sense, they were to be "as a City upon a Hill." That last image, drawn by Winthrop from the Gospel according to Matthew, was a commonplace among puritans. All Christians, if they lived up to God's wishes, would be an inspiration to others. Winthrop's use of the phrase did not imply that more was expected of the colonists than was expected of other godly communities.

See also: John Winthrop, Great Migration, Massachusetts Bay Colony

Further Reading

Francis J. Bremer, *John Winthrop: America's Forgotten Founding Father* (New York, 2003); Hugh Dawson, "'Christian Charitie' as Colonial Discourse: Reading Winthrop's Sermon in its English Context," *Early American Literature* 33 (1998), 117–148; Edmund S. Morgan, "John Winthrop's 'Model of Christian Charity' in a Wider Context," *Huntington Library Quarterly* 50 (1987), 145–151.

Francis J. Bremer

Moses His Judicials and Mosaic Law

As the modern scholar Theodore Dwight Bozeman has shown, discussion of the relevance of Old Testament Mosaic law for English law emerged in the 1570s between Presbyterian Thomas Cartwright and Anglican John Whitgift. Whitgift, affirming the status quo of English law, held that Mosaic law had been abrogated by the Christian dispensation, thereby leaving judicial law to the discretion of Christian princes and magistrates. Cartwright acknowledged that much of Mosaic law was not universally applicable, but he argued that its underlying principles should inform and instruct civil law; further, certain Mosaic laws (e.g., idolatry as capital offense) were unalterable and should be used directly or as a pattern by which to reform latter-day law in accordance with Mosaic law. Others of the Puritan stripe, such as William Perkins, held similar positions, but their arguments had little weight in legal reform. Later, in Massachusetts Bay, where the General Court passed its own laws, the situation was different. At first, the magistrates ruled with broad discretionary powers and passed laws only as necessary, but by the mid-1630s pressure was mounting to curb discretionary powers by codifying and publishing the colony's laws. Although the process did not culminate until 1648 with *The Laws and Liberties*, an important early document was Boston minister John Cotton's *Moses His Judicials,* first drafted in 1636. The original title alone indicates indebtedness to the discussion of Mosaic law as source for judicial law; slightly earlier, related documents, such as the "Modell of Church and Civill Power" and "How Far Moses Judicials Bind Mass[achusetts]," reflect ongoing discussion of the question.

Although never officially accepted as the colony's law, *Moses His Judicials* was published anonymously in London in 1641, under the title *An Abstract of the Lawes of New England, As they are now established*, a somewhat accurate title, even though the draft was never formally implemented. Despite its title and plentiful biblical references, the *Abstract* does not simply transcribe Mosaic law for a theocratic regime but uses it as a pattern, both to describe existing law that accords with Mosaic law and to point toward reform according to that pattern. Organized in ten chapters, the *Abstract* both describes the existing government of Massachusetts Bay (more or less as laid out in the charter) and provides scriptural citations for most elements of the government; the latter feature has sometimes misled commentators into supposing that

Cotton's design too much ignored English law and was too theocratic even for the Massachusetts Puritans. But in substance, the *Abstract* does not depart from the charter (or its colonial modifications). When it comes to matters not specifically addressed in the Bible (such as "free burgesses and free inhabitants" and military protection) there are few or no scriptural references. Cotton's document certainly influenced both Nathaniel Ward's *Body of Liberties* and the final *Laws and Liberties;* it also was influential in the formation of New Haven and again in Southampton plantation. Cotton's document was reprinted by William Aspinwall in 1655 during Fifth Monarchist agitation.

See also: Law in Puritan New England
Further Reading
P. S. Atiyah and R. S. Summers, *Form and Substance in Anglo-American Law: A Comparative Study of Legal Reasoning, Legal Theory, and Legal Institutions* (Oxford, 1991); Cornelia Hughes Dayton, *Women before the Bar* (New Haven, 1995); George Lee Haskins, *Law and Authority in Early Massachusetts* (New York, 1961); Edgar J. McManus, *Law and Liberty in Early New England: Criminal Justice and Due Process, 1620–1692* (Amherst, 1993); Christopher L. Tomlins and Bruce H. Mann, eds., *The Many Legalities of Early America* (Chapel Hill, 2001).

Michael G. Ditmore

Music

The attitude of the godly to music has been subject to a bad press. The caricature of the joyless, leisure-hating Puritan (an inaccurate picture) and the forcible removal of organs from cathedral churches in the 1640s (a well-documented and accurate one) have combined to produce a common misconception of Puritan opposition to music in all its forms. I propose to deal with two different types of musical activity: that in the home, and that in the church.

There is ample evidence of the use of music for domestic recreation by Puritan figures. The moderate Jacobean divine Andrew Willet is reported to have recreated himself at dinnertime by playing upon a small organ and singing to it. The radical Elizabethan Separatist Robert Browne was also a talented lutenist, and he taught his son Timothy to play the viol. There is, however, a distinction to be made between vocal and instrumental music. It is difficult to be absolutely certain, but it is very likely that the vocal music sung in Puritan homes was overwhelmingly the metrical Psalms, rather than any secular songs, for fear of the moral corruption caused by "ribald" songs (an issue we shall consider below).

Perhaps the single most common concern expressed in writers on music as used in church, and worship more generally, was its effect on the engagement of the understanding of the worshipper. The Directory of Public Worship, the archetype of truly reformed worship, stipulated that the "chief care must be, to sing with the understanding, and with Grace in the heart, making melody unto the Lord." To this end, each was to have a book of psalms from which to read, in order that all could be involved. In addition, if it were not possible for all to have a book, the psalms would be intoned line by line, in order that all could then follow.

One of the key problems diagnosed by Puritan writers was therefore the kind of church music that obscured the meaning of the words being sung. In 1628 the Durham cathedral clergyman Peter Smart accused the Laudian John Cosin of overloading the service with choral singing and organs, so that the congregation could understand it no better than if it had been in Greek or Hebrew.

A closely connected theme was that of the need for edification—if the worshipping community, the living stones of the church, were to be built up (a literal translation of "edified"), they needed to be able to discern and feed on the words, and to participate in their worship. The lack of this kind of edification was a constant feature in the rhetoric of reforming writers about the music of the church in England. Unintelligible music, the "dumb" rumbling of organs, and the separation of singers from congregation were all part of the corrupt popish order of the church, which for at least some radical writers needed to be swept away and the church built again from the roots upwards. It was largely for this reason that the use of music (in those churches under strong Puritan influence) was largely restricted to the unaccompanied congregational singing of metrical psalms.

Despite all of this, it is in fact extremely difficult to identify an entirely distinctive "Puritan" position on the "right" use of music in worship. It is in fact possible to find examples of the rhetoric that we have examined in writings from all parts of the ecclesiastical spectrum. The more radical Puritan position can in part be identified by tone, rather than substance, tending to focus on the association of music with popish corruption and adopting a "safety first" approach to music. In doctrinal terms, it is almost impossible to distinguish Puritans from the vast Calvinist middle ground of the English church. The difference in tone has much to do with the fact that most writing on music is to be found in polemical writings, concerned with attacking perceived abuse in the church, rather than in systematic reflection on the issues from first principles.

Some of the confusion at the heart of the debate over church music was a deep ambiguity, universal in the church, over the power of music to move and elevate the worshipper, but also to deprave, corrupt, and lead to vice. Calvin, standing in a long line of Christian thinkers stretching back to St. Augustine and beyond, had been acutely aware of the power of singing to amplify the effect of a text, good or bad, on the heart of the singer, using, after Plato, the metaphor of a funnel. It was the case that almost every writer on music in Elizabethan and Stuart England could agree that only "good" music ought to be used, as it would be too dangerous to the soul to use "bad" music. Few, however, were able to define the difference between the two. It was also the case that little practical guidance was to be gained from scripture, the center of all Puritan piety. The clearest stipulation in the New Testament was in Colossians 3:16, which suggested that "psalms and hymns and spirituall songs" were to be sung, with the stipulation that this was to be done "with grace in your hearts to the Lord." All writers could agree that some form of music could and should therefore be sung, as long as it engaged the heart.

However, there was one specific theoretical issue on which the godly were largely united, and that was the use of musical instruments in church. The debate centered over whether the instruments described in the Old Testament (and absent from the New) were part of the old covenant and now obsolete. The majority of Puritan commentators argued that instruments were part of the old order, and were now disallowed. However, this was not a uniquely Puritan position, as there were also non-Puritan writers who took the same view.

See also: Psalms

Further Reading

Horton Davies, *Worship and Theology in England: From Andrewes to Baxter and Fox, 1603–1690* (Princeton, 1975); Peter Le Huray, *Music and the Reformation in England, 1549–1660* (London, 1967); Percy Scholes, *The Puritans and Music* (London, 1934); Nicholas Temperley, *The Music of the English Parish Church* (Cambridge, Eng., 1979).

Peter Webster

N

National Covenant

A Scottish manifesto of about 4,000 words embracing issues both political and religious, first signed in the Greyfriars Kirkyard, Edinburgh, on 28 February 1638, the "glorious marriage day between God and Scotland." The introduction of the long-awaited *Booke of Common Prayer, and Administration of the Sacraments* (Edinburgh, 1637) on 22 July 1637 had led to premeditated riots and the institution of a provisional government called the Tables.

Until about the middle of 1637, Scottish divines had adhered to a rather conservative political ideology that eschewed rebellion, even in the face of the reintroduction of popery. But this changed as men like Sir Archibald Johnston of Wariston, a young lawyer, began to read Althusius and the French Protestant monarchomachs. At the behest of the aristocratic leadership of the rebellion, Johnston and the minister of Leuchars in Fife, Alexander Henderson, began to write a document that would serve as apology and manifesto for what was fast becoming a national revolt against the now colonial rule of England and its anglicized monarchy.

The essence of the National Covenant lies in the King's Confession (also known as the Negative Confession), first signed in 1581 in the midst of an outbreak of fears of rampant popery. Johnston and Henderson began with this document, quoted verbatim, making it the first of three parts of the National Covenant. Earlier Presbyterians had argued that the signing of this confession meant that Scotland was bound forever to God in a national covenant, and so the actions of 1638 were actually a renewal of something more than fifty years old. The second part identifies those acts of Scottish parliaments against popery, along with acts that had been passed as bulwarks of the Reformed Kirk. The third part confirms the Reformed substance of the Church of Scotland, and it also upholds loyalty to King Charles I. The affirmations were, of course, incompatible, as the next five years revealed.

The National Covenant could never have come about without the aristocracy and the Presbyterian clergy. The frequent incompatibility of their goals were likewise manifested in the next decade, but for now the aristocrats, fearing the king's encroachments upon their title to church lands redistributed under James VI (the so-called Revocation), led the way in signing the National Covenant and embraced the republicanism of presbytery, leading to the Glasgow general assembly in November, which provided a forum for the expression of numerous grievances in the language of an evangelical puritan theology.

The clerical leadership, including Henderson, Robert Blair, and David Dickson, were dedicated to the removal of all "innovations": the restoration of diocesan episcopacy (1610); liturgical changes, and especially kneeling at communion, imposed by the Five Articles of Perth (1618); the arbitrarily introduced *Canons and constitutions ecclesiasticall* (1636), and the new service book (1637).

The National Covenant cast a lengthy shadow over the next fifty years of Scottish, and to some extent, insular history, and even in the mid-nineteenth century its presence might still have been felt.

See also: Solemn League and Covenant
Further Reading
Maurice Lee Jr., *The Road to Revolution: Scotland under Charles I, 1625–37* (Urbana, 1985); Allan I. Macinnes, *Charles I and the Making of the Covenanting Movement, 1625–1641* (Edinburgh, 1991); David George Mullan, *Scottish Puritanism, 1590–1638* (Oxford, 2000).

David Mullan

New Haven

New Haven was the last and least successful of the Puritan colonies in New England. It was founded in the belief that the Bible was a sufficient rule for the creation of a church and state, and in the expectation that New Haven would become a prosperous seaport. Neither hope was realized, and the colony winked out of existence less than thirty years after its founding.

New Haven began with the repudiation of the Church of England by its founders, men like Theophilus Eaton and John Davenport, who had tried in vain for years to reform the church from within. The rise of William Laud in the 1630s cast them into despair, and when they left England in 1637, it was with the intention of establishing a congregational form of worship.

In 1638 the group built New Haven at the mouth of the Quinnipiac River, a site that they thought would give them immediate access to fur-trading Indians, and pondered the Bible for a year before a mass meeting in a large barn finally laid down the rules for church and state. By 1643, the neighboring towns of Branford, Guilford, Milford, Stamford, and Southold (on Long Island) had joined New Haven town to form the colony of New Haven, governed by a general court composed of magistrates and deputies elected by the towns. In the same year, New Haven Colony was admitted into the Confederation of New England.

When the original New Haven settlers began their construction of a church and state in 1639, Davenport began the proceedings by asking if the Bible was a perfect rule for civil and ecclesiastical government, and everyone agreed that it was. From the very beginning, however, the Bible was supplemented with English law and practical experience. It was agreed, for example, that the Bible restricted full church membership to those who could profess a conversion experience, and that only church members should have the right to vote, but the New Haven colonists knew that these practices had already been adopted in Massachusetts Bay. When New Haven adopted Deuteronomy as its code of laws in 1643, it was a temporary and limited arrangement, made necessary by the absence of a set of colony-wide laws. When the laws actually being enforced were finally codified in 1656, it became evident that magistrates had routinely gone beyond scripture in their rulings. While the capital laws referred to specific passages in the Bible, the rules governing the militia, the longest section of the code, made no claim whatever to divine inspiration.

It is not even certain that the most original of New Haven's actions were given a biblical sanction. At the urging of Theophilus Eaton, jury trials were eliminated in New Haven, perhaps because it was preferred that godly magistrates determine guilt and innocence, as they supposedly did in ancient Israel. So far as we know, however, Eaton defended the innovation by reference to the civil law system that he came to know during his residence in Denmark. The layout of New Haven town was also strikingly different from English or New England models. It was designed as nine squares, the middle one of which was to remain an open space for such public uses as a marketplace. The plan may have been inspired by the visions of Ezekiel, or it may have been copied from a pagan Roman manual. The matter is in dispute. What is certain is that we cannot agree with Perry Miller's assertion: "New Haven was the essence of Puritanism, distilled and undefiled, the Bible Commonwealth and nothing else."

New Haven Colony adapted its ideals in its struggle for survival, just as other colonies did, but it suffered extraordinary bad luck and paid dearly for bad decisions. It was very quickly realized that settlement on the Quinnipiac River had been a mistake, and the colony would have relocated to the Delaware Valley if it had not been for the opposition of the Dutch in New Netherland. New Haven tried for years, in vain, to persuade the New England Confederation and the government of Oliver Cromwell to drive the Dutch out of America.

New Haven cannot be blamed for the depression that fell over New England in 1640, but her attempts to cope with hard times were misdirected. New Haven merchants rapidly opened trade with New Amsterdam, Virginia, the West Indies, and elsewhere, and this trade, though small, should have been encouraged. Instead, Eaton and others foolishly attempted, in 1646, to open a direct trade with London by outfitting a "great ship" at enormous cost. The ship went down somewhere in the Atlantic.

Despite its problems, New Haven in 1660 was a considerable colony, and its demise could not have been predicted. In population and the extent of inhabited territory, New Haven was larger than Rhode Island, and nearly as large as Connecticut. There was always some opposition to a government that was always exclusive, and often intrusive, but the colony collected taxes and drafted men into the militia without significant protest. The "burgesses," the only ones who could vote for the colonial government, hardly bothered to do so, apparently content with being ruled by the same few men who were elected year after year. Eaton was annually elected magistrate of the town, and governor of the colony, from 1639 until his death in 1658.

And yet, New Haven Colony in 1660 was doomed, not by its Biblicism, but by the determination of Connecticut to destroy it. Connecticut and New Haven had often cooperated, and the two were allies in the New England Confederation, but New Haven's growth threatened Connecticut's, and the Restoration gave Connecticut a chance to annex its rival. When John Winthrop Jr. secured a royal charter for Connecticut in 1662, he made sure its boundaries included New Haven, and Connecticut immediately began to subvert New Haven's authority in the peripheral towns. In December 1664, the general court of the New Haven

Colony voted itself out of existence, and in January 1665, a New Haven town meeting conceded defeat. A few diehards, like Davenport, held out against Connecticut for a few more years, but the union had been consummated, and New Haven Colony had ceased to exist.

See also: John Davenport, Theophilus Eaton, Connecticut

Further Reading

Charles Andrews, *The Rise and Fall of the New Haven Colony* (New Haven, 1936); Isabel Calder, *The New Haven Colony* (New Haven, 1934); Gail Sussman Marcus, "A 'Due Execution of the Generall Rules of Righteousness': Criminal Procedures in New Haven Town and Colony, 1638–1658;" and John M. Murrin, "Magistrates, Sinners, and a Precarious Liberty: Trial by Jury in Seventeenth-Century New England," in David D. Hall, John M. Murrin, and Thad Tate, eds., *Saints and Revolutionaries: Essays on Early American History* (New York, 1984).

James P. Walsh

New Model Army

The principal army of Parliament in the English Civil Wars. Following the removal of peers and members of Parliament (MPs) from military command under the Self-Denying Ordinance of December 1644, Parliament on 17 February 1645 ordered the formation of a professional army of 22,000 soldiers, financed through central taxation. Supreme command was bestowed upon a moderate Presbyterian, Sir Thomas Fairfax—a compromise choice but also a highly competent soldier. Another Presbyterian, Philip Skippon, was appointed to command the infantry, while the cavalry was belatedly entrusted to a leading Independent, Oliver Cromwell.

The officer corps was an uneasy alliance of moderate and radical Puritans, while their regiments consisted of orthodox Puritans, sectaries, republicans, unwilling conscripts, and even a large number of former royalist prisoners-of-war. Desertion was rife, and the royalists were contemptuous of their new opponents. This, however, was to underestimate the religiously inspired commitment and

Oliver Cromwell and his New Model Army sing the 117th Psalm prior to the Battle of Dunbar. (North Wind Picture Archives)

competence of officers appointed on the basis of merit and experience, and the superb quality of Cromwell's cavalry—the so-called Ironsides. The first major clash with the royalist army at Naseby in June 1645 resulted in a spectacular victory for the New Model. There followed a series of military successes, culminating in the surrender of royalist forces and the end of the first Civil War in 1646.

Peace brought calls for the disbandment of the New Model, not least because of the huge financial burden on the civilian population. With their pay in arrears, the soldiers faced the prospect of disbandment or service in Ireland. The army mutinies of 1647 led to a politicized soldiery, increasingly alienated from a Presbyterian-dominated Parliament. Despite these tensions, the New Model was easily able to defeat the royalists and their new Scottish Presbyterian allies during the Second Civil War of 1648. In December 1648 the New Model purged

Parliament, engineering the trial and execution of King Charles a month later.

Parliamentarian forces in Ireland, struggling to defeat an alliance of royalists and Irish Catholics, were joined by Cromwell and New Model units in the summer of 1649. A ruthless campaign was marked by particularly brutal examples of bloodshed at Drogheda and Wexford.

Fairfax, already unnerved by the king's execution, refused to command a preemptive strike against Scotland and resigned in 1650. He was replaced as Lord General by Cromwell. Cromwell's decisive victories at Dunbar (1650) and Worcester (1651) brought the wars to an end. From then until Cromwell's death, the New Model acted as an armed police force, keeping the Lord Protector in power and enforcing godly rule—most famously under the sixteen-month rule of Cromwell's major-generals. During this time, regiments were dispatched to campaign against the Spanish in Jamaica, and even hired out to Louis XIV of France.

After Cromwell's death in 1658, disunity between his generals threatened anarchy. In 1660 General George Monck occupied London with his regiments, restoring order and facilitating the restoration of the monarchy. After the Restoration, most New Model regiments were disbanded, while a select few, such as Monck's personal regiment (today's Coldstream Guards) became the basis of the modern British Army.

See also: Oliver Cromwell, Independency, Major-Generals, Soldier's Bible
Further Reading
Charles H. Firth, *Cromwell's Army* (London, 1902); Ian Gentles, *The New Model Army in England, Ireland and Scotland, 1645–1653* (Oxford, 1992); Mark Kishlansky, *The Rise of the New Model Army* (Cambridge, Eng., 1979).

David J. Appleby

Nonconformity

A refusal to conform fully to the doctrine, discipline, and liturgy of the Church of England. The term had (and has) several distinct uses. In the sixteenth and seventeenth centuries, *nonconformity* and *nonconformist* were occasionally used to describe any individual refusal. After 1662, the term came into more general use to refer to the whole community of lay and clerical Protestants (also known as Dissenters) who would not conform to the Act of Uniformity. In that sense, the term is generally capitalized.

The earlier use of *nonconformity* was quite indiscriminate. It was applied to lay sectaries and to clergy such as those involved in the Vestiarian and Subscription controversies. Clerical nonconformity generally concerned vestments and rituals (such as the sign of the cross in baptism, the use of the ring in marriage, and kneeling at the sacrament), but by the 1620s and 1630s doctrine and preaching were also becoming issues of conformity. The Elizabethan and early Stuart Church contained numerous ministers who had made initial declarations of conformity but then tailored their routine worship

and preaching to their own principles. In this sense there was a lot of partial conformity within the church.

The Nonconformity created in the wake of the 1662 Uniformity Act was an artificial community. Separatists, Quakers, Baptists, Independents, and Presbyterians were all Nonconformists. Although they might now all fall into the same legal category, they had little else in common: learned, university-educated, and conservative Presbyterian ministers shared nothing with Baptist ex-soldiers or wandering Quaker preachers. And they resented being lumped together: "It is a palpable injury to burden us with the various parties with whom we are now herded by our ejection in the general state of dissenters." John Corbet, the author of this complaint, saw himself as a Nonconformist—a subtle but significant distinction. For while their adversaries labeled them all as Dissenters, those, mainly the Presbyterians, who could not bring themselves to conform to the church as it now stood, but who hoped that things might change, preferred to describe themselves as Nonconformists. Between 1662 and 1689, however, these distinctions were often challenged and in many cases eroded. Common suffering as a harassed minority forced the different denominations to cooperate, and it has been said that in time the separate nonconformities coalesced into a single "Dissent."

See also: Clarendon Code, Dissenters, Toleration, Toleration Act
Further Reading
Neil H. Keeble, *The Literary Culture of Nonconformity in Later Seventeenth-Century England* (Leicester, Eng., 1987).

John Spurr

Nonjurors

The Anglican clergymen who refused to take the oath of allegiance to William III and Mary in 1689. Although laymen, including the Earl of Clarendon, refused the oath, it was the failure of Archbishop Sancroft, seven other bishops, and about 400 (or 4 percent) of the Anglican clergy to swear allegiance, that created a Nonjuring movement. Despite the obvious reluctance of Sancroft and other bishops, it seemed at first that parliamentary negotiations would allow the scrupulous clergy to avoid the oaths in return for concessions to Dissent. The failure of this plan resulted in the Act of 1689 (1 William and Mary ca. 8) that imposed the oaths of supremacy and allegiance on all beneficed clergy. Those who refused were suspended from their benefices for six months. If they remained obdurate, they were to be deprived of their benefices. The difficulty for many of the Nonjurors was a simple one of conflicting oaths. Having sworn solemn allegiance to James II, they feared the sin of perjury, or false swearing, if they now swore allegiance to another ruler. Perhaps the majority of Nonjurors were motivated by this scruple of conscience and their belief in the "divine right" of monarchy, rather than by an underlying "Jacobitism," or devotion to the person of James II. Indeed, five of the Nonjuring bishops (William Sancroft, Francis Turner, Thomas Ken, Thomas White, and John Lake) had been among the "Seven Bishops" who had defied James over the reading of the Declaration of Indulgence.

In any case, at first William stayed his hand. For more than a year the deprived bishops were allowed to draw their revenues and retain their palaces. There was a distinct possibility of compromise and many cases of clerical evasion. It was suggested that the oath could be sworn in a "lower" sense than the preexisting oath as recognition of the de facto rather than de iure authority of the new monarchs. The discovery late in 1690 of a compromising letter from Bishop Turner to James II undermined William's patience. In April 1691 John Tillotson was nominated as Sancroft's successor, and William began to replace the deprived bishops. This brought a new issue to the fore. Did the civil magistrate have the right to remove bishops? In the face of the exercise of naked political power, the Nonjurors denied that monarch or parliament possessed such authority. In their eyes, the Church of England had broken with its rightful pastors and was in schism. Nonjurors took up a range of positions. Some, like Ken and Frampton, retired but maintained their communion with the church as laymen; others, like Henry Dodwell and Francis Cherry's circle at Shottesbrooke, argued that the church's schism would cease with the death of the deprived bishops.

The more extreme Nonjurors not only separated but took steps to perpetuate their own ministry. In 1691 Sancroft had conveyed his archiepiscopal powers to William Lloyd, deprived bishop of Norwich, and in 1693, with James II's approval, Lloyd consecrated George Hickes, deprived dean of Worcester, as suffragan bishop of Thetford, and Thomas Wagstaff as bishop of Ipswich. Hickes was a moving force in all this. In 1713, with the help of Scottish bishops, he consecrated more Nonjuring bishops, including Jeremy Collier. Yet the Nonjurors rapidly became a political irrelevance. Some drifted back to the Church of England, others into outright Jacobitism. Internal dissension took its toll. In 1716 they were split over the "usages," a series of eucharistic rituals. The Nonjurors' significance came to lie in their intellectual distinction, as displayed in the works of theologians like Dodwell and Charles Leslie, devotional writers like John Kettlewell and William Law, and liturgical scholars such as John Johnson, Robert Nelson, and Thomas Brett.

Further Reading

Craig Rose, *England in the 1690s* (Oxford, 1999); Gordon Rupp, *Religion in England, 1688–1791* (Oxford, 1981).

John Spurr

O

Old Age

As part of the Atlantic world, Puritans shared many characteristics and cultural assumptions with non-Puritans, including the theoretical belief in a gerontocratic world. This position was universally honored. In theory, the attributes of male old age were considered critical components of a valuable leader or adviser. The old were thought to be beyond lust, and thus beyond the distractions of physical pleasure. They were thought to be levelheaded and wise, capable of considered choice and unflappable in times of crisis. Similarly, they were considered repositories of knowledge and wells of experience. Increase Mather's old age was described as "How bright! How wise! How strong! And in what an uncommon measure serviceable!" And in his eightieth year he published "An Hoary Head found in the Way of Righteousness," which described all the things that he was yet able to do and accomplish. Nevertheless, English civic officials were typically middle-aged, most of them between forty and fifty years of age. In New England, on the other hand, the elderly had a strong position in all areas of society, with the highest offices typically held by the oldest members. This was the result of the cult of age among New England Puritans, coupled with New England's demographics: only 2 percent of New England's population was over the age of sixty-five, while roughly 8 percent of England's population was over the age of sixty. Respect for the aged also rested on a firm economic and material base. The aging parent typically retained control over the family's property until close to death, thus delaying the independence of most male heirs until sometime in their thirties.

The notion of respect, if not veneration, of the elderly was woven into the very fabric of Puritan social thought and theology. Raised up on a steady diet of the fifth commandment to honor one's mother and father, Puritans learned from an early age to rise up and honor the hoary head. Commentators, such as Cotton Mather, made plain that the fifth commandment was not restricted to one's natural parents, but was to be extended to the leaders of the Commonwealth, the church, and the schools, just as he instructed: "Remember, O Servants, thy Master, is thy Father, and thy Mistress, is thy Mother." Mather was typical of many early modern writers when he instructed his readers that they would reap in old age what they had sown in youth. At the same time, he offers a distinctively Puritan stance on the horrors of the disrespectful child: "Undutiful Children soon become horrid Creatures, for Unchastity, for Dishonesty, for Lying, and all manner of Abominations: And the Contempt which they cast upon the Advice of their Parents, is one thing that pulls down this Curse of God upon them." Mather goes on, adding: "Yea, an Early Death, and a Woeful Death, is not seldom the Curse of God upon Undutiful Children for their being so. It is the Tenour of the Precept, Honour thy Father and thy Mother, that thy Days may be long upon the Land. Mind it, Children; Your days are not like to be long upon the Land, if you

Set Light by your Father or Mother." Care for one's aged parents, conversely, brought glory in the eyes of God and man: "That Aged Father or Mother, in thy House, is not only the Glory of thy House, but a better and a richer Thing than a Mine of Silver there." One overt manifestation of this "natural law," and one that carried with it huge cultural import, was the seating of the eldest members of a congregation in the front of the church, nearest to the pulpit.

Puritan theology further enhanced the cultural position of the aged man and woman. First, church membership was restricted to those old enough to have examined themselves. While that did not mean membership was limited to the elderly, this practice did put a premium on age. Second, the road to Puritan election was framed in terms of a pilgrimage, a series of spiritual stages in which one grew toward—but never reached—the stature of God. Older Puritans were generally thought to have traveled far in this journey toward sanctification and glory, possessing "a peculiar acquaintance with the Lord Jesus." Living into old age, according to Increase Mather, was thought to be a sign of election: "If any man is favored with long life it is God who has lengthened his days." Calvin himself characterized this stage of life as having "a good heart, filled with love and peace of God and the soul of an Abraham." Because Calvinist thought granted women and men the same standing before God as "elder-saints," old women, too, were considered worthy of respect and veneration, even if "Mothers do more frequently by their Fondness, and Weakness, bring upon themselves, the Contempt of their Children, and Lay themselves Low, by many Impertinencies." Male saints, however, do not seem to have suffered from the host of negative old age attributes current in early modern society, such as drunkenness, boasting, vanity, and gluttony.

Old age was regarded as the final stage of life, ending only with death. Puritan writers were quick to remind the elderly that death would come soon, and that they should properly arrange their affairs, and order their behavior to ensure a peaceful death. "Elder People," wrote one New England minister, "are so near their End, so soon to dye, and to give up their Account, that surely they above any shou'd be very careful about their Behaviour." Seventy years, "three score and ten," was considered the normal life span, while the particularly fit might live to eighty. Yet the aged Puritan, just like his less godly counterpart, knew how quickly the years passed and how short the time to get right with God. "Now ask any man," wrote Cotton Mather in *Life Swiftly Passing and Quickly Ending* (1716), "that may be Seventy years old; my Father, How long does the Time of your past Life now seem to you? He will say, 'indeed, when I look'd forward, it seem'd long; but now I look backward, Oh! how swiftly it is passed; how quickly ended'." The aging Puritan was surrounded by a set of social conventions, theological beliefs, signs, and symbols that placed old age in an esteemed position, and though a lifetime may have swiftly passed, the elderly Puritan would have spent his or her final years at the pinnacle of personal authority.

See also: Death and Dying, Family Piety
Further Reading
Thomas R. Cole, *The Journey of Life: A Cultural History of Aging in America* (New York, 1992); David Hackett Fischer, *Albion's Seed: Four British Folkways in America* (New York, 1989); David Hackett Fischer, *Growing Old in America* (New York, 1978); Cotton Mather, *The Duties of Children to Their Parents* (1699); Daniel Scott Smith and J. David Hacker, "Cultural Demography: New England Deaths and the Puritan Perception of Risk," *Journal of Interdisciplinary History* 26 (1996), 367–392.

Lynn A. Botelho

P

Pequot War (1636–1637)

The first major armed conflict between Puritan colonists and Native Americans in New England. Rapid English expansion into the Pequot region of Connecticut in the mid-1630s, coupled with the destabilizing effects of a 1633 Indian smallpox pandemic, sharply strained Euro-Indian relations. The murder of trader John Stone in 1633, and the death of a second trader, John Oldham, two years later, led the English to launch retaliatory strikes against Indians on Block Island, burning their homes and fields. Pequot warriors killed English settlers in Wethersfield and at Saybrook, torturing captives and taunting garrisoned survivors. The climax of the conflict came on 26 May 1637, when Puritan soldiers under the command of John Mason torched a palisaded Pequot village on the Mystic River, slaughtering up to 500 men, women, and children. The English were supported by the Pequots' native rivals, Mohegans under Uncas, and Narragansetts. These Indian allies were appalled by the English troops' wholesale slaughter of the Pequots, just as the English had been shocked by the Pequot's public torture of English captives. The brutality of the English at Mystic established Puritan dominance for nearly two generations. The remaining Pequot combatants were either killed in battle at New Haven (28 July) or captured and enslaved. Noncombatant Pequots were made tributary slaves to the Mohegans or Narragansetts. Sassacus, the Pequot sachem (leader), eluded English capture but was later executed by the Mohawks of eastern New York.

The Treaty of Hartford in 1638 declared that the Pequot tribe and name was to be permanently extinguished, but a later alliance between New London's founder, John Winthrop Jr., and the Pequot sachem Robin Cassacinnamon helped ensure the group's continuity.

See also: Indian Bible, King Philip's War, Praying Towns

Further Reading

Alfred Cave, *The Pequot War* (Amherst, 1996); Neal Salisbury, *Manitou and Providence: Indians, Europeans, and the Making of New England, 1500–1643* (New York, 1982); Alden T. Vaughan, *New England Frontier: Puritans and Indians, 1620–1675* (Norman, OK; 1995 edition).

Laura Luder

Pilgrims
See Plymouth Colony

Pinners' Hall

The London guildhall of the livery company of the pin makers, or pinners, was the site of a joint lectureship of the Congregationalist and Presbyterian Dissenters, established in 1672. During the troubled years of the Interregnum and even before, many Puritans had divided into Presbyterian and Independent (Congregationalist) factions. With the restoration of the monarchy in 1660 and then the Bartholomew Ejections of 1662, about 2,000

Puritans lost their positions in the Church of England. Now alike Dissenters from the established church, Presbyterians and Congregationalists sought union with each other, as common suffering under the Clarendon Code brought them together. Their differences had been initially over church government, but after 1660 they also differed over the desirability of comprehension within a more inclusive Church of England, the Presbyterians favoring it, unlike the Congregationalists. But theological differences also intruded, the Congregationalists tending toward high Calvinism and the Presbyterians toward a more moderate Calvinism. Various efforts toward achieving harmony had been made by Richard Baxter and John Owen, as leaders of the two dissenting factions, but agreement eluded them.

In 1669 a lecture (a name commonly given to a regular weekday sermon) was undertaken at Hackney near London, and the lecturers included the Presbyterians William Bates and Thomas Watson and the Independents Owen, Philip Nye, George Griffith, Thomas Brooks, and Peter Sterry. In 1672, the year of the Declaration of Indulgence, a Tuesday morning lecture was established at Pinners' Hall, which brought together notable preachers of both factions for the common purpose of defending the Reformation faith against the threats of "Popery" and Socinianism. Also known as the Merchants' Lecture, it was financed by London merchants of Dissenting sympathies, and paid the lecturers twenty shillings for each sermon. Among those chosen as lecturers were Bates, Baxter, William Jenkyn, and Thomas Manton from the Presbyterians, and Owen and John Collins from the Independents. As lecturers passed from the scene on account of age or death, they were replaced, John Howe replacing Manton in 1677 and Matthew Mead replacing Owen in 1683. However, controversy soon appeared, notably with Baxter's four sermons, given either at the end of 1673 or the beginning of the next year, in which he seemed to breach the walls of Calvinist orthodoxy. In Baxter's words, "When I had preached there but four sermons, I found the Independents so quarrelsome with what I said that all the city did ring of their backbiting

and false accusations." Baxter felt that the high Calvinist teaching on justification by the imputed righteousness of Christ rendered the Dissenters vulnerable to the Anglican accusation that they were antinomian. Manton rebuked Baxter's accusers in one of his lectures, and Baxter published a defensive *An Appeal to the Light* in 1675. But not all Pinners' Hall sermons were controversial: Mead used the lecture to plead for money to aid impoverished ministers, and Howe used it to decry controversy in a sermon published in 1693 as *The Carnality of Religious Contention.*

In 1677 the lord mayor of London sought to suppress the lecture, but it survived until the Toleration Act of 1689, after which it was clearly legal. What it did not survive was the differences of the two factions. In 1690, sermons of Tobias Crisp (d. 1642), who, though favored by some Independents, was reputed to have been an antinomian, were published by his son Samuel. Baxter, in a Pinners' Hall sermon in 1690, condemned Crisp's teaching. Baxter died the next year and was replaced as lecturer by Daniel Williams, who continued the assault on antinomianism in his *Gospel Truth Stated* (1692). In response, the Congregationalists Isaac Chauncy, Thomas Cole (another Pinners' Hall lecturer), Nathaniel Mather, and Stephen Lobb charged Williams with Arminianism. In 1694 Williams was expelled as a Pinners' Hall lecturer, and he and other Presbyterian lecturers (Bates, Howe, and Vincent Alsop) withdrew to found a lecture at Salters' Hall. They were replaced at Pinners' Hall with Lobb, Mather, and others, and the Congregationalists continued at Pinners' Hall throughout the next century.

See also: Dissenters, Happy Union, Independency, Lectures and Lectureships, Salters' Hall
Further Reading
Peter Toon, *The Emergence of Hyper-Calvinism in English Nonconformity, 1689–1765* (London, 1967); Dewey D. Wallace Jr., *Puritans and Predestination* (Chapel Hill, 1982); C. E. Whiting, *Studies in English Puritanism from the Restoration to the Revolution, 1660–1688* (London, 1931).

Dewey D. Wallace Jr.

Plain Style

The puritan preaching style that stressed scriptural interpretation, a strict form of organization and presentation, language understandable by "common people," and the application of doctrines to the lives of the hearers. Plain style was popular among puritan preachers of all persuasions from the 1560s through the mid-seventeenth century. For example, the Presbyterian "Bill and Book" reform program offered to the 1584 Parliament called for the adoption of a plain style of preaching that was "spirituall, pure, proper, simple, and applied to the capacity of the people, not such as humane wisdom teacheth, nor favoring of new fangledness, nor either so affectate as it may serve for pompe and ostentation or so careless, and base, as becometh not ministers of the Word of God." The puritan concern for the education of the public through sermons dictated these rules: "humane wisdom," that is, the classical education available to the upper classes and frequently employed in sermons at the royal court or the universities, was meaningless to the "vulgar" people who flocked to hear puritans preach. *Plain style* is the term most puritans and their contemporaries used to describe the method of structuring the language and meaning of the sermon so that complex doctrines and their "uses" could be easily apprehended by the audience.

William Perkins, puritan preacher and author of the influential manual for preachers, *Arte of Prophesying* (1607), laid out the puritan approach to plain style in four principles. First, learned preparation was essential: "plainness" did not mean what puritans termed "negligent rudeness" or a sermon spoken extempore without careful planning of the content, structure, or language. Many puritans preached from prepared notes that listed the general topics of the sermon, or "heads," and committed the rest to memory. Perkins's second principle is the danger of "humane learning" for an uneducated audience, as rhetorical flourishes, classical allusions, and traditional examples from the church fathers would be meaningless, or worse, confuse the truth and lead to false belief. Accordingly many puritans avoided classical references and confined their examples and illustrations to biblical texts and more popular metaphors and allegories based on the life experiences of the hearers.

Third, Perkins stressed the importance of a formal structure and plain style of delivery. Puritan sermons followed a "doctrine, reason, use" pattern, which began with (1) the reading of the central biblical text of the sermon, (2) the "collection" of doctrines contained within the central text and the definition of the terms of the text, (3) the "opening" of these doctrines, or explanation of their meaning according to the principles of Ramist logic (movement from general truths to the more particular), with illustrations from common experience, and (4) specific instructions on how the doctrines could be applied to the hearers' lives. This formal structure should avoid "new fangled" words or rhetorical flourishes and use only words that had clear meanings that the hearers could understand. Fourth, Perkins stressed the sermon's focus on the use or application of the doctrines. The goal of puritan preaching was not only to provide systematic instruction, but to move people to account for their sins, come to a greater understanding of their own condition, and find assurance of salvation.

Plain style did not necessarily mean dry or boring. Delivery was also a key aspect of puritan preaching. The preacher's style of delivery—tone of voice, hand gestures, and body movements—also helped the hearers to understand and persuaded them to be moved to action. The legendary "hellfire and brimstone" sermons of New England puritans like Jonathan Edwards were above all calls to hear the word and be stirred to a sense of sin and faith. Plain style also did not mean that no rhetoric was allowed, rather that rhetorical figures could only be used as they helped to illustrate an example of the text, not to show the preacher's own learning, skill, or wit. Rhetoric was meant to persuade the audience, not give fame to the preacher. Plain style was thus an exercise in self-discipline for puritan preachers, who had to submit their prodigious learning to the capacity of their hearers.

Puritans (and their detractors) often compared and contrasted plain style with other popular styles of preaching, especially during the early Stuart,

Civil War, and Interregnum periods. The style used in the Church of England liturgy was standardized homilies read aloud, which puritans argued carried none of the accommodation to the audience they so favored and did not inspire the hearers to repent. Puritans believed that read homilies also did not befit the scriptural injunction to ministers of the word of God to expound scripture. Second, puritans criticized the so-called metaphysical preachers like John Donne for overelaborate use of rhetorical tropes and figures, often referred to as witty conceits, harmful because they confused rather than edified the audience. Third, especially during the Civil War and Interregnum, the "mechanick preachers," or independent sectarian preachers with little formal education, preached sermons without any preparation or notes (*ex tempore*) and were the scorn of all educated clergymen because they claimed the inspiration of the Holy Spirit and denied the necessity of the minister's special education and status. Like many aspects of puritanism, discussion of plain style was not detached from other issues, but was also a political statement about clerical and popular education and the further reform of the church in doctrine, liturgy, organization, government, and discipline.

See also: Preaching, Ramist Logic
Further Reading
J. W. Blench, *Preaching in England in the Late Fifteenth and Sixteenth Centuries: A Study of English Sermons 1450–c. 1600* (Oxford, 1964); Horton Davies, *Worship and Theology in England, 1500–1700*, 2 vols. (Princeton, 1975); N. H. Keeble, *Richard Baxter: Puritan Man of Letters* (Oxford, 1982); John Morgan, *Godly Learning: Puritan Attitudes toward Reason, Learning, and Education, 1560–1640* (Cambridge, Eng., 1986).

Stephanie Sleeper

Plymouth Colony

The Plymouth Colony was established by the Leiden Separatists (traditionally known as the Pilgrims) in 1620 in what is now southeastern Massachusetts; it lasted independently until 1691, when it was subsumed in the new Province of Massachu-

setts. Most of the first settlers, including all the leaders, were from Leiden, with other passengers from England joining them on the *Mayflower*. Aiming for the Hudson River, they made landfall instead on Cape Cod, an area not covered by their charter. They consequently signed a mutual civil covenant to abide by English laws and any further bylaws they themselves would enact. Later augmented by charters (1621, 1630), this covenant brought all under a democratic government, including "strangers" who had asserted their potential independence outside the originally agreed territory (perhaps "strangers" were Walloon or Dutch, not by birth subject to English law). Later ships brought more colonists from Holland and England. A constitution elaborating specific details of governance was enacted in 1636, in accordance with the principles of the Mayflower Compact of 1620. This constitution gave no formal role in government to the clergy, the assumption being that magistrates were Christians who fulfilled a God-given task. Suffrage was not made dependent on congregational membership, although a lack of orthodoxy was used later to disenfranchise supporters of Quakers.

Elder William Brewster and Deacon Samuel Fuller provided religious leadership in early years; Pastor John Robinson remained with the majority in Leiden, hoping to come later. On Robinson's advice, Brewster was not ordained by the Plymouth congregation, which was not considered distinct from that of Leiden. John Lyford, sent over at the request of non-separating Puritans among colony investors, intended to suppress the colonists' separatism, but he was exposed when he preached on the strength of his "episcopal calling" (instead of local congregational ordination) and was returned to England. Ralph Smith became the first minister to serve (1629–1636), assisted briefly by Roger Williams in 1633. Smith was succeeded by John Rayner (1636–1654).

Without ministers, in 1621 the Pilgrims instituted civil marriage registration before magistrates, citing the Dutch legal precedent they had experienced in Leiden, besides the absence of biblical indication that marriage is an ecclesiastical matter. In 1629 and 1630, Deacon Fuller and others from Ply-

Depiction of the Plymouth Colony in 1622. (Library of Congress)

mouth advised at the establishment of congregations in Salem and Charlestown, contributing to sentiment favoring what became known as the New England Way, with independence (within limits) for each congregation. The Plymouth congregation was also involved in the establishment of the churches at Duxbury, Scituate, and Marshfield, and all other towns established by Plymouth's court. In 1633, following advice from Roger Williams, Plymouth's court established legal practices recognizing Indian title to land, in an attempt to follow biblical injunctions to treat the "stranger" equally under law.

Reorganization of colony finances allowed expansion beyond the bounds of the town of Plymouth, starting in 1628. New towns sprang up rapidly. By midcentury, the largest and most important was Scituate, north of Plymouth along the coast, consistently assessed for taxes at around 60 percent more than Plymouth. Just before King Philip's War (1675–1676), Rehoboth, west on the boundary with Rhode Island, was assessed at about 40 percent more than Plymouth, but that assessment dropped

drastically after wartime destruction. Barnstable, Duxbury, Sandwich, and Taunton remained about equal to Plymouth. Ministers for the new towns included John Lathrop, who came to serve the congregation already formed at Scituate by people dismissed in 1634 from Plymouth. Lathrop, just released from prison in London, had been Henry Jacob's successor as pastor in Southwark. About five of his London members accompanied him to Scituate, three of them having been jailed with him. Lathrop was invested into office in January 1635, a couple of weeks after the congregation had mutually (re)covenanted itself. Deacons were chosen later. In 1639, Lathrop led a migration of farmers dissatisfied with Scituate's stony ground to settle Barnstable on Cape Cod and establish its church, which did not consider a new covenant necessary.

After William Blackford, active a few months, Scituate's pastor was Charles Chauncy, who had been in Plymouth with John Rayner but caused trouble by insisting on baptism (of infants) by immersion. Chauncy's rigidity split Scituate's church; he excommunicated members who would not enter into a new covenant when he arrived, and he refused their children baptism. Excommunication could lead to exclusion from future land distribution, if being a covenanted member of the local congregation were to be made a requirement for the status of freeman, as Chauncy seems to have intended. Led by William Vassall, the remnant of Scituate's first congregation called William Wetherell to be their minister, and Scituate had two congregations thereafter. Vassall's experience with Chauncy was an aspect of his participation in similar issues in neighboring Hingham, supporting Robert Child's petition for Presbyterian reform in Massachusetts Bay Colony (mid-1640s). In 1645, Vassall, as a Plymouth Colony magistrate, proposed that the court grant religious toleration to all sects. Governor William Bradford prevented a vote being taken, convinced the motion would pass. Chauncy left to become president of Harvard in 1654, succeeded in Scituate by Henry Dunster, who was praised for opposing persecution of Quakers.

Plymouth Colony's relative tolerance can be seen in its refusal to pursue accusations of witchcraft and in its treatment of Quakers at Sandwich, who suffered severe fines but not capital punishment. Magistrate James Cudworth of Scituate (philosopher Ralph Cudworth's brother) was coauthor with George Fox and John Rous of a plea against persecution, *Secret Workes Of a Cruel People Made Manifest* (London, 1659), for which he suffered disenfranchisement (later rescinded). Baptists could meet at Rehoboth from 1649 on, led by John Myles who arrived from Swansea, Wales, in 1663. In 1667, the Plymouth Court fined and expelled Myles with his followers to prevent competition with Rehoboth's existing congregation, but allowed them to establish a Baptist church in a new town they called Swansey.

See also: William Bradford, William Brewster, Law in Puritan New England, Mayflower Compact, Separatists, Thanksgiving
Further Reading
Jeremy Dupertuis Bangs, ed., *The Seventeenth-Century Town Records of Scituate, Massachusetts,* 3 vols. (Boston, 1997, 1999, 2001); William Bradford, *Bradford's History "Of*

Plimouth Plantation" (Boston, 1901); Eugene A. Stratton, *Pilgrim Colony* (Salt Lake City, 1986).

Jeremy Bangs

Poor Relief

Puritanism had a significant effect on English poor relief, although its influence was seldom direct and rarely undiluted. The general outlines of early modern poor relief are well known. In its mature form, essentially set out in the statues of 1598 and the minor adjustments of 1601, England established a national system of relief, funded by local rate (tax), and organized by appointed, secular officers of the state. It addressed four areas of poverty: children, beggars and vagabonds, the poor, and parish relief administration. The program called for the apprenticing of pauper children between the ages of five and fourteen. Rogues under fourteen were to be placed in the stocks, while those over fourteen caught begging were to be jailed until the next Sessions and then tried for vagrancy. Beggars convicted of vagrancy, the second theme of the statute, were to be whipped, unless an "honest" person would take them into service for one year. Convicted beggars caught running away from service were to be declared vagrants. All those guilty of vagrancy were to be whipped and an inch-wide hole burned "through the gristle of the right Ear with a hot iron." Those convicted twice for vagrancy were to be declared felons unless service could again be found, this time for two years. A third offense was to result in felony charges and execution. For the "aged decayed and impotent poor People . . . forced to live upon Alms," the Justices of Peace were to record their names into a "Register Book." Those listed were then to be provided with "convenient Habitations and Abiding Places throughout the Realm to settle themselves upon to the end that they nor any of them should hereafter beg or wander about."

Further, the employable poor were to be set to work according to their abilities. The completely helpless were to be provided for, and those who worked were to have their efforts supplemented from the parish fund. Each parish was to appoint Overseers of the Poor to assess and collect a local poor tax. Individuals refusing to pay their weekly rate were to be jailed until they complied. Those on relief who wandered from their parish-appointed place were deemed and declared vagrant, regardless of their age or physical condition (39 Eliz. 1. C. 30; 39 Eliz. 1. C. 40; and 43 Eliz. 1. C. 2).

Equally well known are the roots of the Poor Laws in Christian Humanism, the draft statue of William Marshall of 1535, and the parliamentary borrowing and codifying of individually and autonomously established local practices, especially that of Norwich. Norwich hosted a fair number of godly men on its municipal government, with John Aldrich serving as mayor in 1570, and member of Parliament (MP) in 1572 and 1576. Norwich's goal was a thorough reformation of the city, first by establishing a bridewell in 1565, then by conducting a census of the poor in 1570 and establishing work schemes for the able-bodied poor and children, regular surveys of the poor community, and a compulsory assessment for the relief of the poor. In doing so, Norwich sought quite deliberately to become an English Geneva, and England's premiere city of reforming Calvinism. It was indeed hailed as the model of social reform, and Norwich men were recruited by the councils of cities such as Oxford and Nottingham to run their bridewells. Parliament, too, deliberately built on Norwich's scheme when drafting its statutes. As the implementation of the Elizabethan poor laws spread, the distinctively Puritan associations faded, and the Puritan approach merged with local practice and regional need to form an organic and distinctively English approach to a pan-European problem.

A renewed interest in the use of poor relief to reform English society was arguably instigated and driven by Puritans in the creation of "godly cities." These communities were clustered around two geographical areas and came into being during two distinctive periods. The first, beginning in the 1570s, was in East Anglia, running roughly between Norwich and Colchester, and including villages as small as 300 in population, such as Crat-field, Suffolk. The second, between 1610 and 1630, was in the west, forming a triangle whose points were Plymouth, Southampton, and Gloucester. These schemes typically included a bridewell, a work scheme, public food stocks, municipal poor relief, and in the western country, a municipal brew house. Their explicit goal was the spiritual reform and material relief of the poor. The similarity of schemes was in part driven by a shared network of co-religious. In the west, for example, the Puritan father of Dorchester, John White, was a colleague of Peter Thatcher of Salisbury, the town's most influential preacher. Henry Sherfield was the Recorder of Salisbury, and a known Puritan iconoclast, as well as the Recorder of Southampton. He was also an MP who sat on committees with other western Puritans, such as Ignatius Jorden, an alderman of Exeter. The mayor of Exeter was a regular correspondent of the mayor of Plymouth, thus completing this particular circle. The spark that ignited this western reform was a series of plague visitations, and the Puritan interpretation of the same as a sign of God's displeasure and his call to reform.

It is this period that has generated a sizable historiographical debate about the nature of Puritanism, poor relief, and the reformation of society. In line with a position influentially put forth by Keith Wrightson as early as 1974, by 1987 Margo Todd could assume that the theory "that puritan concern with discipline led to a stereotypically bourgeois disdain for the idle as social parasites and the poor as justly condemned by God has become an historiographical commonplace" (Todd, p. 118). The idea implicit here is that Puritans withheld poor relief unless the poor conformed to Puritan standards of behavior. This theory has been challenged, most notably by Margaret Spufford. Spufford questions whether Puritanism was "a necessary condition for a greater enforcement of moral behaviour on the poor," calling the notion that Puritanism was an explanatory mechanism for the reformation of manners a "gigantic red herring" (Spufford, pp. 41–57). Instead, she argues that economic circumstances produced bouts of reform, be it in 1600 or 1300 (her counterexample). Current consensus seems to be summed up in the words of

Paul Slack: "action cannot be separated from motivation, and motivation may be powerfully influenced by ideology" (Slack, *From Reformation*, p. 35). In other words, local circumstances and economic conditions certainly did play a role in the implementation of poor relief, but they were not the mechanism that drove it forward. That mechanism was often—although it is important to note, not always—the godly leader responding to the iniquities of the world.

Puritanism's particular contribution to poor relief was not in the development of new means and methods, but in their maintaining of the zeal and momentum of reform: "occasionally ratcheting up the regulatory machinery by another notch, more often creating a new spurt of local reform when earlier bursts of energy had flagged." (Slack, *From Reformation*, p. 44). Their willingness to inject life into a stagnating program came as a direct result of Puritan ideology, which required constant vigilance to detect God's displeasure and to deliberately create a renewed sense of reforming urgency. Such zeal was always temporary, as it depended upon the activities of a small group of local leaders, if not sometimes on the drive of just one man. In fact, such activity lasted rarely more than a decade, yet its effects had a long half-life.

The frailty of godly rule during the Interregnum led to a shift of interest away from wholesale civic reform toward the politics of political power. The following generation of Puritans showed a greater interest in "the wider 'propagating of the gospel,' into the counties, into Wales, to the American Indians; and that may have dispersed energies which might otherwise have gone into internal civic reform" (Slack, *From Reformation*, pp. 50–51).

Puritan New England made a concerted effort to block the migration of England's lower orders to the colonies. New England poor were faced with strict settlement criteria and a "warning out" system that ensured that only the homegrown poor would be relieved by the community.

See also: Bridewell, Crime and Punishment, Reformation of Manners
Further Reading
Paul Slack, *From Reformation to Improvement. Public Welfare in Early Modern England* (Oxford,

1999); Paul Slack, *Poverty & Policy in Tudor and Stuart England* (London, 1988); Margaret Spufford, "Puritanism and Social Control?" in A. Fletcher and J. Stevenson, eds., *Order and Disorder in Early Modern England* (Cambridge, Eng., 1985), pp. 41–57; Margo Todd, *Christian Humanism and the Puritan Social Order* (Cambridge, Eng., 1987); Keith Wrightson, *English Society, 1580–1680* (London, 1982); Keith Wrightson, "The Puritan Reformation of Manners, with Special Reference to the Counties of Lancashire and Essex 1640–1660" (Ph.D. diss., Cambridge University, 1974); Keith Wrightson, "Two Concepts of Order," in J. Brewer and J. Styles, eds., *An Ungovernable People: The English and Their Law in the Seventeenth and the Eighteenth Centuries* (London, 1980).

Lynn A. Botelho

Popish Plot

A spurious, but almost universally credited, plot to assassinate King Charles II and install a Roman Catholic regime. The Popish Plot was revealed in August 1678 and thereafter antipopish fever gripped England for many months. The plot set in train, first, the trial and execution of some three dozen Catholics; second, an attempt by the Whig opposition to exclude the king's Catholic brother, James, duke of York, from succeeding to the throne; and, third, a counterattempt by Tories to destroy not only the Whigs but also the Dissenters, as being "fanatics" who fomented a new civil war under the guise of purging popery.

The plot was "revealed" by unscrupulous perjurers, several of whom harbored paranoid resentments, but who gained public acclaim for their services to the Protestant nation. Principal of these were Titus Oates, Israel Tonge, William Bedloe, Miles Prance, Stephen Dugdale, John "Narrative" Smith, and Edward Turberville. Two factors ensured widespread belief in the plot revelations. The first was that the examining magistrate, Sir Edmund Berry Godfrey, was found murdered, a crime never yet solved, but one that was immediately imputed to the papists, and for which three Catholics were executed. The second was the discovery of the correspondence of Edward Coleman, a Catholic lawyer who acted as secretary to the Duke and Duchess of York, with Father La Chaise, confessor to the French king, Louis XIV. This was at a time when Louis was increasingly seen as preparing a Catholic crusade against the "Northern heresy." Coleman's letters could readily be construed as treasonable, and he was duly executed.

Through the winter of 1678–1679 Protestants panicked at the prospect of imminent Catholic massacre; town gates were guarded; people armed themselves. Edmund Calamy was eight years old, and he later said the plot was "the first public matter I can remember." Spectacular antipopish carnivals were held, culminating in pope burnings. Accusations of popish treason readily convinced juries, vigorously pressed on by Chief Justice Sir William Scroggs. In some localities, such as Monmouthshire, which had a significant Catholic population sheltered by the Marquess of Worcester, bitter rivalries were manifested in the activities of vicious priest hunters like John Arnold. All in all, over 70 priests were arrested, and upwards of 35 Catholic priests and laymen were executed or died in jail. Some were convicted of murder, some of treason, some under the Act of 1585, which forbade the presence of Catholic priests in England. The victims included one peer, Viscount Stafford, impeached in Parliament; Richard Langhorne, a prosperous lawyer who acted as the English Jesuits' steward; and the leading Irish bishop, Oliver Plunket, archbishop of Armagh. Four other Catholic peers (Arundel, Belasyse, Petre, and Powis) languished in the Tower for several years. Those who died were the last of the English Catholic martyrs, who number in all some 250, beginning with Thomas More and John Fisher in 1535. A representative 40 of these were canonized by the pope in 1970, including 6 from the plot era.

Riding the wave of the plot, the parliamentary opposition launched a campaign to pass a Bill of Exclusion, which would have prevented any but Protestants from succeeding to the throne. This movement was led by the Earl of Shaftesbury and soon acquired the name Whig. Though they won three general elections during 1679–1681, the Whigs were outmaneuverd by the king, who held the constitutional trump cards: the right to prorogue and dissolve Parliament, and the power to overawe the House of Lords, which voted down the proposal.

The Whigs also failed because the tide of public feeling turned against them. Plot fever waned as the perjurious fabrications of the "witnesses" became apparent. In the courts, the acquittal of Sir George Wakeman in July 1679 was a turning point. The Whigs overreached themselves by accusing Protestants of crypto-popery, among them Samuel Pepys. Gradually, public fear of popery gave way to fear of "presbytery," a label signifying revolutionary puritanism. It was common for Tories to say of the Exclusion Parliaments that they were "filled with Presbyterians." The Whigs began to seem too like the incendiaries of the Civil War, who had overthrown the constitution and the monarchy on the back of ferocious scaremongering about popery. On London bonfires, effigies of "Jack Presbyter" began to be burnt. Another fake plot was revealed in October 1679, this time a Presbyterian Plot, also known as the Meal Tub Plot, fabricated by Catholics, including Elizabeth Cellier, the "popish midwife."

In 1681 Charles II felt strong enough to dismiss the third Exclusion Parliament (also known as the Oxford Parliament) after a mere one week's sitting; he never summoned another. Soon Sir Roger L'Estrange was trumpeting high monarchist principles in his newspaper, *Observator.* The Anglican hierarchy rallied to the crown and repulsed Whig attempts to provide toleration or comprehension, that is, inclusion in the Church of England, for the Dissenters. On the same day that the last Catholic victim, Plunket, was executed, 1 July 1681, the first victim of the Tory revenge, Edward Fitzharris, also went to his death.

During the early 1680s the persecution of Dissenters was more severe than at any time since the passage of the Act of Uniformity in 1662. The purge aimed at nothing less than the destruction of Dissent, and it was the final attempt in English history to coerce people to be of one religion. The extremity of the reversal of mood since 1678 was remarkable, sufficient to ensure that the Catholic

James II inherited the throne in 1685 with remarkable ease. It was his conduct on the throne that once more turned events another full circle, renewing deep-seated anxieties about popery and arbitrary power. The aims of the Exclusionists were finally achieved: by the overthrow of James in 1688, through foreign invasion, and by the entrenching of the Protestant Succession in the Act of Settlement of 1701, which today still determines the religion of the British monarch.

See also: Antipopery, Comprehension, Dissenters
Further Reading
J. P. Kenyon, *The Popish Plot* (London, 1974).

Mark Goldie

Prayer

Prayer is a means of communication between man and supernatural beings. Rejecting medieval Catholic practices of addressing prayers to Mary and the saints, Protestants argued that prayer should only be addressed to God. This still left room for Reformers to disagree about the forms and function of prayer.

The established Church of England believed that it was appropriate for worship to include set prayers. In the Book of Common Prayer (1549 and 1552), Thomas Cranmer set forth English forms of prayer for communal worship in a graceful language that was to remain unchanged for over four hundred years. But from the start there were Reformers who were dissatisfied with the liturgical recitation of set prayers.

Puritans believed that the use of set forms of prayer was a human invention that rested on tradition rather than scripture, and they sometimes even criticized such forms as idolatrous images of the kind forbidden by the second commandment. Set prayers were likely to be recited by rote with little thought connected to their utterance. In contrast, all prayer should arise spontaneously from the heart under the inspiration of the Holy Spirit. Most puritans even questioned the recitation in the liturgy of the Lord's Prayer, believing it to be a model offered by Christ as to how men should pray, but not a form to be blindly repeated.

Rejection of set forms did not mean that puritans were insensitive to the importance of prayer. Rather, they urged on the faithful the responsibility to raise their hearts and voices to God in prayer privately in moments of meditation, while working, or while traveling; together with members of their family in household devotions; and as members of a congregation in church worship.

Private, or "secret," prayer was a form of devotion or conversation with God that brought the individual closer to God. Puritan diaries abound with records of individuals meditating and praying to God, and with the feeling of God's caress that often blessed the prayerful believer. In this respect prayer was often referred to as a means of grace. Clergy recommended devotional manuals to aid their congregants in developing the habit of prayer.

The family was often referred to as a small congregation, and family heads were urged to lead the members of their household in morning and evening religious exercises that included scripture reading, prayer, and occasionally the singing of psalms. The family would also offer prayers of thanks to God at meals. On special occasions, such as when one of its members was ill, the family would gather to offer special prayers. All such gatherings for prayer usually began with an admission of the sinfulness of those gathered and proceeded with thanks to God for the blessings he had bestowed on the family and its individual members.

Public worship often began with the minister offering a prayer that would last a quarter of an hour or more. Prior to the sermon, the preacher uttered a prayer that he might be inspired in his preaching and the congregation in their hearing. A longer prayer typically followed the sermon.

Despite believing that nothing could alter the will of God, puritans offered up petitions in their prayers. They asked God for blessings in this life as well as salvation in the next. They prayed for the salvation of loved ones and neighbors. They asked God to assist them in warding off threats to their churches and to the commonwealth. They requested the healing of loved ones who were ill. In all of this, they believed that what they asked for was in keeping with God's will—and were it not, they prayed for the grace to accept God's will.

See also: Book of Common Prayer, Family Piety, Predestination, Puritan Prayer Books
Further Reading
Francis J. Bremer and Barbara A. Bremer, "Thomas Cobbett's Practical Discourse of Prayer," Essex Institute Historical Collections 111 (1975), 138–150; Horton Davies, The Worship of the English Puritans (Westminster, Eng., 1948); Charles Hambrick-Stowe, The Practise of Piety: Puritan Devotional Disciplines in Seventeenth-Century New England (Chapel Hill, 1982).

Francis J. Bremer

Praying Towns

Soon after its formation in 1643, The Society for the Propagation of the Gospel in New England organized settlements for Native American proselytes, or "Praying Indians." These settlements were known as Praying Towns. While maintaining some syncretist cultural and religious practices, the Praying Town required Native Americans to conform to English customs and religion. As leading missionary John Eliot explained, the first task of the Praying Town was to construct "a very sufficient Meeting-House of fifty foot long, twenty five foot broad." Private homes and footbridges across the Charles River accompanied the meetinghouse, though many Praying Indians continued to reside in wigwams. In August 1646, Puritan minister Thomas Shepard composed a list of twenty-nine "orders," each requiring inhabitants of the Praying Towns to "conform themselves to the civil fashions of the English." The Society felt that such "civilizing" institutions and laws were necessary preconditions for the conversion of Native Americans.

In 1644 the Massachusetts General Court ordered that Native American tribes in the southeastern part of the Massachusetts Bay Colony be "instructed in the knowledge and worship of God." Two years later, John Eliot went to Nonantum, where he preached his first Algonquian sermon in Waban's wigwam. The court then appointed a committee to buy land for the Praying Towns. Land was

purchased from the Native Americans at Watertown Mills and at Nonantum. The missionary experiment was then tried at Natick, the first Praying Town. John Eliot's goal was to generate native missionaries from the structure of the Praying Town. He appointed Cutshamekin, a sachem, or leader, of the Massachusetts, to rule over approximately 150 people in Natick. Totherswamp and Waban adjudicated legal matters, and Monequassun, whom Eliot had already instructed to read and write, started as the teacher of the Indian proselytes. As such, the missionaries called upon native people to introduce English standards of "cohabitation and labor, government and law, and church covenant" within the Praying Town. After a series of setbacks, the first Indian Church was officially formed in Natick in 1660.

Two years after the settlement of Natick, Eliot discovered the need to expand. Natick was not a suitable place to gather converts from other villages, in part because the growing number of proselytes wanted to stay closer to their traditional homelands. The General Court's original land grant was also not large enough, and it was too near the English, causing tensions between Natick's Praying Indians and the English settlers in the neighboring town of Dedham. Eliot obtained tracts of land approximating 6,000 acres each and created five other Praying Towns nearby: Punkapoag, Wamesit, Hassanamesit, Okommakamesit, and Nashobahh. Magunkog followed in 1669, completing the cluster that Daniel Gookin in 1677 referred to as the "old praying towns." With the exception of the Pennacook Indians in Wamesit, most of these Praying Towns were inhabited by Massachusett and Nipmuck Indians.

The relocation of native peoples through the Praying Town system irreparably damaged kinship structures and undermined the social and political structures of native villages. While missionaries incorporated the political authority of sachems, they also greatly augmented the power traditionally accorded this figure within the governmental structure of the Praying Town. Conversely, the Puritans rejected the powwow, or spiritual leader's authority, reflecting their deliberate efforts to supplant native religious customs with Christianity. Eighty percent of the native people originally inhabiting the land where the Praying Towns were located lived by agriculture. They were not nomadic hunters, but they were significantly more mobile than the British because they moved to gather and fish between harvest seasons. The English criticized the natives' relationship to the land, characterizing them as "lazy savages" who did not understand the proper use of the environment.

Despite the missionary tactics of "coercion and rigidity," the native populations were able to incorporate some of their traditional beliefs and practices within the culture of the Praying Towns. The Algonquian language remained relatively intact among the proselytes, as Eliot used it as a tool for missionary work. Powwows could be admitted into the towns provided that they would submit to the authority of the Puritans. Native interest in Christianity was often rooted in parallels between Massachusett creation myths and biblical stories. Praying Indians had to alter their culture and lifestyle to subsist on the marginalized land of the Praying Town, but the settlement system also provided a limited avenue through which natives could maintain a hold on ancestral land. Since the arrival of the English, Massachusetts Bay tribes had been devastated by waves of disease. The Praying Towns presented many of them with a viable option for protecting their people and culture from further destruction.

The number of Praying Towns continued to expand through the 1660s. Motivated by desire for English protection from their Narragansett enemies, the eight Nipmuck sachems requested Praying Towns. This request resulted in the formation of Quantisset, Pakachoog, Chabanakongdomun, Wabquisset, Manchage, Maaexit, and Waeuntug. The Mayhew family settled Praying Towns on Martha's Vineyard, home to 300 Wampanoag proselytes. Richard Bourne founded Mashpee in Plymouth Plantation, where John Cotton Jr. also preached and studied Algonquian from 1667 to 1697. The Mohegans in Connecticut and the Narragansetts in Rhode Island were generally resistant to the mission.

During the height of the mission's success, there were between 3,600 and 4,000 residents in Praying Towns and thirty Indian congregations in the southern part of Massachusetts alone. The escalating tensions between the English and the Native Americans on the eve of King Philip's War quickly and radically changed this model of relatively peaceful colonial coexistence. In June 1675, Praying Indians were relocated to only five towns. In October of that same year, the General Court moved them to Long Island and Deer Isle. There was much hardship, sickness, and death during the long, cold winter of the war. Eliot and Gookin were harshly criticized for defending the Praying Indians, even though one-fourth of the Native Americans maintained their allegiance to the English. After the war, roughly 40 percent of the Massachusett proselytes retained their Christian faith, but more hostile English laws and attitudes toward the Native Americans had all but permanently destroyed the Praying Town system.

See also: John Eliot, Thomas Mayhew, Waban, Indian Bible, King Philip's War, Society for the Propagation of the Gospel in New England
Further Reading
Michael P. Clark, *The Eliot Tracts* (Westport, CT, 2003); Richard W. Cogley, *John Eliot's Mission to the Indians before King Philip's War* (Cambridge, MA, 1999); William Cronon, *Changes in the Land: Indians, Colonists, and the Ecology of New England* (New York, 1983); Daniel Gookin, *An Account of the Doings and Sufferings of the Christian Indians in New England* (1677); Dane Morrison, *A Praying People: Massachusett Acculturation and the Failure of the Puritan Mission, 1600–1690* (New York, 1995).

Sarah Rivett

Preaching

Preaching, as a sacred address, is one of the most ancient practices in the Christian Church, and indeed it predates Christianity, as it has its origins in the Jewish tradition of reading portions of scripture from the Torah scrolls to the congregation in the synagogue and commenting upon them each Sabbath. By reading from Isaiah in the synagogue in

Nazareth, and by sending out his apostles to preach two by two, Jesus himself elaborated upon time-honored observances. Sermons are among the greatest legacies of the early Greek and Latin Fathers in the centuries following Christ, including Saints John Chrysostom and Jerome. The homily, a type of scriptural exegesis that was offered during the Mass in those ritual moments when the priest imitated Christ's life and teaching, evolved from such ancient beginnings.

Preaching has always been closely connected with the life of the soul, and its changing traditions have reflected contemporary concerns for the soul's health. In England by the end of the fifteenth century, preaching was supplemental in devotional life, subordinate to the sacrifice of the Mass. Preaching's importance stemmed from its ability to break the cycle of sin that most people's lives were locked into, and also to be a moralizing force for the suppression of wrongdoing and the elevation of virtue. Three different (albeit complementary) forms of preaching composed the spiritual fare: the homily, the quarter sermon, and the outdoor sermon. By the late Middle Ages, the homily had been adapted from its chief role as a scriptural commentary to include readings on the lives of the saints, and it retained its place as a brief interlude during the Mass. From the early 1400s, four sermons each year (one each quarter) were supposed to be delivered at every parish church (under the terms of canon law) as an antidote to the Lollard heresy, and their form was heavily influenced by the innovations of the mendicant friars. In denouncing sin and inculcating virtue, they preached on the Ten Commandments and other fundamentals in as many churches as their extensive itineraries could reach. The outdoor sermon too had been promoted by the friars, and by 1500 many pulpit crosses had been built in the cemeteries of cathedrals and religious houses for long afternoon sermons that were preached (especially in the case of Paul's Cross in London) by the best available and finest orators of the day. During the Middle Ages, the outdoor sermon was dominated by the intense allegorical style of Scholasticism, until the Humanists began to raise new standards for preaching from the end of the fourteenth century.

This transformation was sponsored by senior churchmen, including Bishop John Fisher (as chancellor of Cambridge University), Dean John Colet of St. Paul's, and especially Erasmus, who came repeatedly to Cambridge to teach Greek. Heavily influenced by the preaching styles of his friends (especially Colet and the French Franciscan Jean Vitrier), Erasmus printed several works on the value and techniques of preaching, culminating in his final major book, the *Ecclesiastes* (1535). By the continual study of scripture, and through the mysterious workings of the Holy Spirit, the heart of the preacher would be transformed and cleansed. Through his voice, and through his teachings, he would kindle in his listeners a renewed desire for pious lives. Erasmus's reliance upon understanding scripture in light of its meanings, as recorded from the mouths of the evangelists, spelled the extinction of the Scholastic style of preaching in Western Europe. The *Ecclesiastes* was a landmark in the history of preaching, and it was influential across what were widening doctrinal fissures, for the rest of the sixteenth century and beyond.

The early evangelical Reformers, from Martin Luther onward, redefined the role of the sermon in light of their contention that salvation proceeded from faith alone. Christ was the sole mediator between a sinful humanity and a reconciling God, and faith meant placing active confidence in Christ's promises. Reformers redefined the balance between faith and works and argued that good works in themselves were not a means to salvation (as the medieval Church had taught), but rather were the attributes of any good Christian. Thus as they undermined the traditional economy of salvation, they enhanced the importance of preaching, in accordance with their understanding of "faith cometh by hearing" (Romans 10:8–17). While Erasmus had taught that preaching was one office among many that the priest must exercise, the reformers established preaching as the premier office of any clergyman or minister, beyond other duties. In the *Book of Homilies*, Archbishop Thomas Cranmer lifted the ideal of the patristic homily to exquisite new heights, especially as pulpit readings for clergy who were not already strong preachers.

The Reformers also elevated the sermon beyond many of its ancient connections with the Mass. The followers of John Calvin redesigned churches in the Netherlands in imitation of Solomon's Temple. As in Geneva, many English parish churches were adapted to focus on the sermon. The rood screen was removed, and the pulpit was brought out into the nave as a dominating feature. Afternoon sermons continued to be delivered in England at surviving pulpit crosses (those that were not dismantled with the friaries), and especially at Paul's Cross, which remained the foremost public preaching place in the realm.

Among the most important developments in the style of preaching, beginning during Edward VI's reign (and continuing for at least two centuries thereafter, and on both sides of the Atlantic), was the prophetic mode. Sermons attempted to discern the special patterns of God's providence for each believer's life, as well as for society as a whole. Preachers encouraged their hearers to engage in a critical, inward-seeking self-exploration of their consciences as the means to determine whether they were predestined by God to salvation, as members of the elect. The doom-laden jeremiad, which warned society of its moral failings, and raised the awful specter of the possibility of God's wrathful judgment, is the best-known example of the prophetic mode.

Preaching "exercises" began to develop according to the model of prophesying established first in the Grossmünster in Zürich, through the influence of the "Dutch Stranger Church" in London. In the English experience, prophesying took the form of learned scriptural exegesis, conducted by the delivery of several sermons on the same biblical text, in the presence of local clergy and laity, presided over by a senior cleric as moderator, followed by a discussion (usually, but not always private) by the attending ministers of the doctrines that had been preached. Prophesying precipitated a crisis in 1577, when Queen Elizabeth, confident that the reading of homilies was a safer means to inculcate faith among the people, ordered the suppression of prophesyings, even though she had to undermine the authority of Archbishop Edmund Grindal to achieve her aims.

Prophesying was replaced by "lectures by combination." Ministers from local parishes assembled weekly in their central town to preach to the crowds who came to market. Though the size of the combination varied, thirteen was the ideal because of its apostolic resonance, as well as for practical purposes, so that each member took his turn once every quarter. After the sermon, the ministers took a meal together, for the sake of good fellowship, to confer on matters of doctrine, and also to encourage each other in their learning. At least eighty-five combination lectures are known in late Tudor and early Stuart England, and their attempts to raise standards in preaching were necessary when clerical attainments in many parts of the realm were still low, especially in a church that had not been fully reformed (in the opinion of many Calvinist theologians). The combination lectures (and Emmanuel College, Cambridge) were important seedbeds for the preachers who migrated to New England in the seventeenth century to escape the ceremonials of the Laudian church.

The fire-and-brimstone style of the jeremiad, with its prophetic warnings and denunciations of indifference and sin, was the staple of sermons in Massachusetts, as well as Hartford and New Haven colonies (later Connecticut), from the earliest days of their settlement to the mid-eighteenth century. The influence of the formidable dynasty of preachers in the Cotton and Mather families was profound and lasting, and the establishment of Harvard (and later Yale) ensured the training of New England's preachers in the prophetic tradition.

See also: Hourglasses in the Church, Lectures and Lectureships, Prophesyings

Further Reading

Francis J. Bremer, *John Winthrop: America's Forgotten Founding Father* (New York, 2003); Patrick Collinson, "Lectures by Combination: Structures and Characteristics of Church Life in 17th-Century England," in Patrick Collinson, *Godly People: Essays on English Protestantism and Puritanism* (London, 1983), pp. 466–498; Patrick Collinson, John Craig, and Brett Usher, eds., *Conferences and Combination Lectures in the Elizabethan Church: Dedham and Bury St. Edmunds, 1582–1590*, Church of England Record Society, vol. 10 (Woodbridge, Eng., 2003); Andrew Spicer, "Rebuilding Solomon's Temple? The Architecture of Calvinism," in R. N. Swanson, ed., *The Holy Land, Holy Lands, and Christian History*, Studies in Church History, vol. 36 (Woodbridge, Eng., 2000), pp. 275–287; Susan Wabuda, *Preaching during the English Reformation* (Cambridge, Eng., 2002); Alexandra Walsham, *Providence in Early Modern England* (Oxford, 1999).

Susan Wabuda

Predestination

The doctrine in Christian theology that affirms that God from eternity has chosen some persons for salvation. It was a very important doctrine in the theology of the Puritans because it emphasized the sovereignty of God and salvation as an unmerited gift of God's grace to sinful humans rather than an achievement for which persons could claim credit. Predestination was also appealing to Puritans because it accentuated the spiritual nature of the relationship between the divine and the human, thereby undermining the authority of church hierarchy and of ritual efficacy. Predestination refers to the eternal divine decree that determines the final supernatural end of rational creatures (humans and angels) and not to the divine decree governing all that should come to pass in nature and history, which the Puritans considered under the topic of providence. Predestination is thus distinguished from the providence of God, by which the creation is governed and directed to divinely appointed natural ends.

The doctrines of predestination and providence both differ from fatalism insofar as, according to most Puritan theologians, all that God has decreed occurs without, as the Westminster Confession of Faith put it, taking away "the liberty or contingency" of secondary causes. Accordingly the human will is never forced by God but acts willingly, without compulsion, so that sinners are responsible for their sins. Predestination is also distinguished from fatalism because it represents the will of a benevolent God, even though that will is often beyond human understanding. Predestination subdivides into election and reprobation, the former referring to God's will to save some (the elect) and the latter to God's passing by and condemnation of others (the reprobate). When both election and reprobation are affirmed, the doctrine is sometimes referred to as double predestination. Election is an act of God's mercy and grace; reprobation an act of justice and judgment against sin. Both illustrate the divine glory and are hidden in the mystery of God's will. Puritan theologians typically described election as being "in Christ," thereby placing God's forgiving grace in a Christological context. Puritan theologians sometimes disputed the logical priority in the divine mind of God's decrees: did predestination follow upon God's decree to create humanity and permit the fall of Adam (so that those reprobated were reprobated with a view to their sin), or did it precede it, in the latter case being a pure act of divine sovereignty? The former position is called infralapsarianism and the latter supralapsarianism. In infralapsarianism, election presupposes the fall and the reprobate are left to the punishment due their sin. Supralapsarianism is more emphatically double predestination. But in both cases it was denied that God was in any way the author of sin. While certain theologians important to Puritans, such as William Perkins and William Ames and later in New England Samuel Willard, were supralapsarians, the various confessions of faith honored by the Puritans, including the Canons of the Synod of Dort and the Westminster Confession of Faith, were infralapsarian.

Roots and History of the Puritan Doctrine of Predestination

The teaching and preaching of predestination by the Puritans was a part of their Calvinist (or more properly, Reformed) theological heritage, sharpened by their own theological and devotional commitment to the freedom of God's grace. Reformed theology drew on such biblical roots of the doctrine as the Old Testament teaching of God's free choice of Israel as his people and the various statements about predestination in the Pauline epistles in the New Testament. It also depended heavily upon the predestinarian writings of St. Augustine against the Pelagian heretics of the fifth century and on medieval anti-Pelagian theologians such as Thomas Bradwardine, an Englishman who had ended his life as archbishop of Canterbury, whom English Calvinists particularly cited. Puritans also especially admired John Wycliffe, who had taught predestination. More important to the Puritans, however, was the predestinarian theology of many Protestant reformers, beginning with Huldrych Zwingli, Martin Luther, and John Calvin. And although later Lutherans backed away from some of the strong predestinarian assertions of Luther, the Reformed, or Calvinist, theologians tended to place even more emphasis on predestination as time went on, drawing from many Reformed theologians in addition to Calvin, including Theodore Beza, Martin Bucer, and Peter Martyr Vermigli, the latter two of whom taught theology at the English universities during the reign of Edward VI.

Predestinarian theology was influential in the Church of England from the beginning of its Reformation, appearing in such early English Protestant martyrs as William Tyndale and John Frith, as well as in such Protestant leaders in the Church of England as archbishop of Canterbury Thomas Cranmer (also martyred). The doctrine of election is affirmed in the Thirty-nine Articles of the Church of England. There was extensive Calvinist influence in England after the accession of Queen Elizabeth in 1558, with predestinarian Reformed theology becoming the prevailing outlook in the Church of England during the reigns of Elizabeth I and James I, the latter having imbibed it from the Scottish Presbyterians among whom he had been raised. William Perkins, perhaps the greatest of Elizabethan theologians, gave a central position to predestination in a number of writings published in the 1590s that placed predestination in the framework of the divine decrees and divided it into election and reprobation.

In the same decade of the 1590s, there arose a countercurrent in English Protestant theology soon dubbed Arminianism, and only then did the doctrine of predestination become controversial in England. Perkins and other English Calvinists had attacked the Dutch theologian Jacobus Arminius, after whom this theological party was named, for making predestination depend upon God's foreknowledge of those who would have faith. The predestinarian Lambeth Articles of 1595, drawn up as a guide for correct teaching in the University of Cambridge, indicate the thoroughly Calvinist character of the leadership of the English church at that date. In 1618 delegates from the Church of England participated in the Synod of Dort in the Netherlands, which strongly endorsed the doctrine of predestination, and King James agreed with the synod's view that the Dutch Arminians were Pelagian heretics. But after 1625 an Arminian theology opposed to the Calvinist teaching on predestination gained the patronage of King Charles I and of archbishop of Canterbury William Laud.

The defense of predestinarian theology in the Church of England was led by those of Puritan outlook, and the doctrine remained on the defensive until the 1640s, the years of civil war and parliamentary and Puritan hegemony. During the Interregnum and the ascendancy of Oliver Cromwell, predestinarian theology prevailed in church and university. The Westminster Confession of Faith, drawn up to be a statement of faith for a Puritan-controlled Church of England, treated both predestination and the covenant as an unfolding of the divine decree. This confession was eventually adopted in the Church of Scotland and, along with its accompanying catechisms, was widely influential in New England, especially in its later Congregationalist form known as the Savoy Confession of Faith. With the restoration of the monarchy in 1660, however, an anti-predestinarian theology came to prevail in the Church of England, with Calvinism flourishing primarily among the Dissenters of Puritan background, though there never ceased to be Church of England Calvinists. Thus the doctrine of predestination came to be especially associated in England with the Puritans, represented importantly by the great Puritan theologians William Ames, in exile in Holland before the Civil Wars, and John Owen, during the Restoration one of the principal theological leaders of Dissent. This predestinarian theology was carried to New England, the Pilgrim pastor John Robinson (who never himself went to Plymouth) being a strong opponent of Arminianism. John Davenport, who came to New England in 1637, confided to a correspondent before leaving England that Arminianism corrupted the Church of England far more than any flaws in liturgy or polity. The doctrine of predestination became a staple of New England Puritan teaching and was given extended treatment in the theological writings of Samuel Willard. In *A Seasonable Testimony to the Glorious Doctrines* (1702), Cotton Mather urged that the doctrine should be preached.

Puritan Differences about the Doctrine and Devotional Implications

Throughout the seventeenth century, Puritan theologians, as a consequence of controversy with Arminians and Roman Catholics, and in accord with the increasing prevalence of Scholastic method in Protestant theology, gave the doctrine of predestination more logical precision and elaboration than it had earlier had and also engaged in more speculative and metaphysical discussions about it. Predestination also became controversial among the Puritans themselves. Some high Calvinists took the position that predestination meant that persons were justified prior to their actual believing, but this was rejected as an erroneous inference leading to antinomian error by the generality of Puritan theologians. A few extremists, designated hyper-Calvinists, took the doctrine of predestination to mean that one should be reserved in proclaiming offers of salvation. Others, moderate Calvinists typified by Richard Baxter and John Howe, fearful of antinomian and hyper-Calvinist excess, began to soften the doctrine, affirming only a single predestination (election) and avoiding what they regarded as Scholastic subtleties. But with all of these controversies and Scholastic refinements, it must not be forgotten that the reason predestination was at the heart of Puritan piety was because it was the guarantor of God's free grace and mercy, the essence of the Christian gospel as they understood it.

The devotional and experiential aspects of predestination were given expression in countless sermons and published treatises on the Christian life that poured forth from the pens of Puritan writers. In these treatises, predestination appears not as a source of anxiety, but of the assurance for believers that their redemption did not depend on their virtue and constancy, but rested securely in the divine will. For them predestination was a source of comfort and an aspect of that soteriology in terms of which they probed the Christian life. Among the Puritan writers of devotional and imaginative literature whose works presuppose a strongly predestinarian theology, John Bunyan is preeminent.

See also: Anti-Calvinism, Arminianism, God, Grace, Soteriology

Further Reading

R. T. Kendall, *Calvin and English Calvinism to 1649* (Oxford, 1979); Nicholas Tyacke, *Anti-Calvinists: The Rise of English Arminianism, c. 1590–1640* (Oxford, 1987); Dewey D. Wallace Jr., *Puritans and Predestination: Grace in English Protestant Theology, 1525–1695* (Chapel Hill, 1982).

Dewey D. Wallace Jr.

Primitive Episcopacy

An attempt to return to an apostolical model of the episcopacy. The term refers to an effort to create a less worldly and authoritarian office and covers a spectrum, rather than a single position, with supporters at different places among the Reformers over time. In the mid-sixteenth century, the idea of "reduced" episcopacy, with smaller dioceses where the bishop acted as a superintendent or supervisor, an idea based on the reformer Martin Bucer's *De Regno Christi*, had a fairly broad spread, and it was only with the rise of *iure divino* episcopacy (that is, the claim that episcopacy was ordained by divine law) that it became a more exclusively puritan model. John Reynolds offered reduced episcopacy as a via media at the Hampton Court Conference of religious leaders with James I in 1604.

There were cautious expressions in favor of primitive episcopacy over the first forty years of the seventeenth century, explicitly by puritan clergy

Cornelius Burges and John Preston, less so by other puritan clergy such as Thomas Taylor and William Gouge. In 1641 it was, momentarily, a greater possibility, being a major concern of the Scottish Commissioners and raised in Parliament by moderates such as Sir Edward Dering. Such a proposal was promoted by James Ussher, archbishop of Armagh and primate of the Church of Ireland. His scheme was withdrawn when he feared that it might be used as a stepping stone for more radical options. The pragmatic politics of the 1640s encouraged continued adherents to primitive episcopacy like the minister Thomas Gataker to accept Presbyterianism, and after the Restoration it remained as a theoretically possible but politically unattainable means to achieve reconciliation between Presbyterians and the established church.

See also: Hampton Court Conference
Further Reading
Patrick Collinson, *Archbishop Grindal, 1519–1583: The Struggle for a Reformed Church* (Berkeley, 1979); Patrick Collinson, *The Religion of Protestants: Church in English Society, 1559–1625* (Oxford, 1984); Diarmaid MacCulloch, *Thomas Cranmer: A Life* (New Haven, 1997).

Tom Webster

Prophesyings

In England, prophesyings were clerical gatherings designed to enhance the expertise of the clergy. The prophesyings might have fared better if they had been called something else. To those who chose to be ignorant of what they were about (like Queen Elizabeth I), the word carried alarming chiliastic resonances. But in fact prophesying took its name from matters discussed by St. Paul in his letters to the church at Corinth (I Corinthians 14:26–33; see also I Thessalonians 5:20); and as an institution reinstated in the early years of the Reformation in Huldrych Zwingli's Zürich, *Prophezei* was a sober academic exercise, conducted in Latin, but expounding the text from the other biblical languages, devoted only to exposition of the Old Testament, and related to the production of the Zürich

Bible. But to anyone more interested in order and conservation than evangelism, the exercise was inherently and alarmingly participatory, seeking to involve as many as possible in the task of defining biblical truth. At Zürich, although *Prophezei* was conducted by the most learned of the city's ministers and intended primarily for the edification of divinity students, all who could cope with its exacting academic standards, women as well as men, were encouraged to attend. And in other churches, notably the "Stranger Church" of religious refugees organized in Edwardian London by the émigré Polish evangelical John a Lasco, prophesying was a congregational affair, a weekly opportunity for lay members of the church to question what they had heard from the pulpit; although as Calvinism matured in the later sixteenth century, steps were everywhere taken to discourage these more demotic tendencies.

Much of the episcopal leadership of the early Elizabethan Church was in the hands of bishops who had spent the reign of the Catholic Mary Tudor in exile on the continent, where they had encountered "prophesying" in more than one city of refuge. (The most Zwinglian of English reforming bishops, John Hooper of Gloucester, had already introduced a form of prophesying exercise into his diocese in Edward VI's reign.) In the first fifteen years of Elizabeth's reign, in the 1570s especially, the prophesyings were sanctioned by the bishops in many parts of the southern province of Canterbury, including East Anglia, several centers in Essex, a number of towns in the extensive diocese of Lincoln, Sussex, and the West Country. They were even set up in four market towns in Archbishop Matthew Parker's diocese of Canterbury, although Parker, who had not been a Marian exile, was not especially sympathetic.

The early prophesyings built upon, or incorporated, the written exercises on theological topics prescribed by authority to be undertaken by unlearned, nongraduate clergy, the dead weight of the mid-Tudor clergy inherited from the pre-Reformation church. The pattern most often followed consisted of two or three sermons on the same text, delivered in the presence of all the ministers "tied to the exercise," and in the presence of a lay audience. This was followed by more private conference among the clergy, which included formal "censure" of the doctrine preached. Where most of the attendant clergy were still, as it were, serving their apprenticeships, the structure of the exercise was top-down, with the authority to convene and regulate vested, by the bishop, in one or more permanent moderators: the model of devolved episcopacy. As things progressed, a greater collegiality came to be enjoyed. The value of the prophesyings was not only that they constituted a kind of seminary without bars for the unlearned clergy, but that they provided sermons, typically on a market day, for large numbers of people who were still without preaching in their own parishes. They also represented a show of strength for the Reformed religion in social and political contexts in which it still needed all the support and credit it could get. These exercises were also good for the business of a market town. The people who attended prophesyings needed to eat and drink.

Although the various "orders of prophesying" that have survived were formally sanctioned by sympathetic bishops and some bishops claimed to have preached in the exercise themselves, it is far from certain that it was the bishops who were responsible in all cases for setting them up. Rather most orders are couched in terms that suggest that it was the participating ministers who took the initiative. Prophesyings were in any case no part of the formal and legally defined infrastructure of the Elizabethan Church. The first occurrence of the word *prophesying* in any official document of the Church of England came after Elizabeth's death, when no. 72 of the Canons of 1604 forbade any minister to appoint or hold meetings for sermons, "commonly termed by some prophecies or exercises," without episcopal license and direction, given under the bishop's hand and seal. Such permission, as we have seen, was often forthcoming, but Elizabeth had denied that the bishops had any authority to approve such proceedings. There were prophesyings in the 1570s of which the bishops were probably ignorant, and such irregularities as puritan ministers suspended for nonconformity continuing to preach in

the exercises and, here and there, some lay participation. From 1574 there was a tussle between those who wanted the prophesyings suppressed (who included the queen) and those who supported their continuance, not only many of the bishops but several Privy Counsellors. When Bishop John Parkhurst of Norwich was ordered by Archbishop Parker (himself under royal orders) to suppress "those vain prophesyings," he asked whether only "vain" exercises were meant, and Parker told him not to be so pedantic. But sympathetic Privy Counsellors were advising the bishop to pay no attention. The truth is that it was the prophesyings that, above anything else, gave the Elizabethan Church the appearance of a Reformed church and promised to make it in reality what in principle it was.

This was where matters stood in the summer of 1576, when reports reached the court of dangerous developments at Southam in Warwickshire, where there was an exercise that some Puritans regarded as one of the best in all England, but which, by the same token, the enemies of the prophesyings, as well as of the advanced, progressive Protestantism that they symbolized, would have considered the worst. The upshot was that Archbishop Edmund Grindal, who had succeeded the conservative Parker a few months before and was the white hope for all "forward" Protestants, was ordered by the queen in a face-to-face interview to convey an order suppressing the prophesyings and to curtail the number of preachers in the church. Grindal, shocked, sat down to write a letter in which he refused to transmit such an order and reminded Elizabeth, with words borrowed from St. Ambrose in his letters to the Emperor Theodosius, of the limits of her authority in matters of religion and even of her own mortality. Meanwhile, Grindal obtained reports on the prophesyings from the bishops and drew up orders for reform of the practice. These orders insisted, before everything, that no layman be allowed to speak in an exercise. But on the matter of lay attendance, Grindal dug in his heels and refused the terms of a compromise deal that would have restricted the exercises to the clergy, a compromise that many, including Sir Francis Bacon, thought was the right way to proceed. In consequence, Grindal was effectively sacked. Although his status was formally one of sequestration, and the politicians made sure that the affair would not lead to the ultimate scandal of deprivation, so that the archbishop died in office, this was the end of the false dawn that was Grindal's archiepiscopate. Elizabeth had already taken the matter of prophesying into her own hands and had ordered an end to the practice.

This was not, however, the end of the prophesyings. In the years immediately following Grindal's disgrace, something very like the southern prophesyings was set up in many places in the northwest of England. The only difference from the prophesyings of the 1570s was that a single sermon now took the place of a conference in public conducted by two or three preachers; or rather one sermon preached to the clergy only and another, later in the morning, to the people. That was to minimize the risk of open disagreement between the preachers in the full light of day. But everything else remained the same, including the note taking and examination of "the meaner sort," and learned conference. Much the same pattern was to be followed in the "combination lectures," which took the place of the prophesyings in very many market towns in the south, and which were a characteristic and defining institution of the Jacobean church.

But Elizabeth's diktat of 1576 had consequences that were more threatening to the peace of the Church of England. In Norwich in 1575, in the vacancy of the episcopal see, the preachers set up a prophesying on their own authority with an essentially Presbyterian constitution. It was "judged meet by the brethren" that things should be managed in the way that they were, and the orders were adopted "by the consent of the brethren only, and not by one man's authority." This form of prophesying still took place publicly, in Norwich Cathedral. But with the intensification of the post-Grindal reaction, in Norwich and elsewhere, such activities were driven underground. The consequence was the Conference Movement, which was secret. The Dedham Conference was set up by refugees from the anti-puritan reaction in Nor-

wich, which followed the arrival of Bishop Edmund Freke.

See also: Edmund Grindal, Dedham Conference, Lectures and Lectureships, Marian Exiles, Preaching

Further Reading

P. Benedict, *Christ's Churches Purely Reformed: A Social History of Calvinism* (New Haven, 2002); Patrick Collinson, *The Elizabethan Puritan Movement* (London, 1967); Patrick Collinson, *Archbishop Grindal, 1519–1583: The Struggle for a Reformed Church* (Berkeley, 1979); B. Gordon, *The Swiss Reformation* (Manchester, Eng., 2002).

Patrick Collinson

Protectorate

The name given to the period of the Commonwealth during which Oliver and Richard Cromwell served (successively) as heads of state with the title Lord Protector (December 1653 to May 1659). Following the regicide (the execution of Charles I, 30 January 1649), the abolition of monarchy (March 1649), and the military conquest by armies under Oliver Cromwell of Ireland and Scotland, the whole of Britain and Ireland was, for the first time, united into a single Commonwealth. In April 1653 Cromwell used the army to dissolve the Rump of the Long Parliament, tiring of its failure to promote constitutional, religious, social, and legal reform. He and his fellow officers handpicked 140 "godly men" from the four nations of England, Ireland, Scotland, and Wales and entrusted them with finding a way to prepare the peoples for self-government and the fruits of religious liberty. When they failed to find a way forward and resigned their power back into his hands, he reluctantly agreed to serve as head of state under a paper constitution (the Instrument of Government) with the title Lord Protector.

The new constitution was based on a strong commitment to the separation of powers. Cromwell himself as Lord Protector had limited personal authority—he was required to act on the advice of a Council of State, albeit one packed with close friends and long-term colleagues. The constitution provided for a national church along loosely Congregationalist lines, with enormous devolution of responsibility for forms of worship and discipline to a parish level. Many—perhaps half—reverted to a simplified form of the old Anglican worship. Cromwell appointed a group of men of Presbyterian, Congregationalist, and Baptist backgrounds to ordain men for service in this church, their "trying" of candidates being restricted to tests of their biblical knowledge and soundness of morals (they were forbidden to examine doctrinal matters); and he appointed local commissioners of godly gentlemen to evict clergy who became "scandalous" in their way of life. But no one was required to attend the parish church (although they did have to pay tithes to maintain it). Those who kept their views to themselves were free to gather in private; those who preached licentiousness or denied the Trinity in public were harried and imprisoned. Cromwell may have given the people liberty, but all too many abused that liberty, and for the godly all hope of imposing discipline at a local level evaporated. The Quakers not only preached against the priestcraft and the forms of worship in "steeple houses," but organized tithe strikes; and some challenged the authority of scripture and emphasized the authority of the Holy Spirit in the heart of each believer. An extreme example was James Nayler's proclamation of the presence of Christ in every man in his symbolic ride into Bristol reenacting Christ's entry into Jerusalem (September 1656). The godly were convinced that in the face of such blasphemies, the Protectorate was too weak.

After trying to use his senior army colleagues (the major-generals) to instill a "reformation of manners," Cromwell came under pressure to regularize his position by taking the Crown. He refused, but agreed to a redefinition of his powers under a revised parliamentary constitution (The Humble Petition and Advice), which reintroduced the idea of doctrinal tests (essentially acceptance of the Apostles Creed) for those who would be allowed to minister in public, and toughened the laws against blasphemy and licentiousness. Oliver was uncomfortable with these changes, but he accepted them, while grumbling that instead of working to share

their part of the truth that would build God's kingdom, they were bent on bitter rivalries and feuds. His son Richard, who became Lord Protector on Oliver's death (3 September 1658), had more natural sympathy with orthodox Calvinist programs; but this in turn destroyed such goodwill as he enjoyed from the religious libertarians in the army, and after a few months he was forced to resign (May 1659), leading to a period of increasing anarchy, which culminated in the recall of the king within a year of the fall of the Protectorate.

See also: Oliver Cromwell, Major-Generals, Reformation of Manners, Triers and Ejectors
Further Reading
Barry Coward, *The Cromwellian Protectorate* (Manchester, Eng., 2002).

John Morrill

Providence

To believe in God's providence was to believe that the world and history follow a preordained pattern, established by God for the benefit of the elect. The doctrine, thus conceived, is a characteristic of Puritan piety, and it can be seen as based on the desire for security. It could be manipulated to assert the danger of sin and used as an inducement for good behavior. On a larger scale, belief in God's providence helped to reinforce the concepts of a theocentric universe and the teleological order.

Divine Action

Puritans emphasized the sovereignty of God. This meant that they did not interpret the visible world to be the final outcome of the act of creation. It was demeaning to an omnipotent and sovereign God to argue that the world was a machine set in motion by God at the beginning of time. Therefore they maintained that, once the world had been created, an emanation of divine power continually sustained it. Only when this power was withdrawn could the world no longer exist. In this the Puritans were the inheritors of the Augustinian belief that matter must continually depend on spirit.

In the sixteenth century, European Reformers increasingly denied the belief of the medieval church that it was possible to understand and harness this power. On the Continent there was a growth of books that attacked the belief in and use of astrology. William Fulke wrote the first English attack on the subject in 1560, entitled *Antiprognosticon*. In the New World, Increase Mather's *An Essay for the Recording of Illustrious Providences* (1684), following the European example, also denounced "magical" belief, such as the use of words or spells to ward of devils and disease, as superstitious.

Protestants such as John Calvin did allow that divine will was manifest in daily life, but they argued that the action of that will, of providence, should be attributed to God alone; it could not be manipulated by human beings. Calvin contrasted providence with the fatalism of Stoicism. God's sovereignty was paramount. It was vital though, for Puritans to avoid identifying God with creation, because that could lead to undesirable pantheistic tendencies.

Workings

Although most laymen probably did not consider the mechanics of providence, theologians spent a great deal of time discussing it. The debate centered upon the discussion of primary and secondary causes, and the question of whether God acted through nature or above it. God was certainly not the remote, transcendent God of later Jewish tradition. He was rather the angry God of the earlier parts of the Old Testament. Although the majority of people believed that miracles had ceased after the Apostolic Age, it was still expected that should God desire, the world could be subject to the physical disasters described in the Old Testament. Many of the early modern interpretations of the weather as portents of things to come were based on classical sources, such as Pliny, Seneca, Josephus, and also the biblical texts of Psalms 144:6, Matthew 24, and Revelation 8:5 and 10:4.

Disease was also seen as a providential occurrence. Lack of morality was assumed to have been the cause of venereal disease. Even plague deaths where attributed to supernatural causes as a consequence of sin. It was argued by some that such deaths occurred by the direct stroke of a ministering angel. Conversely, if one was beyond reproach and had sufficient faith in God, one was protected from the effects of the plague. In England, Henoch Clapham, a prominent preacher, argued this in *An Epistle Discoursing upon the Present Pestilence* (1603). Obviously this belief was discouraged, and he retracted the view from prison in *Henoch Clapham, his Demaundes and Answeres touching the Pestilence* (1604). He was also imprisoned in 1603 for asserting the widely held position that it was unnecessary for the clergy to visit infected houses, since every man was allotted a certain life span, and once it was over, there was nothing more one could do (Psalms 91:3).

Benefits

The conciliatory value of the belief in providence was tremendous. It offered security from the randomness of life. No event could occur without a reason. Although the doctrine of providence makes free will seem illusory, it was also taught that, as rational beings, human beings could make their own choices, which themselves brought about preordained consequences. The Puritan was comforted by the thought that God had willed every event, although why was not always clear. A believer was surely protected from adversity, and if misfortune did occur it could easily be interpreted as the will of God taking the form of a test, or as punishment. It is true, then, that the doctrine of providence was a self-confirming one. Indeed suffering was seen as evidence of God's continuing interest in one, and temporal afflictions were often seen as signs of God's affection. Nicholas Bernard's *The Life and Death of . . . Dr James Usher* (1656) shows that at fifteen, the future archbishop thought that God did not love him because he had not been troubled enough.

The Elect

One problem of the doctrine of providence was the discrepancy between the God of everyday events, and the God of supernatural grace, dispensed according to his will, and resulting in regeneration for the elect. In the former, God is diffused through the world in order to govern and sustain it. In the latter, he is infused into the heart of man. God created everything, therefore his spirit is present in sinners as well as the godly. This means that the presence of God in the latter requires a re-creation, a re-formation, which is carried out by grace. After this regeneration, the elect are brought under the government and protection of providence. Puritanism relied on this special contact between God and his elect.

National Identity

Rather than being a preserve of the Puritans, belief in providence was current in every area of English society, and indeed was so to such an extent that it helped form the myth of nationhood. The idea that the English were an elect nation, based on the model of Israel, brought with it the idea that it was also governed by its own guardian angel, and indeed the most important angel of all, Michael (Daniel 10:13). Perhaps evidence of this view can be found in the belief that when natural disasters occurred, such as a failed harvest, it was thought to be because of the collective sins of the English people.

In the New World, this connection between collective and communal responsibility and providence is also evident. When Increase Mather studied the history of the world, he looked at the military success of the Greeks and Romans and attributed it to divine providence: to the assistance of the angels. It was natural for Puritans to read the past in this way. History was a chronicle of God's providence. It was like a play, directed by an omnipotent and omniscient God.

It was the belief of the colonists that all that had happened in history elsewhere in the world was a prologue to the establishment of their communities in the New World. Indeed, the diaries of John Winthrop show how strong the belief was that divine providence played an important and essential part in this establishment. In March 1648 he described the sinking of the ship sailed by a late governor of the Dutch colonies, William Kieft, when he left for Holland in 1647. This sinking was a just reward for a man who, during his time in office, had harangued the English colonies of Hartford and New Haven. Winthrop kept his journal in order to record the providential occurrences that reflected the colonials' status as elect, and not out of private curiosity. The general argument was that if individuals put self-interest ahead of the good of the whole community, terrible things would occur to them. Portents therefore reaffirmed the moral order.

The colonists believed that they were not leaving England in order to establish a new country, but rather in order to save the old. The occurrence of the Civil Wars in England was interpreted as evidence that they had succeeded, and from their vantage point across the Atlantic, the New World Colonists prayed both individually and corporately for the support of either side: most New Englanders for Parliament, and most Virginians for the monarchy. At the same time, the Puritans did not think only of England. The ideal of internationalism was strong, envisioning a Protestant elect throughout the world. This internationalism is exemplified by the desire of the colonists to spread their brand of Puritanism throughout the New World, for example, by founding another colony, in the middle of the Catholic Caribbean, called Providence Island. The name itself is suggestive. The New World could be said to have had a providential role in the developments of Puritanism.

Decline

The 1690s in America saw the beginning of a tendency to move away from the doctrine of providence, an intellectual movement that included figures such as Increase Mather, John Hall, Samuel Willard, and Thomas Battle. This tendency continued a move already begun in England in the mid-1600s, and it continued into the eighteenth century. While early writers in England, such as Thomas Beard and Samuel Clarke, were interested in interruptions to world order, later theories of providence emphasized its regularity. There was also a separation between the beliefs of the educated and the "superstition" of the uneducated, with the educated coming to reject the common lore of the wonders of providence.

See also: Antipopery, God, Grace, Gunpowder Plot, Predestination

Further Reading

Richard S. Dunn and Laetitia Yeandle, eds., *The Journal of John Winthrop, 1630–1649* (Boston, 1996); David D. Hall, *Worlds of Wonder, Days of Judgment* (New York, 1990); S. K. Heninger Jr., *A Handbook of Renaissance Meteorology* (Durham, NC, 1960); Perry Miller, *The New England Mind: The Seventeenth Century* (Cambridge, MA, 1939); Alexandra Walsham, *Providence in Early Modern England* (Oxford, 1999).

Kate Harvey

Psalms

The singing and reading of psalms formed a central part of Puritan devotion, and in a sense, the history of the metrical psalm in Scotland and New England as well as England revolves around the "Old Version" of the metrical psalms, that of Thomas Sternhold, completed by John Hopkins and others. Compiled over several years, the definitive version was first published in London in 1562, and subsequently appeared in perhaps some 470 editions. Of the 156 Sternhold-Hopkins texts, 131 were in the easily memorable common meter—the "fourteener"—and it provided a basic compendium of forty-eight tunes to match them. The Scottish Psalters of 1564 and 1650 drew on this publication, as did the 1640 Bay Psalm Book used in New England. These simple unison tunes, mostly without accompaniment, were used extremely widely, although not universally, in both parish churches and cathedrals, usually before the sermon, and before Morning Prayer, and before and after Evening Prayer. This use was sanctioned (or at least assumed to have been so) by the Elizabethan Injunctions of 1559, and by the binding of the psalms with many later editions of the Book of Common Prayer. Its popularity is indicated by the fact that the advent of Nahum Tate and Nicholas Brady's "New Version" in 1696 failed to displace the Sternhold and Hopkins version from many parishes in England, as had numerous other attempts to versify some or all of the psalms.

It would be a mistake, therefore, to suggest that these metrical psalms were used only in churches under Puritan influence. What was, however, dis-

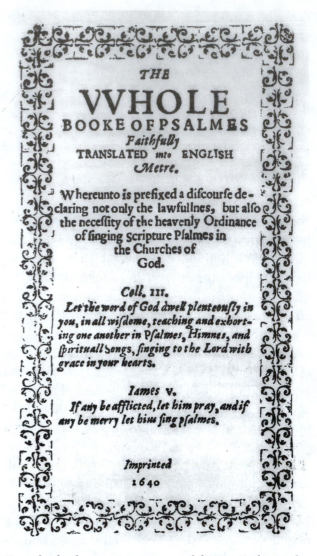

One of only eleven existing copies of the Bay Psalm Book, the first book to be published in America, 1640. (MPI/Getty Images)

tinctive about Puritan use of these godly songs was their particular place in the covenant relationship between God and the godly. There was a sense that the Book of Psalms was distinct from other parts of scripture in that it consisted of words addressed *to* God, and therefore that singing them was a peculiarly appropriate way to worship him. A key to this is the treatise appended to the front of the 1606 edition of Sternhold-Hopkins. The Psalms were to sinful man a storehouse of God's own words, able to teach the proper way to worship. Therefore the pilgrim, if he felt that "evill men lay snares for" him, should sing the fifth psalm, or, if he "wilt sing of obedience praysing God Alleluia," any of a list of sixteen would suffice. These godly songs were the "battle hymns" with which the godly fortified themselves for the spiritual struggle.

The Psalms also played a central role in Puritan private and family devotion. The twin motivations, both proposed by Calvin, that a family should both worship and learn from the scriptures together, coupled with the particular aptness of the Psalms for expressing the lives of the godly, meant that they were to be used to the exclusion of other ungodly or ribald songs. Thus the godly home was in a sense a temple, in which the spiritual sacrifices of prayer and praise were daily offered up to God.

See also: Bay Psalm Book, Music
Further Reading
Ian Green, *Print and Protestantism in Early Modern England* (Oxford, 2000); Stanley Sadie, ed., *The New Grove Dictionary of Music and Musicians* (London, 1987).

Peter Webster

Puritan Best-Sellers

Books and pamphlets written and read by puritans that were published in multiple editions or versions due to their popularity. The centrality of reading for puritans, especially in matters of conversion and godly living, created a strong market for affordable books that explained doctrine and gave spiritual encouragement and advice. Puritans believed that reading not only complemented the hearing of sermons, prayer, and worship, but was a central way in which the "call" to election could be heard: literacy and reading were central duties of faith. Continual reading of religious works brought knowledge of one's spiritual state, assurance of faith, and comfort in times of tribulation. The scholar David Hall noted that many puritans read "godly living" texts like Lewis Bayly's *Practise of Piety* "100 and 100 times" over the course of their lifetimes. Puritan best-sellers provided both individuals and families with a blueprint for godly living and confirmed them in faith and community.

Many genres of printed texts, such as political treatises, plays and poetry, polemical works, and more "entertaining" texts like ballads and pamphlets were best-selling works in early modern England and New England. However, the term *puritan best-seller* denotes religious handbooks and manuals that were read over and over throughout the course of a puritan's lifetime and passed on to children, such as handbooks for prayer and the examination of conscience, explications of the scriptures and doctrine, or printed sermons. Devotional reading was part of a puritan family's daily routine; reading of psalms or sections of best-selling handbooks was central to familial worship. The reading of best-sellers often occurred in a cyclical pattern over the course of days, weeks, and months, as specific sections were read aloud or privately each day, just as in the cyclical reading of psalms or other scriptures. Nehemiah Wallington, a seventeenth-century puritan artisan, read to his family from the Book of Psalms or the best-selling prayer book *A Garden of Spiritual Flowers* every morning at six o'clock. For puritans, the act of reading brought the word of God to life and the spirit into one's household and daily activities. Puritan minister Richard Baxter noted that books were "domestick, present, constant, judicious, pertinent, yea, and powerfull." Reading was a necessary complement to the hearing of sermons and public worship.

In order to fulfill puritans' need for religious education, devotional guidance, and spiritual uplifting through reading, puritan best-sellers generally contained "helps" to guide people along the path to salvation. Puritan best-sellers contained explication of scriptural texts, such as the discourse on the Lord's Prayer in Henry Scudder's *A Key of Heaven: the Lord's Prayer Opened* (1620), and gave advice on resolving cases of conscience, as in William Perkins's *The Whole Treatise of the Cases of Conscience* (1606). Many of these texts sold thousands of copies in both Old and New England over the sixteenth and seventeenth centuries, demonstrating the importance of the printed word as well as the vitality of the transatlantic book trade in the seventeenth century. Books that were best-sellers among puritans also sold many copies among non-puritans and even radical groups. Some extremely popular texts, such as Arthur Dent's godly living handbook, *A Plaine Man's Pathway to Heaven* (more than seventy editions between 1601 and 1800), or John Bunyan's allegorical call to repentance, *Pilgrim's Progress* (twenty-two editions of the first part between 1678 and 1727), crossed boundaries between nonconformist, conformist, and "Separatist," and later, Anglican and Dissenter.

Puritan best-sellers generally fell into the following genres: (1) treatises on repentance and faith; (2) catechisms explaining the tenets of doctrine; (3) manuals on how to prepare for communion, order one's household, resolve cases of conscience, and pray properly; (4) warnings of God's wrath for national sins, including millennial expectations; (5) treatises on moral issues such as drinking or keeping the Sabbath; (6) printed sermons; and, of course, (7) Bibles or sections of the Bible, especially the Psalms. Some works contained elements of all of these genres, such as Lewis Bayly's best-selling handbook, *The Practise of Piety* (1612), which included dialogues between characters that illustrated morality and the tenets of religion, selections from the Psalms, and examples of morning prayers. Other texts brought together the works of famous ministers, such as Richard Greenham's collected works, which contained a guide to resolving cases of conscience, selected sermons, treatises on specific topics, and a catechism. Greenham's *Works* went through four editions by the end of the sixteenth century. Sermons were particularly popular, as they allowed people to read the words of famous preachers that they could not hear in person and review and study the meaning of sermons during their daily devotions. In New England, treatises on and reports of conversion experiences, such as Thomas Shepard's *Sincere Convert* (1636), were also popular, in addition to the transatlantic best-sellers named above. The existence of so many best-sellers, and the diversity of their genres, highlights the importance of books and reading for the religion and culture of puritanism.

See also: Ballads, Broadsides, Family Piety

Further Reading

Ian Green, *Print and Protestantism in Early Modern England* (Oxford, 2000); David D. Hall, *Worlds of Wonder, Days of Judgment: Popular Religious Belief in Early New England* (New York, 1989); Margaret Spufford, *Small Books and Pleasant Histories: Popular Fiction and Its Readership in Seventeenth-Century England* (London, 1981); Alexandra Walsham, *Providence in Early Modern England* (Oxford, 1999).

Stephanie Sleeper

Puritan Childrearing

Many a puritan blessed God for having been raised in a godly household. And all puritans, whether they had benefited from such an upbringing or not, believed that it was the duty of parents to raise their children to godliness.

Puritans rejected the idea that children were innocent. All who entered the world carried with them the taint of original sin. The earliest care of children fell to their mothers. In these first years, nurturing involved trying to discipline the child away from the selfish impulses that puritans associated with sin and to help the child develop self-mastery. This effort also included portraying God as someone worthy of all love. It was important for parents to set a good example for their children.

As the child grew older, considerable emphasis was placed on education, and many children began to learn to read as early as three years old. Being able to read was vital if the youth was to be able to eventually read the scriptures. But as they grew they would be exposed to other literature. Some puritans remembered early exposure to the tales of Christian martyrdom contained in John Foxe's *Acts and Monuments*, popularly known as the Book of Martyrs. The tales of young Christians of exemplary faith and character became more popular as the seventeenth century went on.

Household devotions were also an important part of nurturing the faith of all family members, children included. Morning and evening prayer, scripture reading, and psalm singing might be found as regular, even daily, occasions in many households. Many heads of household undertook catechetical instruction of youth and servants as part of their responsibilities.

In England these types of activities were left to the decision of parents. Clergy might preach and write about the responsibilities of household government, but the responsibility was on the actual fathers and mothers. In New England, colony governments required parents to educate their children. In 1642 the Massachusetts General Court required the selectmen of every town to check that parents and masters fulfilled their responsibility to teach their children and servants "to read and understand the principles of religion and the capital laws of this country." Connecticut passed similar legislation in 1650, New Haven in 1655, and Plymouth in 1671. Though most children were taught to read and write in the home, the General Court of Massachusetts in 1647 passed another law that addressed the situation of households where this might not be easily accomplished. Citing concerns that "that old deluder Satan" sought "to keep men from the knowledge of the Scriptures," the Court required that every town of fifty or more households appoint a schoolteacher to teach those who resorted to him how to read and write, and that all towns of a hundred or more families provide a grammar school where area youth could be prepared for university.

See also: Domestic Relations, Family Piety, Puritan Best-Sellers

Further Reading

Judith Graham, *Puritan Family Life: The Diary of Samuel Sewall* (Boston, 2000); Philip Greven, *The Protestant Temperament: Patterns of Child-Rearing, Religious Experience, and the Self in Early America* (New York,1977); Alan Macfarlane, *The Family Life of Ralph Josselin* (Cambridge, Eng., 1970); Edmund S. Morgan, *The Puritan Family: Religion and Domestic Relations in Seventeenth-Century New England* (Boston, 1944); C. John Sommerville, *The Discovery of Childhood in Puritan England* (Athens, GA, 1992).

Francis J. Bremer

Puritan Historians

From the beginning of their experiences in America, the Puritans recognized something new and special in themselves and their undertaking. Their endeavors, they believed, deserved recording; they would not leave it to others to judge or define them. Self-definition was an imperative task to the Puritans. Their faith demanded it, as they sought to learn if they were saved or not. Their roles as immigrants, founders, and self-appointed new Israelites also made it mandatory. As toilers in a new wilderness, they needed to assign some meaning to themselves and their endeavors. One of the most significant ways in which the Puritans sought to define themselves was by writing histories.

The Uses of History

Ostensibly, from their theocentric perspective, the Puritans believed that the best histories were providential, that is, they explained the entire course of the world as dictated by God, not determined by individuals. The purpose of writing history was to show the progress of piety. The Bible remained their primary text and the best explanation for the beginning and end of sacred time, and though histories could not equal the sacred texts, they picked up where those stories left off. The Puritans' task was especially important: considering themselves as the new Israelites, the New England settlers wrote histories to continue and indeed place themselves in holy time. In spite of their best intentions, the Puritans did not succeed in writing strictly providential histories. Though they had initially set out to show the hand of God working in New England, to locate themselves along the spectrum of holy time, and to ascertain where they stood in relation to the millennium, the Puritans transformed providential history to enable their chronicles to serve and define them. From the start, their historical writings reflected their sense of both their secular and sacred pursuits. Although they acknowledged the Divine Hand in their work, humans took center stage.

Christian and English Historical Precedents

The Puritans looked back on a long tradition of Christian history writing. Two early historians, Eusebius and St. Augustine, had influenced historical sensibilities for centuries. Eusebius, the fourth-century bishop of Caesarea, believed that ever since the apostles had established the pure church, the course of history had witnessed the struggle of God's elect to protect the church from enemies and traitors within. The history of the church was the history of the faithful risking persecution and martyrdom, always anticipating the glorious Final Judgment. Writing only fifty years later, St. Augustine approached history differently, in part because the sacking of Rome had taken place in the interim. Augustine created the idea of a City of Man and a City of God. Whereas the City of Man was one of nature and reprobation, the City of God was one of grace and election. Humans should strive to create a City of God, and history writing must reflect their efforts. Writing in the sixth century in Britain, Gildas equated the British with the new Israelites, stressing that the nation's past might be understood as part of the history of salvation and God's providence.

With the Reformation and the persecutions of Protestants under the Catholic Queen Mary, history writing assumed a new urgency. Nationalism and salvation became inexorably and necessarily linked. In contrast to earlier historians who chronicled the persecutions of all Christians, English Protestants brought light to the sufferings of their own compatriots. John Bale located the origins and sacrifices necessitated by the Reformation in Britain. Of all nations "beyond the immediate empire of Christ," England had found the true faith first. Polydore Vergil affirmed, "The kingdom of England was the kingdom of God." John Aylmer declared unequivocally, "God is English."

New England Puritan Uses of History

More than any other history, John Foxe's *Acts and Monuments* (popularly known as the Book of Martyrs) dominated Reformation historiography in both Old and New England. The Puritans brought his text, second only in significance to the Bible, to America. Foxe told the Puritans that the English Protestants were the New Israelites. In terms comprehensible and significant to his eager readers, he showed them that Providence could and did favor a nation. Once in America, the Puritans changed Foxe's terms to accommodate their own concep-

tions. They disagreed that God privileged England in its seventeenth-century state, one that was controlled by a corrupt ecclesiastical and civil bureaucracy. Desiring to believe that God favored them exclusively, the New England Puritans borrowed heavily from the idea that a people—they—could be elected. Under this premise, they entered the wilderness with the idea that their story deserved recording. For all that they gained from earlier historical writings, the Puritans ultimately found that their predecessors' works could not provide an appropriate model. Although the Puritans had not forgotten their English past, their histories addressed concerns unique to their own experiences.

Seventeenth-century New England Puritans wrote histories not so much as a forum to glorify God but as a means of explaining their decisions, justifying their actions, and ultimately trying to understand what they had done and who, in the process, they had become. Rather than each of the three generations writing a monolithic story, the histories reflect the concerns and sensibilities of the times in which their authors wrote. The first generation, whose members include Governor William Bradford of Plymouth, Governor John Winthrop of the Massachusetts Bay Colony, and Edward Johnson, strove to establish the terms in which the founding of New England would be memorialized. The second generation, the children of the founders, were constantly being reminded that they lacked the same commitment as their parents, and thus historians William Hubbard and Nathaniel Morton sought to write themselves into history and to prove that they were continuing the worthy endeavors of the founders. The third generation belonged to Cotton Mather. In his monumental *Magnalia Christi Americana,* he marshaled abundant evidence—saintly lives and godly institutions, supported by divine providences—to prove the Puritans' success in creating a New Israel. Though their interpretations vary, each historian in his own way shows how the Puritans took up the important task of self-definition and myth creation. Their work continues to influence the way history is written about the Puritans and the way early New England's history continues to be sentimentalized.

First-Generation Historians

Though *Of Plymouth Plantation* reflects Governor Bradford's hopes and misgivings, above all, writing this history assured that his name and the names of his company would be remembered. Bradford began his history in 1630, ten years after the Separatist Pilgrims had arrived on the *Mayflower,* and the same year Winthrop's Puritans landed in Massachusetts. Though Bradford had been planning to chronicle his experiences, the decision to start writing in 1630 was more than a coincidence. The planting of Massachusetts was proof that the Errand was succeeding and that a history of Plymouth was warranted.

The governor's optimism was cautious, however. He portrayed the Separatists as a godly, honest flock seeking a peaceful place to live and worship. As newcomers to the wilderness, they worked hard to create a New Israel. Memories of the voyage and the initially difficult years, including internal conflicts, economic problems, and starvation, pervade Bradford's account. Bradford became consumed with defending the Pilgrims' actions and decisions and musing on the colony's progress, temporal as well as spiritual. As the years went on, the problems multiplied. Foremost among them were success and acculturation: the settlers and their children were losing sight of the sect's initial goals and were leaving the confines of Plymouth and its church as they became overpopulated. Such reflection led the governor to conclude that the Pilgrims were their own worst enemies. Of Plymouth Bradford wrote, "Thus, she that had made many rich became herself poor."

To a great extent a lament over the colony's trials, *Of Plymouth Plantation* shows its author developing an allegiance to America, or perhaps rather an identity as an American Puritan; the history quickly became a history of Plymouth rather than a chapter in a bigger Christian history. When the story became too sad to continue, Bradford stopped writing, leaving the pages he had labeled 1647 and 1648 blank, except for a list of *Mayflower* passengers. Still, in the end, the history that Bradford created suggests that he still believed in the Pilgrims' virtue and election and that their experiences and names (hence the list of passengers) were worthy of remembrance.

If, initially, John Winthrop aimed to place the Puritans into holy time and write the official record of the Massachusetts Bay Colony, the governor ultimately wrote his *Journal* to codify the terms in which the colony's founding and early years should be remembered. Winthrop is best remembered for his classic lay sermon, "Model of Christian Charity," in which he exhorted the Puritans aboard the *Arbella* to create a "City upon a Hill." His *Journal,* written at irregular intervals as he had the time and inclination, and covering the years between 1630 and 1649, recorded the course of the colony's history as he saw it. Though Winthrop wished to present the Puritans in terms that would prove their favor in God's eyes, he, like Bradford, used his journal to justify his own actions and decisions, which often put him at odds with other members of the community.

More than a personal means of defense, the *Journal* illustrates the transformation of Winthrop—and those who identified with his vision of the colony—from one searching for an English Christian outpost to one who had found an American home. Winthrop never lost his hope that Massachusetts would become a "City upon a Hill." He soon found himself developing a growing attachment to the colony as more than a temporary home. The change reflected in the *Journal* was subtle and perhaps unconscious on Winthrop's part. He described the everyday physical, social, and political events as well as the special providences he believed were sent by God. In such descriptions Winthrop showed his new identity, that of American Puritan, celebrating the Puritans' accomplishments and memorializing them in mythic terms. If Winthrop's *Journal* lacks the same coherent themes as *Of Plymouth Plantation* (the Bay Colony governor died before having time to revise his history into a single story), it does create the themes by which Winthrop wanted the colony's founding to be remembered. Later memorialists have adopted Winthrop's ideas, including the Puritans' divinely chosen status and their transformation of the land into hallowed ground.

Edward Johnson (1598–1672), one of the staunchest defenders of Massachusetts, defined his vision in *The Wonder-Working Providence of Sion's Savior in New England*. This work, in contrast to those written by William Bradford and John Winthrop, was not intended as an official record of a colony's founding. Rather, Johnson wanted his history to be a record of the battle between the forces of good and evil in New England.

The Wonder-Working Providence combined fact and vision. The history, first published in 1654, attempted to provide a year-by-year account of the history of Massachusetts. Johnson often confused the course of events and reported them incorrectly. More important is the way in which Johnson expressed his sense that the Puritans were soldiers of Christ engaged in a real fight against Satan's forces who wished to destroy the New Jerusalem. As such, the work is better considered allegory than history. At the same time as describing New England as a millennial battlefield, *The Wonder-Working Providence* suggests that Johnson had developed a sense of pride in his new home—without Bradford's apprehensions—and that he believed that its history warranted memorialization. Johnson offers another voice that helps in comprehending the first-generation Puritan experience, one freed from the constraints that limited Governors Bradford and Winthrop.

Second-Generation Historians

The sons of the founders, New England's second generation, felt the imperative to define themselves, as had their fathers before them. Their task was all the more difficult, as they had grown up hearing of their parents' virtues and sacrifices. As adults, they were repeatedly told that theirs was an era of "declension" and that they alone would bring about the doom of the Covenant. Nonetheless, they did write their own histories, celebrating the founders and chronicling their own achievements. All the while, they risked disobeying their fathers by disagreeing with them. The question confronting the second generation was not whether to write history but how to write it. Some members of the second generation were content to look back and celebrate their forebears, in terms the founders had used. Others recognized and acknowledged the founders' virtue but wished to move forward and write in their own terms.

As a result of such conflicting ideals, second-generation histories were neither as numerous nor as original and passionate as those of the founders had been. Besides a few narratives of Indian wars, only two general histories were written by the children of the founders: William Hubbard's *General History of New England* (1680) and Nathaniel Morton's *New England's Memorial* (1669). These works relied heavily on earlier works. Hubbard "borrowed" in large part from Winthrop and Morton from his uncle Bradford and other histories of Plymouth. Although such "borrowing" was a well-accepted practice, it suggests that neither historian was quite sure of how to express himself and found it easier to repeat what others had written.

Still, we see second-generation Puritan sensibilities at work. Both historians were responding to the ways in which New England was maturing after the mid-seventeenth century, including economic, political, and religious changes. If a theological orthodoxy had ever existed, it was less powerful now, and the Puritans sought to make changes to the system to ensure that some version of religious homogeneity would continue. As doubts about New England's future emerged, second-generation historians needed to set the record straight.

Morton, while devoting most of his history to the period from the founding to 1647 (the years Bradford covered), offered his own interpretation. In part, this was for political reasons; at the time Morton wrote, Plymouth was trying to obtain a new charter for the colony. Even more, he sought to redefine the myth of Plymouth. He chose not to recall the bitterness as his uncle had, which suggests that Morton was more at home in America and regarded earlier struggles as best relegated to the past. Morton was selective in the events he presented; he omitted examples that presented Plymouth in a poor light. He was more certain of the Puritans' hegemony and right to be in New England, as his disdain for the Indians shows. "God had made way for his people," Morton wrote, "by removing the heathen, and planting them [the Puritans] in the land." At the same time, however, Morton seems less committed to and more emotionally detached from the colony than Plymouth's founder did; his vision is less grandiose than his uncle's. As a result, Morton did not find the Pilgrims guilty of abandoning their mission as his uncle had. In part, the way in which Morton constructed his history stemmed from his differing definition of the colony: in contrast to Bradford, he did not regard a single community a prerequisite for a Christian commonwealth. From the younger historian's perspective, the colony had not failed simply because his concept of its origins was not as lofty. At the same time, Morton's work departs from contemporary literary expressions, jeremiads, which lacked a sense of optimism.

In taking up the task of writing the *General History*, Hubbard intended both to redefine and continue what first-generation Bay Colony historians had written. Hubbard's work suggests that he was hopeful that the second generation would remain among God's chosen people. Yet he did convey a sense of uncertainty over what to write and how to portray the founders and their children. The posture he assumed lacked the passion and commitment of his Puritan predecessors, suggesting that he was uncertain of the ultimate meaning of the Errand. As one integrally involved in the affairs of midcentury Massachusetts—he was a member of Harvard's first graduating class and a minister in Ipswich, and he had been paid by the General Court to write a history—Hubbard could authoritatively speak about the 1660s and 1670s. Still, the founding attracted Hubbard's attention; he devoted nearly three-quarters of his work to the period from the founding to 1650. Hubbard believed that the New England past was the proper concern of history; moreover, compared to his own problematic times, the colony's early years seemed, if not idyllic, then more illustrative of the Puritans' capacity to be architects of the New Israel.

Hubbard was not content to replicate the founders' view of history; subtly he reinterpreted often-treated subject matter. He did not present events with the same sense of urgency. At times, his tone suggests that he was an aloof bystander or observer. He sketched New England's geography and listed its commodities as an anthropologist might. Hubbard continued by describing the founding with detached reverence. The founders deserved praise for their sacrifices, piety, and accomplishments, but he would not raise the exaltation of these people to a level of worship. Providence did play a role in the colony's events, but it did not provide a wholly suitable explanation of history. Hubbard recognized that history was cyclical. He brought a perspective unavailable to the first generation and saw that the colony had survived (and even succeeded). Praising the founders without apotheosizing them, Hubbard had difficulty castigating his own generation. Hence, Hubbard, like Morton, wrote his own era into history. The second generation still needed to write history, finding meaning in the endeavor. The use of history—to memorialize themselves—remained constant. The myth continued, but gone were the terms their fathers had imported.

Third-Generation Puritan History: The *Magnalia Christi Americana*

When Mather began to write his masterful history in the 1690s, the status of New England was much in doubt. Mather sought to demonstrate that despite appearances, New England had not been defeated and was worthy of a grand history illustrating its glory. Indeed, at over one thousand pages, the *Magnalia Christi Americana* (1702) gave Mather the opportunity not only to write a history of New England but also to express his family's version of history. It constitutes a grand history of the New Israel, one that could only have been written after several decades of ebbs and flows in News England. Although Mather discussed many of the same themes as his first- and second-generation predecessors did, the *Magnalia* differs from other histories both quantitatively and qualitatively. More than any other Puritan historian, he demonstrated his extraordinary, unparalleled passion for New England. At the heart of Mather's story was New England itself, rather than a colony with a connection, however tentative, to England.

The *Magnalia* expressed a sense of New England's role, potential, uniqueness, and wonder unlike any other Puritan writing. In part, Mather wrote because his prominent family was often on the wrong side of popular issues, and Cotton thought it necessary to explain their controversial positions. Even more, as the supreme defender of the Errand, he wrote to defend it and to show that the experiment was succeeding. As evidence of this success, Mather included myriad details. He recounted the lives of clergy and rulers, the history of Harvard, and stories of remarkable providences. With its innumerable accounts of ordinary and extraordinary events as well as famous and infamous individuals, it is the most comprehensive, original, and visionary seventeenth-century American Puritan history. Together, all of this evidence supports Mather's idea that New England had already become worthy of merit in the eyes of God and that it still held great potential to become a New Israel.

At the same time, Mather could not be completely certain that America would become the elect nation he hoped for. Writing at the end of the seventeenth century when the Massachusetts charter had been annulled, and Puritans were enduring the tyrannies of Dominion Governor Edmund Andros, Mather and many of his colleagues were experiencing a crisis of confidence. Moreover, he was especially concerned that his generation and their children were less pious than their forebears and lacked respect for the clergy. Mather showed how God responded to this declension: the colonists were punished harshly with various misfortunes. Despite such misgivings, Mather desired to write his own generation into history and indicated that they might reform themselves and revive their dying piety. Given this message, scholars have seen the *Magnalia*, unlike the work of Morton and Hubbard, as having some of the characteristics of a jeremiad. Ultimately, Mather concluded his work unsure whether he should be optimistic or pessimistic about the Puritans' prospects in America, and he thus had much in common with first-generation New England historians. Though he identified himself more as a New England Puritan than the historians who preceded him, he did not end the

Magnalia on the confident note on which he had begun it. As original and as grand as the *Magnalia* may seem, it shows how deeply Mather had imbibed the founders' myths as well as their trepidations about New England's future. Yet it is a grand work, set apart by Mather's imagination and the eighty years of history behind him, as well as by a motivating passion unseen in any other Puritan.

Legacies of the Puritan Histories

With the end of the Puritan era, history writing also shifted. The founders and the two succeeding generations canonized the particular traits by which they wished to be remembered: the virtue, religiosity, and sacrifices, for example. In the eighteenth century, histories concentrated more on chronicling worldly events, especially after the American Revolution, when it became imperative to mythicize the United States. Historians still found Puritan myths compelling and returned to the themes the founders had created. Subsequent chroniclers imbibed the sense of the Puritans that the early New Englanders themselves had originated. No longer compelled to write history as defensively as the Puritans had, and without the same sense of urgency that often informed seventeenth-century work, they gave new life to the idea of Puritan sanctity and sacrifice well beyond the founders' era. Mercy Otis Warren's *History of the Rise, Progress, and Termination of the American Revolution* (1805) and Abiel Holmes's *American Annals* (1805) both looked to New England for early examples of virtue and democracy.

The influence of the Puritans and the values they proffered in their histories reverberated into the nineteenth century with greater resonance than ever before. Writers were fascinated by the Puritans, especially Ralph Waldo Emerson, Henry Wadsworth Longfellow, and James Russell Lowell. No one was more troubled by the Puritan legacy than Nathaniel Hawthorne, and no one placed them more at the center of his literary output. Late nineteenth-century historians continued to employ the terms in which the Puritans defined themselves. John Gorham Palfrey in his five-volume *History of New England* (1858–1890) borrowed themes from the early historians and even sounded like the founders, at the same time that he criticized their intolerance. The Puritans would have recognized much in George Bancroft's ten-volume *History of the United States* (1834–75). Bancroft believed that history must be written (as Mather believed) on a grand scale. He, too, found that America had been favored by Providence.

Rejecting the intolerance of the Puritans, Bancroft nonetheless exalted them in familiar terms: "Puritanism was a life-giving spirit. . . . As for courage, a coward and a Puritan never went together."

In the late nineteenth century, the Puritans' reputation suffered. In both popular culture and scholarly circles, the values they privileged fell into disfavor. As history became professionalized, however, the Puritans, though carefully scrutinized, also offered a usable past. Twentieth-century historians took seriously the terms of the Puritan myth. Samuel Eliot Morison, a scion of the founders, wrote: "My attitude toward seventeenth century Puritanism has passed through scorn . . . to a warm interest and respect. The ways of the puritans are not my ways . . . nevertheless they appear to me a courageous, humane, brave, and significant people." The literary historian Perry Miller, more than any other scholar (except, perhaps, Cotton Mather) has helped to continue the myth that the Puritans themselves originated. As the Puritan historians had hoped, and helped to ensure, we do recall the myths they created, in the terms by which they defined themselves. Bradford's fears were unfounded; the Puritans, along with their names, have not been buried.

See also: William Bradford, Book of Martyrs, *Magnalia Christi Americana*, Massachusetts Bay Colony, "Model of Christian Charity," Plymouth Colony, Providence

Further Reading

Stephen Carl Arch, *Authorizing the Past: The Rhetoric of History in Seventeenth-Century New England* (De Kalb, 1994); Sacvan Bercovitch, *The American Jeremiad* (Madison, 1978); Sacvan Bercovitch, *The Puritan Origins of the American Self* (New Haven, 1975); Andrew Delbanco, *The Puritan Ordeal* (Cambridge, MA, 1989); Richard Dunn, "John Winthrop Writes His Journal," *William and Mary Quarterly* 41, 185–212; Katharine R. Firth, *The Apocalyptic Tradition in Reformation Britain, 1530–1645* (New York, 1979); Frank Smith Fussner, *The Historical Revolution: English Historical Writing and Thought, 1580–1640* (Westport, CT, 1962); Peter Gay, *A Loss of Mastery: Puritan Historians in Colonial America* (Berkeley, 1966); David Levin, *Cotton Mather: The Young Life of the Lord's Remembrancer, 1663–1703* (Cambridge, MA, 1978); James G. Moseley, *John Winthrop's World: History as a Story, the Story as History* (1992); Kenneth Silverman, *The Life and Times of Cotton Mather* (New York, 1984); Avihu Zakai, *Exile and Kingdom: History and Apocalypse in the Puritan Migration to America* (Cambridge, Eng., 1992).

Rachelle E. Friedman

Puritan Prayer Books

Popular printed texts that served as manuals or guides for family and individual prayer, often containing explication of the proper times for praying; the steps, types, proper disposition, and goals of prayer; and samples of prayers to be said on different occasions. The reading of devotional prayer books either in a family setting or in private provided puritans with the means to fulfill the duty of daily prayer and to achieve its primary goals—to atone for sin, speak with the voice of the spirit, and receive grace.

Prayer, whether in public worship, with one's household, or in the privacy of the "closet" (as small rooms meant for privacy were called), was one of the primary religious duties for puritans. Prayer was not only the way in which puritans could petition God for help or give thanks for success or good health, but the primary means of moving the heart toward feelings of repentance, forgiveness, and reconciliation with God. Hearing sermons and attending weekly worship could begin the process of conversion, but daily prayer cemented it by turning the heart toward repentance and awareness of sin. Authors of puritan prayer books such as Henry Scudder, whose manual *The Christians Daily Walke* was published in more than eleven editions from 1627 to 1690, stressed the importance of daily prayer for families and the need for householders to provide religious instruction to their spouses, children, and servants. Daily readings from the Bible and devotional books, followed by family prayer, aided in the religious instruction of families and formed the basis of family piety.

The very act of reading the Bible, prayer books, and other devotional manuals was central to puritan religion because it opened the heart to receive grace. Reading was also central to private, or solitary, prayer undertaken in one's closet. Puritan prayer books described private prayer as a solemn duty requiring preparation and extreme care—after all, prayers were spoken directly to God and had to be appropriately approached and phrased. The primary goal of private prayer was to re-create the conversion experience: to bring feelings of awareness of sin, repentance, acceptance by God, and finally the joy of salvation. In prayer, puritans asked for forgiveness, petitioned God to help them, their neighbors, or their country, and gave thanks for God's blessings.

Puritan prayer books aided puritans' daily prayers by providing topical scriptural passages to read in preparation for prayer and themes for meditation that put the puritan in the right frame of mind to approach God. These two steps—reading and meditation—were essential preparations for "continual" prayer, or a sustained session of prayer that should be undertaken daily in a private place. First, reading the scriptures, or God's own words, gave a puritan the right forms of language to address God. Meditation led to the examination of conscience and brought awareness of a puritan's true self—the sincerity necessary for prayer. These two steps would ensure that prayer took place with the right disposition. According to Scudder, preparation led puritans to pray "in the Spirit of adoption" and made sure that they held God "in their mind" as they prayed, made only lawful requests, were sincere, and kept their attention toward God, not worldly business. Puritan prayer books provided both the knowledge of specific steps of preparation and the texts to read and meditate upon.

Because the proper structure and content of prayers were so essential, many puritan clergy noted that people were unsure of and anxious about how they should speak to God. Therefore, puritan prayer books often provided some examples of prayers that could be said on different occasions. Morning prayers, like those found in Lewis Bayly's best-selling manual, *The Practise of Piety* (first published 1612), stressed repentance, asked for forgiveness, and gave thanks for passing through the night unharmed. Puritan authors meant these examples of prayers to be introductory guides or templates for those who were new to prayer and needed additional help to choose appropriate topics or to phrase their speech properly. The ultimate, ideal form of prayer was extemporaneous and "from the heart," not static, repeated prayers that were composed for an occasion wholly separate from the immediacy of each individual puritan's prayer session. Puritans believed prayer books were useful not because they told people exactly *what* to pray by providing a "liturgy" of prayers, such as those found in the Book of Common Prayer or non-puritan books of prayers, but because they taught people *how* to pray "freely and extemporaneously" to strengthen their assurance of adoption.

See also: Book of Common Prayer, Prayer, Puritan Best-Sellers

Further Reading

David Hall, *Worlds of Wonder, Days of Judgment: Popular Religious Belief in Early New England* (New York, 1989); Charles E. Hambrick-Stowe, *The Practise of Piety: Puritan Devotional Disciplines in Seventeenth-Century New England* (Chapel Hill, 1982); Geoffrey F. Nuttall, *The Holy Spirit in Puritan Faith and Experience*, 3rd ed. (Chicago, 1992); Paul S. Seaver, *Wallington's World: A Puritan Artisan in Seventeenth-Century London* (London, 1985).

Stephanie Sleeper

Puritan Revolution

One of many titles given to the multiple crises in the Stuart monarchies in the mid-seventeenth century—others include "the English Civil War," "the English Civil Wars," "the Great Civil War," "the Great Rebellion," "the English Revolution," "En-

Charles I at the Battle of Naseby, 14 June 1645. The Puritan Army under Fairfax and Cromwell won a decisive victory over the Royalists under Charles I and Prince Rupert. (Hulton Archive/Getty Images)

gland's Wars of Religion," "The war [or wars] of the three kingdoms." The term *Puritan Revolution* seems to have been coined by the great Victorian historian Samuel Rawson Gardiner in 1876, and he used it for his seminal collection, *Documents of the Puritan Revolution, 1625–1660,* but not for his great narrative account of the period. It was little used until adopted by American historians of Puritanism from the 1930s—headed by William Haller (*Tracts on Liberty in the Puritan Revolution* [1934], *Liberty and Reformation in the Puritan Revolution* [1955]), and Don M. Wolfe (*Milton in the Puritan Revolution* [1941], *Leveller Manifestoes of the Puritan Revolution* [1944]). It remained in vogue, mainly on the American side of the Atlantic, until the 1970s, but it is now little used. "Puritan Revolution" has its uses as a description of a process but

not of an outcome. Whatever the consequences of the turmoil, it did not see the triumph of Puritanism, but its disintegration and defeat. Indeed it could be argued that it has inoculated the English against religious enthusiasm and especially against millennial politics ever since.

The case for calling the crisis a Puritan Revolution has two main supporting points. First, in its initial phase (1640–1646), it was those who believed themselves empowered by God to complete the reformation in England, to rid the land of the dregs of popery and to answer God's call to make the English nation a model godly commonwealth, who were the driving force in a rainbow coalition of otherwise timid groups of alienated lawyers and politicians who took up arms against the king. Second, after 1646 the most important dynamic within the victorious parliamentarian cause was the nuclear fission engendered by struggles within Puritanism. These struggles took different forms—between the advocates of a strong clerical authority and of an equally strong Erastianism; between the advocates of a strict confessional settlement based on the examples of Geneva and Scotland and the advocates of the "New England Way"; between the advocates of orthodox Calvinism and advocates of a whole range of heterodox opinions on the nature of the church, the sacraments, and Christian morality. These struggles came to focus on the shape of the state church that was to replace the Elizabethan settlement and on the nature and extent of liberty of conscience for those who did not wish to be part of a national settlement.

The years 1646–1653 were years of "teeming liberty," with the emergence of a myriad Separatist movements, some defined doctrinally (the Particular and the General Baptists, the Fifth Monarchists), others by their charismatic leaders (the Ranters and the Muggletonians). From 1653 onward, the Protectorate under Oliver Cromwell sought to combine a clear and effective parish-based system based on a large measure of local self-determination and godly lay control, with a prudent measure of liberty for those who accepted the authority of scripture, the literal truth of the Apostles' Creed, and the moral code as spelled out in mainstream Protestant teaching. Anti-Trinitarians and those suspected of antinomian beliefs were harried. The major confrontation was with the Quakers, who emerged in 1652 but rapidly became a national movement. The Quakers put more emphasis on the Spirit than on the Word (that is, the actual words of the Bible), denounced a professional clergy and the worship of steeple houses, and organized tithe strikes. Noble suffering in the face of vicious persecution guaranteed increasing support.

The Puritan Revolution is most easily defined by the religious documents and tracts that it generated. The Confession of Faith, the Large and Small Catechism, and the Directory of Worship produced by the Westminster Assembly (1643–1650) were and remain influential documents for evangelical churches throughout the English-speaking world (and elsewhere, as in Korea). Hundreds of published sermons, especially those preached on the monthly Fast Days to the two Houses of Parliament remain epitomes of evangelical preaching from the Reformation era. These sermons (perhaps most notably Stephen Marshall's *Meroz Cursed* [1641] and Thomas Goodwin's *Zerubbabel's Encouragement to finish the Temple* [1642]) had a profound effect on political developments. Many of the great arguments about how the Reformation was to be re-formed, and about the nature and extent of religious liberty have remained deeply influential—such as the tracts denouncing episcopacy written in 1641 by five puritan ministers whose initials make up the acrostic SMECTYMNUUS; the violently anti-priestcraft, libertarian tracts of John Milton and of the Levellers; the passionate writings of Roger Williams (e.g., *The Bloody Tenant of Persecution* [1644]). And many ministers wrote powerful and effective autobiographies (Richard Baxter, Adam Martindale) or records of pastoral experience (Richard Baxter again, or Samuel Rutherford).

Oliver Cromwell, greatest of all the puritan generals, and from 1653 to 1658 head of state under the title of Lord Protector, epitomizes the paradoxes of the Puritan Revolution. He believed passionately that he had been called by God to overthrow tyranny in the state and in the church and to liberate God's new chosen people from bondage, just as God had called Moses to liberate his first chosen people from Egypt. Cromwell believed that all forms of government were "dross and dung in comparison with Christ" and that creating the true church would require input from "the various forms of godliness in this nation." So he believed in religious liberty for all those who were committed to creating that true church. His problem was that too many appeared to him to be abusing liberty to excuse licentiousness of life. Or they simply abused one another verbally or in print. Some Quakers for example would disrupt religious services in parish churches by shouting down the preacher. When he gave local communities the freedom to worship in ways they preferred, they opted to return to the Book of Common Prayer. So he became more and more an authoritarian liberal, insofar as commanding people how to use their liberty. But to the extent that he saw himself as using his authority as head of state to build a godly commonwealth based on Scripture and Providence, he does exemplify what has led some scholars to name England's Time of Troubles the Puritan Revolution.

See also: Oliver Cromwell, Congregationalism, Erastianism, Protectorate, Sects, Separatists, Westminster Assembly
Further Reading
Christopher Hill, *The World Turned Upside Down: Radical Ideas during the English Revolution* (London, 1972); Derek Hirst, *England in Conflict, 1603–1660: Kingdom, Community, Conflict* (London, 1999).

John Morrill

Puritans in Literature

The modern stereotype of the puritan as an austere killjoy, hypocritically pious and joyless, is a literary invention. Nathaniel Hawthorne's works are informed by the stereotype even as they further it. The same is the case for twentieth-century authors ranging from the poet William Carlos Williams to

Frontispiece of The Pilgrim's Progress, *by English writer and Puritan John Bunyan, published in 1684. (Library of Congress)*

the essayist H. L. Mencken to the playwright Arthur Miller. Real puritans, needless to say, were no enemies of joy. In the sixteenth and seventeenth centuries, in fact, the same literary stereotype existed side by side with one remarkably different: the puritan as coarse sensualist: gluttonous, greedy, and lecherous.

If we define the puritan broadly as a sincere believer who desired further reformation of the church as well as of individual morality, the sixteenth and seventeenth centuries saw a sizable body of literature depicting such characters in a positive light. Protestant drama flourished in the

sixteenth century: Reformers such as John Foxe, John Bale, and Stephen Gosson were playwrights as well as polemicists in the cause of reform. In the seventeenth century, Bunyan's *Pilgrim's Progress* and Milton's *Paradise Lost* provide just two of the more prominent examples of the widely varied body of literature involving characters who serve as models of Reformed Christian piety. But of course the word *puritan* was from the start a term of abuse. Its use in literature generally reflects that origin. The following comments will therefore focus on some of the more noteworthy moments in the history of anti-puritan Renaissance literature.

Marprelate and the Sensualist Puritan

The tone was set by a puritan: one "Martin Marprelate," the pseudonym of the anonymous author of the witty, scathing satires that have come to be called the Marprelate tracts. These lively pamphlets made a sensation in London in 1588 and 1589 with their attacks on the hierarchy of the Church of England. So outrageous were the descriptions of the corruption of well-known bishops that the bishops themselves commissioned satiric pamphleteers such as Thomas Nashe, Robert Greene, John Lyly, and Anthony Munday to reply in kind. It is in these pamphlets of the countercampaign that puritans are characterized as grotesque sensualists. In Nashe's phrase, they are "Hipocrites and belli-gods"; Nashe calls Marprelate himself "the Ape, the dronke, and the madde." The invectives hurled against puritans in general and Marprelate in particular were soon the common currency of the stage as well as the tract. Such was the sensationalist lechery and violence of the puritans depicted in plays that in 1589 the Master of the Revels closed the London theaters.

The sensualist puritan was satirized not only on the stage and in pamphlets but also in popular poetry. For example, in some lines by the early seventeenth-century poet Richard Corbett, a pair of puritans walk in the fields, discussing biblical stories "Of David, and Uriahs lovely wife, / Of Thamar, and her lustfull brothers strife; / Then, underneath the hedge that woos them next, / They may sit downe, and there act out the text." By the middle of the century, when jabs at the puritan Roundhead party had become common, one anonymous ballad put the matter less delicately: "What's he that met a holy Sister / And in an Hay-cock gently kist her, / Oh! then his zeal abounded, / Close underneath a shady willow, / Her Bible serv'd her for her pillow, / And there they got a Roundhead." Such light, bawdy verses had their counterpart in increasingly bitter anti-puritan satire, especially as the tensions between the parliamentary and royalist parties began to build. But satire that depicted puritans as too ludicrous to be taken seriously also remained popular.

Puritans in the Theater

It is on the stage that the caricature of the puritan received its lasting form. Patrick Collinson, in fact, has gone so far as to claim—and only half playfully—that the theater invented puritanism. Since a number of puritans had singled out plays as objects of moral assault, and since the acting companies were controlled by the court, it is not surprising that the playwrights and the royal patrons of the theater united in their opposition to their common enemy: the radical Reformer. The playwrights went to work with abandon. Puritans, especially Separatists, presented ready targets. Since their habits of worship deviated from the norm, and since they held themselves to high moral standards, they were susceptible to exaggerations of their peculiarities and to charges of hypocrisy.

At least sixty Renaissance plays satirize puritans directly, and a good many more do so glancingly. Some stage puritans are promiscuous libertines, some are dour moralists, and some are combinations of the two. There is no better example of the combination of grotesque sensuality and hypocritical moralizing than Ben Jonson's Zeal-of-the-Land Busy in *Bartholomew Fair*. When he is asked whether the pregnant Win-the-Fight can eat roast pork at the fair "without offense to the weaker sisters," Busy replies that Win's craving for pork is "a disease, a carnal disease, or appetite incident to women," and that while pork may lawfully be eaten, "in the Fair, and as a Bartholomew-pig, it cannot be eaten, for the very calling of it a Bartholomew-pig, and to eat it so, is a spice of idolatry." When his wealthy puritan patron Dame Purecraft, spokeswoman for "the beauteous discipline," presses the issue, Busy backtracks: "We may be religious in the face of the profane, so it be eaten with a reformed mouth." Then, his own appetite for pork whetted, he declares, "In the way of comfort to the weak I will go and eat. I will eat exceedingly and prophesy. There may be good use made of it too, now I think on't: by the public eating of swine's flesh, to profess our hate and loathing of Judaism, whereof the brethren stand taxed. I will therefore eat, yea, I will eat exceedingly." It is only after Busy has had his fill of pork and ale at the fair that he rails against the festivities: "Thou art the seat of the Beast, O Smithfield, and I will leave thee. Idolatry peepeth out on every side of thee."

Busy embodies several of the standard features of ridicule: the puritan tendency to identify objects of idolatry, to split theological hairs, to "prophesy" in heightened, pseudobiblical cadences, to mask worldly motives with pious talk. Other points of satire in the plays of the period include the length and dullness of puritan prayers and sermons, puritan preachers' high-pitched, nasal tone, offense at bells, crosses, wedding rings, and the word *Christmas*, some extremists' refusal to eat fish on Fridays since it was a Catholic custom to do so, and the pretentiousness of uneducated men and women who become preachers. In Middleton's *The Family of Love,* the character Lipsalve says of a sermon by the wife of a bellows-mender, "she swore that all gallants were persons inferior to bellows-menders, for the trade of bellows-making was very aerial and high; and what were men and women but bellows, for they take wind in at one place and do evaporate it at another." In the same play Mistress Purge says of church organs, "they edify not a whit; I detest 'em: I hope my body has no organs." Another target of satire was the tendency of the godly to give their children Old Testament names or names underscoring the oppression the faithful must overcome. A character in William Cartwright's *The Ordinary* deeply regrets that he was named Credulous, not "Tribulation, / Nor holy Ananias." In taking a stab at some puritans' anti-intellectual tendency to refuse to learn foreign languages or read anything except the Bible, especially the Old Testament, Jonson has his Ananias of *The Alchemist* say, "All's heathen, but the Hebrew."

The above examples are merely illustrative of the tone of a large body of anti-puritan satire. Though radical groups such as Anabaptists, Brownists, and the Family of Love were frequently singled out for ridicule, most playwrights exhibited little knowledge of the differences among them; satiric portraits of the Separatists are generally no different from those of other stereotypical stage puritans.

The Case of Shakespeare

Though there is little doubt about what playwrights like Jonson, Middleton, George Chapman, Thomas Dekker, John Marston, Thomas Heywood, John Webster, and Cyril Tourneur thought about puritans, Shakespeare's attitude presents special problems. Nothing is known for certain about Shakespeare's own religious beliefs, and his characters with puritan tendencies are typically complex. Malvolio of *Twelfth Night* seems to have something of the rigidly austere puritan about him, and the servant Maria at one point says that he is "something of a puritan," but then says that he really is not one at all. Moreover, a good bit of what Malvolio says and does is inconsistent with the language and actions of puritans of any sort, real or staged.

The straight-laced Angelo of *Measure for Measure* is twice called "precise" (a "precisian" was a puritan). Angelo reveals himself as a scheming hypocrite in his lust for the would-be nun Isabella, but he himself is agonized about his behavior and is hardly the transparent libertine of other anti-puritan satire.

Kristen Poole has argued convincingly that, odd as it may seem, Shakespeare's Sir John Falstaff of the *Henry IV* plays is in part a version of the grotesque puritan. Falstaff's original name was Sir John Oldcastle, a historical proto-puritan and martyr. Under pressure from Oldcastle's descendants, Shakespeare changed the name. Falstaff himself is a satirist, but he is also the butt of satire. Like the stage puritans of the Marprelate controversy, Falstaff is repeatedly shown up as a hypocrite despite his pious language. His speeches are full of rhetoric Shakespeare's audiences would have associated with puritanism: Falstaff quotes the Bible no fewer than twenty-six times, refers to himself as a "saint" and as a singer of psalms and anthems, argues that he is entitled to labor in his "vocation" (thievery), worries about his guilty conscience, and on his deathbed refers to the "Whore of Babylon": in puritan jargon, the Church of Rome. Falstaff is, to be sure, more complex than most staged representations of puritans; he is no simple stereotype. Yet one of his facets reflects a prominent sixteenth-century caricature of the puritan.

See also: Marprelate Tracts, Martin Marprelate, Puritan Best-Sellers

Further Reading

Patrick Collinson, "*Bartholomew Fair:* Theatre Invents Puritans," in D. Smith and R. Strier, eds., *The Theatrical City* (Cambridge, Eng., 1999); William P. Holden, *Anti-Puritan Satire, 1572–1642* (New Haven, 1954); Peter Lake with Michael Questier, *The Antichrist's Lewd Hat: Protestants,* *Papists and Players in Post-Reformation England* (New Haven, 2002); Aaron Michael Myers, *Representation and Misrepresentation of the Puritan in Elizabethan Drama* (Philadelphia, 1931); Kristen Poole, "Saints Alive! Falstaff, Martin Marprelate, and the Staging of Puritanism," *Shakespeare Quarterly* 46 (1995) 47–75.

Bryan Crockett

R

Ramist Logic

A dialectical method of analysis and argument developed by the French Protestant Humanist educational reformer Peter Ramus (Pierre de la Ramée, 1515–1572) and adopted by many puritans as a useful means for explaining and understanding scripture and theology. As a Humanist educational method, Ramism stressed the practical application of knowledge rather than the abstract syllogistic debates of medieval Scholasticism. As a logical method, Ramism is based on the observation of nature, human experience, and the "natural" structures of the human mind, not the formal categories of Aristotelian logic. In Ramist logic, truth is not discovered by syllogistic reasoning, but communicated through easily observable "axioms," which lead from the most general to the more particular, illustrated with concrete examples from classical authors or common experience. Thus Ramist logic aids the memory because it is "natural": the mind easily remembers knowledge that is structured by the eternal laws of nature.

Ramist logic is also visual. It is often characterized by the use of bracketed diagrams showing the division of the whole into parts according to categories called "heads," "topics," or "commonplaces." Many English Ramists included bracketed diagrams in their printed works to show the arrangement of topics within the text. In this and other respects, Ramist logic derives from the Humanist rhetorical strategies of invention (the creation of topics, ideas, and categories) and division (of the whole into categories), though Ramus criticized what he perceived as overelaborate Humanist use of rhetorical tropes and figures that concealed rather than revealed truths. Like rhetoric, however, the primary function of Ramist logic is to persuade. In its inception, Ramism was an educational strategy meant to persuade students—it fitted knowledge to students' memories and experiences.

Ramus's primary treatise, *The Logic* (1555), first appeared in English in the translations of Roland MacIlmaine (1574) and the English puritan Dudley Fenner, whose *Artes of Logicke and Rhetoricke* went through several editions from its initial publication in 1584 through the mid-seventeenth century. Fenner's adaptation of Ramus's *Logic* is significant because it explicitly used the Ramist method to explain scripture and, in *Methode in the Government of the Familie* (1590), apply the method to the puritan ideology of godly living. In *Artes of Logicke*, Fenner replaced Ramus's classical Humanist illustrations with examples from scripture and classical aphorisms with examples especially relevant to the late sixteenth-century English church and the cause of puritan reform, such as the syllogism: "Every puritane is a Christian. No Lord Bishop is a puritane. Therefore, no Lord Bishop is a Christian." The prevalence of Ramist diagrams and principles in many puritan texts during the sixteenth and seventeenth centuries in both Old and New England demonstrates the popularity of the method.

Petrus Ramus, founder of Ramist logic. (Bettman/Corbis)

These Ramist principles of the division of the whole into parts, "natural" logic as an aid to memory, and the practical application of knowledge to life, as well as, above all, the ease of learning in the Ramist method, strongly appealed to puritans who strove to educate the "common people" on the scriptures, doctrines, and their duties as Christians. Because it was so suited to the explanation and "opening" of truth, and because it was based on a "natural" system that anyone could understand, many puritans saw Ramism as the educational method par excellence for teaching the difficult doctrines of election, justification, assurance, and sanctification, and, more importantly, for moving people to apply these doctrines to their own lives.

The influence of Ramist logic among puritans is readily apparent in the preferred method for preaching, often called puritan "plain style." The influence of Ramism on puritan styles of preaching is apparent in both the theoretical goal of the sermon and the method used for organizing and expounding it. For puritans, sermons were the key means of educating and moving the audience to both right understanding and right action: "the Word preached" both instructed hearers in the fundamentals of Christianity and in how they could apply these doctrines to their own lives—what they should do to find assurance of salvation.

Puritan sermons therefore followed a specific format that moved in Ramist fashion from the general to the specific. The sermon would begin with a particular text of Scripture, move to the more particular by placing it in the context of its chapter and book of the Bible, then "open" the different words of the text and classify the different doctrines each word or phrase illustrated (with examples from other texts or from common experience), and end with the "uses" of the text, or how it might be applied to the hearer's life. This final aspect—the "use" or application of the text—was the central goal of the sermon; it gave people the means to understand how the abstract doctrines fitted into their own lives, and it moved them to repentance. In this method, both of the key Ramist principles of division and the practical application of knowledge to life are evident.

A third principle of Ramist logic—the relationship of logic to the memory—was also important to the organization and explication of puritan sermons. Puritan preachers generally organized each sermon under different heads, or topics, that would be further defined and illustrated with examples. This approach enabled the preacher to more easily remember the sermon (which was often given only from brief notes, or from memory) and allowed the audience to follow the sermon and take notes themselves in order to study it further.

See also: Plain Style, Preaching, Sermon Notes
Further Reading

William Samuel Howell, *Logic and Rhetoric in England, 1500–1700* (Princeton, 1956); Perry Miller, *The New England Mind: The Seventeenth Century* (Cambridge, MA, 1939); John Morgan, *Godly Learning: Puritan Attitudes Towards Reason, Learning, and Education, 1560–1640* (Cambridge, Eng., 1986); Walter J. Ong, *Ramus: Method and the Decay of Dialogue* (New York, 1958).

Stephanie Sleeper

Ranters

The Ranters were not an organized movement at the radical edge of the puritan movement during the late 1640s and 1650s in England, but a heresiological category with which opponents of religious enthusiasm identified numerous sectaries. These were the outrageous radicals whose antics were the result of the breakdown of church government in the 1640s and the ideological and spiritual free-for-all that followed.

Before the appearance of a loose group of mystical antinomians in the late 1640s, "ranting" described merrily rowdy and belligerent individuals; during the 1640s, the word was attached to melodramatic tub-preachers. The heresiological category, *Ranter*, however, grew out of *Rantism* and *rantizing*, which referred to the baptismal "sprinkling." Abiezer Coppe, for example, was known as "the great Anabaptist from Warwick" after the publication of his "Ranter" *Fiery Flying Roll* in 1649 (*A Perfect Diurnall*, no. 6, 14–21 January 1650, p. 42). The term *Ranter* became attached to him only after it was given polemical credibility as an offshoot of not the Baptist movement, but Gerard Winstanley's Diggers. In 1649, Winstanley defended the Diggers against accusations of "the Ranting Practise," which consisted of indolent and self-indulgent promiscuity, gluttony, and greed (Gerard Winstanley, *A Vindication of Those, Whose Endeavors [sic] is Only to Make the Earth a Common Treasury, Called Diggers*, 1650). This is the first known attack upon "Ranters."

It is unknown whether the group of Ranters attacked by Winstanley included any of the men who were later numbered among the libertines and antinomians who achieved such notoriety in the early 1650s. Though no Ranter "sect" existed, this group was certainly a category, if not a collection of individuals, some of whom were certainly known to and in correspondence with each other. In London, Laurence Clarkson spoke of a group known as My One Flesh, which was associated (as so many radicals were) with the printer of radical literature, Giles Calvert. Clarkson claimed that he became the Captain of the Rant, but this indicates that Clarkson was capable of parodying the Ranter myth for his own self-empowering purposes just as it suggests that the Ranters possessed a congregational structure of sorts. Clarkson himself claimed that the group of antinomians of which he was a part in the 1640s was not an appreciable congregation: "for Church it was none, in that it was but part form, and part none" (Laurence Clarkson, *The Lost Sheep Found*, 1660, p. 10).

Despite the Ranters' loose and amorphous organization, they shared a discernible theological position, which can be sketched with reference to several of the tracts that at the time were attacked as belonging to "Ranters." The libertarian practices of which the Ranters were accused, such as promiscuity, polygamy, blasphemy, and communitarianism, were rooted in their suggestion that sin was an artificial category, subsumed within God's being, which flowed into all things. That God's being saturated all things also meant that external forms of worship and ritual were rendered obsolete and invalid. This monism, however, was predicated upon a sublimated dualism that was expressed in discernibly emanationist accounts of God's universal immanence. This was not only a reaction against a radical conception of Calvinism and the theological basis for the dismantling of sin as a moral category, but the root of "Ranter" pantheism, which identified in all things, including the Ranters themselves, a divine presence. Such thinking encouraged hostile stories of drinking ale as the blood of Christ and eating beef as His flesh.

Such tales were propagated by scandalous pamphlets, which turned the Ranter threat into a social phenomenon rather than a theological position. Between October 1650 and August 1654, fifteen scandalous and sensationalizing anti-Ranter pamphlets were printed. These pamphlets portrayed Ranters as exhibiting a pattern of social deviance, an inverted image of morality, proper conduct, and right religion. Written by penitent ex-Ranters, professional hacks who had previously earned their livings by attacking Cavaliers, and indignant "orthodox" puritans and Quakers, eager to distance their own denomination from Ranter excesses, these pamphlets perpetuated a number of caricatures and accounts of blasphemous and promiscuous

Ranter merrymaking. One of these pamphlets (Gilbert Roulston, *The Ranters Bible*, 1650) even tried to conceptualize the Ranters' apparent dualism by identifying them with early Christian Gnostics—an instance of hostile Ranter propaganda that contributed to the "Ranter" myth by attempting to understand their perceived beliefs rather than by simply deriding them. The Ranters' notoriety ensured that they were also met with severe legal prosecution: Blasphemy Acts were passed by Parliament in 1650, and most of the so-called Ranters were at some point arrested, imprisoned, and released upon the publication of their (often ambiguous) recantations.

Persecuted with such severity, the Ranters themselves soon faded into obscurity, and little is known of their subsequent spiritual careers. Clarkson became a Muggletonian, for example, and died a debtor; Coppe changed his name to Higham and turned his attention to medicine. But in the later 1650s, "Ranters" continued to play a role as a heresiological category in tracts by Quakers, who used accusations of Ranting to police their own ranks, and by Commonwealth propagandists who turned Ranters into boisterous but closet royalists. The effect of this latter strategy was to return the label "Ranter" to its original meaning of declamatory, jovial misbehavior.

See also: Anabaptists, Antinomianism, Puritan Revolution, Sects

Further Reading

J. C. Davis, *Fear, Myth and History: The Ranters and the Historians* (Cambridge, Eng., 1986); Jerome Friedman, *Blasphemy, Immorality and Anarchy: The Ranters and the English Revolution* (Athens, OH, 1987); J. F. MacGregor, "Seekers and Ranters," in J. F. MacGregor and Barry Reay, eds., *Radical Religion in the English Revolution* (Oxford, 1984), pp. 121–139; Nigel Smith, *A Collection of Ranter Writings from the Seventeenth Century* (London, 1983).

Simon Dyton

Reformation of Manners

The "reformation of manners" was a preoccupation not only of the godly, as the puritans were often called, but of many other elements in early modern English society. The term *manners* denoted morality and personal behavior rather than mere politeness. Those whose manners were judged to be in need of reform were more often than not the poor, the young, the rootless, and the marginal. Although historians have occasionally inflated this slogan into a movement, the "reformation of manners" was usually manifest as a short-lived, highly localized crusade against one or several transgressions, such as swearing, drunkenness, tippling or alehouse-haunting, idleness, "night-walking," absence from church, and dancing, football, sports, and other pastimes on a Sunday afternoon. These campaigns were aimed at feasting, wakes, church ales, maypoles, and merrymaking; at the sexuality of young people, at sex before marriage, promiscuity, and adultery; and at strolling players, fiddlers, minstrels, and puppeteers. *Manners* was, then, an elastic term. It covered sins with direct social consequences, such as the bastard children who were a financial burden on the parish, and popular pastimes, such as football on the village green, which had no immediate communal repercussions. The reformers offered several kinds of objection to popular behavior and recreation. Some were practical: it was, for instance, wasteful and inefficient to raise parish funds through the church ales or wakes. Others were purely moral, such as the crackdown on swearing or the increased reporting to the church courts of married couples who had anticipated marriage and gone to bed together before the wedding. In most cases these were complex "moral panics," bringing together a variety of anxieties about a local lack of public discipline and order.

Phases

The first discernible phase of the drive to reform English manners occurred in the late Elizabethan and Jacobean periods. This war "in our streets," as Richard Baxter called it, was fought on several fronts: over daily routines and habits, especially drinking and the sociability of the inn; over the weekly challenge to the sanctity of Sunday from dancing and football or, in London, commercial entertainments; and over the highlights of the festive year such as May Day or Christmas. These were the points of friction between those who sought to impose order, decorum, and responsibility and those who rejoiced in opportunities for good fellowship and neighborliness. In the provinces, oases of godliness, little Zions, were created by godly magistrates and ministers working together. At Rye in Sussex, the council and the local bishop agreed in 1575 to give the minister Richard Fletcher jurisdiction to punish sin and wickedness and to secure "such a civil and virtuous order of living as the Word of God daily taught unto us doth require." Similar attempts were made at Northampton, Dorchester, Exeter, Norwich, Salisbury, and elsewhere.

The second phase of reformation occurred in the late 1640s and 1650s. Now firmly in political control, puritans were at last able to bring about the cultural revolution they had long dreamed of: draconian legislation was enacted against breaches of the Sabbath, adultery, drunkenness, swearing, and the like; and if the local authorities failed to take up the cause of the reformation of manners, the New Model Army and its major-generals could ensure that alehouses were closed down and the ban on Christmas festivity was observed. Anecdotal evidence suggests that central attempts to enforce such policies were both of limited effect and deeply unpopular.

The Revolution of 1688 initiated a third wave of reform. The "Societies for the Reformation of Manners" were established by laymen intent on prosecuting drunkards, whores, swearers, profaners of the Sabbath, and other offenders in the criminal courts. The societies began in London, but spread to the provinces: one was active in Bristol between 1699 and 1705. In London they distributed blank printed warrants for sympathetic justices of the peace (JPs) to sign and published lists of those who were convicted of moral offenses. In forty-four years, the London societies claimed responsibility for 101,683 prosecutions. At the same time they spread edifying literature about the stews and slums of the city in an attempt to wean the people from vice. The Societies for the Reformation of

Manners were at their height in the 1690s and 1700s; thereafter support dwindled, and the last one was disbanded in 1738.

Motives

Did this diverse moral activism share underlying common motives? Was it even new? It had long been the job of a community's elders to watch over the morality of the young and poor, as Marjorie McIntosh's study of the fifteenth century (1998) demonstrated. Yet new forces came into play in Tudor and Stuart England. Protestant zeal was one; so too was the sophistication and ambition of the state and administrators both local and national. Preachers and bureaucrats now enjoyed the inestimable technological advantage of the printing press. And economic pressures were undoubtedly significant.

The most ambitious model of the process was offered by Keith Wrightson and David Levine's study of the Essex village of Terling. This community of 600 people experienced a process of social and economic polarization in the half century after 1580. The elite became richer; they acquired literacy and better education than the poor; they lived more sober and restrained lives; and they were the godly. In other words, the respectable made puritanism their own creed and used it as an ideology of social control. Puritanism rationalized their efforts to discipline the poor, to curb their drunken, promiscuous ways, and to instil in them respect for sobriety, property, and hard work. It promoted a new social ethic. David Underdown (1985) saw the squabbles over maypoles and church ales as an attack on rituals appropriate to traditional communities by those who placed their trust in individual diligence rather than cooperative values. Parallel investigations, however, such as that of the Wiltshire village of Keevil, have complicated the picture. Here, economic pressures led to a harsher line against bastardy and bridal pregnancy, but there was no campaign to enforce religious observance or ban games and celebrations. Whether the fundamental motive was ideological or material, the reality was that religion played a major part in the effort to regulate personal behavior.

This was a phenomenon seen across early modern Europe. The triumph of Lent over Carnival epitomized the suspicion of popular culture and recreation among the educated and authoritarian classes in both Protestant and Roman Catholic countries. In England, it was godly rhetoric and preaching, puritan Sabbatarianism, millenarianism, and concern with "discipline" (conspicuously absent from the Church of England and its courts) that inspired reform. Contemporaries had no hesitation in seeing these as puritan campaigns. The disaffected asked, with Sir Toby Belch in Shakespeare's *Twelfth Night* "Dost thou think, because thou art virtuous, there shall be no more cakes and ale?" (2.3.123), and they mocked Zeal-of-the-Land Busy in Ben Jonson's *Bartholomew Fair* for seeing idolatry in a puppet show. Modern perceptions of what it was to be a puritan have been shaped by this identification of all moral reformers with puritanism. Some reformers were no more than social improvers or altruistic Protestants; others may have been hypocrites; but the "reformation of manners" was undeniably a central element in that diffuse entity that was Tudor and Stuart puritanism.

See also: Churching of Women, Illegitimacy, Leisure Time, Theology of, Major-Generals, Poor Relief, Protectorate, Sexuality, Sports and Recreation
Further Reading
Patrick Collinson, *The Birthpangs of Protestant England* (New York, 1988); Martin Ingram, "The Reformation of Manners in Early Modern England," in Paul Griffiths, Adam Fox, and Steve Hindle, eds., *The Experience of Authority in Early Modern England* (Basingstoke, Eng., 1996); Marjorie K. McIntosh, *Controlling Misbehavior in England, 1370–1600* (New York, 1998); David Underdown, *Revel, Riot, and Rebellion* (Oxford, 1985); Keith Wrightson and David Levine, *Poverty and Piety in an English Village, 1525–1700* (New York, 1979).

John Spurr

Reforming Synod of 1679

For American puritans who believed that their society was in a national covenant with God, the series of reverses that began with the Restoration (the return of the Stuart monarchy in 1660), were viewed as signs of God's displeasure. Economic decline, political threats, epidemic disease, and the devastation of King Philip's War—these and other misfortunes were seen as punishments for the society's sins.

In sermons often labeled jeremiads (in reference to the similar warnings to Israel uttered by the Old Testament prophet Jeremiah), individual clergy called upon their congregations to repent lest God punish them further. In the late 1670s, Increase Mather and other clergy prevailed upon the Massachusetts General Court to call a synod that would address itself to two questions: "What are the evils that have provoked the Lord to bring his judgments on New England?" and "What is to be done so those evils may be reformed?" The idea had been suggested to Mather by one of his English correspondents.

The synod met in September 1679. Following its deliberations, a committee consisting of Mather, Urian Oakes, Solomon Stoddard, and James Allen prepared a report on "The Necessity of Reformation" that was subsequently endorsed by the General Court. It pointed to the neglect of religion in families and churches, intemperance, worldliness, and lack of public spirit as being among the sins of the land and recommended renewals of church covenants, firmer church discipline, and renewed emphasis on education as means of reformation. In addition to these recommendations, the synod also endorsed the Confession of Faith that had been prepared by the English Congregational Savoy Assembly of 1658.

Further Reading
Francis J. Bremer, *The Puritan Experiments: New England Society from Bradford to Edwards*, revised edition (Hanover, NH, 1995).

Francis J. Bremer

Rhode Island

Rhode Island, an accidental colony derided by the rest of Puritan New England as a dung heap, proved that it was possible for a state to govern successfully without divine sanction for its laws.

Rhode Island began in 1636, when Roger Williams fled persecution in Massachusetts and founded Providence at the head of Narragansett Bay, on land given him by friendly Indians. He was followed in the next few years by an exodus of antinomians from Massachusetts, led by Anne Hutchinson and William Coddington, who built a settlement at Portsmouth, at the northern end of Aquidneck Island, where they were joined by the mystic Samuel Gorton. Not surprisingly, the trio soon split up, Coddington moving to what became Newport, and Gorton to the town of Warwick.

From the beginning, the variety of religious expression in the original four towns of Rhode Island was wide and perplexing. Gorton claimed to be in direct communication with God, as perhaps did Hutchinson. Coddington joined the Quakers, and Williams, who had begun as an Anglican priest, had become, first, a Separatist, then a Baptist, and finally, denying the validity of any organized Christian church, a "seeker." It was William's sort of seeker mentality that fundamentally united the founders of Rhode Island. Their own experience told them that divine inspiration had not ended with the apostles, that supernatural "light" might strike anyone, male or female, at any time, that "truth" in any age was only partial and subject to revision, and that the established church and state were as certain to persecute prophets in modern times as they had been in ancient days. It was, therefore, necessary to guarantee "soul liberty" to all, even to those in error.

It might seem difficult to maintain order in a society based on those ideals, but the towns all created local governments, based on covenants that bound all residents to civil obedience and that allowed most adult males to enact laws. The problem was that each town was independent of the others, and the need for a central government seemed urgent as long as Massachusetts lurked in the background, with plans to slice Rhode Island into digestible pieces. Williams met this threat by going to England, where he secured, in 1643, a patent, or charter, from Parliament, giving legal sanction to the colony of Rhode Island and Providence Plantations. In 1647, a general assembly finally met, presided over by a president, and composed after 1648 of assistants and deputies elected by the towns. The form of government was described as "democratical," meaning "a government held by the free and voluntary consent of all or the greater part of the free inhabitants." Women, children, and enslaved Blacks were given no political standing, but the Rhode Island government of 1647 was radically representative for its time. Even so, it was feared that the elected officials would abuse their power, so such safeguards were adopted as frequent elections, term limits, referenda, and recall.

The parliamentary patent was abrogated by the restoration of Charles II in 1660, and Rhode Islanders reverted to the status of squatters in English law. Connecticut tried to take advantage of the situation when it negotiated a royal charter in 1662 that included more than half of Rhode Island's territory, but a Rhode Island agent, John Clarke, persuaded the king, in 1663, to grant Rhode Island its own charter, restoring to it the land lost the previous year. The charter of 1663, which described Rhode Island as "a lively experiment" in religious freedom, validated the government already established, guaranteed that nobody would be persecuted for his or her religious beliefs, and specifically prohibited the neighboring colonies from invading Rhode Island.

The charter did not clearly define the colony's boundaries and did not prevent speculators from Massachusetts and Connecticut from grabbing at Rhode Island's lands, but it did ensure the colony's existence. Allowed to live, Rhode Island became prosperous, politically stable, and less democratic, in the eighteenth century. The towns conceded many of their powers to the general assembly, and Rhode Island even took on a more normal appearance, in British-American terms, when in 1716 it excluded Jews and Catholics from political participation. The central government encouraged the economic growth of Newport, and by issuing bountiful amounts of paper money, practically eliminated taxes. Rhode Islanders so appreciated the charter of 1663 that they did not replace it with a state constitution until 1843.

Rhode Island remained Rhode Island, but did Rhode Island remain Puritan? The founders of the colony had arisen from the Puritan movement, but they had pushed Puritanism to its limits, and perhaps beyond. Their followers, finding their own "light," added even greater complexity to the rich variety of religious expression that they had inherited, but much of that expression was not Puritan. We may exclude from this discussion Anglicans, Jews, Moravians, and such homegrown sects as the one founded by Jemima Wilkinson, none of whom can be reasonably defined as Puritans. We must also omit, with great reluctance, the Society of Friends, the dominant political force in colonial Rhode Island.

Baptists are a more difficult proposition. Many Puritans were tempted to give up infant baptism, which made no sense if the church was supposed to be composed only of saints, and not necessarily their seed. Baptists soon became the largest single community in Rhode Island, but they were always greatly divided, and only some Baptists can be defined as Puritans. General-Redemption Six Principle Baptists were outside the Puritan tradition, but Six Principle Calvinists Baptists were not. These denominational distinctions, however, need to be so highly qualified that they may be useless. Perhaps the more accurate description of Baptist division in the eighteenth century was the widening split between rural and urban Baptists. Country Baptists, who worshiped in barns, or meetinghouses little better than barns, and who listened to ministers whose only qualification for office was divine inspiration, regarded education with suspicion, cared nothing about theology, and assumed free will as a matter of common sense. City Baptists, like those who worshiped at the First Baptist Meeting House in Newport, with its graceful steeple and gold-painted columns, listened to ministers like James Manning, a Princeton graduate, who accepted Calvinist theology and explained its implications in his sermons. It was these Baptists who founded the College of Rhode Island (Brown University) in 1764, with a curriculum that assigned texts by such Puritans as Isaac Watts and Philip Doddridge, to teach students ethics, logic, divinity, and "pneumatology" (or psychology). If Manning had had his way, all Baptists in Rhode Island would have united around the Westminster Confession, the basic statement of Puritan belief.

Even Congregationalists are a problem. They were Puritans almost by definition in New England, but Congregationalists in Rhode Island were few in number and peculiar in practice. Before 1720, when a meetinghouse was built in Newport, Rhode Island, Congregationalists were served, if at all, by visiting ministers, who could not administer the Lord's Supper. By the eve of the Great Awakening, there were still only six Congregational churches, and the revival was a disaster for them, estranging ministers from their congregations, and leading many into Separatist or Baptist churches. Even when people remained members of a Congregational church, they insisted upon practices that would not have been tolerated in Connecticut or Massachusetts. In the Newport Second Church, the pastor, Ezra Stiles, counted 608 members in 1770, but only 57 were communicants. Some of these "congregationalists" insisted that their children be baptized by full immersion, and some refused to have their children baptized at all.

Whatever the difficulty of identifying Puritans in a society as religiously fluid as Rhode Island, we can say with certainty that Protestants had become a small minority in the state by 1900. A generous approximation of Congregationalists, Baptists, and Quakers would put their number below 50,000, while Roman Catholics totaled over 200,000. Demographically at least, Rhode Island had ceased to be Puritan.

Further Reading

Carl Bridenbaugh, *Fat Mutton and Liberty of Conscience: Society in Rhode Island, 1636–1690* (Providence, RI; 1974); Bruce Daniels, *Dissent and Conformity on Narragansett Bay: The Colonial Rhode Island Town* (Middletown, CT, 1974); Edward Field, ed., *State of Rhode Island and Providence Plantations at the End of the Century: A History,* 3 vols. (Boston, 1902); William McLoughlin, *Rhode Island: A History* (New York, 1978).

James P. Walsh

Roundheads

A disparaging term applied to supporters of Parliament during the English Civil Wars, alluding to the supposed shortness of their hair. This pervasive crop-haired image and its associated terminology became virtually synonymous with Puritanism in Victorian literature and painting. Works such as *The Puritan* by John Pettie (1839–1893) and numerous pictures by Ernest Crofts (1847–1911) featuring dour, shorthaired Puritans and romantic, longhaired Cavaliers are largely to blame for a pair of anachronistic stereotypes that still contaminate a surprisingly large number of serious history books, as well as the more populist media offerings of film and television. In actuality, contemporary portraits of leading Parliamentarians show that most, if not all, sported hairstyles virtually indistinguishable from their royalist opponents.

The term *roundhead* first arose in street fighting in London before the outbreak of civil war, as is evident from the text of *The Roundhead Uncovered* (1642) and from Richard Baxter's reminiscences, published as *Reliquiae Baxterianae* in 1696. The term soon spread to the provinces: Baxter noted in Worcester in the late summer of 1642 that strangers with short hair and civil manners were being taunted with the name and sometimes assaulted.

There are various explanations as to why the royalists alluded to their opponents' hair: the London apprentices (frequently the main antagonists of royalist supporters in clashes around Whitehall) were often shorthaired, as, admittedly, were certain members of the Puritan persuasion. As short hair was also often to be found among the poorer members of society, royalist derision may have attempted to invoke social stigma. Baxter suggested that the nickname might have arisen from an incident at the trial of the Earl of Strafford in 1641, when Queen Henrietta-Maria allegedly described John Pym as a "round-headed man."

There is a voluminous body of contemporary literature on the subject, including the work of one pamphleteer, in *The Roundhead Uncovered* (1642), who attempted to make a subtle distinction between Roundheads and Puritans. Other contemporary diatribes were intended either to defend the parliamentarian cause, such as *An Exact Description of a Roundhead and a Long-Head Shag-Poll* (1642), or attack it, such as John Taylor's *Conversion, Confession, Contrition . . . of a Mis-led, Ill-bred Rebellious Roundhead* (1643). The term *shag-poll*, or *shag-poll locust*, was a derisive reference to a supporter of the king, although the term *Cavalier*, with its allusions to the depredations of Spanish soldiery in the Netherlands, was the more usual expression. *Twenty Lookes over all the Roundheads that ever Lived in the World* (1643) was an interesting pro-Parliamentarian guide that purported to be a study of the use of the term *roundhead* throughout history, from biblical times (beginning with Leviticus 19:27) to the seventeenth century. It is unlikely, however, that the Puritans' detractors were quite so scientific in their choice of pejorative language.

See also: Clothing

David J. Appleby

S

Sabbath and Sabbatarianism

The requirement to observe the Sabbath is set forth in the Old Testament. The fourth commandment in Exodus 20 commands the Israelites to "Remember the Sabbath day, to keep it holy. Six days you shall labor, and do all your work; but the seventh day is a Sabbath to the Lord your God; in it you shall not do any work, you, or your son, or your daughter, your manservant, or your maidservant, or your cattle, or the sojourner who is within your gates." Here the command rests upon the example of God, who made the heavens and earth in six days and rested on the seventh. The same commandment in Deuteronomy 5 reads "Observe the Sabbath day, to keep it holy, as the Lord your God commanded you," but is explained as a responsibility owed God for having brought the Israelites out of Egypt. Jewish law came to elaborate the specific ways in which the commandment was to be observed, rabbinical writers identifying as many as thirty-nine specific types of tasks to be avoided on the Sabbath, as well as specifying other aspects of observance.

The early Christian church did not adopt Jewish Sabbath practice and came to specify weekly worship on what was understood to be the first day of the week, Sunday. In the fourth and fifth centuries, aspects of Jewish Sabbath practice were applied to Sunday observances, but recreation and labor were prohibited only to the extent that they might interfere with worship. Over the following centuries, however, the Roman Catholic Church increasingly stipulated what people could and could not do on Sundays and on holy days set in the church calendar. The new restrictions and requirements were justified by reference to the observation of the Old Testament Sabbath and by the fourth commandment. But the new legalism rested on the authority of the papacy, and this authority was challenged by the Reformation.

The early Protestant reformers were agreed in rejecting the authority of Rome, but had different approaches to interpreting the scripture, leading to different views on the Sabbath. Luther emphasized the primacy of the New over the Old Testament, stressed the antithesis between the Law and the Gospel, and rejected the Catholic adoption of Jewish Sabbath observance. Calvin, on the other hand, stressed the unity of the two testaments and, as one scholar put it, "Christianized the Old and Judaized the New Testament." But though he assimilated much of the Mosaic code into his teachings, he allowed amusements and recreation after Sunday worship. Calvin's disciple, John Knox, brought these views to Scotland. The 1561 *Book of Discipline* condemned holy days but referenced the fourth commandment in requiring participation in Sunday worship. Scots were allowed to travel, join in sports, and have dinner parties on Sundays, so long as these did not interfere with worship.

In the early days of the English Reformation, the requirements of Sunday observance rested on the authority of Henry VIII as head of the church, rather than on the fourth commandment, and permitted work on holy days and Sundays "for the speedy performance of the necessary affairs of the prince and the commonwealth, at the command of them that have rule and authority therein." The Edwardian church focused on the problem of those who dishonored holy days, including the Sabbath, by "idleness, pride, drunkenness, quarreling, and brawling," and stipulated that henceforth they should "celebrate and keep their holy day [Sunday] according to God's holy will and pleasure; that is, in hearing the word of God read and taught; in private and public prayers," as well as in good works and "godly conversation." The second Book of Common Prayer (1552) drastically reduced the number of holy days and emphasized the importance of Sunday observance. These trends were reversed during the reign of Queen Mary, but English Protestant discussion of the Sabbath resumed in the reign of Queen Elizabeth.

Early in Elizabeth's reign, a chorus of complaints about the profanation of the Sabbath began to rise, coupled with a growing conviction that God punished those individuals and nations who neglected to properly observe his day. Contributing to this concern was the fact that a growing number of Englishmen could read and had unprecedented access to the Bible, where they could read the Ten Commandments themselves. Though puritans became most closely identified with this new Sabbatarianism, it was a movement that had adherents across the entire spectrum of the church. Thus, Lancelot Andrewes advocated stricter observance of the Sabbath while he was a student at Cambridge, though he later disassociated himself from more extreme forms of Sabbatarianism.

Nicholas Bownd's *The Doctrine of the Sabbath* (1595) was the most comprehensive statement of the new outlook. At the center of the work was the view that the fourth commandment was part of the moral rather than the ceremonial law expressed in the Old Testament and therefore was binding on Christians. But whereas the Israelites observed the command to rest one day each week on the seventh day, it was appropriate for Christians to celebrate the Sabbath, called the Lord's Day, on Sunday in commemoration of the Resurrection. Labor and travel were strictly forbidden. Among tasks specifically identified as proscribed were building, sowing, harvesting, attending markets, buying and selling, and various activities of lawyers, physicians, and court officers. Preparing food and cooking meals was allowed. Certain acts of mercy, such as putting out a fire and tending the sick, were also permitted. Sunday sports—including "honest recreations" such as hunting and bowling—were banned. On the positive side, Christians were to attend morning and afternoon services and to spend the remainder of the day in family psalm singing, scripture reading, and prayer; private prayer; and meditation. This was to be a day devoted to God and not to worldly concerns.

Once again it should be stressed that many Englishmen who would never be identified as puritans read Bownd and similar authors with approval and tried to incorporate those teachings into their lives. And puritans themselves were not agreed on every detail of how the Sabbath was to be observed. A striking example of this is to be found in the recorded debates over the Sabbath in the meetings of the Dedham Conference in the 1580s. The "question touching the right use of the Lord's Day" was raised at the very first meeting of the Conference in December 1582 and was discussed twelve times over the next four years. The debate centered around three issues. The first was whether Christians were bound to observe the Sabbath on the first day of the week or whether the church had the liberty to choose the day. Related to this was the question of whether the commandment was part of the moral law (required of all people at all times) or the ceremonial law (which it was considered the prerogative of the church to modify). The second key issue involved the length of the day—whether a figurative day from dawn to dusk or a natural day of twenty-four hours. This issue also involved the question of when the day began, with some puritans holding that it ran from sundown on Saturday to sundown on Sunday. The third point of contention among the Dedham clergy involved the definition of "rest" and the particular types of work to be allowed and disallowed.

Related to all of these was the question of whether it was the responsibility of the civil government to enforce Sabbath observance.

While divided on some of the details of proper Sabbath observance, many Englishmen, puritan and not, were committed to a more religious observance of the Lord's Day. Because of this, many were affronted by King James I's declaration, generally referred to as the Book of Sports, which permitted a wide range of recreational activities after Sunday services. When King Charles I reissued his father's declaration and ordered that it be read in every church, he widened the gap that had been developing between the king and many of his pious subjects.

It is not surprising that the new, more rigorous concepts of how the Sabbath was to be observed shaped the practice of the New England colonists. Identifying with the ancient Israelites, the colonists saw proper observance of the Sabbath as essential to the fulfillment of their mission to lead exemplary lives. From the earliest days of settlement, the colonists observed the Lord's Day as beginning at sundown on Saturday and continuing for twenty-four hours. All were expected to attend Sunday morning and afternoon services and to devote the rest of the day to family and private devotions. The unique character of the day was underlined by the elimination of all other holy days and feast days such as were still observed in England prior to the Civil Wars. The most elaborate presentation of the colonial viewpoint was offered by Thomas Shepard in his *These Sabbaticae: Or, The Doctrine of the Sabbath* (1649). The Massachusetts *Book of Laws and Liberties* (1648) included four laws regarding the Sabbath: all were required to attend public worship; denying the Sabbath was an offense; Sabbath breaking was illegal; and burglary and theft on the Sabbath were punished more harshly than when committed on other occasions.

During the English Civil Wars, Parliament sought to implement a more thorough observance of the Sabbath. An ordinance of 1644 used the fourth commandment as justification for banning commercial activities, travel, games, sports, and other recreations. Copies of the Book of Sports were ordered to be burned. The "Directory for Public Worship," which Parliament substituted for the Book of Common Prayer in 1645, encapsulated many of the reforms that had been urged by puritans and others.

See also: Book of Sports, Reformation of Manners, Sports and Recreation
Further Reading
Patrick Collinson, "The Beginnings of English Sabbatarianism, in Collinson, *Godly People* (London, 1983); Kenneth Parker, *The English Sabbath: A Study of Doctrine and Discipline from the Reformation to the Civil War* (New York, 1988); John H. Primus, *Holy Time: Moderate Puritanism and the Sabbath* (1989); Winton Solberg: *Redeem the Time: The Puritan Sabbath in Early America* (Urbana, 1977).

Francis J. Bremer

St. Antholin's

A London parish famous for its early morning lectures and for the nonconformity of many of its preachers. It gained its reputation as a radical center early. By 1531 Edward Crome, the rector, was among those accused of preaching against the doctrine of purgatory, the veneration of the saints, and the orthodox ceremonies of the Church of England. His successor as rector, William Tolwin, was charged with Anabaptist beliefs in 1541. The early morning lectures may date from the reign of Edward VI, and they certainly existed in 1559, when a Catholic observer noted that an early morning service in the Geneva fashion preceded the lectures, given in the early Elizabethan years by three nonconformists, Robert Crowley, John Gough, and John Philpott. All three were suspended in 1566 as a consequence of the Vestiarian Controversy, but after various suspensions and deprivations, Crowley was back preaching at St. Antholin's in 1576. Other nonconformists followed: James Stile, who had been suspended from preaching at St. Margaret Lothbury in 1574, served briefly as chaplain to Sir Philip Sidney and then became an early morning lecturer in 1586; Andrew Castleton, a lecturer in 1583, was later in trouble for nonconformity at St. Martin Ironmonger Lane; Edward

Spendlow, who began lecturing in 1594, was cited in 1628 for preaching without a license; Thomas Foxley, who began lecturing in 1622, was questioned by Bishop William Laud in 1630 and by the High Commission five years later; and John Archer, one of the lecturers in 1628, was suspended by Bishop Laud in 1630 for unorthodox catechizing. Not all the lecturers were nonconformists, and Charles Offspring, who served as rector from 1617 until his death in 1659, as well as one of the lecturers, never seems to have been questioned by the authorities, despite the fact that he was one of the clerical Feoffees for Impropriations, which the authorities regarded as an illegal corporation bent on subverting church and state.

The early morning lectures, initially given by three preachers, then four in 1623, and five from the following year, were a major financial undertaking for a single parish and depended on both parish collections and pious bequests, the first by William Parker, Draper, who died in 1567 bequeathing £100, which produced £6 in annual income, and a second in 1581 by Dame Elizabeth Martin; ultimately the parish was to receive twenty-three bequests for that purpose. However, lecturer salaries rose from £6 in the 1560s to £20 per annum by the 1620s, and the parish was only able to balance its books by a £40 annual gift from the City Chamber, which ceased in 1629, and by additional funds raised by the Feoffees for Impropriations from 1626 to 1633. Endowments gave the lectures longevity: the early morning lectures were still preached every day in 1720, although no longer by Puritans, and a St. Antholin's lecture was still given in 1960, long after the parish itself had vanished.

See also: Feoffees for Impropriations, Lectures and Lectureships, Preaching
Further Reading
Seaver, Paul S., *The Puritan Lectureships* (Stanford, 1970).

Paul Seaver

Salem, Massachusetts
The present-day town of Danvers, Massachusetts, site of the witch hunt of 1692, was known then as Salem Village. It was a troubled agrarian town linked to the prosperous and growing mercantile port of Salem. Historians have often cited unique social and economic pathologies afflicting Salem Village at the time of the outbreak as significant factors in the witch panic. Like all other Massachusetts towns, Salem Village was facing the political and economic instability left in the wake of the overthrow of royal governor Edmund Andros in 1689. In addition, Salem Village's proximity to the scenes of combat between English settlers and French and Indian warriors in King William's War (1690–1697), made the area a center for refugees traumatized by their participation in the conflict. Village residents themselves experienced significant internal tensions as a result of differences in their ties to the economic life of the town of Salem. Those who lived closer to and had economic ties with the port town were often at odds with the poorer farmers who lived farther away.

Not surprisingly, a significant amount of the village's internal tension was focused on selecting a minister for Salem Village church. Two leading families—the Putnams and the Porters—were deeply divided over the issue. The Putnams, village leaders whose economic and political fortunes were in decline, favored the selection of Parris, a Harvard trained minister who had previously been a failed Bermudian merchant. The Porters, a wealthy local family with close ties to Salem town's commercial elites, were opposed to Parris's selection and fought against it. It was in this atmosphere of multivalent tensions centered on the Parris household that Parris's young daughter Betty and her cousin Abigail Williams first became afflicted by spectral apparitions. From that incident, the entire witch hunt evolved.

See also: Salem Witchcraft, Witchcraft
Further Reading
Paul Boyer and Stephen Nissenbaum, *Salem Possessed* (Cambridge, MA, 1976); Richard Gildrie, *Salem, Massachusetts, 1626–1682: A Covenanted Community* (Charlottesville, 1975).

Walt Woodward

Salem Witchcraft

Occurring in 1692–1693, what happened in Salem was the largest outbreak of witchcraft accusations in North America. Although the Salem crisis has become synonymous with the history of colonial witchcraft, when examined in the context of previous episodes, it appears anomalous.

Most obviously anomalous are its size, duration, and geographical scope: over a period of seventeen months—from January 1692 to May 1693—at least 144 people faced formal charges, with more being accused informally. The first accusations arose in Salem Village (now Danvers), and trials were held in Salem town, but charges were filed in twenty-three different towns, mainly in Essex County. Andover supplied the largest number of accusations (more than forty). Earlier witchcraft incidents had involved at most eleven accusations (Hartford, 1662) and had been confined to a town or two and a few months.

Less often remarked upon are three other key differences from the norm: the identity of the initial accusers, the content of their accusations, and the fate of those tried. Historically, most colonial witchcraft cases arose from charges of *maleficium*—accusations that a witch had damaged the family or goods of an adult accuser by, for instance, killing or injuring a child or animal or disrupting household processes. In 1692, although such claims supported many accusations, the first charges usually came from young women (aged twelve to twenty-five) who claimed that a specter of the witch had afflicted and tortured them. Moreover, all the accused tried before October 1692 were convicted, and most were executed by hanging. Previously, most witchcraft accusations had not led to trials; those tried were seldom convicted and even more rarely hanged.

Chronology

In mid-January 1692, the daughter and niece of the Reverend Samuel Parris, minister of the sharply divided parish of Salem Village, began to suffer from mysterious fits. Parris consulted the village doctor, who diagnosed witchcraft. After fits spread to the daughters and maidservants of other households

Engraving depicting the arrest of a witch by the Puritan townfolk of Salem, Massachusetts. (Time Life Pictures/ Getty Images)

(most notably that of the doctor and of Thomas Putnam, one of Parris's staunch allies in the village conflicts discussed in the previous entry), adults pressed the girls to identify their afflicters. In late February they began to do so, first naming Parris's Indian slave, Tituba, and two village women with poor reputations. Tituba then confessed to being a witch. By the middle of April, a total of fourteen people had been formally accused of witchcraft, and many others, including Thomas Putnam's wife Ann, had complained of afflictions.

After a fourteen-year-old girl from Topsfield, Abigail Hobbs, confessed that Satan had recruited her as a witch four years earlier on the Maine frontier, the Putnams' afflicted daughter, also Ann, reported a vision in which she saw the specter of the former village minister, George Burroughs, in 1692 a resident of Wells, Maine, who confessed to her that he had killed his first two wives and had bewitched the colonial soldiers currently fighting

Indians on the northern frontier. There followed immediately an explosion of accusations throughout Essex County, spearheaded by the afflicted young women of Salem Village, who began naming as Satan's allies women (and some men) who had long been regarded as witches in their own towns.

In mid-May a new governor, Sir William Phips, arrived from England to constitute a government under a charter issued in 1691. He created a Court of Oyer and Terminer led by his lieutenant governor, William Stoughton, to try the accused. The first person tried, Bridget Bishop of Salem Town, had been acquitted of witchcraft twelve years earlier. This time she was convicted; she was hanged on 10 June 1692. During the second court session, 28 June–2 July, five more women were tried and convicted; all were hanged on 19 July.

Accusations mounted rapidly in mid-July after the confessions of the Andover resident Ann Foster and her daughter and granddaughter. Increasing numbers of accused Andover townspeople confessed their guilt and named additional malefactors. At the court's third session, 2–5 August, six more people, including George Burroughs, were convicted of witchcraft; they were executed on 19 August. The number of accusations and confessions continued to rise, especially in Andover, until, around the middle of September, an Andover magistrate refused to issue any more arrest warrants and thereby essentially ended the accusation phase of the crisis. A few other charges were later filed elsewhere, the last three in early November. The final session of the special court lasted two weeks, 6–17 September. Fourteen people were tried and convicted; on 22 September, eight of them were hanged. Three days earlier, Giles Corey of Salem Village was pressed to death for refusing to enter a plea. Including him, fourteen women and six men were executed in 1692.

By mid-October, criticism of the court's reliance on testimony about spectral tortures had become irresistible, and Governor Phips dissolved the court. That did not, however, end the witchcraft trials, which resumed in January 1693 in regular courts, without the use of spectral evidence. Three more people were convicted, but Phips reprieved both them and those convicted in September but not yet executed.

Interpretations

Historians have developed myriad explanations for these remarkable events. Some emphasize religious, economic, or familial divisions within Salem Village. Many offer psychological explanations for the afflictions or attribute the reputed sufferings to disease or out-and-out fraud. Others focus on the accused witches and the challenges they posed to puritans' gendered norms of behavior. Certainly Essex County residents' longstanding identifications of certain of their neighbors as witches perpetuated and expanded the crisis. The most recent interpretation stresses the importance of the widespread fears generated by two successive Indian wars on the northern frontier (1675–1678; 1688–1699) in generating so many accusations, pointing to the key significance of the charges against George Burroughs, who had lived both on the frontier and in Salem Village.

See also: Law in Puritan New England, Salem, Massachusetts, Witchcraft
Further Reading
Paul Boyer and Stephen Nissenbaum, *Salem Possessed: The Social Origins of Witchcraft* (Cambridge, MA, 1974); Mary Beth Norton, *In the Devil's Snare: The Salem Witchcraft Crisis of 1692* (New York, 2002); Bernard Rosenthal, *Salem Story: Reading the Witch Trials of 1692* (New York, 1993).

Mary Beth Norton

Salters' Hall

Salters' Hall was the London guildhall of the livery company of the salters, which became the site of a Presbyterian lecture in 1694 and remained a center of London Dissenting activity.

In the 1690s, grievances and incidents divided the English Presbyterians and Congregationalists, both descended from the earlier Puritan movement, and both free to form their own institutions separate from the Church of England after the Toleration Act of 1689. By then differences between the two groups in matters of church government and practice were mainly over whether congregations or higher assemblies should ordain clergy and how inclusive participation in the Lord's Supper should be. But theological differences over grace, such as emerged at Pinners' Hall in the 1670s, drove a wedge between the strictly Calvinist Congregationalists and the moderately Calvinist Presbyterians, although these differences did not entirely follow denominational lines. In 1690 Presbyterians and Congregationalists founded the Common Fund for educating ministerial students and aiding congregations, and the next year many of the London ministers of both groups formed a "Happy Union." But incidents such as the putative antinomianism of the Northampton Dissenting minister Richard Davis, who had received money from the fund, again brought differences into the open, the Presbyterians fearing some Congregationalists tolerated antinomianism, while Congregationalists suspected some Presbyterians of Arminianism. Thus the Happy Union broke up in 1693, and the fund was divided along denominational lines. Then in 1694 the Presbyterians left the lectureship at Pinners' Hall, establishing a rival Tuesday morning lecture at Salters' Hall. The original lecturers at Salters' Hall were Daniel Williams, William Bates, John Howe, and Vincent Alsop, all of whom had lectured at Pinners' Hall. Soon added to the Salters' Hall lecturers were Samuel Annesley, maternal grandfather of John Wesley, and Richard Mayo, pastor to a Dissenting congregation that had been meeting at Salters' Hall since 1689. But all harmony did not end: in 1699 Howe preached at the funeral of Matthew Mead, who had continued as a Pinners' Hall lecturer.

Salters' Hall was also important in Dissenting history because of a conference held there in 1719, summoned to consider charges of Arian subordinationism (see Anti-Trinitarianism) made against several Dissenting ministers in Exeter. After vigorous debate, those assembled, representing Baptists as well as Congregationalists and Presbyterians, decided by a slight majority against doctrinal tests other than adherence to the scriptures, no other language for the doctrine of the Trinity being needed than the formulations of scripture. This conclusion was more acceptable to the Presbyterians than the Congregationalists and furthered the division of the two groups, the former becoming increasingly Arminian and occasionally Arian, while the latter persisted in their adherence to Calvinism.

See also: Dissenters, Happy Union, Independency, Lectures and Lectureships, Pinners' Hall
Further Reading
C. G. Bolam, Jeremy Goring, H. L. Short, and Roger Thomas, *The English Presbyterians: From Elizabethan Puritanism to Modern Unitarianism* (London, 1968); Francis J. Bremer, *Congregational Communion* (Boston, 1994); Michael R. Watts, *The Dissenters: From the Reformation to the French Revolution* (Oxford, 1978).

Dewey D. Wallace Jr.

Satan

See Devil

Savoy Assembly

A gathering of Congregational clergy and moderate Presbyterians at the Savoy Palace in Westminster in 1658. In June of that year, Henry Scobell, a clerk of Oliver Cromwell's Council and also a lay elder of the Congregational church that met at Westminster Abbey, sent a letter calling for a "meeting of the elders of the Congregational Churches in and about London" to meet at the home of the George Griffith. Plans were laid for a national gathering, and following further discussion at the Oxford University commencement, Griffith issued a call for representatives of the nation's Congregational churches to gather at the Savoy in September. Responses were to be directed to Scobell. The close association between Cromwell and Scobell, along with the fact that the Savoy was used by Cromwell to house members of his court, has led some to suspect that the call was approved by the Protector and his council.

The assembly convened on 29 September, with about 120 churches represented by slightly fewer than twice that number of delegates. Among those known to have been there were Thomas Goodwin, Philip Nye, William Bridge, William Greenhill,

Joseph Caryl, John Owen, George Griffith, William Hooke, Thomas Jollie, Isaac Loeffs, Comfort Starr, and John Knowles. Some moderate Presbyterians also sat in the assembly, probably including John Howe. Philip Nye was chosen as the chair and Griffith as the clerk. A committee consisting of Nye, Thomas Godwin, Bridge, Caryl, Owen, and Greenhill was chosen to draft articles to be debated by the whole body. Most of these clergymen were veterans of the Westminster Assembly and had long debated the subjects of faith and church order.

The "Declaration of Faith and Order" presented by the committee and adopted by the assembly reiterated the Congregationalists' Calvinist orthodoxy by essentially adopting the Westminster Confession of Faith. In setting forth their views on polity, the clergy explained that "what we have laid down and asserted about churches and their government we humbly conceive to be the order which Christ himself hath appointed to be observed [and] have endeavored to follow Scripture-light and those also that went before us according to that Rule, desirous of nearest uniformity with reforming churches, as with our brethren in new England, so with other that differ from them and us." The details regarding church formation, officers, discipline, and consociation owed much to the New England Cambridge Platform of 1648.

The Congregationalists may have intended this declaration to form the basis for a church settlement, as called for in 1657 "Humble Petition and Advice." If so, they were to be disappointed. Even as they were reaching their conclusions, Oliver Cromwell died. Though Thomas Goodwin did present the assembly's results to the new Protector, Richard Cromwell, the rapid disintegration of the political situation precluded any consideration of it.

Though it did not form the basis for a new and puritan state church, the Savoy Declaration did serve as a guide for English Congregationalists in the years that followed. It was adopted by a synod in Massachusetts in 1680 and incorporated as part of the Saybrook (Connecticut) Platform of 1708.

Further Reading
Francis J. Bremer, *Congregational Communion: Clerical Friendship in the Anglo-American*

Puritan Community, 1610–1692 (Boston, 1994); A. G. Matthews, ed., *The Savoy Declaration of Faith and Order* (London, 1958); Williston Walker, *The Creeds and Platforms of Congregationalism* (Boston, 1960).

Francis J. Bremer

Savoy Declaration
See Savoy Assembly

Seating Customs in the Post-Reformation English Parish Church

Given the emphasis puritans placed on listening to sermons as cenral to the life of faith, the internal arrangement of the church was a matter of great concern to them. Puritans had strong views on the placement of the communion table and the ornamentation of churches. For the most part, however, they shared with fellow Protestants an understanding of how believers should be seated. The custom of sitting in church was not entirely an innovation of the Reformation. Fourteenth-century local celebrities such as patrons of the church or prominent local landowners had been granted permission to build seats for themselves, and very occasionally for their wives, in the privileged east end of the church in the chancel. Fifteenth-century entries in several sets of churchwardens' accounts relating to pew rents show early evidence of seat reservation and appropriation. Nevertheless, during the sixteenth century, the different priorities, beliefs, and practices of Protestantism generated significant changes in the use and appropriation of seating in English parish churches. Firstly, as Protestant churchmen began to think out the principles that should govern reorganization of a building now used for worship according to the Book of Common Prayer, it became established that different services were to be conducted in different parts of the church. Part of this process involved the erection of new and specialized seats in the nave. Pews were set aside for the christening party near the baptismal font, which was generally placed at the west end near the church door. A special pew was also provided for the churching of married women after childbirth, although the precise position of the seat varied according to local custom and to contest between different religious groups.

The major innovation and addition to the interior of the nave after the Reformation was the introduction of seating for the whole congregation. After around 1600, sitting of all parishioners in church became typical rather than exceptional. Although the celebration of Communion remained an important and central ritual for the expression of the Christian community, scripture and sermon were a priority. It was most important that the minister was heard as well as seen reading the lesson, reading the prayers, and preaching the sermon. Movement around the church became a real problem, and the best way of stopping it was to secure everybody safely in a seat.

The process of pewing was often gradual and partial, especially in country areas. After the middle of the sixteenth century, however, entries in churchwardens' accounts regularly record payments for the building, maintenance, and repair of benches or pews. Increasing numbers of the more eminent members of the parish also began to apply to the ecclesiastical courts for licenses or faculties to build private pews for themselves and their wives, families, and servants. These private pews grew both in size and in opulence as time went by and became another sign of the growing affluence of the landed classes. Doors and locks were often fitted. Many seats were magnificently furnished; several had fireplaces, and many had separate entrances. One even had a dog kennel. It also became fashionable to roof and curtain the pew, so that, as Swift so caustically observed, they came to look like four-poster beds. The frequent cases of conflict over the placement of people in church demonstrate the importance of seats as symbols of status. The church became the single most important local arena where hierarchy was visibly defined and displayed.

Disputes give an insight into the problems involved in deciding who was to sit where. The power to place people in the chancel remained with the parson of the church, but in the last quarter of the sixteenth century, the power to place parishioners in the nave came to rest firmly with the churchwardens and the "chief" or "better sort" of the parishioners, with the consent of the ordinary parishioners. Certain pews were exclusively attached to public office, and the allocation of seats could be further disrupted, especially in market towns, by the spread of systems of seat rents charged for a month, for a year, or for life. Systems of allocation were essentially based on three criteria. Precedence of place in church was decided first according to gender. Sexual segregation was the most common arrangement in English parish churches until well into the seventeenth century. Women tended to be grouped together on the north side of the nave, while men sat on the south side, an arrangement apparent in churches from a much earlier date. Male and female parishioners were then ordered into separate status hierarchies.

Being a householder was the fundamental basis of a right to a seat in church for an adult male. His precise position then depended on a locally variable, complex combination of criteria, which reflected varying attitudes of parish elites toward the appropriate social distribution of seating. Consideration could be given to any one or a combination of several factors, including residence in a particular house, levels of wealth, the amount paid by an individual in rates to the church, appointment to public office, moral reputation, religious affiliation, or, more problematically, merely the workings of systems of local patronage.

The status of a woman was judged differently from that of a man. Outside the household, married women had no formal status in their own right other than being someone's wife, daughter, or widow. This position was reflected and reinforced by systems of seat allocation in church. Women could not claim seats independently, but only through their husband's position in the parish. Faculty applications, for example, were typically made by a husband on behalf of his wife or jointly by a married couple. It was in the man, as household head, that the title to a seat was invested. Married women placed by churchwardens were arranged according to perceptions of the status of their husbands. In St. Peter's West Cheap in London, women were seated according to their husband's age and status. In Eccles in Lancashire, women's place in church depended on their husband's rating assessment.

The arrangement of widows was more complex. A widow's right to retain her place in a seat allocated by a churchwarden continued to be derived from the status of her late husband. But the position of wealthy widows resembled those of other male household heads. When seats were held in the right of a house, for example, it might be a widow, as head of a household, in whom a title to a seat was invested. A widow, as head of the household, could also retain control of prescriptively held men's and women's seats on the death of her husband. Where widows' claims to privately held seats were contested, judges frequently found in their favor.

Age, as well as rank and gender, was taken into account when decisions were made about the ordering and allocation of pews. The young and the unmarried were typically seated separately. Servants generally stood at the back of the church or were seated in their own pews. Many parishes also set aside seats or areas of the church for children, although it is also clear that there was a ranking system even among the young. Private seats were built for the exclusive use of children of the elite.

Over time a variety of pressures began to undermine ancient customs of segregation. The Protestant insistence on the central importance of the household as the basis of all religious, social, and moral discipline and stability, most clearly seen in puritans, gradually began to alter attitudes, so that over time it became more acceptable for husbands and wives with their servants and children to sit together in church. But patterns of change were extremely uneven, socially, chronologically, and geographically. Family pews were first adopted by the upper ranks of local society during the first half of the seventeenth century, probably in part because of the powerful visual means of local social and political propaganda they offered through display of a large and deferential household. Laudian bishops were shocked by such "promiscuity" and struggled to reinforce systems of segregation, although mixed seating was clearly creeping in, especially in large urban parishes.

Yet ancient traditions remained entrenched, especially in rural communities, for many years. It is interesting to note that religious radicals perpetuated the Anglican custom of seating their members separately at their meetings. Quaker meetinghouses divided the men from the women, although it is not known if they were arranged into any sort of status hierarchy, and Methodist men and women sat separately.

Over time, most Anglican churches appear to have evolved a combination of mixed- and single-sex pews. In some places the distinction between gender-specific and mixed seating continued to be determined by social standing. In Chesham, Buckinghamshire, in 1606, only 6 women sat with their husbands, all in the superior pews. A further 169 women sat in single-sex pews. At Hackney, as late as 1699, only the most prominent men of the parish sat with their wives, while "the meaner sort" sat in segregated seats. In other parishes, allocation of single-sex seating was determined predominantly by marital status. At St. John's Chester in 1638, young single men were seated separately from single women, but upon marriage they moved with their wives to mixed pews. Servants and young people of both sexes continued to be seated separately in many parishes right up until the first half of the twentieth century.

See also: Family Piety
Further Reading
Amanda Flather, *Politics of Place: A Study of Church Seating in Essex, c.1580–1640* (1999).

Amanda Flather

Sects

The emergence of religious sects during the Puritan Revolution was the natural consequence of men and women pursuing religious liberty and following their private religious consciences. The traditional (and teleological) view of puritanism's development into a "sectarian" phenomenon is that after the fragmentation of the Roman Catholic Church and then the Protestant movement, the urge to continue reforming the Reformation prompted religious separatism and sectarianism.

Thus sects emerged out of the centrifugal momentum of Protestant itself, which turned private meetings into small, self-selecting congregations in which members of the godly often felt divorced from or ostracized by the world at large. But some historians (such as Margaret Spufford and Christopher Marsh) have shown that religious sects were not isolated, introverted groups, but integrated with the "ungodly" communities in which they existed. Their prominent members often held civic and social roles that reflected their broader status. Others (notably Christopher Hill) have suggested that the disintegration of parish communities into smaller, more inclusive conventicles and congregations anticipated the demographics of early industrialization.

During the mid-sixteenth century, Continental sectaries reached London, and in the 1540s and 1550s, England witnessed a proliferation of "Free-Will Men" and Familists. Like the Lollards before them, Familists adopted outward conformity. Early puritans, however, shunned social integration since the emergence of puritanism in England had the effect of gathering "godly" individuals together in a way that could tend towards the formation of a church within a church. While most puritans sought to remain within and reform the national church, relentless catechizing, unrestrained preaching, and the repetition of sermons, together with strict congregational discipline, could produce discernible "sects," small groups of true believers who held that their faith and assembly, even in groups of two or three, constituted the True Church of Christ.

During Elizabeth I's reign, many of the Continental sectaries who had been reported during the reign of Edward VI were no longer to be found. Though they may have been wiped out in the Marian persecutions, adopted the conformity of Familists, or turned into a radical underground that only resurfaced in the 1640s, it is more likely that Elizabethan puritanism proved to be a force for re-

grouping, re-educating, and integrating "puritan" separatists (such as Henoch Clapham) who had grown tired of internecine squabbling among rival congregations. But during this same period until the 1620s, the Separatist followers of Robert Browne (and hence "Brownists") were vigorously attacked by mainstream puritans of the Elizabethan church. It was not until the 1640s that a proliferation of sects threatened to engulf the English church.

In the 1620s and 1630s, the puritan movement was galvanized by the "Arminian" movement in England, and it was the puritan reaction against Laud's Church of England and the subsequent collapse of that reaction that led to a new wave of sectarian activity. Historians have shown that in the 1630s, small groups of radical puritans did exist, meeting clandestinely, circulating esoteric and sometimes seditious manuscripts, and publishing theologically eccentric pamphlets through sympathetic printers. When censorship and episcopacy collapsed in the 1640s, their numbers increased, and their demands for religious toleration grew. They were a very small proportion of the country as a whole, a fraction of the puritan movement. In much hostile propaganda, however, the effect of sectarian labels to describe them was to create a more denominationally distinct sectarian milieu than the amorphous and often anonymous reality. Only the Quakers adopted wholesale an initially hostile label, although Laurence Clarkson parodied the widespread attacks upon Ranters by adopting the mantle "Captain of the Rant," even though the "Ranters" themselves had no congregational organization or discipline.

Beginning in 1593, when a Separatist congregation associated with Henry Barrow, John Greenwood, and John Penry was discovered, a number of Conventicles Acts were passed that attempted to forbid potentially subversive gatherings. Some sectaries joined disillusioned puritans in America, where Separatist communities were tolerated more freely than in England. After the Restoration, sects were suppressed with increasing ferocity. The Conventicles Acts of 1664 and 1670 linked the religious motive to conspiratorial gatherings, which the Act of 1593 and the ecclesiastical canons of 1604 had established. These acts gained momentum from fears of a Presbyterian reaction against the Restoration and Thomas Venner's armed Fifth Monarchist uprisings. Quakers, however, were feared more than Presbyterians, mainly for their refusal to swear oaths such as the Oath of Allegiance.

See also: Roger Brearley, Antinomianism, Arminianism, Dissenters, Family of Love, Fifth Monarchists, Puritan Revolution, Ranters, Seekers, Separatists

Further Reading

Patrick Collinson, "The English Conventicle," in W. J. Sheils and Diana Wood, eds. *Voluntary Religion: Papers Read at the 1985 Summer Meeting and the 1986 Winter Meeting of the Ecclesiastical History Society* (Oxford, 1986), pp. 223–259; Patrick Collinson, "Sects and the Evolution of Puritanism," in Francis J. Bremer, ed. *Puritanism: Transatlantic Perspectives on a Seventeenth-Century Anglo-American Faith* (Boston, 1993), pp. 147–166; Christopher Hill, *The World Turned Upside Down* (London, 1972); J. F. MacGregor and Barry Reay, eds. *Radical Religion in the English Revolution* (Oxford, 1984).

Simon Dyton

Seekers

The Seekers were not a coherent or organized radical group within the puritan movement; a Seeker was a puritan who rejected traditional congregationalism. Seekers considered that ecclesiastical *and* formal congregational church government was unable to claim the same divine dispensation that animated the apostles' sanctity. Thus Seekers accused the Church of England and existing gathered congregations of being spiritually defunct, with irrelevant, invalid rituals. They defected from organized forms of worship and awaited the True Church of Christ with millenarian anticipation.

No real Seeker confessions of faith or explicit manifestoes exist, and their attitude is best understood as a broad psychological disposition, one that most radical puritans experienced on their way to finding a sectarian identity that best expressed their conception of salvation. During the 1630s and early 1640s, several Separatist congregations in London were prompted to adopt spiritual rather than biblical justification of religious worship. The Separatist Praise-God "Barebones" Barbon, for example, attacked adult baptism by immersion, not on the grounds that there was no proper scriptural warrant for it, but because it had no "special and particular warrant from heaven, and a Commission," as John the Baptist had Barbon pointed out that such a "Commission" was imminent, along with Christ's Second Coming. Though Barbon was not a Seeker himself, his views shared the same millenarian enthusiasm and deference to apostolic commission that came to be identified with Seeker doctrine. Indeed, Seekers were often the alienated "puritans" whose disillusionment with congregational practice prompted them to abandon external forms of worship.

By the mid-1640s, Seekers achieved sufficient notoriety to be attacked vigorously in Thomas Edwards's *Gangraena: or A Catalogue and Discovery of Many of the Errours, Heresies, Blasphemies and Pernicious Practices of the Sectaries of this Time, Vented and Acted in England in These Last Four Years* (1646). Edwards was quick to identify several separatists as Seekers, including John Saltmarsh, William Walwyn, and William Erbery. These prominent "Seekers" defended themselves against Edwards's attacks, refuting his accusations that they occupied a despairing spiritual limbo, beyond the salvation of external, formal worship. Rather, they promoted the sufficiency of spiritual illumination and personal grace.

These men, typical of many others at the time, refused to accept that any single denomination, congregation, or religious position possessed exclusive claims upon spiritual truth. They saw a measure of spiritual truth in all religious forms and considered dispute and discussion to be ways of revealing and clarifying it. Accordingly, they held liberty of conscience and worship dear and denied that any single church could or should hold absolute authority. Such a position enraged Presbyterians such as Thomas Edwards.

This position lent itself to the naturally occurring sectarian continuum that characterized the evolution of radical positions. Many radicals whose positions were unclear or fluid were located within this category by their opponents: Richard Coppin, John Webster, Giles Randall, William Dell, Roger Williams, and even John Milton. For others, their identification as a Seeker was just one stage in their spiritual careers. Thomas Edwards remarked that Clement Writer, a Worcestershire clothier, had progressed from Seeking to being an "Anti-Scripturist," a "Questionist," a "Sceptick," and an "Atheist." To be a Seeker was less to belong to a religious denomination than to share a radical state of mind that represented the search for authentic forms of worship. Since it was traditionally a heresiological category, it is perhaps surprising that Laurence Clarkson's self-described spiritual evolution included Seeking as a transitional stage between the congregational worship of Baptists and the looser, less formal ways of the Ranters.

As an indeterminate, "intransitive" category that describes the direction of an individual's spiritual evolution, the term *Seeker* accommodated numerous doctrinal positions, which generally included disillusionment with any single particular church, combined with the millenarian conviction that such dissatisfaction would be banished by an imminent spiritual enlightenment. Some Seekers attached themselves to prophets, such as John Pordage, the vicar of Bradfield, who was a follower of the mystic Jakob Böhme, and pursued individual, sometimes eccentric, forms of worship; others emigrated to America, where the self-proclaimed Seeker Roger Williams, for example, founded Providence, Rhode Island. Some have been accused of becoming the first Quakers, though this is a convenient means of explaining the birth of Quakerism, rather than a verifiable account of the Seekers' demise. Indeed, the Quakers did not emerge out of a discernible body of Seekers, and it is difficult to examine the demise of Seekers, who—as a coherent sect—did not exist. Instead, the Seekers were a heresiological category, expressing a yearning for spiritual truth and a rejection of the congregational discipline that was so critical to puritan church organization; a category, or stage, through which alienated and disillusioned puritans passed on their way to finding other denominational positions or formulating other doctrinal beliefs.

See also: George Fox, Ranters, Sects
Further Reading
Christopher Hill, *The World Turned Upside Down: Radical Ideas during the English Revolution* (London, 1972), esp. pp. 184–197; J. F. MacGregor, "Seekers and Ranters," in J. F. MacGregor and Barry Reay, eds., *Radical Religion in the English Revolution* (Oxford, 1984), pp. 121–139.

Simon Dyton

Separatists

A name applied to Elizabethan and early Stuart radical puritans who effectively renounced their membership in the parish system of the Church of England by establishing independent, congregationally oriented churches of their own based on a voluntary covenant relationship. In so doing, they defied the law of the land, which demanded uniformity of religion, and ran the risk of imprisonment, exile, and even capital punishment. Numerous Separatists were incarcerated for their nonconformity; under pressure by the authorities many others fled to Holland into exile. Three Separatists died on the royal gallows at Tyburn in 1593 for their subversive religious activities.

The origins of separatism are rooted in sixteenth-century left-wing puritanism. Some scholars believe that evidence of Continental Anabaptism in England from as early as the 1530s may have provided the seedbed for Separatist ideals, especially their congregational polity. But the evidence for this is meager and inconsequential. There is no traceable Anabaptist influence on the formation of the Separatist tradition. At the turn of the seventeenth century, when separatism had become well established, Dutch Anabaptism left an imprint on the handful of English Separatists in Amsterdam who embraced believer's baptism in 1609, as it did again among another small group of London Separatists who formed the first English Calvinist Baptists in 1640. But the source of separatism as a clearly identifiable ecclesial movement, especially as it first appeared in the city of Norwich in 1581 under the leadership of Robert Browne, is most likely a result of increasingly radical dynamics within English puritan dissent, not an import from the continent.

Separatism flourished briefly in the early years of Queen Elizabeth's reign within the burgeoning radical puritan party. Dissatisfied with the queen's moderate approach to ecclesiastical reform, which puritans in general believed left the Church of England vulnerable to the corruptions of Rome, some of the more extreme puritans were determined to see the established church fully reformed along the more Presbyterian lines of Calvin's experiment at Geneva.

The first indication of a Separatist impulse within this context of radicalized puritanism occurred in 1567, when a group of some 200 puritan extremists were arrested in London. They had been discovered meeting in secret at the Plumbers' Hall for worship. Under interrogation by Bishop Edmund Grindal, it became evident just how far matters had progressed. According to Grindal, the group had for some time been meeting in private homes and in open fields as a fully functioning and independent church. They had ordained their own ministers, elders, and deacons, administered the sacraments and excommunicated those who had seceded from them.

In 1571, a second Separatist cell appeared in London, under the leadership of the puritan minister Richard Fitz. Several members of this second group had previously belonged to the Plumbers' Hall gathering. From prison, Fitz described the church as an oppressed flock of faithful Christians separated from the false worship of the parish churches. By this time, most of the congregation had been arrested and imprisoned along with their pastor, and some had already died in prison. One member, John Bolton, recanted when arrested and turned state's evidence. He later hanged himself out of shame.

Robert Browne founded the first Separatist congregation of enduring significance at Norwich in the spring of 1581. His writings, which offered a distinctly congregational shape to Separatist eccle-siology, provided a fully developed theological rationale for the movement. Browne's plunge into radical religion began at Cambridge University in the early 1570s, where he came under the influence of Thomas Cartwright, puritan lecturer in divinity who denounced episcopacy in favor of presbyterian polity. Without episcopal authority, Browne began preaching in and around Cambridge and soon clashed with authorities about his own increasingly radical views. Browne had become convinced that only congregations, not bishops, had the right to appoint their own pastors.

Convinced that a true church could not exist in the unreformed parish system, Browne, along with his co-religionist Robert Harrison, founded a Separatist church in Norwich. His vision for a fully reformed church and his justification for separatism appeared in his famous work, *A Treatise of Reformation without Tarrying for Any,* in 1582. There he laid out the essentials of Separatist ecclesiology: a true church was composed of visible believers, separated from the world, and voluntarily joined together by a covenant made with God and one another.

Twice imprisoned for his religious activities, Browne was freed through the intervention of an influential relative, William Cecil, Lord Burghley. The Norwich separatists then fled to Middelburg in the Netherlands. Once there, Browne quarreled with Harrison over several issues. Disillusioned and embittered with the experience in Holland, Browne made his way back to England alone. There he was incarcerated for a third time, before he finally recanted his separatism in 1586. Five years later, he received episcopal ordination and became rector of Thorpe Church, where he remained until his death in 1633, though not without further troubles with the authorities for failing to comply fully with established ecclesial practice.

The next wave of Separatist activity occurred in 1587, after Archbishop Whitgift's suppression of puritan ministers. Deprived of his pulpit, the puritan minister John Greenwood joined a small Separatist congregation meeting in London, which was composed of lay remnants of earlier congregations, including Robert Browne's. Shortly after he became their pastor, Greenwood and twenty others from the congregation were arrested. While in prison, Geeenwood was visited by Henry Barrow, a young, rather impetuous London lawyer with court connections who had recently turned to puritanism. Convinced that Greenwood's separatism offered the only true alternative to a corrupt state church, Barrow soon found himself resident of the same prison. He earned the name "hot-brains Barrow" from Whitgift when, under interrogation, Barrow called the archbishop "a monster, a miserable compound . . . neither ecclesiastical nor civil, even that second beast spoken of in the Revelation."

Barrow and Greenwood managed to smuggle several hundred pages of Separatist propaganda out of prison, now available in a three-volume edition edited by Leland H. Carlson. They became the first Separatist martyrs, hanged by royal decree at Tyburn on 6 April 1593. Six weeks later, a third Separatist, John Penry, met the same fate. All three were accused of writing "seditious books" and executed as "traitors to the state."

While Barrow and Greenwood were in prison, a remnant of the congregation continued to function as a fully constituted church, meeting secretly in private homes or in open country where lay members preached and prayed. Most migrated to Amsterdam following the execution of their leaders, where they remained intact, but without pastoral leadership until 1597, when Francis Johnson joined them. Johnson was another Cambridge-trained puritan, who turned Separatist under the influence of Barrow's writings. After five years of imprisonment in the same London jail, Johnson fled to Holland and became the pastor of the Amsterdam congregation, which at that time numbered about forty members.

The congregation prospered numerically under Johnson's leadership; by 1609 William Bradford reported that there were about 300 communicants. But problems haunted congregational life. Disputes over issues of pastoral authority, divorce, and the expensive clothing worn by Johnson's wife chipped away at the communal bond of these exiled Separatists. By far the most devastating blow,

however, came with the arrival in 1608 of Johnson's own disciple John Smyth.

> *See also:* Henry Barrow, Robert Browne, John Greenwood, John Robinson, John Smyth, Anabaptists, Independency
> *Further Reading*
> Stephen Brachlow, *The Communion of Saints: Radical Puritan and Separatist Ecclesiology, 1570–1625* (Oxford, 1988); Murray Tolmie, *The Triumph of the Saints: The Separate Churches of London, 1619–1649* (Cambridge, Eng., 1977); B. R. White, "The English Separatists and John Smyth Revisited," *Baptist Quarterly* 30 (1984), 344–347; B. R. White, *The English Separatist Tradition from the Marian Martyrs to the Pilgrim Fathers* (Oxford, 1971).

Stephen Brachlow

Sermon Notes

Not only did Reformation preachers typically speak from notes rather than sermons written out in full, but their parishioners were avid note takers. Sometimes, in fact, members of the audience produced more complete written versions of sermons than did the preachers themselves. Because of the importance they placed on sermons, puritan laity were especially likely to take such notes. Both types of notes will be considered below.

Three preliminary matters bear mentioning. First, even where we have manuscript notes, whether recorded by preachers or their auditors, and can compare those notes with printed versions of the sermons, it is impossible to reconstruct any sermon as it was actually performed: one never knows whether either the manuscript or the printed version reflects the preacher's actual words—despite claims to the contrary by printers (and occasionally by the preachers themselves). Second, sixteenth- and seventeenth-century European culture was still profoundly oral as well as literary and documentary: people of the Reformation had by today's standards an astounding capacity for memorization. A relatively sketchy set of notes, then, may have effectively served a preacher as reminders of the main points of a sermon fully conceived and committed to memory but never fully

A page from the sermon notebook kept by John Winthrop when he was living in England. (Courtesy Francis J. Bremer)

form-minded preachers preferred original sermons and delivered them whenever possible. More than one divine expressed the opinion that preachers were less able to move their audiences when they spoke by rote than when they spontaneously allowed their own immediate affections and the audience's reactions to influence their choices of words. The preacher who penned his sermon and then read it from the pulpit was the exception. Robert Sanderson was exceptional in this way; the seventeenth-century biographer John Aubrey reported that Sanderson "had no great memorie" and that he "always read his sermons and lectures." Generally, though, it was a point of pride to refer to one's notes sparingly or not at all during a sermon. Since sermons typically lasted an hour (two hours for Paul's Cross sermons), this meant that a preacher needed to develop his skills of memorization, his ability to phrase ideas extemporaneously, or both.

Highly poetic, word-conscious preachers like Lancelot Andrewes, who became a significant theologian and bishop in the English Church, took great care in crafting their sermons and preserving their wording during delivery. In his funeral sermon for Andrewes, John Buckeridge said that "most of his Solemne Sermons he was most carefull of, and exact; I dare say, few of them, but they passed his hand, and were thrice revised before they were preached." Joseph Hall, though less concerned with exactness in his recitation, also wrote complete drafts of his sermons. According to John Lightfoot, Hall "never durst clime up into the Pulpit to preach any Sermon, whereof he had not penn'd every word in the same order, wherein he hoped to deliver it: although in his expression he was no slave to syllables, neither made use of his Notes." At the other extreme is Thomas Bilson, who said of a printed version of a Paul's Cross sermon, "In setting downe the summe of that which I preached, I neither do, nor can promise . . . the same words which I spake; I wrote them not."

On both sides of the Atlantic, the seventeenth century saw a vogue, especially among the more radical reformers, for fully composed and then fully memorized sermons. The Massachusetts puritan Cotton Mather, though, defended notes in the pul-

penned. And note takers often relied on their own memories to fill out their notes after the performance itself. Third, practices for making notes on sermons, both the preacher's notes and those of his hearers, varied widely. Some preachers prided themselves on speaking entirely extemporaneously; others used notes of varying degrees of completeness; and others wrote out their sermons in full, either memorizing them before delivery or simply reading them from the pulpit. Notes taken by sermon goers ranged from skeletal outlines of a sermon's main points to complete transcriptions taken in shorthand.

Preachers' Notes

Simply reading sermons from the pulpit was generally frowned on during the English Reformation. Queen Elizabeth attempted to assert a degree of control over preachers by appointing the official *Book of Homilies* to be read in the churches, but re-pit, making a distinction between "the *reading* of *Notes,* and the *using* of Notes. . . . It is not the want of our Abilities, that makes us use our Notes; but it's a Regard unto our Work, and the good of our Hearers. I use Notes as much as any Man."

Parishioners' Notes

The practice of taking notes during sermons was extremely widespread during the Reformation. Young schoolchildren were commonly encouraged to take down a sermon's main points, and older ones to transcribe sermons as fully as possible, sometimes to memorize and recite them a few days later. Prefaces to printed sermons often expressed gratitude to parishioners for their notes, which helped the preachers prepare accurate manuscripts for printing. Symon Presse, for example, thanked six of his hearers for taking notes, conferring, and penning a good manuscript version of a 1596 sermon.

The 1580s and 1590s witnessed the development of two systems of shorthand put to frequent use in transcribing sermons: Timothy Bright's "Charactery" and Peter Bales's "Brachygraphy." Both systems produced reasonably good results for those who took the pains to learn them. Some preachers used their hearers' transcriptions of shorthand notes as bases for printed sermons, but others objected to the practice: too many shorthand transcribers were not practiced enough to produce acceptable results. Some note takers pirated sermons, selling their versions to printers without the preacher's knowledge. The sixteenth century English clergyman Thomas Playfere complained of a 1595 sermon's pirating: "I had rather have my head broken, then my Sermon so mangled. For this Sermon hath beene twice printed already without my procurement or privity any maner of way. Yea to my very great griefe and trouble." Playfere's consternation is understandable, but generally Reformation sermon goers took notes for the sake of piety rather than profit.

See also: Plain Style, Preaching

Further Reading

Lori Anne Ferrell and Peter McCullough, eds., *The English Sermon Revised: Religion, Literature, and History, 1600–1750* (Manchester, Eng., 2000);

Alan F. Herr, *The Elizabethan Sermon: A Survey and Bibliography* (Philadelphia, 1940); W. Fraser Mitchell, *English Pulpit Oratory from Andrewes to Tillotson: A Study of Its Literary Aspects* (London, 1932).

Bryan Crockett

Sexuality

Puritans had stringent views on the circumstances in which sex should be considered legitimate, but they were not as sexually repressed or repressive as persistent stereotypes would suggest. The sweeping "reformation of manners" they advocated included an assault on all unmarried sex as immoral and disorderly. Yet Puritans encouraged and celebrated sexual intimacy between husband and wife, not only for reproductive purposes but also as an expression of marital love. Puritan pastors taught that believers could envisage two marriages, one with an earthly partner and the other with Jesus Christ, their heavenly bridegroom. They characterized both as romantic, sensual, and passionate.

Puritan theologians did not conceive of sex as a distinct realm of identity. Nor did they define people in terms of a specific sexuality or sexual orientation. Though ministers distinguished between different forms of illicit sex, they did not see any of these as unique in terms of causation. They explained all sinful thoughts and actions, sexual and nonsexual, as a product of the innate depravity that men and women inherited from Adam and Eve. Thus, laziness, disobedience, premarital sex, and sodomy all had the same cause. Because the impulse to engage in illicit sexual relations originated in universal corruption, the temptation to commit such offenses was not specific to any one group of people. "Every child of Adam," declared one Puritan pastor, was "pregnant with the seeds of all sin, though all do not shoot forth together, or in every individual." Sexual and nonsexual sins fed on each other, since any illicit behavior acted as a stimulant to other kinds of sin. Ministers taught that youthful experimentation with masturbation or premarital sex could set malefactors on a course toward adultery, sodomy, or bestiality, especially if early sexual lapses were conjoined with other forms of depravity such as laziness or disobedience. Each person's sexual history thus fit into a larger developmental framework of moral orientation.

The frequent use of words such as *uncleanness* and *defilement* in Puritan discussions of sexual sin reflected their conception of the human body as an arena in which was fought the cosmic struggle between virtuous and wicked impulses. The body was ordained as a temple for the human soul, and believers should take care not to subvert any part of that body for sinful ends. Misuse of the body was a form of desecration as well as evincing immorality, disorder, and disobedience to God's law; it endangered the soul and delighted the devil. Through sermonic exhortation, mutual surveillance, disciplinary measures against errant church members, and legal prosecution for sexual activity other than between husband and wife, Puritans sought to protect each other from self-pollution.

Sex within marriage was not only acceptable, Puritans argued, but even essential. They characterized marital sex as "due benevolence," in which duty converged with pleasure. Sex between husband and wife, they insisted, was as much an expression of love as it was a means to reproduction. Private writings leave no doubt as to the passionate and intensely physical nature of the love that lay at the center of many Puritan marriages. Men were taught that it was a husband's duty to satisfy his wife sexually. A Bostonian in Massachusetts was excommunicated for offenses that included his having abstained from sex with his wife for a period of two years as a self-imposed penance for engaging in premarital sex. According to New England law, male impotence constituted grounds for divorce. The principal issue here was not fertility: a barren man who could perform sexually was still conferring "due benevolence," yet even a woman who could no longer produce children had the right to divorce an impotent man.

The Puritans' validation of marital sex was complicated by their belief that original sin was transmitted from one generation to another through the act of intercourse that led to conception. Sex as an expression of ordained love was thus compromised by sex as the purveyor of sin. Puritans also worried that the physical passion between husband and wife ceased to be sanctified if it became an end in itself or distracted the couple from their devotion to God. Sexual passion must always serve to reinforce emotional and spiritual passion.

The emphasis placed by Puritans upon their prospective marriage to Christ helped to counteract these misgivings about even marital sex. Instead of portraying spiritual marriage as a mystical transcension of earthly unions, Puritan ministers encouraged their flocks to envisage these two forms of marriage as closely analogous and symbiotic. Rather than thinking of marriage as the legacy of Adam and Eve, who were in some respects far from ideal models, they should view human marriage as a foretaste of union with Christ, the second and flawless Adam. This perspective enabled a less equivocal affirmation of marriage and sex within it.

Pastors often depicted marriage with Christ in unabashedly passionate and even erotic language. This was especially the case in New England during the later decades of the seventeenth century and into the early eighteenth century: as ministers sought to convert young people who had not chosen to live in a Puritan colony and who had to be persuaded to join the covenanted community, they sought to do so by describing not only the torments awaiting sinners but also the voluptuous delights that the saved could anticipate once they were resurrected and wedded to their savior. Young converts could thus anticipate fulfillment as passionate sexual beings in both this world and the world to come.

See also: Espousal Imagery, Illegitimacy, Marriage
Further Reading

Richard Godbeer, *Sexual Revolution in Early America* (Baltimore, 2002); Edmund Leites, *The Puritan Conscience and Modern Sexuality* (New Haven, 1986); Roger Thompson, *Sex in Middlesex: Popular Mores in a Massachusetts County, 1649–1699* (Amherst, 1986).

Richard Godbeer

Sin

Sin was defined in the Westminster Shorter Catechism (1648), an instructional tool used by Puritans in Old and New England, as "any want of conformity unto, or transgression of, the law of God." Most of what Puritans thought and said about sin echoed common Christian views, particularly those of St. Augustine and the Protestant reformers, which stressed the power of sin and the greatness of God's grace in overcoming it.

Original Sin

Puritan theologians followed Christian tradition in explaining the origin of sin by reference to the biblical story of Adam's fall. Adam and Eve, in their pre-fall state good by nature like the rest of creation, by free choice rebelled against God and forfeited their original righteousness and communion with God, entailing on their posterity sin, misery, and both physical and spiritual death. This original sin was at first a sin of the will rather than the intellect, the sin of pride and disobedience, the sin for which Satan was cast out of heaven. Puritans particularly emphasized that it was a breach of covenant with God. Original sin was not only propagated through natural generation, but was also imputed to all humankind, insofar as all were in Adam as their "federal" head (the *New England Primer* famously started the alphabet with the rhyme "In Adam's fall, we sinned all"). According to William Ames, all were created in the beginning in Adam; William Perkins described Adam as not just a private but a representative person; Adam, said Samuel Willard, was a common name for the whole human species. This breach of a covenant of works made with humankind in Adam was a central element in a "Federal Theology" that became increasingly important to Puritans throughout the seventeenth century.

Original sin meant that all human beings shared in Adam's guilt, were corrupted by sin, and inherited a propensity to sin, with the earthly misery attendant thereupon. Consequently, humans suffer from a guilty and tormenting conscience defiled and numbed by sin; a will in bondage to sin, unable to obey God and do the good; and an intellect so blinded and impaired that it lacked clear knowledge of God. This defacing of the image of God in humankind and impairment by sin of every human

faculty is the meaning of *total depravity*, a term often connected to Calvinist theology. Some Puritan theologians, however, granted, as did Calvin, that vestiges of free will and reason sufficient for matters of ordinary life and even capable of notable earthly achievement remained, and that even the fallen conscience was sufficiently active to render the sins of human beings inexcusable.

Puritans joined the whole Christian tradition in denying that God was the author of sin. Adam, who had received both righteousness and grace from God, freely chose sin and disobedience; all humankind, whom he represented, thereby participated in his sin. Even after the fall, the will acted without compulsion (a notion deriving from St. Augustine that was a commonplace among many medieval and later Protestant theologians). According to this version of free will, sinners freely sinned even when they could not do otherwise, as they willingly succumbed to the disposition to sin that was their legacy from Adam. Such sinners were therefore morally responsible for their misdeeds. Many Puritan theologians also followed St. Augustine in arguing that sin and evil were privative, that is real but not substantive, created entities; evil was a defect in something otherwise good, since every created thing was good to the extent that it participated in being. Puritans also maintained that God did not ordain evil but permitted it, even the strictest predestinarians denying that God was the author of sin, arguing that in the case of sin, God's will was not a cause but a willing not to prevent. Furthermore, Puritans sometimes argued that God in permitting sin purposed it for his own glory, bringing out of it the greater good of redemption and holiness through Christ. In the last book of Milton's *Paradise Lost*, Adam seems to reflect this view when he rejoices at the future redemption shown him by the archangel Michael, and even wonders whether he should repent his sin when so much good will come of it.

Actual Sin

Puritan and Calvinist theology distinguished actual sin from original sin. According to Ames, actual sins derive from original sin in the same way that acts follow a habit. Actual sins were considered to be of various kinds and degrees of sinfulness, aggravated by reason of the age, experience, or office of those sinning and by the deliberateness or circumstances of the sin. Sins were classified as those of omission and commission, and also as sins of thought, word, or deed. Sins were also divided into those against God and those against other persons, though ultimately the latter were also against God. Although Protestants and Puritans rejected the Roman Catholic distinction of mortal and venial sins, they still held that graver sins would be punished in greater degree. Some Puritans also maintained (for example Willard) that there was no guilt for actual sins until one had come of sufficient age to be morally responsible.

Sin as a Topic in Puritan Spiritual Writings

Books of Puritan spirituality dealt with sin as a devotional consideration as well as a theological topic. A notable example was *The Sinfulnesse of Sinne* (1632) by Edward Reynolds, which developed the main theological points typical of Puritan and Calvinist thinking but then treated the topic in a devotional and homiletic fashion. Thus Reynolds sketched the pollution and loathsomeness of sin and expressed amazement at the patience of God in not casting sinners such as himself immediately into hell. But sin was also regarded as its own punishment, being an evil in the life of the sinful, since it entailed disorders of will and intellect, terrors of guilt, and a state of horror of God's wrath. Such wrath was, according to the Puritans, divine justice acting against sin. For the unrepentant sinner, sin continues even after this life as the perpetual hatred and envy experienced in hell. (For the redeemed, however, past sins, covered by the righteousness of Christ, will not come into judgment after this life, and in heavenly beatitude, believers will be perfected and no longer able to sin.)

But the Puritan focus was not primarily on the punishment of sin, but on sin as that which drives persons to the wonders of forgiving grace. Sin and grace thus stood in a dialectical relationship to each other: the magnitude of sin rendered yet greater the magnitude of that grace that pardoned sin and

worked to overcome it in the lives of believers. Calvinist and Puritan theology, however, insisted that in earthly life sin would always remain in the believer; sinless perfection in this life was regarded as a Roman Catholic error. According to the Calvinist theology of the Puritans, the righteousness of Christ, the sacrificed mediator, was imputed to believers and clothed them in a righteousness not their own. This did not imply, however, as some antinomians claimed, that God saw no sin at all in believers, since the Puritan mainstream felt that the Christian life was a continual struggle, with God's help, against sin. Puritans discussed the growth that came during this struggle as sanctification and described it as involving the continual mortification of sin and vivification of the sinner by the grace of God and the power of the Holy Spirit. Mortification (used in the sense of "making dead," the literal meaning of the Latin word) of sin became an important category in Puritan theology and spiritual writing; John Owen in particular gave a classic statement of the teaching in several treatises devoted to it, including *Of the Mortification of Sin in Believers* (1656). Owen described mortification as the impairment of the principle of sin within believers that warred with its opposite, the principle of grace. Such mortification could overcome the power and strength of sin so that sin lost its dominion over the believer. But sin in the believer ever strives to regain dominion and can only be defeated through the work of the Holy Spirit and the union of the soul with Christ. Reynolds described the fellowship of the believer with Christ as a daily dying to sin.

In spite of their reputation as moralistic, Puritans probably had more to say about sin as a condition than about sins. Indeed, contemporary opponents of the Puritans often charged them with indifference to morality rather than excessive moralism; they were accused of so emphasizing salvation from sin by grace that they undermined morality. But Puritans also had much to say about sins and often did so in their consideration of God's law in the Ten Commandments. The exposition of the Ten Commandments in the Westminster Longer Catechism listed in detail the sins forbidden and the duties enjoined by each commandment. Analyses of this type could be quite searching in their designation of sinful behavior, including not only such personal sins as fornication and drunkenness, but also such social sins as fraud, cruelty, and oppression.

See also: Antinomianism, Federal Theology, Grace, Soteriology, Westminster Catechisms
Further Reading
Randall C. Gleason, *John Calvin and John Owen on Mortification* (New York, 1995); Ernest Benson Lowrie, *The Shape of the Puritan Mind: The Thought of Samuel Willard* (New Haven, 1974); John Von Rohr, *The Covenant of Grace in Puritan Thought* (Atlanta, 1986).

Dewey D. Wallace Jr.

Smectymnuus

Smectymnuus was an acronym based on the initials of Stephen Marshall, Edmund Calamy, Thomas Young, Matthew Newcomen, and William (since *w* was often spelled as two *u*'s) Spurstowe. These ministers cowrote *An Answer to a Book entituled, An Humble Remonstrance* (1641), which was a point-by-point rebuttal of an anonymous tract by Joseph Hall defending *iure divino* episcopacy (that is, arguing that episcopacy was ordained by divine law). Hall's *Episcopacy by Divine Right Asserted* (1640), written with William Laud and his colleagues as advisors, is also criticized. In the consequent exchange, Smectymnuus was defended with a vituperative pamphlet by the poet John Milton.

Given the later careers of Smectymnuus, this and its sequel, *A Vindication of the Answer to the Humble Remonstrance* (1641), are seen as Presbyterian manifestoes. In fact they are masterpieces of ambiguity and opaqueness. In delivering a contrapuntal engagement with Hall's work, there is space for a great deal of spleen against the policies and practices identified with archbishop of Canterbury William Laud and a condemnation of Theodore Beza's *episcopus diabolicus*, the bishop with sole powers of ordination and jurisdiction, but there is deliberate ambiguity in its proposed replacement. The Christian leaders of the apostolic church, Timothy and Titus, were contrasted to their Stuart equivalents, and scriptural bishops and presbyters

were shown to have shared a name (as Hall admitted) and not to have been distinct in their offices. There are hints of support for Presbyterianism, but a reading supportive of primitive episcopacy can also be extracted. There is, for instance, a recurrent reference to bishops as overseers, or superintendents. This ambiguity displays a desire to recruit more moderate readers in addition to established Presbyterians.

See also: Thomas Edwards, William Laud, Stephen Marshall, John Milton, Matthew Newcomen, William Spurstowe, *Antapologia, Gangraena,* Primitive Episcopacy
Further Reading
Ann Hughes, *Gangraena and the Struggle for the English Revolution* (Oxford, 2004); Tom Webster, *Stephen Marshall and Finchingfield* (Chelmsford, Eng., 1999).

Tom Webster

Society for the Propagation of the Gospel in New England

The Society for the Propagation of the Gospel in New England was established on 27 July 1649 by act of Parliament, drafted by Edward Winslow, the "Ordinance for the Advancement of Civilization and Christianity Among the Indians." How best to encourage that "advancement" was debated. In tracts called *The Day-Breaking, If Not the Sun-Rising of the Gospell with the Indians in New-England* (London, 1647), *The Clear Sun-shine of the Gospel Breaking Forth upon the Indians in New-England* (London, 1648), and *The Glorious Progress of the Gospel amongst the Indians in New England* (London, 1649), Winslow had published accounts of conversion and education reported by missionaries John Eliot and Thomas Mayhew, together with John Dury's indications that the Indians could be the lost ten tribes of Israel. These reports inspired enthusiasts of Last Days speculation, recently stimulated by the execution of King Charles I, with the prospect of converting the Jews (believed to be a necessary prelude to the coming of Christ's reign on earth) by converting the Indians, fitting in with the mounting excitement also expressed in the

Fifth Monarchy movement. Excitement soon waned, and collecting money in England for missionary activity slowed. New Englanders suspected misuse of funds by the society headed by William Steele in London, while the English became suspicious of the accounting sent to explain what had happened to donations sent, in the form of clothing and tools.

The society's most important project was the support of the salaries of Eliot and Mayhew. Besides preaching, the most efficient way to improve the conditions of Indians was, thought Winslow, to send agricultural tools they could use. Officials in New England evidently wanted the corporation to send goods that could be sold to colonists so that the funds could be employed to reimburse the expense of acquiring land for Christian Indian settlements, as well as for construction of an Indian school at Harvard, where Indian youths could be trained for the ministry, eventually to evangelize in Algonquian. Eliot, assisted by Job Nesutan and John Sassamon, began translation and publication of the New Testament in the Massachusetts language, of which 1,500 copies were printed in 1661 by Samuel Green, his Nipmuck apprentice James the Printer, and Marmaduke Johnson, a printer sent over to New England by the corporation, which also in 1654 sent the press and materials for the project. Translations of the Old Testament (finished in 1663–1,000 copies), of Richard Baxter's *A Call to the Unconverted,* and of *The Practise of Piety* by Lewis Bayly followed.

Eliot envisioned remaking Indian society following Old Testament models. This drastic alteration was intended to prepare Indians for the divine work of conversion and also protect them from colonists' territorial expansion. Eliot helped establish numerous Praying Towns, of which the most important was at Natick, founded in 1650. Others included Punkapoag (1653–1657), Hassanamesit, Okommakamesit, and Nashobahh (1653–1654), Wamesit (1656–1664), and Magunkog (1669). Changes in Indian social relationships brought complaints from leaders not receiving accustomed tribute, as well as incomprehension from Indians unconvinced of the superiority of new rules. May-

hew less drastically established an Indian congregation on Martha's Vineyard, with a consistory like a tribal council. In England, impatience for quantifiable results led to complaints that the numbers of converts failed to meet expectations.

King Philip's War (1675–1676) disrupted the work, since colonists interned Christian Indians. In declining health after the war, Eliot saw the Natick Indians ordain Daniel Tokkohwompait to be their minister (1683). The corporation had been given a new charter at the Restoration, and it continued its work throughout New England after King Philip's War. Samuel Sewall was the committee's secretary for twenty years. In the mid-eighteenth century, Samson Occum was supported by the corporation. After the Revolutionary War, the corporation moved to Canada.

See also John Eliot, Thomas Mayhew, Indian Bible, King Philip's War, Praying Towns
Further Reading
Richard W. Cogley, *John Eliot's Mission to the Indians before King Philip's War* (Cambridge, MA, 1999).

Jeremy Bangs

Socinianism
See Anti-Trinitarianism

Soldier's Bible
Sometimes erroneously known as "Cromwell's Soldier's Bible," *The Souldier's Pocket Bible* (1643) was a sixteen-page pamphlet of inspirational biblical extracts, published during the first English Civil War. The image of the New Model Army as a godly host infused with Puritan radicalism has been fostered in no small part by the belief that every soldier carried a Bible in his knapsack. Historians skeptical of this claim have sometimes argued that the Bible in question may actually have been *The Souldier's Pocket Bible.* There is no evidence, however, that Cromwell had any hand in its creation, and it should be noted that *The Souldier's Pocket Bible* was published two years before the formation of the New Model.

Supervised by Edmund Calamy senior, who was named on the frontispiece, *The Souldier's Pocket Bible* was clearly intended to fortify Parliament's troops against the psychological stresses of combat, as well as to reassure them of the religious and ideological propriety of their cause. Short biblical texts, almost exclusively taken from the Old Testament, were arranged under eighteen different headings, intended as an exhortation to fight God's enemies and as a checklist of moral instruction. The source of the texts appears to have been the Geneva Bible rather than the Authorized Version. Whether this soldier's Bible was intended to be issued free to all parliamentary troops, or whether it was simply offered for general sale is a matter of debate. It was certainly available to the London public from the outset, as shown by George Thomason's purchase of a copy on 3 August 1643. It is known, however, that Bibles of some description were ordered for free issue to parliamentary units (albeit not to individual soldiers) in later campaigns in Ireland, the West Indies, and France in the 1650s.

Although *The Souldier's Pocket Bible* is the most notable book of devotion intended for the Parliamentary armies, similar publications of the time included *The Christian Soldier, or a Preparation for Battle* (1642) and *The Soldier's Catechism* (1644) by Robert Ram. Ram's *Catechism* ran to two more editions in 1645, and was reprinted again in 1686. By the time he was appointed major-general of the New Model infantry in 1645, Philip Skippon had published no less than three pamphlets of religious advice intended specifically for military use. The royalist forces in turn published their own "soldier's Bible," entitled *Certain Prayers Fitted to Severall Occasions and Are to be Used in His Majesty's Armies and Garrisons* (1645). This pamphlet even suggested psalms to be sung at the changing of the garrison guard—a feature omitted from the pages of the second edition in 1648. Either this royalist title, or the original *Souldier's Pocket Bible* appear to have influenced later versions of the genre, such as *The Christian Soldier's Penny Bible*, a collection of scriptural texts arranged under twenty headings, published in 1693 with the intention that it should be carried by English soldiers and sailors campaigning against France.

See also: Bible, Geneva Bible, New Model Army
Further Reading
Cromwell's Soldier's Bible (facsimile of the original 1643 ed.; Pryor, Eng., 1997); Charles H. Firth, *Cromwell's Army* (London, 1902).

David J. Appleby

Solemn League and Covenant

An alliance between Scotland and the English parliamentary faction subscribed about one year after the beginning of the first English Civil War. The basis of the document was shaped by the Scottish minister Alexander Henderson, and after about ten days of negotiation in Edinburgh, Scottish and English representatives signed it on 17 August 1643. It consisted of six articles: (1) maintenance of the Reformed religion, defined "according to the word of God, and the example of the best reformed churches"; (2) "the extirpation of popery"; (3) defense of loyalty to the king, and a pact to defend political liberties; (4) rooting out of "incendiaries" who promote division; (5) maintenance of peace between Scotland and England; (6) defense of the unity of leaguers. Article 1 committed the signatories to "indeavour to bring the churches of God in the three kingdoms, to the neerest conjunction and uniformity in religion," and led to the sending of Scottish representatives to the Westminster Assembly.

There were significant tensions between the parties, and only the military emergency faced by the English parliament was able to produce this league. Gilbert Burnet was under no illusions, pointing out that the two parties did not share a common set of religious aims in what was a decidedly religious document, the Scots believing that they could use the covenant to press their Presbyterian system on the English, while the English believed that they had fortified themselves against any such eventuality. In Scotland, the Solemn League and Covenant (SLC) was approved by both a convention of estates (an informal parliament) and the general assembly of the Kirk, and after approval in England, the Scottish committee of estates, on 22 October, issued an edict that called on all Scots to subscribe the league, under penalty of confiscation of goods or worse. In England the Commons and the Westminster Assembly subscribed it on 25 September 1643; the upper chamber followed on 15 October, followed by London congregations the next Sunday. Parliament, in February 1644, ordered that everyone in England over the age of eighteen must subscribe.

The rise of the New Model Army, the purging of parliament, and the Cromwellian years meant that the Solemn League and Covenant was to have an abbreviated life. In Scotland, however, it was, in evangelical Presbyterian minds, joined inseparably with the National Covenant, the two providing a beacon in the darkness of prelacy and other, later, religious decay.

See also: National Covenant, Westminster Assembly
Further Reading
Edward J. Cowan, "The Solemn League and Covenant," in R. A. Mason (ed.), *Scotland and England 1286–1815* (Edinburgh, 1987); David G. Mullan, "'Uniformity in Religion': The Solemn League and Covenant (1643) and the Presbyterian Vision," in W. Fred Graham, ed., *Later Calvinism: International Perspectives* (1994); David Stevenson, *The Scottish Revolution 1637–1644* (1973).

David Mullan

Soteriology

A term in Christian theology that refers to the study of a scheme or doctrine of salvation, usually specifically the doctrine that salvation comes through Christ. Soteriological concerns were at the very core of the Puritan movement, as they were for the Protestant Reformation in general. In Christian theology and in particular the Reformed, or Calvinist, theology of the Puritans, soteriology dealt both with God's willing and effecting of salvation through Christ and with the application of salvation to those who were its beneficiaries. As a plan of salvation, then, soteriology includes the person and work of Christ: Christ as both human and divine and therefore as mediator between God and hu-

manity through his offices of prophet, priest, and king. Puritan theology, following Reformed theology generally as it developed in the sixteenth and seventeenth centuries, articulated soteriology through two main schemes, the covenant and the *ordo salutis,* "order of salvation." Both schemes were rooted in the Bible and in the writings of early Reformed theologians such as Martin Bucer, Heinrich Bullinger, John Calvin, and Peter Martyr Vermigli; both were sequential in form, the covenant scheme providing a history of salvation as it unfolded in scripture and the order of salvation presenting salvation analytically as a process. The Westminster Confession of Faith (1648) melded covenant theology and the order of salvation. In addition to covenant and order, Calvinist and Puritan soteriology also developed the concept of the means of grace. Insofar as covenant (Federal Theology), Christology, and atonement are described elsewhere, this entry will focus on the order of salvation and the means of grace.

The Order of Salvation

Based on Romans 8:30, the order of salvation appeared in the writings of Bucer and Peter Martyr, two Continental Reformed theologians active in England during the Edwardian Reformation, and in the works of such early English Protestants as John Ponet and John Bradford. The order of salvation consisted of a number of stages in the work of salvation, although different theologians offered slightly different versions of the order. Romans 8:30 laid out four stages: predestination, calling (vocation), justification, and glorification. William Perkins's *A Golden Chaine* (first edition 1590; revised 1592), an early Puritan classic of soteriology, laid out the order of election, effectual calling, justification, sanctification, glorification, eternal life. William Ames's scheme inserted adoption between justification and sanctification. The Westminster Confession of Faith treated perseverance as prior to glorification, and other schemes included conversion and regeneration among the elements of the order.

Thus the order of salvation included a number of elements. Predestination, or more properly, election, as predestination to eternal life, began the order, referring to God's gracious will from eternity to save the undeserving; it was typically described as being election in Christ. Vocation, or effectual calling, unlike the outward call by the word of the gospel common to elect and reprobate alike, was an effectual work of grace, an inward call by the Holy Spirit that drew believers to Christ and renewed them, spiritually uniting them to Christ. Sometimes regeneration and conversion were treated as aspects of the order separate from vocation, regeneration as the renewal of the fallen mind and will through the power of the Holy Spirit, and conversion as the actual turning of the renewed person toward God. Justification involved God's forgiveness of sinners and his acceptance of Christ's righteousness in their stead. The saving faith that accompanied justification was itself a gift of God's grace, enabling the believer to trust in Christ for the forgiveness of sin, and it was ordinarily regarded as preceding justification, even though God had purposed the justification of the elect from eternity. But actual justification from eternity was seen as antinomian heresy. Some theologians insisted that vocation, regeneration, and justification were simultaneous, lest it be thought that God was forgiving regenerated persons on account of their regeneration, and not accepting them as sinners.

Those effectually called and justified were also adopted into the privileges of the children of God; according to Ames, by grace in adoption believers received the dignity of sonship and the inner witness of the Holy Spirit. But it was by sanctification that the believer became actually holy, increasingly freed from the power of sin, and obedient to God. Perseverance of the Saints was often discussed in relation to the order of salvation as the promise of God to complete in elect believers what had been begun in them. Perseverance was grounded in God's grace and indefectible. This did not, however, mean that the elect could not fall into grave sins, thus incurring God's displeasure, depriving themselves of the comforts and assurance of grace, and bringing upon themselves temporal punishments. Of course some might falsely assume that they were among the elect who would then not persevere to salvation. Glorification came last in the order of salvation and referred to the final beatitude and heavenly rest to which the elect would come. This order of salvation was never just a theological scheme for Puritan writers and preachers; it was also a pattern for analyzing and encouraging the devout life, in which many grounds of assurance were found.

The Means of Grace

Another aspect of Puritan and Calvinist soteriology was consideration of the instruments, known as the means of grace, by which persons actually came to redemption. These were ways through which God graciously accommodated himself to human weakness to bring persons to faith and salvation. By the means of grace, God worked through the secondary causality of things in the world to effect divine purposes. Classically in Reformed theology the means of grace were Word and Sacrament, the verbal proclamation of the gospel through scripture and sermon and the symbolic proclamation through baptism and the Lord's Supper. But other instruments were described as means of grace: Richard Sibbes considered prayer, meditation, and even godly conversation as also means of grace, and many considered the Sabbath among them. These means of grace were effective both at the beginning and throughout the lives of believers. But of course none were effective apart from the working of the Holy Spirit.

See also: Assurance of Salvation, Atonement, Christology, Conversion Process, Federal Theology, Glorification, Grace, Predestination
Further Reading
Charles Lloyd Cohen, *God's Caress: The Psychology of Puritan Religious Experience* (New York, 1986); John Von Rohr, *The Covenant of Grace in Puritan Thought* (Atlanta, 1986); Dewey D. Wallace Jr., *Puritans and Predestination: Grace in English Protestant Theology, 1525–1695* (Chapel Hill, 1982).

Dewey D. Wallace Jr.

Spiritual Healing
Puritan clergy of the seventeenth century were often called upon to serve as physicians of the soul

in attempting to heal individuals suffering from an extreme form of melancholy or spiritual depression. In particularly difficult cases, such as that of Mrs. Joan Drake, a number of clergy might attempt to aid the afflicted individual, sometimes acting in concert. Success in curing such an individual could significantly enhance a clergyman's reputation, as was the case when Thomas Hooker succeeded with Mrs. Drake. In cases where a variety of clergymen were engaged in ministering to an individual, the efforts helped to strengthen godly communications.

See also: Joan Drake
Further Reading
Tom Webster, *Godly Clergy in Early Stuart England: The Caroline Puritan Movement, c. 1620–1643* (Cambridge, Eng., 1997).

Francis J. Bremer

Sports and Recreation
Sports

A person's position in the social structure of medieval or early modern England determined to a substantial degree the kinds of sports available to him or her. The most celebrated sporting events of the late Middle Ages, ritualistic fights among military men, had moved from the wild melees of the twelfth and thirteenth centuries, in which large numbers of men from all classes bashed each other senseless, to the formal jousting tournaments of the fourteenth and fifteenth centuries, which took place primarily between knights who were members of an elite. Well-placed ladies served as patrons of these tournaments—perhaps the equivalent of modern cheerleaders—and common men and women attended in large and often drunken numbers as wildly roaring partisans of one jouster or another. Monarchs and nobles organized these great spectacles, and the church continually opposed them as unchristian and cruel. Although jousting tournaments died out in the half century before Puritanism emerged in Elizabethan England, the church's assertion of its role as the arbiter of appropriate sporting conduct did not. Thus, when the reformers who became known as Puri-

tans developed views on theology, organizational structure, and practices of worship, it seemed natural for them also to assert views on sport, which they freely did.

Three major categories of sports provided much diversion to the English at mid-sixteenth century and furnished possibilities for Puritan reformers to approve of or condemn: hunting and fishing, ball games, and blood sports. English men of all ranks loved hunting, but increasingly over the previous several centuries, legal codes had restricted access to forests where game was available to members of the nobility and their friends. Nobles often granted access to the clergy and gentry and occasionally to the landed peasantry, but much of the hunting was done by poor poachers who loved both the thrill of the kill and its fruits. Access to fishing proved somewhat easier but still was restricted. Less equipment was needed for fishing, however, and women as well as men of all ranks took advantage of the opportunity afforded by a land crisscrossed with streams and dotted with ponds to have fun and catch supper while doing so. Ball games had been enjoyed primarily by women and children in England until the fourteenth century, but under the influence of a contrary French example, English men began to play also. Here, too, class lines fragmented the experience. The elite played tennis and handball, and those lower down the social ladder played bowls, stone-hurling, and football. As for the blood sports, they truly deserved their name: almost all of them did indeed require blood to be shed. Some pitted animal against animal—dog- or cockfighting; some pitted man against animal—bull or bearbaiting; and some pitted man against man—cudgel fighting or boxing.

Thus the stockpile of sporting recreations that presented itself to the Puritan reformers for commentary was rife with class divisions, historical associations, and violence. Puritans endorsed hunting and fishing because they liked the productive potential inherent in each, and they resented the historic attempts of the idle nobility to reserve the land for their own selfish purposes. Reformers condemned virtually all ball games. Tennis and handball, Puritans associated historically with the courtyards of monasteries and the Catholic clergy. Football usually pitted whole villages against each other and engendered frequent limb-breaking violence. Bowling lent itself too easily to gambling and indolence. One did not have to be a religious reformer to despise the blood sports: anyone with even the slightest pretence of morality would have to be horrified by their cruelty. Puritans thus joined their efforts to the voices of all respectable English men and women who condemned making sport of injuring God's creatures, whether man or beast.

Puritan attitudes toward sports became famously entangled in their theological debates within the Church of England and their political battles with the monarchy when James I issued the Book of Sports in 1616 and his son, Charles I, reissued it in 1633. Required to be read from every pulpit, the Book of Sports became one of the greatest symbols of royal repression to the Puritans because it offended their commitment to Sabbatarianism by encouraging people to play games on Sundays. Puritans regarded the Book of Sports as an invitation to sin, and it exponentially increased their association of sporting activities with the Anglican apostasy and monarchical despotism. However, their railing against the Book of Sports has given their historical image more of an anti-sport and anti-pleasure reputation than it deserves.

Sports fared much better in Puritan practice in New England than they had in Puritan rhetoric in the old world. Ball games and blood sports were generally proscribed, but a tolerance of nine-pin bowling developed by mid-seventeenth century. With an entire region committed to godliness, New England's saints did not have to worry as much as ones in the home isles that any ball sport would inevitably lead to ancillary vice. All able-bodied males in New England between the ages of sixteen and sixty had to take part in militia training exercises, which invariably produced contests and games associated with martial skills befitting warriors training to defend Zion. Foot and horse races and marksmanship contests were commonplace and much fun by all accounts, and they honed military skills at the same time. Wrestling contests became extremely popular and, unlike boxing or cudgel fights, produced few injuries and drew no blood.

Hunting was widespread in Puritan America and pursued by many, but some of the unsavory connotations that had become associated with hunting in England still clung to it in New England. It often seemed wasteful because of the vast assortment of props that the nobility had used—horses, dogs, hawks, falcons, and gamekeepers. And, although New England teemed with wild game, the early settlers found their muskets to be inadequate for bringing down most animals with the exception of birds. Hence, fowling became the most practiced and respectable New England form of hunting because it was the least wasteful. Fishing, however, became the mania of the region because it was so remarkably productive, available virtually everywhere, and open to all. Women and girls occasionally fished, but more frequently they accompanied men and boys on fishing outings—picnics for everyone that produced as much food as was consumed. Fishing had associated virtues that commended it to Puritans: depending upon the circumstances, it could be either very companionable or contemplative. Unlike in England, where fishing and hunting remained much regulated, New England guaranteed "free fishing and fowling" to all.

After Charles II assumed the throne in England, sports took on a new prominence and a decidedly modern cast. Ball games moved from their hitherto irregular status to a new level of organization with advance advertising, paying crowds and paid players, record keeping, and betting. Cricket, boxing, and horse racing became spectator sports, and cudgel fighting became bloodier and more frequent. Track and field events standardized distances, weights, and rules. Freak shows with races between dwarfs or men with wooden legs or scantily clad women joined the panoply of events that drew large crowds. The vulgarization and violence associated with sport in Restoration England confirmed the New England Puritans in their beliefs that most sport should be avoided, and the attitudes and practices of the founding generation persisted to a remarkable degree throughout the colonial era. During the American Revolution, soldiers from the southern and middle colonies were surprised that New England boys had never played ball games and introduced many of them to new sports. Nathaniel Hale, the hero-to-be, discovered that he loved football and was good at it.

Recreation

Despite their historical reputation as dour killjoys, the reformers in England who hammered out alternative theologies and advocated lives of piety were sophisticated men and women who fully appreciated the need for recreation. They asked only that recreations not be contrary to scripture, despoil others, become addictive, waste much time, consume great resources, or incline one toward collateral sins. They liked especially recreations that were educational or instructive, truly did relax body and soul, and could be pursued in groups. Puritans also, of course, were English and shared many of the habits, thoughts, traditions, and antipathies of their fellow subjects.

A few recreational subjects have become so negatively associated with the historical image of the Puritans on both sides of the Atlantic that they require specific myth-debunking discussion. Puritans were not hostile to music or musical instruments, though they were, indeed, opposed to any instruments or organized choral arrangements during church services. This use of music smacked far too much, they thought, of Roman Catholic practice, which they associated with the anti-Christ. Puritans were not against all forms of dancing but were opposed to men and women dancing together as partners, "gynecandrical dancing" as Increase Mather termed it, because this might easily arouse inappropriate sexual passions. Not only did Puritans not proscribe the drinking of alcohol, they endorsed the consumption of beer and wine as a positive good, though of course they condemned drunkenness and punished it severely. Card games, which took England by storm in the sixteenth and seventeenth centuries, did pose a dilemma to Puritans. They associated cards with the Italians and French, both of whom they assumed were usually depraved in their pursuit of amusements. Additionally, cards lent themselves easily to

gambling and indolence. On the other hand, card games were cheap, easily accessed, great fun, and could teach arithmetic skills. In general, most Puritan moralists never explicitly condemned card games but remained uneasy about them. In New England, however, during the late seventeenth century, whist became an extremely popular card game and enjoyed widespread social acceptability. Whist parties became commonplace and often had more than a dozen participating couples.

The communal impulse that lay at the heart of reformers who emphasized a congregational polity inclined Puritans to pursue recreations in groups—to have congregational fun. Quiet socializing over food, conversation, and good fellowship played a major role in their entertainments. Family meals were usually gregarious affairs, even if only members of the household were present, and often local guests or traveling visitors added an extra measure of conviviality. On Sundays, Puritans customarily gathered between the morning and afternoon services to chat about crops, friends, and news, and to enjoy "the good fare of brown bread and the Gospel," as one Connecticut man wrote. They celebrated great events with thanksgiving meals—the first historical Thanksgiving in Plymouth was part of an ongoing tradition—or they commemorated sad events with communal fasts. They liked tea parties, celebrated weddings with feasting, and had weekend-long parties to celebrate the ordination of a new minister. In New England, they frequently held house and barn raisings, wood cuttings, corn harvests, and sewing, quilting, and spinning bees. Young men and women often got together in mixed or in same-sex parties to read aloud to each other or to pick berries. Puritans regarded themselves as their brothers' and sisters' keepers and also as members of a special network of friends knit together in common purpose.

Some of the recreations that Puritans denounced may surprise us today. They hated theater for valuing public lying on stage and because they believed it to be unduly sensual, subversive of authority, frivolous, and addictive. They celebrated no holidays on a regular basis because they associated the practice with Catholic idolatry and superstitious worship of false saints: in particular, they hated Christmas because they believed it was ahistorical—no evidence existed to suggest that Jesus had been born on 25 December—and because that date had once been a pagan holiday. New England's most famous (infamous) recreation, bundling, did not begin to be practiced until the early eighteenth century and was confined primarily to the lower classes. Always controversial throughout its short life span, bundling came to be vigorously attacked at mid-eighteenth century and disappeared shortly after the American Revolution.

In sum, Puritans enjoyed diversions from daily labor, as do most people. They did not believe in a life of self-denying asceticism, but they did scrutinize all recreations carefully to ensure that they were consistent with God's wishes and with the public good. They did betray a deep-seated fear, born primarily of their own reading of history, that recreation, while essential to human existence, could easily lead one astray from the central purpose of living a godly life. This produced in Puritans an unusual wariness that the devil may be lurking near the most innocent of recreations in order to pounce on an unsuspecting soul.

See also: Ballads, Book of Sports, Leisure Time, Theology of, Music, Reformation of Manners, Theater and Opposition

Further Reading

Bruce C. Daniels, *Puritans at Play: Leisure and Recreation in Colonial New England* (New York, 1995); Alice Morse Earle, *Stage Coach and Tavern Days* (New York, 1900); Allen Guttmann, *From Ritual to Record: The Nature of Modern Sports* (New York, 1978); Robert Malcolmson, *Popular Recreations in English Society, 1700–1850* (London, 1973); Robert Blair St. George, *Material Life in America, 1600–1860* (Boston, 1988); Nancy L. Struna, *People of Prowess: Sport, Leisure, and Labor in Early Anglo-America* (Urbana, 1996).

Bruce C. Daniels

Star Chamber

The Star Chamber, named for the room at Westminster Palace in which it sat, was a law court presided over by members of the Privy Council, the two Chief Justices, and the Lord Chancellor. Star Chamber was a court of "criminal equity": it dealt with public misdemeanors, and its jurisdiction covered offenses against the enforcement of the law (such as riot, perjury, conspiracy, and forgery). It was clearly distinguished from courts of common law: in Star Chamber, trials were not by jury but proceeded on the examination and depositions of witnesses under oath. It could not, therefore, prosecute felonies nor impose the death penalty. It could levy fines, order whippings and the pillory, and imprison at pleasure. Because of its origins in the king's council, it brought to these pronouncements and punishments the authority of the monarch.

By the seventeenth century, the government's use of Star Chamber proved a matter for puritan concern. It was the venue for the prosecution of the Presbyterian party in Elizabeth's reign, prosecution that contributed to that party's political demise by the 1590s. In the reign of the early Stuarts, Star Chamber fell increasingly into disrepute, in part due to the hostile polemic of its major competitors, the common lawyers; in part due to its reputation for repressive and tyrannical exercise of its jurisdiction. Star Chamber prosecution was one of the important instruments of Charles I's rule without Parliament, and his reign witnessed a rash of prosecutions for refusal to pay ship money, an assessment in 1636 the legitimacy of which was widely questioned, and for political criticism of his religious policy.

The most famous conflict between puritans and the state conducted in Star Chamber was the trial and conviction of Henry Burton, John Bastwick, and William Prynne in 1637. Convicted of anti-episcopal pamphleteering, the three men were sentenced to ear dockings and stints in the pillory, which made them visible symbols of the king's abuse of his legal power. Puritans regarded Star Chamber with increasing fear and contempt as relations between them and the Church of England, and between king and Parliament, broke down in the late 1630s. The Long Parliament abolished Star Chamber in 1641.

See also: Crime and Punishment

Further Reading
J. H. Baker, *An Introduction to English Legal History* (London, 1979); G. R. Elton, *Star Chamber Stories* (London, 1958).

Lori Anne Ferrell

Subscription

Subscription to the doctrine of royal supremacy, that is, acknowledging that the monarch of England was the head of the Church of England, by all clergy was required under the Act of Supremacy of 1559, and in 1571 Parliament required that those clergy with cure of souls should subscribe to the Thirty-nine Articles, though there was some debate on this requirement, and subscription was confined to their doctrinal content. Subscription normally took place on entry to a parochial charge, so that a number of positions in the established church, including prestigious college fellowships, did not require it. In this context several puritan clergy were able to find posts within the church, and sympathetic bishops such as Edmund Grindal were willing to accept conditional subscription from preaching ministers in the years up to 1580. The arrival of John Whitgift at Canterbury in 1583 tightened the subscription procedure significantly. His Three Articles of 1583 extended subscription to holders of all ecclesiastical posts and, in addition to the royal supremacy and the Thirty-nine Articles, required the clergy to subscribe to the Book of Common Prayer as containing nothing contrary to the word of God. This struck at the heart of the doubts that moderate puritans held over ceremonies and occasioned a vigorous response from the puritan clergy and their lay supporters, with petitions issuing from several countries. Whitgift was forced to modify the second article, accepting a promise from puritan ministers simply to use the Book of Common Prayer; a major crisis was averted and only a small number of clergy were deprived.

Whitgift's articles remained in place, but subscription was not enforced consistently until, in 1604, the Canons tightened up procedures considerably. Canon 36 insisted that both episcopacy and the Book of Common Prayer contained nothing contrary to the word of God and set out a required form of subscription that closed down those opportunities for equivocation that had hitherto existed. The canon applied to all clergy, in whatever posts, and also included censures against bishops and other authorities who did not enforce it. A further canon, 77, applied the same test to schoolmasters, thereby closing down an alternative route for puritan clergy. The enforcement of the Canons, despite Richard Bancroft's determination, was marked by the same sort of negotiation as had taken place in 1584–1585, and some bishops were forced to accept equivocal submissions from clergy in the puritan heartlands, especially in Northamptonshire and East Anglia. Nevertheless, in the years following 1604, some eighty clergy appear to have been deprived for failure to subscribe, though some, like John Dod, found posts in the homes of their gentry patrons, and others were replaced by men of similar views if of more compliant temperament. With the universities turning out more graduates, and requiring subscription to the Book of Common Prayer from those wishing to progress to higher degrees, access to the early Stuart church became more difficult for the radical puritan, and this was even more so in the 1630s, when episcopal policy became more uniform and closely supervised.

Subscription to the Solemn League and Covenant was never a requirement for clergy during the Civil Wars and Interregnum, though many did subscribe, but the failure of comprehension at the Restoration and the Act of Uniformity of 1662 once again required subscription from the clergy: in this case a declaration of "assent" to the Book of Common Prayer, an acknowledgment that it was unlawful to take up arms against the king, and a repudiation of the Solemn League and Covenant. In addition, those without episcopal orders (that is, those who had not been ordained by a bishop) were required to seek them. The act allowed a mere fourteen weeks to fulfill these requirements, and August 1662 marked a watershed for Puritanism, as over 2,000 clergy left the Church of England, and Dissent was born.

See also: Clarendon Code, Comprehension, Dissenters, Ejections of Clergy, Solemn League and Covenant, Swearing
Further Reading
Patrick Collinson, *The Elizabethan Puritan Movement* (London, 1967); Kenneth Fincham, ed., *The Early Stuart Church* (Basingstoke, Eng., 1993).

William Sheils

Surplice

A knee-length white linen tunic worn by clergymen officiating at all religious services. It was the one vestment that the 1552 and 1559 Book of Common Prayer required English clergy to use. From the beginning many reformers protested the use of this "papist" garb, claiming that it distinguished the clergy from believers and implied that they held special powers. This opposition precipitated a number of "vestiarian controversies." While some puritan ministers managed to successfully evade the requirement, others were suspended or deprived for their failure to wear the surplice. In New England the use of the vestment was discarded.

See also: Vestments
Further Reading
John Primus, *The Vestments Controversy* (Kampen, 1960).

Francis J. Bremer

Swearing

Swearing in early modern England meant calling on God to witness the truth of what one said. English puritans were acutely sensitive to the dangers inherent in swearing, due to the third commandment's ban on taking the name of God in vain. They were horrified by "profane swearing and cursing," the rash use of God's name in trivial or dissolute circumstances, and they were wary of the misuse of solemn oaths in legal proceedings and elsewhere.

Profane Swearing

Puritans were characterized by their intolerance of profane swearing. Lucy Hutchinson recalled that whoever could not endure a blasphemous oath was immediately dubbed puritan by opponents. In accounts of their own conversions, many puritans recalled a misspent youth when they were addicted to swearing, among other vices. After conversion, puritans not only found it impossible to take God's name in vain but recoiled at the casual profanities of their neighbors and associates. So wary were they of blasphemy, puritans adopted a distinct mode of speech and avoided all asseverations. Their language not only made them socially distinctive, but it also rendered them excellent targets for ridicule by satirists and playwrights. Several godly ministers were also troubled by the persistence of popular forms of swearing, such as "By Our Lady," that implied a residual Roman Catholic belief.

Puritan preaching and moralizing stressed the spiritual dangers of profane swearing. It was the work of the devil, a sin without pleasure or profit, a certain route to damnation, and a provocation to God to visit divine wrath upon the land. In 1606 James I banned profane swearing in plays, and a statute of 1624 imposed a fine on those who swore in public of twelve pence per oath. Fines were levied on swearers in several parts of the country during the Interregnum, and the proposed constitution of 1655 suggested that no "profane swearer, nor curser" should be allowed to serve in Parliament. This concern with the personal and public dangers of swearing did not abate. In 1695 the Jacobean statute was replaced by an act that made convictions easier by reducing the number of witnesses required from two to one. Swearing was a central concern in the recurrent campaigns for the "reformation of manners."

Solemn Oaths

Solemn oaths were widely used in law courts and in the appointment of officials in early modern England. Solemn oaths were either "promissory," as when one promised to keep a bargain or tell the truth, or "assertory," as when one asserted or denied a matter of fact. Puritans, like most Protestants, recognized the utility of oaths to end controversies and to bind consciences, and they acknowledged that scripture authorized such a use of the name of God. They did not wish to be identified with groups such as the Lollards, Baptists, and Quakers, who refused all oaths on the grounds of Matthew 5:34. Like most of their contemporaries, they regarded Roman Catholics as duplicitous in the matter of oaths and despised the Jesuit teaching that equivocation and mental reservation could be used to subvert a solemn oath. English puritans were scornful of their society's easy reliance on oaths and particularly critical of the way that churchwardens were routinely required to swear to the truth of returns of which they could not possibly have personal knowledge.

There were several solemn oaths that caused acute difficulties for puritans. The "ex officio" oath or oath of inquiry, had a long history in the church courts. It required a defendant to swear to tell the truth before knowing what she or he was to be questioned about. It had been used against Lollards and early Protestants, but from the 1580s until its abolition along with the Court of High Commission in 1641, the "ex officio" oath was one of the government's most despised weapons against puritans. It was regarded as inquisitorial and alien to the fundamental principle that one should not be compelled to incriminate oneself.

There were repeated attempts to bind the loyalty of clergymen and others by oaths. The 1606 Oath of Allegiance had been aimed at Roman Catholics, but similar oaths were designed against dissident Protestants. The Canons of 1640 included an oath of loyalty to the Church of England to be imposed on all clergy. It included a fatally ambiguous "etcetera," which led many puritan ministers to object to it as an open-ended oath. The Puritan Revolution saw the widespread imposition of oaths as tests of religious and political loyalty. The Protestation (1641) and the Solemn League and Covenant (1643) were explicit promises to defend a certain interpretation of the country's religious and political constitution. Many of those who swore these sacred oaths believed that their solemn commitment was unbreakable. Thus at the Restoration, despite the changed circumstances, they could not bring themselves to repudiate these oaths. The legislation known as the Clarendon Code demanded that

those seeking public office or a clerical benefice should declare the Solemn League and Covenant was in itself an unlawful oath. Many of the "ejected clergy" found this impossible. A similar scruple of conscience motivated the Anglican "nonjurors" of the 1690s.

See also: Clarendon Code, Crime and Punishment, Ejections of Clergy, Reformation of Manners, Solemn League and Covenant, Subscription
Further Reading
Christopher. Hill, *Society and Puritanism in Pre-revolutionary England* (London, 1964); John Spurr, "A Profane History of Early Modern Oaths," *Transactions of the Royal Historical Society*, 6th series, XI. (2001).

John Spurr

Synod of Dort

The Synod of Dort (Dordrecht, Netherlands), which met from 13 November 1618 to 9 May 1619, was a national synod of the Dutch churches—attended also by theologians from Germany, Switzerland, and Britain—called to pass judgment against Reformed ministers known as Remonstrants, who in 1610 had signed a Remonstrance to the Dutch parliament (States General) in which they formulated five points concerning the doctrine of predestination in ways that differed from the form of Calvinism that was developing among the followers of the French Reformer Theodore Beza, who were led by Leiden professor Franciscus Gomarus. Jacobus Arminius and his followers (the Remonstrants) defined God's predestination as the decree before Creation that those who believed would be saved, which left a degree of individual active choice to accept or reject the grace of belief. Such free will as this implied was considered by their opponents to be inconsistent with philosophical conceptions of God's majesty, omnipotence, and omniscience. Contra-Remonstrants believed that God had foreordained specific individuals to salvation or damnation before Creation, which the Remonstrants considered an idea that necessarily made God the author of sin. In England, such ideas were represented by William Perkins's pamphlet *De praedestinationis mode et ordine* (1598; i.e., "How Predestination Works"), which was specifically answered by Arminius in his *Examination of Perkins' Pamphlet*, first published (posthumously) in 1612, and then reissued in Dutch translation, together with Perkins's piece, in 1617, when Dutch controversial tension was increasing.

The Remonstrants, following the thought of Arminius, acknowledged the Bible as sole requisite for faith, thus offending those who considered the Belgic Confession and Heidelberg Catechism to be binding formulations of doctrine. The 1610 Remonstrance had been part of a request that the government call a national synod that would examine and revise that confession and catechism. At that time, the Gomarists opposed such government participation, changing their attitude after the military coup staged by Prince Maurice, commonly known as Maurice of Nassau, in 1618 resulted in the ejection of Arminians from all government posts. At the Synod of Dort, the Remonstrants were not allowed to present their arguments, merely being summoned to hear judgment against themselves. Nor were they allowed to allege conscientious objections to pronouncements made by the synod delegates, who claimed the authority of the civil government to enforce their opinions. Finally around two hundred Remonstrant ministers were banished or imprisoned. In English the synod's answers to the Remonstrants' five articles have been summarized with the acronym TULIP: T for total depravity; U for unconditional election; L for limited atonement; I for irresistible grace; P for perseverance of the saint(s). The response to the charge that the theology so summarized makes God the author of sin has been that God's wisdom is unsearchable. Joseph Hall warned the Synod in his speech of 29 November 1618 to avoid the self-destruction that would come from attempting to know too much, preaching on the text Ecclesiastes 7:16 and describing the Puritans as modern Pharisees. In later years the Synod of Dort has been much praised as a defining point in the codification of orthodox doctrine by Calvinists, most of whom have not read its deliberations.

See also: Jacobus Arminius, Arminianism, Grace, Predestination

Further Reading

Carl Bangs, *Arminius: A Study in the Dutch Reformation* (Nashville, 1971); Richard Muller, *God, Creation and Providence in the Thought of Jacobus Arminius* (Grand Rapids, 1991).

Jeremy Bangs

T

Test Acts

Two statutes enacted in the 1670s that sought to exclude Roman Catholics from public life by imposing oaths and other "tests" on officeholders, but that also had the effect of making full participation in public life difficult for puritans who had become Dissenters. The 1673 Test Act, *an Act for preventing dangers which may happen from Popish recusants* (25 Charles II. c.2), required anyone, commoner or peer, who held any office, military or civil, or who received any pay or fees under the Crown, to take the oaths of supremacy and allegiance in the open court of King's Bench or the Quarter Sessions and to furnish a certificate signed by an incumbent and churchwarden that they had received the sacrament in the Church of England. Finally officeholders had to declare that "I do believe that there is not any transubstantiation in the sacrament of the Lord's Supper." Among the casualties of this legislation were the leading minister Lord Clifford and, most spectacularly, the king's brother and heir, James, Duke of York, whose resignation of the office of Lord Admiral confirmed the widespread suspicion that he was a Roman Catholic. Thus the 1673 Test Act not only demonstrated the long-standing anti-Catholicism of seventeenth-century English politics, but it initiated a decade of political instability by exposing the heir to the throne as a Catholic.

The second Test Act, *An Act for the more effectual preserving the King's person and government by disabling Papists from sitting in either House of Parliament* (30 Charles II, st. 2, c.1), was enacted in November 1678 in the midst of revelations about the supposed "Popish Plot" against Charles II. This statute added to the oaths of allegiance and supremacy a long declaration against the Roman Catholic doctrines of transubstantiation and veneration of the Virgin Mary and an explicit renunciation of equivocation, mental reservation, or papal absolution for false swearing. Although this act did drive a handful of Roman Catholic peers from the House of Lords, the explicit exclusion of the Duke of York from its provisions left the underlying political problem unresolved. When the duke came to the throne as James II in 1685, one of his goals was the repeal of the Test Acts, along with other earlier anti-Catholic legislation, but he failed to convince a largely Anglican parliament and political class to support him. The "Three Questions" posed to the justices and lieutenants of the counties in 1687 asked whether they would vote for repeal if elected to Parliament. Those who indicated they would not were removed from office.

James II did not succeed in repeal of the Test Acts, and the Toleration Act of 1689 allowed only limited religious freedom rather than full civil participation to non-Anglicans. Protestant Dissenters increasingly saw that the Test Acts were an obstacle to their own ambitions. The requirement to have received Anglican communion was as onerous for Dissenters as Catholics and was disliked by many Anglicans for encouraging the hypocrisy of "occasional conformity." From 1727 annual "indemnity acts" were passed to protect officeholders from the consequence of not receiving the sacrament in the Church of England. These acts helped only Protestants, and Roman Catholics had to wait until 1828–1829 for the repeal of the Test Acts.

See also: Dissenters
Further Reading
John P. Kenyon, ed., *The Stuart Constitution, 1603–1688* (2nd ed., Cambridge, Eng., 1986).

John Spurr

Thanksgiving

Christian days of thanksgiving had been proclaimed by governments since Constantine; puritans announced such days of thanksgiving (as well as days of humiliation or penitence) as Bible-based replacements for the recurrent festivals of the medieval liturgical calendar. Thomas Wilson's *A Christian Dictionarie* (London, 1612) defines "thanksgiving" as "An acknowledging and confessing, with gladness, of the benefits and deliverances of God, both towards our selves and others, to the praise of his Name," consisting of "1. Remembrance of the good done to us. 2. Mention of it. 3. Confessing God to be the Author and giver of it. 4. Cheerfulness, being glad of an occasion to praise him, and doing it gladly, with joy." The Book of Common Prayer, as established by Edward VI and reestablished by Elizabeth I, provided set prayers of thanksgiving for rain, for fair weather, for plenteous harvests, for peace and military victory, and for deliverance from the plague. These "collects" were inserted in the liturgy in church services preceding further festivities.

Days of thanksgiving celebrated royal events, such as the accession of a monarch or birth of an heir. Recurrent thanksgivings commemorated the failure of Guy Fawkes's attempt to blow up Parliament in 1605. In New England, in the summer of 1623, the Pilgrims held a day of humiliation. Soon after, gentle rain relieved a lengthy drought; the colonists responded with a day of thanksgiving. On 8 July 1630, a day of thanksgiving throughout Massachusetts Bay Colony responded to the safe arrival of John Winthrop's fleet. In 1637, similar thanksgiv-

ing marked the victorious end of the Pequot War following the massacre of Indians who had been perceived as a threat to the territorial ambitions of the Massachusetts Bay and Connecticut colonies.

The New England pattern of such thanksgivings is described for that at Scituate, Massachusetts, held for unknown reasons on 22 December 1636: "in ye Meetinghouse, beginning some half an hour before nine continued until after twelve a clock, the day being very cold, beginning with a short prayer, then a psalm sang, then more large in prayer, after that another Psalm, & then the Word taught, after that prayer B & then a psalme, B, Then making merry to the creature, the poorer sort being invited of the richer." A religious service was followed by feasting (in contrast to the fasting that was an aspect of days of humiliation).

Obviously the Pilgrims' harvest festival in Plymouth, Massachusetts, in 1621 was not a first. Was it was even a thanksgiving? That word is not explicitly mentioned in Edward Winslow's description of the event, our only source. Furthermore, the length of the feast differed from the one-day pattern customary later in New England. However, when Winslow described the Pilgrims' intention, "after a more special manner [to] rejoice together, after we had gathered the fruit of our labours," he was alluding to John 4:36 and to Psalm 33. His intended readers were familiar with such allusions, where thanksgiving is both assumed and mentioned. The first passage, as found in the Geneva Bible, is, "And he that reapeth, receiveth wages, & gathereth fruit unto life eternal, that both he that soweth, & he [that] reapeth, might rejoice together." From Psalm 33, the same version, the most relevant verses are 1, 4–5, 18–19: "Rejoice in the Lord, O ye righteous: for it becometh upright men to be thankful. . . . For the word of the Lord is righteous and his works are faithful. He loveth righteousness & judgment: the earth is full of the goodness of ye Lord. . . . Behold, the eye of the Lord is upon them that fear him, & upon them, that trust in his mercy, To deliver their souls from death, and to preserve them in famine." Half the Pilgrims had died, but the survivors rejoiced in the hope of their resurrection and of continuing sustenance.

A Thanksgiving Dinner among the Puritans, *by John Whetton Ehninger. (Corbis)*

Rejecting traditional prayer book practice (still obligatory in England), the Pilgrims' celebration lasted several days, like the annual Reformed thanksgiving commemorating the relief of Leiden on 3 October 1574, ending a siege in which half the town had died. Doubtless the Plymouth colonists devised the form of their celebration by combining sources—traditional harvest festivities common to all agricultural societies, the Dutch Reformed practice they had experienced in Leiden, and the description of the Old Testament Feast of Tabernacles (Deuteronomy 16:13–14). The biblical injunction was to hold a harvest festival lasting "seven days," when everyone was to rejoice, including "the stranger, and the fatherless, and the widow, that are within thy gates." The biblical command to include the "stranger" may have led to the Pilgrims' inviting their Native neighbors to rejoice with them.

In recent years, a spurious Thanksgiving Proclamation for 29 November 1623 has been attributed to Plymouth's Governor William Bradford.

See also: Plymouth Colony, Pilgrim Thanksgiving (in Primary Sources)
Further Reading
Richard Gildrie, "The Ceremonial Puritan Days of Humiliation and Thanksgiving," *New England Historical and Genealogical Register,* 136 (1982), 3–16.

Jeremy Bangs

Theater and Opposition

It is a half-truth that the puritans systematically opposed the stage. Undeniably, fervent denunciations of the theater resounded from English pulpits and poured from English presses, albeit sporadically, from the middle of the sixteenth century until the middle of the seventeenth. Such outcries were no doubt an index of real enmity toward plays and players. The treatment of that opposition in this entry, however, should be understood in the context provided by the following preliminary observations.

First, the opposition to the theater has deep roots in human culture, Eastern as well as Western; certainly the animus against the stage cannot be limited to puritans. It is doubtful that the term *puritan* is even an appropriate description of all the antitheatrical writers of the sixteenth century. There is some reason to include neither Stephen Gosson nor Anthony Munday, two of the most important antitheatrical writers, in that category; both were at times vehement anti-puritan polemists. Second, even puritans hardly spoke about the theater with one voice. People of widely divergent views about the theater's legitimacy can reasonably be called puritans; the strident voices were hardly the only ones. Third, hostile exchanges were the order of the day. The heat of the screeds against the theater was often no higher than that of high-minded denunciations of all sorts of other common practices. Fourth, the likenesses between preaching and playing should not be underestimated. One reason the player and the preacher competed so fiercely was that they were such close kin.

Grounds of Opposition

Objections to the theater ranged from the ethical and theological to the hygienic and political—hardly watertight categories in early modern England. As sixteenth-century English theater took its turn from the decidedly religious and didactic to the secular and mimetic, opposition grew among the magistrates of London. The argument was that professional actors were notoriously unruly and that their plays inspired all manner of depravity and disorder. The theaters were sites of seduction and prostitution, luring the citizenry from sober lives and fruitful work. For decades the lord mayor struggled against the defenders of the theater in Queen Elizabeth's Privy Council to keep the professional playhouses closed. When an act of the city's common council (undated, but probably from the early 1580s) permanently prohibited plays in London, the Privy Council responded by investing the master of the revels with wide powers of control over licensing and production. Despite the city's continued opposition, and despite frequent closures of the theaters during times of plague, the drama of Shakespeare and his contemporaries flourished in and around London.

The acting companies' expedient of circumventing the city's control by erecting public playhouses in the "liberties," as the disreputable suburbs of London were called, instigated a storm of protests from preachers and pamphleteers. After the construction of the Theatre and the Curtain in 1576 and 1577, Paul's Cross sermons such as those by Thomas White, John Stockwood, John Walsall, Robert Sparke, Francis Marbury, William Holbrooke, and Robert Milles denounced the theater. White's 1576 Paul's Cross sermon is typical: in inveighing against the "prodigalitie and folly" of the playhouses, White put the danger in a simple syllogism: "the cause of plagues is sinne, if you looke to it well: and the cause of sinne are playes: therefore the cause of plagues are playes." A few years later the lord mayor echoed the sentiment, claiming that while playing in times of plague spread the infection, playing at other times invited God to revisit the plague on the city.

Writers of religious treatises, like the preachers, denounced the theater on theological as well as ethical grounds. John Northbrooke's 1577 tract denouncing dicing, dancing, and "vain playes or enterludes" not only doggedly rehearsed the lurid modes of immorality to which playgoers were exposed, but invoked the Bible to sanction the author's animosity to the stage. In addition to failing to honor the sacredness of the Sabbath (and, not incidentally, providing competition for the Sunday performances from the pulpit), plays violated the Deuteronomic law forbidding men to dress as women, and they inspired idolatry. The imputation of idolatry, no uncommon accusation in the sixteenth century, was urged with particular force and frequency against the stage.

Stephen Gosson, himself a playwright who had seen the error of his ways, performed his penance by writing two lively antitheatrical tracts, *The*

Schoole of Abuse (1579) and *Plays Confuted in Five Actions* (1582). The latter treatise employed rhetoric typical of the antitheatricalists in its refusal to posit any middle ground for free will between the activities of God and Satan. Plays, said Gosson, being "consecrated to idolatrie . . . , are not of God [, and] if they proceede not from God, they are the doctrine and inventions of the devill."

In 1580 Anthony Munday followed Gosson's *The Schoole of Abuse* with *A second and third blast of retrait from plaies and Theaters;* Gosson's was the first blast. Munday, like Gosson a playwright but unlike Gosson, one who kept writing plays after his diatribe against them, claims that in a Christian land plays are "not sufferable. My reason is, because they are publike enimies to virtue and religion; allurements unto sinne . . . meere brothel houses of Bauderie."

Gosson's and Munday's tracts were followed in 1583 by the formidable social reformer Philip Stubbes's *Anatomy of Abuses,* which catalogued the varieties of divine judgment visited upon sinners of all sorts, and which vehemently denounced the theater in the section entitled "Of Stage-Playes and Enterludes, with their wickedness." In 1587 William Rankins published *A Mirrour of Monsters,* the subtitle of which speaks for itself: *Wherein is plainely described the manifold vices, & spotted enormities, that are caused by the infectious sight of playes, with the description of the subtile slights of Sathan, making them his instruments. . . .*

The culmination of antitheatrical rhetoric was a massive diatribe that took years to write and still more to see through the press. William Prynne's *Histrio-Mastix* was finally published in 1633, just ten years before the theaters were closed by the antiroyalists for a combination of political and moral reasons. *Histrio-Mastix,* a screed so vituperative as to appear pathological, had little to do with the theaters' closing. Its eleven hundred pages of rambling, repetitive arguments contained nothing new. The tract is interesting mainly as an index of the depth antitheatrical feeling could reach in an unstable mind.

No doubt some antitheatrical feeling extended to the English settlements in the New World, but since there was no professional theater in the Colonies until the 1760s, no body of antitheatrical rhetoric comparable to that of the English puritans existed among the Americans. Still, there must have been some interest in plays before the professionalization of the American theater, or laws would not have been passed such as the 1750 statute prohibiting them in Boston.

Jonas Barish has convincingly argued that the psychological component of antitheatricalism runs deep in Western culture. Objections to the theater from Plato to postmodernity, Barish argues, may in part be political, economic, ethical, or theological, but underlying these objections is a deep-seated fear of change. The actor's refusal to inhabit a single, stable identity instills in the antitheatrical mind a powerful revulsion, positing a threat to the comforting ideals of order and stability. But the antitheatrical urge, of course, constitutes only one part of the human psyche.

Defenders of the Theater

Early modern defenders of the theater, especially those of a Neoplatonist stripe, saw human creativity as a legitimate enterprise, even a godly one. Sir Philip Sidney, for instance, while no great advocate of the theater, very likely wrote his *Apologie for Poetrie* (in 1581) as a reply to *The Schoole of Abuse,* which Gosson had had the temerity to dedicate to him. Later defenders of the theater echoed Sidney's poetics, similarly arguing for the morally edifying force of fictive presentations of virtue and vice. In holding the mirror up to human nature, the playwright taught us how to behave.

An index of the political strength of the antitheatricalists is that Thomas Lodge's 1579 *A Defence of Poetry, Music, and Stage-Playes,* also apparently a reply to Gosson, had to be published surreptitiously, despite its agreement with Gosson's claim that abuses of the theater were pernicious. Lodge argued that he wished "as zealously as the best that all abuse of playinge were abolished," but that the abuses did not justify abolishing the theater itself.

In *The Anatomie of Absurditie* the lively controversialist Thomas Nashe argued in a similar vein against Stubbes's *The Anatomy of Abuses:* if all the ungodly activities Stubbes listed in his treatise were abandoned, said Nashe, there would be virtually nothing left for people to do. Anticipating Barish, Nashe pointed out that the origin of Stubbes's invectives was psychological: Stubbes and his ilk "make the Presse the dunghill whither they carry all the muck of their melancholicke imaginations."

In *An Apology for Actors,* the playwright Thomas Heywood echoed Lodge's arguments, adding that while the Roman theater reached its height in the first century before the birth of Christ, not a single New Testament verse condemned it. Moreover, Heywood argued that it was only the already corrupt whose corruption could be exposed by the theater; the upright had nothing to fear. Interestingly, in positing a single, unchanging identity for each playgoer, whether vicious or virtuous, this argument belied the claim of the theater's power to change individuals, a claim shared by antitheatricalists and supporters of the theater alike.

See also: Leisure Time, Theology of, Puritans in Literature, Reformation of Manners, Sports and Recreation

Further Reading
Jonas Barish, *The Antitheatrical Prejudice* (Berkeley, 1981); Russell Fraser, *The War against Poetry* (Princeton, 1970); Arthur F. Kinney, *Markets of Bawdrie: The Dramatic Criticism of Stephen Gosson* (Salzburg, 1974); Peter Lake, with Michael Questier, *The Antichrist's Lewd Hat: Protestants, Papists and Players in Post-Reformation England* (New Haven, 2002).

Bryan Crockett

Thirty-nine Articles
See Articles of Religion

Tithes

Tithes, whereby the clergy were paid 10 percent of the produce of the community, were the ancient support of the parochial clergy and survived the Reformation as the mainstay of clerical incomes. They had long been a source of contention, in part due to the wide variation in income that clergy received from tithe, but also because of the compli-

cated distinction between great tithes on corn, hay, and wood, which were due to rectors, and small tithes, on other products, which were due to vicars where these had been established. This distinction, between great and small tithes, itself marked some separation of tithe from the parochial clergy as, where vicarages were established, the great tithes, usually the more significant financially, were appropriated to a monastic house, often located some distance away, which undertook to appoint a vicar to the parish, paying him the less valuable small tithes. Thus in many cases tithe was no longer paid to the individual for whose upkeep it was originally intended. Added to this were the complexities of estimating and collecting the actual produce itself, so that litigation over tithes was widespread before the Reformation, though the institution itself did not come under serious attack.

The Reformation had two important consequences for the debate over tithe: firstly, tithes were included in those assets of the dissolved monasteries sold or granted to laymen, colleges, cathedrals, and senior ecclesiastics, so that the separation of a significant amount of tithe from the pastoral work of the church became even more obvious; and secondly, the emphasis on a learned, preaching, and married clergy made the disparities in the value of parochial incomes even more disputable. Many leading Reformers, including men such as Edmund Grindal who were to take prominent positions in the Elizabethan Church, objected to the structural inequities of the system and blamed the poor quality of clergy and therefore the slowness of reform, on this weakness. Reform of the institution, and in particular the removal of impropriations, which impoverished many livings, especially at key urban centers, such as Halifax, Cirencester, and Bury St. Edmunds, where the need for learned preaching ministers was pressing, became a principal platform of puritan critics of the established church. The difficulty was that both universities and many senior churchmen, not to mention the Crown itself, profited from the income they received from these rectory estates. In response to calls for reform, the bishops could point to the potential damage to important ecclesiastical institutions if radical proposals were adopted, while the threat to the property rights of lay tithe-owners, many of whom were to be found among the Parliamentary supporters of the puritans, meant wholesale reform was impossible. Some bishops, including Grindal, made attempts to divert the income they received from impropriations to increasing the level of preaching in their dioceses by augmenting small livings, but these efforts were piecemeal and largely ineffectual. Bills for augmenting poor livings were introduced in many parliaments but foundered, and puritan schemes such as that introduced in the millenary petition got no further, while James I's offer to hand over the tithe income from his rectory estates was quickly withdrawn.

One significant attempt to address the issue of impropriations by the puritans was the Feoffees for Impropriations, a group of London-based ministers, lawyers, and merchants who set about buying up rectories offered for sale in order to restore the income to an impoverished preaching minister, not necessarily in the parish of the purchased rectory. In this way a number of puritan clergy were given places in populous market towns between 1625 and the suppression of the Feoffees in 1638 by Archbishop William Laud, who was himself encouraging a counter attempt by the bishops and cathedrals to augment poor livings out of their rectory estates and fill those livings with orthodox clergy.

The question of tithes, though it continued to be a source of litigation locally (often between parishioners and lay rather than clerical owners, it must be said) and contentious nationally, remained unresolved at the outbreak of the Civil Wars. Locally it was the financial imposition of the tithe that figured most strongly in the disputes, but nationally controversy focused on the role of the church courts where tithe cases were heard, making the church appear as both plaintiff and judge. Increasingly defendants, especially the wealthier ones, looked to the equity courts to settle tithe disputes, and the Court of Exchequer developed a competence in this area challenging the authority of the ecclesiastical courts.

During the Civil Wars and Interregnum, tithes, together with the whole question of the maintenance of the ministry, remained at the center of debate. With the breakdown of ecclesiastical structures in some areas, the rise of sects, and the presence of competing ministers in parishes, opposition to the tithe became both more vocal and more theologically based. In 1650 Parliament compiled a survey of parochial livings with the intention of augmenting the incomes of the poorer ones and amalgamating those that had modest profits and small congregations. This was the first attempt to address the problem nationally since the Reformation, and Parliament used the profits of the dissolved cathedral chapters to find the necessary funds. Some improvements were made, but the scale of the problem proved intractable and, as the sects gained adherents, so refusal to pay tithes increased. Most notable among those who objected to the tithe were the Quakers who, in 1653, presented a petition to the Rump Parliament with 15,000 signatures called for tithe to be abolished. The House was divided on the issue but, faced by the implications for notions of property consequent on any wholesale reform, voted to maintain tithes as the mainstay of the ministry. Anglican writers such as John Gauden were stimulated into rethinking the justification for tithes in response to criticisms of the sectaries, and tithes survived the Restoration and continued into the nineteenth century as the mainstay of the clergy, though its imposition on Nonconformists continued to make it controversial and a source of litigation.

See also: Feoffees for Impropriations
Further Reading
L. Brace, *The Idea of Property in Seventeenth-Century England: Tithes and the Individual* (Manchester, Eng., 1998); Christopher Hill, *Economic Problems of the Church: from Whitgift to the Long Parliament* (Oxford, 1956); Barry Reay, *The Quakers and the English Revolution* (London, 1986).

William Sheils

Toleration

The relationship between puritanism and toleration is complex and ambiguous. On the one hand, puritanism is associated in the popular imagination with religious intolerance and bigotry. On the other hand, traditional Whig historians linked "puritanism and liberty" and claimed that the puritan movement played a key role in "the rise of toleration."

England

During the reigns of Elizabeth I and James I, few puritans showed any enthusiasm for toleration. As heirs of the magisterial Reformation, mainstream puritans believed in a "godly magistrate" who would support the true church and suppress heresy and schism. Since false religion posed a terrible threat to souls, tolerating it was out of the question. Puritans supported the persecution of Catholics and anti-Trinitarians, and stressed the need for religious unity (even if they themselves sometimes suffered in campaigns for clerical uniformity). Though puritans often called for further reformation, toleration was not part of their program. Even Separatists continued to embrace the traditional Reformed vision—they called for toleration for themselves, but had no intention of giving it to heretics. The one exception to this rule was the General Baptist movement, whose founder Thomas Helwys advocated toleration for all religions.

It was not until the 1640s that the idea of toleration began to take hold more widely among radical puritans. The Presbyterian drive to impose a new system of religious uniformity during that decade provoked a fierce counterattack from Independents and sectarians, who called for toleration. Congregationalists like Thomas Goodwin and Jeremiah Burroughes still supported the ideal of a state church, but they wanted toleration for orthodox Protestant congregations meeting outside the parish system. However, more radical figures such as Roger Williams, John Goodwin, William Walwyn, and Henry Robinson challenged the very principle of religious coercion in a series of pamphlets published between 1644 and 1647. These tolerationist ideas met with a furious response from conservative puritans like Thomas Edwards, Samuel Rutherford, and William Prynne, who unapologetically reasserted the traditional Reformed theory of religious coercion. Meanwhile, toleration was becoming a practical reality for the puritan sects, who worshipped freely in London and other cities, as well as in the New Model Army, where they found a protector in Oliver Cromwell.

The triumph of the New Model Army in the Revolution of 1648–1649 also ensured the triumph of the sects, whose safety was guaranteed by the Commonwealth and Protectorate. Cromwell and his Independent advisors (like John Owen and Philip Nye) favored a limited toleration that would protect the godly, while allowing little room for license or heresy. Cromwell believed that one of his prime duties was to protect "the people of God," and during the 1650s, the sects were able to put down deep roots. Under puritan rule there was no official toleration for Catholics or Anglicans, though occasional harassment rather than persecution was the experience of both. Quakers, by contrast, were on the receiving end of some brutal treatment from local magistrates, and in 1656 the Quaker James Nayler was sentenced by Parliament to mutilation and flogging for blasphemy. Anti-Trinitarians were also at risk, though John Biddle escaped with his life and was exiled to the Scilly Isles.

After the Restoration in 1660, puritans themselves became the victims of persecution. Almost two thousand puritan clergy were ejected from the Church of England, and many thousands of Dissenters were fined and imprisoned over the next twenty-five years. As a result, even the more conservative Presbyterians became less hostile to toleration, though what they really longed for was "comprehension" within a reformed Church of England, a goal shut off by a combination of Anglican intransigence and Dissenting scruples. Some puritans like John Owen published pamphlets in favor of toleration, and puritans took advantage of Charles II's short-lived Declaration of Indulgence in 1672. But it was the so-called Act of Toleration (1689) that finally ended the era of persecution. The act ensured toleration for all Trinitarian Protestant Dissenters, though it did not repeal the Test and Corporation Acts, which excluded Dissenters from civil office.

New England

The Massachusetts colony held firmly to the traditional Reformed vision of a godly magistrate who punished heresy and schism. When Roger Williams mounted a separatist challenge to the Massachusetts establishment, he was expelled from the colony in 1636. Williams migrated to Rhode Island, where he founded a settlement that became a safe haven for religious Dissenters. When Anne Hutchinson and the antinomians were expelled from Massachusetts in 1637–1638, they fled to Rhode Island. Williams became a leading proponent of toleration, arguing in *The Bloudy Tenent of Persecution* (1644) that magistrates were responsible only for the bodies and goods of their subjects, not for their souls. His views were condemned by John Cotton and other Massachusetts puritans, who denounced the fashionable notion of toleration and continued to defend traditional Reformed theories of the godly magistrate. Massachusetts did tolerate a certain amount of diversity on the issue of law and grace, church membership, and even baptism. But the colony would not tolerate open assaults on its system. Baptists, who were enjoying freedom under Cromwell, were flogged and expelled from Massachusetts, and several Quakers were hanged in 1659–1660 for returning to the colony after their expulsion. Persecution of Baptists and Quakers persisted during the 1660s and 1670s. Only gradually, as a result of increasing pressure from England and the growing complexity of the colony itself, did Massachusetts start to relax its strictures against dissent. In 1681, the General Court gave permission to the Baptists to worship in their own church in Boston. After the loss of the colony's charter in 1684, Anglican worship was also permitted in Boston. Slowly but surely, Massachusetts was being forced to come to terms with religious pluralism.

Conclusion

In both England and New England, the seventeenth century saw the growth of religious diversity and toleration. Conservative puritans were appalled by this phenomenon and lamented the demise of a religiously unified society, where everyone worshipped one God in one truly reformed church. Yet puritanism itself was partly responsible for the new diversity and toleration. Firstly, seventeenth-century puritanism had proved extraordinarily fissile, generating an array of new movements, including Separatists, General and Particular Baptists, Seekers, Congregationalists, Presbyterians, Quakers, and Socinians. The radical Protestant pluralism of England and America by the late seventeenth century owed much to the puritan drive for "further reformation." Secondly, radical puritans had been at the forefront of the campaign for toleration since the 1640s and had developed theories of toleration in numerous pamphlets. Finally, the resilience of English puritans during the persecutions of the Restoration era demonstrated the sheer difficulty of restoring uniformity and helped prepare the way for the Toleration Act of 1689.

See also: An Apologeticall Narration, Clarendon Code, Comprehension, Crime and Punishment, Dissenters, Sects, Toleration Act

Further Reading

John Coffey, *Persecution and Toleration in Protestant England, 1558–1689* (Harlow, Eng., 2000); Philip Gura, *A Glimpse of Sion's Glory: Puritan Radicalism in New England, 1620–1660* (Chapel Hill, 1984).

John Coffey

Toleration Act

An Act passed by the English Parliament in May 1689 granting orthodox Protestant Dissenters freedom of public worship. Officially entitled "An Act exempting their Majesties Protestant subjects, dissenting from the Church of England, from the penalties of certain laws," it exempted Dissenters from the penalties imposed by the Clarendon Code and allowed them to apply for licenses to open legally approved places of worship. The Act confirmed the end of "the Great Persecution," which Dissenters had experienced from 1660 to 1686.

The origins of the act lay in the common front formed by Anglicans and Dissenters against the

Catholic James II in 1688. The threat of an aggressive Catholic monarchy revealed Dissent to be the lesser of two evils in Anglican eyes, and after the overthrow of James, many Anglicans were willing to contemplate conciliatory measures. In March 1689, two bills were introduced into the Convention Parliament. The first, a Comprehension Bill, proposed to reincorporate Dissenters within the church by making certain alterations to its terms of communion. The bill was supported by Anglican Latitudinarians who wanted a broad church and by Presbyterians who wished to belong once more to the established church. The second was an Indulgence Bill, based on the Toleration Bill of 1680 and intended to offer protection to sects who would not rejoin the Church of England. Fierce opposition from High Churchmen forced William III to abandon the Comprehension Bill, but in exchange for its demise the church party agreed to allow the Indulgence Bill to proceed, and it became law on 24 May.

Although the act was warmly welcomed by most Dissenters, it was a strictly limited measure. Firstly, although it became known as the Toleration Act, the term *toleration* was pointedly omitted from both its title and its text. In contrast to James II's Declaration of Indulgence, the preamble to the act merely spoke of giving "some ease to scrupulous consciences in exercise of religion," and offered no principled justification of toleration. One member of Parliament remarked that the Committee that had drawn up the bill "though they were for Indulgence, were for no Toleration." The Act of Uniformity and other elements of the Clarendon Code were not repealed; Dissenters were simply exempted from their penalties. Secondly, the act explicitly excluded anti-Trinitarians and Catholics and offered nothing to Jews, atheists, or other non-Christians. Even Quakers had to go out of their way to persuade Parliament that they did not deny the doctrine of Trinity. Everyone was still required by law to attend a place of worship on Sunday. Thirdly, in order to take advantage of the new law, Dissenters were required to take the oaths of allegiance and supremacy; their ministers had to subscribe to the Thirty-nine Articles of the Church of England (though an exception was made for the articles on church government and—in the case of the Baptists—the article on infant baptism); and their meetinghouses had to be registered. Finally, the act ensured that Dissenters remained second-class citizens. With the Test and Corporation Acts still on the statute books, public office was restricted to those willing to take communion in the Church of England—Dissenters were only able to run for public office if they practiced "occasional communion."

Yet for all its limitations, the Toleration Act was a significant turning point in English religious history. It marked the reluctant acceptance that religious pluralism was here to stay and that religious uniformity was unenforceable. Although High Churchmen campaigned for its repeal, especially during the reign of Queen Anne, the act survived. By 1710 Dissenters had registered over 2,500 licensed meeting places. Never again were they prosecuted by the state for worshipping outside the established church. Even Catholics benefited from the act, since discreet Catholic worship was clearly tolerated. For some historians, the Toleration Act marks the end of the heroic age of militant Puritanism and the beginning of the more prosaic age of moderate Nonconformity.

See also: Comprehension, Dissenters, Nonconformity, Toleration
Further Reading
John Spurr, "The Church of England, comprehension and the Toleration Act of 1689," *English Historical Review*, 104 (1989), 927–946.

John Coffey

Triers and Ejectors

The two commissions established by the Protectorate government to regulate the placement and dismissal of clergy in the parishes of the Church of England. Together the Triers and Ejectors represented an attempt by Cromwell to reshape the national church in line with a broad Calvinist consensus along the lines that had earlier been proposed by John Owen. The commissions did not have jurisdiction over congregations that were separate from the structure of the national church and whose clergy were not paid tithes.

The Triers were a commission of thirty-eight clergymen appointed by Cromwell in March 1654 to examine (or "try") the qualifications of candidates nominated by patrons for ministerial posts. The members of the commission were predominantly Congregationalists, but included Presbyterians and Particular Baptists, reflecting the Calvinist orthodoxy that characterized the Cromwellian church. Members of the more radical sects complained about what they saw as the narrow doctrinal bounds that the Triers used as a test.

The Ejectors were commissions established by Cromwell in August of 1654 and charged with expelling from livings those clergy and schoolmasters who were considered scandalous, ignorant, or otherwise insufficient. A separate commission was established for each county. Each local board had about twenty lay members and fourteen clerical assistants. Trials were held to judge the complaints lodged against those brought to the commission's attention.

See also: Protectorate
Further Reading
Robert Paul, *The Lord Protector: Religion and Politics in the Life of Oliver Cromwell* (London, 1955); John Spurr, *English Puritanism, 1603–1689* (Basingstoke, Eng., 1998).

Francis J. Bremer

V

Vestments

Ecclesiastical dress worn by clergy performing liturgical and other church services. The requirement to wear the surplice (a loose white robe with wide sleeves) provoked the *adiaphoric* dispute (that is, dispute about *adiaphora,* "things indifferent," matters not specifically spoken of in the Bible) of longest standing and plainest visibility between puritan clergy and their more conforming brethren in the Church of England. Concerns over wearing the surplice, therefore, can be gauged as a reliable cultural marker to determine the extent of puritan leanings: generally speaking, the more recalcitrant to the wearing, the less conformable the individual.

The puritan objection to vestments was that they recalled the priestly garb worn in the pre-Reformation Church, when (in their opinion) the sacrament was celebrated superstitiously as altar sacrifice rather than table communion. In 1550, John Hooper refused to be consecrated in the surplice prescribed in the Ordinal (the requirements for worship set forth in the book of Common Prayer). With the presumed backing of his Privy Council, Edward VI issued a dispensation allowing Archbishop Thomas Cranmer to consecrate an un-vestmented Hooper. But Cranmer and the bishop of London, Nicholas Ridley, refused. The bishop and archbishop did not believe that the wearing of such garments was theologically prescribed, but they did believe in governmental authority over matters adiaphoric and in the maintenance of good order in the church. And so, the following year, worn down by a stint in the Fleet (to which he was sent by archiepiscopal order), Hooper finally put away his scruples and put on his surplice, after which he was duly consecrated bishop of Gloucester.

Elizabeth I's restoration of vestments in her religious settlement of 1559 led to strong condemnations of the same in the 1563 Convocation. Unable to effect a working compromise with hotter Protestants, Archbishop Matthew Parker nonetheless issued his *Advertisements* (1566), which required the wearing of a "four-cornered cap," gown and surplice, and a cope in cathedrals and collegiate churches. The *Advertisements* provoked bitter controversy in the Church of England, and a war of words commenced. Vestments were referred to in "A view of popish Abuses yet remaining in the English Church" (attached to *An Admonition to Parliament* of 1572) as "the garments of the idol, to which we should say, avaunt and get thee hence . . . they keep the memory of Egypt still amongst us, they bring the ministry into contempt, they offend the weak, they encourage the obstinate."

The *Advertisements* and "A view of popish abuses," however, mark two extremes in a broad and varied ecclesiopolitical approach to the archiepiscopal mandate to conformity. In many parishes and dioceses, sympathetic bishops winked at vestiarian offenses, and (as Hooper's case demonstrates) even clerics opposed in principle were reconciled in practice to donning the "garments of the idol" when occasion demanded. Those who could not abandon their scruples, however, did separate from the established church.

Their retreat from the field of this particular ecclesiastical battle did not spell the end of controversies over clerical dress in the Church of England. The importance both sides continued to grant this supposedly indifferent issue is charted in episcopal visitations and churchwarden's accounts up to the 1640s. In 1638, Richard Montagu, bishop of Norwich, included in his articles of visitation pointed questions about the number of surplices a parish kept at the ready (two were required, so that no minister could duck the requirement by using the excuse his surplice happened to be in the wash the day the bishop dropped by). He also inquired into the quality of the cloth, as "not cheapness but decentness [was] to be respected in the things of God." Archbishop William Laud's visitation records for Leicestershire include a number of presentments for breach of clerical dress. The careful watch over matters of dress kept by the Laudian regime in the reign of Charles I marks the end of the local compromises made in earlier reigns. It bears witness, therefore, to the breakdown of negotiations over matters adiaphoric that caused the estrangement of many puritans from the established church to which they were once conformable, the church that they once thought they could transform.

See also: Adiaphora, Surplice, Visitation
Further Reading
David Cressy and Lori Anne Ferrell, eds., *Religion and Society in Early Modern England* (London, 1996); J. H. Primus, *The Vestments Controversy* (Kampen, 1960).

Lori Anne Ferrell

Visitation

Visitation was the administrative cornerstone of episcopal authority within the Church of England and a survivor from its pre-Reformation structure. As such it was a major battleground between puritans and their episcopal opponents, for it was chiefly through visitation that the hierarchy—bishops, archdeacons, and cathedral chapters—were empowered to impose uniformity and discipline nonconforming clergy and laity. Episcopal visitations were normally held triennially, while archdeaconry visitations, covering a more restricted range of offenses, were held each year. All clergy and churchwardens were required to attend at visitation, the former being asked to show their letters of ordination and such licenses as they held, and the latter to answer a series of articles that had been compiled by the authorities in advance.

The chief purpose of these articles was to enforce ecclesiastical policy as defined in Convocation and other central agencies of church and state, but they also reflected the particular concerns of individual bishops and were directed at the perceived problems of particular dioceses. Such visitation records provide historians with one of the key sources for both the progress of the Reformation generally and the growth of puritan support in provincial England. In addition to questions about church fabric, attendance at worship, and the moral conduct of the laity, the visitors asked about the conduct and provision of services and the existence of extraparochial or extraliturgical worship and preaching, and it was on these issues that conflict between diocesans and the puritans was potentially most direct. Visitation was also the area in which bishops sympathetic to the reforming impulse of some puritans could exercise discretion. Thus we can see in the articles inquired of by successive bishops of the northern province in the early seventeenth century, following the lead of the evangelical archbishop Tobie Matthew, the concern for a preaching clergy that many bishops shared with moderate puritan ministers. These sets of articles dominated visitation in the north until the arrival of the Arminian Richard Neile, whose articles for Durham in 1624 concentrated not on preaching but on the ceremonial and sacramental role of the clergy. Thereafter the articles compiled by bishops of differing persuasions, Calvinist and anti-Calvinist, reflected the competing views of the church held by members of the hierarchy, and priorities and policy varied from diocese to diocese.

Such diversity did not assist enforcement, always a difficult area, as the visitors were dependent largely upon the answers of churchwardens for the discovery of nonconformity. Where nonconformist practices had the support of the laity, as they did in the diocese of Peterborough for the half century following the suppression of the prophesyings in 1574, they were concealed from authority for much of the period except when national events, such as the Marprelate controversy and the discovery of the puritan classes or conferences around 1590, made the hierarchy especially vigilant and local opponents of the puritans bolder. For much of the time, puritan clergy of a moderate stance could be concealed by sympathetic church wardens beneath returns of *omnia bene* (all is well).

Not only was discovery piecemeal, but discipline also varied. Many bishops of the Elizabethan period and a number under James shared the concern for preaching that was a hallmark of the puritans, and so the full rigor of the law was rarely enforced, and accommodation by both parties enabled moderate puritan critics to remain in post, or at least active in their neighborhoods, in several dioceses, at least until the 1620s. Visitation was, of course, a vital tool of anti-puritans such as Archbishop John Whitgift and a considerable source of concern and harassment to nonconformists, but of itself it was rarely the instrument for their removal from the church.

It was when visitation became allied to other campaigns, such as the enforcement of the Canons of 1604, that the livelihoods of puritan ministers became threatened. Even here the number of clergy who were deprived was modest, but the disputes between the puritans and the bishops over visitation transcended its practical implications. To the puritans the whole system, with its courts, its lay officials, and its powers of excommunication and deprivation, represented the most offensive nonscriptural survival of the unreformed church, which militated against that pastoral discipline that lay at the heart of the Reformed discipline and was to be found in Presbyterian-style order. From the 1570s and the *Admonition to Parliament*, the legitimacy of visitation, in which the bishops and other authorities were seen as both prosecutor and judge, was regularly challenged by puritan preachers in both pulpit and press.

From the 1620s, these conflicts were aggravated as the Arminians gained control of the church leadership. They sought a more rigorous application of church law as laid down in the Canons, stricter adherence to the Book of Common Prayer, and a more uniform approach from the bishops in the matter of visitation. Both Laud at Canterbury and Richard Neile at York sought to override diocesan variations in both the articles enquired of and the degree of their enforcement by a greater use of their powers of metropolitan visitation and other disciplinary instruments of the church courts. The articles produced in the 1630s required parishes to rearrange and refit their churches, often at considerable expense, to accommodate a form of churchmanship that the parishioners and their clergy did not embrace. Furthermore, prosecution of nonconforming ministers was pursued with a determination not previously seen, so that many puritans, both lay and clerical, were forced out of the church, some to emigration, and the middle ground of moderate puritan conformity became untenable. In this context, visitation itself became the center of controversy once again, and the arguments about its legitimacy were revived. To radicals like Prynne, the abuse, as he saw it, of Laud and Neile raised fundamental questions about authority in church and state and, in 1636 he asked rhetorically whether visitation articles had been ratified by king or Parliament, suggesting that, if not, they should be used "as waster paper, or to stop mustard pots." Vistiations ceased during the mid-seventeenth century with the dismantling of episcopacy, but resumed with the Restoration of the monarchy and church in 1660.

Further Reading

Kenneth Fincham, ed., *Visitation Articles of the Early Stuart Church*, 2 vols. (Woodbridge, Eng., 1994, 1998); W. P. M. Kennedy, *Elizabethan Episcopal Administration*, 3 vols. (London, 1924).

William Sheils

W

Westminster Assembly

The Westminster Assembly (1643–1652) was initially a gathering of English divines and governing laity to settle the government and liturgy of the English church, and to establish its doctrine, that is, to bring to fruition the desires of puritans for decades to achieve a further reformation of the English church and, since August 1643, to attain this goal in such a way as to embrace the British Isles, including, in particular, Scotland. The assembly's historical context was first the gathering storm clouds and then the raging storm itself of civil war (beginning in August 1642), heavily influenced with religious ideologies. Agitation for religious reform had hardly been entirely quiet since the Elizabethan Settlement. Again under James I of England (VI of Scotland), who called the Hampton Court Conference shortly after his arrival (1603) in England, and then under Charles I, there was a rising tide of discontent from the puritan left, with all manner of diatribes about the rise of Arminianism and popery, signaled especially by the emergence of the Anglo-Catholic William Laud, elevated to the see of Canterbury in 1633. Right from the beginning of the Long Parliament in November 1640, attention was directed to the question of the English church, and on 1 December 1641 the Commons sent the Grand Remonstrance to Charles, calling for a synod to settle matters in the Church of England. In April following, Parliament undertook the task of selecting suitable delegates, but the project was frustrated by the king for the time being. On 12 June 1643 the Lords and Commons passed an ordinance to this effect and called for the further reformation of the church, presupposing that diocesan episcopacy was evil, offensive, and burdensome, inhibited the advancement of true religion, and imperiled the state. The criterion was the Bible and agreement thereupon with other Reformed churches.

The assembly was to advise Parliament. The first meeting place was the Henry VII Chapel at Westminster Abbey; the date of first convocating was 1 July 1643, and the quorum was set at forty. The assembly sat at the pleasure of Parliament. William Twisse was named as chair, and his deputy was also to be named by Parliament. Parliament ordered payment of 40 shillings per day during sitting, and members were protected from all litigation that might conceivably arise from nonresidence in their parishes. The ordinance also contained a list of the original appointees, naming 10 peers, 20 members of Parliament (MPs), and 121 divines, for a total of 151, and 3 clerks. They represented Parliament, the universities, and the counties. Most of these appointees did actually participate for greater or longer periods; replacements were in due course named for those who dropped out. The vast majority were Presbyterians (a rather complex and sometimes conflicted group), but there were also five vocal Independents, a few Erastians, and some episcopalians, who for the most part did not sit. However, the Presbyterianism of the English was not exactly that of the Scots, being less dogmatic and not so independent-minded with regard to the state; indeed the assembly was Parliament's creature, something that Scottish Presbyterians would never have countenanced; hence Robert Baillie's famous comment about "a lame, Erastian, presbytery."

Given the close concurrence between puritans on both sides of the Tweed, it was not long before a sense of united destiny brought Scotland into the same picture. The Scottish puritans, or Covenanters, had already defied the king by rioting against the new Scottish prayer book in July 1637, signing the National Covenant on 28 February 1638, and then in November that year continuing to meet in the Glasgow general assembly, despite the departure of Hamilton, the king's commissioner, and passing acts dismantling the hierarchical and liturgical edifices of James and Charles. If earlier the proximity of the two countries had bred Scotland's hostility, now it was apparent that the success of "further reformation" depended upon cooperation.

In 1642, after the outbreak of civil war, the English parliament had called upon the commissioners of the Scottish general assembly to send ministers to participate in a forthcoming synod. Nothing came of these plans until the following year, and before the Scots could participate in the Westminster Assembly, an agreement had to be negotiated between the parliaments of the two countries. This was concluded on 17 August 1643 as the Solemn League and Covenant, and its subscription prepared the way for a number of Scottish commissioners, appointed two days later, to join their English brethren in the Westminster Assembly on 15 September. Though others were similarly appointed, those joining the proceedings that day were the divines Robert Baillie, George Gillespie, Alexander Henderson, and Samuel Rutherford; and the lay elders John, Lord Maitland, and Archibald Johnston of Wariston. The Scots were not actual members of the assembly, equivalent to the English who participated. They preferred to remain commissioners from their own church, that is, not state appointees, advising and indeed participating in debates, without formal membership; in fact they were highly overrepresented on the committee that produced the final version of the Westminster Confession.

The English commissioners covered a broad spectrum of ecclesiastical opinion and commitment, but it did exclude Laud and his disciples, and few royalists appointed to sit actually did so, the longest to sit being Daniel Featley. James Ussher, archbishop of Armagh and primate of the Church of Ireland, was not among the commissioners, rather surprising in view of his reputation and the influence of his Irish Articles (1615) on the assembly's confession. They represented a high quality, quantity, and breadth of scholarship, theological and beyond. They were not innovators, and they were not at all interested in the changing currents of European thought then beginning to exercise their influence. The Bible was their primary source, viewed through the lenses of Augustine and Calvin, and they were imbued with the spirit of federal, or covenant theology. In fact there was a great theological consensus; some other practical matters would evoke controversy. The Independents were fond neither of the notion of powerful Presbyterian structures nor of a governing national church. Their preferred structure would have focused ecclesiastical power at the congregational level, high bodies generally functioning in an advisory capacity.

First the New Model Army and then the Restoration mitigated the English impact of the assembly's achievements, but they became standards for English Dissent and the Church of Scotland (after the Glorious Revolution), and they were eventually carried around the world, wherever such people traveled, whether to settle or to evangelize. The best-known achievements were the Westminster Confession and the Catechisms, both treated separately.

In addition, there were provisions for church government and worship. *A Directory of Church Government,* though not published until 1644, was produced in Elizabethan times when Walter Travers drafted a church discipline, that is, a manual of church government. It was finished in May 1587 and was circulated in Latin as *Disciplina Ecclesiae Dei Verbo Descripta.* There may also have been an English translation not long after, but no publication in either language until 1644. The *Directory* addressed the work of the ministry and defined what may be referred to as the presbyterian, or classical, system of church government proper; it is similar to the Scottish second Book of Discipline.

Work on the Directory of Public Worship was commissioned by Parliament on 12 October 1643, but drafts were considered by the assembly only beginning on 24 May 1644. The assembly gave more than seventy sessions to the directory. It was finished on 27 December 1644, approved by English parliament on 3 January 1645 and by the Scottish general assembly and parliament on 3 and 6 February. It explicitly replaced the Book of Common Prayer and its unpalatable ceremonies with what was nothing more than a guide for worship, prayer, sermon, and pastoral care, altogether eschewing set forms.

A collection of metrical psalms made by Francis Rous, MP, was proposed to Parliament, and the process of its adoption was initiated by the Commons on 20 November 1643. The Scots commissioners had a preference for the work of Sir William Muir of Rowallan, while another English version by the minister William Barton was also set forth; it was known for its superior versification. A lengthy process of revision followed (against the will of the Independents, who were unconvinced of the theological propriety of set forms and the use of the Psalms in such a manner) and on 26 January 1646, the Commons authorized the publication of the Rous edition. The Lords were less willing, and so authorization for public usage was delayed, though in some respects that was of little significance, since the English already had a number of editions, besides the Psalms for chanting in the Book of Common Prayer, for congregational singing. In the end the Scots adopted the Rous edition, but with some changes authorized by the General Assembly on 28 August 1647, to be made by four appointees and drawing upon earlier work by Muir, Zachary Boyd, and the Kirk's own Psalter.

Historian Gordon Donaldson concluded: "It is a little curious that the Confession of Faith of Scottish Presbyterians, the Larger and Shorter Catechisms, their Directory of Public Worship and their Form of Church Government are all plainly marked on their title-pages 'Made in England'" (Donaldson, p. 85). And it has been observed that the Presbyterian gibe that it was unpatriotic of Scottish bishops to seek consecration at Westminster is a little inappropriate. The other view of the matter is that, with particular reference to the confession, the Scot Alexander Henderson's outstanding creative role at Westminster "will account for the readiness and unanimity with which the General Assembly of Scotland adopted these formularies of the English Assembly. They were in substance, their own" (*History*, p. 78).

The last numbered session (1163) of the Westminster Assembly convened on 22 February 1648, but it sat to discuss several issues until June. Thereafter it continued to function, though only as a body for the examination of ministers, until its demise, without formal dissolution, on 25 March 1652.

Further Reading
Ian Breward, ed., *The Westminster Directory* (Bramcote, Eng., 1980); S. W. Carruthers, *The Everyday Work of the Westminster Assembly* (Philadelphia, 1943); Gordon Donaldson, *Scotland: Church and Nation through Sixteen Centuries* (London, 1960); *History of the Westminster Assembly of Divines* (Philadelphia, 1841); John H. Leith, *Assembly at Westminster: Reformed Theology in the Making* (Richmond, VA, 1973); Alexander F. Mitchell, *The Westminster Assembly: Its History and Standards, being the Baird Lecture for 1882* (London, 1884).

David Mullan

Westminster Catechisms

The Westminster Catechisms, the Shorter and the Longer, were intended to serve the educational needs of the church, the Longer Catechism for public instruction from the pulpit, while the Shorter was for the catechizing of children. They were printed, separately, in 1647 as *The Humble Advice of the Assembly of Divines now by Authority of Parliament sitting at Westminster, concerning a Larger/Shorter Catechisme*. They were published together, in the same year, in Edinburgh. The Shorter Catechism was presented on 5 November 1647, and the Longer Catechism in April 1648. The published form was given English parliamentary approval, with a few reservations, on 15 September 1648. In Scotland, the Longer Catechism was approved in Edinburgh by general assembly on 2 July 1648, and the Shorter Catechism on 28 July.

Both of the catechisms rested on the foundation of the Westminster Confession. In order of composition, the Shorter Catechism was first, with 107 questions, preceding the Longer Catechism, consisting of 196 questions. The Longer Catechism, also often referred to as the Larger Catechism, was shaped by Anthony Tuckney, while John Wallis, a remarkable mathematician, did final work on the Shorter. The assembly had before it a productive past of catechetical invention and refinement, proceeding from England, Scotland, and the Continent, and in fact a dozen or more participants in the assembly, including Samuel Rutherford, the Scottish divine, had already turned their hands to such work.

John Calvin's 1545 Genevan catechism probably supplied the first question of the Shorter Catechism. It commences with the question, "What is the chief end of human life?" The question is practically the same as the Shorter Catechism's "What is the chief end of man?" but the answer is not quite the same, Calvin pointing to knowledge of the Creator, the Shorter Catechism to that most famous of responses, "Man's chief end is to glorify God, and to enjoy him for ever." This notion is supplied by Calvin in the next answer. Beyond this the form diverges significantly, with Calvin incorporating the Apostles' Creed, while this is relegated to an appendix in the Shorter Catechism. From this point the Shorter Catechism passes to "the decrees of God" made manifest in creation and providence. Sin intervened in creation, and through the Adamic covenant all humanity fell into "an estate of sin and misery" (17). Then God came to the rescue with the covenant of grace, and the Shorter Catechism proceeds to discuss the work of the Redeemer Christ. Effectual calling is the means of access to justification, adoption, and sanctification, and finally the resurrection. Obedience is required of humankind, and here the Shorter Catechism introduces a lengthy section (41–81) on the Decalogue.

Thereafter the Shorter Catechism turns to faith, repentance, "the outward means whereby Christ communicateth to us the benefits of redemption," that is, preaching and the two Reformed sacraments. The final questions (98–107) treat of prayer, attending to each of the petitions of the Lord's Prayer.

The Shorter Catechism has enjoyed a long and lively history among churches of the Reformed tradition; the Longer Catechism has, however, been relatively neglected. Based upon the Shorter Catechism, it is substantially longer, not only in the number of questions, but also in the substance of the answers, which would hardly be amenable to memorization. It addresses more ecclesiastical issues (61–65, 158–159). Even more than the Shorter Catechism, the Longer Catechism is dwarfed by the scripture proofs attached to it.

Both Westminster Catechisms were thoroughly intellectualized descriptions of the Christian religion, and neither restricted itself to the traditional usage of the Apostles' Creed. The Shorter Catechism in particular was of seminal influence in the communication of Reformed Christianity to generations of English-speaking peoples.

See also: Catechisms, Westminster Confession of Faith

Further Reading

Ian Breward, ed., *The Westminster Directory* (Bramcote, Eng, 1980); S. W. Carruthers, *The Everyday Work of the Westminster Assembly* (Philadelphia, 1943); John H. Leith, *Assembly at Westminster: Reformed Theology in the Making* (Richmond, VA, 1973); Alexander F. Mitchell, *The Westminster Assembly: Its History and Standards, being the Baird Lecture for 1882* (London, 1884).

David Mullan

Westminster Confession of Faith

The Westminster Confession of Faith is one of the more enduring achievements of the Westminster Assembly, a statement in thirty-three articles of the Reformed religion then in the ascendancy in England and Scotland. The title is more a popular one than an official designation, at least in the seventeenth century. In England it was known as the *Articles of Christian Religion,* and in Scotland as *The Confession of the Church of Scotland.*

As early as 1641 Alexander Henderson, a leader among Scottish Presbyterians, had written *Our Desires concerning Unitie in Religion,* expressing his hope that common theological and ecclesiological standards, including a confession, might be established for England and Scotland. Indeed the assembly went far to achieving this dream. The first work assigned to the assembly in 1643 was a revision of the doctrinal standard of the English church, the Thirty-nine Articles. The work of revision proceeded as far as the fifteenth article, whereupon a new confessional project was taken on with the arrival of the Scottish commissioners. Though there might be arguments about polity and the magistrate, the assembly's theology per se was without exception Reformed; that is, there were no Arminians, antinomians, or Pelagians, and the earlier revisionary work made changes to the Thirty-nine Articles that moved toward an even clearer or stricter uniformity with Reformed theology. For example, the revised sixth article, "Of the Sufficiency of the Holy Scripture for Salvation," deleted all reference to the Apocrypha; and the revised ninth article, "Of Original or Birth-Sin," strengthened the phrase "whereby man is very far gone from original righteousness" to "whereby man is *wholly deprived* of original righteousness."

The committee appointed to draft an outline was formed on 20 August 1644. It consisted of William Gouge, Thomas Temple, Joshua Hoyle, Thomas Gataker, John Arrowsmith, Jeremiah Burroughes, Cornelius Burgess, Richard Vines, and Thomas Goodwin. On 4 September they asked for more members and received, among others, Edward Reynolds, Charles Herle, and Anthony Tuckney. A report followed on 12 May 1645 describing the possible structure of a confession. A portion of the committee, along with the Scottish commissioners, was then charged with the task of generating a first draft. Subcommittees dealt with particular items, as assigned on 16 July. One was to address God and the Holy Trinity, the decrees, creation, and providence, and the fall. A second was assigned the

heads of sin and its punishment, free will, the covenant of grace, and the role of Christ the Mediator. Finally, a third subcommittee was given effectual vocation, justification, adoption, and sanctification. Many revisions and drafts were produced, delayed by debates and disputes over the directories of worship and church government. At the behest of Parliament, delivered on 25 September 1646, the assembly sent, on 9 October 1646, a total of nineteen articles to the Commons for approval. Then, in early December a complete draft was sent to the Commons and the Lords for consideration. On 11 December the members of the assembly attended Parliament to present their work. The Commons required the addition of "scripture proofs," and the new version was presented on 29 April 1647 and sent for printing (not publication) on 11 May. The parliamentary process of revision was not concluded until March 1648. The English parliament was not entirely impressed, the Commons insisting on the deletion of chapters 30 and 31, and portions of 20 and 24. In the summer 1648 this version was published as *Articles of Christian Religion approved and passed by both Houses of Parliament after advice had with the Assembly of Divines,* a title deemed closer to the Thirty-nine Articles and not including the term *confession,* since the document did not contain such definitive words as, for example, "I believe." Parliament also had reservations about the second paragraph of chapter 31, "Of Synods and Councils," which provided for the magistrate calling ministerial synods (referring to Isaiah 49:23).

In Scotland, however, it was the April version of the confession that was approved by the Edinburgh general assembly on 27 August 1647, then by Parliament on 7 February 1649, then once more by Parliament in 1690, following the Glorious Revolution and the restoration of Presbyterian government in the Church of Scotland. The Confession of Westminster has remained the symbol of Scottish Presbyterianism to the present day. However, the act of general assembly apologized for the confession's failure to treat church polity and referred the faithful to the Directory of Government. As for chapter 31, the Kirk advised that it referred only to churches not yet properly provided with the true ecclesiastical government, that is, the Presbyterian. As for ministerial gatherings, it was good that these might be held with magisterial approval, but the church possessed the intrinsic power to meet whether or not such permission might be forthcoming.

The theology of the Westminster Confession has been described as a modified Protestant Scholasticism, and its dogmatic roots lie in the Continental Reformation, without being dependent upon any particular formula. Those who drafted it were themselves highly capable theologians and religious controversialists steeped in Reformed theology, and they had before them the Irish Articles of Religion (1615) and its strongly Calvinistic emphases, set forth by James Ussher, who was at that time the head of the theological faculty at Dublin. The Westminster Confession follows the order of the Irish Articles quite closely and sometimes adopts the very wording of the earlier work. The confession is deeply rooted in the sixty-six books of the Protestant Bible, and like the catechisms that are its progeny, the articles are heavily laden with scripture proofs.

The confession has a decidedly systematic and dogmatic tone, beginning not with human experience per se, but with the foundation of Reformed epistemology, the Holy Scripture. Thereafter it addresses the God and the Trinity, and then, with chapter 3, enters upon soteriology, first addressing the matter of predestination. Chapter 7 speaks of the two covenants that identify this document with the theology called federal (from Latin *foedus,* meaning covenant). The final chapter in this doctrinal area is 18, on assurance. From 19 to 24 civil matters, including liberty, Sabbath observance, the magistrate, and marriage and divorce, are addressed. With 25 the confession enters upon the church and the sacraments, without touching upon the details of the presbyterian system, whence the Scottish assembly's comment on that deficiency. The final two chapters, 32 and 33, deal with eschatology.

The Westminster Confession has served Presbyterians and others as the basis for subsequent statements of faith on both sides of the Atlantic Ocean and beyond.

See also: Articles of Religion, Irish Articles, Cambridge Platform, Westminster Assembly
Further Reading
John MacPherson, *The Westminster Confession of Faith,* 2nd ed. (Edinburgh, 1882).

David Mullan

Witchcraft

The belief that certain individuals have powers thought to destroy society from within has been present in almost all societies at certain times. Although the stereotypical images of the puritan and the witch-hunter share many characteristics, witchcraft has little to do with puritanism per se. Persecution was widespread in early modern Europe, with some 50,000 executions throughout the period, in both Protestant and Catholic areas. Between 80 and 90 percent of those executed were women, a proportion relatively stable in areas of differing theology. There was a tendency for the evangelical of all major churches to become involved in persecutions. Belief in witchcraft was extensive at popular and elite levels in England, Scotland, Ireland, and America. America should be considered alongside England, as a result of shared legal structures. Scotland, where Roman law was practiced, had greater levels of persecution, and the use of torture was permitted in witchcraft cases. In Ireland, there was very little persecution despite strong popular belief. The crime of witchcraft was prosecuted by secular, not ecclesiastical, authorities under the Acts of 1563 and 1604. The 1563 Act defined witchcraft in terms of *maleficium,* the harm it caused to persons and property, rather than of the relationship between Satan and the witch, the preferred definition of the godly, including the sixteenth-century prelates of the Church of England, bishop of Salisbury John Jewel and archbishop of Canterbury Edmund Grindal. The 1604 Act extended the crime to include death, rather than imprisonment, for the conjuration of spirits. The crime of witchcraft was abolished by statute in 1736, though popular belief in it remained strong.

The difcouerie of witchcraft,

Wherein the lewde dealing of witches *and witchmongers is notablie detected,* the knauerie of coniurors, the impietie of inchar-tors, *the follie of foothfaiers, the impudent falf-* + hood of coufenors, the infidelitie of atheifts, *the peftilent practifes of Pythonifts,* the curiofitie of figurecafters, the va-*nitie of dreamers, the begger-* lie art of Alcu-myftrie,

The abhomination of idolatrie, the hor-*rible art of poifoning, the vertue and power of* naturall magike, and all the conueiances *of Legierdemaine and iuggling are deciphered:* and many other things opened, which haue long lien hidden, howbeit verie neceffarie to be knowne.

Heerevnto is added a treatife vpon the *nature and fubftance of fpirits and diuels,* &c : all latelie written *by Reginald Scot,* Efquire. 1. Iohn, 4, 1. *Beleeue not euerie fpirit, but trie the fpirits, whether they are* *of God; for manie falfe prophets are gone* out into the world, &c. 1584

Title page of The Discoverie of Witchcraft, *by Reginald Scot, London, 1584. (Fortean Picture Library)*

Puritan Ideas of Witchcraft

Puritans accepted the reality of witchcraft but rarely had distinctive demonological ideas. However, the majority of writers in the English language who promoted belief in and prosecution of witchcraft were puritans. Their ideas were rational and cogent, part of a coherent system of theology, written as a reaction to a perceived threat rather than from malice. In England, proponents included prominent puritan theologians such as William Perkins, whose *A discourse of the damned art of witchcraft* (1610) was influential in encouraging prosecution. He argued in favor of a godly state and regarded witches along with traitors as enemies of the state who were in league with the devil. Other important works were Henry Holland's *A treatise against witchcraft* (1590), George Gifford's *A dialogue concerning witches* (1593),

and Richard Bernard's influential witchfinding manual, *A Guide to Grand Jury-men with respect to Witches* (1627). Puritan demonologies tended to be written by trained clergymen, whose zeal formed part of a wider effort to achieve "reformation of manners." In Scotland, the key book was *Daemonologie* (1597) by James VI (from 1603 also James I of England), which viewed witchcraft as an attack on the godly commonwealth. American puritan texts repeated the themes of the English Jacobean works. The most notable was Cotton Mather's *A Discourse of the Wonders of the Invisible World* (1692). Puritans also preached against witchcraft, and some demonologies were reconstructed from sermons. Though the printed works contain many differences, and though some puritans argued belief in witchcraft was a delusion, one that detracted from God's providence, their similarities make it possible to identify, tentatively, a puritan idea of witchcraft.

The Protestant Reformation strengthened the importance of Satan by emphasizing the conception of personal sin. As it presented the apocalypse as imminent, the struggle between God and the devil, at its height in the Last Days, became more important, and this importance was reflected in Protestant ideas of witchcraft. Puritan ideas, driven by biblicism, emphasized the importance of the key witch-hunting biblical texts, Isaiah 28:15 and Exodus 22:18, though these were important to all Christians. The puritan conception of witchcraft was narrower than Catholic ones that highlighted the importance of the sabbat, or witches meetings. The idea of the demonic pact, signed by the witch to confirm an association with Satan, was particularly menacing to puritans, as it inverted their covenant theology, in which the promise was between God and the Christian. To avoid accusations of Manichaeism, Puritan authors argued that witchcraft was possible only by divine permission. They rejected the views of skeptics, arguing, as did Richard Greenham, that "it is a policy of the Devil to persuade us there is no Devil." Puritan diarists, such as Lady Margaret Hoby and Nehemiah Wallington, described their lives as a constant struggle with Satan. Puritan Decalogue morality categorized witchcraft as a sin against the first commandment, and, as Puritans taught a second commandment against images, they tended to be more concerned with the idolatry of image worship than of devil worship, the focus of Catholics and Lutherans.

Puritan authors were distinctive in that they saw all forms of magic, not just *maleficium*, as harmful magic. This resulted in the religious polarization of remedies for witchcraft, especially white magic. Puritanism had removed much of the therapeutic healing repertoire of the Catholic and more orthodox Protestant Churches. Puritan authors were strongly hostile to magical healers. William Gouge criticized those who resorted to sorcerers and cunning folk. George Gifford condemned healing in absolute terms, arguing that "the charmer . . . is the instructor of the enchanter." Although Perkins and others argued that the best protection was to remain within the covenant of God's grace, some puritans used traditional countermeasures, as did the puritan cleric who advocated "scratching" in the case of the witches of Warboys in 1593. Unlike European Calvinists, English puritans did not deny the reality of exorcism. There were many puritan and dissenting cases of possession. John Darrell, the puritan cleric involved in a number of high-profile cases in the 1590s, used fasting and prayer to demonstrate the power of the puritan ministry in dispossession. He was supported by puritans such as Richard Bernard and Arthur Hildersham, but his supposedly feigned "dispossession" of William Somers was seized upon by the anti-puritans Richard Bancroft and Samuel Harsnett, who undermined puritanism, as did later Laudians, by associating it with fraudulent exorcism.

The Decline of Belief in Witchcraft

The decline of witchcraft beliefs at the elite level was opposed by puritans, who continued to promote the reality of a corporeal devil and advocated belief in witchcraft well into the eighteenth century. The Cambridge Platonist Henry More harnessed belief in witchcraft in the late seventeenth century as ammunition against a rising tide of "atheism." The Yorkshire Nonconformist Oliver Heywood readily believed in witchcraft, as did

Richard Baxter, who wrote *The certainty of the world of spirits* (1691). Their opponents combined scientific rationalism with virulent anti-Calvinism, equating belief in witchcraft with puritanism. Sir Robert Filmer, a royalist, gave a stinging critique of Perkins's proofs of witchcraft, in his *Advertisement to the Jurymen of England* (1653), his skepticism forming part of an anti-Calvinist agenda. Orthodox ideas, such as those of Francis Hutchinson's *An Historical Essay Concerning Witchcraft* (1718), rejected puritan demonologies and consigned belief in witches to the superstitious past.

Persecution of Witches

The persecution of witches in puritan areas was no more intensive than elsewhere. Of around 500 executions in England, only a minority might be seen as partially puritan. Without the achievement of a godly state, persecution was sporadic and relied more on village tensions and reputations than on the enthusiasm of central or local government. Puritans were involved in a number of important cases, including that of the witches of Warboys (1593), whose story was spread through a popular pamphlet and an annual commemorative sermon in Cambridge. Political attempts to ascribe witchcraft beliefs to puritan delusion can be seen in the Darrell case and in Lancashire in 1633. The most intense persecution occurred in East Anglia in 1645–1647, when at least 250 people were tried as witches and over 100 executed, under the semiprofessional witch-hunter Matthew Hopkins and his puritan associate John Stearne. The panic was also encouraged by godly communities and clergymen, including Samuel Fairclough and Edmund Calamy. The witch-hunters had an unusually strong concern to discover sexual pacts with the devil, which may have been derived from puritan authors, in particular Perkins. It would be wrong, however, to polarize even this outbreak, which was opposed by some puritans, benefited from the breakdown of local government, and relied on local support and existing suspicions.

In Scotland, there were more than 1,000 executions, with national panics in 1590–1591, 1597, 1629–1630, 1649, and 1661–1662. These persecutions can be associated with puritanism and the desire of the Kirk to educate and Christianize. It is plausible that persecutions, considered as a whole, relied for their impetus on the political drive for a godly state, but in individual cases, accusations appear to have stemmed from local suspicions and social and economic problems.

In the American colonies, persecution was sporadic, though geographically widespread. The panic at Salem Village in 1692, in which over 100 people were arrested, 19 hanged, and 1 pressed to death, was only its most famous manifestation. The puritanism of Salem Village was just one aspect of the social separation between it and the richer Salem Town. The Independent church in the village was established in 1689. The minister, Samuel Parris, spurred on the panic in his sermons, but prosecution relied on a breakdown in colonial government and a feud between the Parris and Putnam families. Puritan ministers from Massachusetts were important in stopping the panic: they denounced the executions, arguing that the accusers were possessed, not bewitched.

See also: Devil, Salem Witchcraft
Further Reading
Stuart Clark, *Thinking with Demons: The Idea of Witchcraft in Early Modern Europe* (Oxford, 1997); John Demos, *Entertaining Satan: Witchcraft and the Culture of Early New England* (New York, 1982); Christina Larner, *Enemies of God: The Witch-Hunt in Scotland* (Baltimore, 1981); Brian Levack, *The Witch-Hunt in Early Modern Europe* (London, 1995); James Sharpe, *Instruments of Darkness: Witchcraft in England, 1550–1750* (Philadelphia, 1996); Keith Thomas, *Religion and the Decline of Magic* (Oxford, 1971).

Andrew Cambers

Glossary

Advowsons
The right of nomination or presentation to an ecclesiastical living. An advowson was a property right that could come into the hands of a lay patron through the purchase of church land. By exercising this right, lay patrons had the opportunity to shape the character of local religion.

Agitators
During the English Civil Wars of the 1640s, this formal term was used to describe representatives of the rank-and-file soldiers of the New Model Army who were chosen to negotiate with the officers of the army.

Alienation
The transfer of property, as in a church benefice.

Altar
The term used in the early church to refer to the table where the priest celebrated the sacrament of the Eucharist. The term carried connotations of sacrifice and thus fit with the church's view of the sacrament as a reenactment of Christ's sacrifice on the cross. The principal altar in a church was located at the east end of the church, in the chancel. The altar tended to be made of stone and could be plain or ornate. With the Reformation, many sought to redefine the sacrament to evoke the communion of Christ with his disciples at the Last Supper. They preferred to call the table a communion table and to reposition it so as to allow those receiving communion to gather around it.

Archdeacon
A church official to whom a bishop has granted administrative responsibilities for parishes within a geographical area called an archdeaconry. The archdeaconry may be further subdivided into deaneries, each with a dean reporting to the archdeacon.

Archpriest
The title given by the pope in 1598 to the clergyman placed over those English Catholic priests who were not members of a religious order such as the Jesuits.

Assurance
The certainty of salvation achieved by those who believed themselves to be God's elect.

Athanasian Creed
An ancient Trinitarian creed, not actually written by the fourth-century church father Athanasius but later, perhaps in the sixth century. Its occasional use was prescribed by the liturgy of the Church of England.

Barebone's Parliament
One of the names given to the parliament of 1653, also referred to by some as the Nominated Parliament. The Council of the Army selected 140 members from nominations that came from puritan congregations. One of the members was named Praise-God Barebone. The parliament was called the Barebones Parliament by mockers, and the name stuck. The parliament divided over radical reform proposals and dissolved itself in December 1653.

Bartholomew Ejections
On St. Bartholomew's day, 24 August 1662, about a thousand clergy of Puritan sympathies were ejected from their positions in the Church of England because of their refusal to accept the 1662 Act of Uniformity, which required them by that date to publicly agree to use the Book of Common Prayer and to submit to reordination by bishops if they had not been so ordained. Perhaps nearly another thousand had been ejected in 1660 with the restoration of the monarchy, or shortly thereafter.

Benefice
An ecclesiastical office such as a rectory, deanery, or vicarage.

Bible Commonwealths
A term referring to the New England puritan colonies that reflects the goal of the founders to create godly societies, in accord with the will of God as expressed in the Bible.

Cambridge Platonists
A group of English scholars and thinkers, centered at Cambridge University, who developed a Christian Platonism in the middle of the seventeenth century as a philosophical defense of the Christian faith and of the reality of the spiritual realm. Notable among them were Benjamin Whichcote, John Smith, Ralph Cudworth, and Henry More.

Canons
Laws legislated for the governance of the Church of England by the convocations (assemblies of bishops and representative clergy) of Canterbury and York.

Casuistry
The branch of ethics that seeks to apply general rules of religion and morality to resolve particular cases of conscience. Sometimes used in a negative sense, almost as a synonym for *rationalization.*

Chancel
The area of the church where, prior to the Reformation, the priest would conduct the sacrifice of the Mass. Believed to be holier than the rest of the church, it was sometimes also referred to as the Sanctuary. The chancel was often physically separated from the body of the church by a screen.

Chantry
A place, usually a side altar, where a priest said masses for the release of a deceased soul from purgatory. It also referred to the office held by the priest, which was funded by an endowment created for the purpose of having masses said for the particular individual. The chantries were dissolved in 1547 as part of the English Reformation.

Chaplain
A priest who officiated at a chapel, serving the religious needs of a private family. Noble families often hired a chaplain to be sure of getting the religious counsel they desired.

Church Ales
Community festivals to raise funds for the parish church.

Church Papist
This is a term used to refer to Roman Catholics who chose to fulfill the legal requirements of attending religious services in a Church of England parish while retaining loyalty to Catholicism in conscience. They were thus distinguished from those who openly recused themselves from Church of England services. See "Recusants."

Churching
Sometimes referred to as purification, this was a ceremony required by the church whereby a woman was allowed back into the church following childbirth.

Churchwardens
Lay officers of the parish who administered church property, including bequests to the parish; staged entertainments such as church ales to raise funds; collected fees for bell ringing and burials; and were responsible for the maintenance of the church. Most often there were two wardens for a parish, chosen by the parishioners at Easter. Surveys of English parishes in the early modern period suggest that individuals from the highest and lowest strata of society were unlikely to be chosen, meaning that the wardens tended to come from the middling ranks of society. Wardens were expected to report moral offenders to the archdeaconry courts and to respond to the visitation inquiries of the bishop. Their influence in a parish could be considerable.

Classis and Classes
In the system of presbyterian government proposed by the Westminster Assembly, England was to be divided into provinces (roughly the same as counties), with each province divided into *classes* (the plural of *classis*). Each classis included a group of parishes, and they were to be governed by clergymen and lay elders, known collectively as *presbyters,* from the Greek term for "elders," from the constituent parishes.

Combination lecture
A voluntary arrangement by a group of clergy to provide regular preaching, usually in a market town.

Comprehension
The proposal that the post-Restoration Church of England be broadly based to include a variety of beliefs and practices.

Consistory Court
The court in the Church of England that administered ecclesiastical justice within a diocese. In a presbyterian system, it is a court of lay elders and clergy that regulates the moral life of a congregation.

Conventicle
A term used in a variety of ways to refer to prohibited religious meetings.

Convocations
The clerical assemblies of the two provinces of the English church, Canterbury and York. By the end of the thirteenth century, the bishops, abbots, archdeacons, and representatives of the clergy of each diocese met in convocation to legislate for the province.

Court of Augmentations
The court established in 1535 that administered the lands and possessions of the dissolved religious houses, such as the monasteries. One of its purposes was to augment the royal income through the sale of those properties and possessions.

Curate
A clergyman who was a deputy appointed to serve a parish by the individual who held the living.

Decalogue
An alternative name for the Ten Commandments.

Degradation
The depriving a clergyman of his holy orders, benefice, and privileges.

Deprivation
The removal of a clergyman from his ecclesiastical living.

Directory of Public Worship
Adopted by Parliament in 1645 on the recommendation of the Westminster Assembly; a document that called for a new liturgy that would have replaced the Book of Common Prayer. It was seen as the first step in establishing a presbyterian system, but was ignored in much of the country.

Dissenting Academies
Schools for the training of young men, especially for the ministry, that were established by Protestant dissenters from the Church of England after the restoration of the monarchy in 1660 and the exclusion of Dissenters from the universities of Oxford and Cambridge.

Ecclesiology
The theological study of the nature and characteristics of the church. It was a hotly contested subject in the Reformation period, as individuals sought to determine what the shape of the true church was.

Elect
In a religious context, a term used to refer to those whom God had selected (elected) for salvation.

Erastianism
The philosophy that claimed that the state should maintain responsibility for the church.

Eschatology
The branch of theology that deals with the Last Things (that is, the events that were expected to accompany the end of the world).

Et Cetera Oath
The "et cetera oath," required of all clergy by Convocation in 1640, was an oath never to undertake alteration of the church's government "by Archbishops, bishops, deans, archdeacons, etc." It was one of the canons intended to codify Archbishop William Laud's innovations, and it was seen by puritans and their supporters as another step in reintroducing Catholicism to England.

Ex Officio Oath
The *ex officio* oath was employed in prerogative courts such as the Court of High Commission; by it, a person could be compelled to indict himself on his own evidence.

Excommunication
A penalty whereby an individual is cut off from the church and denied participation in its affairs.

Exorcism
The process of expelling devils or evil spirits from a possessed person by means of prayer. Exorcisms could be public events in which clergy enhanced their reputations by means of a successful exorcism.

First Fruits and Tenths
Beneficed clergy in England were required to pay the Exchequer (Crown treasury) the first year's revenue ("first fruits") from their living as assessed by the Crown, and then a tenth of their income thereafter.

Five Articles of 1618
Articles passed by the General Assembly of the Church of Scotland in 1618 at the insistence of King James VI (of

Scotland) and I (of England). They provided for the observance of holy days, stipulated that the sacrament of confirmation be administered by bishops, required kneeling at Holy Communion, and allowed for private baptism and communion. They were perceived by many as signaling a drift back toward Catholic practice.

Font
A receptacle for holding the water used in the sacrament of baptism. In the pre-Reformation church, the font was most often made of stone and set on a carved stone pedestal located in the nave of the church, near the entrance. Some reformers wished to replace the font with a movable basin, which could be brought to the area near the communion table for the sacrament.

Freewillers
A sect in the sixteenth century that believed in the exercise of free will in achieving salvation and that generally supported religious toleration. The sect existed in the country of Essex and elsewhere during Edward's reign. A group of Freewillers was arrested by the religious authorities under the Roman Catholic Mary Tudor.

Gathered Church
A church or congregation that is organized by the voluntary coming together of the members, as distinguished from a parish church where membership is determined by virtue of one's geographical location. Such congregations of churches are usually self-governing.

General Assembly
The governing body of the Church of Scotland. Originally composed of members of the three estates, by the seventeenth century it consisted of clergy and elders chosen by local presbyteries.

General Baptists
English and later colonial American Baptists who were not Calvinists, but adhered to an Arminian theology, so named because of their belief in a general offer of salvation to all. General Baptists go back to John Smyth and Thomas Helwys at the beginning of the seventeenth century.

Grammar School
A school in which someone who had already received an elementary education in reading and writing would pursue a classical curriculum, preparatory to entering a university.

Guilds
Also referred to as confraternities, guilds were associations of local Christians in the pre-Reformation era.

They were designed to further piety and to support the members in tangible ways. In the nonreligious context, the term *guild* refers to associations of craftsmen or others who regulated the business conduct of the members.

Homily
Another term for a sermon. From the 1540s on, the Church of England issued an official *Book of Homilies,* which offered packaged sermons for clergymen not licensed to preach or unable to preach their own sermons.

Host
The wafer of consecrated bread that was distributed in Holy Communion. Catholics and Protestants disagreed over the nature of the host.

Incumbent
The individual who holds an office. In a religious context this was the individual who held a benefice, such as a rector or a vicar.

Induction
There were various stages leading to clergyman receiving a benefice in the Church of England. *Ordination* was the first stage, in which the individual was admitted to the ministry through a ceremonial laying on of hands. After an ordained minister was chosen to hold a living (benefice), he was *instituted* by a bishop, empowering him to exercise the spiritual responsibilities of the living. *Induction,* usually by an archdeacon, then followed, whereby the minister acquired legal possession of the rights, tithes, and other endowments of the parish.

Infralapsarianism
The term *infralapsarian* comes from Latin words that mean, roughly, "after the fall," in this case the fall of Adam. Infralapsarianism was a further definition of the doctrine of predestination, according to which God's decrees of election and reprobation are logically subsequent in the divine mind to God's decree of creation and permission of the Fall. To put that in lay language, God was believed to have decided first that he would create the world and human beings and allow Adam and Eve to fall; only then did God decide that he would save only some of those who were born of Adam and Eve (and thus inherited their guilt), leaving the rest to the just punishment of the sins they would commit. For the other main interpretation of the doctrine of predestination, see Supralapsarianism. For more discussion, see the entry on predestination.

Inns of Court

Located in Westminster, these were the residential inns in which men trained for the practice of the law. Four of them—Gray's Inn, Lincoln's Inn, the Inner Temple, and the Middle Temple—licensed those who were admitted to plead in the national courts. Some attended the Inns to be admitted to the bar; others used attendance to acquire knowledge useful in managing their estates, to acquire social polish, or to form friendships that would be useful in later life. A number of prominent puritan clergy, such as Richard Sibbes, were preachers at the Inns.

Institution

See Induction.

Interregnum

An interregnum is any period between two reigns. When capitalized, the term refers to the period between the execution of King Charles I in 1649 and the return of the monarchy with his son King Charles II in 1660.

Latitudinarian, Latitudinarianism

These were general terms used in the later seventeenth century to refer to liberalized forms of Christianity both within and outside the Church of England. Latitudinarians emphasized reason and individual judgment over prescribed church doctrines.

Lecturer

A minister hired specifically to preach, without obligation to administer the sacraments or officiate in church services. Puritans saw the holding of such a post as a means of preaching God's word without being faced with the requirement to use ceremonies or practices that they considered unscriptural. A lecturer might be hired to supplement the ministry of a rector or vicar who was not prepared to preach or who preached infrequently. Lecturers were also hired by towns to offer regular sermons on market days. A combination lectureship brought a number of lecturers together to take turns preaching.

Liturgy

A prescribed form or set of forms for public worship, which included the gestures and words used in acts of worship.

Living

See Benefice.

Millenarianism

The belief that at some point in the future there will be a *millennium,* a thousand-year rule of Christ and the saints. There are a variety of nuances that were not always clearly developed or discussed in the sixteenth and seventeenth centuries. One concerns the timing of the millennium in reference to the second coming of Christ, with one position (later referred to as *premillennialism*) seeing the second coming as the event that was going to transform earthly existence and begin the millennium, and the other (*postmillennialism*) seeing the second coming as the climax of the thousand-year rule of the saints. Closely associated with this is a difference over the role of human beings. One position sees the transformation precipitated by a cataclysmic and cleansing devastation of the world (an apocalypse), with human beings passive. Another view is that human beings, with the grace of God, have a role in perfecting society and ushering in the millennium. During the English conflicts of the mid-seventeenth century, some groups, such as the Fifth Monarchists, felt called upon to engage in bringing about the millennium.

Nave

The main body of the church in which the members of the congregation stood (in the Middle Ages) or sat (which became more common in the early modern era). In larger churches seating areas were separated by aisles.

New England Way

The system of New England church organization and practice as developed in the colonies in the 1630s and 1640s, whose essential characteristics were relative independence for each congregation and membership in the congregation only for those who were convinced they were saved. In the debates over English church reform during the 1640s and 1650s, the Dissenting Brethren and others often pointed to the "New England Way" as a model worth considering. Presbyterians frequently were critical of the system.

Nonjurors

The term refers to the four hundred or so Church of England clergymen who refused to take the oath of allegiance to William and Mary following the Glorious Revolution of 1688. They justified their refusal on the basis that James II was still *de jure* (by law) the monarch of England and William and Mary were not. These Nonjurors were consequently deprived of their livings.

Non-Separating Congregationalism

A term employed by some to distinguish those Congregationalists, such as the New Englanders of the 1630s, who maintained that they had not left the Church of England, as well as other Congregationalists who sought a position within a larger church, from the Separatists, who also advocated congregational polity but who severed ties with the national church.

Ordination

Ordination was the rite that empowered bishops, priests, and deacons. The Church of England adopted most of the ceremonies of the Roman Catholic Church in this regard. Those submitting themselves for ordination were to be examined by a bishop or his representative on their knowledge and vocation and regarding their behavior. In the ceremony itself, the bishop placed his hands on the head of the candidate and charged him to be a faithful preacher and minister of the sacraments.

Overseers of the Poor

Parish officials appointed by the vestry and charged with administering the poor laws.

Parish Chest

In 1538 Thomas Cromwell directed that each parish obtain a "secure coffer" to hold its records. These chests can often be seen in English churches today.

Particular Baptists

Calvinistic Baptists who believe in predestination, that is, God's choice of particular persons for salvation. They first appeared as a group in England in the 1640s.

Patristic

Pertaining to the church fathers, a group of early Christian writers who lived after the New Testament period but preceded the medieval theologians, in other words, non-biblical writers of Christian antiquity. Their authority carried weight with both Protestants and Roman Catholics. Prominent among the Latin fathers were Tertullian, Cyprian, Augustine, and Ambrose, and among the Greek fathers, Irenaeus, Basil, and Chrysostom.

Pelagianism

A viewpoint associated with the heretic Pelagius (d. 419), an opponent of St. Augustine, who was accused of teaching that man earned salvation by his own efforts and possessed free will.

Pluralism

The practice of a clergyman holding two or more livings simultaneously. The impetus to pluralism came from the difficulties caused by the poor remuneration provided by many livings and the need to provide an educated preaching ministry. The objection was that clergy in these circumstances neglected their pastoral responsibilities.

Practical Divinity

Preaching, writing, and counsel designed to apply the doctrines of faith to the everyday lives of believers, counseling them on how to pray and meditate and how to detect signs of their spiritual state. It became a central concern of puritans such as Richard Rogers in the late sixteenth and early seventeenth centuries.

Practical Syllogism

A term often used to describe the spiritual logic of those Protestants, including puritans, who held that good behavior was the logical consequence of spiritual election. In other words, believers were assured that, if they exhibited good behavior, this was evidence of the transformation of their souls that was taking place because God had "elected" them for salvation and was now acting in their lives.

Precentor

The director of music in the church.

Pulpit

The pulpit is an elevated platform in the church from which lessons may be read and sermons preached. They began to appear in the fourteenth century with the popularity of itinerant Franciscan preachers. With the greater emphasis on preaching following the Reformation, Edward VI ordered that every church should have a "comely and honest pulpit." Many of these became towering, elaborate structures.

Purgatory

In Catholic belief, purgatory was a place where the souls of the departed went to be purged of the consequences of their sins before being able to enter heaven. The time one spent in purgatory could be reduced by indulgences one received for one's actions while still living, and by the application to the individual in purgatory of credits earned through the efforts of those still on earth. Protestants rejected the belief in purgatory.

Rector

The rector was the incumbent of a parish to whom the tithes were owed. The rector was responsible for maintenance of the church chancel and the rectory and for providing service books and vestments for the conduct of religious services. When the right to tithes was appropriated to a layperson or corporate body, a vicar was appointed to perform the tasks of the rector.

Recusants

Recusants were those, primarily Roman Catholics, who recused themselves from (refused to attend) services of the Church of England, attendance at which was required by law. From 1552 they were subject to weekly fines, which were substantially increased in 1581.

Regicides

The fifty-nine commissioners who signed the death warrant for Charles I in 1649 and thus became king-killers (the literal translation of *regicides*).

Reredos

A decorative screen made of stone or timber that traditionally covered the wall behind and above the altar. The reredos could be decorated with painted panels or statues in its various niches.

Root and Branch Petition

In 1640 Parliament was presented with this petition, signed by over 15,000 London laypeople and clergy, calling for the abolition of episcopacy "with all its dependencies, roots and branches." In response a bill was introduced in May 1641 that would have abolished bishops, deans, and chapters and replace them with regional commissions of clergy and laymen to organize church affairs, but the bill was passed over in favor of other proposals.

Sacraments

A sacrament is an outward and visible sign, or rite, that is held by some to bestow, by others (most puritans among them) to symbolize the bestowing of inward grace. In the Catholic Church there are seven sacraments: baptism, confirmation, the Eucharist (or Holy Communion), matrimony, ordination, penance, and the last rites. Protestant churches, including the Church of England in the sixteenth and seventeenth centuries, reduced the official sacraments to two, baptism and the Eucharist.

Sanctification

This term may refer to the process whereby God makes a sinner whom he has elected holy, or it may refer to the state of holiness of the elect, which enables them to better follow God's will.

Sect

A congregation or group of congregations that has split from an established church because of a strongly held and distinctive spiritual insight.

Select Vestry

See Vestry.

Solifidianism

The belief that man is justified, or saved, by faith alone, a position taken by most Protestant theologians.

Star Chamber

A prerogative court (that is, a court established on the king's authority) that met in the Star Chamber of the Palace of Westminster. It was used in the sixteenth century for political cases and cases involving public order. It operated outside the provisions and restrictions of the common law. It was used by Charles I to deal with his opponents and was abolished by the Long Parliament.

Supralapsarianism

The term *supralapsarianism* comes from the Latin words meaning "before the fall," in this case the fall of Adam. It was used to describe an elaboration of the doctrine of predestination in which the decrees of election and reprobation are said to logically precede in the divine mind the decree of creation and the divine permission of the fall. In effect, the belief was that God had decided first that some human beings would be saved and some damned, and that he had decided which would meet which fate, simply by his inscrutable will; afterwards he decided to create the world and human beings and to allow Adam and Eve to fall. For the other main interpretation of the doctrine of predestination, see Infralapsarianism. For more discussion, see the entry on predestination.

Surplice

A white linen robe that was part of the vestments worn by priests while officiating at religious services. Protestants wished to do away with this article of dress, which they associated with Roman Catholic practice, but the Church of England, while discarding other vestments, insisted on its use.

Tithes

Tithes were payments of a tenth of one's personal income, profits, or agricultural produce to the church. These traditional payments were intended for the support of the local parish clergyman. In the Middle Ages, the legal right to tithes was impropriated (taken over) by a monastery or a bishop, who paid a portion of the tithes to the clergyman whom they installed in the parish. With the Reformation, impropriation rights that had belonged to monasteries were acquired by the laymen who acquired monastic lands. A common complaint was that many of these laymen kept the bulk of the tithes as personal income while paying the parish clergyman a pittance. In Scotland the term used was *teind*.

Transubstantiation

The Roman Catholic belief that the consecration of bread and wine by a priest during Mass transforms those "elements" into the body and blood of Jesus Christ.

Unitarians
Those who rejected the doctrine of the Trinity and insisted on the unity of the Godhead.

Universalism
Belief in the ultimate salvation of all human beings; sometimes used to designate the Arminian belief that rejected the election of particular persons to salvation and taught that salvation was universally *available* for all human beings.

Vestments
The clothing worn by clergy in performing religious services. In the pre-Reformation church these included an alb, cassock, chasuble, cope, girdle, stole, and surplice. Protestants saw these as symbolic of the Roman Catholic doctrine that ordination to the priesthood conferred special powers and rejected their use. The insistence of the Church of England that the surplice continue to be used was a source of contention between the leaders of that church and the puritan reformers.

Vestry
Originally, a room in the church where vestments were stored. The term also came to refer to the members of the parish gathered there to make decisions on the government of the church. In most parishes the vestry was composed of all householders in the parish. During the sixteenth century, in some parts of England, responsibilities were shifted to a "select vestry" composed of some of the wealthier members of the community. Such select vestries might fill vacancies by their own choice rather than by vote of the parish as a whole, thus contributing to an oligarchic shift in those communities.

Vicar
In a parish where the tithes were in the control of a layperson or corporate body, the clergyman who served the parish was referred to as a vicar rather than as a rector.

Visitation
A required inspection of a diocese by a bishop (diocesan visitation) or of an archdiocese by an archbishop. Visitation articles were items of inquiry that were distributed to parish officials preparatory to the actual visit.

Wall Paintings
In the Middle Ages, the walls of many parish churches were adorned by paintings that depicted scenes from scripture, episodes in the lives of saints, and images of the Last Judgment. At the Reformation, these paintings were generally covered over with whitewash.

Works
In discussions of the process of salvation, the term *works* was shorthand for acts of human agency—such as observances of ritual, acts of charity, and the like—that some believed could help an individual earn, or merit, salvation. Most puritans believed that one could never be saved by works, only by faith.

Primary Sources

Anne Hutchinson's Statement

In the course of her trial before the General Court, Anne Marbury Hutchinson told the magistrates and those assembled how God had come to her and how she had reached the conclusions that had brought her to the attention of the authorities. Assuming that this is an accurate account of what she said, it is the closest we have to an account of her beliefs in her own words. This statement was used as ground to convict her, both for her claim of immediate revelations from God, and the threat to the colony she made at the end of it.

> Source: John Winthrop, *A Short Story of the Rise, reign, and ruine of the Antinomians, Familists & Libertines that infected the Churches of New England* (London, 1644).

When I was in old England, I was very much troubled at the constitution of the churches there, so far as I was ready to have joined the Separation [Separatists]. Whereupon I set aside a day for humiliation by myself to seek direction from God. And then God did discover unto me the unfaithfulness of the churches, and the dangers of them, and that none of those ministers could preach the Lord Jesus aright, He had brought to mind that [passage] in 1 John 4:3, *Every spirit that confesseth not that Jesus Christ is come in the flesh, is the spirit of Antichrist.* I marveled what this should mean, for I knew that neither Protestants nor Papists did deny that Christ was come in the flesh, and are the Turks then the only Antichrists?

Now I had none to open the scripture to me but the Lord. He must be the prophet. Then he brought to my mind another scripture [Hebrews 9:16–17], *He that de-*

nies the testament, denies the death of the testator. From whence the Lord did let me see that everyone that did not preach the new covenant denies the death of the testator. Then it was revealed to me that the ministers of England were these Antichrists. But I knew not how to bear this. I did in my heart rise up against it. Then I begged of the Lord that this atheism might not be in my heart. After I had begged this light a twelve month together, at last he let me see how I did oppose Christ Jesus, and he revealed to me that place in Isaiah 46:12–13, and from thence showed me the atheism of my own heart, and how I did turn in upon a covenant of works, and did oppose Christ Jesus.

From which time the Lord did discover to me all sorts of ministers, and how they taught, and to know what voice I heard—which was the voice of Moses, which of John Baptist, which of Christ, the voice of my beloved—from the voice of strangers. And thenceforth I was the more careful whom I heard, for after our teacher Mr. Cotton, and my brother Wheelwright were put down, there was none in England that I durst hear. Then it pleased God to reveal himself to me in that of Isaiah 30:20, *Though the Lord give thee the bread of adversity, etc., yet thine eyes shall see thy teachers.* After this, the Lord carrying Mr. Cotton to New England (at which I was much troubled) it was revealed to me that I must go thither also, and that there I should be persecuted and suffer much trouble.

I will give you another scripture, Jeremiah 46 [:28], *Fear not, Jacob my servant, for I am with thee, I will make a full end of all the nations, etc.* The Lord did reveal himself to me, sitting upon a throne of justice, and all the world appearing before him. And though I must come to new England, yet I must not fear nor be dismayed. The Lord brought another scripture to me, Isaiah 8:11, *The Lord spake this to me with a strong hand, and instructed me that I should not walk in the way of the people, etc.* I will give you one place more which the Lord brought to me by immediate revelations, and that doth concern you all. It is in Daniel 6 [:4–5]. When the presidents and princes could find nothing against him, because he was faithful, they sought matter against him concerning the law of God, to cast him into the lion's den. So it was revealed to me that they should plot against me. But the Lord bid me not to fear, for he that delivered Daniel and the three children his hand was not shortened. And see this scripture fulfilled this day in mine eyes.

Therefore take heed what ye go about to do unto me, for you have no power over my body, neither can you do me any harm, for I am in the hands of the eternal Jehovah, my Savior. I am at his appointment. The bounds of my habitation are cast in heaven. No more do I esteem of any mortal man than creatures in his hand. I fear none but the great Jehovah, which hath foretold me of these things, and I do verily believe that he will deliver me out of your hands. Therefore, take heed how you proceed against me, for I know that for this you go about to do to me, God will ruin you and your posterity, and this whole state.

Book of Sports

The declaration issued by Charles I in 1633, which incorporates the declarations issued by his father, King James I, in 1617 and 1618. See the entry for "Book of Sports."

Source: *The King's Majesty's declaration to his subjects concerning lawful sports to be used* (London, 1633).

Our dear father of blessed memory, in his return from Scotland, coming through Lancashire, found that his subjects were debarred from lawful recreations upon Sundays after evening prayers ended, and upon Holydays; and he prudently considered that, if these times were taken from them, the meaner sort who labor hard all the week should have no recreations at all to refresh their spirits: and after his return, he further saw that his loyal subjects in all other parts of his kingdom did suffer in the same kind, though perhaps not in the same degree: and did therefore in his princely wisdom publish a Declaration to all his loving subjects concerning lawful sports to be used at such times, which was printed and published by his royal commandment in the year 1618, in the tenor which hereafter follows:

Whereas upon our return the last year out of Scotland, we did publish our pleasure touching the recreations of our people in those parts under our hand; for some causes us thereunto moving, we have thought good to command these our directions then given in Lancashire, with a few words thereunto added, and most applicable to these parts of our realms, to be published to all our subjects.

Whereas we did justly in our progress through Lancashire rebuke some Puritans and precise people, and took order that the like unlawful carriage should not be used by any of them hereafter, in the prohibiting and unlawful punishing of our good people for using their lawful recreations and honest exercises upon Sundays, and other Holy-days, after the afternoon sermon or service, we now find that two sorts of people wherewith that country is much infected, we mean Papists and Puritans, have maliciously traduced and calumniated those our just and honorable proceedings: and therefore, lest our reputation might upon the one side (though innocently) have some aspersion laid upon it, and that upon the other part our good people in that country be misled by the mistaking and misinterpretation of our meaning, we have therefore thought good hereby to clear and make our pleasure to be manifested to all our good people in those parts.

It is true that at our first entry to this Crown and kingdom we were informed, and that too truly, that our county of Lancashire abounded more in Popish Recusants than any county of England, and thus hath still continued since, to our great regret, with little amendment, save that, now of late, in our last riding through our said country, we find both by the report of the Judges, and of the Bishop of that Diocese, that there is some amendment now daily beginning, which is no small contentment to us.

The report of this growing amendment amongst them made us the more sorry, when with our own ears we heard the general complaint of our people, that they were barred from all lawful recreations and exercise upon the Sunday's afternoon, after the ending of all divine service, which cannot but produce two evils: the one the hindering of the conversion of many, whom their priests will take occasion hereby to vex, persuading them that no honest mirth or recreation is lawful or tolerable in our religion, which cannot but breed a great discontentment in our people's hearts, especially of such as are peradventure upon the point of turning: the other inconvenience is, that this prohibition bars the common and meaner sort of people from using such exercises as may make their bodies more able for war, when His Majesty or his successors shall have occasion to use them; and in place thereof sets up filthy tippling and drunkenness, and breeds a number of idle and discontented speeches in their alehouses. For when shall the common people have leave to exercise, if not upon the Sundays and Holy-days, seeing they must apply their labor and win their living in all working days?

Our express pleasure therefore is, that the laws of our kingdom and canons of the Church be as well observed in that county, as in all other places of this our kingdom: and on the other part, that no lawful recreation shall be barred to our good people, which shall not tend to the breach of our aforesaid laws and canons of our Church: which to express more particularly, our pleasure is, that the Bishop, and all other inferior churchmen and churchwardens, shall for their parts be careful and diligent, both to instruct the ignorant, and convince and reform them that are misled in religion, presenting them that will not conform themselves, but obstinately stand out, to our Judges and Justices: whom we likewise command to put the law in due execution against them.

Our pleasure likewise is, that the Bishop of that Diocese take the like strait order with all the Puritans and Precisians within the same, either constraining them to conform themselves or to leave the county, according to the laws of our kingdom and canons of our Church, and so to strike equally on both hands against the condemners of our authority and adversaries of our Church; and as for our good people's lawful recreation, our pleasure likewise is, that after the end of divine service our good people be not disturbed, letted or discouraged from any lawful recreation, such as dancing, either men or women; archery for men, leaping, vaulting, or any other such harmless recreation, nor from having of May-games, Whitsun-ales, and Morris-dances; and the setting up of May-poles and other sports therewith used: so as the same be had in due and convenient time, without impediment or neglect of divine service: and that women shall have leave to carry rushes to the church for the decorating of it, according to their old custom; but withal we do here account still as prohibited all unlawful games to be used upon Sundays only, as bear and bull-baiting, interludes and at all times in the meaner sort of people by law prohibited, bowling.

And likewise we bar from this benefit and liberty all such known Recusants, either men or women, as will abstain from coming to church or divine service, being therefore unworthy of any lawful recreation after the said service, that will not first come to the church and serve God: prohibiting in like sort the said recreations to any that, though conform in religion, are not present in the church at the service of God, before their going to the said recreations. Our pleasure likewise is, that they to whom it belongs in office, shall present and sharply punish all such, as in abuse of this our liberty, will use these exercises before the end of all divine services for that day: and we likewise straightly command that every person shall resort to his own parish church to hear divine service, and each parish by itself to use the said recreation after divine service: prohibiting likewise any offensive weapons to be carried or used in the said times of recreation: and our pleasure is, that this our Declaration shall be published by order from the Bishop of the Diocese, through all the parish churches, and that both our Judges of our circuit and our Justices of our Peace be informed thereof.

Given at our Manor of Greenwich the four and twentieth day of May, in the sixteenth year of our Reign, of England, France and Ireland; and of Scotland the one and fiftieth.

Now out of a like pious care for the service of God, and for suppressing of any humors that oppose truth, and for the ease, comfort and recreation of our well-deserving people, His Majesty doth ratify and publish this our blessed father's Declaration: the rather, because of late in some counties of our kingdom, we find that under pretence of taking away abuses, there hath been a general forbidding, not only of ordinary meetings, but of the Feasts of the Dedication of the Churches, commonly called Wakes. Now our express will and pleasure is, that these Feasts, with others, shall be observed, and that our Justices of the Peace, in their several divisions, shall look to it, both that all disorders there may be prevented or punished, and that all neighborhood and freedom, with manlike and lawful exercises be used: and we further command all Justices of Assize in their several circuits to see that no man do trouble or molest any of our loyal and dutiful people, in or for their lawful recreations, having first done their duty to God, and continuing in obedience to us and our laws: and for this we command all our Judges, Justices of Peace, as well within liberties as without, Mayors, Bailiffs, Constables, and other officers, to take notice of, and to see observed, as they tender our displeasure. And we further will that publication of this our command be made by order from the Bishops, through all the parish churches of their several dioceses respectively.

Given at our Palace of Westminster, the eighteenth day of October, in the ninth year of our Reign.

God save the King

Description of Boston, 1638

John Wiswall emigrated to Massachusetts in the late 1630s. In 1638 he wrote to George Rigby, an English friend and benefactor, to describe the new land in which he had settled. The following description of Boston and the Massachusetts colony is from that letter.

Source: *Historical Record Commission: Mss of Lord Kenyon* (London, 1894).

There is a pretty castle and fort to which the ships lower their top gallants before they pass into Boston, and divers there shoot two or three cannons, and then the fort will welcome and salute them with one. For the land, it is a fine land, good for corn, especially Indian (which is a very precious grain for divers uses besides bread), good for pasture, and good hay land, plenty of wood. It is a pleasant country to look upon. Truly, sir, I like it very well, and so I think any godly man God calls over will, when he sees Moses and Aaron—I mean magistrate and minister—in church and commonwealth to walk hand in hand, discountenancing and punishing sin in whomsoever, and standing for the praise of them that do well.

Our sovereign Lord and King is King Charles, whose crown and honor is daily prayed for in all the churches. Under him we have a Governor, Deputy, and Council, and men called Assistants, in power, much like your justices. Constables we have in every town. Men we call Committees [deputies] we send from every town to the general Court.

Plantations there are divers, and they succeed and prosper well. Boston is a pretty town. In it there are fine houses and some six or seven shops finely furnished with all commodities. There is a pretty quay and a crane, as at Bristol, to lade and unlade goods. There is a warehouse wherein strangers' and passengers' goods may be put. Newtown now is called Cambridge. There a university house [is] reared, I hear, and a pretty library begun. There is also Roxbury, Dorchester, Salem, and divers towns. At Connecticut there are some pretty plantations. But to wind up all in one word, things prosper well, and men of pretty parts God sends over, both for church and commonweal. The Indians are a pretty active, ingenious people in kind, yet loving to us.

Catholic Worship before the Reformation

Not all Englishmen welcomed the Protestant Reformation launched by King Henry VIII. Roger Marten (c.1527–1615) was a parishioner in the Suffolk parish of Long Melford who was deeply devoted to the forms of worship of the pre-Reformation church. In this excerpt from a memoir he wrote late in Elizabeth's reign, he remembers the appearance of the church in the days of his youth, and its brief restoration during the reign of Queen Mary.

He makes reference to having saved one of the statues dispensed with at the Reformation, which he moved to his home.

Source: William Parker, *The History of Long Melford* (London, 1873), pp. 70–71.

At the back of the high altar in the said church there was a goodly mount, made of one great tree, and set up to the foot of the window there, carved very artificially with the story of Christ's passion, representing the horse-men with their swords and the footmen, etc. as they used Christ on the mount of Calvary, all being fair gilt, and lively and beautifully set forth. To cover and keep clean all the which, there were very fair and painted boards, made to shut to, which were opened upon high and solemn feast days, which then was a very beautiful show. Which painted boards were set up again in Queen Mary's time. At the north end of the same altar, there was a goodly tabernacle, reaching up to the roof of the chancel, in the which there was one large fair gilt image of the Holy Trinity, being patron of the church; besides other fair images. The like tabernacle was at the south end.

There was also in my aisle, called "Jesus aisle," at the back of the altar, a table with a crucifix on it, with two thieves hanging, on every side, one [of which] which is in my house, decayed. And the same I hope my heirs will repair and restore again one day. There was also two fair [gilt] tabernacles, from the ground up to the roof, with a fair image of Jesus in the tabernacle at the north end of the altar, holding a round ball in his hand, signifying I think that he containeth the whole round world. And in the tabernacle at the south end there was a fair image of Our Blessed Lady, having the afflicted body of her dear son, as he was taken down off the cross, lying along on her lap, the tears as it were running down pitifully upon her beautiful cheeks, as it seemed bedewing the said sweet body of her son, and therefore named the image of Our Lady of Pity.

There was a fair rood loft with the rood; Mary and John of every side, and with a fair pair of organs standing there by; which loft extended all the breadth of the church. And on Good Friday a priest then standing by the rood sang the Passion. The side thereof towards the body of the church, in twelve partitions in boards, was fair painted with the images of the twelve apostles. All the roof of the church was beautified with fair gilt stars. Finally, in the vestry where there were many rich copes and suits of vestments there was a fair press with fair large doors to shut to, wherein there were made devices to hang on all the copes, without folding or crumpling of them, with a convenient distance the one from the other.

Conversion Narratives

It was common for puritans to record their progress towards grace in diaries or other forms of journals. On occasion, they shared these narratives with others to help those who would hear or read the story to achieve a better understanding of their own religious pilgrimage. There are many such accounts. The following are by two lay believers, one male and one female.

I. John Winthrop's Conversion Narrative

John Winthrop was the first governor of the Massachusetts Bay Colony. He emigrated to New England in 1630, at the age of forty-two. In 1637 he reviewed his lengthy spiritual diary to compile this summary of his relationship with God.

> Source: *The Winthrop Papers, Volume III: 1631–1637* (Boston, 1943), pp. 338–344.

In my youth I was very lewdly disposed, inclining unto and attempting (so far as my years enabled me) all kind of wickedness, except swearing and scorning religion, which I had no temptation unto in regard of my education. About ten years of age I had some notions of God, for in some great frighting or danger, I have prayed unto God, and have found manifest answer; the remembrance whereof many years after made me think that God did love me, but it made me no whit the better.

After I was 12 years old, I began to have some more savor of Religion, and I thought I had more understanding in Divinity then many of my years, for in reading of some good books I conceived that I did know divers of those points before, though I knew not how I should come by such knowledge (but since I perceived it was out of some Logical principles, whereby out of some things I could conclude other). Yet I was still very wild, and dissolute, and as years came on my lusts grew stronger, but yet under some restraint of my natural reason; whereby I had the command of myself that I could turn into any form. I would, as occasion required, write letters etc. of mere vanity; and if occasion were, I could write others of savory and Godly counsel.

About 14 years of age, being in Cambridge, I fell into a lingering fever, which took away the comfort of my life. For being there neglected, and despised, I went up and down mourning with my self; and being deprived of my youthful joys, I betook my self to God, whom I did believe to be very good and merciful, and would welcome any that would come to him, especially such a young soul, and so well qualified as I took my self to be; so as I took pleasure in drawing near to him. But how my heart was affected with my sins, or what thoughts I had of Christ I remember not. But I was willing to love God, and therefore I thought he loved me. But so soon as I recovered my perfect health, and met with somewhat else to take pleasure in, I forgot my former acquaintance with God, and fell to former lusts, and grew worse then before. Yet some good moods I had now and then, and sad checks of my natural Conscience, by which the lord preserved me from some foul sins, which otherwise I had fallen into. But my lusts were so masterly as no good could fasten upon me, otherwise then to hold me to some task of ordinary duties, for I cared for nothing but how to satisfy my voluptuous heart.

About 18 years of age, (being a man in stature, and understanding as my parents conceived me) I married into a family under Mr. Culverwell his ministry in Essex; and living there sometimes I first found the ministry of the word to come home to my heart with power (for in all before I found only light), and after that I found the like in the ministry of many others. So as there began to be some change which I perceived in myself, and others took notice of. Now I began to come under strong exercises of Conscience: (yet by fits only). I could no longer dally with Religion. God put my soul to sad tasks sometimes, which yet the flesh would shake off, and outwear still. I had withal many sweet invitations which I would willingly have entertained, but the flesh would not give up her interest. The merciful Lord would not thus be answered, but notwithstanding all my stubbornness and unkind rejections of mercy, he left me not till he had overcome my heart to give up it self to him, and to bid farewell to all the world, and until my heart could answer, Lord what wilt thou have me to do?

Now came I to some peace and comfort in God and in his ways. My chief delight was therein, I loved a Christian, and the very ground he went upon, I honored a faithful minister in my heart and could have kissed his feet. Now I grew full of zeal (which outran my knowledge and carried me sometimes beyond my Calling), and very liberal to any good work. I had an insatiable thirst after the word of God and could not miss a good sermon, though many miles off, especially of such as did search deep into the Conscience. I had also a great striving in my heart to draw others to God. It pitied my heart to see men so little to regard their souls, and to despise that happiness which I knew to be better than all the world besides, which stirred me up to take any opportunity to draw men to God, and by success in my endeavors I took much encouragement hereunto. But those affections were not constant, but very unsettled. By these occasions I grew to be of some note for religion (which did not a little puff me up), and divers would come to me for advice in Cases of Conscience; and If I heard of any that were in trouble of mind I usually went to comfort them. So that upon the bent of my spirit this way, and the success I found of my endeavors, I gave up my self to the study of Divinity, and intended to enter into the ministry If my friends had not diverted me.

But as I grew into employment and credit thereby, so I grew also in pride of my gifts, and under temptations which set me on work to look to my evidence more narrowly than I had done before (for the great change which God had wrought in me, and the general approbation of good ministers and other Christians, kept me from making any great question of my good Estate,) though my secret Corruptions, and some tremblings of heart (which was greatest when I was among the most Godly persons), put me to some plunges; but especially when I perceived a great decay in my zeal and love, etc. And hearing sometimes of better assurance by the seal of the spirit, which I also knew by the word of God, but could not nor durst say that ever I had it; and finding by reading of Mr. Perkins and other books that a reprobate might (in appearance) attain to as much as I had done. Finding withal much hollowness and vainglory in my heart, I began to grow very sad, and knew not what to do. I was ashamed to open my case to any minister that knew me. I feared it would shame my self and religion also, that such an eminent professor as I was accounted should discover such Corruptions as I found in my self, and had in all this time attained no better evidence of salvation, and I should prove a hypocrite. It was too late to begin anew: I should never repent in truth, having repented so oft as I had done. It was like Hell to me to think of that in Hebrews 6. Yet I should sometimes propound questions afar off to such of the most Godly ministers as I met, which gave me ease for the present, but my heart could not find where to rest. But I grew very sad and melancholy; and now to hear others applaud me was a dart through my liver, for still I feared I was not sound at the root, and sometimes I had thoughts of breaking from my profession, and proclaim my self an Hypocrite. But those troubles came not all at once but by fits, for sometimes I should find refreshing in prayer, and sometimes in the Love that I had had to the saints, which, though it were but poor comfort (for I durst not say before the Lord that I did love them in truth), yet the Lord upheld me, and many times outward occasions put these fears out of my thoughts. And though I had known long before the Doctrine of free Justification by Christ, and had often urged it upon my own soul and others, yet I could not close with Christ to my satisfaction. I have many times striven to lay hold upon Christ in some promise, and have brought forth all the Arguments that I had for my part in it. But instead of finding it to be

mine, I have lost sometimes the faith of the very general truth of the promise. Sometimes, after much striving by prayer for faith in Christ, I have thought I had received some power to apply Christ unto my soul, but it was so doubtful as I could have little comfort in it, arid it soon vanished.

Upon these and the like troubles, when I could by no means attain sure and settled peace, and that which I did get was still broken off upon every infirmity, I concluded there was no way to help it, but by walking more close with God and more strict observation of all duties. And hereby, though I put my self to many a needless task, and deprived my self of many lawful Comforts, yet my peace would fail upon every small occasion. And I was held long under great bondage to the Law (sin, and humble my self; and sin, and to humiliation again; and so day after day), yet neither got strength to my sanctification, nor bettered my Evidence, but was brought to such bondage as I durst not use any recreation, nor meddle with any worldly business, etc., for fear of breaking my peace (which, even such as it was, was very precious to me). But this would not hold neither, for then I grew very melancholy and mine own thoughts wearied me, and wasted my spirits.

While I wandered up and down in this sad and doubtful estate (wherein yet I had many intermissions, for the flesh would often shake of this yoke of the law, but was still forced to come under it again), wherein my greatest troubles were not the sense of Gods wrath, or fear of damnation, but want of assurance of salvation, and want of strength against my Corruptions. I knew that my greatest want was faith in Christ, and fain would I have been united to Christ, but I thought I was not holy enough. I had many times comfortable thoughts about him in the word, prayer, and meditation, but they gave me no satisfaction, but brought me lower in mine own eyes, and held me still to a constant use of all means in hope of better things to come. Sometimes I was very confident that he had given me a hungering and thirsting soul after Christ, and therefore would surely satisfy me in his good time. Sometimes again I was ready to entertain secret murmurings that all my pains and prayers, etc., should prevail no more. But such thoughts were soon rebuked. I found my heart still willing to Justify God. Yea, I was persuaded I should love him though he should cast me off.

Being in this Condition, it pleased the Lord in my family exercise to manifest unto me the difference between the Covenant of Grace and the Covenant of Works (but I took the foundation of that of works to have been man in innocency, and only held forth in the Law of Moses to drive us to Christ). This Covenant of Grace began to take great impression in me. I thought I had now enough. To have Christ freely, and to be justified freely was very sweet to me, and upon sound warrant (as I conceived), but I would not say with any confidence. It had been sealed to me, but I rather took occasion to be more remiss in my spiritual watch, and so more loose in my Conversation.

I was now about 30 years of age, and now was the time come that the Lord would reveal Christ unto me, whom I had long desired, but not so earnestly as since I came to see more clearly into the Covenant of free grace. First, therefore, he laid a sore affliction upon me, wherein he laid me lower in mine own eyes than at any time before, and showed me the emptiness of all my gifts and parts, left me neither power nor will, so as I became as a weaned child. I could now no more look at what I had been, or what I had done, nor be discontented for want of strength or assurance. Mine eyes were only upon his free mercy in Jesus Christ. I knew I was worthy of nothing, for I knew I could do nothing for him or for my self. I could only mourn and weep to think of free mercy to such a vile wretch as I was. Though I had no power to apply it yet, I felt comfort in it. I did not long continue in this estate, but the good spirit of the Lord breathed upon my soul, and said I should live. Then every promise I thought upon held forth Christ unto me, saying I am thy salvation. Now could my soul close with Christ and rest there with sweet content, so ravished with his Love as I desired nothing nor feared any thing, but was filled with joy unspeakable and glorious, and with a spirit of Adoption. Not that I could pray with more fervency or more enlargement of heart than sometimes before, but I could now cry my father with more confidence. Me thought this Condition and that frame of heart which I had after, was in respect of the former like the reign of Solomon—free, peaceable, prosperous, and glorious; the other more like that of Ahaz—full of troubles, fears, and abasements. And the more I grew thus acquainted with the spirit of God, the more were my corruptions mortified, and the new man quickened. The world, the flesh, and Satan, were for a time silent. I heard not of them. But they would not leave me so. This estate lasted a good time (divers months), but not always alike. But if my comfort and joy slackened awhile, yet my peace continued, and it would return with advantage. I was now grown familiar with the Lord Jesus Christ. He would oft tell me he loved me. I did not doubt to believe him. If I went abroad he went with me, when I returned he came home with me. I talked with him upon the way, he lay down with me, and usually I did awake with him. Now I could go into any company and not lose him, and so sweet was his love to me as I desired nothing but him in heaven or earth.

This estate would not hold. Neither did it decline suddenly, but by degrees. And though I found much spiritual strength in it, yet I could not discern but my hunger after the word of God, and my love to the saints had been as great (if not more) in former times. One reason might be this, I found that the many blemishes and much hollow-heartedness which I discerned in many professors, had weakened the esteem of a Christian in my heart. And for my comfort in Christ, as worldly employments, and the Love of Temporal things did steal away my heart from him, so would his sweet Countenance be withdrawn from me. But in such a condition he would not long leave me, but would still recall me by some word or affliction, or in prayer or meditation. And I should then be as a man awakened out of a dream, or as if I had been another man. And then my care was (not so much to get pardon for that was sometimes sealed to me while I was purposing to go seek it, and yet sometimes I could not obtain it without seeking and waiting also but) to mourn for my ingratitude towards my God, and his free and rich mercy. The Consideration whereof would break my heart more, and wring more tears from mine eyes, then ever the fear of Damnation or any affliction had done. So as many times, and to this very day, a thought of Christ Jesus and free grace bestowed on me melts my heart, that I cannot refrain.

Since this time I have gone under continual conflicts between the flesh and the spirit, and sometimes with Satan himself (which I have more discerned of late then I did formerly). Many falls I have had, and have lain long under some, yet never quite forsaken of the Lord. But still, when I have been put to it by any sudden danger or fearful Temptation, the good spirit of the Lord hath not failed to bear witness to me, giving me Comfort and Courage in the very pinch when of my self I have been very fearful, and dismayed. My usual falls have been through dead heartedness and presumptuousness, by which Satan hath taken advantage to wind me into other sins. When the flesh prevails, the spirit withdraws, and is sometimes so grieved as he seems not to acknowledge his own work. Yet in my worst times he hath been pleased to stir when he would not speak, and would yet support me that my faith hath not failed utterly.

The Doctrine of free justification lately taught here took me in as drowsy a condition as I had been in (to my remembrance) these twenty years, and brought me as low (in my own apprehension) as if the whole work had been to begin anew. But when the voice of peace came, I knew it to be the same that I had been acquainted with before, though it did not speak so loud, nor in that measure of joy that I had felt sometimes. Only this I found, that I had defiled the white garments of the Lord Jesus, That of Justification in undervaluing the riches of the

Lord Jesus Christ and his free grace, and setting up Idols in mine own heart, some of them made of his Silver, and of his gold, and that other garment of sanctification, by many foul spots which Gods people might take notice of. And yet the inward spots were fouler than those.

The Lord Jesus who (of his own free grace) hath washed my soul in the blood of the everlasting Covenant, wash away all those spots also in his good time. Amen, even so do Lord Jesus.

II. The Conversion of Anna Trapnel

Anna Trapnel was a puritan laywoman who came to depend on the free grace of God for her salvation. Like Winthrop she had intense mystical experiences of God's love. She believed that the Spirit talked to her and in the mid-1650s began to have visions and to prophesy. She was accused of being antinomian, and became associated with the Fifth Monarchist movement.

Source: Anna Trapnel, *A Legacy for Saints; being Several Experiences of the Dealings of God with Anna Trapnel* (London, 1654).

When I was about 14 years of age, I began to be very eager and forward to hear and pray, though in a very formal manner. Thus I went on for some years, and then I rose to a higher pitch, to a more special condition, as I thought, and I followed after that ministry that was most pressed after by the strictest professors. And I ran with great violence, having a great zeal, though not according to knowledge, and I appeared a very high-grown Christian in the thoughts of many. I had great parts, in prayer great enlargements, and in discoursing and repeating of sermons I was very forward, and did it with great delight and affection, and much trembling of spirit . . .. But I was in all this very legal, and yet more legal.

Providence ordered that I should hear Mr. [Hugh] Peters speak from those words in the 26th of Isaiah, the 20th verse, "Come my people, enter thou into thy chambers, and shut thy doors about thee, bide thyself as it were for a little moment, until the indignation be overpast." From these words he opened the marriage covenant that is between God and his spouse. From that word, "Come," he showed the sweet compellation of God to his covenanted people. Then I was convinced of the excellency of that condition, to be in covenant and to have it upon good grounds, which I was very ignorant of. And though I thought myself in a very good condition before, yet now it seized upon my spirit that surely I was not in the covenant, and that if I was I should know it. And I still cried out, "Oh, what shall I do to know it? Without the knowledge of God to be my God I am undone." My spirit was filled with horror, and the terrors of the Lord exceedingly oppressed me. I ran from minister to minister, from sermon to sermon, but I could find no rest. I could not be contented to hear once or twice in the week; but I must hear from the first day to the last, and thought that not enough either. And if I had not shed some tears at a sermon I then went home full of horror, concluding myself to be that stony ground Christ spoke of in the parable of the sower. I apprehended divine displeasure against me, leaving me in a fearful condition, giving me over to blindness of mind and hardness of heart forever. And when I have been hindered from hearing a sermon which I desired to hear, I have concluded that I might have received Christ in that sermon. . . .

Such bondage I was under that had I neglected a duty or an opportunity of hearing (though a lawful occasion hindered and I could not be said to be neglectful), yet it sorely seized upon me that I had been neglectful and that I was damned, one set apart for destruction. I was strongly tempted to destroy myself, and had not divine power prevented it, I had been a murderer of my own life, and of their lives that I loved most entirely. I have been wakened in the night by the devil for this very purpose, and directed where to have the knife, and what kind of knife I should take. And these assaults followed me not seldom, but very often, which made my poor soul and body exceedingly to tremble. . . .

I was now as a cripple who, when his crutches are taken away from him, he falls. So my spirit was laid flat on the ground. I was convinced that it was the Spirit alone that witnesseth to the creature its good condition, and all witnesses were nothing if the Spirit did not witness. I was as if I had never heard of a Spirit, though I had professed much some years before. But because I went about to establish a righteousness of my own, as it were, by the works of the Law, therefore I was left in the dark concerning the righteousness of the Lord Jesus, which I thought I had not denied. If any of them that were Gospel-enlightened saints had said to me that you rest in your good works and expect to be saved some other way than alone by Jesus Christ, I looked upon them as doing me great wrong and speaking very false. I thought, and I would say to them, I am not ignorant to look upon my works as anything. But I was made to acknowledge afterwards that I had set up my own works in the room of Christ. And the Lord stripped me at last of all gifts and enlargements in duty, and I was stricken dumb, or else fast asleep, when I have set myself to pray.

It was indeed self that the Lord struck dumb, though I then beheld it not, but was sore wounded, being persuaded that I was forever shut out from the presence of God, which weight I could hardly bear. It was so burdensome that I still cried out, "what shall I do?" And all my prayer that was left was this, "Give me Christ, or else I die." Now nothing but a Christ would serve my turn. Before if I could have had tears or any relenting for sin, or enlargements in duty, I was well enough, but the only wise God knew it was best for me to be deprived of these, which I so much built upon and made idols of. . . .

And many that were enlightened in the doctrine of free grace took a great deal of pain with me, persuading me to bear those ministers that taught most upon the doctrine of free grace. But I could not relish that doctrine. It was such a cold, lean, poor discovery, I thought. I, being under the flashes of hell, delighted in the thunderings of the Law, and they pleased me best that preached most upon the Law, and that pressed legal qualifications which I strove to come up to. I thought I should never have Christ unless I was so qualified, as I was taught, but unto which I could not attain for all my struggling and striving after it. This made me conclude that I was not elected. If I were, I thought I should be made conformable to his image, who is holy, which I was not. Therefore I was none of Christ's flock, which condition was very dreadful to me to be without Christ. I could not receive a word of satisfaction from any, though some would say to me, "dost thou not love Christ?" I would say, "But how shall I know whether my love be true love?" . . .

But the great and glorious God at length thoroughly convinced me that he justified ungodly ones, and that he sent Christ not to call the righteous, but sinners, and he came to save the chiefest sinners. And now I began to hearken to free grace, and I saw nothing else could revive me. And I found my spirits a little stayed in listening to the free tenders of Christ. And then I was put upon arguing with God, entreating him to give me Christ, which he had given as the only object for sinners to fly to, being stung with sin. . . . And now, though I could not come to God as a righteous one, I could come as a sinner and beg of God to receive me, being such an object that he sent forth his love to, commending it to sinners and to rebels. And I desired that I might be one of those rebels that might have a pardon, were it upon ever so hard terms. And truly I found God trying me to purpose: it was a very hard thing to me to be ranked among the vilest miscreants in the world, and to behold myself as bad as the greatest adulterer or blasphemer in the world, whom I looked upon as a great deal viler than I and further from God's accepting. But this conceit free grace laid in the dust, and divine light showed me the spawn and seed of all sin within my corrupt nature, which made me to lie in the dust and to cry out, "Lord, let free grace own me, else I am undone." When the Law of the Spirit came, then sin revived, and I died. It showed me every secret sin that I saw not before, so that all my sins were set in order before me, and I beheld them innumerable. Oh, what a deplorable condition I was in, forlorn and without hope. Nothing now could comfort me but the true comforter, and nothing could speak peace to my soul but Christ. . . .

I could speak much concerning the time of my sorrow, of my terrors and perplexities, and sore plunges. I could make a large rehearsal, telling you much of the sad apprehensions I had of my eternal condition, whereas I have but a little hint of my condition in the times of my bonds. But my desire now is rather to tell you of my freedom, unto which I hasten, though I know that these mourning experiences may be of great use to the sorrowful and troubled spirit that lieth languishing for lack of the light of assurance which God doth see good for a time to conceal from his beloved that he hath loved with an eternal love, and who in time he draweth with loving kindness. Therefore, let not any poor soul despair. There is free grace enough, an ocean, to swallow up not my sins only, but many more; a fountain open for all manner of sins, be they never so great.

Poor souls, you cannot out-sin mercy. Your sins are finite, but grace is infinite. Do not think that any sin can shut thee out of divine love. If it could, it would have shut me out, for certain I am that no heart could be more desperately wicked than mine, no one's sins could be of a more scarlet dye than mine. . . . Oh, let sinners admire free grace with me, that hath freed me from as stony, as feared, benumbed, senseless a condition as any could or can be in. Hearing or reading, or saints speaking to me was as to one deaf. I still concluded my condition to be like those that the scriptures speak of, that were given up by the Lord to blindness of mind and hardness of heart. I thought confidently that God had given me to know that I should perish forever, but God's thought at length appeared higher than mine, as the heavens are higher than the earth. And when my spirit had thus been upon the rack for a season, and tossed up and down with the waves of a continual accusing troubled conscience. And none spoke any word that did in the least measure revive me, till that voice sounded that I could not contradict. But I did withstand it and repulse it as long as I could. And when it spoke as a still small voice, I rejected it a week before I felt, heard, and saw that glorious light and power sounded into my spirit, which caused an echo or answer from my spirit in believing the testimony of the Spirit. But that small voice made such a report in my soul which made me to listen. It was such a speaking that I had not heard before, therefore it was very strange to me. The word I had was this, "Christ is thine, and thou art his." And no word was spoken to my spirit for six or seven days but this. It followed me wherever I went. . . .

Now I shall, by the assistance of the Spirit, tell the time when my heart was brought to believe the pardon of my sins past, present, and to come by an act of grace through the blood of the Lord Jesus, which I clearly saw by the light of the Spirit, bearing witness to my spirit that Christ was mine, and I was his.

The time, the year 1642. The day, the first of the first month, called January, it being the first day of the week, commonly called the Sabbath day, which was indeed a Lord's day to my soul. It was when Mr. John Simpson was preaching from that scripture, in the 8th of the Romans. The words are these, "Now if any man have not the spirit of Christ, he is none of his." . . .

My spirit was under much trembling for fear it should still be said that I had none of the Spirit, which often was a terrible sound within me which I still dreaded. And my spirit cried out to the Lord when this sermon was almost ended. I said, "Lord I have the Spirit" in this confused manner, as I found a witness within me that I had the Spirit in those particulars that were declared. But my spirit strongly ran out to the Lord for a clear manifestation of his love in Christ. And suddenly my soul was filled with joy unspeakable, and full of glory in believing, the Spirit witnessing that word, Christ is thy well-beloved, and thou art his. My soul was now full of joy as it could hold. Now I saw all my sins fall upon Jesus Christ, and when he was sacrificed all my sins were sacrificed with him. Oh, what triumphing and songs of Hallelujah were in my spirit. I knew not where I was, nor how to get out of the place where I sat. I apprehended nothing but a clothing of glory over my whole man. I never beheld saints as I did then; I saw their faces as the faces of Angels. Oh, what angelical creatures did they appear before me, full of shining brightness. Oh, what a heart inflamed now was mine, filled with the flame of divine love! There appeared now no smoke, but a clear flame, nothing now before me but christal [original spelling retained for the sake of the double meaning] appearances. Oh, how my soul was enamored with Christ! Earth was now gone, and heaven come; the unclean spirit dispossessed, the pure spirit now possessed, taking my soul from the dunghill and setting it upon the throne. My natural food I tasted not till now, it was bitter to my taste. But, oh, now, every bit of bread I ate, how sweet was it to my taste! Christ sweetened every creature to me. Oh, how sweet was the feast of love, that my soul was made partaker in every creature! Oh, what a rebound doth divine love make in the soul! I could not keep love in it, it would flame forth into a declaration. I must now tell saints what I had now received from the Spirit's testimony, that they might praise with me, having mourned with me. I told them I had now seen him whom my poor spirit doubted I should never have beheld. I called others to come and taste how sweet and loving Christ is to sinners. Now sermons appeared living to me. Where Christ was preached most to sinners, I delighted most in such a ministry, and still went away with melody in my heart. For a whole year hereafter I was sealed up to the day of Redemption. I had exceeding raptures of joy very frequently, little or no intermissions, no questions or doubtings in the least measure, but my seat was still for constancy, a seat of joy and spiritual mirth. Though sometimes the golden trumpet sounded higher, and sometimes lower, yet it was still sounding and caused an echo to follow it.

Cotton's Catechism

John Cotton's Milk for Babes, Drawn Out of the Breasts of Both Testaments *is typical of seventeenth-century English puritan catechisms. It summarized the doctrines to be known by all Christians in simple question-and-answer form. The following modernized version does not include the numerous scriptural references that Cotton used to buttress his positions.*

Source: John Cotton, *Milk for Babes, Drawn Out of the Breasts of Both Testaments. Chiefly for the spiritual nourishment of Boston babes in either England, but may be of like use for any Children* (London, 1646).

Q. What hath God done for you?
A. God hath made me, He keepeth me, and He can save me.
Q. Who is God?
A. God is a Spirit of Himself and for Himself.
Q. How many gods be there?
A. There is but one God in three persons, the Father, the Son, and the Holy Ghost.
Q. How did God make you?
A. In my first parents holy and righteous.
Q. Are you then born holy and righteous?
A. No, my first father sinned, and I in him.
Q. Are you then born a sinner?
A. I was conceived in sin and born in iniquity.
Q. What is your birth-sin?
A. Adam's sin imputed to me and a corrupt nature dwelling in me.
Q. What is your corrupt nature?
A. My corrupt nature is empty of grace, bent unto sin, and only unto sin, and that continually.
Q. What is sin?
A. Sin is the transgression of the Law.
Q. How many commandments of the Law be there?

A. Ten.

Q. What is the First Commandment?

A. Thou shalt have no other gods but me.

Q. What is the Second Commandment?

A. Thou shalt not make to thyself any graven image, etc.

Q. What is the meaning of this commandment?

A. That we should worship the true God with true worship such as God hath ordained, not such as man hath invented.

Q. What is the Third Commandment?

A. Thou shalt not take the name of the Lord thy God in vain, etc.

Q. What is here meant by the name of God?

A. God Himself and the good things of God, whereby He is known, as a man by his name, as His attributes, worship, Word, and works.

Q. What is not to take His name in vain?

A. To make use of God and the good things of God to His glory and our good, not vainly, not unreverently, not unprofitably.

Q. What is the Fourth Commandment?

A. Remember that thou keep holy the Sabbath day, etc.

Q. What is the meaning of this commandment?

A. That we should rest from labor and much more from play on the Lord's day, that we may draw nigh to God in holy duties.

Q. What is the Fifth Commandment?

A. Honor thy father and thy mother, that thy days may be long in the land which the Lord thy God giveth thee.

Q. Who are here meant by father and mother?

A. All our superiors, whether in family, school, church, and commonwealth.

Q. What is the honor due to them?

A. Reverence, obedience, and (when I am able) recompense.

Q. What is the Sixth Commandment?

A. Thou shalt do no murder.

Q. What is the meaning of this commandment?

A. That we should not shorten the life or health of ourselves or others but preserve both.

Q. What is the Seventh Commandment?

A. Thou shalt not commit adultery.

Q. What is the sin here forbidden?

A. To defile ourselves or others with unclean lusts.

Q. What is the duty here commanded?

A. Chastity, to possess our vessels in holiness and honor.

Q. What is the Eighth Commandment?

A. Thou shalt not steal.

Q. What is the stealth here forbidden?

A. To take away another man's goods without his leave, or to spend our own without benefit to ourselves or others.

Q. What is the duty here commanded?

A. To get our goods honestly, to keep them safely, and to spend them thriftily.

Q. What is the Ninth Commandment?

A. Thou shalt not bear false witness against thy neighbor.

Q. What is the sin here forbidden?

A. To lie falsely, to think or speak untruly of ourselves or others.

Q. What is the duty here required?

A. Truth and faithfulness.

Q. What is the Tenth Commandment?

A. Thou shalt not covet, etc.

Q. What is the coveting here forbidden?

A. Lust after the things of other men and want of contentment with our own.

Q. Whether have you kept all these commandments?

A. No, I and all men are sinners.

Q. What is the wages of sin?

A. Death and damnation.

Q. How look you then to be saved?

A. Only by Jesus Christ.

Q. Who is Jesus Christ?

A. The eternal Son of God, who for our sakes became man that He might redeem and save us.

Q. How doth Christ redeem and save us?

A. By His righteous life and bitter death and resurrection to life again.

Q. How do we come to have part and fellowship with Christ in his death and resurrection?

A. By the power of his Word and Spirit, which bring us to Christ and keep us in Him.

Q. What is his Word?

A. The Holy Scriptures of the prophets and apostles, the Old and New Testament, Law and Gospel.

Q. How doth the ministry of the Law bring you towards Christ?

A. By bringing me to know my sin and the wrath of God against me for it.

Q. What are you thereby the nearer to Christ?

A. So I come to feel my cursed estate and need of a savior.

Q. How doth the ministry of the Gospel humble you more?

A. By revealing the grace of the Lord Jesus in dying to save sinners and yet convincing me of my sin in not believing on Him and of mine utter insufficiency to come to Him, and so I feel myself utterly lost.

Q. How then doth the ministry of the Gospel raise you up out of this lost estate to come unto Christ?

A. By teaching me the value and the virtue of the death of Christ and the riches of his grace to lost sinners, by revealing the promise of grace to such and by ministering the Spirit of grace to apply Christ and His promise of grace unto myself and to keep me in Him.

Q. How doth the Spirit of grace apply Christ and His promise of grace unto you and keep you in Him?

A. By begetting in me faith to receive Him, prayer to call upon Him, repentance to mourn after Him, and new obedience to serve Him.

Q. What is faith?

A. Faith is a grace of the Spirit whereby I deny myself and believe on Christ for righteousness and salvation.

Q. What is prayer?

A. It is a calling upon God in the name of Christ by the help of the Holy Ghost, according to the will of God.

Q. What is repentance?

A. Repentance is a grace of the Spirit whereby I loathe my sins and myself for them and confess them before the Lord and mourn after Christ for the pardon of them and for grace to serve Him in newness of life.

Q. What is newness of life or new obedience?

A. Newness of life is a grace of the Spirit whereby I forsake my former lusts and vain company, and walk before the Lord in the light of His Word and in the communion of His saints.

Q. What is the communion of saints?

A. It is the fellowship of the church in the blessings of the Covenant of Grace and the seals thereof.

Q. What is the church?

A. It is a congregation of saints joined together in the bond of the Covenant to worship the Lord and to edify one another in all His holy ordinances.

Q. What is the bond of the Covenant in which the church is joined together?

A. It is the profession of that Covenant which God hath made with His faithful people to be a God unto them and to their seed.

Q. What doth the Lord bind His people to in this Covenant?

A. To give up themselves and their seed first to the Lord to be His people and then to the elders and brethren of the church to set forward the worship of God and their mutual edification.

Q. How do they give up themselves and their seed to the Lord?

A. By receiving, through faith, the Lord and His Covenant to themselves and to their seed, and accordingly walking themselves and training up their children in the ways of His Covenant.

Q. How do they give up themselves and their seed to the elders and brethren of the church?

A. By confession of their sins and profession of their faith and of their subjection to the Gospel of Christ. And so they and their seed are received into the fellowship of the church and the seals thereof.

Q. What are the seals of the Covenant now in the days of the Gospel?

A. Baptism and the Lord's Supper.

Q. What is done for you in baptism?

A. In baptism the washing with water is a sign and seal of my washing with the blood and Spirit of Christ and thereby of my ingrafting into Christ, of the pardon and cleansing of my sins, of my rising up out of affliction, and also of my resurrection from the dead at the last day.

Q. What is done for you in the Lord's Supper?

A. In the Lord's Supper the receiving of the bread broken and the wine poured out is a sign and seal of my receiving the communion of the body of Christ broken for me, and of His blood shed for me, and thereby of my growth in Christ, of the pardon and healing of my sins, of the fellowship of His Spirit, of my strengthening and quickening in grace, and of my sitting together with Christ on His throne of glory at the Last Judgment.

Q. What is the resurrection from the dead, which was sealed up to you in baptism?

A. When Christ shall come to His Last Judgment, all that are in the graves shall rise again, both the just and the unjust.

Q. What is the Last Judgment which is sealed up to you in the Lord's Supper?

A. At the last day we shall all appear before the judgment seat of Christ to give an account of our works and to receive our reward according to them.

Q. What is the reward that shall then be given?

A. The righteous shall go into life eternal, and the wicked shall be cast into everlasting fire with the devil and his angels.

Covenants—Church Covenants

The early churches of New England were not established by the initiative of the Church of England, but rather were formed by the settlers of the towns. The authority of the church derived from its members, who prepared and signed covenants binding themselves to the common goals. The first three examples show the evolution of New England covenants from basic to more elaborate. This aspect of the New England Way was adopted by English and Irish Congregationalists. The fourth example is the covenant adopted by the church in Great Yarmouth in England. The fifth is from the congregation of John Rogers in Dublin, Ireland.

I. The Original Salem Covenant of 1629

We covenant with the Lord and one with another; and do bind ourselves in the presence of God to walk together in all his ways, according as he is pleased to reveal himself unto us in his Blessed word of truth.

II. The Covenant of the Boston Church as first gathered in Charlestown in 1630

In the name of our Lord Jesus Christ, and in obedience to his holy will and divine ordinance, we whose names are here underwritten, being by his most wise and good providence brought together into this part of America in the Bay of Massachusetts, and desirous to unite ourselves into one congregation or church under the Lord Jesus Christ our head, in such sort as becometh all those whom he hath redeemed, and sanctified to himself, do hereby solemnly and religiously (in his most holy presence) promise and bind ourselves to walk in all our ways according to the rule of the Gospel, and in all sincere conformity to his holy ordinances, and in mutual love and respect each to other, so near as God shall give us grace.

III. The Revised Salem Covenant of 1636

We covenant with our Lord, and with one another; and we do bind ourselves in the presence of God, to walk together in all his ways according as he is pleased to reveal himself unto us in his blessed word of truth; and do explicitly, in the name and fear of God, profess and protest to walk as follows, through the power and grace of our Lord, Jesus Christ.

We avouch the Lord to be our God, and ourselves to be his people, in the truth and simplicity of our spirits.

We give ourselves to the Lord Jesus Christ, and the work of his grace for the teaching, ruling, and sanctifying of us in matters of worship and conversion, resolving to cleave unto him alone for life and glory, and to reject all contrary ways, canons, and constitutions of men in his worship.

We promise to walk with our brethren with all watchfulness and tenderness, avoiding jealousies and back-bitings, censurings, provokings, secret risings of spirit against them, but in all offences to follow the rule of our Lord Jesus, and to bear and forbear, give and forgive, as he hath taught us.

In public or private, we will willingly do nothing to the offence of the church, but willing to take advice for ourselves and ours, as occasion shall be presented.

We will not in the congregation be forward either to show our own gifts and parts in speaking or scrupling, or there discover the weakness or failings of our brethren, but attend an orderly call thereunto, knowing how much the Lord may be dishonored and his gospel, and the profession of it, slighted by our distempers and weaknesses in public.

We bind ourselves to study the advancement of the gospel in all truth and peace, both in regard of those that are within or without; no way slighting our sister churches, but using their counsel as need shall be; not laying a stumbling block before any, no, not the Indians, whose good we desire to promote; and so to converse as we may avoid the very appearance of evil.

We do hereby promise to carry ourselves in all lawful obedience to those that are over us in church or commonwealth, knowing how well pleasing it will be to the Lord that they should have encouragement in their places by our not grieving their spirits through our irregularities.

We resolve to approve ourselves to the Lord in our particular callings, shunning idleness as the bane of any state; nor will we deal oppressingly with any, wherein we are the Lord's stewards.

Promising also unto our best ability to teach our children and servants the knowledge of God, and of his will, that they may serve him also, and this not by any strength of our own, but by the Lord Jesus Christ, whose blood we desire may sprinkle this our covenant made in his name.

IV. Yarmouth (England) Church Covenant: June 1643

It is manifest out of God's word, that God was pleased to walk in a way of Covenant with his people, he promising to be their God & they promising to be his people. . . . We, being in the fear of God, desirous to worship & fear him according to his revealed will, do freely, solemnly & jointly covenant with the Lord in the presence of his saints & angels

1. First. That we will forever acknowledge & avouch God to be our God in Jesus Christ.
2. Secondly. That we will always endeavor, through the grace of God assisting us, to walk in his ways & ordinances & according to his written word, which is the only sufficient rule of good life for every man.
3. Thirdly. Neither will we suffer our selves to be polluted by any sinful ways either public or private, but will abstain from the very appearance of

evil, giving no offence to the Jew or to the Gentile, or to the Churches of Christ.

4. Fourthly. That we will in all love improve our communion as brethren by watching over one another, & as need shall be to counsel, admonish, reprove, comfort, relieve, assist & bear with one another, humbly submitting our selves to the government of Christ in his church.

5. Lastly. We do not promise these things in our own but by Christ his strength, neither do we confine ourselves to the word of this Covenant but shall account it our duty at all times to embrace any further light or truth that shall be revealed to us out of Gods word.

V. Covenant of Christ Church Cathedral, Dublin (c. 1650)

We whose names are hereunder written do freely give up our hands and hearts to God the Father and his Son Christ Jesus, our only Lord and lawgiver; and do unanimously engage in the fear of the Lord every one of us, to our utmost powers, through the gracious assistance of Gods Holy Spirit, that we will walk together in one body with one mind, in all sweetness of Spirit, and Saint-like love each to other, (as the Disciples of Jesus Christ) and all to the Church.

Jointly to contend and strive together in all good and lawful ways, both by doing and by suffering for the purity of the Gospel, the truth of Christ, his ordinances and orders, the honor and liberty, and privileges of the Church against all opposers.

With all care and conscience to study and labor to keep up the unity of the spirit in the bond of peace, both in the church in general, and in particular, between one another.

Carefully to avoid all causes and causers of divisions (as much as in us lies) and to shun seducers, false teachers of errors or Heresies., [sic]

Partaking and fellow feeling to our power with one another, in every condition, bearing each other burdens.

To forbear and bear with one another's weaknesses and infirmities in much pity, tenderness, meekness, and patience, not ripping up the weakness of any one to any other without our Church, nor yet to any within, unless according to Christ's rule and Gospel order, endeavoring all we may for the glory of the Gospel and the credit of his church to hide and cover one another's slippings and failings.

And that we will (as the Lord our God shall enable us) to our utmost, cleave close one to another, and every one to the Lord, and cheerfully undergo the condition and lot the Lord shall lay upon this his Church, whether in persecution or in prosperity, without any willful drawing back or falling away from the fellowship or faith which we possess together.

If any one brother or sister be afflicted, &c, fellow-feelingly to be afflicted with that brother or sister, and, in all Christian ways we can, to counsel, comfort, or assist, and to pray hard for such a member.

Freely to contribute and communicate of things temporal and spiritual according to our abilities out of our abundance, both to particular members in want and also into the public treasury or church-stock.

Vigilantly to watch over each other's conversation so as to counsel, comfort, or correct according to Christ's rules in such cases; provoking one another to love and good works, with brotherly bowels and affections.

Carefully walking together in all holiness, godliness, and humility of mind (to our utmost) every day and often, and orderly meeting together to the edifying of the body, for the glory of the Gospel, credit of the Church, convincing of our adversaries, and them that are without.

Praying continually for the prosperity of this Church, for God's presence in it, and protection of it, against all the gates of hell.

And lastly, because differences have formerly arose about a Pastor, we do freely declare to embrace and own our brother—our Pastor—according to the order of the Gospel; to submit with all ready obedience in the Lord to Christ's ordinances dispensed by him; to pray for assistance from the Lord in the administration to him committed; and to esteem of him as the Lord requires; and to adhere and cleave to him in the Lord.

All which we do in the sincerity of our souls declare, promise, purpose, and engage to, as our God shall enable us by his own gracious Spirit.

Covenants—Covenants of Private Christians
I. Wethersfield 1588

During the Elizabethan Age, some puritans began to form private groups to assist each other in sustaining their faith and advancing their piety. In his book Seven Treatises, containing such direction as is gathered out of the Holy Scriptures, leading and guiding to true happiness, etc. *(1603), Richard Rogers described the formation of one such group in his parish of Wethersfield, in Essex. This account became a guide for other groups attempting the same thing.*

In the year 1588 there met in a Christian man's house certain well minded persons, which dwelt in one town together, with whom also the Preacher of the place did meet at the same time. Their meeting was for the continuance of love, and for the edifying one of another, after some bodily repast and refreshing. And yet know, that they were no Brownists, for they were diligent and ordinary frequenters of public assemblies of the people of God. Neither were their meetings Conventicles, for the disturbing of the state of the Church and peace thereof, as many imagine that there can be no private fellowship among Christians, but it is to such ends: the contrary may be seen by their conference. These with one consent fell into communication, how the case stood betwixt God and themselves.

Some accusing and complaining of themselves, that they had not used their long continued peace and liberty of the Gospel, to the end for which God did send both, but that they had been dim lights. The rest consenting, and by occasion offered among them all (well nigh twenty persons) sundry reasons and proofs were set down to make their complaints more weighty, and also to show, what evil fruit they did see to proceed from such a dead and unprofitable course of living: and yet the persons spoken of, did as far exceed the common sort of them that professes the Gospel, as the common professors do exceed them in Religion which know not the Gospel.

When they proceeded thus far, it was demanded, whether there were no way to come out of this wearisome and unprofitable life, which (in their own judgment) did not beseem such as embraced the Gospel. The conclusion was this, they did covenant faithfully and seriously, to set up these remedies forthwith and speedily; thinking that such a weighty matter had need of no delay; and thereupon, desired the Preacher to set down the sum of their conference and communication together, for the better parting of them in remembrance of it to practice it; as also that they might see what the sum of their conference was; which, seeing they agreed unto, was called a Covenant.

Now it may be, ye look to hear what fruit there came of this; surely even this meeting was a great whetting them on to enjoy the public ministry more cheerfully and fruitfully afterwards: and this mean with others, both public and private, did knit them in that love, the bond whereof could not be broken, either on their part which now sleep in the Lord, while they here lived, nor in them which yet remain, by any adversary power unto this day.

The true report of a conference, had betwixt certain well-minded Christians, (Anno 1588) who saw they had not lived according to the knowledge which they had, nor to have answered to their profession, as they might and ought to have done: containing a complaint of their coldness and negligence, with remedies against the same, and a covenant to turn to God by repentance, profitable for these days.

We weighing advisedly, and by due consideration here of late, the glorious and goodly beauty of a Christian life, as it is commended and set forth in the word of God, how full of heavenly comfort it is said to be unto all such as make it their treasure and how amiable, and how fruitful also it is (in whomsoever it bee) unto others which truly know the price and excellency of it, and we so dimly and darkly beholding the image of this in our selves, who yet had hope, and that not small, that we had a part therein: we [saw] just cause why we should confess, that we had been much wanting herein, and that the pattern of our life was far unlike this rule, when we compared the one with the other, and therefore complained with bitterness, that we had fallen into a deep slumber, being rather ready to think our selves in safety, than carefully looking to those testimonies in our selves, which might indeed assure us of it.

Concerning God, we have not purchased such glory to his name, and showed forth his loving kindness to the sons of men, as we ought and might have done; neither glorified his Gospel, as, if it should have been taken from us, we would have promised to do. Further, it may appear hereby; that we see we have not profited in the knowledge of the will of God answerably to our time, and to the helps which we have enjoyed for that purpose. for many of us are as yet but weakly settled in the chief points of Christian religion, much less are we fit hearers, with ready minds to put in use any doctrine which shall be necessarily, soundly and faithfully delivered unto us. Nay, we must needs confess to our shame, that the means to come by knowledge, have been very negligently used of us: as, seldom reading, and in hearing, not usually preparing our hearts before we came, with casting off the sins which might hinder us, and coming with meekness; neither in hearing, have been diligently attending and hearkening to the voice of God, neither after our hearing have usually meditated or communed with other of that which we have heard. So that this hath not been our delight, but with much irreverence (for so holy and heavenly a service) gone about. Moreover, we have not so tamed our corrupt nature, and so set our selves against the same in many particulars, so as we have prevailed over it in our temptations: (for we have thought it too tedious and irksome for us:) but we have favored exceedingly, and given too much liberty to our selves in our sins; not ready to mislike and withstand the same, as either some of us sometime have done, or as we have seen other of gods servants to have done, as *Joseph* (*Gen.* 39) did in one time; *Moses* (*Heb.* 11.24.) in another, yet the means which we use sometimes to obtain grace, if they were continued, would bring to pass some effects this way not to be complained of; therefore seeing we thus fail herein, we must needs complain bitterly. and what is like to be a greater hinderer of true godliness in us, than this tender bearing with our selves in our sins, as being hardly brought to offer any violence unto them: when yet we know, that the smallest even of our evil lusts, do fight against our souls, are rank poison unto us, and have need to be driven out with most strong medicines?

And as concerning the danger of favoring our selves in our sins, though secret and smaller than many sins seem, these fearful effects have followed, that having winked at the smaller, we have rushed and been plunged into greater: and not chasing away light and wandering desires, we have fallen into deeper and more dangerous delighting in them, which having once taken hold of us, could not with ten times so much ado be removed. Now when these and such like unsavory fruits have come from us, and that we have in such like manner (as hath been said) walked in the world, what hath been our estate and condition, but that which might well enough be seen such as have in no careful sort been professors of religion.

But yet we living (through Gods goodness) under the ministry of the word, could not be so forgetful of that which had been in us, nor so blockish in remembering and considering of that which had been taught us, neither all religion so utterly extinguished in us, but that the sparks of zeal which were in us, must needs be kindled one time or other: by means whereof, we were informed to see a marvelous decay of godliness, and a change from that which hath been in us; and thereby were driven into exceeding heaviness, to behold from what we had fallen, and yet utterly unable to recover our selves again for the time.

In our afflictions and trials we have not felt our selves contented, that the Lord should exercise us as it hath been seen good to him: we have not overcome impatience in them, much less rejoiced in bearing them. We have not taken occasion by Gods blessings, of liberty, peace, health, fellowship one with another, prosperity and such like to be more fruitful and cheerful in doing all good duties, as occasion hath been offered: lowliness, meekness, kind-heartedness, faithfulness to men, sincerity to God in the good things which we have done, have oft and much been wanting; very spare and niggardly in prayer, meditation, trial of our selves, and laboring to know sin better, and confessing against our selves, that which we know, soon weary of well-doing, yet sometime not grieved at it; but unwearied in things needless, if we should have given place thereto. We so hardly and slightly saw the necessity of practicing many duties and precepts, which by doctrine are commended unto us, that we rested in that which hath been, and coldly rose up to any new or further proceeding. Our crucifying of our selves to the world, that we might be content to be despised and of little account in it: or our crucifying of the world unto our selves, that it might not blear our eyes with the vanity and deceivable enticements and baits of it, hath been very faintly gone about of us.

And from these accusations arises another, that we have taken too liberal an use of lawful things; never suspecting that any hurt or danger can thereby come unto us; as in diet, apparel, sleep, the use of marriage, dealings in the world and talking thereof: forgetting that which the holy Ghost hath taught us; that is, that these lawful things, namely, pleasures and profits, are called snares, and therefore easily able to entangle men and hold them fast; so as it shall be hard for them to run the race of Christian duty required of them: and that they are said to press them down, that by means of them, they cannot with such cheerfulness and fruit live unto God. Wherein to be directed, they may serve us for a rule, that as every one of us can see what is sufficient, so we bestow no more time about the world than we needs must, neither in talk nor other dealings, fearing withal, lest we should be carried to love it too much: wherein the more that every man labors to overcome himself, that his cheerfulness in good duties may not be hindered, so much the more he shall rejoice, that he hath been content to abridge his own delight for better things.

Another proof of this our complaint, is; that we have had little feeling of the wants and miseries of others to see how many thousands walk ignorantly; other many, in security, hypocrisy, superstition, &c, many to have fallen away utterly, after they had received a taste of the Gospel: Oh, who should not be moved at the beholding of it? and pity them, as much as in him should lye? and not to be content, that we our selves should do well, while we see so many in calamity? But it cannot be denied, but that their estate, either of the desolate beyond the seas, in many countries, or of the distressed ones amongst us, doth little touch or come near us: whereby as our prayers are weak which are made in their behalf, so are the other fruits of our compassion small and few.

The cause hereof was not one, but yet chiefly our evil hearts which for all the taste of holy doctrine, and light which we had of the life to come, yet being cleansed and renewed but in part, were evermore in respect of our corruption prone to evil, and unapt to goodness: so that, not only after good means using, they carried us to a forgetfulness of that good which was offered us, either in prayer, conference, or the ministry of the word, and to a sensible desire at least of some declining, but even in the time of our enjoying of them, our hearts deceived us, that we could not make (I speak of the most times) any great use or profit of them at all.

Earthly-mindedness is another stream running from this fountain, when we are drawn to the love of the commodities of this world, and are led with a desire of growing rich, which snares us, and calls back our minds from living holy, and cause such as wisely resist it not, to have their treasure in the earth. In prayer great coldness and weariness possesses (as it were) this heart of ours when by any occasion we have attempted it; anger, malice and revenge, in degree one exceeding the other, do easily appear to have their abode in this heart. Pride, though sometime privy, is one among the rest, which poisons our best actions, and soon arises when any good hath been done of us; the repining at the gifts of others, doth many times assault us; and what barrenness and emptiness of Gods grace is too commonly found in us; our woeful experience doth cause us to remember. Unclean desires (among the rest) are here; an innumerable rabble of other unsavory, dangerous, and carnal thoughts do swarm in us: and temperance and moderation is so meanly reached unto, that we can hardly be merry without lightness; sad without unfruitful dumpishness, believing God without presuming, or fear him without some doubts and inclining to despairing.

But now, when these shall be let loose in us, when they are not held in as it were with bit and bridle, when they shall govern us; and not we them; but we become slaves and servants unto them, how can it be otherwise, but that our lives should give little light unto men and glory to God, and for all our profession of the Gospel, and the account that we make of it, yet that the forementioned offences should be found in us? And this is the second cause why we bring forth no greater fruits of amendment. For when our hearts which in themselves are too evil, shall wander where they will without check, and feed themselves by occasions without control, little watching over them, or keeping in of them with diligent care and observing of them, full easily and right soon is the unsettledness and unprofitableness, which we complained of, engendered in us: and so brings forth fruit accordingly, even like unto it self, as hath been said.

And yet another cause why so little good hath been done, we may remember to have been that we have looked so narrowly to the lives of others to gather hurt thereby, not remembering that we should follow Christ. Of which, some being of the better sort, and others of the common, we have taken exceeding great hurt to them both. For these latter, when we saw how they have many times, continuance in outward peace & prosperity, so that they are merry, and take no thought about providing for the judgment day, neither are withheld from

any intemperance of living; though we become not like unto them, yet as men not so fully persuading our selves of their misery, we began to think that it is but vain for us to labor greatly after innocence, and to shine as lights, which (we see) is little regarded. And so we have grown to justify our own course of life, as very sufficient, and well liking to the Lord, yea, and besides this, we gathered some rubbish and scurf from them, by beholding, by dealing, & being too conversant with them. And if of these, some be less evil than others, and retain some points of honesty, and of better behavior in them; yet what a gross bewitching of our selves it is to compare our selves with those, of whose happiness we have persuasion? Now as the lives of this bad sort of men were laid too near us, and we may see that we were weakened in our course by them: so the lives of the first sort, even right good men, we either little or not at all profited by, or (that which more is) we many times took hurt by them.

And these are the special causes, that so much fault may be found in our lives; unto the which briefly these may be added, that we have not been careful to be strangers to such companies; where we might be easily corrupted, or cooled and discouraged: neither taken occasion to be in good company, or to have made profit of the same when we were in it, but in a common manner spent such times, either in endless or needless worldly talk, or some other way unprofitably; rather framing our selves to their humors, and to approve of their evil custom, than bethinking our selves how to stop them by giving better example unto them.

Now forasmuch as in the weighing of the truth of these things, we could not but be grieved heartily, (as who can behold so great depth of corruption and the fruit of the same, so many ways with deadly uncomfortableness threatening his confusion, but he must needs seek and use all possible means, speedily to pull himself out again?) therefore immediately after the due consideration of our woeful condition, we turned our selves to bethink us, what remedies we might apply to this fall, if thereby we might possibly recover our selves again: and also make them help hereafter, that we may as well continue in a fruitful and cheerful course unto the end of our lives; as, to return into the right way again. First therefore, we thought thus, and took order as followeth: that such of us, as did find our falls to be so great, and our offences so dangerous, that either for our too great delight in them, or long lying therein we could not by our usual prayers and humiliation, or by help of any ordinary and daily practices of repentance, (as by hearing the word and preparing our selves for the Lords Supper;) come to peace of conscience, by the remission of our sins, and obtain confidence and godly boldness with the Lord; such of us (I say) should humble our selves before him with fasting and prayer, without which means such devils are hardly cast out. Especially our purpose was in such a case that our fasting should tend to this, that we might forcibly pray for the recovery of our faith, and clear beholding of Gods loving kindness restored to us again.

After this, our covenant was, to know our hearts better, how evil they are; what falsehood, fickleness, lightness, and such like naughtiness, and variety of corrupt affections we carry about us; that thereby we be enforced to take more pain to weaken them daily, for we saw that if we be not diligent to search them out, as by occasion we shall be moved to do, we shall both walk in continual unsettledness, and in an uncomfortable estate, because we can go about nothing, but some one of these or other shall be espied to carry us some way amiss in the same. And thus we purposed to note and find them out in us, by a diligent view of, and taking heed unto our ways, that so we may be in daily combat with them. A worthy work therefore and commendable we saw it, to take knowledge of them; and not to be content to be blind in the beholding of them; (and yet that he which hides them should not prosper:) that so we may behold more filth and venom in them, than we would have thought could have been in us.

Now further, because the knowledge of our hearts, (if we stay here) I mean, of the manifold evil lusts of them, doth make us the more heady and greedy to fulfill them, when we know them by the Law of God to be condemned in us: we have further faithfully determined to watch over them with all diligence, that neither any of those which have already been mentioned, neither any other (as far as we may know them) may lurk or have their abode with us with our liking, but that we may purge them out; and not those only which are apparently gross, but even such as are more secret, being not yet come near their ripeness: and therefore wheresoever we become, or in whatsoever we have to do, not to neglect this part of Christian duty, but especially there to be most vigilant, where we suspect or see cause to fear more danger thereby: as in vehement and strong temptations, and grievous and long continuing afflictions, there to stand the more upon our watch, &c. So that whether we be in company, or alone; in dealings abroad, or matters at home; by one occasion or by other, yet still to have this purpose fixed in us, that as far as our frail memory will suffer us to remember, it, we may go forward in the watching and observing of them. Which must the rather be done, because, as the heart is the fountain of life, and from thence we have it, that we live; so from thence we must fetch the beginning of well living: for from an evil and unclean heart, comes no part of good life, no more than good fruit from an evil tree.

All which shall have their part in this covenant, or have already desired to have, must be renewed in their mind, and have their hearts purged and made clean by faith in the Son of god; whereby their sins may be defaced, and all their old conversation pardoned, their souls through the same with most comfortable and sound peace enlightened, and so their hearts purified, both to will and also to live well and godly, so they must have learned it, and have attained to it, who are here mentioned, that is, such as have covenanted unfeignedly to watch and observe the same.

We wean our hearts from earthly delights, which oftentimes tickling it with a pleasant sweetness, steal it away from heavenly things, and hold it here below, and so by little and little bring it to find a contentation here, and breed a wearisomeness in that godly life. And further, that we be very wary, that our hearts be not stolen from a liking of good ways, neither brought out of frame by loathing our duties, and so deprived of their peace: especially, that we be not hurt nor wounded that way where there is greatest cause of fear and danger, nor brought into subjection to those sins, to the which by nature we be most inclined, as to the love of the world, uncleanness, breaking off of brotherly affection, &c.

And to the end that in this work we may more happily go forward, and this watch be the better kept, our purpose was, to avoid carefully all outward hindrances, and occasions of quenching God's Spirit in us as we shall have wisdom to see them: as, too far entering into dealings or talk about the world, to call our selves back from all excess that way, also unprofitable and dangerous company and acquaintance, any unnecessary and idle talk, and whatsoever else like unto these. And contrarily, to be careful to continue with diligence and delight, not only in the exercise and use of such holy means of meditation, prayer, reading, hearing and conference, &c. but also to do it with minds to reap fruit by the same; which is not always intended nor sought for, so oft as the things themselves are used. As for example, seeing the readiest and best way to nourish and continue this holy desire, and careful watching over our hearts, is increase of knowledge, by the help of hearing and reading, (for zealous and holy affections are like a flame of fire, which without the adding and putting to of wood, as new matter, will soon be quenched and extinguished; so will our looking to our hearts and observing of them, be loosely and lightly continued:) it is our purpose to stir up our selves with more earnestness hereunto, because we know that we shall otherwise frustrate and make vain our whole covenant.

And to sharpen our desire to hear and read the more willingly, seeing there is much untowardness in our nature to such exercises, and we have strong temptations to persuade us that it is as needless as we feel it irksome: we have seen it necessary for us to stir up our dullness, not only by the Commandment of God, that we should fear the Scriptures, (and so read them) & that we should give care daily to the Apostles doctrine, (and therefore hear the same in season and out of season, that by both the word of God may dwell plentifully in us;) but also to have in fresh memory the power of the Scriptures: which, besides that they are able to save our souls, so they can fill us with goodness, and comfort every way, as we shall have need, and have done so often in times past unto us.

And further, because experience hath taught us that we easily lose that in the world amongst the manifold encumbrances, discouragements and dealings thereof, which we learned of the Lord by any means; we have faithfully covenanted for the better keeping of our hearts watchful, and safe from evil, once in the day (if it be possible) to set apart a time from all other lawful and necessary duties, for meditation and private prayer, to the seasoning of our hearts with grace, and to the establishing of them against all temptations, afflictions and other hindrances. Not, to free our selves hereby from other times of communing with the Lord, as occasions shall be offered, and necessity shall require: but because our untoward hearts would otherwise draw us altogether to break off this duty, if we should not determine of some special time; therefore one quarter of an hour, or as every one shall find himself able, we have seen meet to appoint hereunto, if we can have good opportunity; that is to say, if God give us minds fitly disposed thereto, and minister profitable and plentiful matter accordingly, or if we fail in both, so much the more to take occasion by our present wants and infirmity, to repair unto God.

And because the morning when we arise, is both most meet to be employed that way, as wherein our minds are best able to think upon heavenly matters, when we have not yet been about our worldly affairs; and for the most people which are at their own hand, the best time that may be spared: therefore we have purposed to allot (as we shall be able) the first part of the day thereunto, with this proviso, that if through necessary occasions we should be hindered from it, we may yet carefully perform it on some other part of the day.

And because it is hard, especially for us private persons, to have always, matter in a readiness, which is profitable to mediate upon, (for he that shall be furnished herewithall, must be one which hath a daily observation of his life, without the which grace even the more learned sort shall be to seek:) therefore we intend for this purpose to draw matter out of the 119. Psalm and others; some points are set down for those which are least able to help our selves; that by some few of those which are very fit and available, we may set our selves on work, and by them learn to find out others like unto them, which do most nearly tend to the well ordering of the life.

Lastly, we concluded to observe, what fruit we reap by these remedies: what release of our strong and usual maladies and diseases, what weakening of any such lusts as sometimes had strongly prevailed against us. Also, what liking we find of this manner of dealing with our selves; or contrarily, whether we feel any watchfulness over our hearts throughout the day, since we entered into this covenant, and whether any bettering of our ways by the same: whether in company we have been more wary of taking or doing good according to the occasion offered; in our dealings more careful not to be found offensive. And weekly and by days to mark it, and to communicate our estate with some faithful brother, with whom we may freely and faithfully open and impart our whole course, as what means we use, what we see cause most to complain of, and what is more required of us than that which we do: that thus we may be set forward, counseled, and confirmed; and seeing what course we ought to take for the bringing of this to pass, we may be established in a Christian life: For it doth not a little help to have this communion with some. Also, that we our selves should be helpers of others, where either any do require the same duty of us, or through bashfulness dare not be bold, or through simplicity cannot do it: yet we seeing that they stand in need of such counsel and direction; should through love show them what we can, and what we have learned in this behalf. And here we purposed for the hope of the great fruit of this communion, to avoid strangeness, which as it breaks off all profit betwixt us, so it gives fear of some secret conceitedness, and that much love is wanting. This direction, if it be read over (as we shall see cause, and as, we may do it conveniently) with a mind desirous as well as to see what is amiss in us, as also in faithfulness to use these remedies: we may be bold: (the Lord working by means) to assure our selves that we shall not labor herein in vain. And when we have attained hereto, we determined not to rest in that, but to be directed full by such rules as Gods Word doth minister to us.

Howsoever this endeavoring after a godly life, hath ever of the world been little regarded; yet the happiest and men of greatest commendation for godliness, have always preferred it, and made it as the flower of their garland, and the crown of their rejoicing: we have a cloud of witnesses, and not all in one age, who have walked with God, even from *Enoch* and thereabout to this day, who testified this daily looking to their lives, to be the best thing of all. Now if by these and such like persuasions we be brought to like of it, we faithfully covenanted with our selves, to use these remedies which have been set down for continuance, and to make our beginnings sound and substantial; so as they may be able to bear and uphold the weight of all that shall press us down. For although our temptations are strong and many, yet may none of them prevail thus far, as to make us break off this our happy covenant.

II. John Winthrop and his friends

In his spiritual diary John Winthrop recorded a covenant made by lay and clerical friends in the Stour Valley region surrounding Groton in which the individuals pledged themselves to pray for each other on a regular basis and to meet to discuss their spiritual progress.

September 17, 1613. There met at Mr. Sandes', Mr. Knewstub, Mr. Bird & his wife, Mr. Chambers, John Garrold & his wife, John Warner & his wife, Mr. Stebbin, Barker of the Priory, & I with my company, where we appointed all to meet again the next year on that Friday which should be nearest to the 17 of September, &, in the meantime, every of us each Friday in the week to be mindful one of another in desiring God to grant the petitions that were made to him that day, &c.

Covenants—Town Covenants

Just as they bound themselves together to form churches, so too the New England colonists joined in social fellowship through the drawing up and agreeing to written covenants. Similar to the Pilgrim's Mayflower Compact, these agreements committed the community members to accept the decisions they made as a corporate body. There was, however, a precedent for this in the similar articles drawn up by certain English parishes. There follow an example of one such English set of articles and the town covenant of Dedham, Massachusetts.

I. The Swallowfield (England) Articles of 1596

Source: modernized from the transcription by Steve Hindle of Huntington Library Ms Ellesmere 6162, folios 34–36.

In the parish of Swallowfield in the country of Wiltshire.
The 4 day of December 1596 & in the 38 year of the reign of our Sovereign lady Queen Elizabeth

Made the day & year above written. We whose names are hereunto subscribed, being the chief inhabitants in Sheperig Magna & Sheperidge Parva, Fowleigh Hill, & Didenham, in the county of Wiltshire, have firmly agreed to observe & keep all & singular of the articles here set down, and for that the Justices are far off, this we have done to the end we may the better & more quietly live together in good love & amity, to the praise of God, and for the better serving of her Majesty when wee meet together about any assessments or other designs of her Majesty's whatsoever, or any other matter or cause concerning the Church, the poor or the parish as followeth.

[1] First, it is agreed that every man shall be heard at our meeting quietly, one after another, and that none shall interrupt another in his speech. And that every man shall speak as he is first in account, & so in order, that thereby the depth of every man's Judgment with reason may be considered.

[2] And that no man shall scorn another's speech, but that all that shall be spoken may be quietly taken & heard of all, be it against any man or with him, his reason or defense that is aggrieved, only allowed when the other hath ended.

[3] And that every man shall submit himself to the censure of the whole company, or to the most in number, so that no man in our meeting shall think himself wisest or greatest.

[4] And to bring all things the better to pass, & that we may the better continue in good love & liking, one of another, every one doth promise for himself to the whole company & to every of them, that they will not fall out one with another, nor offer to go to law one with another, before the whole company or the most part thereof for that cause be made privy to this grievance, that by them all strife may be ended before any malice take root, for pacifying of which grievances every of us promises to do the best he can, and altogether do promise the same one to another.

[5] And he that shall refuse to be ordered in such matters as neighbors shall be able to consider of & to decide, so it be no matter of the Crown & touch no man's freehold, shall not be accounted one of our company, as one worthy to be accounted of amongst us, because he refuseth his promise which was made & received by us all, for our better quiet & ordering of ourselves, & the whole inhabitants aforesaid.

[6] And that no man shall do any thing one against another, nor against any man, by word nor deed, upon affection, or malice, in our meeting, nor to be discontented, one with another, since none of us is ruler of himself, but the whole company or the most part is ruler of us all.

[7] And that none of us shall disdain one another, nor seek to hinder one another, neither by words nor deeds, but rather to be helpers, assisters & councilors of one another, and all our doings to be good, honest, loving and just one to an other.

[8] And that whosoever doth take in to his house ether wife or other woman with child, & suffer her to be brought abed in his house that thereby the parish shall be charged with a child or children there born, everyone upon knowledge thereof shall give warning to the Constable, that thereby some present order may be taken & due presentment made by the Churchwardens.

[9] And that every man whatsoever, if he be upon denial of his duty by any assessment, or that doth not pay it when he is asked or appoint not some day or time to pay it to him that shall be appointed to gather the same, shall after have no favor, & yet be complained on to the Justice to force him thereunto.

[10] And that all officers whatsoever concerning her Majesty's service, & all other officers for the public affairs of the tithings & the inhabitants thereof shall be countenanced & born out of us all.

[11] And that there be a paper book to register all our doings, & by what authority or warrant we do it concerning her Majesty's service, & one other book for the church & the poor.

[12] And every one of us doth promise one to an other, & to the whole company, that whatsoever suit shall grow or arise in the said tithings or in any of them amongst the inhabitants thereof, which toucheth the whole tithings, or in any of them & the inhabitants therein, that then we agree to join together in purse, travel & credit in defense of all such wrongs and not otherwise.

[13] And if any single or unmarried woman shall be brought to bed or be gotten with child, then presently to find out the supposed father & force him, by the help of the Justice, to put in good surety for the discharge of the parish if she be a common born child, if not to banish her from the parish.

[14] And all the Company prayeth & beseecheth all officers before they go to any court to present any offence, to make the whole company privy to such faults as are to be presented, that some good order may be taken by us all for the remedy thereof before any presentment be made, that thereby we may live in lawful manner together without any discord or disliking one of another.

[15] And every one promiseth to do his best to end all strife which shall happen between neighbor & neighbor, be they poor or rich, and that such as be poor & will malapertly compare with their betters & set them at nought, shall be warned to live & behave themselves as becometh them; if such amend not, then no man to

make any other account of them than of common disturbers of peace & quietness, and the Justices of the Shire to be made privy of such misdemeanors, that at the Sessions or assizes such persons may be reformed by the severity of the law in such case provided.

[16] And that the officers shall not be disliked of, for the doing of their office, & in furthering of her Majesty's service, or any other business of the tithings aforesaid, but shall be used with all gentleness, both in word and deed.

[17] And that hereafter, if any man remember an article or matter whereby the tithings aforesaid may be benefited or otherwise saved from harm or danger, that shall be by the whole company or the most part of them be set in this book, wherefore our desire is that in charity & truth every one of us shall take all honest care one of another, and of the wrongs, that may arise amongst us or against us, especially of our duties or service towards her Majesty.

[18] And that all shall do their best to suppress pilferers, backbiters, hedge breakers, & mischievous persons, & all such as be proud, dissentious & arrogant persons.

[19] And that all shall do their best to help the honest poor, the blind, the sick, the lame, & diseased persons.

[20] And that all of us have an especial care to speak to the minister to stay the marriage of such as would marry before they have a convenient house to live in, according to their calling, that thereby, the parish shall not be troubled with such inmates.

[21] And that every man shall be forbidden to keep inmates, & whosoever doth keep any inmates, to complain of them to the Justice & by no means to relieve the householder, nor inmates during the time of the inmates abiding with the householder.

[22] And for the better observation to see that the Sabbath day [be observed] with more reverence & less profaning thereof, then there shall be appointed two of us to see that all the tipplers shall after the second ring of the bell, as well before morning prayer as evening prayer, shut in their doors & so come to the Church, and if they shall neglect, or suffer any to come within their house to eat or drink, the party so offending to pay to the lame blind & poor for every time two shillings & the parties taken drinking or eating in time of public service six pence a man to the same use, & to be registered in the book, but it shall be lawful for the traveler to call for drink & drink at the door & go away.

[23] And he or she that shall be found to be drunk being warned once before & will not take warning shall for every time so offending as he is of wealth to be punished by the purse; those that be poor and not able, to be put in to the stocks till he or she shall be sober & be ashamed of their drunkenness.

[24] And also that all the inhabitants shall henceforth see that all his servants shall come to the church in due time to learn & put in practice that which shall there be delivered by the minister out of the word of God for their edification, & not to send them on that day on their worldly business as is too much practiced, but that they shall set them in the Church except it be those that dress dinner at home & see to the house.

[25] And further, by the consent of us all & at the request of every of us, it is agreed that two of us (if need be) shall be appointed to every Sessions to make the Justices privy to the misorders & to present the defaults that are amongst us, if upon warning to the offenders they persist in their willful & vile sins, for which cause & to keep men from harm the whole company promiseth to meet once in every month to hear the complaints of such as have been wronged or are moved to discover the disorders of any, & upon their complaints to appoint two of the company to examine the matter & to make report. that the unruly may be reformed, or else that two of us shall be present at Sessions, Leet & Law days for to use the best means for to keep down sin, & all of us to be contributory to the charges hereof, if those parties shall be willful & stubborn against the peace.

[26] Moreover it is agreed by us all, & every of us for himself doth promise to each other & to the whole company that whatsoever shall by any of us done or said in our meetings to the effect of the former Articles mentioned shall be kept secret, & not to be revealed further than our own company, and that none of us all shall use any communication or means concerning our meetings or anything therein done or said which may tend to, or procure, the discredit or disgrace of our meetings & good intent, or of any of our company.

And this article with all the rest to be truly observed by every of us, as we will be esteemed to be men of discretion, good credit, honest minds, & Christian like behavior one towards another.

In the name of God, amen, so be it.

Our father, which art in heaven, hallowed be thy name, kingdom come.

II. The Dedham, Massachusetts, Covenant of 1636

Source: *Early Records of the Town of Dedham*, 6 volumes (Dedham, 1886–1936), III, 2–3.

One: We whose names are hereunto subscribed do, in the fear and reverence of our Almighty God, mutually and severally promise among ourselves and each to profess and practice one truth according to that most perfect rule, the foundation whereof is everlasting love.

Two: That we shall by all means labor to keep off from us all such as are contrary minded, and receive only such unto us as may be probably of one heart with us, [such] as that we either know or may well and truly be informed to walk in a peaceable conversation with all meekness of spirit, [this] for the edification of each other in the knowledge and faith of the Lord Jesus, and the mutual encouragement unto all temporal comforts in all things, seeking the good of each other out of which may be derived true peace.

Three: That if at any time differences shall rise between parties of our said town, that then such party or parties shall presently refer all such differences unto some one, two, or three others of our said society to be fully accorded and determined without any further delay, if it possibly may be.

Four: That every man that shall have lots in our said town shall pay his share in all such . . . charges as shall be imposed on him . . ., as also become freely subject unto all such orders and constitutions as shall be . . . made now or at any time hereafter from this day forward, as well for loving and comfortable society in our said town as also for the prosperous and thriving condition of our said fellowship, especially respecting fear of God, in which we desire to begin and continue whatsoever we shall by his loving favor take into hand.

Five: And for the better manifestation of our true resolution herein, every man so received into the town is to subscribe hereunto his name, thereby obliging both himself and his successors after him, as we have done.

Death and Dying

The following is a description of the death of Thomasine Winthrop, the wife of John Winthrop, later the governor of Massachusetts, taken from his spiritual diary. John Winthrop's first wife, Mary Forth, had died in 1615, leaving him with four children under the age of ten. As was customary, Winthrop married again soon thereafter, choosing as his bride Thomasine Clopton, whom he had known for most of his life. Whereas his first marriage had occasionally been troubled by the different personalities of John and Mary, Thomasine shared Winthrop's religious commitments and intellectual curiosity. Her death a year after they were wed was a hard blow to John. His account of her last days is one of the most complete and most moving accounts of death and dying in a puritan household.

On Saturday, being the last of November 1616, Thomasine, my dear & loving wife, was delivered of a daughter, which died the Monday following, in the morning. She took the death of it with that patience that made us all to marvel, especially those that saw how careful she was for the life of it in her travail. That day, soon after the death of the child, she was taken with a fever which shaked her very much, & set her into a great fit of coughing, which by Tuesday morning was well allayed. Yet she continued aguish & sweating, with much hoarseness, & her mouth grew very sore, & much troubled with blood falling from her head into her mouth & throat.

On Wednesday morning those which were about her, & herself also, began to fear that which followed, whereupon we sent for my Cousin Duke,[1] which, when she understood, she told me that she hoped when he came he would deal plainly with me, & not feed me with vain hopes. Whereupon I, breaking forth into tears, she was moved at it, & desired me to be contented, for you break mine heart (said she) with your grieving. I answered that I could do no less when I feared to be stripped of such a blessing. She replied, God never bestows any blessing so great on his children but still he hath a greater in store, & that I should not be troubled at it, for I might see how God had dealt with Mr. Rogers before me in the like case.[2] And always, when she perceived me to mourn for her, she would entreat & persuade me to be contented, telling me that she did love me well, & if God would let her live with me, she would endeavor to show it more, &c. She also desired me oft, that so long as she lived I would not cease praying for her, neither would be absent from her, but when I had necessary occasions.

On Thursday at noon my Cousin Duke came to her, & took notice of her dangerous estate, yet expecting a farther issue that night, he departed, saying that before Saturday we should see a great change. After his departure she asked me what he said of her, which when I told her, she was no whit moved at it, but was as comfortably resolved whether to live or die.

On Thursday in the night she was taken with death, & about midnight or somewhat after called for me, & for the rest of her friends. When I came to her she seemed to be fully assured that her time was come, & to be glad of it, & desired me to pray, which I did, & she took comfort therein, & desired that we would send for Mr. Sandes, which we did.[3] In the meantime, she desired that the bell might ring for her, & divers of the neighbors came into her, which, when she perceived, she desired me that they might come to her one by one, & so she would speak to them all, which she did, as they came, quietly & comfortably. When the bell began to ring, some said it was the 4 o'clock bell, but she, conceiving that they sought to conceal it from her, that it did ring for her, she said it needed not, for it did not trouble her. Then came in Mr. Nicolson, whom she desired to pray, which he did.[4]

When Mr. Sandes was come she reached him her hand, being glad of his coming (for she had asked often for him). He spake to her of diverse comfortable points, whereunto she answered so wisely & comfortably, as he & Mr. Nicolson did both marvel to hear her, Mr. Sandes saying to me that he did not look for so sound Judgment in her. He said he had taken her always for a harmless young woman, & well affected, but did not think she had been so well grounded. Mr. Nicolson, seeing her humbleness of mind & great comfort in God, said that her life had been so innocent & harmless as the Devil could find nothing to lay to her charge. Then she desired Mr. Sandes to pray, but not pray for life for her. He answered that he would pray for grace. After prayer she desired me that I would not let Mr. Sandes go away, but when he showed her the occasion he had, she was content, upon promise that he would come again. This was about 5 of the clock on friday morning.

Friday morning, about 6 of the clock, my Cousin Duke came to us again, & when he had seen how things fell out that night, he told us that that was the dismal night, wherein she had received her death's wound, yet she might languish a day or 2. Yet after he had felt her pulse, he said that if the next night were a good night with her, there was some hope left.

Friday morning she began somewhat to cheer, & so continued all that day, & had a very good night that night following, & began herself to entertain some thought of life, & so did most of us that were about her. But on Saturday morning she began to complain of cold, & a little after awaking out of a slumber, she prayed me to set my heart at rest, for now (said she) I am but a dead woman, for this hand (meaning her left hand) is dead already. And when we would have persuaded her that it was but numb with being under her, she still constantly affirmed that it was dead, & that she had no feeling in it, & desired me to pull off her gloves that she might see it, which I did. Then, when they would have wrapped some clothes about it, she disliked it, telling them that it was in vain, & why should they cover a dead hand. When I prayed her to suffer it, she answered that if I would have it so she would, & so I pulled on her gloves, & they pinned clothes about her hands. When they had done, she said, O what a wretch was I, for laying my leg out of the bed this night, for when I should pull it in again it was as if it had come through the coverlet, (yet it seemed to be but her imagination or dream for the women could not perceive it).

The fever grew very strong upon her, so as when all the time of her sickness before she was wont to say she thanked God she felt no pain, now she began to complain of her breast, & troubles in her head, & after she had slumbered a while & was awaked, she began to be tempted, & when I came to her she seemed to be affrighted, used some speeches of Satan's assaulting her, & complained of the loss of her first love, &c. Then we prayed with her, as she desired. After prayer she disliked that we prayed for life for her, since we might see it was not God's will that she should live.

Her fever increased very violently upon her, which the Devil made advantage of to molest her comfort, but she, declaring unto us with what temptations the devil did assault her, bent herself against them, praying with great vehemence for God's help, & that he would not take away his loving kindness from her, defying Satan, & spitting at him, so as we might see by her setting of her teeth, & fixing her eyes, shaking her head & whole body, that she had a very great conflict with the adversary.

After, she a little paused, & that they went about to cover her hands, which lay open with her former striving, she began to lift up herself, desiring that she might have her hands & all at liberty to glorify God, & prayed earnestly that she might glorify God, although it were in hell. Then she began very earnestly to call upon all that were about her, exhorting them to serve God, &c (& whereas all the time of her sickness before she would not endure the light, but would be careful to have the curtains kept close, now she desired light, & would have the curtain towards the window set open, & so to her end was much grieved when she had not either the daylight or candlelight. But the firelight she could not endure to look upon, saying that it was of too many colors, like the rainbow.)

Then she called for her sisters, & first for her sister Mary, & when she came she said, "sister Mary, thou hast many good things in thee, so as I have cause to hope well of thee, & that we shall meet in heaven, &c."

Then she called for her sister Margery, whom she exhorted to serve God, & take heed of pride, & to have care in her matching, that she looked not at riches & worldly respects, but at the fear of God, for that would bring her comfort at her death although she should meet with many afflictions.

To her Elizabeth she said, "serve God, take heed of lying. I do not know that you do use it, but I wish you to beware."

Her sister Sampson she exhorted to serve God, & to bring up her children well, not in pride & vanity, but in the fear of God.

To her mother she said that she was the first child that she should bury, but prayed her that she would not be discomforted at it. When her mother answered that she had no cause to be discomforted for her, for she should go to a better place, & she should go to her father, she replied that she should go to a better father than her earthly father.

Then came my father & mother, whom she thanked for all their kindness & love towards her.

Then she called for my children & blessed them severally, & would needs have Mary brought that she might kiss her, which she did.

Then she called for my sister Luce, & exhorted her to take heed of pride & to serve God.

Then she called for her servants: to Robert she said, "you have many good things in you, I have nothing to accuse you of. Be faithful & diligent in your service."

To Anne Pold she said that she was a stubborn wench, &c, & exhorted her to be obedient to my mother.

To Elizabeth Crouff she said, "take heed of pride & I shall now release you, but take heed what service you go into."

To Anne Addams she said, "thou hast been in bad serving, long in an Alehouse, &c. Thou make no conscience of the Sabbath; when I would have had thee go to Church thou would not, &c."

Then came Mercy Smith to her, to whom she said "thou art a good woman. Bring up thy children well, you poor folks commonly spoil your children in suffering them to break God's Sabbaths, &c."

To another she said, "you have many children, bring them up well, not in lying, &c."

To another she said, "God forgive your sins whatsoever they be."

To goodwife Cole she said, "you are a good woman, I thank you for all your pains towards me, God reward you."

To Henry Pease she said, "be diligent & faithful in your work, or else when death come, it will be laid before you. I pray God send your wife good deliverance, she may do well. Though I die, bring up my goddaughter well, let her not want correction."

To her keeper she said, "be not discouraged, although I die, thou hast kept many that have done well. Thou hast but one child, bring it up well."

Her pain increased very much in her breast, which swelled so as they were forced to cut the ties of her waistcoat to give her ease. Whilst she lay in this estate she ceased not (albeit she was very hoarse, & spoke with great pain) one while to exhort, another while to pray. Her usual prayer was Come Lord Jesus; When Lord Jesus, &c. Her exhortation was to stir up all that saw her, to prepare for death, telling them that they did not know how sharp & bitter the pangs of death were, with many like speeches.

In this time she prayed for the Church, &c, & for the ministry, that God would bless good ministers, &

convert such ill ones as did belong to him, & weed out the rest. After this we might perceive that God had given her victory by the comfort which she had in the meditation of her happiness, in the favor of God in Christ Jesus. Towards afternoon her great pains remitted, & she lay very still, & said she saw her time was not yet come, she should live 24 hours longer. Then, when any asked her how she did, she would answer pretty well, but in her former fit, to that question she would answer that she was going the way of all flesh. Then she prayed me to read by her. When I asked her where, she answered, in some of the holy gospels. So I began in John the 14, & read on to the end of the 17th Chapter. And when I paused at the end of any sweet sentence, she would say this is comfortable. If I stayed at the end of any Chapter for her to take rest, she would call earnestly to read on—then she desired to take a little rest.

She often prayed God to forgive the sins of her youth, &c, & desired me often to pray for her, that God would strengthen her with his holy spirit. After, she desired me again to read to her the 8th to the Romans, & the 11th to the Hebrews, whereby she received great comfort. Still calling to read on, then I read the 116 psalm. This is a sweet psalm (said she). Then I read the 84 Psalm, the 32, 36, 37, & other places.

In the evening Mr. Sandes came again & prayed, & soon after she took him by the hand & told him she would bid him farewell, for she knew it was a busy night with him. After, we went to prayer, & when he had done, "O what a wretch am I (said she) to lose the end of this prayer, for I was asleep."

After we had continued in reading, etc, until late in the night, she asked who should watch with her, & when we told her, she was satisfied, & disposed herself to rest.

In the night she prayed one of the women that watched with her to read unto her. Whilst I was gone to bed, she asked often for me, & about 2 of the clock in the morning I came to her. Now it was the Sabbath day, & she had now & then a brunt of temptation, bewailing that she could not then be assured of her salvation, as she had been. She said that the devil went about to persuade her to cast off her subjection to her husband, &c.

That Sabbath noon, when most of the company were gone down to dinner, when I discoursed unto her of the sweet love of Christ unto her, & of the glory that she was going unto, & what an holy everlasting Sabbath she should keep, & how she should sup with Christ in Paradise that night, &c, she showed by her speeches & gestures the great joy & steadfast assurance that she had of those things. When I told her that her Redeemer lived,

& that she should see him with those poor dim eyes, which should be bright & glorified, she answered cheerfully, she should. When I told her that she should leave the society of friends which were full of infirmities, & should have communion with Abram, Isaac, & Jacob, all the prophets & apostles & saints of God, & those holy martyrs (whose stories when I asked her if she remembered, she answered yea) she would lift up her hands & eyes, & say, yea she should. Such comfort had she against death that she steadfastly professed that if life were set before her she would not take it.

When I told her that the day before was 12 months she was married to me, & now this day she should be married to Christ Jesus, who would embrace her with another manner of love than I could, Oh husband (said she, & spake as if she were offended, for I perceived she did mistake me) I must not love thee as I love Christ.

Her hearing still continued, & her understanding very perfect, her sight was dimmed, yet she knew everybody to the last. If I went from her she would call for me again, & once asked me if I were angry with her that I would not stay with her.

While I spake to her of anything that was comfortable, as the promises of the Gospel & the happy estate she was entering into, she would lay still & fix her eyes steadfastly upon me. And if I ceased awhile (when her speech was gone), she would turn her head towards me, & stir her hands as well as she could, till I spake, & then would be still again.

About 5 of the clock, Mr. Nicolson came to her & prayed with her, & about the end of his prayer, she fetched 2 or 3 sighs, & fell asleep in the Lord.

The Wednesday following, being the 11 of December, she was buried in Groton chancel by my other wife, & her child was taken up, & laid with her.

She was a woman wise, modest, loving, & patient of injuries. But her innocent & harmless life was of most observation. She was truly religious, & industrious therein; plain hearted, & free from guile, & very humble minded; never so addicted to any outward things (to my judgment) but that she could bring her affections to stoop to God's will in them. She was sparing in outward show of zeal, &c, but her constant love to good Christians & the best things, with her reverent & careful attendance of God's ordinances, both public & private, with her care for avoiding of evil herself, & reproving it in others, did plainly show that truth & the love of God, did lie at the heart. Her loving & tender regard of my children was such as might well become a natural mother. For her carriage towards myself, it was so amiable & observant as I am not able to express; it had this only inconvenience, that it made me delight too much in her to enjoy her long.

Notes

1. John Duke was the brother-in-law of John's mother, Anne Browne Winthrop, and was a physician who resided in Colchester, Essex.

2. A reference to the Reverend Richard Rogers of Wethersfield, who, after the death of his first wife, had married the widow of the Reverend John Ward of Haverhill.

3. Henry Sandes was a local clergyman, lecturer at the neighboring village of Boxford, and a close family friend of the Winthrops.

4. The Reverend Thomas Nicholson had been appointed to the living of Groton by John's uncle, John Winthrop. He was not known as a puritan and there is little evidence of his preaching.

Declaration of Breda, 4 April 1660

The declaration made by Charles II explaining how he intended to deal with religion following his restoration to the English throne.

> Source: Samuel Rawson Gardner, editor, *The Constitution Documents of the puritan Revolution, 1625-1660,* third edition, revised (Oxford, 1906), pp. 465–467.

Charles R.

Charles, by the grace of God, King of England, Scotland, France and Ireland, Defender of the Faith, &c. To all our loving subjects, of what degree or quality soever, greeting.

If the general distraction and confusion which is spread over the whole kingdom doth not awaken all men to a desire and longing that those wounds which have so many years together been kept bleeding, may be bound up, all we can say will be to no purpose; however, after this long silence, we have thought it our duty to declare how much we desire to contribute thereunto; and that as we can never give over the hope, in good time, to obtain the possession of that right which God and nature hath made our due, so we do make it our daily suit to the Divine Providence, that He will, in compassion to us and our subjects, after so long misery and sufferings, remit and put us into a quiet and peaceable possession of that our right, with as little blood and damage to our people as is possible; nor do we desire more to enjoy what is ours, than that all our subjects may enjoy what by law is theirs, by a full and entire administration of justice throughout the land, and by extending our mercy where it is wanted and deserved.

And to the end that the fear of punishment may not engage any, conscious to themselves of what is past, to a perseverance in guilt for the future, by opposing the quiet and happiness of their country, in the restoration of King, Peers and people to their just, ancient and fundamental rights, we do, by these presents, declare, that we do grant a free and general pardon, which we are ready, upon demand, to pass under our Great Seal of England, to all our subjects, of what degree or quality soever, who, within forty days after the publishing hereof, shall lay hold upon this our grace and favour, and shall, by any public act, declare their doing so, and that they return to the loyalty and obedience of good subjects; excepting only such persons as shall hereafter be excepted by Parliament, those only be excepted. Let all our subjects, how faulty soever, rely upon the word of a King, solemnly given by this present declaration, that no crime whatsoever, committed against us or our royal father before the publication of this, shall ever rise in judgment, or be brought in question, against any of them, to the least endamagement of them, either in their lives, liberties or estates, or (as far forth as lies in our power) so much as to the prejudice of their reputations, by any reproach or term of distinction from the rest of our best subjects; we desiring and ordaining that henceforth all notes of discord, separation and difference of parties be utterly abolished among all our subjects, whom we invite and conjure to a perfect union among themselves, under our protection, for the re-settlement of our just rights and theirs in a free Parliament, by which, upon the word of a King, we will be advised.

And because the passion and uncharitableness of the times have produced several opinions in religion, by which men are engaged in parties and animosities against each other (which, when they shall hereafter unite in a freedom of conversation, will be composed or better understood), we do declare a liberty to tender consciences, and that no man shall be disquieted or called in question for differences of opinion in matter of religion, which do not disturb the peace of the kingdom; and that we shall be ready to consent to such an Act of Parliament, as, upon mature deliberation, shall be offered to us, for the full granting that indulgence.

And because, in the continued distractions of so many years, and so many and great revolutions, many grants and purchases of estates have been made to and by many officers, soldiers and others, who are now possessed of the same, and who may be liable to actions at law upon several titles, we are likewise willing that all such differences, and all things relating to such grants, sales and purchases, shall be determined in Parliament, which can best provide for the just satisfaction of all men who are concerned.

And we do further declare, that we will be ready to consent to any Act or Acts of Parliament to the purposes aforesaid, and for the full satisfaction of all arrears due to the officers and soldiers of the army under the command of General Monk; and that they shall be received into our service upon as good pay and conditions as they now enjoy.

Given under our Sign Manual and Privy Signet, at our Court at Breda, this 4 day of April, 1660, in the twelfth year of our reign.

Directions for Godly Living

As part of their practice of piety, many puritan clergy and laity prepared guidelines that they sought to follow in their everyday lives. These directions give us an insight into how puritans viewed the godly lives they felt called by God to lead.

I. Reverend John Rogers

This compendium of "Sixty Memorials for a Godly Life" *was prepared by John Rogers, the famous preacher of Dedham, England, who was referred to as "Roaring Rogers" because of his dramatic preaching style. They were published by Cotton Mather in his* Magnalia Christi Americana *from a manuscript he had that had been passed to him from Rogers's son Daniel Rogers, who migrated to New England*

A Covenant

I. I have firmly purposed, (by God's grace,) to make my whole life, a meditation of a better life, and godliness in every part; that I may from point to point, and from step to step, with more watchfulness, walk with the Lord. Oh, the infinite gain of it! No small help hereto is daily meditation and often conference. Therefore, since the Lord hath given me to see in some sort the coldness of the half-service that is done to his majesty, by the most, and even by myself, I renew my covenant more firmly with the Lord, to come nearer unto the practice of godliness, and oftener to have my conversation in heaven, my mind seldomer and more lightly set upon the things of this life, to give to my self less liberty in the secretest and smallest provocations to evil, and to endeavor after a more continual watch from thing to thing, that as much as may be I may walk with the Lord for the time of my abiding here below.

A Form of Direction

II. This I resolutely determine, That God be always my glory through the day; and, as occasion shall be offered, help forward such as shall repair to me, or among whom, by God's providence, I shall come: and these two being regarded, that I might tend to my own good, going forward (my own heart, I mean, calling and life, and my family and charge) looking for my *change*, and preparing for the cross yea, for death itself: and to like little of mine estate, when I shall not sensibly find it thus with me: and whiles God affordeth me peace, health, liberty, an heart delighting in him, outward blessings with the same, to beware that godliness seem not pleasant to me, for earthly commodity, but for it self: if in this course, or any part of it, I should halt, or mislike, not to admit of any such deceit: and for the maintenance of this course, to take my part in all the good helps, appointed by God for the same; as these, first, to begin the day with meditation, thanksgiving, confession and prayer: to put on my armor: to watch and pray earnestly in the day for holding fast this course: to hearten on my self hereto by mine own experience (who have ever seen, that it goeth well with those which walk after this rule, 1 Peter 3:13; Galatians 6:16) and by the example of others (Hebrews 8:7). And for the better helping myself forward, still in this course, my purpose and desire is, to learn humility and meekness more and more, by God's chastisements, and encourage myself to this course of life, by his daily blessings and mercies: and to make the same use of all exercises in my family. And faithfully to peruse and examine the several parts of my life every evening, how this course has been kept of me, where it hath to keep it still, where it hath not, to seek pardon and recovery; and all behavior that will not stand with this, to hold me from it, as from *bane*.

A form for a Minister's Life

III. In solitariness to be least solitary: in company, taking or doing of good; to wife, to family, to neighbors, to fellow-ministers, to all with whom I deal, kind; amiable, yet modest; low in mine own eyes; oft with the sick and afflicted; attending to reading; painful for my sermons; not easily provoked unto anger; not carried away with conceits hastily; not wandering in fond dreams about ease and deceivable pleasures; not snared in the world, nor making lawful liberties my delight; helpful to all that need my help, readily, and all those that I ought to regard; and all this, with continuance, even all my days.

IV. Chief corruptions to be watched against be sourness, sadness, timorousness, forgetfulness, fretting, and inability to bear wrongs.

V. I am very backward to private visiting of neighbors' houses, which doth much hurt: for thereby their love to me cannot be so great as it would be. And I know not their particular wants and states so well, and therefore cannot speak so fitly to them as I might.

VI. A minister had need look that he profit from his preaching himself, because he knows not what others do. Many, he knows, get no good. Of many more he is uncertain. So that if he gets no good himself, his labor and travail shall be in vain.

VII. Begin the day with half an hour's meditation and prayer. And let me resolutely set myself to walk with God through the day. If anything fall out amiss, recover again speedily by humble confession, hearty prayer for pardon, with confidence of obtaining. And so proceed.

VIII. Oh! Mildness and cheerfulness, with reverence, how sweet a companion art thou!

IX. Few rare and worthy men continue so to their end, but one way or other fall into coldness, gross sin, or the world. Therefore, beware!

X. Count not the daily direction nor Christian life to be bondage, but count it the sweetest liberty and the only way of true peace. Whensoever this is counted hard, that state that is embraced instead thereof shall be harder.

XI. Worldly dealings are great lets to fruitfulness in study and cheerful proceeding in our Christian course.

XII. One can never go about study or preaching if anything lie heavy on the conscience.

XIII. The worst day wherein a man keeps his watch and hold to the daily rules of direction is freer from danger and brings more safety than the best day wherein this is not known or practiced.

XIV. I am oft, I confess, ashamed of myself when I have been in company and seen gifts of knowledge in many careless, unconscionable, and odd ministers, which (with better reasons) hath stirred up a desire oft-times in me that I could follow my studies. Yet I would never have been willing to have changed with them. For what is all knowledge without a sanctified and comfortable use of it through love, and without fruit of our labor in dong good, and winning and building up of souls, or at least a great endeavor after it.

XV. Many ministers set their minds upon this world, either profit or preferment, for which they venture dangerously, and some of them are "soon snatched way." Therefore, God keep me from ever setting my foot on such a path as hath no continuance and is not without much danger in the end.

XVI. It is good for a man to delight in that wherein he may be bold to delight without repentance: and that is, to be always doing or seeking occasion to do some good. The Lord help me herein!

XVII. When God hedgeth in a man with many mercies, and gives him a comfortable condition, it is good to acknowledge it often and be highly thankful for it. Else God may soon bring a man so low as he would think that state happy he was in before if now he had it again. Therefore, God make me wise!

XVIII. Right good men have complained that they are oft-times in very bad case, their hearts disordered and distempered very sore for want of taking to themselves a certain direction for the government of their lives.

XIX. Idle and unprofitable talk of by-matters is a canker that consumeth all good, and yet our heart much lusteth after it; therefore resolve firmly against it.

XX. A necessary and most comely thing it is for a minister to carry himself so wisely and amiably unto all, as he may do good unto all sorts; to bring back them that be fallen off in meekness and kindness; to pass by an offence in those that have wronged them, which is an high point of honor, and not to keep from them and estrange himself from their acquaintance, and so suffer them to fall further, to be lowly towards the meaner sort of Christians; to keep the credit of his ministry with all. I am persuaded if my light did shine more clearly, and mine example were seen more manifestly in these and such things (which are of no small force to persuade the people), that both my ministry would be of more power and that I should draw them also to be better.

XXI. Look that I lie not down in bed but in peace with God any night, and never my heart rest until it relent truly for anything that has passed amiss in the day.

XXII. It is good for a minister not to deal much with his people about worldly matters, yet not to be strange to them, nor to be a stumbling block unto the people by worldliness or any other fault, else he deprives himself of all liberty and advantage of dealing with them in their errors.

XXIII. Buffetings of Satan, though they be grievous, yet they are a very good medicine against pride and security.

XXIV. Christ's death and God's mercy is not sweet, but where sin is sour.

XXV. It is an hard thing for a man to keep the "rules of daily direction" at times of sickness and pain. Let a man labor to keep out evil when he wants fitness, strength, and occasion to do good, and that is a good portion for a sick body. Also in sickness that is sore and sharp, if a man can help himself with short and oft prayers to God for patience, contentment, meekness, and obedience to his holy hand, it is well, though he can't bend the mind much or earnestly upon anything.

XXVI. Innocence is a very good fence and fort against impatience in false accusations or great afflictions. Let them that be guilty fret and vex themselves, and show bitterness of stomach against such as speak ill of them. But they that look carefully to their hearts and ways (without looking at men's eye) let them be still and of a "meek and quiet spirit."

XXVII. Besides the use of the "daily direction," and following strictly the rules thereof, yet there must be now and then the use of fasting to purge our weariness and commonness in the use of it.

XXVIII. 'Tis a rare thing for any man so to use prosperity as that his heart be drawn nearer to God. Therefore, we had need in that estate to watch diligently, and labor to walk humbly.

XXIX. Oh, frowardness [contrariness, obstinacy]! How unseemly and hurtful a thing to a man's self and others. Amiable cheerfulness, with watchfulness and sobriety, is the best estate, and meetest to do good, especially to others.

XXX. Follow my calling: lose no time at home or abroad, but be doing some good. Mind my going homeward. Let my life never be pleasant to me when I am not fruitful and fit to be employed in doing good, one way or other.

XXXI. It is a great mercy of God to a minister, and a thing much to be desired, that he be well moved with the matter that he preaches to the people, either in his private meditation or in his public delivery, or both; better hope there is then that the people will be moved therewith, which we should ever aim at.

XXXII. If the heart be heavy at any time, and wounded for anything, shame ourselves and be humbled for our sin before we attempt any good exercise or duty.

XXXIII. It's a very good help, and a most present remedy, when one feels himself dull and in ill condition, to confess it to God, accuse himself, and pray for quickening. God sends redress.

XXXIV. There is as much need to pray to be kept in old age, and unto the end, as at any time. And yet a body would think that he that hath escaped the danger of his younger, should have no great fear in his latter days, but that his experience might prepare him against anything. However, it is not so, for many that have done well, and very commendably for a while, have shrewdly fallen to great hurt. This may moderate our grief when young men of great hopes be taken away. Oh! How much rather had I die in peace quickly, than live to disgrace the gospel and be a stumbling block to any, and live with reproach!

XXXV. What a sweet life it is when every part of the day hath some work or other allotted unto it, and this done constantly, but without commonness or customariness of spirit in the doing it!

XXXVI. When a man is in a drowsy, unprofitable course, and is not humbled for it, God oft lets him fall into some sensible sin to shame him with, to humble his heart, and drive him more thoroughly to God, to bewail and repent of both.

XXXVII. A true godly man hath never his life joyful unto him any longer than his conversation is holy and heavenly. Oh! Let it be so with me!

XXXVIII. It is some comfort for a man whose heart is out of order if he seeth it, and that with hearty mislike, and cannot be content until it be bettered.

XXXIX. I have seen of others (which I desire to die rather than it should be verified of me!) that many ministers did never seem grossly to depart from God until they grew wealthy and great.

XL. How much better it is to resist sin when we are tempted thereunto, than to repent of it after we have committed it!

XLI. Whatsoever a justified man doth by direction of God's word, and for which he hath either precept or promise, he pleases God in it, and may be comfortable in whatsoever falls out thereupon. But where ignorance, rashness, or our own will carry us, we offend.

XLII. Let no man boast of the grace he hath had, for we stand not now by that, but it must be daily nourished or else a man shall become as other men, and fall into noisome evils: for what are we but a lump of sin of ourselves?

XLIII. If God in mercy arm us not, and keep us not in compass, Lord, what stuff will break from us! For what a deal of poison is in our hearts if it may have issue! And therefore what need of watchfulness continually?

XLIV. The worst day (commonly) of him that knoweth and endeavoreth to walk by the "daily direction" is freer from danger and passed in greater safety than the best day of a godly man that knows not this "direction."

XLV. Many show themselves forward Christians in company abroad, that yet where they should show most fruits (as at home) are too secure, either thinking they are not marked, or, if they be, do not much regard it. This ought not to be.

XLVI. Be careful to mark what falls out in the day, in heart or life. And be sure to look over all at night that hath been amiss in the day, that so I might lie down in peace with God and conscience. The contrary were a woeful thing, and would cause hellish unquietness. Be sure, therefore, that none of the malicious subtleties of the devil, nor the naughtiness of my own heart, do carry me further than at night I may sleep with quiet to God-ward.

XLVII. When God saith (Deuteronomy 12:7) "That his may rejoice before him, in all that they put their hands unto," it is a great liberty, and enjoyed by few. No doubt many of our sorrows come through our own default, which we might avoid. And as for godly sorrow, it may stand with this rejoicing. If, therefore, we may in all things rejoice, then from one thing to another, from our waking to our sleeping: first, in our thoughts of God in the morning; then in our prayer; after, in our calling, and while we are at it; then at our meat, and in company, and alone, at home and abroad, in prosperity and adversity, in meditation, in dealings, and affairs; and lastly, in shutting up the day in examination, and viewing it over. And what hinders? if we be willing and resolved to do the will of God throughout the day, but that we might "rejoice before him in all we put our hand unto."

XLVIII. He that makes conscience of his ways, and to please God his only way, is to take him up a "daily direction" and some set rules, thereby looking constantly to his heart all the day, and thus, for the most part, he may live comfortably, either not falling into anything that should much disquiet him, or soon returning by repentance to peace again. But if a man tie not himself thus to rules, his heart will break from him and be disguised one way or another, which will breed continual wound unto his conscience, and so he shall never live any time together in peace. The cause why many Christians also give themselves great liberty in not accusing themselves for many offences is the want of some certain direction to follow in the day.

XLIX. When we feel unfitness to our ordinary duties we either begin to be discouraged, or else yield to corruption and neglect our duties, neither of both which should be, but without discouragement we should resist our untowardness and shake it off, and flee to God by prayer, even force ourselves to pray for grace and fitness to pray. And being earnest, and praying in faith, we may be assured that we shall obtain life and grace.

L. When the mind is distracted any way, unsettled, unquiet, or out of order, then get alone and muse, and see what hath brought us to this pass. Consider how irksome a state this is, and unprofitable. Pray to God, and work with thy own heart till it be brought in frame. An hour or two alone shall do a man more good than any other courses or duties.

LI. Aim (if it be possible) to spend one afternoon in a week visiting the neighbors' houses. Great use there is of it. Their love of me will be much increased. Much occasion will be ministered unto me for direction to speak the more fitly in my ministry. I am exceedingly grieved that I am so distracted with journeyings about that I cannot bring this to pass.

LII. I never go abroad (except I season my mind with good meditations by the way, or read, or confer) but beside the loss of my time, neglecting my ordinary task at home, at my study, I come home weary in body, unsettled in mind, untoward in study. So that I have small cause to rejoice in my goings forth, and I desire God to free me more and more from them. So may I also attend my own neighbors more diligently, which is my great desire; and the contrary has been and is my great burden.

LIII. I have ever observed that my journeyings and distractions of divers kinds, in these my latter times, and by too often preaching in my younger years, I have been held from using means to get knowledge, and to grow therein; which I counted ever the just punishment of God upon me for the neglect of my young time, when I should and might have furnished myself.

LIV. When I am in the best estate myself, I preach most zealously and profitably for the people.

LV. It breeds an incredible comfort and joy when one hath got power over some such corruption as in former times hath been used to get the mastery over him. This is a good provocation to strive hard to do so, and a cause of great thankfulness when it so comes to pass.

LVI. If we be at any time much dejected for sin, or otherwise disquieted in our minds, the best way that can be is to settle and quiet them by private meditation and prayer. *Probatum est.*

LVII. The humble man is the strongest man in the world and surest to stand, for he goes out of himself for help. The proud man is the weakest man and surest to fall, for he trusts to his own strength.

LVIII. It is good in all the changes of our life, whatever they be, to hold our own and be not changed therewith from our goodness; as Abraham, wheresoever he came (after his calling) still built his altar to the true God, and "called upon his name." He changed his place, but never changed his God.

LIX. Our whole life under the gospel should be nothing but thankfulness and fruitfulness. And if we must judge ourselves for our inward luster and corruptions of pride, dullness in good duties, earthliness, impatience. If we make not conscience of, and be not humbled by these, God will and doth oft give us up to open sins that stain and blemish our profession.

LX. The more we judge ourselves daily, the less we shall have to do on our sick-beds, and when we come to die. Oh, that is an unfit time for this! We should have nothing to do then but bear our pain wisely and be ready to die. Therefore, let us be exact in our accounts every day!

II. John Winthrop

The following list is drawn from the spiritual diary of John Winthrop. Here the puritan layman explains the conditions that led him to reconsider how he was leading his life, the behaviors he committed himself to reform, and his description of a meeting with fellow laymen and laywomen and with local clergy to covenant together to lead better lives.

Source: Francis J. Bremer, editor, *Winthrop Papers: Religious Writings* (forthcoming from the Massachusetts Historical Society).

May 23, 1613. When my condition was much straitened, partly through my long sickness, partly through want of freedom, partly through lack of outward things, I prayed often to the Lord for deliverance, referring the means to himself, & withal I often promised to put forth myself to much fruit when the Lord should enlarge me. Now that he hath set me at great liberty, giving me a good end to my tedious quatrain, freedom from a superior will, & liberal maintenance by the death of my wife's father (who finished his days in peace the 15 of May, 1613), I do resolve first to give myself, my life, my wit, my health, my wealth, to the service of my God & Savior, who by giving himself for me, & to me, deserves whatsoever I am or can be, to be at his Commandment, & for his glory:

2. I will live where he appoints me.

3. I will faithfully endeavor to discharge that calling which he shall appoint me unto.

4. I will carefully avoid vain & needless expenses, that I may be the more liberal to good uses.

5. My property, & bounty, must go forth abroad, yet I must ever be careful that it begin at home.

6. I will so dispose of my family affairs as my morning prayers & evening exercises be not omitted.

7. I will have a special care of the good education of my children.

8. I will banish profaneness from my family.

9. I will diligently observe the Lord's Sabbath, both for the avoiding & preventing worldly business, & also for the religious spending of such times as are free from public exercises, viz: the morning, noon, & evening.

10. I will endeavor to have the morning free for private prayer, meditation, & reading.

11. I will flee Idleness, & much worldly business.

12. I will often pray & confer privately with my wife.

I must remember to perform my father's will faithfully, for I promised him so to do, & particularly to pay Mr. Meges 40 a year till he should otherwise be provided for.

Directions for Daily Life

Puritan authors often suggested checklists to guide believers through their daily lives. The following list is drawn from Richard Rogers's Seven Treatises, containing such direction as is gathered out of the Holy Scriptures, leading and guiding to true happiness, etc. *(1603).*

Sundry necessary observations for a Christian, fit also to meditate upon.

1. That we keep a narrow watch over our hearts, words, and deeds continually.

2. That with all care the time be redeemed, which hath been idly, carelessly, and unprofitably spent.

3. That once in the day at the least, private prayer and meditation (if it may) be used.

4. That care be had to do and receive good company.

5. That our family be with diligence and regard, instructed, watched over and governed.

6. That no more time or care be bestowed in matters of the world, than must needs.

7. That we stir up ourselves to liberality to God's Saints.

8. That we give not the least bridle to wandering lusts and affections.

9. That we prepare ourselves to bear the cross, by what means soever it shall please God to exercise us.

10. That we bestow some time not only in mourning for our own sins, but also for the sins of the time and age wherein we live.

11. That we look daily for the coming of our Lord Jesus Christ, for our full deliverance out of this life.

12. That we use (as we shall have opportunity, at least as we shall have necessity) to acquaint our selves with some godly and faithful person, with whom we may confer of our Christian estate, and open our doubts, to the quickening up of God's graces in us.

13. That we observe the departure of men out of this life, their mortality, the vanity and alteration of things below, the more to contemn the world, and to continue our longing after the life to come. And that we meditate and muse often of our own death and going out of this life, how we must lie in the grave, all our glory put off, which will serve to beat down the pride of life that is in us.

14. That we read somewhat daily of the Holy Scriptures, for the further increase of our knowledge, if it may be.

15. That we enter into covenant with the Lord to strive against all sin, and especially against the special sins and corruptions of our hearts and lives, wherein we have most dishonored the Lord, and have raised up most guiltiness to our own consciences, that we carefully see our covenant with God be kept and continued.

16. That we mark how sin dies and is weakened in us, and that we turn not to our old sins again, but wisely avoid all occasions to sin.

17. That we fall not from our first love, but continue still our affections to the liking of God's Word, and

all the holy exercises of religion, diligently hearing it, and faithfully practicing the same in our lives and conversations: that we prepare our selves before we come, and meditate and confer of that we hear, either by ourselves or with other, and so mark our daily profiting in religion.

18. That we be often occupied in meditating on God's benefits and works, and sound forth his praises for the same.

19. That we exercise our faith by taking comfort and delight in the great benefit of our redemption by Christ, and the fruition of God's presence, in his glorious and blessed Kingdom.

20. Lastly, that we make not these holy meditations, and such like practices of repentance common in time, neither use them for course.

These I have set down to help thee to meditate, gentle Reader. And who sees not now, by that which hath been said, that a good heart may be able to mediate? That as the exercise it self is both very needful for all Christians, and many ways gainful; so none may have just cause to complain, that they cannot tell how to make use of it. But let us remember, that besides the benefit and gain of it, it is one of the private helps that God in his wise and merciful providence ordained for his dear children to make their life sweet and comfortable here, which otherwise would be irksome and painful, even to them who are best able to pass it well. And therefore to neglect it, shall not only be gross unthankfulness, but a charging of the Lord with a work merely needless.

Mary Dyer's Challenge to the Massachusetts Bay Colony

William and Mary Dyer emigrated to Boston in late 1634 or early 1635 and were admitted as members of the Boston church in December 1635. The Dyers were friends of the Hutchinson family and shared some of the controversial views associated with Anne Hutchinson. In November 1637 William Dyer was disenfranchised and disarmed, along with others who had supported Hutchinson and the Reverend John Wheelwright. When Anne Hutchinson was excommunicated from the Boston church, Mary Dyer followed her out, and the Dyers joined the Hutchinsons in migrating to the unsettled region that became Rhode Island.

I.

In 1652 the Dyers returned to England, where Mary at least was convinced by the teachings of George Fox, the leader of the Religious Society of Friends, or Quakers. When she returned to New England, she felt called to bring the Quaker message of the inner light to the puritans of Massachusetts. The Bay Colony had passed laws that fined shipmasters who brought Quakers to the colony, and passed further fines against any possessing Quaker writings. On her arrival in Boston in 1657, Mary Dyer was imprisoned. She was released by Governor John Endecott, presumably on the promise of her husband that she would not return to the colony.

In 1658 the Bay colony passed a new law banishing Quakers under pain of death. The first attempt to pass the law had been defeated by the deputies; with the magistrates urging the need for it, the law was passed by a single vote. Informed of the arrest of two of her fellow Quaker friends in 1659, Mary traveled to Boston to visit them. She herself was arrested and placed in prison. The following letter is an appeal by William Dyer to the Massachusetts magistrates, calling on them to release his wife.

Source: Worthington C. Ford, ed., *Mary Dyer, Quaker: Two Letters of William Dyer of Rhode Island* (Cambridge, MA; 1902).

To the Court of Assistants now assembled at Boston, this 6 September 1659, delivered unto the court by his wife, Mary Dyer, September 7, 1659.

Gentlemen,

Having received some letters from my wife, I am given to understand of her commitment to close prison, to a place (according to description) not unlike to Bishop Bonner's rooms,[1] not a place to sit or lie upon but dust. It is a sad condition that New England professors are come unto, in exercising such cruelties towards their fellow creatures . . . [who were] sufferers in old England upon the same account under the bishops as yourselves were. Had you no consideration of a tender [conscience] that, being wet to the skin, you cause her to be thrust into a room where [there] was nothing to . . . or lie down [upon] but dust (as is said)? Had your dog been wet you would have afforded it the liberty of a chimney corner to dry itself. Or had your hogs been penned in a sty you would have afforded them some dry store, or else you would have wanted mercy to your beast. But, alas, Christians now with you are used worse than hogs or dogs! Oh! Merciless cruelty!

What doth [this] evince but a ratification of that book recently come over to Mr. Cunnigrave from his wife in England, entitled *The Popis Inquisition Erected in New England,* which . . . may be resented by the supreme authority of England and its dominions. Time will declare [this] and I believe you will be made sensible of [it]. The [stories] . . . therein expressed doth relent the hearts of the rudest of men, besides abominating the carriages of men called magistrates in your seat of justice, withal relating that you have done more in persecution in one year than the worst bishops did in seven. And now [you] . . . add more towards a tender woman in that condition, that gave you no just cause against her. For did she come to your meetings to disturb them, as you call it, or did she come to reprehend the magistrates? [She] only came to visit her friends in prison, and when dispatching that [she was] . . . intent on returning to her family, as she declared in her [statement] the next day to the Governor. Therefore it is you that disturbed her, else why was she not let alone? What house entered she to molest, or what did she, that like a malefactor she must be haled to prison, or what law did she transgress?

She was about a business justifiable before God and all good men. . . . The worst of men, the bishops themselves, denied not the visitations and reliefs of friends to their prisoners, which myself have often experienced, by visiting Mr. Prynne, Mr. Smart, and other excellent [men]. Yea, when he was commanded close in the Tower, I had resort once or twice a week, and [I was] never fetched before authority to ask me wherefore I came to the Tower, or King's Bench, or the Gatehouse. Sure, it argues yourselves little to [have] practiced that duty when you were there in England . . . . Had there not been more adventurous, tender hearted professors than yourselves, many of them you call godly ministers and others might have perished, for ought I know. Doubtless the authority there might quickly have filled the prisons with such as came upon such errands out of a tender conscience if that course you take had been in use with them, to send for a person [visiting prisoners] and asking wherefore they came hither. What, hath not people in America the same liberty as beasts and birds have to pass the land or air without examination, or are you of the fearful mind as the barbarous Chinese, that would not permit others to come into their country? . . .

And when she had declared her business. Then for those that sit in the seat of justice to charge her that she was a quaker—what! A judge and an accuser both, just as did the Spanish Inquisitors in Spain to Mr. Lithgow. "You are a spy," say they, notwithstanding he showed his commission. But . . . a spy they say he was, and into such a

place as you have put my wife so did they thrust him, and did not give him so much straw as to lie on, but kept him close. According as my wife writes me word and information, . . . she has been there above a fortnight, and had not trode on the ground, but saw it out at the windows. What inhumanity is this? Had you never wives of your own? [How] can man that is born of a woman, or ever had any tender affection to a woman, deal so with a woman? What, is nature forgotten if refreshment be debarred? Bennington, the Lady Elizabeth's dogged keeper, would admit the liberty of the garden to her, though a condemned heretic (as they called her). Oh! cruel unheard of dealings! Where was her accuser that she was a quaker? Only Mr. Bellingham, a magistrate and an accuser! What hath magistrates (in the simplicity of justice) to do to make inquisition upon persons, innocent persons that are brought before them? Or, what precedent is there but the Romish inquisitors and the bishops' oath *ex officio?*

For did she not say [that] when she had finished her visitation of friends her business was done for aught she knew, and so should return to her family? But some of you would charge her to [have] come to foment her errors. Wisdom would have stayed till some such thing had been done, that so colorable transgression might have appeared for proceedings, and not [just] upon your own suggestions to draw up and stuff a [writ] with . . . . All the standers by could not but own by their silence that . . . she gave a good account of her coming, and that she said no such things as you expressed in your first [writ], a copy of which I have . . . .

It is not to be forgotten the former cruelties you used towards her, when she came from England having been tossed at sea all winter . . ., clapped up into a prison and kept there . . . for no transgression at all, only Mr. Bellingham (then as now) said she was a quaker—just as Bonner, Gardiner, and the rest of the bloody crew said to the poor saints in Queen Mary's day, when they sent their bloodhounds about . . . with their everlasting commission, to spy out and bring them before their thrones. Commonly the first or second word to them was, "You are an heretic."

It may be those days are forgotten. Yet surely you, or some of you, if you ever had the courage to look a bishop in the face, cannot but remember that first, second, or third word from them was, "You are a Puritan, are you not?" And is it not so in New England? The magistracy having, contrary to God's law, affirmed a coercive power over the conscience, the first or next word after [one's] appearance is, "You are a quaker." See the steps you follow, and let their misery be your warning. And then, if answer be not made according to the ruling will, "Away with them to the Coal hole, or new prison, or house of correction." And never any of the three ages have [lacked] railing, scurrilous terms to make the innocent saints odious in the peoples' eyes, especially when they are not able to gainsay their righteous profession. And all [this] borrowed from the nursery of devils, the persecutors of the poor Waldenses.

And now, gentlemen, consider their ends, and believe it. It was certain the bishops' ruin suddenly followed after their pursuit of some godly people by them called Puritans, especially when they proceeded to suck the blood of Doctor Leighton's and John Lillburne's backs (no more do I remember [whom] they proceeded to whip) and the blood of Mr. Prynne, Mr. Burton, and Doctor Bastwick's ears (only to them three, but three). And these were as odious to them as the quakers are to you.

And let me appeal to your own consciences, and to your own [word], whether ever two witnesses came against any person you have either imprisoned or [made to] suffer this [way] in general. And now, in particular, I do demand what witness, or whether legal testimony was given or taken that my wife, Mary Dyer, was a quaker? If no, before God and man how can you clear yourselves and [your] seat of justice from cruelty, persecution, yea, and so far as in you lies murder as to her, and to myself and family oppression and tyranny? The God of truth knows all this, and believe it is in remembrance with him. And of you will it be required who have kept her to the utmost (that is to this present court or sitting) to bring her into or under the capacity of your cruel law of banishment, and that this is the sum total of your law titled "Quakers." That a law titled "Quakers" should be a law is [strange]. That she is guilty of a breach of a law titled "Quakers" is as strange. That she is lawfully convicted by two witnesses is not yet heard of. That she must be banished by a law titled "Quakers," being not convicted by law, but convented by surmise and condemned to close prison by Mr. Bellingham's suggestion is so absurd and ridiculous that the meanest pupil at law will hiss at such proceeds in old lawyers. What branch of the law titled "Quakers" hath she broke? Or will you say she is vehemently suspected to be a Quaker? Is your law titled "Quakers" felony or treason, that vehement suspicion renders [the accused] capable of suffering?

Look now upon all the tyrannical and persecuting governments in the world, and give the like instance, but for mine own part I never heard or read of any. To Rome, I being an Englishman and known not to be of their profession, I may see and visit, and yet not be banished because I am suspected to be a protestant. And now you that profess the law of God is your rule, where is your law or rule to keep a man's wife from him seven or eight weeks, and mother from her children, in a capacity of close prison which admits of no bail? Is not this

your endeavor, and fact of a divorcement what you may? And is not this little less than murder by your own catechisms, to bring in a guiltless person into a little chamber in such a contagious time as God shakes his rod over you in? And hath not offered her the benefit of fresh air? Truly, this is a non pareil. And that she has broken no law your [writ] do sufficiently witness, which saith by virtue hereof you are to take unto your custody the person [torn] who upon examination before authority professeth her coming into these parts was to visit the prisoners [torn] fair account of her coming. Have you a law, or doth your law titled "Quakers" prohibit any from visiting such as you call Quakers in hold (besides, she asked not to go in to them, but stood without the doors in all the rain till she was wet to the skin), then had you some color. And yet her ignorance of that law or clause, had there been one, might have pleaded a sufficient excuse for the first time among merciful men.

Secondly, your [writ] saith that she professed herself of the same religion that Humphrey Norton was of. I dare engage _500 she never spoke such a word. But that she might say H. N. was in the truth I deny not. Yet have you a law to commit such to close prison as shall say they were of H. Norton's religion?

Thirdly, that she refused to give a direct answer to what was proposed to her on any other occasion. You might as well with the high priest condemn our savior! Besides, that savors so much the oath *ex officio* so much formerly damned by your own selves!

Fourthly, for affirming the light within her to be the rule. Have you a law that saith the light in Mary Dyer is not Mary Dyer's rule? If you have for that or any, the forenamed a law, she then may be made transgressor for words, and your [writ] hold good. But if not, then have you imprisoned her and punished her without the law and against the law of God and man, I mean yourselves? For if you be men, I suppose your fundamental law is that no person shall be imprisoned or molested but upon the breach of a law, yet behold my wife without law, and against law, imprisoned and punished, and so highly punished as intended to a step next unto death, and that for which you practice yourselves in part, as she is condemned for saying the light in her is the rule! Is not your light within your rule, by which you make and act such laws—for you have no rule of God's word in the Bible to make a law titled "Quakers," nor have you any order from the supreme state of England to make such laws. Therefore it must be your light within that is your rule you walk by.

And then remember what Jesus Christ said, "If the light that be in you is darkness." The Lord of his grace dispel it from you, that you may come to see and say as Adonibezech did, "Three score and ten kings, having their thumbs and toes cut off, gathered their feet under my table. As I have done to others, so God hath done to me." And they carried him to Jerusalem, and there he died. I have written thus plainly to you, being exceeding sensible of the unjust molestation and detaining of my dear yoke fellow. Mine and my family's want of her will cry loud in your ears, together with her sufferings on your part, but I question not mercy, favor, and comfort from the most high to her own soul, though at present myself and family by you deprived of the comfort and refreshment we might have enjoyed by her. So saith her husband, William Dyer. Newport, this 30 August 1659.

II.

Mary herself addressed the magistrates from prison.

Source: Massachusetts Archives

Whereas I am by many charged with the guiltiness of my own blood: if you mean in my coming to Boston, I am therein clear, and justified by the Lord, in whose will I came, who will require my blood of you, be sure, who have made a law to take away the lives of the innocent servants of God, if they come among you who are called by you, "Cursed Quakers," although I say, [I] am a Living Witness for them and the Lord, that he hath blessed them, and sent them unto you: Therefore, be not found fighters against God, but let my counsel and request be accepted with you, to repeal all such laws, that the truth and servants of the Lord may have free Passage among you, and you be kept from shedding innocent blood, which I know there are many among you would not do, if they knew it so to be. Nor can the enemy that stirs you up thus to destroy this holy seed, in any measure contervail the great damage that you will by thus doing procure. Therefore, seeing the Lord hath not hid it from me, it lieth upon me, in love to your souls, thus to persuade you. I have no selfish ends, the Lord knoweth, for if my life were freely granted by you, it would not avail me, nor could I expect it of you, so long as I shall daily hear and see of the sufferings of these people, my dear brethren and seed, with whom my life is bound up. . . .

Was ever the like laws heard of, among a people that profess Christ come in the flesh? And have [you] . . . no other weapons but such laws to fight with against spiritual wickedness, as you call it? Woe is me for you! Of whom take you counsel? Search with the light of Christ in you, and it will show you of whom, as it hath done me, and many more, who have been disobedient and deceived, as now you are. Which light, as you come into and obey what is made manifest to you therein, you will not repent that you were kept from shedding blood, though [it] be a woman's. It's not my own life I seek (for I chose rather to suffer with the people of God, than to enjoy the pleasures

of Egypt), but the life of the seed, which I know the Lord hath blessed, and therefore seeks the enemy thus vehemently the life thereof to destroy, as in all ages he ever did. Oh! hearken not unto him, I beseech you, for the seed's Sake, which is one in all, and is dear in the sight of God . . . . Whereof I, having felt, cannot but persuade all men that I have to do withal, especially you who name the name of Christ, to depart from such Iniquity, as shedding blood, even of the saints of the Most High.

Therefore let my Request have as much Acceptance with you, if you be Christians as Esther had with Ahasuerus,[2] whose relation is short of that that's between Christians, and my request is the same that hers was. And he said not that he had made a law, and it would be dishonorable for him to revoke it. But when he understood that these people were so prized by her, and so nearly concerned her (as in truth these are to me) . . . you may see what he did for her. Therefore I leave these lines with you, appealing to the faithful and true witness of God, which is one in all consciences, before whom we must all appear [and] with whom I shall eternally rest, in everlasting joy and peace, whether you will hear or forebear. With him is my reward, with whom to live is my joy, and to die is my gain. . . .

And know this also, that if through this enmity you shall declare yourselves worse than Ahasueras, and confirm your Law, though it were but the taking away the life of one of us, that the Lord will overthrow both your law and you, by his righteous judgments and plagues poured justly upon you, who now, whilst you are warned thereof, and tenderly sought unto, may avoid the one, by removing the other. If you neither hear nor obey the Lord nor his servants, yet will he send more of his servants among you, so that your end shall be frustrated . . . . [You] think to restrain them [that] you call "Cursed Quakers" from coming among you by any thing you can do to them. Yea, verily, he hath a seed here among you, for whom we have suffered all this while, and yet suffer . . . . The Lord of the Harvest will send forth more laborers to gather (out of the Mouths of the Devourers of all sorts) into his fold, where he will lead them into fresh pastures, even the paths of righteousness, for his name's sake. Oh! let none of you put this day far from you, which verily in the light of the Lord I see approaching, even to many in and about Boston, which is the bitterest and darkest professing place, and so to continue as long as you have done, that ever I heard of . . . In Love and in the spirit of meekness, I again beseech you, for I have no enmity to the persons of any; but you shall know, that God will not be mocked, but what you sow, that shall you reap from him, that will render to everyone according to the deeds done in the body, whether good or evil. Even so be it, saith Mary Dyer.

III.

Following this, Mary and her fellow Quakers were released by the Massachusetts authorities on condition that should they return they would be sentenced to death. Within a month William Robinson and Marmaduke Stevenson violated the terms of their release and returned to Massachusetts, where they were again arrested for proselytizing their Quaker views. Mary Dyer also returned, and at the October 1659 meeting of the General Court the three were sentenced to be executed. On the twenty-seventh of that month the three were taken to Boston Common. Robinson and Stevenson were hung, while Dyer was made to watch with a halter around her neck. Reluctant to hang a woman, the authorities released her into the custody of her son, who had come to Boston to plead for his mother's life and who pledged that she would not return again.

The following spring, Dyer, who had spent the intervening time spreading her faith among the residents of Shelter Island and along the Narragansett Bay, returned yet again to Boston. Once again, her husband pleaded for her life in a letter to Governor Endecott.

Honored Sir,

It is with no little grief of mind and sadness of heart that I am necessitated to be so bold as to supplicate your honored self, with the honorable assembly of your general Court, to extend your mercy and favor once again to me and my children. Little did I dream that I should have occasion to petition you in a matter of this nature, but so it is that through the divine providence and your benignity my son obtained so much pity and mercy at your hands as to enjoy the life of his mother.

Now my supplication, your honor, is to beg affectionately the life of my dear wife. It is true I have not seen her above this half year, and therefore I cannot tell how in the flame of her spirit she was moved thus again to run so great a hazard to herself and perplexity to me and mine, and all her friends and well wishers. So it is from Shelter Island about by Pequod, Narragansett, and to the town of Providence she secretly and speedily journeyed, and as secretly came to your jurisdiction. Unhappy journey, may I say, and woe to that generation (says I) that gives occasion thus of grief and trouble (to those that desires to be quiet) by helping one another (as I may say) to hazard their lives for I know not what end or to what purpose.

If her zeal be so great as thus to adventure, Oh let your favor and pity surmount it, and save her life. Let not your forwonted compassion be conquered by her inconsiderate madness. And how greatly will your renown be spread if by so conquering you become victorious.

What shall I say more? I know you are all sensible of my condition, and let the reflection be, and you will what my petition is and what will give me and mine peace. Oh, let mercy's wings once more seem above justice's balance, and then whilst I live I shall exalt your goodness. But other ways it will be a languishing sorrow, yea, so great that I should gladly suffer the blow at once, much rather. I shall forbear to trouble your honor with words. Neither am I in a capacity to expatriate myself at present. I only say this, yourselves have been and are, or may be husbands to wife or wives. So am I, yea to one most dearly beloved. Oh, do not deprive me of her, but I pray give her me once again, and I shall be so much obliged forever that I shall endeavor continually to utter my thanks and render your love and honor most renowned. Pity me. I beg it with tears, and rest your most humbly suppliant, William Dyer.

27th May 1660.

IV.

Imprisoned one again, Mary Dyer defended her position and defied the authorities.

Once more [to] the General Court, assembled in Boston, speaks Mary Dyer, even as before. My life is not accepted, neither availeth me, in comparison of the lives and liberty of the truth and servants of the living God, for which in the bowels of love and meekness I sought you . . .. With wicked hands have you put two of them to death, which makes me to feel that the mercies of the wicked is cruelty. I rather choose to die than to live, as from you, as guilty of their innocent blood. Therefore, seeing my request is hindered, I leave you to the righteous judge and searcher of all hearts, who, with the pure measure of light he hath given to every man to profit withal, will in his due time let you see whose servants you are, and of whom you have taken counsel, which [I] desire you to search into.

But all his counsel hath been slighted, and you would [heed] none of his reproofs. Read your portion, Proverbs 1:24 to 32. For verily the night cometh on you apace, wherein no man can work, in which you shall assuredly fall to your own master, in obedience to the Lord, whom I serve with my Spirit, and to pity to your Souls, which you neither know nor pity. I can do no less than once more to warn you to put away the evil of your doings, and kiss the Son, the Light in you, before his wrath be kindled in you . . .. Nothing without you can help or deliver you out of his hand at all. And if these things be not so, then say there hath been no prophet from the Lord sent amongst you. Yet it is his pleasure, by things that are not, to bring to naught things that are.

When I heard your last order read, it was a disturbance unto me, that was so freely offering up my life to him that give it me, and sent me hither to do, which obedience being his own work. He gloriously accompanied [me] with his presence, and peace, and love in me, in which I rested from my labor, till by your order, and the people, I was so far disturbed, that I could not retain anymore of the words thereof, than that I should return to prison, and there remain forty and eight hours. To which I submitted, finding nothing from the Lord to the contrary, that I may know what his pleasure and counsel is concerning me, on whom I wait therefore. For he is my life, and the length of my days, and, as I said before, I came at his command, and go at his command.

Mary Dyer refused an offer to release her yet again if she would promise to never more enter Massachusetts. She was hung on 1 June 1660.

Notes

1. A reference to the rooms in which Bishop Edmund Bonner kept Protestants captive during the persecutions of the reign of Queen Mary (1553–1558).

2. Mary here referred to the Old Testament, comparing Gov. Endicott to King Ahasuerus and herself to Esther. Esther persuaded the king not to execute the Jews in his kingdom, and Mary wanted Endicott to change the laws and free the Quakers.

Massachusetts—An Account of the First Year of the Great Migration

Thomas Dudley migrated to Massachusetts in 1630 as the colony's deputy governor. Dudley had formerly been steward to the Earl of Lincoln, and in March 1631 he sent a lengthy letter to the Countess of Lincoln describing the first year of the settlement. The following is excerpted from that letter.

Source: Alexander Young, editor, *Chronicles of the First Planters of the Colony of Massachusetts Bay* (Boston, 1846), 301–341.

For the satisfaction of your Honor, and some friends, and for the use of such as shall hereafter intend to increase our plantation in New England, I have in the throng of domestic, and not altogether free from public business, thought fit to commit to memory our present condition, and what hath befallen us since our arrival here; which I will do shortly, after my usual manner, and must do rudely, having yet no table, nor other room to write in, than by the fireside upon my knee, in this sharp winter; to which my family must have leave to resort, though they break good manners, and make me sometimes forget what I would say, and say what I would not.

In April 1630, we set sail from old England with four good ships. And in May following, eight more followed; two having gone before in February and March, and two more following in June and August, besides another set out by a private merchant. These 17 ships arrived all safe in New England for the increase of the plantation here this year 1630, but made a long, troublesome and costly voyage, being all wind-bound long in England, and hindered with contrary winds, after they set sail and so scattered with mists and tempests that few of them arrived together. Our four ships which set out in April arrived here in June and July, where we found the Colony in a sad and unexpected condition, above 80 of them being dead the winter before, and many of those alive were weak and sick.

All the corn and bread amongst them all, hardly sufficient to feed upon a fortnight, insomuch that the remainder of 180 servants we had the two years before sent over, coming to us for victuals to sustain them, we found ourselves wholly unable to feed them by reason that the provisions shipped for them were taken out of the ship they were put in, and they who were trusted to ship them in another, failed us, and left them behind; whereupon necessity enforced us to our extreme loss to give them all liberty *(to our provisions, to them)* who had cost us about £16 or £20 a person furnishing and sending over. But bearing these things as we might, we began to consult of the place of our sitting down; for Salem, where we landed, pleased us not. And to that purpose, some were sent to the Bay to search up the rivers for a convenient place. We were forced to . . . plant dispersedly, some at Charlestown which stands on the North side of the mouth of Charles river; some on the south side thereof, which place we named Boston; (as we intended to have done the place we first resolved on) some of us upon Mystic, which we named Medford; some of us westwards on Charles River, four miles from Charlestown, which place we named Watertown; others of us two miles from Boston, in a place we named Roxbury; others upon the river of Saugus between Salem and Charlestown; and the western men *(of the Mary & John)* four miles South from Boston, at a place we named Dorchester. This dispersion troubled some of us, but help it we could not; wanting ability to remove to any place fit to build a town upon, and the time too short to deliberate any longer, least the winter should surprise us before we had built our houses. The best counsel we could find out was, to build a fort to retire to, in some convenient place, if an enemy pressed thereunto, after we should have fortified ourselves against the injuries of wet and cold. So ceasing to consult further for that time, they who had health to labor fell to building, wherein many were interrupted with sickness and many died weekly, yea almost daily.

Insomuch that the ships being now upon their return, some for England, some for Ireland, there was, as I take it not much less than a hundred (some think many more) partly out of dislike of our government which restrained and punished their excesses, and partly through fear of famine, not seeing other means than by their labor to feed themselves, which returned back again. And glad were we so to be rid of them. Others also afterwards hearing of men of their own disposition, which were planted at Piscataway, went from us to them, whereby though our numbers were lessened, yet we accounted ourselves nothing weakened by their removal.

Before the departure of the ships, we contracted with Mr. Pierce, master of the *Lyon* of Bristol, to return to us with all speed with fresh supplies of victuals, and gave him directions accordingly. The ships being gone, victuals wasting, and mortality increasing, we held diverse fasts in our several congregations, but the Lord would not yet be deprecated; for about the beginning of September, died Mr. Gager, a right godly man, a skilful surgeon, and one of the deacons of our congregation; and Mr. Higginson, one of the ministers of Salem, a zealous and a profitable preacher; this of a consumption, that of a fever, and on the 30th of September, died Mr. Johnson (the Lady Arbella, his wife, being dead a month before). This gentleman was a prime man amongst us, having the best estate of any, zealous for religion and greatest furtherer of this plantation. He made a most godly end, dying willingly, professing his life better spent in promoting this plantation than it would have been any other way. He left to us a loss greater than the most conceived. Within a month after, died Mr. Rossiter, another of our assistants, a godly man, and of a good estate, which still weakened us more; so that there now were left of the five undertakers but the Governor [John Winthrop], Sir Richard Saltonstall and myself, and seven other of the Assistants. And of the people who came over with us, from the time of their setting sail from England in April, 1630, until December following, there died by estimation about 200 at the least—so low hath the Lord brought us! Well, yet they who survived were not discouraged, but bearing God's corrections with humility and trusting in his mercies.

I should also have remembered how the half of our cows, and almost all our mares and goats, sent us out of England died at sea in their passage hither, and that those intended to be sent us out of Ireland were not sent at all; all which together with the loss of our six months building, occasioned by our intended removal to a town to be fortified, weakened our estates, especially the estates of the undertakers, who were £3000 or £4000 engaged in the joint stock, which was now not above many hundreds; yet many of us labored to bear it as comfortably as we could, remembering the end of our coming hither and knowing the power of God who can support and raise us again, and useth to bring his servants low that the meek may be made glorious by deliverance. Psalms 112.

But now having some leisure to discourse of the motives for other men's coming to this place, or their abstaining from it, after my brief manner I say this: That if any come hither to plant for worldly ends that can live well at home, he commits an error, of which he will soon repent him. But if for spiritual, and that no particular obstacle hinder his removal, he may find here what may well content him, viz: materials to build, fuel to burn, ground to plant, seas and rivers to fish in, a pure air to breathe in, good water to drink, till wine or beer can be made; which, together with the cows, hogs and goats brought hither already, may suffice for food; for as for fowl and venison, they are dainties here as well as in England. For clothes and bedding, they must bring them with them, till time and industry produce them here. In a word, we yet enjoy little to be envied, but endure much to be pitied in the sickness and mortality of our people. And I do the more willingly use this open and plain dealing, lest other men should fall short of their expectations when they come hither, as we to our great prejudice did, by means of letters sent us from hence into England, wherein honest men out of a desire to draw over others to them, wrote somewhat hyperbolically of many things here. If any godly men, out of religious ends, will come over to help us in the good work we are about, I think they cannot dispose of themselves nor of their estates more to God's glory, and the furtherance of their own reckoning; but they must not be of the poorer sort yet, for diverse years; for we have found by experience that they have hindered, not furthered the work. And for profane and debauched persons, their oversight in coming hither is wondered at, where they shall find nothing to content them. If there be any endowed with grace and furnished with means to feed themselves and theirs for 18 months, and to build and plant, let them come over into our Macedonia and help us, and not spend themselves and their estates in a less profitable employment; for others I conceive they are not yet fitted for this business.

Touching the discouragements which the sickness and mortality which every first year hath seized upon us, and those of Plymouth as appeared before, may give to such who have cast any thoughts this way (of which mortality it may be said of us almost as of the Egyptians, that there is not an house where there is not one dead, and in some houses many) the natural causes seem to be in the want of warm lodging, and good diet, to which Englishmen are habituated at home; and in the sudden increase of heat which they endure that are landed here in summer, the salted meat at sea having prepared their bodies thereto, for of those only 2 last year died of fevers who landed in June and July; as those of Plymouth who landed in the winter died of the scurvy, as did our poorer sort, whose houses and bedding kept them not sufficiently warm, nor their diet sufficiently in heart. Other causes God may have, as our faithful minister Mr. John Wilson (lately handling that point) showed unto us, which I forbear to mention, leaving this matter to the further dispute of physicians and divines. Wherefore to return, upon the third of January died the daughter of Mr. Sharpe, a godly virgin, making a comfortable end, after a long sickness. The plantation here received not the like loss of any woman since we came hither, and therefore she well deserves to be remembered in this place.

Amongst those who died about the end of this January, there was a girl of 11 years old, the daughter of one John Ruggles of whose family and kindred died so many, that for some reason it was matter of observation amongst us; who in the time of her sickness expressed to the minister and to those about her, so much faith and assurance of salvation, as is rarely found in any of that age, which I thought not unworthy here to commit to memory; and if any tax me for wasting paper with recording these small matters, such may consider that little mothers bring forth little children, small commonwealths; matters of small moment, the reading whereof yet is not to be despised by the judicious, because small things in the beginning of natural or politic bodies are as remarkable as greater things in bodies full grown.

Upon the 5th of February, arrived here Master Pierce with the ship *Lyon* of Bristol with supplies of victuals from England, who had set forth from Bristol the first of December before.

Upon the 22nd day of February, we held a general day of Thanksgiving throughout the whole Colony for the safe arrival of the ship which came at last with our provisions.

Upon the 8th of March, from after it was fair day light until about 8 of the clock in the forenoon, there flew over all the towns in our plantations so many flocks of doves [passenger pigeons, a species now extinct], each flock containing many thousands, and some so many that they obscured the light, that passeth credit, if but the truth should be written. And the thing was the more strange, because I scarce remember to have seen ten doves since I came into this country. They were all turtle doves, as appeared by diverse of them we killed flying, somewhat bigger than those of Europe, and they flew from the north east to the south west; but what it portends I know not.

The ship now waits but for wind, which when it blows, there are ready to go aboard therein for England Sir Richard Saltonstall, Mr. Sharpe, Mr. Coddington, and many others, the most whereof purpose to return to us again, if God will. In the mean time, we are left a people poor and contemptible, yet such as trust in God and are contented with our condition, being well assured that he will not fail us nor forsake us.

Massachusetts Body of Liberties of 1641

After a decade of debating the virtues of codification, the Massachusetts General Court adopted what was in effect a law code for the colony. The 96th article specifically stated that these were not laws, undoubtedly to protect the colonists from violating their charter, which had denied them the right to pass any law that was in violation of the laws of England. Yet that same article stipulated that the articles were to be treated as if they were law. Though this document was influenced by the religious values of the puritans, the colonists rejected a more direct adoption of the Mosaic Code, which some, including John Cotton, had argued for.

The Massachusetts Body of Liberties adopted as law by the General Court of the Commonwealth of Massachusetts Bay December, 1641

1. No man's life shall be taken away, no man's honor or good name shall be stained, no man's person shall be arrested, restrained, banished, dismembered, nor any ways punished, no man shall be deprived of his wife or children, no man's goods or estate shall be taken away from him, nor in any way damaged under color of law, or countenance of authority, unless it be by virtue or equity of some express law of the Country warranting the same established by a General Court and sufficiently published, or in case of the defect of a law in any particular case by the word of God. And in capital cases, or in cases concerning dismembering or banishment, according to that word to be judged by the General Court.

2. Every person within this jurisdiction, whether inhabitant or foreigner, shall enjoy the same justice and

law, that is general for the Plantation, which we constitute and execute one towards another, without partiality or delay.

3. No man shall be urged to take any oath or subscribe any articles, covenants or remonstrance, of a public and civil nature, but such as the General Court hath considered, allowed and required.

5. No man shall be compelled to any public work or service unless the press be grounded upon some act of the General Court, and have reasonable allowance therefore.

7. No man shall be compelled to go out of the limits of this plantation upon any offensive wars which this Commonwealth or any of our friends or confederates shall voluntarily undertake. But only upon such vindictive and defensive wars in our own behalf, or on the behalf of our friends, and confederates as shall be enterprised by the Council and consent of a General Court, or by authority derived from the same.

8. No man's cattle or goods of what kind soever shall be pressed or taken for any public use or service, unless it be by warrant grounded upon some act of the General Court, nor without such reasonable prices and hire as the ordinary rates of the Country do afford. And if his cattle or goods shall perish or suffer damage in such service, the owner shall be sufficiently recompensed.

9. No monopolies shall be granted or allowed amongst us, but of such new inventions that are profitable to the Country, and that for a short time.

10. All our lands and heritages shall be free from all fines and licenses upon alienations, and from all heriots, wardships, liveries, prime seisens, year-day and waste, escheats and forfeitures [deeply resented burdens on estates, often left over from feudal customs], upon the death of parents or ancestors, be they natural, casual or judicial.

12. Every man, whether inhabitant or foreigner, free or not free, shall have liberty to come to any public Court, Council, or town-meeting, and either by speech or by writing, move any lawful, seasonable and material question, or to present any necessary motion, complaint, petition, Bill or information, whereof that meeting hath proper cognizance, so it be done in convenient time, due order and respective manner.

14. Any conveyance or alienation of land or other estate whatsoever, made by a woman that is married, any child under age, idiot, or distracted person, shall be good, if it be passed and ratified by the consent of a General Court.

Rites and Rules Concerning Judicial Proceedings
18. No man's person shall be restrained or imprisoned by any authority whatsoever, before the law hath sentenced him thereto, if he can put in sufficient security, bail, or mainprise, for his appearance and good behavior in the meantime, unless it be in capital crimes, and contempt in open Court, and in such cases where some express act of Court doth allow it.

20. If any which are to sit as Judges in any other Court shall demean themselves offensively in the Court, the rest of the Judges present shall have the power to censure him for it. If the cause be of a high nature it shall be presented to and censured at the next superior Court.

22. No man in any suit or action against another shall falsely pretend great debts or damages to vex his adversary. If it appear that any doth do so, the Court shall have power to set a reasonable fine on his head.

23. No man shall be adjudged to pay for detaining any debt from any creditor above eight pounds in the hundred for one year [8 percent simple interest], and not above that rate proportionable for all sums whatsoever, neither shall this be a color or countenance to allow any usury amongst us contrary to the law of God.

25. No summons pleading judgment, or any kind of proceeding in Court or course of Justice shall be abated, arrested or reversed upon any circumstantial errors or mistakes, if the person and cause be rightly understood and intended by the Court.

26. Any man that findeth himself unfit to plead his own cause in any Court, shall have the liberty to employ any man against whom the Court doth not except, to help him provided he give him no fee or reward for his pains. This shall not except the party himself from answering such questions in person as the Court shall think meet to demand of him.

27. If any plaintiff shall give into any Court a declaration of his cause in writing, the defendant shall also have liberty and time to give his answer in writing. And so in all proceedings between party and party, so it doth not hinder the dispatch of justice such as the Court shall be willing unto.

29. In all actions at law it shall be the liberty of the plaintiff and defendant by mutual consent to choose whether they will be tried by the bench or by a jury, unless it be where the law upon just reason hath otherwise determined. The like liberty shall be granted to all persons in criminal cases.

30. It shall be in the liberty of both the plaintiff and defendant and likewise every delinquent (to be judged by a jury) to challenge any of the jurors. And if this challenge be found just and reasonable by the bench or the rest of the jury, as the challenger shall choose, it shall be allowed him, and *tales de circumstantibus* [such persons as are standing around] impaneled in their room.

31. In cases where evidence is so obscure or defective that the jury cannot clearly and safely give a positive ver-

dict, whether it be Grand or Petit Jury, it shall have liberty to give a *non liquet* ["it is not clear": a verdict given by a jury that defers the matter to another day], or a special verdict, in which last, that is in a special verdict, the judgment of the cause shall be left to the Court. And all jurors have liberty in matters of fact if they cannot find the main issue, yet to find and present in their verdict so much as they can. If the bench and the jurors shall so disagree at any time that either of them cannot proceed at peace of conscience the case shall be referred to the General Court, who shall take the case from both and determine it.

34. If any man be judged a common Barrator vexing others with unjust and frequent suits, it shall be in the power of the Courts both to deny him the benefit of the law, and punish him for his barratry.

36. It shall be the liberty of any man, cast condemned or sentenced in any cause in any inferior Court, to make their appeal to the Court of Assistants, provided they tender their appeal and put in security and prosecute it before the Court [session] be ended wherein they were condemned, and within six days next ensuing put in good security before some Assistant to satisfy what his adversary shall recover against him, and if the cause be of a criminal nature, for his good behavior and appearance (at the Court). And every man shall have liberty to complain to the General Court of any injustice done him at any Court of Assistants or other.

37. In all cases where it appears to the Court that the plaintiff hath willingly and wittingly doth wrong to the defendant in commencing and prosecuting any action or complaint against him, they shall have power to impose upon him [the plaintiff] a proportionable fine to the use of the defendant or accused person, for his false complaint or clamor.

39. In all actions both real and personal between party and party, the Court will have power to respite execution for a convenient time, when in their prudence they see just cause to do so.

41. Every man that is to answer for any criminal cause, whether he be in prison or under bail, his cause shall be heard and determined at the next Court that hath proper cognizance thereof, and may be done without prejudice of justice.

42. No man shall be twice sentenced by civil justice for one and the same crime, offense, or trespass.

43. No man shall be beaten with above 40 stripes, nor shall any true gentleman, nor any man equal to a gentleman, be punished with a whipping, unless his crime be very shameful, and his course of life vicious and profligate.

44. No man condemned to die shall be put to death within four days next after his condemnation, unless the Court see special cause to the contrary, or in case of martial law, nor should the body of any man so put to death be left unburied 12 hours, unless it be in cause of [the study of] Anatomy.

45. No man shall be forced by torture to confess any crime against himself nor any other unless it be in some capital case where he is first fully convicted by clear and sufficient evidence to be guilty. After which, if the cause be of that nature, that it is very apparent that there be other conspirators or confederates with him, then he may be tortured, yet not with such tortures as be barbarous and inhumane.

46. For bodily punishments we allow amongst us none that are inhumane, barbarous, or cruel.

47. No man shall be put to death without the testimony of two or three witnesses, or that which is equivalent thereunto.

49. No free man shall be compelled to serve upon juries above two Courts in a year, except Grand Jury men, who shall hold two Courts together at the least.

50. All jurors shall be chosen continually by the Freemen of the town where they dwell.

51. All Associates selected at any time to assist the Assistants in inferior Courts shall be nominated by the towns belonging to that Court by orderly agreement among themselves.

52. Children, idiots, distracted persons, and all that are strangers or new-comers to our Plantation shall have such allowances and dispensations in any cause, whether criminal or other as religion and reason require.

53. The age of discretion for passing away of lands or such kind of herediments, or for giving votes, verdicts or sentence in any civil Courts or causes, shall be one and twenty years.

57. Whensoever any person shall come to any very sudden untimely and unnatural death, some Assistant or the Constables of that town shall forthwith summon a jury of twelve Freemen to inquire of the cause and manner of their death, and shall present a true verdict thereof to some near Assistant, or the next Court to be held for that town, upon their oath.

58. Civil authority hath power and liberty to see the Peace, ordinances, and rules of Christ observed in every church according to His word, so it be done in a civil and not in an ecclesiastical way.

59. Civil authority hath power and liberty to deal with any church member in a way of civil justice, notwithstanding any church relation, office, or interest.

60. No church censure shall degrade or depose any man from any civil dignity, office or authority he shall have in the Commonwealth.

62. Any shire or town shall have liberty to choose their Deputies whom and where they please for the General

Court, sobeit they be Freemen and have taken the oath of fealty, and inhabit the jurisdiction.

65. No custom or prescription shall ever prevail amongst us in any moral cause; our meaning is [there shall not be a custom that will] maintain anything that can be proved to be morally sinful by the word of God.

66. The Freemen of every township shall have power to make such bylaws and constitutions as shall concern the welfare of their town, provided they be not of a criminal but only of a prudential nature, and that their penalties exceed not 20 shillings for one offense, and that they be not repugnant to public laws and orders of the Country. And if any inhabitant neglect or refuse to observe them, they [the townships] shall have power to levy the appointed penalties by distress.

67. It is the constant liberty of the Freemen of this plantation to choose yearly at the Court of Election out of the Freemen all the general officers of this jurisdiction. If they please to discharge them at the day of election by way of vote, they may do it without showing cause. But if at any other General Court, we hold it due justice that the reasons thereof be alleged and proved. By general officers, we mean our Governor, Deputy-Governor, Assistants, Treasurer, General of our wars, and our Admiral at sea, and such as are or hereafter may be of the like general nature.

68. It is the liberty of the Freemen to choose such Deputies for the General Court out of themselves, either in their own towns or elsewhere as they judge fittest. And because we cannot foresee what variety and weight of occasions may fall into future consideration, and what counsels we may stand in need of, we decree: That the Deputies to attend the General Court in the behalf of the Country shall not any time be stated or enacted but from Court to Court, or at the most but for one year; That the Country may have an annual liberty to do in that case what is most behooving for the best welfare thereof.

69. No General Court shall be dissolved or adjourned without the consent of the major part thereof.

71. The Governor shall have a casting vote whensoever an equal vote shall fall out of the Court of Assistants, or general assembly; so shall the president or moderator have in all civil Courts or assemblies.

74. The Freemen of every town or township shall have full power to choose yearly or for less time out of themselves a convenient number of fit men to order the planting or prudential occasions of that town, according to instructions given them in writing, provided nothing be done by them contrary to the public laws and orders of the Country, provided also the number of such select persons be not above nine.

79. If any man at his death shall not leave his wife a competent portion of his estate, upon just complaint made to the General Court she shall be relieved.

80. Every married woman shall be free from bodily correction or stripes by her husband, unless it be in his own defense upon her assault. If there be any just cause of correction, complaint shall be made to authority assembled in some Court, from which she shall receive it.

81. When parents die intestate, the elder son shall have a double portion of his [the father's] whole estate real and personal, unless the General Court upon just cause alleged shall judge otherwise.

82. When parents die intestate, having no heirs male of their bodies, their daughters shall inherit as co-partners, unless the General Court upon just reason shall judge otherwise.

83. If any parents shall willfully and unreasonably deny any child timely or convenient marriage, or shall exercise any unnatural severity towards them, such children shall have free liberty to complain to authority for redress.

84. No orphan during their minority which was not committed to tuition or service in their lifetime, shall afterward be absolutely disposed of by any kindred, friend, executor, township, or church, nor by themselves without the consent of some Court, wherein two Assistants at least shall be present.

85. If any servants shall flee from the tyranny and cruelty of their masters to the house of any freeman of the same Town, they shall be there protected and sustained till due order be taken for their relief. Provided due notice thereof be speedily given to their masters from whom they fled, and the next Assistant or Constable where the party flying is harbored.

86. No servant shall be put off for above a year to any other [masters] neither in the lifetime of their master nor after their death by their Executors or Administrators unless it be by consent of Authority assembled in some Court or two Assistants.

87. If any man smite out the eye or tooth of his manservant, or maid servant, or otherwise maim or much disfigure him, unless it be by mere casualty, he shall let them go free from his service, and shall have such further recompense as the Court shall allow him.

88. Servants that have served diligently and faithfully to the benefit of their masters seven years, shall not be sent away empty. And if any have been unfaithful, negligent or unprofitable in their service, notwithstanding the good usage of their masters, they shall not be dismissed till they have made satisfaction according to the Judgment of Authority.

91. There shall never be any bond slavery, villainage or captivity amongst us unless it be lawful captives taken

in just wars, and such strangers as willingly sell themselves or are sold to us. And these shall have all the liberties and Christian usages which the law of God established in Israel concerning such persons doth morally require. This exempts none from servitude who shall be judged thereto by Authority.

92. No man shall exercise any tyranny or cruelty towards any brute creature which are usually kept for man's use.

93. If any man shall have occasion to lead or drive cattle from place to place that is far off, so that they be weary, or hungry, or fall sick or lame, it shall be lawful to rest or refresh them, for competent time, in any open place that is not corn, meadow, or enclosed for some peculiar use.

94. Capital Laws

1. If any man after legal conviction shall have or worship any other god, but the Lord God, he shall be put to death.

2. If any man or woman be a witch (that is, hath or consulteth with a familiar spirit), they shall be put to death.

3. If any person shall blaspheme the name of God, the Father, Son or Holy Ghost, with direct, express, presumptuous or high handed blasphemy, or shall curse God in the like manner, he shall be put to death.

4. If any person commit any willful murder, which is manslaughter committed upon premeditated malice, hatred, or cruelty, and not in a man's necessary and just defense, nor by mere casualty against his will, he shall be put to death.

5. If any person slayeth another suddenly in his anger or cruelty of passion, he shall be put to death.

6. If any person shall slay another through guile, either by poisoning or other such devilish practice, he shall be put to death.

7. If any man or woman shall lie with any beast or brute creature by carnal copulation, they shall surely be put to death. And the beast shall be slain, and buried and not eaten.

8. If any man lieth with mankind [with another man in homosexual intercourse] as he lieth with a woman, both of them have committed abomination, and they both shall surely be put to death.

9. If any person commits adultery with a married or espoused wife, the adulterer and adulteress shall surely be put to death.

10. If any man steal [kidnap] a man or mankind, he shall surely be put to death.

11. If any man rise up by false witness, wittingly and of purpose to take away any man's life, he shall be put to death.

12. If any man shall conspire and attempt any invasion, insurrection, or public rebellion against our Commonwealth, or shall endeavor to surprise any Town or Towns, fort or forts therein, or shall treacherously and perfidiously attempt the alteration and subversion of our frame of polity or government fundamentally, he shall be put to death.

95. A Declaration of the Liberties the Lord Jesus hath given to the Churches

1. All the people of God within this jurisdiction who are not in a church way, and be orthodox in judgment, and not scandalous in life, shall have full liberty to gather themselves into a Church Estate. Provided they do it in a Christian way, with due observation of the rules of Christ revealed in his word.

2. Every Church hath full liberty to exercise all the ordinances of God, according to the rules of scripture.

3. Every Church hath free liberty of election and ordination of all their officers from time to time, provided they be able, pious and orthodox.

4. Every Church hath free liberty of admission, recommendation, dismission, and expulsion, or deposal of their officers, and members, upon due cause, with free exercise of the discipline and censures of Christ according to the rules of his word.

5. No Injunctions are to be put upon any Church, Church officers or member in point of doctrine, worship or discipline, whether for substance or circumstance besides the Institutions of the Lord.

6. Every Church of Christ hath freedom to celebrate days of fasting and prayer, and of thanksgiving according to the word of God.

7. The Elders of Churches have free liberty to meet monthly, quarterly, or otherwise, in convenient numbers and places, for conferences, and consultations about Christian and Church questions and occasions.

8. All Churches have liberty to deal with any of their members in a church way that are in the hand of Justice. So it be not to retard or hinder the course thereof.

9. Every Church hath liberty to deal with any magistrate, Deputy of Court or other officer whatsoever that is a member in a church way in case of apparent and just offense given in their places, so it be done with due observance and respect.

10. We allow private meetings for edification in religion amongst Christians of all sorts of people. So it be without just offense for number, time, place, and other circumstances.

11. For the preventing and removing of error and offense that may grow and spread in any of the Churches in this jurisdiction, and for the preserving of truth and peace in the several churches within themselves, and for the maintenance and exercise of brotherly communion, amongst all the churches in the Country, it is allowed and ratified, by the authority of

this General Court as a lawful liberty of the Churches of Christ:

- That once in every month of the year (when the season will bear it) it shall be lawful for the ministers and Elders of the Churches near adjoining together, with any other of the brethren, with the consent of the churches to assemble by course in each several Church one after another.

- To the intent after the preaching of the word by such a minister as shall be requested thereto by the Elders of the church where the Assembly is held, the rest of the day may be spent in public Christian conference about the discussing and resolving of any such doubts and cases of conscience concerning matter of doctrine or worship or government of the church as shall be propounded by any of the brethren of that church, will leave also to any other Brother to propound his objections or answers for further satisfaction according to the word of God. Provided that the whole action be guided and moderated by the Elders of the Church where the Assembly is held, or by such others as they shall appoint.

- And that no thing be concluded and imposed by way of authority from one or more churches upon another, but only by way of brotherly conference and consultations.

- That the truth may be searched out to the satisfying of every man's conscience in the sight of God according his word.

- And because such an Assembly and the work thereof cannot be duly attended to if other lectures be held in the same week, it is therefore agreed with the consent of the Churches, that in that week when such an Assembly is held, all the lectures in all the neighboring Churches for that week shall be forborne. That so the public service of Christ in this more solemn Assembly may be transacted with greater diligence and attention.

96. Howsoever these above specified rites, freedoms, immunities, authorites and privileges, both Civil and Ecclesiastical are expressed only under the name and title of Liberties, and not in the exact form of Laws or Statutes, yet we do with one consent fully authorize, and earnestly entreat all that are and shall be in Authority to consider them as laws, and not to fail to inflict condign and proportionable punishments upon every man impartially, that shall infringe or violate any of them.

97. We likewise give full power and liberty to any person that shall at any time be denied or deprived of any of them, to commence and prosecute their suit, complaint or action against any man that shall so do in any Court that hath proper cognizance or judicature thereof.

98. Lastly because our duty and desire is to do nothing suddenly which fundamentally concerns us, we decree that these rites and liberties shall be audibly read and deliberately weighed at every General Court that shall be held, within three years next ensuing, and such of them as shall not be altered or repealed they shall stand so ratified, that no man shall infringe them without due punishment. And if any General Court within these next three years shall fail or forget to read and consider them as above said, the Governor and Deputy Governor for the time being, and every Assistant present at such Courts, shall forfeit 20 shillings a man, and every Deputy 10 shillings a man for each neglect, which shall be paid out of their proper estate, and not by the Country or the Towns which chose them, and whensoever there shall arise any question in any Court among the Assistants and associates thereof about the explanation of these rites and liberties, the General Court only shall have power to interpret them.

New Englanders Contemplate England's Wars of Religion

New Englanders had migrated to the New World to create godly forms of civil and religious government. Some, at least, hoped that their example would inspire reform in their mother country. The colonists understood why the Scots would challenge the efforts of Charles I and Archbishop William Laud to impose what they viewed as popish innovations in the king's northern kingdom. The colonists viewed with hope the English Parliament's challenge to Charles I and his policies. But however much they understood the conflict as God's will, they were concerned over the outbreak of war and how it might affect their friends and families across the Atlantic.

I. Reactions to the Bishops Wars between the Scots and Charles I

In this first selection, William Hooke, minister of Taunton, expressed some of the colonists' sentiments in a fast-day sermon preached on July 23, 1640. In the course of the sermon Hooke evokes the horrors of seventeenth-century warfare. It was later published in England as New England's Tears for Old England's Fears, *perhaps with the assistance of Hooke's kinsman, Oliver Cromwell.*

Source: William Hooke, *New England's Teares for Old England's Feares* (London, 1641), pp. 7–22.

The use that I do principally intend is of exhortation to you all, as you desire to approve yourselves the true friend and brethren of your dear countrymen in old England, to condole with them this day in their afflictions. Job's friends, you see, did it for him seven days and seven nights . . .. Let us do it then this one day, at least . . ..

Indeed, when we look upon ourselves at this time in this land, the Lord hath given us great cause of rejoicing, both in respect of civil and spiritual peace. God hath at once subdued the proud Pequots [in the Pequot War] and the proud opinions that rose up in this land [the antinomian controversy], and for plenty never had the land the like. Yea, which is much better, the Word of God grows and multiplieth; the churches have rest throughout the land, and are edified and, walking in the fear of the Lord and in the comfort of the Holy Ghost, are multiplied. This is much, and more it would be if the edge of these and other comforts were not in this day turned by the fear of civil strifes and combustions in the land of our nativity . . ..

Let us therefore, I beseech you, lay aside the thoughts of all our comforts this day, and let us fasten our eyes upon the calamities of our brethren in old England, . . . imminent calamities dropping, swords that have hung a long time over their heads by a twine thread, judgments long since threatened as forseeen by many of God's messengers in the causes . . ..

If you should but see war described to you in a map, especially in a country well known to you, nay dearly beloved of you, where you drew your first breath, where once—yea, where lately—you dwelt, where you have received ten thousand mercies, and have many a dear friend and countryman and kinsman abiding, how could you but lament and mourn?

War is a conflict of enemies enraged with bloody revenge, wherein the parties opposite carry their lives in their hands, every man turning prodigal of his very heart's blood, and willing to be killed to kill. The instruments are clashing swords, rattling spears, skull-dividing halberds, murdering pieces, and thundering cannons from whose mouths proceed the fire, and smell, and smoke, and terror—death, as it were—of the very bottomless pit. We wonder now and then at the sudden death of a man. Alas, you might there see a thousand men—not only healthy but stout and strong—struck down in the twinkling of an eye, their breath exhales without so much as: "Lord have mercy on us." Death

hews its way through a wood of men in a minute of time. O, the shrill piercing clangs of the trumpets, noise of drums, the animating voices of horse captains and commanders, learned and learning to destroy! There is the undaunted horse whose neck is clothed with thunder, and the glory of whose nostrils is terrible. How does he lie pawing and prancing in the valley, going forth to meet the armed men? He mocks at fear, swallowing the ground with fierceness and rage . . .. He smells the battle afar off, the thunder of the captains and the shouting. Here ride some dead men swaying in their deep saddles. There fall others alive upon their dead horses. Death sends a message to those from the mouth of the muskets, these it talks with face to face and stabs them in the fifth rib. In yonder file there is a man who hath his arm struck off from his shoulder; another by him has lost his leg. Here stands a soldier with half a face. There fights another upon his stumps, and at once both kills and is killed. Not far off lies a company wallowing in their sweat and gore. . . . A man while he charges his musket is discharged of his life, and falls upon his dead fellow . . .. Death reigns in the field, and is sure to have the day which side soever falls. In the meanwhile . . . the infernal fiends follow the camp to catch after the souls of rude nefarious soldiers . . . who fight themselves fearlessly into the mouth of hell for revenge, a booty, or a little revenue. . . . A day of battle is a day of harvest for the devil.

All this while, the poor wife and tender children sit weeping together at home, having taken their late farewell of the harnessed husband and father (O! It was a sad parting if you had seen it!), never looking to see his face again, as indeed many, and the most of them, never do. Anon comes Ely's messenger from the camp, saying, "There is a great slaughter among the people, and your husband is dead, your father is dead. He was slain in an hot fight. He was shot dead in the place and never spoke a word more." Then the poor widow, who fed yet upon a crumb of hope, tears her hair from her head, rends her clothes, wrings her hands, lifts up her voice to heaven, and weeps like Rachel that would not be comforted. Her children hang about her crying and saying, "O! my father is slain, my father is dead. I shall never see my father more." And so they cry and sob and sigh out their afflicted souls, and break their hearts together. Alas, alas! This is yet but war through a crevice. Beloved, but do consider, there is many times fire without war, and famine and pestilence without war, but war is never without them. And there are many times robberies without war, and murdering of passengers, ravishing of matrons, deflowering of virgins, cruelties and torments, and sometimes barbarous and inhuman practices without war, but war seldom or never without them.

. . .

[There are] no wars so cruel, so unnatural, so desolating, as civil wars. . . . A kingdom at war with a foreign enemy may stand, but a kingdom divided against itself can never . . . .

To this end, you may think upon these particulars.

Of our civil relation to that land, and the inhabitants therein. There is no land that claims our name, but England . . . . There is no potentate breathing, that we call our dread sovereign, but King Charles, nor laws of any land have civilized us but England's. . . . Did we not there draw in our first breath? Did not the sun first shine there upon our heads? Did not that land first bear us, even that pleasant island—but for sin I would say, that garden of the lord, that paradise? . . .

Is it not meet that we should bear a part with them in their sorrows, who have borne a part with them in their sins? Have we conferred so many sins as we have done to speed on their confusion, and shall we bestow no sorrow on them? Shall we not help to quench the fire with our tears, that we have kindled with our sins? O cruel! How know we but that the Lord is at this instant visiting our transgressions there acted, which polluted the land? Beloved, did we not commit there ten thousand millions of sins and more amongst us during our abode there? There, O there, we played the ungodly atheists. There it was we halted between God and Baal, swore by the Lord and by Malchom [the god of the Ammonites]. [There we] were neither hot nor cold . . . . There some of us blasphemed the dreadful name of the ever blessed God, polluted his sabbaths, despised his messengers, contemned his holy ways, profaned and abused his mercies, and his good creatures. [There we] ran with others to the same excess of riot, etc. And however some may say they have repented hereof, yet little do they know what evil examples they have left there behind to fill up the measure both of sin and wrath. If thy sins committed there be pardoned, yet thy sins may be punished . . . .

Neither let this be forgotten, that of all the Christian people in the world, we in this land enjoy the greatest measure of peace and tranquility. We have beaten our swords into ploughshares, and our spears into pruning hooks, when others have beaten their pruning hooks into spears, and their ploughshares into swords . . . .

II. The Outbreak of Civil War

This selection is from another sermon preached by William Hooke, also preached on a fast day, and published in England with the assistance of Joseph Caryl in 1645. In it Hooke calls upon New Englanders to join with the Scots and Parliament in fighting the forces of the English prelates and Charles I, using their prayers and fasts as potent weapons against God's enemies.

Source: William Hooke, *New-Englands Sence of Old-England and Ireland's Sorrowes* (London, 1645), pp. 4–19.

. . . The prelates of England do this day stink in the nostrils of God's people, yea, of many such as have little religion in them. Their indignities and abuses offered to the Lord's ambassadors have been infinite and intolerable . . . .

This should make us this day more earnest with God for England, that he would purge the land of this filth. For otherwise how noisome will that country be when there are so many unsavory creatures . . . .

The wonderful goodness of God [is now revealed] in four particulars, which should melt our hearts this day.

First, in uniting the honorable nation of the Scots by covenant against the prelates, in their late defense against their tyranny . . . .

Secondly, in the firm brotherly union of England and Scotland . . . .

Thirdly, in uniting both houses of Parliament . . . . It is such a knot that the very sword of Alexander, we hope, shall not easily cut asunder. A kingdom united into one body will endure a mighty shock. Men standing single are soon jostled down; [it is] most difficulty, when they are all embodied in one.

Fourthly, in uniting the hearts of all the churches in this land [New England] to one another, and all of them this day to our dear country in opposing the common adversaries. For what has England said to us of late? "If the papists, prelates, and atheists be too strong for us, then you shall help us; and if at any time the enemy be too strong for you, we will help you." . . .

When religion and policy, church and commonwealth, lie at stake, God's people had need to encourage themselves, and one another. . . .

Beloved! I cannot but look upon the churches in this land [New England] this day, as upon so many several regiments, or bands of soldiers, lying in ambush here under the fern and brushes of the wilderness . . . . I know we are little dreamt of at this time in any part of Christendom, our weapons being as invisible to the eyes of flesh as our persons are to the world. So much the better. We shall fight this day with greater safety to ourselves, and danger to our enemies, among whom, I am confident in the Lord, thousands shall fall and never know who hurt them. We arrogate nothing to ourselves, for if the weapons of our warfare are mighty it is not through us, but through God . . . . [We have been sent] to lie in wait in the wilderness, to come upon the backs of God's enemies with deadly fastings and prayer, murderers that will kill point blank from one end of the world to the other.

III. Regicide

New Englanders continued to support the Parliamentary cause of their English puritan allies. Despite this support, the news of the execution of King Charles I came as a shock to the colonists. John Cotton preached a sermon to reiterate support for the Parliament and to justify the regicide.

Source: Francis J. Bremer, "In Defense of Regicide: John Cotton on the Execution of Charles I," *William and Mary Quarterly*, 3rd series, 37 (1980), 103–124.

[In the Covenant taken by the leaders of Parliament] the article containing the king's safety cometh but in the third place. The first article of the Covenant was to provide for the worship of God and purity of religion against popery and prelacy. And the second article was to preserve the liberty and safety of the people against tyranny. And the third is to provide for the king's safety and honor. Now if this be an article in the third place, then the two former must have precedence and pre-eminence. And if the king cannot be restored but with prejudice to the purity of religion, and restoring of prelacy or inclination to popery, or if he cannot be restored without prejudice to the liberty and safety of the people, they must now of necessity be excused from maintaining in the third article . . .. And take all the concessions which the king was pleased to grant, it was still with [his] reservation of restoring prelacy and liturgy and having the militia in his own hands, or his son's, after so many years, which still left things in the same state as they were . . ..

Our intelligence here at so great a distance and small acquaintance is but shallow to wade through these great difficulties. Notwithstanding, let me tell you what to my best observation is, that which most satisfieth my own soul in this case . . ..

When the Parliament sent forth their commissioners to treat with the king's commissioners at Newport, at the same time the commissioners of Scotland were sent to join in [negotiating] the treaty. At that time the Parliament was full and the commissioners were sent forth with full power . . .. But when they met there and argued and reasoned according to the wisdom of statesmen, and when they had done all and driven matters as far and as close as they could go by any argument of religion or state, the king condescended so little to them that both the commissioners of England and Scotland agreed in this—that the king's concessions were not safe to center upon and to settle a firm peace . . .. Parliament was full and thereupon an act passeth to have no more addresses to the king. Now this was done by the act of that state body which represented the whole kingdom.

And all the godly ministers in both city and country did encourage the Parliament and army to [continue] to undertake the war against the king for the maintenance of those things which the king would not grant. And [they] were also ready to assist them, not only with their money, but their plate also to carry on this design against the king. Now when it came to this, . . . sundry people were offended at that, and they supply the house with more burgesses [sixteen new members elected to the Long Parliament in 1648], for ends best known to themselves did reverse this act [of no further addresses to the king], and devise how they may restore the king again on his own concessions. . . . They kept up the rest of the house the most part of the night. Wearied with long watching and tedious and impetuous speeches, they began to think the king's concession was safe to be rested on . . .. And then the army, knowing a full vote had passed before to the contrary, and discerning that if this was [changed] it was hazardous not only to themselves, but to many others of the parliament, and destructive also to the commonwealth, . . . they went and secluded sundry members of the house [Pride's Purge] . . ..

It was a wise speech of Trajan when he committed the sword to any: use it for me, saith he, when I rule according to law and justice, but against me when otherwise.

Suppose among us it be concluded by the general court as unsafe to the church and commonwealth to receive a general governor over us. And afterwards a sudden confluence of deputies and some magistrates shall reverse that act, and conclude a safety in receiving him. May not the major general in such a case, with the consent of his trained bands (which are, through God, the strength of the country) may not he, I say, seclude such of the magistrates and deputies as were ready to betray the safety of the church and commonwealth? What if now the major part of the people of the kingdom should now dislike the act both of parliament and the army, and in their hearts turn back again, both to the wonted pollutions in the church and state? Shall the parliament and army and godly party in the kingdom (who were studious of reformation), shall they follow the multitude to lose all that which they have wrought?

. . .

[Cotton goes on to point to God's approbation of the army's action by his granting them victory in the battle of Dunbar]

It is a great and wonderful deliverance of the English army in that great battle. . . . They were so weather beaten with rain and cold, and charged upon with such advantage by a double number to their own. And upon that charge, when the English army began to recoil and fall, soon after . . . the general's regiment came in. In one hour god had so ended the dispute that so many were fain to flee, and so many slain, and their general himself fain to retreat to Edinburgh with a few with him. We may stand and wonder at the salvation of God, especially considering that if they had been beaten in that battle a great part of the kingdom of England would have risen up in a combustion and been ready to give up on all that which had been purchased by so much blood and charge. They that do write the most certain intelligence certify that now scarce one in ten in England are found true to the Parliament, and therefore it is a matter of just praise and of the wonderful goodness of god. Both armies and nations appealed to the justice and truth of god in that cause, and god cast the scale. Just and righteous are thy ways Christ, king of saints.

Pilgrim Thanksgiving

Though historians recognize that the urge to give thanks to God was common throughout the history of Christianity, and that prior to 1620 there were many such occasions in colonial America—Spanish colonists along the Rio Grande offering their thanks to God for their deliverances, and the Jamestown settlers who survived thanking the Lord, are examples—the thanksgiving observance and feast held by the Pilgrims in November 1621 have become hallowed parts of the American tradition. The following accounts offer us insight into that event, though they do not actually refer to the act of giving thanks to God.

William Bradford's Account

> Source: William Bradford, *History of Plymouth Plantation, 1620–1647,* edited by Worthington C. Ford (Boston, 1912).

[November 1621] They began now to gather in the small harvest they had, and to fit up their houses and dwellings against winter, being all well recovered in health and strength, and had all things in good plenty. As some were thus employed in affairs abroad, others were exercised in fishing about cod and bass and other fish, of which they took good store, of which every family had their portion. All the summer there was no want; and now began to come in store of fowl, as winter approached, of

which the place did abound . . .. And besides waterfowl there was a great store of wild turkeys, of which they took many, besides venison, etc. Besides they had about a peck of meal a week to a person or now, since the harvest, Indian corn to that proportion. Which made many afterwards write so largely of their plenty here to friends in England. . . .

Edward Winslow's Account

> Source: *A Relation or Journal of the Beginning and Proceedings of the English Plantation settled at Plimoth in New England* (London, 1622), pp. 60-61.

Our corn did prove well, and, God be praised, we had a good increase of Indian corn, and our barley indifferent good, but our pease not worth the gathering for we feared they were too late sown. . . . Our harvest being gotten in, our governor sent four men on fowling, that so we might, after a more special manner, rejoice together after we had gathered the fruits of our labors. They four, in one day, killed as much fowl as, with a little help besides, served the company almost a week. At which time, amongst other recreations, we exercised our arms, many of the Indians coming among us. And among the rest their greatest king, Massasoit, with some ninety men whom, for three days, we entertained and feasted.

Providences

Puritans saw God's hand in everyday matters. Throughout the sixteenth and seventeenth century, English and New England Puritans would publish collections of providential events—stories of how God had sent a message through his treatment of certain individuals. Henry Burton's A Divine Tragedy Lately Acted *(1636) was one such collection.*

> Source: *Henry Burton's* A Divine Tragedy Lately Acted *(1636).*

A Collection of sundry memorable examples of God's judgments upon Sabbath-breakers
These examples of God's judgments hereunder set down, have fallen out within the space of less than two years last past, even since the Declaration for Sports (tolerated on the Lord's day) was published, and read by many ministers in their congregations. For here upon ill-disposed people (being as dry fuel, to which fire being put quickly flameth forth; or as waters pent up and re-

strained being let loose, break forth more furiously) were so encouraged, if not enraged, as taking liberty dispensed, thereby so provoked God, that his wrath in sundry places hath broken out to the destruction of many, would to God to the instruction of any.

Example 1:
A woman about Northampton, the same day that she heard the book for sports read, went immediately, and having three pence in her purse, hired a fellow to go to the next town to fetch a minstrel, who coming, she with other fell a-dancing, which continued within night; at which time she was got with child, which at the birth she murdering, was detected and apprehended, and being convented before the justice, she confessed it, and withal told the occasion of it, saying it was her falling to sport on the Sabbath, upon reading of the book, so as for this treble sinful act, her presumptuous profaning of the Sabbath, which brought her adultery and that murder. She was according to the law, both of god and man, put to death; much sin and misery followeth upon the Sabbath-breaking.

Example 23:
In the edge of Essex near Brinkley, two fellows working in a chalk pit, the one was boasting to his fellow how he had angered his mistress with staying so late at their sports the last Sunday night, but he said he would anger her worse the next Sunday. He had no sooner said this, but suddenly the earth fell down upon him, and slew him outright, with the fall whereof his fellow's limb was broken, who had been also partner with him in his jollity on the Lord's day, escaping with his life, that he might tell the truth, that God might be glorified, and that by this warning he night repent of his sin and reform such his profaneness, and remain as a pillar of salt, to season others with fear by his example.

Example 43:
At Glastonbury in Somersetshire, at the setting up of a maypole, it miscarrying, fell upon a child, and slew it, and it is reported that it was the churchwarden's child, who was the chief stickler in the business. Also when the maypole in the same town was again the second time a-setting up, a fire took in the town, so as all the people about the maypole were forced to leave it and to run to the quenching of the fire.

A Puritan "Holy Fair"

One of the hallmarks of Puritanism was a thirst for preaching, which led the godly to travel to market towns and other locations to listen to preachers. The historian Patrick Collinson, borrowing a phrase from a study of Scottish religious exercises by Eric Leigh Schmidt, referred to these gatherings as "holy fairs." They featured preaching, sociability, and occasionally the reception of the sacrament of the Lord's Supper. The participants fasted through the day and then ended the gathering with a supper of sorts. One description of such gatherings is to be found in the writings of Father William Weston, a Catholic priest imprisoned at Wisbech Castle in the diocese of Ely in the 1580s. There he witnessed a number of such gatherings. While he clearly had little sympathy for what he witnessed, the details he offers provide a clear description of what such gatherings might entail.

Source: "The Life of Father William Weston," in John Morris, editor, *The Troubles of Our Catholic Forefathers Related by Themselves*, volume II (London, 1875).

From the beginning [of his captivity] the prison had been beset by a great multitude of Puritan visitors . . . partly from the town itself, partly from the villages near. For as the gaoler was himself a Puritan, together with all his family, and had the justices also for supporters, they used to come in crowds, flocking from all quarters to be present at their exercises. These they used to begin with three or four sermons, preached one after the other. Then they went to communion, not receiving it either on their knees or standing, but moving by, so that it might be called a Passover in very truth. They had likewise a kind of tribunal of their own, and elders who had power to investigate and punish at will the misdemeanors of their brethren. They all had their Bibles, and looked diligently for the texts that were quoted by their preachers, comparing different passages to see if they had been brought forward truly and to the point, in such a manner as to confirm their own doctrine. They held arguments, also, among themselves about the meaning of various Scripture texts, all of them, men and women, boys and girls, laborers, workmen, and simpletons; and these discussions were often wont, as it was said, to produce quarrels and fights. All these things could be seen by the Catholic prisoners from the windows of their cells, for they took place not in a temple of house, but within the enclosure of the prison walls, on a large space where a thousand or more persons were reported sometimes to assemble, and occasioned laughter to such as beheld or heard them by the multitude of their Bibles, the number of their horses, and the medley of their voices. When the congregation was dismissed, after the long fast that had been imposed upon them all, and after the whole day had been consumed in these exercises, they ended the farce with a plentiful supper.

Root and Branch Petition, 1640

In 1640 Londoners signed a petition to Parliament expressing their hopes for the reform of the Church of England, and specifically calling for the abolition of episcopacy, "with all its dependencies, roots and branches." The petition became a platform for those hoping that the chance had at last come to stem the tide of Anticalvinism and further the perfection of the national church. The following selections offer a taste of the puritan complaints and their reform program.

Source: S. R. Gardiner, ed., *Constitutional Documents of the Puritan Revolution, 1625–1660,* 2nd ed. (Oxford, 1889), pp. 137–144.

A particular of the manifold evils, pressures and grievances caused, practiced and occasioned by the prelates and their dependents:

1. The subjecting and enthralling all ministers under them and their authority, and so by degrees exempting them from the temporal power; whence follows,
2. The faint-heartedness of ministers to preach the truth of God, lest they should displease the prelates; as namely, the doctrine of predestination, of free grace, of perseverance, of original sin remaining after baptism, of the Sabbath, the doctrine against universal grace, election for faith foreseen, free will against Antichrist, non-residents, human inventions in God's worship; all which are generally withheld from the people's knowledge, because not relishing to the bishops.

. . .

4. The restraint of many godly and able men from the ministry, and thrusting out of many congregations their faithful, diligent and powerful ministers, who lived peaceably with them, and did them good, only because they cannot in conscience submit unto and maintain the bishops; needless devices; nay, sometimes for no other cause but for their zeal in preaching, of great auditories.

5. The suppressing of that godly design set on foot by certain saints, and sugared with many great gifts by sundry well-affected persons for the buying of impropriations, and placing of able ministers in them, maintaining of lectures, and founding of free schools, which the prelates could not endure, lest it should darken their glories, and draw the ministers from their dependence upon them.
6. The great increase of idle, lewd and dissolute, ignorant and erroneous men in the ministry, which swarm like the locusts of Egypt over the whole kingdom; and will they but wear a canonical coat, a surplice, a hood, bow at the name of Jesus, and be zealous of superstitious ceremonies, they may live as they list, confront whom they please, preach and vent what errors they will, and neglect preaching at their pleasures without control.
7. This discouragement of many from bringing up their children in learning; the many schisms, errors, and strange opinions which are in the church; great corruptions which are in the universities; the gross and lamentable ignorance almost everywhere among the people; the want of preaching ministers in very many places both of England and Wales; the loathing of the ministry; and the general defection to all manner of profaneness.

. . .

. . .

10. The publishing and venting of popish, Arminian, and other dangerous books and tenets; as namely, "That the Church of Rome is a true church, and in the worst times never erred in fundamentals;" "that the subjects have no propriety in their estates, but that the king may take from them what he pleaseth;" "that all is the king's, and that he is bound by no law," and many other, from the former whereof hath sprung,
11. The growth of popery and increase of Papists, priests and Jesuits in sundry places, but especially about London since the Reformation; the frequent venting of crucifixes and popish pictures both engraven and printed, and the placing of such in bibles.

. . .

. . .

14. The great conformity and likeness both continued and increased of our church to the Church of Rome, in vestures, postures, ceremonies and administrations, namely as the bishops' rochets and the lawn-sleeves, the four-cornered cap, the cope and surplice the tippet, the hood, and the canoni-

cal coat; the pulpits clothed, especially now of late, with the Jesuits' badge upon them every way.

15. The standing up at *Gloria Patri* and at the reading of the gospel, praying towards the east, the bowing at the name of Jesus, the bowing to the altar towards the east, cross in baptism, the kneeling at the communion.

16. The turning of the communion table altar-wise, setting images, crucifixes, and conceits over them, and tapers and books upon them, and bowing or adoring to or before them; the reading of the second service at the altar, and forcing people to come up thither to receive, or else denying the sacrament to them; terming the altar to be the mercy-seat, or the place of God Almighty in the church, which is a plain device to usher in the mass.

Setting Up the Churches of Christ in New England

Freed from the supervision of bishops by their emigration to the New World, the colonists had to decide how to shape their religious life, starting with the formation of local institutions. The following contemporary account describes the process and includes the covenant drawn up for one such congregation.

> Source: J. Franklin Jameson, ed., *Johnson's Wonderworking Providence . . .,* Original Narratives of Early American History (New York, 1910), pp. 214–218.

Now to declare how this people [of Woburn] proceeded in religious matters, and so consequently all the Churches of Christ planted in New England. [Once there were enough people to support a minister,] this people went about placing down a town [and then] began the foundation stone [for a church] with earnest seeking of the Lord's assistance, by humbling of their souls before Him in days of prayer, and imploring His aid in so weighty a work. Then they addressed themselves to attend counsel of the most orthodox and ablest Christians, and more especially of such as the Lord had already placed in the ministry, not rashly running together themselves into a church before they had hopes of attaining an officer to preach the Word and administer the seals unto them, choosing rather to continue in fellowship with some other church for their Christian

watch over them till the Lord would be pleased to provide.

They after some search met with a young man named Mr. Thomas Carter, then belonging to the Church of Christ at Watertown, a reverend, godly man, apt to teach the sound and wholesome truths of Christ. Having attained their desires, in hopes of his coming unto them were they once joined in Church estate, he exercised his gifts of preaching and prayer among them in the meantime, and more especially in a day of fasting and prayer. Thus these godly people interest their affections one with the other, both minister and people. After this they make ready for the work, and the 24th of the 6th month, 1642, they assemble together in the morning about eight of the clock. After the reverend Mr. Syms had continued in preaching and prayer about the space of four or five hours, the persons that were to join in covenant, openly and professedly before the congregation and messengers of divers neighbor churches—among whom were the reverend elders of Boston, Mr. Cotton, Mr. Wilson; Mr. [Thomas] Allen of Charlestown; Mr. Shepard of Cambridge [and] Mr. Dunster; of Watertown, Mr. Knowles; of Dorchester, Mr. Mather. [It is] also . . . the duty of the magistrates (in regard of the good and peace of the civil government) to be present, at least some one of them, not only to prevent the disturbance [that] might follow in the Commonwealth by any who under pretense of church covenant might bring in again those cursed opinions that caused such commotion in this and the other colony, to the greatest damage of the people, but also to countenance the people of God in so pious a work, that under them they may live a quiet and peaceable life, in all godliness and honesty. For this cause was present and honored Mr. Increase Nowell.

The persons stood forth and first confessed what the Lord had done for their poor souls, by the work of His Spirit in the preaching of His Word, and providences, one by one. And that all might know their faith in Christ was bottomed upon Him, as He is revealed in His Word, and that from their own knowledge, they also declare the same, according to that measure of understanding the Lord had given them. The elders, or any other messengers there present, question with them, for the better understanding of them in any points they doubt of, which being done, and all satisfied, they in the name of the churches to which they do belong hold out the right hand of fellowship unto them, they declaring their covenant in words expressed in writing to this purpose.

The Church Covenant

We that do assemble ourselves this day before God and His people, in an unfeigned desire to be accepted of Him as the Church of the Lord Jesus Christ, according to the rule of the New Testament, do acknowledge ourselves to be the most unworthy of all others, that we should attain such a high grace, and the most unable of ourselves to the performance of anything that is good, abhorring ourselves for all our former defilements in the worship of God, and other ways, and resting only upon the Lord Jesus Christ for atonement, and upon the power of his grace for the guidance of our whole after course, do here in the name of Christ Jesus, as in the presence of the Lord, from the bottom of our hearts agree together through His grace to give up ourselves, first unto the Lord Jesus as our only King, Priest, and Prophet, wholly to be subject unto Him in all things, and therewith one unto another, as in a church body, to walk together in all the ordinances of the Gospel, and in such mutual love and offices thereof, as toward one another in the Lord. And all this, both according to the present light that the Lord hath given us, as also according to all further light, which He shall be pleased at any time to reach out unto us out of the Word by the goodness of His grace, renouncing also in the same covenant all errors and schisms, and whatsoever byways that are contrary to the blessed rules revealed in the Gospel, and in particular the inordinate love and seeking after the things of the world.

Every church hath not the same for words, for they are not for a form of words.

The 22nd of the 9th month following, Mr. Thomas Carter was ordained pastor in presence of the like assembly. After he had exercised in preaching and prayer the greater part of the day, two persons in the name of the church laid their hands upon his head and said, "We ordain thee, Thomas Carter, to be pastor unto this Church of Christ." Then one of the elders present, being desired of the church, continued in prayer unto the Lord for His more especial assistance of this His servant in His work, being a charge of such weighty importance, as is the glory of God and salvation of souls, that the very thought would make a man to tremble in the sense of his own inability to the work. The people having provided a dwelling house, built at the charge of the town in general, welcomed him unto them with joy that the Lord was pleased to give them such a blessing, that their eyes may see their Teacher's.

After this there were divers added to the church daily in this manner: the person desirous to join with the church cometh to the pastor and makes him acquainted therewith, declaring how the Lord hath been pleased to work his conversion, who discerning hopes of the person's faith in Christ, although weak, yet if any appear he is propounded to the church in general for their approbation, touching his godly life and conversation, and then by the pastor and some brethren heard again, who make report to the church of their charitable approving of the person.

But before they come to join with the church, all persons within the town have public notice of it; then publicly he declares the manner of his conversion and how the Lord hath been pleased by the hearing of His Word preached, and the work of His Spirit in the inward parts of his soul, to bring him out of that natural darkness which all men are by nature in and under, as also the measure of knowledge the Lord hath been pleased to imbue him withal. And because some men cannot speak publicly to edification through bashfulness, the less is required of such, and women speak not publicly at all, for all that is desired is to prevent the polluting [of] the blessed ordinances of Christ by such as walk scandalously, and that men and women do not eat and drink their own condemnation in not discerning the Lord's body.

After this manner were many added to the Church of Christ, and those seven that joined in church fellowship at first are now increased to seventy-four persons or thereabout, of which, according to their own confession, as is supposed, the greater part having been converted by the preaching of the Word in New England, by which may appear the powerful efficacy of the Word of Christ in the mouth of His ministers, and that this way of Christ in joining together in church covenant is not only for building up of souls in Christ, but also for converting of sinners and bringing them out of the natural condition to be engrafted into Christ. For if this one church have so many, then assuredly there must be a great number comparatively throughout all the churches in the country. After this manner have the Churches of Christ had their beginning and progress hitherto. The Lord continue and increase them the world throughout.

Social Order

Puritans shared with their contemporaries a belief that each individual had his or her place in a social order that was designed by God. While spiritually equal in the eyes of God, everyone was created to fit into certain defined roles. This opening to John Winthrop's lay sermon "Model of Christian Charity" sets forth this vision of social order and the reasons for God having created such differences between men.

Source: Francis J. Bremer, editor, *Winthrop Papers: Religious Writings* (forthcoming from the Massachusetts Historical Society).

God Almighty in his most holy and wise providence hath so disposed of the Condition of mankind, as in all times some must be rich, some poor, some high and eminent in power and dignity, others mean and in subjection.

THE REASON HEREOF.

I. REASON: *First*, to hold conformity with the rest of his works, being delighted to show forth the glory of his wisdom in the variety and difference of the Creatures, and the glory of his power in ordering all these differences for the preservation and good of the whole, and the glory of his greatness that as it is the glory of princes to have many officers, so this great King will have many Stewards, counting himself more honored in dispensing his gifts to man by man, then if he did it by his own immediate hand.

2. REASON: Secondly, That he might have the more occasion to manifest the work of his Spirit: first, upon the wicked, in moderating and restraining them. So that the rich and mighty should not eat up the poor, nor the poor and despised rise up against their superiors and shake off their yoke; 2ly in the regenerate, in exercising his graces in them, as in the great ones, their love, mercy, gentleness, temperance, etc., in the poor and inferior sort, their faith, patience, obedience, etc.

3. REASON: Thirdly, That every man might have need of other, and from hence they might be all knit more nearly together in the Bond of brotherly affection. From hence it appears plainly that no man is made more honorable then another, or more wealthy, etc., out of any particular and singular respect to himself, but for the glory of his Creator and the Common good of the Creature, Man. Therefore God still reserves the property of these gifts to himself, as Ezekiel 16:17, he there calls wealth his gold and his silver, etc. Proverbs 3:9, he claims their service as his due, honor the Lord with thy riches, etc. All men being thus (by divine providence) ranked into two sorts, rich and poor, under the first are comprehended all such as are able to live comfortably by their own means duly improved; and all others are poor according to the former distribution.

Thirty-nine Articles, 1563

These articles, established by Convocation in 1563, represent the official stand of the Church of England on matters of doctrine and discipline. Efforts to establish such standards date back to the Ten Articles of 1536, at the start of the English Reformation. From the beginning puritans accepted the doctrinal formulations but objected to the articles dealing with discipline. Efforts to require all clergy to subscribe to the articles were in part an effort to force puritans to conform and to identify those who would not.

Source: *Articles Whereupon it was Agreed by the Archbishoppes and Bishoppes* (London, 1571).

1 *Of faith in the Holy Trinity*

There is but one living and true God, everlasting, without body, parts, or passions; of infinite power, wisdom, and goodness; the maker and preserver of all things both visible and invisible. And in unity of this Godhead there be three persons, of one substance, power, and eternity; the Father, the Son, and the Holy Ghost.

2 *Of the word or Son of God, which was made very man*

The Son, which is the word of the Father, begotten from everlasting of the Father, the very and eternal God, of one substance with the Father, took man's nature in the womb of the Blessed Virgin, of her substance: so that two whole and perfect natures, that is to say, the godhead and manhood, were joined together in one person, never to be divided, whereof is one Christ, very God and very man; who truly suffered, was crucified, dead, and buried, to reconcile his Father to us, and to be a sacrifice, not only for original guilt, but also for all actual sins of men.

3 *Of the going down of Christ into hell*

As Christ died for us, and was buried, so also it is to be believed that he went down into hell.

4 *Of the resurrection of Christ*

Christ did truly arise again from death, and took again his body, with flesh, bones, and all things appertaining to the perfection of man's nature; wherewith he ascended into heaven, and there sitteth, until he return to judge all men at the last day.

5 *Of the Holy Ghost*

The Holy Ghost, proceeding from the Father and the Son, is of one substance, majesty, and glory, with the Father and the Son, very and eternal God.

6 *Of the sufficiency of the Holy Scriptures for salvation*

Holy Scripture containeth all things necessary to salvation: so that whatsoever is not read therein, nor may be proved thereby, is not to be required of any man, that it should be believed as an article of faith, or be thought requisite or necessary to salvation. In the name of the Holy Scripture we do understand those canonical books of the Old and New Testament, of whose authority was never any doubt in the church.

Of the names and number of the canonical books: *Genesis, Exodus, Leviticus, Numbers, Deuteronomy, Joshua, Judges, Ruth, the First Book of Samuel, the Second Book of Samuel, the First Book of Kings, the Second*

Book of Kings, the First Book of Chronicles, the Second Book of Chronicles, the First Book of Esdras, the Second Book of Esdras, the Book of Esther, the Book of Job, the Psalms, the Proverbs, Ecclesiastes or Preacher, Cantica or Songs of Solomon, Four Prophets the greater, Twelve Prophets the less.

And the other books (as Jerome saith) the church doth read for example of life and instruction of manners; but yet doth not apply them to establish any doctrine: such are there following: *the Third Book of Esdras, the Fourth Book of Esdras, The Book of Tobias, the Book of Judith, the rest of the Book of Esther, the Book of Wisdom, Jesus the Son of Sirach, Baruch the Prophet, the Song of Three Children, the Story of Susanna, Of Bel and the Dragon, the Prayer of Manasses, the First Book of Maccabees, the Second Book of Maccabees.*

All the books of the New Testament, as they are commonly received, we do receive and account them canonical.

7 Of the Old Testament

The Old Testament is not contrary to the New: for both in the Old and New Testament everlasting life is offered to mankind by Christ, who is the only mediator between God and man, being both God and man. Wherefore they are not to be heard which feign that the old fathers did look only for transitory promises. Although the law given from God by Moses, as touching ceremonies and rites, do not bind Christian men, nor the civil precepts thereof ought of necessity to be received in any commonwealth: yet notwithstanding, no Christian man whatsoever, is free from the obedience of the commandments which are called moral.

8 Of the three Creeds

The three creeds, Nicene Creed, Athanasius's Creed, and that which is commonly called the Apostles' Creed, ought thoroughly to be received and believed: for they may be proved by most certain warrants of Holt Scripture.

9 Of original or birth-sin

Original sin standeth not in the following of Adam (as the Pelagians do vainly talk), but it is the fault and corruption of the nature of every man, that naturally is engendered of the offspring of Adam: whereby man is very far gone from original righteousness, and is of his own nature inclined to evil, so that the flesh lusteth always contrary to the spirit: and therefore in every person born into this world, it deserveth God's wrath and damnation. And this infection of nature doth remain, yea in them that are regenerated; whereby the lust of the flesh . . . is not subject to the law of God. And although there is no condemnation for them that believe and are baptized, yet the apostle doth confess, that concupiscence and lust hath of itself the nature of sin.

10 Of Free-Will

The condition of man after the fall of Adam is such that he cannot turn and prepare himself, by his own natural strength and good works, to faith and calling upon God: Wherefore we have no power to do good works pleasant and acceptable to God, without the grace of God by Christ preventing us, that we may have a good will, and working with us, when we have that good will.

11 Of the justification of man

We are accounted righteous before God, only for the merit of Our Lord and Savior Jesus Christ, by faith, and not for our own works or deservings: Wherefore, that we are justified by faith only is a most wholesome doctrine, and very full of comfort, as more largely is expressed in the Homily of Justification.

12 Of good works

Albeit that good works, which are the fruits of faith, and follow after justification, cannot put away our sins, and endure the severity of God's judgment; yet are they pleasing and acceptable to God in Christ, and do spring out necessarily of a true and lively faith; insomuch that by them a lively faith may be as evidently known as a tree discerned by the fruit.

13 Of works before justification

Works done before the grace of Christ, and the inspiration of his Spirit, are not pleasant to God, forasmuch as they spring not of faith in Jesus Christ, neither do they make men meet to receive grace, or (as the school-authors say) deserve grace of congruity: yea rather, for that they are not done as God hath willed and commanded them to be done, we doubt not but they have the nature of sin.

14 Of works of supererogation

Voluntary works besides, over and above God's commandments, which they call works of supererogation, cannot be taught without arrogancy and impiety: for by them men do declare, that they do not only render unto God as much as they are bound to do, but that they do more for his sake than of bounden duty is required: whereas Christ saith plainly, When ye have done all that are commanded to you, say, We are unprofitable servants.

15 Of Christ alone without sin

Christ in the truth of our nature was made like unto us in all things, sin only except, from which he was clearly void, both in his flesh, and in his spirit. He came to be the Lamb without spot, who, by sacrifice of himself once made, should take away the sins of the world, and sin (as St John saith) was not in him. But all we the rest (although baptized, and born again in Christ) yet offend in many things; and if we say we have no sin, we deceive ourselves and the truth is not in us.

16 *Of sin after baptism*

Not every deadly sin willingly committed after baptism is sin against the Holy Ghost, and unpardonable. Wherefore the grant of repentance is not to be denied to such as fall into sin after baptism. After we have received the Holy Ghost, we may depart from grace given, and fall into sin, and by the grace of God we may arise again, and amend our lives. And therefore they are to be condemned, which say, they can no more sin as long as they live here, or deny the place of forgiveness to such as truly repent.

17 *Of predestination and election*

Predestination to life is the everlasting purpose of God, whereby (before the foundations of the world were laid) he hath constantly decreed by his counsel secret to us, to deliver from curse and damnation those whom he hath chosen in Christ out of mankind, and to bring them by Christ to everlasting salvation, as vessels made to honor. Wherefore, they which be endued with so excellent a benefit of God be called according to God's purpose by his Spirit working in due season: they through grace obey the calling: they be justified freely: they be made sons of God by adoption: they be made like the image of his only-begotten Son Jesus Christ: they walk religiously in good works, and at length, by God's mercy, they attain to everlasting felicity.

As the godly consideration of predestination, and our election in Christ, is full of sweet, pleasant, and unspeakable comfort to godly persons, and such as feel in themselves the working of the spirit of Christ, mortifying the works of the flesh, and their earthly members, and drawing up their mind to high and heavenly things, as well because it doth greatly establish and confirm their faith of eternal salvation to be enjoyed through Christ, as because it doth fervently kindle their love towards God: So, for curious and carnal persons, lacking the spirit of Christ, to have continually before their eyes the sentence of God's predestination, is a most dangerous downfall, whereby the Devil doth thrust them either into desperation, or into wretchlessness [recklessness] of most unclean living, no less perilous than desperation.

Furthermore, we must receive God's promises in such wise, as they be generally set forth to us in Holy Scripture: and in our doings, that will of God is to be followed, which we have expressly declared unto us in the word of God.

18 *Of obtaining eternal salvation only by the name of Christ*

They also are to be had accursed that presume to say, That every man shall be saved by the law or sect which he professeth, so that he be diligent to frame his life according to that law, and the light of nature. For Holy scripture doth set out unto us only the name of Jesus Christ, whereby men must be saved.

19 *Of the church*

The visible church of Christ is a congregation of faithful men, in the which the pure word of God is preached, and the sacraments be duly ministered according to Christ's ordinance in all those things that of necessity are requisite to the same. As the church of Jerusalem, Alexandria, and Antioch, have erred; so also the church of Rome hath erred, not only in their living and manner of ceremonies, but also in matters of faith.

20 *Of the authority of the church*

The church hath power to decree rites or ceremonies, and authority in controversies of faith: And yet it is not lawful for the church to ordain any thing that is contrary to God's word written, neither may it so expound one place of scripture, that it be repugnant to another. Wherefore, although the church be a witness and a keeper of holy writ, yet, as it ought not to decree any thing against the same, so besides the same ought it not to enforce any thing to be believed for necessity of salvation.

21 *Of the authority of general councils*

General councils may not be gathered together without the commandment and will of princes. And when they be gathered together (forasmuch as they be an assembly of men, whereof all be not governed with the spirit and word of God), they may err, and sometimes have erred, even in things pertaining unto God. Wherefore things ordained by them as necessary to salvation have neither strength nor authority, unless it may be declared that they be taken out of Holy Scripture.

22 *Of purgatory*

The Romish doctrine concerning purgatory, pardons, worshipping and adoration as well of images as of relics, and also invocation of saints, is a fond thing, vainly invented, and grounded upon no warranty of scripture, but rather repugnant to the word of God.

23 *Of ministering in the congregation*

It is not lawful for any man to take upon him the office of public preaching, or ministering the sacraments in the congregation, before he be lawfully called and sent to execute the same. And those we ought to judge lawfully called and sent, which be chosen and called to this work by men who have public authority given unto them in the congregation, to call and send ministers into the Lord's vineyard.

24 *Of speaking in the congregation in such a tongue as the people understandeth*

It is a thing plainly repugnant to the word of God, and the custom of the primitive church, to have public prayer in the church, or to minister the sacraments in a tongue not understood of the people.

25 Of the sacraments

Sacraments ordained of Christ be not only badges or tokens of Christian men's profession, but rather they be certain sure witnesses and effectual signs of grace and God's good will towards us, by which he doth work invisibly in us, and doth not only quicken, but also strengthen and confirm our faith in him.

There are two sacraments ordained of Christ Our Lord in the gospel, that is to say, baptism, and the supper of the Lord. Those five commonly called sacraments, that is to say, confirmation, penance, orders, matrimony, and extreme unction, are not to be counted for sacraments of the gospel, being such as have grown partly of the corrupt following of the apostles, partly are states of life allowed in the scriptures; but yet have not like nature of sacraments with baptism and the Lord's Supper, for that they have not any visible sign or ceremony ordained of God.

The sacraments were not ordained of Christ to be gazed upon, or to be carried about, but that we should duly use them. And in such only as worthily receive the same they have a wholesome effect or operation: but they that receive them unworthily, purchase to themselves damnation, as St Paul saith.

26 Of the unworthiness of the ministers, which hinders not the effect of the sacrament

Although in the visible church the evil be ever mingled with the good, and sometime the evil have chief authority in the ministration of the word and sacraments, yet forasmuch as they do not the same in their own name, but in Christ's, and do minister by his commission and authority, we may use their ministry, both in hearing the word of God, and in the receiving of the sacraments. Neither is the effect of Christ's ordinance taken away by their wickedness, nor the grace of God's gifts diminished from such as by faith and rightly do receive the sacraments ministered unto them; which be effectual, because of Christ's institution and promise, although they be ministered by evil men.

Nevertheless, it appertaineth to the discipline of the church, that enquiry be made of evil ministers, and that they be accused by those that have knowledge of their offences; and finally being found guilty, by just judgment be deposed.

27 Of baptism

Baptism is not only a sign of profession, and mark of difference, whereby Christian men are discerned from others that be not christened, but it is also a sign of regeneration or new birth, whereby, as by an instrument, they that receive baptism rightly are grafted into the church; the promises of forgiveness of sin, and of our adoption to be the sons of God by the Holy Ghost, are visibly signed and sealed; faith is confirmed, and grace increased by virtue of prayer unto God. The baptism of young children is in any wise to be retained in the church, as most agreeable with the institution of Christ.

28 Of the Lord's Supper

The supper of the Lord is not only a sign of the love that Christians ought to have among themselves one to another; but rather it is a sacrament of our redemption by Christ's death: insomuch that to such as rightly, worthily, and with faith, receive the same, the bread which we break is a partaking of the body of Christ; and likewise the cup of blessing is a partaking of the blood of Christ.

Transubstantiation (or the change of the substance of bread and wine) in the supper of the Lord, cannot be proved by holy writ, but is repugnant to the plain words of scripture, overthroweth the nature of a sacrament, and hath given occasion to many superstitions. The body of Christ is given, taken, and eaten, in the supper, only after an heavenly and spiritual manner. And the mean whereby the body of Christ is received and eaten in the supper is faith.

The sacrament of the Lord's supper was not by Christ's ordinance reserved, carried about, lifted up, or worshipped.

29 Of the wicked which do not eat the body of Christ in the use of the Lord's Supper

The wicked, and such as be void of a lively faith, although they do carnally and visibly press with their teeth (as St Augustine saith) the sacrament of the body and blood of Christ, yet in no wise are they partakers of Christ: but rather, to their condemnation, do eat and drink the sign or sacrament of so great a thing.

30 Of both kinds

The cup of the Lord is not to be denied to the lay-people: for both the parts of the Lord's sacrament, by Christ's ordinance and commandment, ought to be ministered to all Christian men alike.

31 Of the one oblation of Christ finished upon the cross

The offering of Christ once made is the perfect redemption, propitiation, and satisfaction, for all the sins of the whole world, both original and actual: and there is none other satisfaction for sin, but that alone. Wherefore the sacrifices of masses, in the which it was commonly said, that the priest did offer Christ for the quick and the dead, to have remission of pain or guilt, were blasphemous fables, and dangerous deceits.

32 Of the marriage of priests

Bishops, priests, and deacons, are not commanded by God's law, either to vow the estate of single life, or to abstain from marriage: therefore it is lawful also for them, as for all other Christian men, to marry at their own discretion, as they shall judge the same to serve better to godliness.

33 *Of excommunicate persons, how they are to be avoided*

That person which by open denunciation of the church is rightly cut off from the unity of the church, and excommunicated, ought to be taken of the whole multitude of the faithful, as an heathen and publican, until he be openly reconciled by penance, and received into the church by a judge that hath authority thereunto.

34 *Of the traditions of the church*

It is not necessary that traditions and ceremonies be in all places one, or utterly like; for at all times they have been divers, and may be changed according to the diversity of countries, times, and men's manners, so that nothing be ordained against God's word. Whosoever through his private judgment, willingly and purposely, doth openly break the traditions and ceremonies of the church, which be not repugnant to the word of God, and be ordained and approved by common authority, ought to be rebuked openly (that other may fear to do the like) as he that offendeth against the common order of the church, and hurteth the authority of the magistrate, and woundeth the consciences of the weak brethren.

Every particular or national church hath authority to ordain, change, and abolish ceremonies or rites of the church ordained only by man's authority, so that all things be done to edifying.

35 *Of homilies*

The second Book of Homilies . . . doth contain a godly and wholesome doctrine, and necessary for these times, as doth the former Book of Homilies, which were set forth in the time of Edward the Sixth; and therefore we judge them to be read in churches by the ministers, diligently and distinctly, that they may be understanded of the people. . . .

36 *Of Consecration of bishops and ministers*

The book of Consecration of Archbishops and Bishops, and Ordering of Priests and Deacons, lately set forth in the time of Edward the Sixth, and confirmed at the same time by authority of parliament, doth contain all things necessary to such consecration and ordering: neither hath it any thing, that of itself is superstitious or ungodly. And therefore, whosoever are consecrated or ordered according to the rites of that book, since the second year of the aforenamed King Edward unto this time, or hereafter shall be consecrated or ordered according to the same rites; we decree all such to be rightly, orderly, and lawfully consecrated and ordered.

37 *Of the civil magistrates*

The queen's majesty hath the chief power in this realm of England and other her dominions, unto whom the chief government of all estates of this realm, whether they be ecclesiastical or civil, in all causes doth appertain, and is not, nor ought to be, subject to any foreign jurisdiction.

Where we attribute to the queen's majesty the chief government, by which titles we understand the minds of some slanderous folks to be offended, we give not to our princes the ministering either of God's word, or of the sacraments, the which thing the Injunctions also lately set forth by Elizabeth our queen do most plainly testify; but that only prerogative, which we see to have been given always to all godly princes in Holy Scriptures by God himself; that is, that they should rule all estates and degrees committed to their charge by God, whether they be ecclesiastical or temporal, and restrain with the civil sword the stubborn and evil-doers.

The Bishop of Rome hath no jurisdiction in this realm of England. The laws of the realm may punish Christian men with death, for heinous and grievous offences. It is lawful for Christian men, at the commandment of the magistrate, to wear weapons, and serve in the wars.

38 *Of Christian men's goods which are not common*

The riches and goods of Christians are not common, as touching the right, title, and possession of the same, as certain Anabaptists do falsely boast. Notwithstanding, every man ought, of such things as he possesseth, liberally to give alms to the poor, according to his ability.

39 *Of a Christian man's oath*

As we confess that vain and rash swearing is forbidden Christian men by Our Lord Jesus Christ, and James his apostle, so we judge, that Christian religion doth not prohibit, but that a man may swear when the magistrate requireth, in a cause of faith and charity, so it be done according to the prophet's teaching, in justice, judgment, and truth.

Works and Salvation

The relationship between works and salvation was a contested one in the Christian world in general, and among puritans. While denying that works had any role in determining if one was saved—all men merited only damnations and God's selection of those who would be saved had no connection to actual behavior—most puritans did believe that redemption carried with it sanctification, so that a good life signified the likelihood that one was saved. Anne Hutchinson believed that such beliefs undermined the doctrine of free grace and attacked those who espoused such views as in essence arguing a form of the Covenant of Works.

Perhaps no one better expressed the mainstream puritan position than Robert Keayne. Keayne, a merchant in London and then in Massachusetts, had been criticized by many for his business practices. In the opening pages of his lengthy will, often referred to as his "Apologia," he set forth his understanding of the relationship between works and salvation

Source: modernized from the transcribed text in Bernard Bailyn, editor, *The Apologia of Robert Keayne: The Self-Portrait of a Puritan Merchant* (New York, 1964).

I do further desire from my heart to renounce all confidence or expectation of merit or desert in any of the best duties or services that ever I have, shall, or can be able to perform, acknowledging that all my righteousness, sanctification, and close walking with God, if it were or had been a thousand times more exact than ever yet I attained to, is all polluted and corrupt and falls short of commending me to God in point of my justification or helping forth my redemption or salvation. They deserve nothing at God's hand but hell and condemnation if he should enter into judgment with me for them. And though I believe that all my ways of holiness are of no use to me in point of justification, yet I believe they may not be neglected by me without great sin, but are ordained by God for me to walk in them carefully, in love to Him, in obedience to His commandments, as well as for many other good ends. They are good fruits and evidences of justification. Therefore, renouncing though not the acts yet all confidence in those acts of holiness and works of sanctification performed by me, I look for my acceptance with God and the salvation of my soul only from the merits or righteousness of the Lord Jesus Christ, and from the free, bountiful, and undeserved grace and love of God in him.

Worship in Massachusetts

Thomas Lechford arrived in Boston, Massachusetts in 1638. He had some training in the law, perhaps in one of England's Inns of Chancery, and tried to support himself as an attorney and solicitor, drawing up legal documents. He was at odds with the civil authorities over his efforts to practice law, and his religious views clashed with some of the clergy. He left the colony in 1641, returning to England, where he published Plain Dealing: or, Newes from New England *(1642). Despite his criticisms of New England, he is generally considered to have been a fair reporter of the colonial practices. The following is one of the few contemporary descriptions of church worship.*

Source: Thomas Lechford, *Plain Dealing: or, Newes from New England* (1642).

The public worship is in as fair a meetinghouse as they can provide, wherein, in most places, they have been at great charges. Every Sabbath or Lord's Day, they come together at Boston by ringing of a bell, about nine of the clock or before.

The pastor begins with solemn prayer, continuing about a quarter of an hour. The teacher then reads and expounds a chapter [in the Bible]. Then a psalm is sung, whichever one of the ruling elders dictates. After that the pastor preaches a sermon, and sometimes extemporaneously exhorts. Then the teacher concludes with prayer and a blessing.

Once a month is a sacrament of the Lords Supper, whereof notice is given usually a fortnight before, and then all others departing save the Church, which is a great deal less in number than those that go away, they receive the sacrament, the ministers and ruling elders sitting at the table, the rest in their seats, or upon forms. . . . The one of the teaching elders prays before, and blesseth, and consecrates the bread and wine, according to the words of institution; the other prays after the receiving of all the members. . . . The ministers deliver the brad in a charger [platter] to some of the chief, . . . and they deliver the charger from one to another, till all have eaten; in like manner the cup, till all have drank. Anyone, though not of the church, may, in Boston, come in and see the sacrament administered if he will. But none of any church in the country may receive the sacrament there without leave of the congregation, for which purpose he comes to one of the ruling elders, who propounds his name to the congregation before they go to the sacrament.

About two in the afternoon they repair to the meetinghouse again. The pastor begins, as before noon, and a psalm being sung, the teacher makes a sermon. He was wont, when I first came, to read and expound a chapter [of scripture] also before his sermon in the afternoon. After and before his sermon, he prays.

After that ensues Baptism, if there be any, which is done by either pastor or teacher in the Deacon's seat, the most eminent place in the church, next under the elders seat. The pastor most commonly makes a speech or exhortation to the church and parents concerning baptism, and then prays before and after. It is done by washing or sprinkling. One of the parents being [a member] of the church, the child may be baptized, and the baptism is in the name of the Father, and of the Son, and of the Holy Ghost. No sureties [godparents] are required.

[Baptism] being ended, [there] follows the contribution, one of the deacons saying, "Brethren of the congregation, now there is time left for contribution. Wherefore as God hath prospered you, so freely offer." Upon some extraordinary occasions, as building and repairing of churches and meetinghouses, or other necessities, the ministers press a liberal contribution, with effectual exhortations out of Scripture. The magistrates and chief gentlemen first, and then the elders, and all the congregation of men and most of them that are not of the church, all single persons, widows, and women in absence of their husbands, come up one after another one way and bring their offerings to the deacon at his seat, and put it into a box of wood [provided] for the purpose,

if it be money or papers. If it be any other chattel, they set it or lay it down before the deacons, and so pass another way to their seats again . . .. I have seen a fair gilt cup with a cover, offered there by one [of the congregation, probably John Winthrop], which is still used at the communion. Which moneys and goods the deacons dispose towards the maintenance of the ministers and the poor of the church, and the church's occasions, without making account ordinarily . . . .

This done, then follows admission of members, or hearing matters of offence, or other things, sometimes till it be very late. If they have time, after this is sung a psalm, and then the pastor concludes with a prayer and a blessing.

Upon the weekdays there are lectures in divers towns, and in Boston upon Thursdays, when Master Cotton teaches out of the [Book of] Revelation. There are days of fasting, thanksgiving, and prayers upon occasions, but no holydays, except the Sunday.

Bibliography

The literature on puritanism is vast, and listing every relevant work would require doubling the size of this encyclopedia. This bibliography concentrates on works published since 1990, though some earlier works of particular value are also included. Discussions of earlier work on American Puritanism may be found in Michael McGiffert, "American Puritan Studies in the 1960s," *William and Mary Quarterly,* 3rd series, 27 (1970), 36–67; David D. Hall, "On Common Ground: The Coherence of American Puritan Studies," *William and Mary Quarterly,* 3rd series, 44 (1987), 193–229; and Charles L. Cohen, "The Post-Puritan Paradigm of Early American Religious History," *William and Mary Quarterly,* 3rd series, 54 (1997), 695–722. Good places to start to review the literature on British themes are Ronald Hutton, *Debates in Stuart History* (2004); Christopher Haigh, "The Recent Historiography of the English Reformation," in Margo Todd, ed., *Reformation to Revolution: Politics and Religion in Early Modern England* (London, 1995); and the relevant sections of Michael Bentley, ed., *Companion to Historiography* (London, 1997).

Achinstein, Sharon, *Literature and Dissent in Milton's England* (Cambridge, Eng., 2003).

Adair, John, *Puritans: Religion and Politics in Seventeenth-Century England and America,* new edition (Stroud, Eng.,1998).

Adams, Simon, "A Godly Peer? Leicester and the Puritans," *History Today* 40 (1990), 14–19.

Alsop, James Douglas, "Revolutionary Puritanism in the Parishes? The Case of St Olave, Old Jewry," *London Journal* 15 (1990), 29–37.

Aston, Margaret, "Puritans and Iconoclasm, 1560–1660," in Christopher Durston and Jacqueline Eales, eds., *The Culture of English Puritanism, 1560–1700* (Basingstoke, Eng., 1996).

Baker, Norman, "Going to the Dogs – Hostility to Greyhound Racing in Britain: Puritanism, Socialism, and Pragmatism," *Journal of Sport History* 23 (1996), 97–119.

Baskerville, Steven, "The Family in Puritan Political Theology," *Journal of Family History* 18 (1993), 157–177.

Baskerville, Steven K., "Puritans, Revisionists, and the English Revolution," *Huntington Library Quarterly* 61 (2000), 151–171.

Bellany, Alastair, "A Poem on the Archbishop's Hearse: Puritanism, Libel, and Sedition after the Hampton Court Conference," *Journal of British Studies* 34 (1995), 137–164.

Bendall, A. Sarah, Christopher Nugent Lawrence Brooke, Patrick Collinson, *A History of Emmanuel College, Cambridge* (Woodbridge, Eng., 2000).

Black, Joseph, "The Rhetoric of Reaction: the Martin Marprelate Tracts (1588–89) and anti-Martinism," *Sixteenth century Journal,* 28 (1997), 717–725.

Blackwood, B. G., "Parties and Issues in the Civil War in Lancashire and East Anglia," in Roger Richardson, ed., *The English Civil Wars: Local Aspects* (Stroud, Eng., 1997).

Boran, Elizabeth Anne, "An Early Friendship Network of James Usher, Archbishop of Armagh, 1626–1656," in Helga Hammerstein, ed., *European Universities in the Age of Reformation and Counter-Reformation* (Dublin, 1998).

Botelho, Lynn A., *Old Age and the Enklish Poor Law, 1500–1700* (Woodbridge, Eng., 2004).

Botonaki, Effie, "Seventeenth-Century Englishwomen's Spiritual Diaries," *Sixteenth Century Journal* 30 (1999), 3–21.

Bozeman, T. D., "The Glory of the 'Third Time': John Eaton as Contra-Puritan," *Journal of Ecclesiastical History* 47 (1996), 638–654.

Braddick, Michael J., and John Walter, "Introduction. Grids of Power: Order, Hierarchy and Subordination in Early Modern Society," in Michael J. Braddick and John Walter, ed., *Negotiating Power in Early Modern Society: Order, Hierarchy and Subordination in Britain and Ireland* (Cambridge, Eng., 2001).

Brautigam, Dwight, "Prelates and Politics: Uses of 'Puritan' 1625–40," in Laura Lunger Knoppers, ed., *Puritanism and Its Discontents* (Newark, DE, 2003).

Breen, Louise A., *Transgressing the Bounds: Subversive Enterprises mong the Puritan Elite in Massachusetts, 1630–1692* (New York, 2001).

Bremer, Francis J., *Congregational Communion: Clerical Friendship in the Anglo-American Puritan Community* (Boston, 1994).

———, "The County of Massachusetts: the Governance of John Winthrop's Suffolk and the Shaping of the Massachusetts Bay Colony," in Francis J. Bremer and Lynn Botelho, eds., *The World of John Winthrop: England and New England, 1588–1649* (Boston, 2005).

———, *John Winthrop: America's Forgotten Founding Father* (New York, 2003).

———, *The Puritan Experiment: New England Society from Bradford to Edwards*, rev. ed. (Hanover, NH, 1995).

———, "Puritan Studies: the Case for an Atlantic Approach," in Francis J. Bremer, ed., *Puritanism: Transatlantic Perspectives on a Seventeenth-Century Anglo-American Faith* (Boston, 1994).

———, ed., *Puritanism: Transatlantic Perspectives on a Seventeenth-Century Anglo-American Faith* (Boston, 1994).

———, "Remembering—and Forgetting—John Winthrop and the Puritan Founders," *Massachusetts Historical Review* 6 (2004), 38–69.

———, *Shaping New Englands: Puritan Clergymen in Seventeenth-Century England and New England* (New York, 1994).

———, "William Winthrop and Religious Reform in London, 1529–1582," *London Journal* 24 (1999).

Bremer, Francis J., and Lynn A. Botelho, "Atlantic History in the World of John Winthrop," in Francis J. Bremer and Lynn Botelho, eds., *The World of John Winthrop: England and New England, 1588–1649* (Boston, 2005).

———, eds., *The World of John Winthrop: England and New England, 1588–1649* (Boston, 2005).

Bremer, Francis J., and Ellen Rydell, "Performance Art? Puritans in the Pulpit," *History Today* 45 (1995), 50–54.

Breslaw, Elaine, *Tituba: Reluctant Witch of Salem* (New York, 1996).

Brown, Sylvia, "The Eloquence of the Word and the Spirit: The Place Of Puritan Women's Writings in Old and New England," in Susan E. Dinan and Debra Meyers, ed., *Women and Religion in Old and New Worlds* (New York, 2001).

Bruhn, Karen, "Pastoral Polemic: William Perkins, the Godly Evangelicals, and the Shaping of a Protestant Community in Early Modern England," *Anglican and Episcopal History* 72:1 (2003), 102–127.

Burgess, Glenn, "Was the Civil War a War of Religion? The Evidence of Political Propaganda," *Huntington Library Quarterly* 61 (2000 for 1998), 173–201.

Bush, Sargent, Jr., "Epistolary Counseling in the Puritan Movement: The Example of John Cotton," in Francis J. Bremer, ed., *Puritanism: Transatlantic Perspectives on a Seventeenth-Century Anglo-American Faith* (Boston, 1994).

———, "Satisfying Cromwell's Curiosity: John Wilson on John Cotton and New England Fauna," *New England Quarterly* 76 (2003), 108–115.

Carlin, Norah, "Toleration for Catholics in the Puritan Revolution," in Ole Peter Grell and Robert Scribner, eds., *Tolerance and Intolerance in the European Reformation* (Cambridge, Eng., 1996).

Carpenter, John, "New England's Puritan Century: Three Generations of Continuity in the City upon a Hill," *Fides et Historia* 35 (2003), 41–58.

Carson, John T., "From Thomas Cartwright to John Howe: Some Puritans who came among us," *Bulletin of the Presbyterian Historical Society of Ireland* 19 (1990), 3–28.

Coffey, John, *Persecution and Toleration in Protestant England, 1558–1689* (Harlow, Eng., 2000).

Cogley, Richard, "The Fall of the Ottoman Empire and the Restoration of Israel in the 'Judeo-Centric' Strand of Puritan Millenarianism," *Church History* 72 (2003), 304–332.

———, *John Eliot's Mission to the Indians before King Philip's War* (Cambridge, MA, 1999).

Cohen, Charles L., "Conversion among Puritans and Amerindians: A Theological and Cultural Perspective," in Francis J. Bremer, ed., *Puritanism: Transatlantic Perspectives on a Seventeenth-Century Anglo-American Faith* (Boston, 1994).

———, *God's Caress: The Psychology of Puritan Religious Experience* (New York, 1986).

Cohen, Matt, "Morton's Maypole and the Indians: Publishing in Early New England," *Book History* 5 (2002), 1–18.

Collinson, Patrick, *The Birthpangs of Protestant England* (Basingstoke, Eng., 1988).

———, "Christian Socialism in Elizabethan Suffolk: Thomas Carew and his *Caveat for Clothiers*," in

Richard G. Wilson et al., eds., *Counties and Communities: Essays on East Anglian History* (Norwich, Eng., 1996).

———, "The Cohabitation of the Faithful with the Unfaithful," in O. P. Grell, Jonathan Israel, and Nicholas Tyacke, eds., *From Persecution to Toleration: The Glorious Revolution and Religion in England* (Oxford, 1991).

———, "Ecclesiastical Vitriol: Religious Satire in the 1590s and the Invention of Puritanism," in John Guy, ed., *The Reign of Elizabeth I* (Cambridge, Eng., 1995).

———, "Elizabethan and Jacobean Puritanism as Forms of Popular Religious Culture," in Christopher Durston and Jacqueline Eales, eds., *The Culture of English Puritanism, 1560–1700* (Basingstoke, Eng., 1996).

———, *Elizabethan Essays* (London, 1994).

———, *The Elizabethan Puritan Movement* (London, 1987).

———, *Godly People* (1983).

———, "Puritanism and the poor," in Rosemary Horrox and Sarah Rees Jones, ed., *Pragmatic Utopias: Ideals and Communities, 1200–1630* (Cambridge, Eng., 2001).

———, *The Religion of Protestants* (Oxford, 1982).

———, "Sects and the Evolution of Puritanism," in Francis J. Bremer, ed., *Puritanism: Transatlantic Perspectives on a Seventeenth-Century Anglo-American Faith* (Boston, 1994).

———, "The Shearman's Tree and the Preacher: the Strange Death of Merry England in Shrewsbury and Beyond," in Patrick Collinson and John Craig, eds., *The Reformation in English Towns, 1500–1640* (Basingstoke, Eng., 1998).

———, "The Theatre Contructs Puritanism," in David L. Smith, Richard Strier, and David Bevington, eds., *The Theatrical City* (Cambridge, Eng., 1995).

———, "The Vertical and the Horizontal in Religious History: Internal and External Integration of the Subject," in Alan Ford, James McGuire, and Kenneth Milne, eds., *As By Law Established: the Church of Ireland since the Reformation* (Dublin, 1995).

Collinson, Patrick, John Craig, Brett Usher, ed., *Conferences and combination lectures in the Elizabethan church: Dedham and Bury St Edmunds, 1582–1590* (Woodbridge, Eng., 2003).

Como, David R., "The Kingdom of Christ, the Kingdom of England, and the Kingdom of John Traske," in Muriel McClendon, et al., *Protestant Identities* (Stanford, 1999).

———, "Predestination and Political Conflict in Laud's London," *Historical Journal* 46:2 (2003), 263–94.

———, "Puritans, Predestination and the Construction of Orthodoxy in Early Seventeenth-Century England," in Peter Lake and Michael Questier, eds., *Conformity and Orthodoxy in the English Church, c. 1560–1660* (Woodbridge, Eng., 2000).

———, "Women, Prophecy, and Authority in Early Stuart Puritanism," *Huntington Library Quarterly* 61 (1998), 203–222.

Como, David R., and Peter Lake, "Puritans, Antinomians in Caroline London," *Journal of Ecclesiastical History* 50 (1999), 684–715.

Cooper, Trevor, ed., *The Journal of William Dowsing: Iconoclasm in East Anglia during the English Civil War,* Ecclesiastical Society (Woodbridge, Eng., 2001).

Coster, William, "Purity, Profanity, and Puritanism: the Churching of Women, 1500–1700," in William J. Sheils and Diana Wood, eds., *Women in the Church on the Eve of the Dissolution,* Studies in Church History, vol. 27 (Oxford, 1990).

Coulton, Barbara, "The Establishment of Protestantism in a Provincial Town: a Study of Shrewsbury in the Sixteenth-Century," *Sixteenth Century Journal* 27 (1996), 307–335.

———, "Rivalry and Religion: The Borough of Shrewsbury in the Early Stuart Period," *Midland History* 28 (2003), 28–50.

Coward, Barry, *Oliver Cromwell* (London, 1991).

Cox, Geoffrey, *The Rediscovery and Renewal of the Local Church: The Puritan Vision* (London, 1992).

Craig, John, "The Bury Stirs Revisited: an Analysis of the Townsmen," *Proceedings of the Suffolk Institute of Archaeology and History* 37 (1991), 208–224.

———, "The 'godly' and the 'froward': Protestant Polemics in the Town of Thetford, 1560–590," *Norfolk Archaeology* 41 (1992), 279–293.

———, *Reformation, Politics, and Polemics: the Growth of Protestantism in East Anglian Market Towns, 1500-1610* (Aldershot, Eng., 2001).

Cressy, David, "The Vast and Furious Ocean: The Passage to Puritan New England," *New England Quarterly* 57 (1984), 511–532.

Cross, Claire, "A Man of Conscience in Seventeenth-Century Urban Politics: Alderman Hoyle of York," in John S. Morrill, Paul Slack, and Daniel Woolf, eds., *Public Duty and Private Conscience in Seventeenth-Century England* (Oxford, 1992).

———, "Religion in Doncaster from the Reformation to the Civil War," in Patrick Collinson and John Craig, eds., *The Reformation in English Towns, 1500–1640* (Basingstoke, Eng., 1998).

Cust, Richard, "Anti-Puritanism and Urban Politics: Charles I and Great Yarmouth," *Historical Journal* 35 (1992), 1–26.

Damrosch, Leopold, *The Sorrows of the Quaker Jesus: James Naylor and the Puritan Crackdown* (Cambridge, MA, 1996).

Danner, Dan G., *Pilgrimage to Puritanism: History and Theology of the Marian Exiles at Geneva, 1555–1560* (New York, 1999).

Davies, Bernard, *Samuel Collins of Braintree* (Braintree, Eng., 1997).

Davies, Horton, *Worship and Theology in England*, 3 vols. (Princeton, 1996).

Davies, Julian, *The Caroline Captivity of the Church: Charles I and the Remoulding of Anglicanism* (Oxford, 1992).

Davis, J. C., "Cromwell's Religion," in John S. Morrill, ed., *Oliver Cromwell and the Puritan Revolution* (London, 1990).

Dever, Michael, "Moderation and Deprivation: Reappraisal of Richard Sibbes," *Journal of Ecclesiastical History* 43 (1992), 396–413.

———, *Richard Sibbes: Puritanism and Calvinism in Late Elizabethan and Early Stuart England* (Macon, GA, 2000).

Donagan, Barbara, "The York House Conference Revisited: Laymen, Calvinism, and Arminianism," *Historical Research* 64 (1991), 312–330.

Duffy, Eamon, "The Reformed Pastor in English Puritanism," *Nederlands Archief voor Kerkgeschiendeis* 83 (2004), 216–234.

Durston, Christopher, *Cromwell's Major Generals: Godly Government during the English Revolution* (Manchester, Eng., 2001).

———, "Puritan Rule and the Failure of Cultural Revolution, 1645–1660," in Christopher Durston and Jacqueline Eales, eds., *The Culture of English Puritanism, 1560–1700* (Basingstoke, Eng., 1996).

Durston, Christopher and Jacqueline Eales, eds., *The Culture of English Puritanism, 1560–1700* (Basingstoke, Eng., 1996).

———, "The Puritan Ethos, 1560–1700," in Christopher Durston and Jacqueline Eales, eds., *The Culture of English Puritanism, 1560–1700* (Basingstoke, Eng., 1996).

Eales, Jacqueline, "Iconoclasm, Iconography, and the Altar in the English Civil War," in Diana Wood, ed., *The Church and Sovereignty, c. 590–1918* (Oxford, 1991).

———, "Patriarchy, Puritanism and Politics: The Letters of Lady Brilliana Harley (1598–1643)," in James Daybell, ed., *Early Modern Women's Letter Writing, 1450–1700* (Basingstoke, Eng., 2001).

———, *Puritans and Roundheads: The Harleys of Brampton Bryan and the Outbreak of the English Civil War* (Cambridge, Eng., 1990).

———, "The Rise of Ideological Politics in Kent, 1558–1640," in Michael Zell, ed., *Early Modern Kent, 1540–1640* (Woodbridge, Eng., 2000).

———, "A Road to Revolution: The Continuity of Puritanism, 1559–1642," in Christopher Durston and Jacqueline Eales, eds., *The Culture of English Puritanism, 1560–1700* (Basingstoke, Eng.,1996).

———, "Samuel Clarke and the 'Lives' of Godly Women in Seventeenth-Century England," in William J. Sheils and Diana Wood, eds., *Women in the Church on the Eve of the Dissolution*, Studies in Church History, vol. 27 (Oxford, 1990).

———, "Thomas Pierson and the Transmission of the Moderate Puritan Tradition," *Midland History* 20 (1995), 75–102.

Ferrell, Lori Anne, *Government by Polemic: James I, the King's Preachers, and the Rhetoric of Conformity* (Stanford, 1998).

———, "Kneeling and the Body Poilitic," in Donna B. Hamilton and Richard Strier, eds., *Religion, Literacy and Politics in Post-Reformation England* (Cambridge, Eng., 1996).

———, "Transfiguring Theology: William Perkins and Calvinist Aesthetics," in Christopher Highley and John King, eds., *John Foxe and His World* (Aldershot, Eng., 2002).

Ferrell, Lori Anne, and Peter McCullough, "Revising the Study of the English Sermon," in Lori Anne Ferrell, ed., *The English Sermon Revised: Religion, Literature and History, 1600–1750* (Manchester, Eng., 2001).

Fielding, John, "Arminianism and the Localities: Peterborough Diocese, 1603–1642," in Kenneth Fincham, ed., *The Early Stuart Church* (Basingstoke, Eng., 1993).

Fincham, Kenneth, "Clerical Conformity from Whitgift to Laud," in Peter Lake and Michael C. Questier, ed., *Conformity and Orthodoxy in the English Church, c. 1560–1660* (Woodbridge, Eng., 2000).

———, "William Laud and the Exercise of Caroline Ecclesiastical Patronage," *Journal of Ecclesiastical History* 51 (2000), 69–93.

Fincham, Kenneth, and Peter Lake, "Popularity, Prelacy, and Puritanism in the 1630s: Joseph Hall Explains Himself," *Historical Review* 111 (1996), 856–881.

Fletcher, Anthony, "Oliver Cromwell and the Godly Nation," in John S. Morrill, ed., *Oliver Cromwell and the Puritan Revolution* (London, 1990).

———, "The Protestant Idea of Marriage in Early Modern England," in Anthony Fletcher and Peter Roberts, eds., *Religion, Culture and Society in Early Modern Britain* (Cambridge, Eng., 1994).

Ford, Alan, "The Church of Ireland, 1558–1634: A Puritan Church?" in Alan Ford, James McGuire, and Kenneth Milne, eds., *As By Law Established: The Church of Ireland since the Reformation* (Dublin, 1995).

Foster, Andrew, "Archbishop Richard Neile Revisited," in Peter Lake and Michael C. Questier, eds., *Conformity and Orthodoxy in the English Church, c. 1560–1660* (Woodbridge, Eng., 2000).

Foster, Stephen, *The Long Argument: English Puritanism and the Shaping of New England Culture, 1570–1700* (Chapel Hill, 1991).

———, "Not What but How – Thomas Minor and the Ligatures of Puritanism," in Francis J. Bremer, ed., *Puritanism: Transatlantic Perspectives on a Seventeenth-Century Anglo-American Faith* (Boston, 1994).

Francis, Richard, *Judge Sewall's Apology: The Salem Witch Trials & the Forming of an American Conscience* (New York, 2005).

Freeman, Thomas, "Demons, Deviance and Defiance: John Darrell and the Politics of Exorcism in Late Elizabethan England," in Peter Lake and Michael C. Questier, eds., *Conformity and Orthodoxy in the English Church, c. 1560–1660* (Woodbridge, Eng., 2000).

George, C. H., "Parnassus Restored, Saints Confounded: The Secular Challenge to the Age of the Godly, 1560–1660," *Albion* 23 (1991), 409–437.

Gildrie, Richard P., "Visions of Evil: Popular Culture, Puritanism and the Massachusetts Witchcraft Crisis of 1692," *Journal of American Culture* 8 (1990), 17–33.

Godbeer, Richard, *Escaping Salem: The Other Witch Hunt of 1692* (New York, 2004).

———, "Performing Patriarchy: Gendered Roles and Hierarchies in Early Modern England and Seventeenth-Century England," in Francis J. Bremer and Lynn Botelho, eds., *The World of John Winthrop: England and New England, 1588–1649* (Boston, 2005).

———, *Sexual Revolution in Early America* Baltimore, 2002).

Grace, Frank, "'Schismaticall and Factious Humours': Opposition in Ipswich to Laudian Church Government," in David Chadd, ed., *History of Religious Dissent in East Anglia, III: Proceedings of the Third Symposium* (Norwich, Eng., 1996).

Gragg, Larry Dale, "A Puritan in the West Indies: the Career of Stephen Winthrop," *William and Mary Quarterly*, 3rd series, 50 (1993), 768–786.

Graham, Judith S., *Puritan Family Life: The Diary of Samuel Sewall* (Boston, 2000)

Greaves, Richard, *John Bunyan and English Nonconformity* (London, 1992).

Green, Ian, "'Puritan Prayer Books' and 'Geneva Bibles': An Episode in Elizabethan Publishing," *Transactions of the Cambridge Bibliographical Society* 11 (1998), 313–349.

Grell, O. P., Jonathan Israel, and Nicholas Tyacke, eds., *From Persecution to Toleration: The Glorious Revolution and Religion in England* (Oxford, 1991).

Gribben, Crawford, "Defining the Puritans? The Baptism Debate in Cromwellian Ireland, 1654–56," *Church History* 73 (2004), 63–89.

Haigh, Christopher, "The Taming of Reformation: Preachers, Pastors and Parishioners in Elizabethan and Early Stuart England," *History* 85:280 (2000), 572–588.

Hall, David D., *Worlds of Wonder, Days of Judgement* (Cambridge, MA, 1990).

Hall, David D., and Alexandra Walsham, "Communication in the Anglo-American World of John Winthrop," in Francis J. Bremer and Lynn Botelho, eds., *The World of John Winthrop: England and New England, 1588–1649* (Boston, 2005).

Hall, Timothy D. "Assurance, Community, and the Puritan Self in the Antinomian Controversy, 1636–38" in Laura Lunger Knoppers, ed., *Puritanism and Its Discontents* (Newark, DE, 2003).

———, *Separating Church and State: Roger Williams and Religious Liberty* (Chicago, 1998).

Hambrick-Stowe, Charles, *The Practice of Piety: Puritan Devotional Disciplines in Seventeenth-Century New England* (Chapel Hill, 1982).

Hamilton, Gary D., "Smectymnuans, Antiquarians, and Milton: Nationhood in 1641," *Prose Studies* 23 (2000).

Hansford-Miller, Frank, *Elizabethan Puritanism*, vol. 11 of *A History and Geography of English Religion* (Canterbury, Eng., 1992).

Hill, Christopher, *The English Bible in the Seventeenth-Century Revolution* (London, 1993).

Hirst, Derek, "The Failure of Godly Rule in the English Republic," *Past & Present* 132 (1991), 33–66.

Holland, Susan, "Archbishop Abbot and the Problem of 'Puritanism'," *Historical Journal* 37 (1994), 23–43.

Holstun, James, *Ehud's Dagger: Class Struggle in the English Revolution* (New York, 2000).

Hornback, R., "Staging Puritanism in the early 1590s: The Carnivalesque, Rebellious Clown as Anti-Puritan Stereotype," *Renaissance and Reformation*, 24 (2000), 31–68.

Houlbrooke, Ralph, "The Puritan Death-Bed, c. 1560-c. 1660," in Christopher Durston and Jacqueline Eales, eds., *The Culture of English Puritanism, 1560–1700* (Basingstoke, Eng., 1996).

Hudson, Elizabeth K., "The Challenge to Puritan Piety, 1580–1620," *Catholic Historical Review* 77 (1991), 1–20.

———, "The *Plaine Mans* Pastor: Arthur Dent and the Cultivation of Popular Piety in Early Seventeenth-Century England," *Albion* 25 (1993), 23–35.

Hughes, Ann, "Building a Godly Town: Religious and Cultural Division in Stratford-upon-Avon, 1560–1640," in Roberet Bearman, editor, *The History of an English Borough: Stratford-upon-Avon, 1196–1996* (Stroud, Eng., 1997).

———, *The Causes of the English Civil War* (London, 1991).

———, "The Frustrations of the Godly," in John S. Morrill, ed., *Revolution and Restoration: England in the 1650s* (London, 1992).

———, "Local History and the Origins of the Civil War," in Margo Todd, ed., *Reformation to Revolution: Politics and Religion in Early Modern England* (London, 1995).

———, "The Meanings of Religious Polemic," in Francis J. Bremer, ed., *Puritanism: Transatlantic Perspectives on a Seventeenth-Century Anglo-American Faith* (Boston, 1994).

Ingram, Martin, "Puritans and the Church Courts, 1560–1640," in Christopher Durston and Jacqueline Eales, eds., *The Culture of English Puritanism, 1560–1700* (Basingstoke, Eng., 1996).

———, "Reformation of Manners in Early Modern England," in Paul Griffiths, Adam Fox, and Steve Hindle, eds., *The Experience of Authority in Early Modern England* (Basingstoke, Eng., 1996).

Innes, Stephen, *Creating the Commonwealth: Economic Culture of Puritan New England* (New York, 1995).

Jinkins, M., "John Cotton and the Antinomian Controversy, 1636–1638: A Profile of Experiential Individualism in American Puritanism," *Scottish Journal of Theology* 43 (1990), 321–349.

Jones, Gwynfor J., "Some Puritan Influences on the Anglican Church in Wales in the Early Seventeenth Century," *Journal of Welsh Religious History* 2 (2002), 19–50.

Kamensky, Jane, *Governing the Tongue: The Politics of Speech in Early New England* (New York, 1997).

———, "Words, Witches, and Women Trouble: Witchcraft, Disorderly Speech, and Gender Boundaries in Puritan New England," *Essex Institute Historical Collections* 128 (1992), 286–307.

Karr, Ronald Dale, "The Missing Clause: Myth and the Massachusetts Bay Charter of 1629," *New England Quarterly* 77 (2004), 89–107.

Kastan, David Scott, "Performances and Playbooks: The Closing of The Theatres and the Politics of Drama," in Kevin M. Sharpe and Steven N. Zwicker, eds., *Reading, Society and Politics in Early Modern England* (Cambridge, Eng., 2003).

Kaufman, Peter Iver, "Fasting in England in the 1560s: 'A Thinge of Nought'?, *Archiv fur Reformationsgeschichte* 94 (2003), 176–193.

———, "How Socially Conservative Were the Elizabethan Religious Radicals?" *Albion* 30 (1998).

———, *Thinking of the Laity in Late Tudor England* (South Bend, IN, 2004).

———, "Putting Elizabethan Puritans in 'The New Paradigm'", *Anglican and Episcopal History*, 74 (2005), 158-179.

Knapp, Henry M., "John Owen's Interpretation of Hebrews 6:4–6: Eternal Perseverance of the Saints in Puritan Exegesis," *Sixteenth Century Journal* 34:1 (2003), 29–52.

Knoppers, Laura Lunger, ed., *Puritanism and Its Discontents* (Newark, DE, 2003).

Knott, John R., "'A Suffering People': Bunyan and the Language of Martyrdom," in Francis J. Bremer, ed., *Puritanism: Transatlantic Perspectives on a Seventeenth-Century Anglo-American Faith* (Boston, 1994).

Kupperman, Karen Ordahl, *Providence Island, 1630–1641: The Other Puritan Colony* (New York, 1994).

Kusunoki, Akiko, "'Their testament at their apron-strings': The Representation of Puritan Women in Early Seventeenth-Century England," in S. P. Cerasano and Marion Wynne-Davies, eds., *Gloriana's Face* (Detroit, 1992).

Lake, Peter, *Anglicans and Puritans?* (London, 1988).

———, *The Boxmaker's Revenge: "Orthodoxy," "Heterodoxy," and the Politics of the Parish in Early Stuart London* (Manchester, Eng., 2001).

———, "Business as Usual? The Immediate Reception of Hooker's *Ecclesiastical Polity*," *Journal of Ecclesiastical History* 52:3 (2001), 456–486.

———, "Calvinism and the English Church 1570–1635," in Margo Todd, ed., *Reformation to Revolution: Politics and Religion in Early Modern England* (London, 1995).

———, "'A Charitable Christian Hatred': The Godly and Their Enemies in the 1630s," in Christopher Durston and Jacqueline Eales, eds., *The Culture of English Puritanism, 1560–1700* (Basingstoke, Eng., 1996).

———, "Defining Puritanism—Again?" in Francis J. Bremer, ed., *Puritanism: Transatlantic Perspectives on a Seventeenth-Century Anglo-American Faith* (Boston, 1994).

———, "Joseph Hall, Robert Skinner and the Rhetoric of Moderation at the Early Stuart Court," in Lori Anne Ferrell and Peter McCullough, eds., *The English Sermon Revised: Religion, Literature and History, 1600–1750* (Manchester, Eng., 2001).

———, "The Laudians and the Argument from Authority," in B. Y. Kunze and D. Brautigam, eds., *Court, Country and Culture* (Rochester, NY, 1992).

———, "The Laudian Style: Order, Uniformity and the Pursuit of the Beauty of Holiness in the 1630s," in Kenneth Fincham, ed., *The Early Stuart Church* (Basingstoke, Eng., 1993).

———, *Moderate Puritans and the Elizabethan Church* (Cambridge, Eng., 1983).

———, "Moving the Goal Posts? Modified Subscription and the Construction of Conformity in the Early Stuart Church," in Peter Lake and Michael C. Questier, eds., *Conformity and Orthodoxy in the English Church, c. 1560–1660* (Woodbridge, Eng., 2000).

———, "Order, Orthodoxy and Resistance: The Ambiguous Legacy of English Puritanism or Just how moderate was Stephen Denison?" in Michael J. Braddick and John Walter, eds., *Negotiating Power in Early Modern Society: Order, Hierarchy and Subordination in Britain and Ireland* (Cambridge, Eng., 2001).

———, "Popular Form, Puritan Content? Two Puritan Appropriations of the Murder Pamphlet," in Anthony Fletcher and Peter Roberts, eds., *Religion, Culture and Society in Early Modern Britain* (Cambridge, Eng., 1994).

———, "Puritanism, Arminianism, and a Shropshire Axe-Murderer," *Midland History* 15 (1990), 37–64.

———, "Puritans, Popularity and Petitions: Local Politics in National Context, Cheshire, 1641," in Thomas Cogswell, Richard Cust, and Peter Lake, eds., *Politics, Religion and Popularity in Early Stuart Britain: Essays in Honour of Conrad Russell* (Oxford, 2002).

Lake, Peter, and David Como, "'Orthodoxy' and Its Discontents," *Journal of British Studies* 39 (2000), 34–70.

Lake, Peter, and Michael C. Questier, "Agency, Appropriation, and Rhetoric under the Gallows: Puritans, Romanists and the State in Early Modern England," *Past & Present* 153 (1996), 64–107.

———, *The Anti-Christ's Lewd Hat: Protestants, Papists and Players in Post-Reformation England* (New Haven, 2002).

———, "Puritans, Papists, and the 'Public Sphere' in Early Modern England: the Edmund Campion Affair in Context," *Journal of Modern History* 72 (2000), 587–627.

Lamont, William, *Puritanism and Historical Controversy* (London, 1996).

———, "Puritanism, Liberty and the Putney Debates," in Michael Mendle, ed., *The Putney Debates of 1647: The Army, the Levellers and the English State* (Cambridge, Eng., 2001).

———, "The Religious Origins of the English Civil War," in G. J. Schochet et al., *Religion, Resistance, and Civil War* (Washington, 1990).

Lander, J. M., "Martin Marprelate and the Fugitive Text," *Reformation* 7 (2002), 135–186.

Lane, Belden C., "Two Schools of Desire: Nature and Marriage in Seventeenth-Century Puritanism," *Church History* 69:2 (2000), 372–402.

Laurence, Anne, "Daniel's Practice: The Daily Round of Godly Women in Seventeenth-Century England," in Robert Norman Swanson, ed., *The Use and Abuse of Time in Christian History* (Woodbridge, Eng., 2003).

Lee, Colin, "'Fanatic magistrates': Religious and Political Conflict in Three Kent Boroughs, 1680–1684," *Historical Journal* 35 (1992), 43–61.

Lindley, Keith, "Irish Adventurers and Godly Militants in the 1640s," *Irish Historical Studies* 29 (1994), 1–12.

Loewenstein, David, *Representing Revolution in Milton and His Contemporaries: Religion, Politics, and Polemics in Radical Puritanism* (New York, 2001).

Longstaffe, Stephen, "Puritan Tribulation and the Protestant History Play," in Andrew Hadfield, ed., *Literature and Censorship in Renaissance England* (2001).

Love, Harold, "Originality and the Puritan Sermon," in Paulina Kewes, ed., *Plagiarism in Early Modern England* (Basingstoke, Eng., 2003)

Lovejoy, D. S., "Plain Englishmen at Plymouth," *New England Quarterly* 63 (1990), 232–248.

Luttmer, Frank, "Persecutors, Tempters and Vassals of the Devil: The Unregenerate in Puritan Practical Divinity," *Journal of Ecclesiastical History* 51:1 (2000), 37–68.

Lyall, Roderick J., "Alexander Montgomerie, Anti-Calvinist Propagandist?" *Notes and Queries* 49:2 (2002), 210–215.

MacCulloch, Diarmaid, *Building a Godly Realm: the Establishment of English Protestantism, 1558–1603* (London, 1992).

———, *The Later Reformation in England* (Basingstoke, Eng., 1990).

———, "Richard Hooker's Reputation," *English Historical Review* 117:473 (2002), 773–812.

———, *Thomas Cranmer: A Life* (New Haven, 1998).

MacDonald, Michael, "*The Fearefull Estate of Francis Spira:* Narrative, Identity, and Emotion in Early Modern England," *Journal of British Studies* 31 (1992), 32–61.

Maclear, J. F., "Restoration Puritanism and the Idea of Liberty: The Case of Edward Bagshaw," *Journal of Religious History* 16 (1990), 1–17.

Maddux, H. C., "Ruling Passion: Consent and Covenant Theology in Westfield, Massachusetts, August 1679," *Early American Literature* 38 (2003), 9–29.

Main, Gloria L., *Peoples of a Spacious Land: Families and Cultures in Colonial New England* (Cambridge, Eng., 2001).

Marsh, Christopher W., "'Common prayer' in England 1560–1640: The View from the Pew," *Past & Present* 171 (2001), 66–94.

———, *Popular Religion in Sixteenth-Century England* (Basingstoke, Eng., 1998).

———, "Order and Place in England, 1580–1640: The View from the Pew," *Journal of British Studies* 44 (2005), 3–26.

———, "Sacred Space in England, 1560–1640: The View from the Pew," *Journal of Ecclesiastical History* 53 (2002), 286–311.

McGee, J. Sears, "On Misidentifying Puritans: the Case of Thomas Adams," *Albion* 30 (1998), 401–418.

Mears, Natalie, "Counsel, Public Debate, and Queenship: John Stubbs's *The discoverie of a gaping gulf,* 1579," *Historical Journal* 44:3 (2001), 629–650.

Merritt, Julia F., "The cradle of Laudianism? Westminster Abbey, 1558–1630," *Journal of Ecclesiastical History* 52:4 (2001), 623–646.

———, "The Pastoral Tightrope: A Puritan Pedagogue in Jacobean London," in Thomas Cogswell, Richard Cust, and Peter Lake, eds., *Politics and Religion in Early Stuart Britain: Essays in Honour of Conrad Russell* (Oxford, 2002).

Milton, Anthony, "The Creation of Laudianism: A New Approach," in Thomas Cogswell, Richard Cust, and Peter Lake, eds., *Politics, Religion and Popularity in Early Stuart Britain: Essays in Honour of Conrad Russell* (Oxford, 2002).

Moody, Joanna, ed., *The Private Life of an Elizabethan Lady: The Diary of Lady Margaret Hoby, 1599–1605* (1998).

Moore, Susan Hardmann, "Popery, Purity and Providence: Deciphering the New England Experiment," in Anthony Fletcher and Peter Roberts, eds., *Religion, Culture and Society in Early Modern Britain* (Cambridge, Eng., 1994).

———, "Sexing the Soul: Gender and the Rhetoric of Puritan Piety," *Studies in Church History* (1998), 175–186.

Morrill, John S., "The English Church in the Seventeenth Century," *History Review* 30 (1998), 18–23.

———, ed., *The Impact of the English Civil War* (London, 1991).

———, "The Impact of Puritanism," in John S. Morrill, ed., *The Impact of the English Civil War* (London, 1991).

———, "A Liberation Theology? Aspects of Puritanism in the English Revolution," in Laura Lunger Knoppers, ed., *Puritanism and Its Discontents* (Newark, DE, 2003).

———, "The Making of Oliver Cromwell," in John S. Morrill, ed., *Oliver Cromwell and the Puritan Revolution* (London, 1990).

———, *The Nature of the English Revolution* (1993).

———, ed., *Oliver Cromwell and the Puritan Revolution* (London, 1990).

———, *Oliver Cromwell and the English Revolution* (London, 1990).

———, "William Dowsing, the Bureaucratic Puritan," in John S. Morrill, Paul Slack, and Daniel Woolf, eds., *Public Duty and Private Conscience in Seventeenth-Century England* (Oxford, 1992).

Morrill, John S., Paul Slack, and Daniel Woolf, eds., *Public Duty and Private Conscience in Seventeenth-Century England* (Oxford, 1992).

Morrissey, Mary, "Scripture, Style and Persuasion in Seventeenth-Century English Theories of Preaching," *Journal of Ecclesiastical History* 53:4 (2002), 686–706.

Mullan, David, *Scottish Puritanism: 1590–1638* (Oxford, 2000).

Myles, Anne G., "From Monster to Martyr: Re-Presenting Mary Dyer," *Early American Literature* 36 (2001), 1–30.

Newell, Margaret Ellen, *From Dependency to Independence: Economic Revolution in Colonial New England* (Ithaca, NY, 1998).

Newman, Christine, "'An Honourable and Elect Lady': the faith of Isobel, Lady Bowes," in Diana Wood, ed., *Life and Thought in the Northern*

Church, c. 1100–c. 1700 (Woodbridge, Eng., 1999).

Newman, Simon, "Nathaniel Ward, 1580–1652: An Elizabethan Puritan in a Jacobean World," *Essex Institute Historical Collections* 127 (1991), 313–326.

Newton, Diana, *Papists, Protestants and Puritans, 1559–1714* (Cambridge, Eng., 1998).

Norbrook, David, "'Words more than civil': Republican Civility in Lucy Hutchinson's 'The Life of John Hutchinson,'" in Jennifer Richards, ed., *Early Modern Civil Discourses* (Basingstoke, Eng., 2003).

Norton, Mary Beth, *In the Devil's Snare:The Salem Witchcraft Crisis of 1692* (New York, 2002).

Oldridge, Darren, *Religion and Society in Early Stuart England* (Aldershot, Eng., 1998).

Olive, Barbara, "The Fabric of Restoration Puritanism: Mary Chudleigh's *The Song of the Three Children Paraphras'd*," in Laura Lunger Knoppers, ed., *Puritanism and Its Discontents* (Newark, DE, 2003).

Parker, Kenneth L., *"Practical Divinity": the Works and Life of Reverend Richard Greenham* (Aldershot, Eng., 1998).

———, "Richard Greenham's 'spiritual physicke': The Comfort of Afflicted Consciences in Elizabethan Pastoral Care," in Katharine Jackson Lualdi and Anne T. Thayer, eds., *Penitence in the Age of Reformations* (Aldershot, Eng., 2000).

Peaccy, Jason, "Seasonable Treatises: A Godly Project of the 1630s," *English Historical Review* 113 (1998), 667–679.

Pestana, Carla Gardina, *The English Atlantic in an Age of Revolution, 1640–1661* (New York, 2004).

Peterson, Mark, "The Practice of Piety in Puritan New England: Notes on Contexts and Consequences," in Francis J. Bremer and Lynn Botelho, eds., *The World of John Winthrop: England and New England, 1588–1649* (Boston, 2005).

———, *The Price of Redemption: The Spiritual Economy of Puritan New England* (Stanford, 1998).

———, "Puritanism and Refinement in Early New England: Reflections on Communion Silver," *William and Mary Quarterly*, 3rd series, 58 (2001), 307–346.

———, "The Selling of Joseph: Bostonians, Antislavery, and the Protestant International, 1689–1733," *Massachusetts Historical Review* 4 (2002), 1–22.

Petrie, Sue, "The Religion of Sir Roger Twysden (1597–1672): A Case Study in Gentry Piety in Seventeenth-Century England," *Archaeologia Cantiana* 124 (2004), 137–162.

Pointer, Richard, "From Imitating Language to a Language of Imitation: Puritan-Indian Discourse in Early New England," in Laura Lunger Knoppers, ed., *Puritanism and Its Discontents* (Newark, DE, 2003).

Pointer, Steven R. "The Emmanuel College, Cambridge, Election of 1622: The Constraints of a Puritan Institution," in Laura Lunger Knoppers, ed., *Puritanism and Its Discontents* (Newark, DE, 2003).

Poole, Kristen, *Radical Religion from Shakespeare to Milton: Figures of Nonconformity in Early Modern England* (New York, 2000).

Porterfield, Amanda, *Female Piety in Puritan New England* (New York, 1992).

Prall, Stuart E., *The Puritan Revolution and the English Civil War* (London, 2002).

Primus, John H., *Richard Greenham: Portrait of an Elizabethan Pastor* (Macon, GA, 1998).

Puglisi, Michael J., *Puritans Besieged: The Legacies of King Philip's War in the Massachusetts Bay Colony* (Lanham, MD, 1991).

Questier, Michael C., and Simon Healey, "'What's in a Name?' A Papist's Perception of Puritanism and Conformity in the Early Seventeenth Century," in Arthur F. Marotti, ed., *Catholicism and Anti-Catholicism* (Basingstoke, Eng., 1999), 137–153.

Racaut, L., "The 'Book of Sports' and Sabbatarian Legislation in Lancashire, 1579–1615," *Northern History* 33 (1997), 73–87.

Ramsbottom, J. D., "Presbyterians and 'partial conformity' in the Restoration Church of England," *Journal of Ecclesiastical History* 43 (1992), 249–270.

Rath, Richard Cullen, *How Early America Sounded* (Ithaca, NY, 2003).

Rehnman, Sebastian, *Divine Discourse: The Theological Methodology of John Owen* (Grand Rapids, MI, 2002).

Reis, Elizabeth, *Damned Women: Sinners and Witches in Puritan New England* (Ithaca, NY, 1997)

Roberts, Stephen, "Welsh Puritanism in the Interregnum," *History Today* 41 (1991), 36–41.

Rosenmeier, Jesper, "'Eaters and Non-Eaters': John Cotton's *A Brief Exposition of Canticles* (1642) in Light of Boston (Lincs.) Religious and Civil Conflicts, 1619–22," *Early American Literature* 36 (2001), 149–181.

———, "John Cotton on Usury," *William and Mary Quarterly*, 3rd series, 47 (1990), 548–565.

Ross, Richard, and James Hart, "The Ancient Constitution in the Old World and the New," in Francis J. Bremer and Lynn Botelho, eds., *The World of John Winthrop: England and New England, 1588–1649* (Boston, 2005).

Russell, Conrad, *The Causes of the English Civil War* (Oxford, 1990).

Sacks, D. H., "Bristol's Wars of Religion," in Roger C. Richardson, ed., *Town and Countryside in the English Revolution* (Manchester, Eng., 1992).

Sanders, Glenn, "'A plain Turkish Tyranny': Images of the Turk in Anti-Puritan Polemic," in Laura Lunger Knoppers, ed., *Puritanism and Its Discontents* (Newark, DE, 2003).

Schneider, Carol G., "Roots and Branches: From Principled Nonconformity to the Emergence of Religious Parties," in Francis J. Bremer, ed., *Puritanism: Transatlantic Perspectives on a Seventeenth-Century Anglo-American Faith* (Boston, 1994).

Schnucker, R. V., "Puritan Attitudes towards Childhood Discipline, 1560–1634," in Valerie Fildes, ed., *Women as Mothers in Pre-Industrial England* (London, 1990).

Scott, David, "Motive for King-Killing," in Jason Peacey, ed., *The Regicides and the Execution of Charles I* (Basingstoke, Eng., 2001).

——, "'Yorkshire's Godly Incendiary: the Career of Henry Darley during the Reign of Charles I," in Diana Wood, ed., *Life and Thought in the Northern Church, c. 1100–c. 1700* (Woodbridge, Eng., 1999).

Seaver, Paul S., "Laud and the Livery Companies," in Charles Carlton et al., eds., *State, Sovereigns, and Society in Early Modern Europe* (Stroud, Eng., 1998).

Semler, L. E., "The Creed of *Eliza's babes* (1652): Nakedness, Adam, and Divinity," *Albion* 33:2 (2001), 185–217.

Sharpe, Kevin, "Archbishop Laud," in Margo Todd, ed., *Reformation to Revolution: Politics and Religion in Early Modern England* (London, 1995).

——, *The Personal Rule of Charles I* (New Haven, 1992).

Shaw, Barry, "Thomas Norton's Devices for a Godly Realm: An Elizabethan Vision for the Future," *Sixteenth Century Journal* 22 (1991), 495–509.

Sheils, William J., "Erecting the Discipline in Provincial England: The Order of Northampton, 1571," in James Kirk, ed., *Humanism and Reform: The Church in Europe, England, and Scotland* (London, 1991).

——, "Reformed Religion in England, 1520–1640," in Sheridan Gilley and William J. Sheils, eds., *A History of Religion in Britain* (Oxford, 1994).

Sievers, Julie, "Refiguring the Song of Songs: John Cotton's 1655 Sermon and the Antinomian Controversy," *New England Quarterly* 76 (2003), 73–107.

Slack, Paul, "The Public Conscience of Henry Sherfield," in John S. Morrill, Paul Slack, and Daniel

Woolf, eds., *Public Duty and Private Conscience in Seventeenth-Century England* (Oxford, 1992).

Smith, David L., "Catholic, Anglican, or Puritan? Edward Sackville, Fourth Earl of Dorset and the Ambiguities of Religion in Early Stuart England," *Transactions of the Royal Historical Society*, 6th series, 2 (1992), 105–124.

——, *Oliver Cromwell: Politics and Religion in the English Revolution, 1640–1658* (Cambridge, Eng., 1991).

Smith, J. R., "Early Stuart Essex: Seedbed of American Democracy and Independence," in Kenneth Neale, ed., *"Full of Profitable Things": Essays Presented to Sir John Ruggles-Brise* (Oxford, 1996).

Sommerville, John C., *The Discovery of Childhood in Puritan England* (Athens, GA, 1992).

——, "Interpreting Seventeenth-Century English Religion as Movements," *Church History* 69 (2000), 749–769.

Song, Young Jae Timothy, *Theology and Piety in the Reformed Theology of William Perkins and John Preston* (Lewiston, NY, 1998).

Spicer, Andrew, "'Laudianism' in Scotland? St Giles' Cathedral, Edinburgh, 1633–1639—a reappraisal," *Architectural History* 46 (2003), 95–108.

Spinks, Bryan D., Sacraments, *Ceremonies and the Stuart Divines: Sacramental Theology and Liturgy in England and Scotland 1603–1662* (Aldershot, Eng; 2002).

Spraggon, Julie, *Puritan Iconoclasm during the English Civil War* (Woodbridge, Eng., 2003).

Sprunger, Keith L., *Trumpets from the Tower: English Puritan Printing in the Netherlands, 1600–1640* (Leiden, 1994).

Spurr, John, *English Puritanism, 1603–1689* (Basingstoke, Eng., 1998).

——, "From Puritanism to Dissent, 1660–1700," in Christopher Durston and Jacqueline Eales, eds., *The Culture of English Puritanism, 1560–1700* (Basingstoke, Eng., 1996).

Stachniewski, John, *The Persecutory Imagination: English Puritanism and the Literature of Religious Despair* (Oxford, 1991).

Staloff, Darren, *The Making of an American Thinking Class: Intellectuals and Intelligentsia in Puritan Massachusetts* (New York, 1998).

Stavely, Keith W. F., "Roger Williams and the Enclosed Gardens of New England," in Francis J. Bremer, ed., *Puritanism: Transatlantic Perspectives on a Seventeenth-Century Anglo-American Faith* (Boston, 1994).

Stocker, Margarita, "From Faith to Faith in Reason? Religious Thought in the Seventeenth Century," in

T. Cain and Ken Robinson, eds., *Into Another Mould: Change and Continuity in English Culture, 1625–1700* (London, 1992).

Stout, Harry S., *The New England Soul: Preaching and Religious Culture in Puritan New England* (New York, 1986).

Tennant, Philip Ernest, "Parish and People: South Warwickshire in the Civil War," in Roger Richardson, ed., *The English Civil Wars: Local Aspects* (Stroud, Eng., 1997).

Thompson, Roger, *Cambridge Cameos: Stories of Life in Seventeenth-Century New England* (Boston, 2005)

———, *Divided We Stand: Watertown, Massachusetts, 1630–1680* (Amherst, MA, 2001)

Thurley, Simon, "The Stuart kings, Oliver Cromwell and the Chapel Royal, 1618–1685," *Architectural History* 45 (2002), 238–274.

Tittler, Robert, "Henry Hardware and the Face of Puritan Reform in Chester," in Robert Tittler, *Townspeople and Nation: English Urban Experiences, 1540–1640* (Stanford, 2001).

Todd, Margo, *The Culture of Protestantism in Early Modern Scotland* (New Haven, 2002).

———, "'All One with Tom Thumb': Arminianism, Popery, and the Story of the Reformation in Early Stuart Cambridge," *Church History* 64 (1995), 568–579.

———, "Anti-Calvinists and the Republican Threat in Early Stuart Cambridge," in Laura Lunger Knoppers, ed., *Puritanism and Its Discontents* (Newark, DE, 2003).

———, "Puritan Self-Fashioning: The Diary of Samuel Ward," *Journal of British Studies* 31 (1992), 236–264.

———, ed., *Reformation to Revolution: Politics and Religion in Early Modern England* (London, 1995).

Trueman, Carl R., *The Claims of Truth: John Owen's Trinitarian Theology* (Carlisle, PA, 1998)

———, *Luther's Legacy: Salvation and the English Reformers* (Oxford, 1994)

———, "Puritanism as Ecumenical Theology," *Nederlands Archief voor Kerkgeschiedenis* 81:3 (2001), 326–336.

Twigg, John, *The University of Cambridge and the English Revolution, 1625–1688* (Cambridge, Eng., 1991).

Tyacke, Nicholas, "Archbishop Laud," in Kenneth Fincham, ed., *The Early Stuart Church* (Basingstoke, Eng., 1993).

———, *Aspects of English Protestantism, c. 1530–1700* (2001).

———, *The Fortunes of English Puritanism, 1603–1640* (London, 1990).

———, "Lancelot Andrewes and the Myth of Anglicanism," in Peter Lake and Michael C. Questier, eds., *Conformity and Orthodoxy in the English Church, c. 1560–1660* (Woodbridge, Eng., 2000).

———, "Puritan Politicians and King James VI and I, 1587–1604," in Thomas Cogswell, Richard Cust, and Peter Lake, eds., *Politics, Religion and Popularity in Early Stuart Britain: Essays in Honour of Conrad Russell* (Oxford, 2002).

———, "Puritanism, Arminianism and Counter-Revolution," in Margo Todd, ed., *Reformation to Revolution: Politics and Religion in Early Modern England* (London, 1995).

———, "The 'Rise of Puritanism' and the Legalizing of Dissent, 1571–1719," in O. P. Grell, Jonathan Israel, and Nicholas Tyacke, eds., *From Persecution to Toleration: The Glorious Revolution and Religion in England* (Oxford, 1991).

Ulrich, Laurel Thatcher, "John Winthrop's City of Women," *Massachusetts Historical Review* 3 (2001), 19–48.

Underdown, David, *Fire from Heaven: Life in an English Town in the Seventeenth Century* (New Haven, 1992).

Usher, Brett, "The Deanery of Bocking and the Demise of the Vestiarian Controversy," *Journal of Ecclesiastical History* 52:3 (2001), 434–455.

———, "The Silent Community: Early Puritans and Patronage of the Arts," in Diana Wood, ed., *The Church and Sovereignty, c. 590–1918* (Oxford, 1991).

———, *William Cecil and Episcopacy, 1559–1577* (Aldershot, Eng., 2003).

Valeri, Mark, "Puritans in the Marketplace," in Francis J. Bremer and Lynn Botelho, eds., *The World of John Winthrop: England and New England, 1588–1649* (Boston, 2005).

Van Dixhoorn, Chad B., "Unity and Diversity at the Westminster Assembly (1643–1649): A Commemorative Essay," *Journal of Presbyterian History* 79:2 (2001), 103–117.

Vaughan, Alden, and Virginia Mason Vaughan, "England's 'Others' in the Old and New Worlds," in Francis J. Bremer and Lynn Botelho, eds., *The World of John Winthrop: England and New England, 1588–1649* (Boston, 2005).

Wallace, Dewey, Jr., *Puritans and Predestination: Grace in English Protestant Theology, 1525–1695* (Chapel Hill, NC, 1982).

Walsham, Alexandra, *Providence in Early Modern England* (Oxford, 1999).

———, "'The Fatall Vesper': Providentialism and Anti-Popery in Late Jacobean London," *Past & Present* 144 (1994), 36–87.

————, "'Frantick Hacket': Prophecy, Sorcery, Insanity, and the Elizabethan Puritan Movement," *Historical Journal* 41 (1998), 27–66.

————, "'A Glosse of Godliness': Philip Stubbes, Elizabethan Grub Street, and the Invention of Puritanism," in Susan Wabuda and Caroline Litzenberger, eds., *Belief and Practice in Reformation England* (Aldershot, Eng., 1998).

————, "'Out of the Mouths of Babes and Sucklings': Prophecy, Puritanism, and Childhood in Elizabethan Suffolk," *Studies in Church History* 31 (1994), 285–300.

————, "The Parochial Roots of Ladianism Revisited," *Journal of Ecclesiastical History* 49 (1998), 620–651.

Walter, John, "Confessional Politics in Pre–Civil War Essex: Prayer Books, Profanations, and Petitions," *Historical Journal* 44:3 (2001), 677–701.

Watson, Nicholas, "Fashioning the Puritan Gentry-Woman," in J. Browne et al., *Medieval Women: Texts and Contexts in Late Medieval Britain* (Turnhout, 2000).

Webster, Tom, *Godly Clergy in Early Stuart England: The Caroline Puritan Movement, c. 1620–1643* (Cambridge, Eng., 1997).

————, *Stephen Marshall and Finchingfield* (Chelmsford, Eng., 1994).

————, and Kenneth Shipps, editors, *The Diary of Samuel Rogers* (Woodbridge, Eng., 2004)

————, "Writing to Redundancy: Approaches to Spiritual Journals and Early Modern Spirituality," *Historical Journal* 39 (1996), 33–56.

————, "The Piety of Practice and the Practice of Piety, in Francis J. Bremer and Lynn Botelho, eds., *The World of John Winthrop: England and New England, 1588–1649* (Boston, 2005).

Weir, David A., *Early New England: A Covenanted Society* (Grand Rapids, MI, 2005).

Westerkamp, Marilyn J., "Engendering Puritan Religious Culture in Old and New England," in Nicholas Canny, Gary Nash, and Joseph Illick, eds., *Empire, Society and Labor* (Philadelphia, 1997).

Whalen, Robert, "George Herbert's Sacramental Puritanism," *Renaissance Quarterly* 54:4:1 (2001), 1273–1307.

White, B. R., "The Twilight of Puritanism in the Years before and after 1688," in O. P. Grell, Jonathan Israel, and Nicholas Tyacke, eds., *From Persecution to Toleration: The Glorious Revolution and Religion in England* (Oxford, 1991).

White, Micheline, "A Biographical Sketch of Dorcas Martin: Elizabethan Translator, Stationer, and Godly Matron," *Sixteenth Century Journal* 30 (1999), 775–792.

White, Peter, *Predestination, Piety, and Polemic: Conflict and Consensus in the English Church from the Reformation to the Civil War* (Cambridge, Eng., 1991).

————, "The Via Media in the Early Stuart Church," in Margo Todd, ed., *Reformation to Revolution: Politics and Religion in Early Modern England* (London, 1995).

————, "Godly Women in Early Modern England: Puritanism and Gender," *Journal of Ecclesiastical History*, 43 (1992), 561–80.

Willen, Diane, "'Communion of the Saints': Spiritual Reciprocity and the Godly Community in Early Modern England," *Albion* 27 (1995), 19–41.

Winship, Michael Paul, "Briget Cooke and the Art of Godly Female Self-Advancement," *Sixteenth Century Journal* 33:4 (2002), 1045–1059.

————, *Making Heretics: Militant Protestantism and Free Grace in Massachusetts, 1636–1641* (Princeton, 2002).

————, "'The Most Glorious Church in the World': The Unity of the Godly in Boston, Massachusetts, in the 1630s," *Journal of British Studies*, 39 (2000), 71–98.

————, "Prodigies, Puritanism and the Perils of Natural Philosophy: The Example of Cotton Mather," *William and Mary Quarterly*, 3rd series, 51 (1994), 92–105.

————, *Seers of God: Puritan Providentialism in the Restoration and early Enlightenment* (Baltimore, 1996).

————, "Weak Christians, Backsliders, and Carnal Gospelers: Assurance of Salvation and the Pastoral Origins of Puritan Practical Divinity in the 1580s," *Church History* 70:3 (2001), 462–481.

————, "Were There Any Puritans in New England?" *New England Quarterly* 74 (2001), 118–138.

Wood, Timothy, "Kingdom Expectations: the Native American in the Puritan Missiology of John Winthrop and Roger Williams," *Fides et Historia* 32 (2000), 39–49.

Woolsey, Stephen, "Staging a Puritan Saint: Cotton Mather's *Magnalia Christi Americana*," in Laura Lunger Knoppers, ed., *Puritanism and Its Discontents* (Newark, DE, 2003).

Wooton, David, "Leveller Democracy and the Puritan Revolution," in J. H. Burns and Mark Goldie, eds., *The Cambridge History of Political Thought, 1450–1700* (Cambridge, Eng., 1991).

Worden, Blair, "The 'Dairy' of Bulstrode Whitelocke," *English Historical Review* 108 (1993), 122–134.

————, *Roundhead Reputations: the English Civil War and the Passions of Posterity* (London, 2001).

———, "Whig History and Puritan Politics: The *Memoirs* of Edmund Ludlow Revisited," *Historical Research* 75:188 (2002), 209–237.

Wormald, Jenny, "Ecclesiastical Vitriol: The Kirk, the Puritans and the Future King of England," in John Guy, ed., *The Reign of Elizabeth I* (Cambridge, Eng., 1995).

Wrightson, Keith, and David Levine, *Poverty and Piety in an English Village: Terling, 1525–1700*, rev. ed. (Oxford, 1995).

Wroughton, John, "Puritanism and Traditionalism: Cultural and Political Division in Bath, 1620–1662," *Bath History* 4 (1992), 52–70.

Wykes, David L., "'The Sabbaths . . . spent before in idleness & the neglect of the word': The Godly and the Use of Time in Their Daily Religion," in Robert Norman Swanson, ed., *The Use and Abuse of Time in Christian History* (Woodbridge, Eng., 2002).

Zakai, Avihu, *Exile and Kingdom: History and Apocalypse in the Puritan Migration to America* (Cambridge, Eng., 1992).

Index

About the Editors

Francis J. Bremer is Professor of History and Chair of the History Department at Millersville University of Pennsylvania. He received his B.A. from Fordham, College (1968) and his M. A. (1970) and Ph. D. (1972) degrees from Columbia University. He previously taught at Thomas More College in Kentucky and has been a visiting professor at New York University and a visiting fellow at Oxford and Cambridge Universities.

Dr. Bremer has long been interested in puritanism in the Atlantic world and brings this interest to his position as Editor of the Winthrop Papers for the Massachusetts Historical Society. He has written and edited ten books and numerous articles on aspects of Puritanism in England and America. His most recent book, *John Winthrop: America's Forgotten Founding Father* (2003) won the John C, Pollock Award for Christian Biography. Dr. Bremer is currently working on a study of *Puritans: an Attempt to Build the Kingdom of God in America* and a biography of John Davenport.

Tom Webster is from Great Grimsby, England. He studied at the University of East Anglia and Jesus College, Cambridge. He is the author of *Godly Clergy in Early Stuart England* and editor of *The Diary of Samuel Rogers.* He has also written on spitituality, masculinity, and possession in the early modern world. Dr. Webster is Lecturer in British History at the University of Edinburgh, Scotland.

FOR REFERENCE

Do Not Take From This Room